Core Techniques and Algorithms in Game Programming

Daniel Sánchez-Crespo Dalmau

New Riders

800 E. 96th Street, Indianapolis, Indiana 46240
An Imprint of Pearson Education
Boston • Indianapolis • London • Munich • New York • San Francisco

Core Techniques and Algorithms in Game Programming

International Standard Book Number: 0-1310-2009-9

Library of Congress Catalog Card Number: 2003107185

Printed in the United States of America

First printing: September, 2003

08 07 06 05 04 03   7 6 5 4 3 2 1

Interpretation of the printing code: The rightmost double-digit number is the year of the book's printing; the rightmost single-digit number is the number of the book's printing. For example, the printing code 03-1 shows that the first printing of the book occurred in 2003.

Trademarks

Warning and Disclaimer

Publisher
Stephanie Wall

Production Manager
Gina Kanouse

Development Editors
Chris Zahn
Anne Marie Walker

Project Editor
Michael Thurston

Senior Indexer
Cheryl Lenser

Proofreader
Debbie Williams

Composition
Gloria Schurick

Manufacturing Coordinator
Dan Uhrig

Interior Designer
Kim Scott

Cover Designer
Aren Howell

Marketing
Scott Cowlin
Tammy Detrich
Hannah Onstad Latham

Publicity Manager
Susan Nixon

Higher, Faster, Stronger

Table of Contents

Part III   Appendices

About the Author

 **Daniel Sánchez-Crespo Dalmau** is a professor at Pompeu Fabra University in Barcelona, Spain where he co-organized and serves as the current director of Spain's first Master's Degree in Video Game Creation. He also founded Novarama, an independent game studio in Barcelona that focuses on creating innovative games for the PC/Xbox platform. As a columnist he has been a frequent contributor to *Byte Magazine Spain*, *Game Developer Magazine*, and the Gamasutra web site, publishing more than 40 articles. Send comments about the book to him at dsanchez@novarama.com.

About the Technical Reviewer

This reviewer contributed his considerable hands-on expertise to the entire development process for *Core Techniques and Algorithms in Game Programming*. As the book was being written, this dedicated professional reviewed all the material for technical content, organization, and flow. His feedback was critical to ensuring that *Core Techniques and Algorithms in Game Programming* fits our readers' needs for the highest-quality technical information.

 Wolfgang Engel is a programmer and author, having written *Beginning Direct3D Game Programming* (Premier Press) and written and edited *Direct3D ShaderX: Vertex and Pixel Shader Programming Tips and Tricks* (Wordware Publishing). He has also published articles on game programming in German journals and a number of online tutorials on sites like gamedev.net. During his career in the game industry he has built two game development units from scratch that published online games for the biggest European television show, "Wetten das...?," and has served as either a member of the board or as CEO of several different companies. He is an advisor and a member of the faculty of the Academy of Game Entertainment Technology.

Acknowledgments

Writing a book like this is definitely not a journey on which you want to embark alone. Thus, before we begin I'd like to thank everyone who has, in one way or another, contributed to this book.

First of all, I'd like to thank both Stephanie Wall and Chris Zahn at New Riders, who have been with me all through the process, and also John Neidhart at Prentice Hall, who had the initial idea for this book. We've been through a pretty wild ride together, and their effort and dedication have been indispensable.

I'd also like to thank Josep Blat at Universitat Pompeu Fabra for his vision in developing a game-specific curricula, supporting the creation of this book, and creating Europe's first Master's Degree in Video Game Creation.

Then there are lots of people who shared ideas, contributed source code, and generally helped shape the book you are now holding. In no special order, here are the luminaries that lit the way for me:

Dave Pottinger, Ensemble Studios
Don Hopkins, Maxis
Ismael Noche, PyroStudios
Andrew Worsey, Codeplay
Cass Everitt, NVIDIA Corp.
Juan Guardado, NVIDIA Corp.
Alex Dunne, Game Developer/Gamasutra
Aleks Jakulin, University of Ljubljana, AI Lab
Ken Perlin, NYU
Toni Susín, UPC
Anna Puig, UPC
Carla Brossa, La Salle School of Multimedia Engineering
Adam Valdez, WETA Digital
Ernest Adams
Guillaume Werle
Martijn van Welie
Pere Fort, UPF
Hector Geffner, ICREA/ICREA

Finally, I'd like to thank everyone at Universitat Pompeu Fabra, especially my students, my work colleagues, and so on. A complete set of thank-yous must go to the Novarama people, who provided tons of information for this project. I'd also like to thank CIDEM/Generalitat de Catalunya for supporting Novarama's activities as a game studio. Finally, I'd like to thank all my friends and among those, my family, who have supported me through each and every one of these pages, and through my sometimes long absences. Last, I'd like to thank the beautiful Cecilia, whose unconditional support makes all this happen.

Barcelona, March 2002–June 2003

Tell Us What You Think

As the reader of this book, you are the most important critic and commentator. We value your opinion and want to know what we're doing right, what we could do better, what areas you'd like to see us publish in, and any other words of wisdom you're willing to pass our way.

As an editor for New Riders Publishing, I welcome your comments. You can fax, email, or write me directly to let me know what you did or didn't like about this book—as well as what we can do to make our books stronger. When you write, please be sure to include this book's title, ISBN, and author, as well as your name and phone or fax number. I will carefully review your comments and share them with the author and editors who worked on the book.

Please note that I cannot help you with technical problems related to the topic of this book, and that due to the high volume of email I receive, I might not be able to reply to every message.

Fax: 317-581-4663

Email: chris.zahn@newriders.com

Mail: Chris Zahn
          Editor
          New Riders Publishing
          800 E. 96th Street
          Indianapolis, IN 46240 USA

Introduction

For many years, the best ideas about game programming were handwritten on the back of a napkin. Knowledge was shared informally, with developers sketching ideas at meetings or industry gatherings, or talking with other fellow developers. Our craft was highly unorganized. Years have gone by, and today coding games is more complex than it ever was. The pursuit of realism and immersion have increased team sizes, budgets, and schedules. These are exciting times in which to be a game developer.

But we can no longer be unorganized in an industry of our size and importance. Today, professional game development must be efficient, and developers must be reliable. We simply cannot risk the failure of a project because one feature does not turn out as expected or because we don't know how to code a certain effect.

Our industry needs structured ways to train new professionals. Our attitude is changing. Events like the Game Developer's Conference, magazines like *Game Developer*, organizations like the International Game Developers Association (IGDA), and schools all over the world have begun creating this new consciousness of game development as a viable career alternative with its own training and disciplines. But we need more. The amount of games-related documentation generated per year is simply appalling, and it is very difficult for anyone wanting to learn about games to find reliable reference materials. Lots of books focus on API programming, which too often is not what game programming is all about. Other books come from different disciplines, like artificial intelligence or graphics. These books are often very good in their academic value and depth, but lack game-specific material. As a result, we end up gathering information from lots of different sources, with no central source of information.

This book is born from this unique context. After six years of teaching game programming and as the founder and director of one of Europe's first master's programs in video game development, I have evolved an extensive curriculum for aspiring game developers. I have tried to teach students the core subjects and techniques any serious game developer should take for granted, so they can enter and succeed in game studios quickly with a very short adaptation time. This is exactly the goal of this book—to present the fundamental subjects involved in video game programming in a structured, coherent way. My goal is to provide a good reference work for anyone wanting to learn about how games are currently coded and designed.

Thus, the focus of the book is not case-by-case tricks. Many good books contain that information. It is not a book about a specific game genre because techniques often cross genre boundaries. It is also not a book about theories. Instead, it is about established, well-understood methods that are at the core of many of today's blockbusters. This book is meant to help you build a foundation layer, so you can understand all the base algorithms that, with minimal differences, are found in most game projects.

What You Will Learn

This is a book about game programming. Its purpose is to teach you the fundamental techniques and algorithms that drive most computer and video games on the market. You will learn the theory and study the implementation details behind many AAA titles for the PC and console. The focus will not be on a specific area such as graphics or networks. The goal is to show you the core algorithms in each area, so this book can effectively become an introductory course on game programming.

It is not my intention to make this book a simple collection of algorithms or a long review of technical papers. My objective is to make the techniques easy to understand and code, so you can apply them yourself. Thus, for the most relevant methods, I will provide full explanations, diagrams, and code samples as required, so you can discover what's going on under the hood, how things work, and why. The measure of my success will be your ability to implement the ideas contained in this book, and thus create future generations of games.

Quite likely, you will end the reading of this book with more questions than answers. Game programming is a huge subject, and it is continually evolving. A book covering all techniques from the past and present would be thousands of pages long. Thus, I have provided a bibliography at the end of the book (Appendix E, "Further Reading") so you can read further and focus on the specific subject you are interested in. I have classified the bibliography entries by chapter, so it can be scanned quickly for relevant information.

What You Need to Know

Game programming is a huge interdisciplinary field. It is derived from fields such as mathematics, general-purpose programming, and artificial intelligence. Although you will learn much about these subjects during your journey, there are some materials with which you should already be comfortable.

To begin with, this book assumes you can code fluently in the C or C++ programming languages. You should be able to comfortably code using includes, pointers, classes, data structures, inheritance, and so on. This is not a book about programming, but a book about a specific use of programs. You will find a review of some popular data structures in Chapter 3, "Data Structures and Algorithms," but that is all you should expect. On the other hand, you don't need to know how to program a game at all: That's exactly what this book is all about.

Another prerequisite is some mathematical background that is equivalent to linear algebra and calculus as taught in many universities. You should be familiar with subjects such as vector math, derivatives and integrals, matrices, trigonometry, and so on. For those who have long forgotten this information, I have provided information on these subjects in Appendix D, "Some Math Involved." It includes most formulae and mathematical techniques used in this book. Be sure to give it a quick read.

Additionally, you will need time, and this is more important than you can imagine. Many people think that programming games is extremely difficult, and that the code is written in some arcane syntax understandable only by experts. Although some parts of the process are indeed complex, most of the source code for a game can be easily understood—complexity lies in very specific and easy to spot areas. So, what makes games so hard to code? It's not the difficulty: It's the time required to achieve any decent result. Many games can be created with dedication and discipline. For the most part, it won't be incredibly difficult. But it does take time, so make sure you have plenty of it.

How This Book Is Organized

From a purely technical standpoint, game code can be divided into two large portions. A sizable part of the code deals with gameplay-related issues: controlling the interaction, artificial intelligence, scripts, and so on. This is the game logic section, and I will devote the first half of the book to it. We will then move on to presentation techniques: graphics, audio, and generally speaking, all that makes games a rich multimedia experience. For the first part of the book, we will be mainly working in plain C/C++ code. Then, for the second part, we will use a variety of tools and libraries such as OpenGL or DirectX. What follows is a rundown of the book's contents.

Part I: Gameplay Programming

Chapter 1, "Chronology of Game Programming," provides a bit of historical perspective. It presents a brief overview of how game development technology has evolved since the dawn of the industry and includes platform examples.

Chapters 2 through 4, "Game Architecture," "Data Structures and Algorithms," and "Design Patterns," are all concerned with macro-level code analysis. They cover such topics as the structure of game code, popular data structures, and design patterns.

Chapter 5, "User Input," covers just that—the handling of interaction from the player.

Chapters 6 through 9 "Fundamental AI Technologies," "Action-Oriented AI," "Tactical AI," and "Scripting," deal with artificial intelligence topics. Fundamental algorithms, action and strategic AI, artificial life, and scripting techniques are explained in these chapters.

Chapter 10, "Network Programming," delves into the issues involved with networked games. It addresses multiplayer programming from the client and server perspective, and massively multiplayer games.

Part II: Engine Programming

Chapters 11 to 15, "2D Programming," "3D Pipeline Overview," "Indoors Rendering," "Outdoors Algorithms," and "Character Animation," cover graphics engine topics such as rendering pipelines, starting with generic designs and then later moving on to indoors and outdoors rendering algorithms.

Chapters 16 through 18, "Cinematography," "Shading," and "Texture Mapping," are concerned with look and feel. This includes setting cameras and lighting, and applying different texture techniques to the geometry.

Chapters 19 to 21, "Particle Systems," "Organic Rendering," and "Procedural Techniques," have to do with complex rendering scenarios. These chapters deal with three popular subjects: particle systems, organic rendering techniques for nature simulation, and procedural/shader-based approaches.

Chapter 22, "Geometrical Algorithms," covers geometric tests, tests for collision detection, geometry simplification, and so on.

Part III: Appendices

Appendix A, "Performance Tuning," covers optimization. Performance tuning techniques are discussed in order to ensure maximum performance of your games.

Appendix B, "OpenGL," and Appendix C, "Direct3D," address APIs. Here we will explore OpenGL 1.4 and DirectX 9.

Appendix D, "Some Math Involved," provides an overview and review of some of the math that is used in game programming.

Appendix E, "Further Reading," supplies sources of further information should you want to pursue certain topics in more depth.

Conventions

This book follows a few typographical conventions:

- ➤ A new term is set in *italics* the first time it is introduced.

- ➤ Program text, functions, variables, and other "computer language" are set in a fixed-pitch font—for example, `int state;`.

Chapter 1

A Chronology of Game Programming

"In the beginning the Universe was created. This has made a lot of people very angry and been widely regarded as a bad move."

Douglas Adams

The art and science of game development have experienced a huge progression since the early days. Hardware has improved by orders of magnitude, whereas game complexity and richness have simply exploded. To better understand how games are coded today, and why, it is essential to look back and review the history of game programming. I have divided that lengthy narration into what I consider the eight most defining moments that shaped the current industry. Let's time warp ourselves to those moments and take a look at how things were done back then. This way the reasons behind today's practices will become obvious. I will avoid the trivial and focus on programming practices. Because raw data is useless without perspective, it's also important to provide some context in which to interpret the data and to understand how today's programming practices were developed.

Phase I: Before *Spacewar*

The video game industry didn't begin as part of any established master plan. Rather, it emerged when independent groups of people, working in different countries, came up with the same ideas at approximately the same time. These were traditional game creators looking for a way to diversify their business, technology companies taking advantage of newly discovered solid-state technology, and some isolated visionaries who imagined a new form of entertainment, which would grow with the passing of years into the industry we know today.

As you will soon see, the dawn of the video game age came in the early 1970s. But most of the companies that played a key role in that defining period of time were born much earlier. These companies started in different business sectors, but somehow ended up realizing that games played on electronic devices could effectively make money and become a new business sector.

An illustrative example would be the industry giant Nintendo, which was established as a traditional gaming company in 1889 by Fusajiro Yamauchi. Initially incorporated under the name Marufuku Company, its core business was to manufacture and sell Hanafuda, a type of Japanese playing cards (see Figure 1.1). In the year 1951, Marufuku was renamed The Nintendo Playing Card Company—Nintendo meaning "leave luck to Heaven." Later, as the first electronic games and devices appeared, Nintendo diversified its business by starting an electronic gaming division. As time went by, the traditional gaming business faded away, and Nintendo became the company we all know today. So Nintendo would be the perfect example of an already existing corporation that changed its sector of activity to embrace emerging technologies.

Figure 1.1 Hanafuda card.

Companies such as Sony followed a completely different approach. Created to focus on consumer electronics, the company known as Sony today was founded by Akio Morita and Masaru Ibuka as the Tokyo Telecommunications Engineering Corporation in 1946. The core business of the company was making tape recorders, which were miniaturized with the advent of solid-state transistors. As soon as the company's products began reaching the European and American markets, the founding team decided to change its name to make it easier to remember by non-Japanese customers.

The company was thus renamed Sony (from the Latin word "sonus," which means sound) in an effort to make its brand easily recognizable. Sony quickly became one of the leading vendors in the consumer electronics arena, especially in the audio and visual areas. Brands like Walkman, Trinitron, and many others are a testament to the impressive product line it assembled. But Sony stood away from the gaming business until the late 1980s when work on the first Sony PlayStation began. The rest is history. Today Sony builds consoles and creates games in many studios worldwide. The PlayStation gaming platform is central to its overall business strategy, which has been successfully expanded outside the consumer electronics division.

A third, minor group of companies provided some middle ground between technology and gaming companies. Sega is a classic example of this group. Its story started in 1940 when Martin Bromely, Irving Bromberg, and James Humpert founded Standard Games, a coin-operated machine manufacturer in Honolulu. In 1951, the company moved to Tokyo and was later registered as Service Games (or, simply put, Sega) of Japan in 1952. The move made it easier for the company to supply coin-operated machines to U.S. military units stationed in Japan. Some years later, in 1965, Service Games merged with Rosen Enterprises, another company that dealt with everything from instant photo booths to mechanical arcade games. Rosen Enterprises had been founded in 1954 by Korean War veteran David Rosen. Rosen experienced firsthand the popularity of mechanical coin-operated machines (like the world-popular pinball machine) in U.S. bases stationed in Japan. Rosen began exporting them to Japanese territory under the name Service Games, or Sega. As the business took off, Rosen started producing his own games by purchasing a Tokyo-based slot machine and jukebox company.

The rest is history. Sega began producing arcade machines first and later expanded its operations to home consoles and game development.

However, it wasn't Nintendo, Sony, nor even Sega that led the way to electronic enter-tainment. These companies entered the emerging game industry following the foot-steps of the true pioneers who came up with the initial designs and business model proposals. Clearly, someone with the vision of how games would be played on elec-tronic devices was required to spark the process. That vision came from researchers working for universities and the military because they were the ones with access to cutting-edge hardware (according to the 1950s standards, that is).

The first of these early-day pioneers worked as a nuclear physicist at Brookhaven National Labs in New York. His name was William Higinbotham and he was a self-confessed pinball player. In the 1950s, Brookhaven was a government-supported research facility that focused on nuclear energy. Visitors toured the facilities, where peaceful uses of atomic energy were showcased. These included pictures and equip-ment displays, illustrating everything from power plants to radiation-based medicine.

Higinbotham, who thought those visits were boring, designed a strange device by using spare parts from the lab: an oscilloscope, some capacitors, two potentiometers, and a small analog computer. He dubbed the invention "Tennis for two" (see Figure 1.2). It was a simple two-player table-tennis game where the court and ball were displayed on the oscilloscope. The player could change the angle by which the ball was hit by turning the potentiometer. The game was mostly hard-wired, so it wasn't game programming just yet.

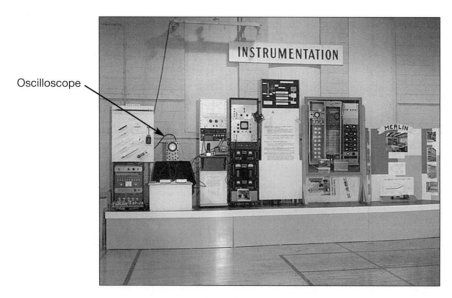

Figure 1.2   Tennis for two.

As with most geniuses, Higinbotham did not realize what he had achieved, not even when people started waiting in line to play the game at Brookhaven. The year was 1958, and by then other people had reached similar results worldwide. As early as 1952, A.S. Douglas presented his Ph.D. thesis on human-computer interaction at Cambridge, UK. As an example, he coded a tic-tac-toe game on an EDSAC computer to illustrate his principles.

Dozens of stories like these have been found relating to the 1950s decade, but Higinbotham's example is one of the best documented complete works from these early days.

Another visionary worth remembering is Ralph Baer, who came up with the home console concept as early as 1951. While working for Loral (an airborne electronics company), Baer got the assignment to create a cutting-edge TV set, which he proposed to enrich by using some kind of playable game. The company management ignored the idea, but 15 years later, while working for a different contractor, Baer gave his idea a second try. He succeeded this second time, and work began on what would become the world's first home console, the Magnavox Odyssey.

As a summary of this early age of development, by the late 1950s/early 1960s, some companies had developed solid positions in classic games (Nintendo, Sega, and so on). Other key players such as Sony and Matsushita were exploiting the benefits of solid-state technology. Additionally, some early pioneers were already aware of the potential of technology as a tool for play. Some test games surfaced—all implemented in specific hardware: Machines that effectively *were* the game. Game programming hadn't really appeared yet because programmable devices were rare. By 1960, a catalyst between traditional games, technology providers, and researchers was needed—a single successful game that would show where the three trends would merge to create meaningful business opportunities.

Phase II: *Spacewar* to Atari

The turning point for the games industry came in 1961 when Steve Russell, an MIT student, coded a simple two-player game on a Digital PDP-1 minicomputer. The game was called *Spacewar*, and it displayed two spaceships on a computer screen (see Figure 1.3). Each ship could move laterally while shooting at the other player.

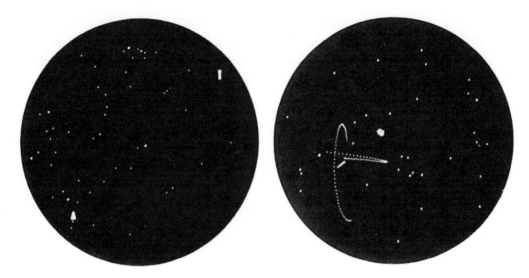

Figure 1.3   *Spacewar.*

The game did not reach consumers but certainly served as an influence on many people. It was a game in the classic sense of the word. It used the new technology, and it defined the path for many others. The game had

- ➤ Competition between two peers

- ➤ Rules of action

- ➤ A clear victory condition

In fact, this structure is not very different from traditional games such as chess. The main difference is the technology layer that supports the gameplay. Through the years, this technology layer has skyrocketed in its complexity, and games have established themselves as a rich, unique media. The overall three-rule structure, however, has remained basically the same.

Many people were deeply influenced by *Spacewar*, but we will focus on two industry pioneers who were illuminated by the elegance of the concept. Nolan Bushnell was exposed to the game while studying engineering at the University of Utah. He envisioned computer games like *Spacewar* filling arcades, where people would pay to play game after game. Some years later, his vision would materialize when he founded Atari and created the first coin-operated (coin-op) machines.

The story of Atari is well known. After seeing *Spacewar*, Bushnell began working on reasonable-cost, dedicated machines where games could be played. His first game, years before the dawn of Atari, was called *Computer Space*, which was a version of *Spacewar* that he hard-wired and plugged into a TV set in his daughter's bedroom. Nutting Associates, a manufacturer of arcade games, bought the *Computer Space* idea, hiring Bushnell to oversee production. In 1971, 1,500 *Computer Space* machines were manufactured and installed in the United States. But players found it too hard to play, so the game received a cold reception. Bushnell tried to create new game ideas, but after some discussions, he left Nutting. As a result, he founded Atari in 1972 with Ted Dabney, taking the name from the Japanese game of *Go*. Atari is the equivalent to a check move in chess.

On the other end of the spectrum stood Ralph Baer, the games-on-TV pioneer from the 1950s. By 1966 he had already left Loral and was working for Sanders Associates, an army contractor. He was given the green light to research his TV set idea, which he patented in 1968. He saw electronic games as secondary uses for TV sets, which already enjoyed a large installed base. At that time, he had succeeded in creating two TV-based games (a chase and a tennis game) as well as a very early light gun design. By 1970, TV manufacturer Magnavox had licensed Baer's technologies. Under Baer's guidance, work on the first game console began. The system, dubbed the *Magnavox Odyssey*, was introduced in 1972, the same year Atari was born.

By the end of 1972, the electronic games business took the world (starting with the West Coast of the United States) by storm. The first Atari game, *Pong*, hit locales, becoming the first successful example of a coin-op machine. Within two weeks, *Pong* machines in California began to break down due to quarters flooding the coin drop mechanism, something Bushnell had never even dreamt of. At the same time, Magnavox sold 100,000 units of the *Odyssey*, a remarkable feat considering distribution was made only through official Magnavox stores.

During this period, two distinct business models appeared: arcade games, paid per play; and home systems, where games could be purchased and played repeatedly. Both have evolved and still subsist today, with the latter being the dominant option. A third trend had yet to appear; one in which games needn't be played on dedicated hardware.

Phase III: Game Consoles and Personal Computers

Electronic games, either for home systems or arcade machines, were an instant success. Different manufacturers such as Coleco (short for Connecticut Leather Company, a clear example of extreme diversification), Fairchild, and many others introduced their own home gaming systems, and competition fostered innovation. Game cartridges were introduced in 1976, trackballs in 1978, and so on.

Game Consoles and Game Developers

It was during this fast growth period, sometime in the 1970s, that the distinction between console manufacturers and game developers was established. Console manufacturers would invest large sums of money in creating the hardware platform and selling it at an attractive price to consumers. Sometimes, the price would hardly cover (or even be below) the real cost of the hardware. Manufacturers would also build tools (very primitive at this stage) that allowed outside companies to create games for the console. The reason why other companies were given access to the business was obvious. As game consoles began to compete against each other for market share, being able to offer many games became the main competitive advantage, and hence the importance of the developer. No manufacturer could ever have the bandwidth to deliver the amount of games required to make its console platform attractive.

Thus, outside companies began coding games for console systems. At this stage, little or no quality control was performed by the console manufacturer; quantity was valued over quality. For each game sold, the developer agreed to pay a royalty fee to the console manufacturer to cover the console development costs and thus generate revenue. Some console manufacturers focused on the hardware business only, whereas others chose to act as developers as well, sometimes causing conflicts of interests. Did the outside developer have the same information as the internal team at the manufacturer? Sometimes first-party teams had access to better information than third parties, which caused complaints. With some variations, this production model still applies today. The main difference with today's model is that consoles are sold way below their manufacturing price, especially when they debut. This is a risky decision, because the hardware manufacturer has to sustain significant losses for some time. Then, as the console manufacturer begins receiving royalties from developers, it is able to recover from the initial losses and finally make money.

The king of programmable consoles at the time became the Atari VCS, also known as the Atari 2600, which was introduced in 1977 with a price tag of $249. Because it became the de facto standard, I will use it to exemplify what coding for a console meant in the 1970s. The console featured a 6507 CPU equipped with 128 bytes of RAM, which were used to store state variables such as the life and ammunition levels. The program was stored in an external, interchangeable cartridge, which was inserted into the console. One side of the cartridge was full of electrical connections. Thus, inserting it into the console integrated the data chips in the cartridge as part of the console's hardware, usually as memory banks where the program code and data were stored.

The memory cartridge method was used with minimal variations until the Nintendo 64 and the Gameboy Advance, whereas more modern systems employ different kinds of disks as storage media. Storing games on CD-ROMs and DVDs makes them much cheaper to manufacture, at the cost of increasing the risk of piracy and having to enhance the memory capabilities of the console to store the program. But for the Atari 2600, 6KB of ROM were usually built into the cartridge and held the game code and data together in a memory chip. The 6507 CPU ran at an incredible 1.19 MHz and had an address space of 8KB.

Assisting the CPU were the television adapter, known as TIA or Stella, and the I/O chip, called RIOT. Stella was accessed through registers and had the extreme limitation of not having a frame buffer or physical memory to hold the screen's contents. Modern adapters (from CGA onward) have a memory region that holds the screen data pixel by pixel, so copying data to that region effectively paints the screen. The Atari 2600 did not have such a buffer. So, the screen was drawn by reading some Stella registers serially, synchronized to the electron beam from the TV set. The CPU had to synchronize itself with the electron beam and write those registers at exactly the right speed, so it looked correct and produced no flicker. As an example of the limitations imposed by the hardware, here is the sequence of a game loop for the Atari 2600:

```
Start the vertical blanking interval
Start the vertical sync interval
     Here is space for 80 micro instructions
End vertical sync
     Perform game computations here
End vertical blank
```

```
Now the screen rendering starts…
      Send each line to the register
      6 instructions can be fit here
Loop lines until the screen is rendered
Go to first step
```

The 2600, as all consoles were at that stage, was coded in machine-specific assembler. Program data and source code were part of a single memory block. Data was just bytes of information trailing after the code, which program code never jumped to. An untested program that began to execute data addresses would simply go mad. Here is an excerpt of a combat game for the 2600, showing how code and data were part of a whole:

```
B15A7          STX    D2
               LDX    #03
B15AB          LDA    L1765,Y
               EOR    D1
               AND    D2
               STA    COLUP0,X
               STA    D6,X
               STA    D8,X
               INY
               DEX
               BPL    B15AB
               RTS
J15BD          LDA    #00
B15BF          INX
               STA    A2,X
               BNE    B15BF
               RTS
L15C5          .BYTE  $0E ,$0A ,$0A ,$0A ,$0E ;   0
               .BYTE  $22 ,$22 ,$22 ,$22 ,$22 ;  11
               .BYTE  $EE ,$22 ,$EE ,$88 ,$EE ;  22
               .BYTE  $EE ,$22 ,$66 ,$22 ,$EE ;  33
               .BYTE  $AA ,$AA ,$EE ,$22 ,$22 ;  44
               .BYTE  $EE ,$88 ,$EE ,$22 ,$EE ;  55
               .BYTE  $EE ,$88 ,$EE ,$AA ,$EE ;  66
               .BYTE  $EE ,$22 ,$22 ,$22 ,$22 ;  77
               .BYTE  $EE ,$AA ,$EE ,$AA ,$EE ;  88
               .BYTE  $EE ,$AA ,$EE ,$22 ,$EE ;  99
```

```
L15F7           .BYTE   $F8 ,$F7 ,$F6 ,$06 ,$06
                .BYTE   $06 ,$16 ,$17 ,$18 ;        $15FC
                .BYTE   $19 ,$1A ,$0A ,$0A ;        $1600
                .BYTE   $0A ,$FA ,$F9 ,$F8 ;        $1604
                .BYTE   $F7 ,$F6 ,$F6 ,$06 ;        $1608
                .BYTE   $16 ,$16 ,$17 ,$18 ;        $160C
                .BYTE   $19 ,$1A ,$1A ,$0A ;        $1610
                .BYTE   $FA ,$FA ,$F9 ,$E8 ;        $1614
                .BYTE   $E6 ,$E4 ,$F4 ,$04 ;        $1618
                .BYTE   $14 ,$24 ,$26 ,$28 ;        $161C
                .BYTE   $2A ,$2C ,$1C ,$0C ;        $1620
                .BYTE   $FC ,$EC ,$EA ;             $1624
```

Most of the time, games were built by a single person who laid down the memory map, wrote the program code, designed the graphics, and even provided the sound. Sometimes an artist helped out, but doing graphics is a relatively straightforward task on such limited hardware. Code reuse, so popular today, was virtually nonexistent. At most, programmers would borrow sequences of microinstructions from a previous title so a new game could be coded faster. But generally speaking, coding for such a machine involved lots of craft and skill, as anyone who has coded assembly programs for a living knows.

Personal Computers

While consumers were busy playing with game consoles, the personal computer revolution was about to begin. Computers appeared as a by-product of the discovery of the integrated circuit by Texas Instruments in 1959. The first computer, the Digital PDP-1, appeared in 1960 and featured a keyboard and a monitor. It debuted at $120,000, clearly positioning computers in the corporate market: Accounting, engineering, and databases were their main uses. By 1964, the BASIC language appeared, allowing intuitive programming.

Douglas Engelbart invented a two-dimensional pointing device called the "mouse," which is now widely used. By 1968 (one year before humanity reached the moon), the first home computer, the Honeywell H316, was introduced at $10,600. The Apollo Guidance Computer, developed specifically for the Apollo 11 spaceship, was an impressive feat. It ran at 2MHz, had 64KB of ROM and 4KB of RAM, and was capable of performing 50,000 additions per second.

In 1972, when Atari and Magnavox became successful, computers were gaining ground. The C programming language was introduced, the first ideas about laptop computers appeared at Xerox's Palo Alto Research Center (PARC), and Intel introduced the 8008, a 16KB, 200kHz, 60,000 instructions-per-second, low cost chip. From this moment on, computers advanced at blazing fast speed. In 1974, Intel unveiled the 8080, a 2MHz, 16KB, 640,000 instructions-per-second chip. That same year, the MITS Altair 8800 was announced in Popular Electronics for about $400.

One year later, Microsoft was founded. Its flagship product was a BASIC interpreter for the Altair. It was the first programmable language for a personal computer. Years later, Microsoft would create the operating system for the IBM PC, and the rest is history.

Then, in 1976, one of the most popular garage startups surfaced, and the personal computer industry was born. Apple was founded by Steven Jobs and Steve Wozniak. Jobs, with an eye on product design and business, had been at Atari since 1974. Wozniak, the hardware genius, worked for Hewlett-Packard. Their first product, the Apple I, sold in kit form for $666, and was introduced at the Homebrew Computer Club. Some simple games began to appear for the Apple I, but they were mainly clones of those existing on game consoles.

But it was with the advent of the Apple][in 1977 when games began to pour in quickly. A decisive factor in this direction was the Apple]['s CPU: a 6502, extremely similar to the one running Atari's own 2600. The computer featured new 16KB RAM modules to reach a theoretical 48KB of total RAM, which was larger than anything on the market at the time. The bundle also included a BASIC interpreter to code your own programs, a QUERTY keyboard, a cassette interface, and a dedicated game I/O connector for paddles, joysticks, and so on. It could display up to 280×192 pixels in 16 colors, making it an ideal delivery platform for games.

The Apple][was state-of-the-art technology, clearly surpassing the products of the competition, including game consoles. It could be programmed, used for games and office applications, had a large memory area, and offered "full" color support (the full 16 colors in the palette, that is). The downside was, obviously, the cost. The base kit cost $600, whereas a full-featured, 48KB "supercomputer" was $2275, which was mainly due to high memory costs of those early days. But Apple][s were sold by the truckload, and hundreds of games were coded for it—a notorious example being the first installments of the popular *Ultima* series.

Five years later, IBM unveiled the IBM PC, which ran on an Intel 8086 CPU and Microsoft's Disk Operating System (MS-DOS). The main advantage of the PC was that the architecture was soon to become open. This enabled other companies to design and sell their own PCs, which were all compatible with the original IBM model. Competition fosters innovation, and an open platform is the best way to enable evolution. The personal computer era had begun.

Phase IV: Shakedown and Consolidation

With the Atari 2600 and Apple][on the market, there was a clear sense of direction in the games business. Thus, the period comprising the late 1970s and early 1980s is sometimes dubbed "The Golden Age." All that was needed was to keep improving these initial products, to create better platforms and games at each iteration. On the console side, Atari reigned supreme for many years, even when Nolan Bushnell left the company in 1978.

Following the departure of its founder, the company enjoyed prosperity due to the huge number of games being published. This period is also characterized by the entrance of Japanese developers into the equation. Taito (a pachinko manufacturer) introduced *Space Invaders*; Nintendo (remember the Hanafuda card company?) began by selling an *Othello* arcade game only to later introduce *Donkey Kong* (the first game by now-celebrity designer Shigeru Miyamoto) in 1981; and Namco (known as the Nakamura Manufacturing Company, maker of merry-go-rounds) introduced such classics as *Galaxian*, *Pac-man*, *Galaga*, and *Pole Position*.

Pac-man, whose initial character concept comes from a pizza with a slice missing, is based on a Japanese folk hero called Paku, known for his appetite. The game was to be called Puckman, but the potential risk of American graffiti artists changing the P to an F made Namco go for *Pac-man* as the final name.

Atari's golden days were about to end. The company did not keep a careful watch on the quality of games for the 2600, and some highly anticipated games for the platform were a flop. *Pac-man* and *E.T.* games were released with great hype, only to see consumers reject them due to their low quality. The legend says that thousands of copies of these games ended up in a massive landfill in New Mexico. By December 7,

1982, Atari announced that 2600 sales had, for the first time, failed to meet predictions, making its parent company, Warner Communications, suffer a 32 percent stock price drop in a day. In early 1983, with Atari still struggling to recover from *E.T.*, a crash occurred in the video game market. Retailers had tons of unsold games on store shelves, and many of them offered very low quality. Game prices dropped sharply. Titles that previously sold for $40 were selling for 99 cents, which resulted in many companies going out of business. Others would survive, but would never quite recover from the hit.

It took a while for the industry to recover from such a bad experience. Luckily, by 1985, some companies introduced a new wave of products and a revised quality policy. Nintendo introduced the Nintendo Entertainment System (NES) (Famicom in Japan), backed by a roster of internally developed, high-quality games. Shortly thereafter, some of the Atari developers such as Namco became Nintendo licensees. By 1988, classics such as *Super Mario Bros* and *Legend of Zelda* had been introduced, making Nintendo the top seller. Sega did not stand still either, introducing the Master System in 1986. Internally, both the NES and Master System were equipped with 8-bit processors (a 6502 and a Zilog Z80, respectively). Spec by spec, the Master System was a slightly better platform: More sprites were supported, and RAM size was increased. But Nintendo had the advantage of being the first mover with an impressive game catalog and reputation.

During these years, the consolidated console business model finally became clear. The console manufacturer created the hardware and produced (internally or through contractors) a first batch of titles, which showcased the hardware's capabilities and helped sell the first units. Then, developers wanting to jump on the bandwagon needed to apply to become licensees, and each game they built had to be tested for quality by the manufacturer. Only by enforcing this policy could consoles offer a consistent-quality game catalog, which made consumers happy with their purchases. Developers still received documentation and sometimes technical support from the console maker. They also had to pay a royalty fee to cover the console's development cost. In the case of Nintendo, there has always been a very strong presence of Nintendo-built games for its game systems, which ensures that a core of high-quality games is always available. By 1988, Nintendo was an established market leader with a well laid out licensing policy.

Let's press the pause button and explore the internals of the flagship product for this era, the NES. To begin with, Nintendo's console was built on top of a customized 6502 MOS CPU, which was enhanced to perform audio waveform computation directly on the CPU. As with all 6502s, the NES could only address 64KB of memory, but some techniques were devised to overcome that limit. Cartridges could implement a paged approach using a memory mapper to increase the addressable memory.

Graphics chores were carried out by the picture processing unit (PPU), whose main feature was support for tile-based backgrounds, sprites, and scrolling on hardware. Contents of the screen were described using four main data structures: the pattern table, the name table, the attribute table, and the sprite table. The *pattern table* was a list holding the definition of each 8×8 tile or pattern. Each tile was defined by a sequence of eight 16-bit values, each one representing one row of the tile. The idea is pretty straightforward. Each pixel in the tile can have one of four possible color values, and thus two bits per pixel are required (hence the 16 bits per row). So one tile in the pattern table could represent four different color values.

The *name table* assigned tiles to screen coordinates. The name table was a two dimensional, 30 row by 32 column matrix, with each position exactly one byte in length (thus selecting from 256 possible tiles). Multiplying the name table dimensions by the tile size would produce the total size of the background: 256 by 240 pixels. This was more than the available screen resolution, so only a portion of the background was visible at any given time. This background could be scrolled by simply changing the value of two offset registers.

An *attribute table* was used to modify how tiles were to be mapped to the screen. Attributes were specified for each 32×32-pixel screen block (which means one block every 4×4 tiles), so all tiles in that area shared the same attributes. Attributes were used to further refine the color scheme to be used. The attribute table provided two high-order bits for the color, whose two low-order bits were taken from the pattern table. This way a maximum of 16 colors could be used.

The *sprite table* was used to overlay sprites—characters, potions, and so on—on top of the background. The PPU could store up to 64 sprites (8×8 or 8×16 pixels each), which could be quickly mapped to the screen. Sprites were prioritized; whichever sequence you decided to paint, lower-number sprites were painted after higher-order ones were processed, thus providing an easy way of layering information onscreen. The main difference between sprites and tiles was that sprites could be blended with the background in a realistic manner; a key value was provided to specify which portions of the sprite were actually transparent and should expose the background.

As these special structures illustrate, the NES was a dedicated game platform. Its structure was clearly limited to what it was supposed to do. This is a common characteristic of all game consoles: They excel at what they were designed to do, but aren't useful for much else due to the system's design decisions.

The evolution of personal computers did not stand still for a decade. The Apple][had marked the course for the industry. Computers that sold at a reasonable cost were useful as working tools, but also kept the door open for home computer gaming. Each new iteration offered more powerful hardware, easier to use programming environments, and a more compelling game experience. The introduction of the IBM PC in 1981, with its open hardware design, fostered innovations by specific peripheral manufacturers. Graphics cards and hard drives began to be manufactured by different companies; each one competing for a piece of the market share. The evolution was enormous: From the crude, 4-color CGA adapter to the 256-color, 320×200 VGA adapter, only five years passed. VGA was the graphics mode that made computer games so popular in the late 1980s. It offered full-screen titles with a resolution similar to game consoles and color depth to display rich game worlds. Masterworks such as *Day of the Tentacle* by LucasArts or the *Alone in the Dark* saga are classic representatives of the VGA days.

Phase V: The Advent of the Game Engine

As soon as file systems appeared on the first home computers, it became obvious that they would be a powerful tool to better organize content in games. Gone were the days of a single file mixing code and data, making projects virtually impossible to maintain. With a decent file system, one file would contain the game code (the executable file), and several files would contain the associated data. This way chaos would be minimized, and work could be divided between different people who would only care about their specific files. A musician need only access the music data, the sprite artists need only work with bitmaps, and so on. Keep in mind that hardware was evolving quickly, and larger games were difficult to create without some proper organization. However, a side effect of this organization soon surfaced: What would happen if you had a single executable file that used data files laid out in a documented format, so you could easily replace the game's data files? Effectively, this enabled the creation of many games that were identical in their gameplay formula, but different in their content. You could do a scroller set in World War II and another one in outer space without touching a single line of the source code. This may seem naïve by today's standards, but try to imagine the revolution it meant for an industry where each game was an indivisible atom with code and data all mixed up. Being able to create different games by modifying the relevant data files was a transformation. Clearly, this was the way to go for the industry; and soon reusable data-driven game engines became ubiquitous because of their obvious economic advantage over hard-coded games.

In these early games, data files were nothing but memory dumps of the data structures, with little or no structure at all. Soon, developers began creating their own file formats, so no one could steal their artwork by looking into the files. Competition fosters innovation, so better systems were devised. At the same time, developers began thinking about more intelligent ways to organize their work using file systems. One of the best ideas they came up with was to use files not only for data, but also for some behavior information. Choreographed trajectories for a scrolling game's AI system could be stored this way. The choreographed AI that made most scrollers famous could be thought of not only as pure data in the form of waypoints, but also as behaviors. Behaviors can be programmed as patterns of movement that actually define the gameplay. Thus, the leap from data files to behavior systems was made. By redefining graphics, sound, and behaviors, game developers and players could quickly derive new games from old ones. Not only did this add flexibility to the development process, but it also enabled the player community to create vast collections of content. Users creating high-quality content were frequently offered jobs at the companies developing their favorite games.

Defining behaviors in the data files brought some changes to the internal game code. What was initially a totally hard-coded gaming system became a bit like an application loader and operating system, providing some internal functionality and interpreting the remainder from the data files. The internal functionality was publicized in an interface that content developers had to learn, and they then used it to implement subsequent games. Thus, game developers began to think not so much in terms of a specific game, but about generic game systems that played different games depending on the data files. The more flexible the engine was the better. Most companies kept their file formats well hidden, partly because of concerns over intellectual property and piracy.

A prototypical example of this first generation would be the Script Creation Utility for Maniac Mansion (SCUMM) system devised by LucasArts. It was a complete authoring system that helped define the game structure, dialogs, locations, and other data needed to implement many popular adventure games. It was first used in games such as *Maniac Mansion* and *Loom*, and was employed (under different versions) in most LucasArts adventures up to *Curse of Monkey Island.*

By the late 1980s/early 1990s, some engine standards began to surface, and their specs were made public, so users could create new missions and content, and thus lengthen the life of the game. The best-known example of this era is the incredibly popular *Doom* engine, introduced by id Software in 1993. After enjoying a first hit with *Wolfenstein*, *Doom* can be considered the game that defined the first-person shooter genre. Its maps and weapons are still venerated by today's standards, and many games have paid tribute to *Doom* in some form or another. Internally, *Doom* was a radical follower of the engine philosophy I have exposed. Both data and behaviors were implemented via external files, so the binary game file was really a level loader. In the case of *Doom*, all engine data was encapsulated in large files using the .wad extension, and were thus called WAD files.

A WAD file was just a collection of data for the game. Data was organized in large blocks; each containing a sequence of one type of information: the level geometry, monster placement, and so on. Each of these blocks was called a lump. Then, the complete WAD file was composed of three main parts:

➤ A 12-byte file header

➤ A directory containing the names, offsets, and sizes of all lumps in the WAD file

➤ One or more lumps with the actual data

The header consisted of a four-byte initialization string, which could be Internal WADs (IWADs) or Patch WADs (PWADs). An IWAD contained all data necessary to play the game, so all entries of the file were full. A PWAD, on the other hand, was just a patch to the core IWAD, so only some of the lumps were present. Logically, all user-created WADs were PWADs, which provided only the lumps required to define a level. Right after the header, four bytes were used to store the number of lumps in the WAD file, and the last four bytes stored a long integer that was the file offset to the beginning of the directory to make file traversal faster.

Then, the directory was just a list of entries; each taking 16 bytes. Here, the first four bytes stored the file offset to the start of the lump. Then, the middle four values stored the lump size in bytes. The last eight bytes were available to store the name of the lump, padded with zeros. To give you an estimate, there are about 2,000 entries in the directory of the main *Doom* WAD file. But only 10 types of lumps are needed to create a new level in a PWAD.

Now we are reaching the interesting part: the lump definition. We will focus on level creation because there are many other lumps that hold information such as menu texts and character sets. A *Doom* level needs several types of lumps. The most interesting are

- ➤ **Linedefs**. A list of two-dimensional line segments that have a meaning for the game engine. These lines are mainly used as walls to block characters, although they can also block sound propagation. Part of the geometry of the level is stored this way (remember that *Doom* was a 2D game internally!).

- ➤ **Sidedef**. A definition of which texture(s) to use with each linedef. This describes how the walls look.

- ➤ **Vertices**. Core vertices use linedefs. The linedefs indirectly refer to the two-dimensional vertices in this list instead of explicitly containing their own coordinates. This way, two adjacent linedefs can share the same vertex, saving memory and making editing easier.

- ➤ **Nodes**. A subdivision of the space according to a two-dimensional Binary Space Partition (BSP). A BSP is a data structure that can efficiently classify geometrical information, such as triangles on a game level.

- ➤ **Things**. A lump that contains positions for relevant items: weapons, poisons, keys, player starting positions, and so on. Thus, it greatly affects the gameplay.

Lumps can define both the contents of the level and gameplay elements as well (for example, the Things lump). This effectively meant that new games could be derived from the base *Doom* product quickly. In fact, *Hexen* is nothing but the *Doom* engine with a new set of data files and some minor additions to the WAD format (such as the capability of some potions to appear only for characters of some special class). *Doom* had a great influence on developers, who followed the trend and began providing complete documentation and even editing tools to encourage user-created modifications. In fact, the popular game *Half-Life* began as a modification to the game *Quake II*, which grew so much that a new, completely different game was born.

Today, the concept of a game engine has evolved a great deal since *Doom*. The core game code is kept to a minimum, providing only the reusable algorithms and functionality that is essential to the game. This includes all time-critical tasks such as the rendering pipeline, networking and audio APIs, and AI interfaces where external modules can be docked. Usually, part of the higher level AI is implemented through structures and scripts in external data files. Lower level, more time critical, and less variable parts of the AI are often implemented in the engine itself. Many games use a mixture of both approaches.

In addition, extensive toolsets are provided to create content for the game. Some products use their own content creation systems (CCS), whereas others have relied on heavily modified versions of off-the-shelf products.

Gmax (see Figure 1.4), for example, is a content creation system built on top of 3d max's core. It can be bundled with your game, so enthusiastic users will be able to create new game content. Coming from max's lineage, Gmax is fundamentally a modeling and texturing package, so it focuses on level creation, characters, and so on. Games such as Microsoft's *Flight Simulator* have included Gmax with their release. The end user gets the software for free (or included in the cost of the game), whereas the developer must have a licensing agreement with the tool manufacturer—discreet in the case of Gmax.

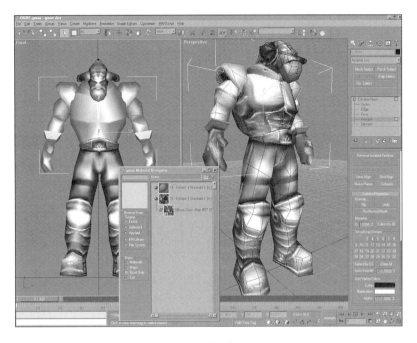

Figure 1.4   Gmax.

Maya hasn't stood still, either.

Maya Personal Edition has been successfully bundled with popular games such as *Unreal Tournament 2003*. In this case, the game developers created a set of plug-ins for Maya PE, so users can export their data sets made with Maya to *Unreal*'s own formats. Again, the software comes at no cost for the end user.

But there is more to game engine content creation tools than modelers. All commercial engines must come with full documentation because the level of complexity and flexibility has skyrocketed with each new iteration. Keep in mind that these engines are not only sold on an "as is" basis: Some developers will choose the advanced track and hard code new features into the core toolset. A typical example is *Half-Life*. Valve, the developers of the game, needed a skeletal animation system that was (at the time) significantly more involved than the key frame-based animation system provided by *Quake*. Thus, after purchasing the engine license, they had to rewrite the animation system from scratch to support the new feature.

Phase VI: The Handheld Revolution

The NES wasn't Nintendo's first electronic device. In the late 1970s, the company became well known for a family of low-cost, simple electronic games called *Game & Watch*. These were handheld devices about the size of a cassette tape, costing between $10 and $25, which came with a single game to play. *Donkey Kong* was introduced on such a platform in split-screen format. Games were just simple combinatorial systems displayed on low-cost LCD screens. But Game & Watch machines were sold by the millions and became extremely popular, especially among young audiences who could take them anywhere and share them with friends.

Interest in Game & Watch faded away as the domestic console market exploded. Such a handheld system could not compete with the color and sound found in the titles that appeared both on the NES and the Sega Master System. But in 1989, when everyone had long forgotten about the Game & Watch, Nintendo released a game console that would become its most profitable product ever: the Nintendo Gameboy. It was a handheld, black-and-white console that could play literally hundreds of games by replacing a cartridge, just like a regular home-based console.

The Gameboy was an instant hit, which can partly be explained by the inclusion of the *Tetris* game with the purchase of the console. The product was targeted at younger audiences, using the same strategy that made Game & Watch so popular in the past. Some Gameboy classics were *Pokemon* and a special version of *Super Mario Bros.* Internally, a Gameboy was inspired by the design of the original NES. It used an 8-bit CPU similar to the Intel 8080 or Zilog Z80 and was armed with 8KB of code RAM and an additional 8KB of video RAM. The CPU ran at approximately 4MHz. Screen resolution was 160×144 pixels (20×18 tiles) but, as with the NES, this was a window of an internal memory representation, which was 256×256 pixels (32×32 tiles) across. This allowed fast scrolling by only changing two registers, SCROLLX and SCROLLY, which defined the offset of the said background to the screen. The background was painted with tiles, which were taken from a tile data table. Thus, the screen (called the Background Tile Map) consisted of only 32 rows of 32 bytes each for a total selection of 256 tiles. Each position held the identifier of the tile to be drawn there.

The Gameboy supported one overlay level, so a menu or scoreboard could easily be drawn on top of the scrolling background. This was achieved with a window that was not scrollable but painted at a fixed onscreen position. Window contents were taken from the tile data table as well, so you could position the window onscreen easily with two registers, `WNDPOSX` and `WNDPOSY`.

As with the NES, a Gameboy could paint keyed sprites on top of the background for characters, enemies, and so on. It could use both 8×8 and 8×16 sprites, and up to 40 were available. As with the NES, only 10 sprites could be displayed per scanline due to a hardware limitation. Sprite patterns were taken from the sprite pattern table and layered on the screen according to some very unintuitive priority rules: Sprites closer to the left end of the screen would have priority, and thus be laid on top of others; if two sprites happened to share the same X coordinate, the one located in lower positions in the sprite table would have priority.

A Gameboy was a pretty powerful piece of hardware by 1989's standards. It was a mini-version of an NES in black and white, which made it cheaper to manufacture. But what set the Gameboy apart from the competition was its lengthy battery life and the vast array of quality games available for the platform. After all, creating titles for the Gameboy was a very profitable business. It was orders of magnitude cheaper than coding for home-based game consoles (especially since the PlayStation and N64 hit the market). But, on the other hand, the price of the games was not that different. In other words, there was a great margin both for the console manufacturer and the software developer.

Among all gaming platforms, the Gameboy has definitely been the console with the longest life cycle (11 years), and some games are still being sold today. The release of the Gameboy Color in 1998, along with new iterations of classic Nintendo titles, breathed new life into the product, making it break all established records. But even great products like the Gameboy grow old, and thus by the year 2000, Nintendo had already decided to release a newer, more powerful machine. The Gameboy Advance (GBA) was designed with the mission of becoming the substitute for the original Gameboy. The GBA specs are living proof of this philosophy. Powered by a 32-bit ARM CPU working at 16.7MHz, the GBA comes with 32KB of RAM, 96KB of VRAM for graphics, and 16KB of sound RAM. The RAM is built directly into the CPU for faster access. This memory can be further expanded with up to 256KB of RAM external to the CPU.

Graphically speaking, the console uses a 244×160 resolution, which is close to half of the resolution of a SuperNES and not very different from the resolution of an Apple][. It can perform tile-based backgrounds, including 4096 maximum sprites (256 of which can be layered on a single scanline). This huge number of sprites is especially useful for special effects such as particle systems, because the GBA supports (to an extent) alpha blending. Sprites can also be hardware scaled and rotated. Color depth is 32,768 colors and is selected from a palette of 16M.

In addition, cartridges can hold as much as 64MB of data, putting this console light years ahead of the initial Gameboy design. The result of this design is that many old-school classics such as *Mario* and *The Legend of Zelda* can easily be ported to the GBA, ensuring Nintendo a great lineup of games people already love to play. In the end, GBA's horsepower is not that different from a reduced-size SuperNES.

Phase VII: The Cellular Phenomenon

Surprisingly, competition for the GBA comes from an unexpected challenger. Which device is sold by the millions, has a low cost, and is also handheld? The cell phone, of course: There are just millions of them, and they keep getting better all the time. When looking for interesting trends, always keep an eye on those devices that have large installed bases. They have a clear potential of becoming "the next big thing." As an example, the ratio between the leading game console and the cell phone is, in most countries, around six to one: There are six cell phones for each game console.

First generation cell phones were big and heavy, and had nothing to do with handheld gaming. They were just pretty simple communications platforms, offering only limited messaging capabilities via Short Message Service (SMS) in some countries. But each new standard brought new features to the market in the typical fast evolution pattern that arises from fierce competition. With so many phone manufacturers and carriers, it is not surprising that cellular telephony and phone-based services have evolved at such speed. For some years, Nintendo could have benefited from the lack of open, world-wide standards in the phone gaming arena. European and American phones had traditionally worked with different systems, which prevented any gaming initiative from reaching the broad consumer base otherwise captured by handheld consoles.

But phones equipped with Java began to surface by the year 2000, and their hardware specs grew accordingly. Today, phones equipped with 64MB of RAM and the processing power of a 486 or Pentium CPU are not uncommon. And what can you do with such a device? You can play *Quake*, *Age of Empires*, and many other games. In fact, playing on a phone has a competitive advantage over the classic PC or console experience. The phone is at the core a communications device, so the path to connected, handheld games is clearly marked.

The first success story on mobile gaming platforms has to be NTT DoCoMo's I-Mode service, launched in Japan in 1999. It is a subscriber service where users pay monthly fees to access different types of mobile content, from small applications like a map service to downloadable games. Fees are small so the use is compulsive, and colorful handsets with large screens offer a relatively sophisticated delivery platform for mobile games. I-Mode was an immediate success, and by April 2002, the service had more than 32M subscribers (with more than 28,000 new users per day). The key to its success is great content, a meaningful business model where content is paid per download (as opposed to connected, per-minute charges), and very low barriers of entry for content developers. I-Mode is based on standards such as HTML and Java, so many companies jumped on the bandwagon from the beginning.

As an example of typical I-Mode content, take *Samurai Romanesque*, a medieval role-playing game (RPG) played on I-mode terminals. Using information from the Japanese weather service, the game is able to sense the current weather right where the user is standing. If it's raining, the gunpowder used by your character in the virtual world will get wet, and you won't be able to use any firearms. Cell phones have access to any online information and also know about the user's location. This is unique to the cell phone medium: No other gaming platform can offer such a rich gaming experience.

Phase VIII: Multiplayer Games

Multiplayer games have been around for longer than you might think. The first examples can be traced back to the early 1980s, with massive adoption starting with the arrival of the Internet and the World Wide Web by the mid 1990s. Multiplayer games can offer the same multimedia values of single-player games while introducing other human players into the mix. That makes them a greater challenge and, in many peoples' opinion, more rewarding to play. Several formulas have evolved through the years, from the squad-based gameplay that was already present in the Essex Multi-User Dungeon (MUD)—one of the first documented massively multiplayer games—to human opponents that can be traced back to games like EA's *Multiple User Labor Element* (M.U.L.E.) from 1983.

The reason why multiplayer games have been so successful is that playing with or against an artificial intelligence cannot be compared to a human opponent. Additionally, the social component of a single-player game is virtually nonexistent.

One of the first viable examples of a multiplayer game was the Essex MUD, which was developed by Richard Bartle and Roy Trubshaw of Essex University in 1979. The original game consisted of about 20 rooms described in prose. Up to 250 players could coexist in this game world, so they could "see" each other in the room. Descriptive texts would state facts like "Peter is here," for example. Players connected to the MUD server using the EPSS network, which connected six British universities; and from 1980, players connected to the MUD server using the ARPA network from the United States. Compared with a modern game, *Planetside* (by Sony) supports more than 3,500 players per server.

The Essex MUD was a great inspiration for many developers. In fact, a very active MUD scene existed during the 1980s and part of the 1990s. MUDs faded away as graphical multiplayer games such as *Everquest* appeared. But for more than 10 years, they ruled the multiplayer arena.

However, MUDs were not the only way to go. Simple competitive games with human opponents created bigger challenges for the player, thus becoming a viable playing experience. A good and early example is M.U.L.E. In M.U.L.E., up to four players competed to conquer a new planet in a way not very distant from today's real-time strategy games. But the success of the game was limited, mainly because network infrastructure circa 1983 was not very well suited for real-time play.

The turning point came around 1993, when the Internet and more specifically the World Wide Web phenomenon exploded. In less than six months, the World Wide Web evolved from zero to infinity, taking the whole planet by storm. As a side effect, connection speeds were greatly improved, from the very early 9600bps modems to somewhere around 56kbps, and from there to ISDN, DSL, and cable. This speed increase was extremely relevant because it allowed developers to transfer all state information from one computer to another while keeping the gameplay fluid. *Age of Empires*, for example, could be played on a 56kbps modem, and that included dozens of units fighting against each other.

Today, multiplayer games have stabilized around two "orbits," which are direct descendants of MUDs and games like M.U.L.E. On one hand, MUDs gave way to graphical RPGs like *Ultima Online* and from there to *Everquest, Asheron's Call*, and many others.

These games are all about immersion and socially interacting with a rich game world. Thousands of people actually live their lives inside each one of these games in a 24-hour alternate reality. In fact, these games are probably the most addictive of them all, with extreme cases counting for more than 1,600 hours of gameplay per year (that's more than four hours a day, even on Sundays). As a very intriguing side effect of the *Ultima/Everquest* phenomenon, real virtual economies have been created. Some fans have sold their properties or characters on auction web sites, often for respectable sums of money. This type of behavior should definitely make us think about the influence of the gaming scene on people's lives.

On the other end of the spectrum, reduced-scale multiplayer games have been successful as well. Here, a distinction has to be made between *competitive* and *cooperative* multiplayer titles. The difference is in the role of other players: Will they be enemies you must defeat, or will they be your teammates on a global mission? A title that clearly shows these two categories is the incredibly popular *Counterstrike*, which is actually a modification to the original *Half-Life* game. In *Counterstrike*, two teams fight each other, so there's competitive gameplay on opposite sides, and cooperative gameplay between members of the same side.

The future looks bright for multiplayer games. Network infrastructure keeps growing, and today most users already have broadband support that allows better interaction. Several middleware companies have emerged in recent years, enabling bigger and better games. Additionally, gameplay innovations are constantly introduced. Some people predict that multiplayer games will eventually engulf all other gaming experiences, so single-player games will just disappear. Although that's probably an overstatement, it clearly shows the level of expectations the industry has put in multiplayer gaming. But remember solo and team sports peacefully coexist in the real world, so there's really no need for single-player games to disappear in favor of multiplayer experiences.

In Closing

The games industry is undergoing a huge transformation. The advent of the PlayStation 2 and Microsoft's Xbox has opened new areas that were unavailable on less powerful devices. A truly cinematic gaming experience seems only years, not decades, away. The evolution is so fast that future consoles will no longer be limited to playing games but will incorporate other features as well. They will offer video-on-demand, online capabilities, and e-commerce integrated into a simple, cost-effective, and easy-to-use solution. The game console will evolve into a completely integrated, general-purpose home entertainment device.

On the other hand, the handheld business is still exploding. There are three contenders (cell phones, palm computers, and handheld consoles), and it now seems clear that they will have to merge and integrate to offer a unified, personal electronics device. After all, consumers don't want to carry three devices in their pockets when their functionality is really not that different. Will one of the three dominate and win the battle, or will new devices surface and take the market by storm? Although the latter seems unlikely, the unexpected awaits where no one is watching.

The ultimate decision will be in the hands of the consumers as to which gaming platforms will succeed. In the last 30 years, we have seen many products flop simply because people didn't embrace them. Other products that did not look very promising became serious hits when consumers accepted and supported them.

To get a glimpse of what the future might bring for the game industry, we need to extract valuable lessons from our past, understanding what made some gaming platforms successful in the first place. The ability to convey a rich, engaging game world is fundamental. Thus, presentation values and the multimedia experience will likely continue to grow for years to come. Excellent gameplay is even more important than sharp graphics and sound. Many games (such as *Tetris*) have triumphed with little presentation values but good gameplay. But no game has ever become a big success if it simply wasn't fun or engaging.

In addition, the ability to break boundaries between the real and the virtual, and between users and developers, is becoming increasingly relevant. From user-created content to games that stream data from the real world, integrating the user more tightly into the game experience is certainly a trend to keep an eye on.

But wait, did we need 20 years to learn this? Wasn't this what the movie *Tron* was all about?

Chapter 2

Game Architecture

"It is a mistake to think you can solve any major problems just with potatoes."

Douglas Adams

In the previous chapter, we explored the evolution of game programming techniques. It is now time to move on and focus on how games are built today. We will begin our journey with a study of games as real-time software applications, and then analyze the internals of a general-purpose game, so the main building blocks of the source code can be identified. These blocks will then be refined in subsequent chapters of the book. Additionally, we will focus on some project management concepts that are specific to game development. We will study the different phases in developing a game, from code planning and scheduling to testing and maintenance. Put together, all these points should help you understand how games are built.

Real-Time Software

Video games are software applications. Specifically, they belong to a class called real-time software applications. This is an important classification because it will help us understand how they behave and why many coding decisions are made. For those unfamiliar with these concepts, I will stop and briefly explain their characteristics.

In a formal definition, real-time software means computer applications that have a time-critical nature or, more generally, applications in which data acquisition and response must be performed under time-constrained conditions. Consider, for example, a computer program that displays information about arrivals on a large screen in an airport terminal; several lines of text display information about flight numbers, status, time of landing, and so on. Clearly, the software responds to timely events—an airplane lands, delays are announced, and so on. The arrival of these bits of information is highly unpredictable, and the application must process and respond to them accordingly. Moreover, this time-dependent information must then be displayed on a screen to provide a visual presentation of the time-dependent data. This is what real-time software is all about.

Now, consider a slightly more involved example—a software application designed to aid in air traffic control (see Figure 2.1). The application senses space with a radar, displays information about planes and their trajectories on a screen, and enables ground personnel to assist pilots in reaching their destination in a timely and safe manner by sending messages to them. Looking at the internals of the system, you will see that it consists of:

> ➤ A data acquisition module—in this case, coupled with physical radar

> ➤ A display/computation module, which helps ground personnel visualize data

> ➤ An interaction module to send signals to planes so they know what to do

Here we are moving one step further from our previous example. We are watching a real-time, interactive application, an application that responds to events that arrive at any point in time, displays information related to those events, and allows the operator to interact with them. Games are not very different from this architecture. Imagine that we eliminate the radar, generate "virtual" air traffic using a software simulator, and tell the user he must make planes land safely. Add a scoreboard to that and a game over screen, and it begins to sound familiar.

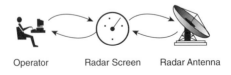

Operator   Radar Screen   Radar Antenna

Figure 2.1   Air traffic controller.

All games are indeed interactive, real-time applications. The operator (henceforth called the player) can communicate with the game world, which itself simulates real-time activity using software components. An enemy chasing us, elevators going up and down, and returning fire are all examples of the kind of "virtual" real time found in games. But there is more time to games than you might think. Games are also time constrained; they must display information at a set pace (usually above 25 frames per second) to allow interaction to become seamless. This certainly limits the scope of both the real-time simulators and the presentation layer found in games. We cannot do more than what the hardware allows in the given time slice. However, games are a bit like magic. The trick is to make the impossible seem possible, crafting worlds that seem larger than what the hardware allows through multimedia presentations well beyond the player's expectations.

As a summary, games are time-dependent interactive applications, consisting of a virtual world simulator that feeds real-time data, a presentation module that displays it, and control mechanisms that allow the player to interact with that world.

Because the interaction rate is fast, there is a limit to what can be simulated. But game programming is about trying to defy that limit and creating something beyond the platform's capabilities both in terms of presentation and simulation. This is the key to game programming and is the subject of this book.

Part I, "Gameplay Programming," deals with the coding of the real-time simulator that implements the game world. Part II, "Engine Programming," covers the presentation layer.

Real-Time Loops

As mentioned earlier, all real-time interactive applications consist of three tasks running concurrently. First, the state of the world must be constantly recomputed (the radar senses space in the airplane example or the virtual world simulator is updated in a game). Second, the operator must be allowed to interact with it. Third, the resulting state must be presented to the player, using onscreen data, audio, and any other output device available. In a game, both the world simulation and the player input can be considered tasks belonging to the same global behavior, which is "updating" the world. In the end, the player is nothing but a special-case game world entity. For the sake of simplicity, I will follow this rule and will thus refer to games as applications consisting of two portions: an update and a render routine.

As soon as we try to lay down these two routines in actual game code, problems begin to appear. How can we ensure that both run simultaneously, giving the actual illusion of peeking into the real world through a window? In an ideal world, both the update and render routines would run in an infinitely powerful device consisting of many parallel processors, so both routines would have unlimited access to the hardware's resources. But real-world technology imposes many limitations: Most computers generally consist of only one processor with limited memory and speed. Clearly, the processor can only be running one of the two tasks at any given time, so some clever planning is needed.

A first approach would be to implement both routines in a loop (as shown in Figure 2.2), so each update is followed by a render call, and so forth. This ensures that both routines are given equal importance. Logic and presentation are considered to be fully coupled with this approach. But what happens if the frames-per-second rate varies due to any subtle change in the level of complexity? Imagine a 10 percent variation in the scene complexity that causes the engine to slow down a bit. Obviously, the number of logic cycles would also vary accordingly. Even worse, what happens in a PC game where faster machines can outperform older machines by a factor of five? Will the AI run slower on these less powerful machines? Clearly, using a coupled approach raises some interesting questions about how the game will be affected by performance variations.

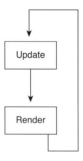

Figure 2.2   Coupled approach.

To solve these problems, we must analyze the nature of each of the two code components. Generally speaking, the render part must be executed as often as the hardware platform allows; a newer, faster computer should provide smoother animation, better frame rates, and so on. But the pacing of the world should not be affected by this speed boost. Characters must still walk at the speed the game was designed for or the gameplay will be destroyed. Imagine that you purchase a football game, and the action is either too fast or too slow due to the hardware speed. Clearly, having the render and update sections in sync makes coding complex, because one of them (update) has an inherent fixed frequency and the other does not.

One solution to this problem would be to still keep update and render in sync but vary the granularity of the update routine according to the elapsed time between successive calls. We would compute the elapsed time (in real-time units), so the update portion uses that information to scale the pacing of events, and thus ensure they take place at the right speed regardless of the hardware. Clearly, update and render would be in a loop, but the granularity of the update portion would depend on the hardware speed— the faster the hardware, the finer the computation within each update call. Although this can be a valid solution in some specific cases, it is generally worthless. As speed and frames-per-second increase, it makes no sense to increase the rate at which the world is updated. Does the character AI really need to think 50 times per second? Decision making is a complex process, and executing it more than is strictly needed is throwing away precious clock cycles.

A different solution to the synchronization problem would be to use a twin-threaded approach (depicted in Figure 2.3) so one thread executes the rendering portion while the other takes care of the world updating. By controlling the frequency at which each routine is called, we can ensure that the rendering portion gets as many calls as possible while keeping a constant, hardware-independent resolution in the world update. Executing the AI between 10 and 25 times per second is more than enough for most games.

Imagine an action game running at 60 fps, with the AI running in a secondary thread at 15 fps. Clearly, only one of every four frames will carry out an AI update. Although this is good practice to ensure fixed-speed logic, it has some downsides that must be carefully addressed. For example, how do we ensure that the four frames that share the same AI cycle are effectively different, showing smoother animation and graphics?

More frames means nothing if all the frames in an AI cycle look exactly the same; animation will effectively run at 15 fps. To solve this problem, AIs are broken down into two sections. The real AI code is executed using a fixed time step, whereas simpler routines such as animation interpolators and trajectory update routines are handled on a per-frame basis. This way those extra frames per second will really make a difference in the player's experience.

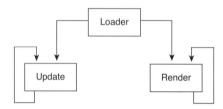

Figure 2.3   Twin-threaded approach.

But the threaded approach has some more serious issues to deal with. Basically, the idea is very good but does not implement well on some hardware platforms. Some single-CPU machines are not really that good at handling threads, especially when very precise timing functions are in place. Variations in frequency occur, and the player experience is degraded. The problem lies not so much in the function call overhead incurred when creating the threads, but in the operating system's timing functions, which are not very precise. Thus, we must find a workaround that allows us to simulate threads on single-CPU machines.

The most popular alternative for those platforms that do not support a solid concurrency mechanism is to implement threads using regular software loops and timers in a single-threaded program. The key idea is to execute update and render calls sequentially, skipping update calls to keep a fixed call rate. We decouple the render from the update routine. Render is called as often as possible, whereas update is synchronized with time.

To achieve this result, we must begin by storing a time stamp for each call performed in the update call. Then, in subsequent loop iterations, we must compute the elapsed time since the last call (using the time stamp) and compare it with the inverse of the desired frequency. By doing so, we are testing whether we need to make an update call to keep the right call frequency. For example, if you want to run the AI 20 times per second, you must call the update routine every 50 milliseconds. Then, all you have to do is store the time at which you perform each call to update, and only execute it if 50 milliseconds have elapsed since then. This is a very popular mechanism because many times it offers better control than threads and simpler programming. You don't have to worry about shared memory, synchronization, and so on. In practical terms, it's a poor man's thread approach, as shown in Figure 2.4

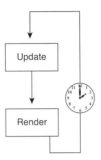

Figure 2.4   Single-thread fully decoupled.

Here is the source code in C for such an approach:

```
long timelastcall=timeGetTime();
while (!end)
    {
    if ((timeGetTime()-timelastcall)>1000/frequency)
        {
        game_logic();
        timelastcall=timeGetTime();
        }
    presentation();
    }
```

Notice how we are using the timeGetTime() call from the Win32 API as our timer. This call returns the time (in milliseconds) elapsed since Windows was last booted. Thus, subtracting the result of two timeGetTime() calls we can measure the period of time between them down to one millisecond of accuracy.

Now, the above code partially addresses our concerns and is a good starting point. Still, it is a bit far away from a professional game loop: We are assuming the logic tick takes 0 time to complete, we are not handling Alt-Tab scenarios, and so on. For completeness, I will now supply a professional-grade game loop. The ideas are basically the same, taken one step further to offer better, finer control. Here is the source code:

```
time0 = getTickCount();
while (!bGameDone)
    {
    time1 = getTickCount();
    frameTime = 0;
    int numLoops = 0;

    while ((time1 - time0) > TICK_TIME && numLoops < MAX_LOOPS)
        {
        GameTickRun();
        time0 += TICK_TIME;
        frameTime += TICK_TIME;
        numLoops++;
        }
    IndependentTickRun(frameTime);

    // If playing solo and game logic takes way too long, discard
    // pending time.
    if (!bNetworkGame && (time1 - time0) > TICK_TIME)
        time0 = time1 - TICK_TIME;
    if (canRender)
        {
        // Account for numLoops overflow causing percent > 1.
        float percentWithinTick = Min(1.f, float(time1 -
time0)/TICK_TIME);
        GameDrawWithInterpolation(percentWithinTick);
        }
    }
```

Now, let's go step by step. The loop has two components: The first (the while controlling the access to GameTickRun) takes care of game logic, while the second (the if controlling access to GameDrawWithInterpolation) is the render portion.

In the game logic portion, we control if the elapsed time since the last logic call has surpassed a `TICK_TIME` (in milliseconds). If you want your AI code to be computed 20 times per second, the `TICK_TIME` is 50. Then, we put this inside a `while` clause because we might want to run several game logic ticks at once, especially if there was a pause, disk swapping slowed the application down, and so on. Notice we incorporate the `TICK_TIME` into the new timing of `time0`. Then, `IndependentTickRun` is called to handle player input, perform general housekeeping, and so on. These routines are rarely time-critical, so they don't need to use precise timing functions.

Finally, we reach the render stage. Notice we begin by computing the percentage of the current tick we have covered. That's stored in `percentWithinTick`. That's interesting, as it allows us to trigger the render call with this factor, which will perform fine interpolation so not all the frames in a given tick look alike.

Let's now move one layer below our initial macro level analysis and explore the components of both the game logic and presentation sections. By doing so, I will present a global game framework that will help you understand which software pieces must be used to make a game, along with their internal relationships.

The Game Logic Section

This first macro block takes care of keeping the world simulator running. For the purpose of our global framework, we will divide it into three main blocks: updating the player, updating the world, and updating the nonplaying characters (NPCs).

Player Update

A game must execute a routine that keeps an updated snapshot of the player state. As a first step in the routine, interaction requests by the player must be checked for. This is achieved differently for many control mechanisms such as joysticks, keyboards, and mice. But the end result is the same—a series of numbers that can be understood by the game code that indicate the state of the player control. It is a good idea to use abstract device controllers so the game code does not actually interact with the physical controller. An abstract device controller handles joysticks and keyboards but uses a common interface so the calling application does not need to. We will talk about input processing and device abstraction in Chapter 5, "User Input."

We will not directly map control decisions to the player's actions because there are some items that can restrict the player's range of actions. He might indicate that he wants to move forward, but a wall may be blocking his path. Thus, a second routine must be designed that implements restrictions to player interaction. These restrictions can be geometric in nature, as in the previous example, or more complex, logic-based combinations. For example, the player can be pressing the "open door" control but because he is not holding the right key, the door won't open. Remember that we are talking about general principles here, which will be applicable to any game you need to code. Thus, we will dub this routine the "player restrictions" handler. A significant part of this routine will be devoted to collision detection, which is discussed in Chapter 21, "Procedural Techniques."

Once we have sensed the player's controller and checked for restrictions, a small update routine must be implemented so players see the result of their interaction; and game state is recomputed. Let's look at two examples to better understand the internals of these three components.

Imagine a game such as Nintendo's classic *The Legend of Zelda*. The three routines mentioned earlier would have the following responsibilities:

1. The "player input" module would effectively read the game controller using specific calls, and then convert the raw data to game world data that makes sense. For example, data such as "left was pushed and button A was active as well" should translate into "request to move the character left while using the currently active weapon."

2. The "player restrictions" routine would access the game world structure because we need to know which level the player is in and what surrounds him or her. This way we can compute both geometrical restrictions, also known as collision detection, and logical restrictions, which basically deal with states the player must be in to be able to perform certain interactions. This second routine is usually the hardest of the three, especially as game complexity increases.

3. The "player update" routine would map the restrictions to the interactions and generate the right world-level responses. If the player was pressing left and there is no obstacle in that direction, we must trigger the moving animation and update his position, and so on.

Some games, such as *Tetris*, do not have a clear onscreen avatar, but still these rules apply. As a rule of thumb, consider your onscreen character as anything you can interact with by pressing the controls. In *Tetris*, clearly, that refers to the bricks falling from the top of the screen. They are not a character in the strict sense of the word, but the principle is the same. We would check for player input in the first stage; in the second stage, we would test brick restrictions; and then we would execute player update to game state current. Restrictions are very easy to determine: Bricks cannot move outside the screen area, cannot fall below ground level, and cannot keep falling if the current brick is directly above any other previously fallen brick. In the player update segment, we simply move or rotate the brick according to the player's input and add a default behavior to the equation, which is that the bricks keep falling regardless of what the player does. This kind of idle, noninteractive behavior is very common in games in which you want to implement a sense of urgency and speed. Some arcades limit the time of your game (except if you find special "extended play" tokens), which is essentially the same formula in a different context.

World Update

The notion of a living game world that displays an active behavior has been present ever since the first games, such as *Pong* and *Space Invaders*. In addition to the player's action, the world keeps its own agenda, showing activity that is generally what the user responds to. For example, the user tries to avoid an incoming rock in *Asteroids*, attempts to return the ball in *Arkanoid*, and so on. Game world updates effectively implement gameplay and make games fun. It is not surprising then that this portion of the game code is especially important and, in modern-day games, complex.

To begin with, a distinction must be made into two broad game world entities. On the one hand, we have passive entities, such as walls and most scenario items. To provide a more formal definition, these are items that belong to the game world but do not have an attached behavior. These items play a key role in the player restriction section, but are not very important for the sake of world updating. In some games with large game worlds, the world update routines preselect a subsection of the game world, so the player restriction portion can focus on those elements, and thus become more efficient. Think of something like a graphics adventure. Somehow, we must store a pointer to the room the player is in, so we check the colliders in that room only.

But the majority of time in the world update section is spent checking the other type of entities, those that have an embedded behavior. From decorative elements such as flying birds to enemies or doors that open and close, these are the items that must be checked to keep a consistent, meaningful playing experience. Some games will divide active elements into simple logical items—such as doors, elevators, or moving platforms— and real enemies with a distinctive behavior. Here the differentiation comes from the complexity of the coding. The logical elements can be solved in a few lines of code, whereas real enemies require artificial intelligence with a higher complexity and computational cost.

In our generic game framework, we will assume there is a large number of these active elements, both logic and AI. So, the process of updating them will consist of four steps. First, a filter will select those elements that are relevant to the gameplay. An enemy 10 miles away from the player does not seem like a very important item from the player's standpoint, nor is a gate placed in a different game level altogether. This filter must not rule out anything. Some games (like real-time strategy titles, for example) will still need to compute the behavior of all entities. But many times level-of-detail (LOD) techniques will be used for distant items, so having them sorted by relevance is always desirable.

Second, the state of the active element must be updated. Here the distinction between logical and intelligent entities will be made obvious. The latter will require a more involved process to update their state.

Generally, within the overall game framework, AI systems will follow a four-step process too. First, goals and current state must be analyzed. For a flight simulator, this means obtaining the position and heading, state of the weapons systems, and sustained damage for both the AI-controlled and the player-controlled planes. The goal in this case is pretty straightforward: Shoot down the player. Second, restrictions must be sensed. This involves both the logical and geometrical restrictions we already sensed for the player. For our flight simulator example, the main restriction is avoiding a collision with the player and keeping an eye on the ground, so we do not crash into a nearby hill. After these two steps, we know everything about our state as AI entities, the player's state, the goal to achieve, and the overall restrictions that apply.

Returning to the overall framework, the third step requires that a decision/plan making engine must be implemented that effectively generates behavior rules. The plane will make a turn, then try to shoot, and so on. Some games implement instantaneous plans, which are recomputed each frame. Take the case of a very simple moving mine that chases the player around. For each frame, it must generate the optimal trajectory to finally blow the player up. But most plan-making routines generate tactics that persist for many clock cycles. A flight simulator might make decisions that span several seconds or even minutes of gameplay, and subsequent AI cycles focus only on refining the plan to adapt to changing conditions.

Fourth, we need to update the world state accordingly. We must store data, such as if the enemy moved, or eliminate it from the data structure if it was shot down by the player. As you will see when we study AI in detail, this four-step process blends extraordinarily well with most game AIs.

That completes the game logic framework. As a summary of the structure that was just exposed, here is the pseudocode for the approach:

```
Player update
    Sense Player input
    Compute restrictions
    Update player state
World update
    Passive elements
        Pre-select active zone for engine use
    Logic-based elements
        Sort according to relevance
        Execute control mechanism
        Update state
    AI based elements
        Sort according to relevance
        Sense internal state and goals
        Sense restrictions
        Decision engine
        Update world
End
```

The Presentation Section

Games would be dull and boring without multimedia programming. As human beings, we are very sensitive to animation, sound, and all the technical features that make a game attractive. Thus, coding a good game certainly involves being very careful with its presentation. You could argue that some really good games can be crafted with little or no presentation values, and you would be right. A game such as *Tetris* does not need much in terms of the audio-visual experience. But it is dangerous to generalize this as a rule. The vast majority of games require a carefully designed multimedia wrapper for the gameplay to become engaging and immersing. We need to see starships and asteroids to get the feeling of space flight, and we need carefully designed ambient sounds to really believe we are in a scary scenario.

The presentation layer helps convey one of the key features of good games—the capability to provoke the willing suspension of disbelief. This happens when good movies, books, and games mentally immerse us in the scenario in which they take place. Take a good movie, for example. In the first 10 minutes, the viewer forgets about the real world. The viewer's job, problems, duties, and so on are simply gone, as he or she gives in to the magic of the narrative. The viewer spends the next hour or two immersed in the story. In fact, the viewer does not feel like he or she is in a movie theatre at all. It feels like he or she is chasing the bad guy, solving the mystery, and so on. That is what willing suspension of disbelief is all about.

Some movies try to tell compelling stories with minimum presentation values. The Dogma movement serves as a good example. Although this trend will undoubtedly emerge in video games as well, and many good games will be created, presentation will still be important for both Dogma and non-Dogma games. Dogma games do not trust the competence of human actors but instead need to resort to synthetic storytelling, which is rooted in technology. Because games are far more technology driven than movies, presentation is still necessary, even for a simple game.

On the other hand, let's not forget that the vast majority of games are produced for the masses, and in this context, presentation is essential. In addition to better gameplay, consumers request better graphics, more and better sound, and production values in a constant progression. It's a catch-22 situation that arises from the constant improvement of computer hardware. So, even in those games where game logic is top priority, you had better keep an eye on the presentation values to ensure that you reach a broad customer base.

Let's now explore the constituent parts of any multimedia pipeline. The focus will be given to graphics and sound as the two main factors in providing a top multimedia experience. Our generic pipeline will be similar to the one used for game logic and be divided into rendering the game world, rendering nonplayable characters, and rendering the player. Keep in mind that this is just a framework to illustrate the constituent parts and does not imply any order of execution. For implementation purposes, elements can be rendered in a different order.

World Rendering

The first step is to render, visually and sonically, the game world. Here we will focus on the passive elements of the world, such as walls and grounds, as well as the simple, logic-based devices such as opening doors. The line will be drawn between objects requiring little or no animation, which will be handled here, and fully animated objects, which will need a different processing scheme altogether.

Rendering complete game worlds in real-time is almost impossible except for simple games like *Tetris*. For any involved title, some filtering must be applied prior to the main render call to decide what should be taken into consideration and what shouldn't. For example, very distant or invisible zones of the world can probably be culled away because they provide little or no information to the player and would just decrease the frame rate due to the added complexity. So, any world-rendering pipeline will more or less consist of two parts: selecting the relevant subset and taking care of the actual rendering.

For the graphics pipeline, the selection routine is implemented via clipping, culling, and computing occlusions, so the resulting representation is just the visible part of the game world from the player's viewpoint. This way we can focus on drawing what actually matters to the player. These routines are the core of any modern-day graphics pipeline and will be analyzed in full in Chapter 12, "3D Pipeline Overview," Chapter 13, "Indoors Rendering," and Chapter 14, "Outdoors Algorithms." An optional, auxiliary process is sometimes applied to the visible data, which computes the relevance of the data and chooses a suitable level of detail to render it. A tree that is seen 500 meters away probably doesn't need 10,000 triangles because each triangle would occupy a tiny fraction of a single pixel. Thus, a low resolution, more efficient representation can be used instead without the detrimental effect on performance.

Now that world geometry has been reduced to the visible part and assigned a suitable level of detail, it is time to actually paint it onscreen. This is achieved in a two-step process. First, geometry is stored in an efficient format in a step usually called *geometry packing*. Second, this packed geometry is sent to the hardware, where it is processed. Graphics hardware is extremely sensitive to packing methods; performance increases tenfold just by selecting the optimal delivery mechanism. We will explore packing and rendering in Chapter 12, "3D Pipeline Overview." If you need API-specific rendering information, Appendix B, "OpenGL," and Appendix C, "Direct3D," should provide you with the information you need.

Audio rendering works in a slightly different way than graphics. We can't just filter what is visible and what is not. An enemy behind you might not be visible, but his footsteps are still audible. However, filtering is also applied, generally by using some distance versus volume metric. Attenuation can be computed in order to know which sound sources are effectively audible to the player. Once these sources are identified, we can focus on sending the audio files to the sound card.

NPC Rendering

Rendering NPCs is quite different from rendering inanimate geometry. They need a specific pipeline due to their animation properties. However, we can still begin by filtering the character lists, so only characters close to the player and affecting him are processed. Again, a visibility step is pretty common. Only characters that survive a clipping and occlusion test will be moved on to the pipeline. This is especially important for fully animated characters. Working with dynamic, animated geometry is more expensive than static, passive elements, and thus must be applied only when needed. Optionally, some games will use an LOD pass to create a simplified representation of characters located in view but far away from the viewer.

Then, the main animation routine must be computed. There are a host of variations, from keyframed to skeletal animations and so on. All of them will be covered in Chapter 15, "Character Animation." But the end result for all of them is the same: static geometry data that represents the current snapshot of how the character must look for a given frame.

At this point, a character has been simplified by a static geometry representation, which can be processed as if it were regular world geometry. It must be packed using an efficient representation and sent to the hardware for display. Notice that, for their internals, some animation methods will require specific rendering algorithms, so characters will need to be rendered separately from passive world geometry.

The Player

The main player is nothing but a very special-case NPC. But its rendering pipeline is simpler than those of secondary characters for two very simple reasons. First, the player is generally visible, so there is no need to allocate time to check him for visibility. After all, he's supposed to be the hero, so it makes no sense for him to remain hidden. Second, there is no need for LOD processing as well. Most games display players in a central role, so they will always use high-resolution meshes.

Thus, the main player will only undergo an animation step, packing, and a render step. The animation will sometimes be of higher quality than that of enemies because the player is in a central role and more details are needed. But there isn't much difference between a player and an NPC.

Our framework for presentation has thus been introduced. It is a very involved process that you should review until it is fully understood, so let's recap for a second, using the following pseudocode:

```
World presentation
   Select visible subset (graphics)
      Clip
      Cull
      Occlude
   Select resolution
   Pack geometry
```

```
      Render world geometry
      Select audible sound sources (sound)
          Pack audio data
          Send to audio hardware
NPC presentation
      Select visible subset
      Animate
      Pack
      Render NPC data
Player presentation
      Animate
      Pack
      Render
```

As a global reminder, use the pseudocode listing at the end of the "World Update" section to review the complete framework. It is a long sequence of operations, but should cover most games on the market. In fact, I recommend that you take some time and decompose one or two commercial games into their constituent parts using the framework. Time spent doing this will be priceless when we start analyzing each of the individual segments. Notice how the following pseudocode can also act as an index to the contents in this book. Pointers to relevant chapters are given for each section, so you know where to look for additional information.

```
Game logic
    Player update
        Sense Player input        (chapter 5)
        Compute restrictions      (chapter 22)
        Update player state
    World update                  (chapters 6 to 9)
        Passive elements          (chapter 4, spatial index)
            Pre-select active zone for engine use
        Logic-based elements
            Sort according to relevance
            Execute control mechanism
            Update state
        AI based elements
            Sort according to relevance
            Sense internal state and goals
```

```
                    Sense restrictions
                    Decision engine
                    Update world
    End

    Presentation
        World presentation          (chapters 11 to 14, 17 to 21)
            Select visible subset   (graphics)
                Clip
                Cull
                Occlude
            Select resolution
            Pack geometry
            Render world geometry
            Select audible sound sources (sound)
            Pack audio data
            Send to audio hardware
        NPC presentation            (chapter 15)
            Select visible subset
            Animate
            Pack
            Render NPC data
        Player presentation (chapter 15)
            Animate
            Pack
            Render
    End
```

Caveat: Networked Games

The previous models do a really good job at depicting most single-player games. But networked titles need to impose some minor changes to the model so they can fit into it. These changes fundamentally affect the game logic section and, specifically, the player control and NPC sections. Just remember that, from another player's standpoint, your character is really just an NPC whose position is updated by another machine through a network connection. Generally, two changes are all that is needed to edit the model.

The player update section must change to make sure every player update is followed by a broadcast message that sends the newly computed position to other gamers through the network. The players receiving the information from the network will then use it to update a special breed of NPCs that actually do represent other game players. Thus, the second change affects the core of the AI system. Networked games can still have AIs for automatic monsters and so on, but a special type of AI must be reserved to represent these other players. This special-case AI module receives data from the communications channel and reflects it to the local gaming environment.

With these two changes in mind, a networked game is not that different from a regular, single-player title. All it takes is a bit of practice to understand that we are the player on a computer screen, but other users just see us as a very particular kind of NPC. We will cover NPCs in depth in Chapter 10, "Network Programming."

The Programming Process

We have examined the building blocks of any game project in some detail, including their potential risks and pitfalls. To complete this overview, we will now focus on today's production techniques and how programming must be planned to ensure timely and complete delivery. Any modern game requires hundreds or thousands of source files, totalling several hundred thousand lines of code. Such a huge data set, coupled with today's budgets and production cycles, makes game programming a very complex task that must be addressed methodically.

Stages

All game projects consist of three basic stages, although some studios consider more by subdividing the base three: preproduction, production, and maintenance (see Figure 2.5). In the first stage, the concept of the game is agreed upon, and different technologies and solutions are tested until a final configuration is reached. It is a highly experimental phase. Gameplay formulae are tested, technologies are evaluated, and some early concept art for the game environments is created. Ideally, preproduction is the only phase where a game company should be allowed to experiment, because subsequent phases must focus on the industrial process of making the game. The result of this first phase is a working prototype of the game—the more similar to the end product, the better. This prototype must be built in order to help establish workflows, test the content and technology production pipelines, and so on. It must also allow the developer to build an accurate picture of the road ahead: budget, milestones, team structure, and so on. In some cases, this demo will also be used to showcase the potential of the game to customers and publishers. The role of preproduction is, then, to analyze alternatives and finally create a detailed plan. Once preproduction is complete, most questions should have been answered because production is really a labor-intensive process. The game design should be final, a gameplay prototype must be working, and some test art should be in place. The trend today is to emphasize the importance of good preproduction as a way to minimize risks in subsequent phases of the development process. With multimillion-dollar budgets, games have become large productions, and the failure of one project due to bad management can cause serious trouble to both the developer and, more importantly, the publisher.

Figure 2.5   Stages of development.

Not surprisingly, one of the key items to study during preproduction is the technology that will be used in creating the game. If the game is created on top of a licensable engine, it should be chosen during preproduction. If, on the other hand, the team is going to create new technology from scratch, a working prototype must be crafted during this phase. From a publisher's/investor's standpoint, technology is always seen as a potential risk. Many games have sold badly (or have never even reached store shelves) due to inappropriate technology choices, so it's a good idea to take care of it as soon as possible to ensure that the game is, to an extent, free of technology risks.

Once preproduction is complete, and funding is secured for the game (either internally or by selling the prototype to a publisher), production begins. This is the longest part of the process and usually takes between one and three years to complete. It is a labor-intensive period in which the game takes shape following the planning that has been laid out during preproduction. Art assets are created in a factory-like fashion, game levels are crafted, and so on. The technology prototype built during preproduction will also mutate to implement all the final features the game needs. Technology prototypes usually focus more on showcasing the key elements of the gameplay, whereas the presentation layer is kept in a very early and crude form. Thus, production is usually where all the eye candy is put in place, and games show their full technological complexity.

Because it is a long process, production is often divided into milestones (both monthly and trimonthly), which mark key moments in the development. These milestones are used to make sure the game development advances at the desired speed and also to show the publisher the rate of progress. The latest build of the game is shown, small corrections on the initial design are made, and so forth. At the end of this iterative process, a final version of the game must be delivered to the publisher for testing and quality assurance. This process ensures that the game is virtually bug-free and also reaches the desired quality standard. In the case of console games, this process is a bit more complex than for a PC title because we need approval not only from the publisher, but also from the console manufacturer who must make sure the game is suitable (both in terms of content and quality) for the target platform. Remember the good old Atari days when lots of poor-quality games remained unsold, causing the console market to crash? Console manufacturers have learned their lesson, and they try to make sure they keep a consistent rate of good games to keep their platform value high.

After this testing process, which usually takes between one and three months, the final version of the game is created. This version, often called the *Gold Master*, is then sent for replication, put in nice boxes, and sent to stores. Because all the physical materials (that is, boxes, manuals, cover art, and so on) are created by a separate team during the testing phase, this final step takes a remarkably short time. Once the Gold Master is agreed upon, it takes about two weeks before games are available in stores.

The final step is the maintenance of the game. Games have a relatively short shelf life except for massively networked games on persistent game worlds. But support must be provided: patches, editing tools for the fan community, and additional missions. Games that encourage this sense of community and post-release enhancements have longer shelf lives because fans see continuous support for the title. As stated earlier, networked games are a whole different world. Lots of content is created after the release, so gamers can visit new game zones, engage in new missions, and so on. For some other games, game servers must be controlled and taken care of, so the player community can enjoy good playing conditions. Clearly, networked games have a long, sometimes almost indefinite, maintenance time. *Ultima Online* by Origin/Electronic Arts, has been around for more than five years now in its different incarnations; it is a testament to good product support from both the developer and publisher sides.

Let's now explore these three phases in more detail.

For the preproduction phase, we will study how games are born, how feature sets and code macro structures are designed, and which prototypes can be built along the way. Next, we will talk about production, which really boils down to calendars and milestones. This is the longest part of the process, so we will explore it thoroughly. In addition, we will analyze the maintenance phase to better understand which tasks must be carried out in order to guarantee long-term player commitment to our title.

Preproduction: Where Do Ideas Come From?

Most promising game projects start with a raw game design—a central idea of what the gameplay will be like. This is usually expressed in a single sentence that defines the genre and gameplay as well as your role in the story. A good example would be, "The game is a first-person shooter, with some outdoors areas and large monsters, where you are a warrior trying to save the princess." This is the best way to start working because you have an initial idea of how the game will be played and which features should make it fun and entertaining. For this method to work, your initial sentence must answer:

➤ Who is the player?

➤ What are his goals?

➤ What's the genre?

➤ How does the game play?

However, there are alternative paths. Sometimes, games start with a strong narrative description, such as, "You are a scientist in a military complex full of soldiers who are trying to conquer the world." Clearly, we are not saying much about the gameplay. It can be a slow-paced graphics adventure, a shooting game, a platform game, and so on. Games created around a narrative tend to be harder to code because you must understand the gameplay elements and formulas, which are what drive the coding process.

Another and even more dangerous game type is started because of some unique and impressive technology, like "let's build a game with this brand new outdoors renderer." Although many good games have been coded this way, you must remember one revealing fact: Only very hard-core gamers are interested in technology. The vast majority of your audience isn't. And technology does not sell games or make them fun.

So starting with the gameplay is a much safer bet. You can make a fun prototype with little or no presentation value and add the technology later. On the other hand, fixing a bad game design buried in a pile of great technology is much harder, and most times ends up in mediocre, formulaic gameplay. As Shigeru Miyamoto puts it:

> *"A lot of people ask me if I start designing games with a story in mind, or a particular scenario, or a particular character, but actually I start on a much more basic level. And really what I do is, I start with some basic core experiments, testing out the action on the screen or a specific gameplay style. When we started with Mario, all we had were some blocks onscreen, and we would try to make those blocks bounce around and jump as we intended them to do using the controller. So it's really at that core element that our game design begins."*
>
> ```
> http://www.techtv.com/extendedplay/videofeatures/story/
> 0,24330,3375049,00.html
> ```

Thus, the safest bet is working from a core gameplay idea and maybe some narrative elements, and discussing with your designers and team the best technological choices to convey the game world you all want to create. By putting technology at the service of gameplay and narrative, a well-balanced, entertaining game is within reach.

As a personal suggestion, I would recommend that teams start working with the "central sentence idea" outlined earlier, so that this sentence becomes the central design idea for the game. For a game such as the classic *Donkey Kong*, the sentence could be, "You are Mario, a plumber who must rescue his girlfriend Pauline, who has been kidnapped by a large ape that has taken her to the top of a skyscraper."

Luckily, you will have a lead game designer who feeds the technology team with great ideas such as this one. Hopefully, he will also create some early gameplay mechanics and sometimes even some keyboard or controller mappings, and so on. Some history elements must also be in place, so you know who you are and what you are supposed to do in the game world. That's the best way to get the project started. Going further than that at this stage often means getting lost in an ocean full of details.

Discussing Feature Sets

The first task any lead programmer should undertake during preproduction is defining a list of features to be implemented into the game both in terms of gameplay and presentation. How many characters should be displayed? Will the user be able to pick objects? This list should be crafted as a team effort between the design and the coding team, so tasks are both meaningful in terms of design and technologically feasible. A good way of getting a reasonable feature set laid out on paper is to use an *expansion-contraction process*.

In the first step, an exhaustive list must be created. Every feature to be added to the game should be written down. At this stage, it does not matter how realistic expectations are. It is a blue-sky research phase, which should be a group effort involving all people in charge of the project. Put all your crazy ideas on a blank sheet of paper. If it takes more than one sheet, that's a good sign. If you end up using a word processor because of the amount of features, that's even better. Whatever the case, number each feature so you can keep track of them in further steps. This completes the first, expansive phase.

Once the list is complete, it is then time for the contraction process. Review the list, merging those features that are similar in terms of coding. For example, the features "poisons" and "power-ups" can be generalized into a single feature called "items that affect the life level," which can be programmed in a single coding effort. As you contract, clusters of features will appear, some larger, some smaller. On the other hand, some highly specific features will remain ungrouped.

Then, review the results of the session. Large clusters will represent groups of many features that are coded similarly. These will generally be the main subsystems for your title: weapons, characters, and so on. As such, they will make it to the final list because they are a very significant part of your design. On the opposite end of the spectrum, single features are somehow risky. These are very specific pieces of code that won't be recycled for any other use. Thus, many of them will simply not make it to the final release.

A good, objective way to choose which clusters to implement is to use the classic *minimax* method. As you know, minimax tries to minimize disadvantages and maximize advantages. This is usually depicted in a 2D matrix of cost versus benefit, which is shown in Figure 2.6. For our feature set, advantages will be

➤ User-perceived value

➤ Generality

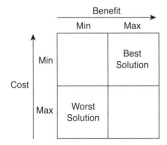

Figure 2.6 Minimax matrix, showing benefit on the horizontal axis and cost in the vertical. It can be suited for any problem, not just game development.

Clearly, we want to code features that will make a difference for the user and also provide general code tools that can be recycled for many uses. As for the drawbacks, here are two that easily come to mind:

➤ Coding size

➤ Coding difficulty

You should worry about the first one if your team is small, whereas the second one should be watched for especially in novice teams. Next, you must qualify each feature cluster according to the different criteria, and then place it in one of the following categories:

➤ **Minimin.** These are features that are not important for the player but are easy to code. They are mainly decorative elements that should be coded at the very end of the project if time allows because they are just icing on the cake. A good example is birds flying by in a 3D adventure. They don't add much to the game but are usually simple to code.

➤ **Maximin.** These are features that offer little or no benefit in terms of the experience but are hard to code. Obviously, they should be dropped immediately. As an example, imagine a car racing game where you can see the driver inside the car. Implementing a skeletal animation system for the character is a significant commitment. But given the specific game you are working on, it is not clear that the effort will pay off in the long run.

➤ **Minimax.** These features are what dreams are made of: simple to code features that add a lot to the player's experience. Obviously, these should all be built into the game, assuming time allows for them. Being able to configure your character's look in a role-playing game (RPG) can sometimes be implemented easily, and it provides a great enhancement for RPG fans—a classic minimax example. Another minimax feature is usually AI communication. In an action game, seeing the AIs cooperate and synchronize themselves greatly enhances the player's experience, and the coding difficulty is moderate.

➤ **Maximax.** These features are generally the cornerstones of the game system. They are hard to code features that define the gameplay experience. An outdoors renderer for a flight simulator can be a huge burden to code, but it really makes the game stand out. For these kinds of features, a twofold analysis must be made. First, is there an easier implementation that converts a maximax feature into a minimax feature? Sometimes a different coding strategy can simplify the algorithm greatly, making the feature a sure hit. Second, is your team capable (considering complexity and size) of handling the feature? And, if so, how many of these features can be built into the game? It is better to realize early what your limitations are than to have to cut features well into the production of the title. So, maybe you will only be able to select some maximax features and forget about the rest for feasibility reasons.

All in all, the end result of this process should be a feature list that makes sense from both a design standpoint and from an efficiency standpoint. The features need to work, and they must be more or less reasonable for the programming team. They must be features that define a great game and can be built by the available personnel in a reasonable time.

Production: Milestones Are King

If your preproduction phase is completed efficiently, chances are you will start the production phase with all the core gameplay in place for your game prototype. During production, you will convert your prototype into a full-blown game. Here rules are much more diffuse, but some advice can still be given. The following list of do's and don'ts have been taken from real-world examples:

➤ **More is not better.** Many times you will feel your team is not capable of pushing the project forward at the right speed. This usually happens in the final stages when pressure starts to build, and you wish you had twice the personnel. In these situations, you might be tempted to hire new personnel so they can assist you in the final months. Think twice. In his classic "The Mythical Man-Month," Frederick P. Brooks states how adding more people in the middle of the battle does not actually improve things, but instead makes them worse. Part of your existing team will be slowed down because developers will need to train the new members, who will need some time to get up to speed. The result? Missed deadlines. Plan your team size conservatively during the preproduction phase, and if you think you might need "emergency personnel" to help out, make sure you choose people who have all the information on the project beforehand, so they can get up to speed and work from day one.

➤ **"On time" is better than "more ambitious."** Game development is driven by ambitious teams that want to create brave new products. But Christmas is in December, no matter how fast or slow you code. And about 50-60 percent of the total number of games sold per year sell at Christmas. Most times, it is better to complete a product "as is" (and then move on to another one that will in turn be better) than to enter a deadly spiral of always trying to improve the current installment. It's a bit like people who do not buy a new computer because next month a new device will appear. Then, next month goes by and they say, "Hey, next month this other piece of equipment is coming out," and the purchase is delayed for months. Coding games is about having products on the market, not about endless tech demos and missed milestones. Work with a closed feature set and, to an extent, try not to add new ideas to it in the middle of the project.

➤ **Surgical teams and key members are a risk**. Let's face it, not all game developers are equally important to a project. In fact, there's always a subset of people who make up the surgical team—the team that the project cannot live without. It can include artists, programmers, or other important personnel. But if one member leaves the team, you're in serious trouble. Some studios pride themselves on these employees, but from a risk assessment standpoint, having such a configuration is not recommended. If you have a key team member, say, the lead programmer, make sure he works closely with at least one other person, so if he leaves the company, you will have a backup plan. Many games have been killed or delayed because a key member left in the middle of production, and no one knew what to do. It is sad, but true. People on your team should be valued, but if the time comes, they should be able to be replaced as quickly as possible.

➤ **Order of execution.** Not all game features are born equal: Some are essential for the game, and others just improve upon a base formula. In a game such as *Quake* or *Unreal*, the indoors renderer is a key component, as is the path finding routine for the AI. On the other hand, rag doll physics for the death animations is great to have but can be disposed of if required. Try to do this kind of exercise with your feature set: Think about which features *must* be included and which *should* be included. Do not forget that coding often takes longer than initially planned. Thus, having a clear distinction between the core features and the accessories is a healthy practice. In the same way, try to think in terms of the order of coding. Some features must be coded early on because they are the pillars of the game, and further advancement cannot be made without them. In *Age of Empires*, for example, path finding is more urgent than most of the graphics engine; without path finding the game simply does not exist. Sometimes it's useful to display the components to code and their order of execution in a graph. Each node represents a component, and each branch represents nodes that need other nodes to be complete before them. Figure 2.7 shows a sample graph for a real-time strategy (RTS) like project.

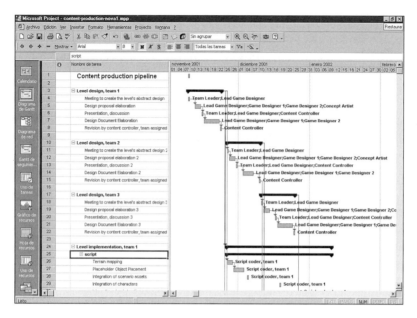

Figure 2.7 Production graph.

Maintenance

Unfortunately, the maintenance phase is too often used as the time when errors from production are fixed, especially if schedules are too tight. It is poor business strategy to have developers release games that are unfinished and have them use patches to solve the remaining bugs. On the other hand, the maintenance phase offers great potential to game developers because it's the moment when relationships with consumers are at their highest point. Thus, the first step to ensure a healthy maintenance relationship is to plan the production phase well, so this last phase does not become a "fix everything you can" scenario.

The goal of maintenance must then be to maximize the enjoyment of the product by the consumer and to make the life cycle as long as possible. It is a time for strong product support so sales increase. Here I will outline some ideas taken from successful projects.

One idea is to release new content for the game, so the user's enjoyment is lengthened. Extra missions or characters are easy to do, and the user-perceived value is very good. These missions can be placed on web sites for easy deployment. Remember that a good data-driven design is the key to success. Being able to plug new missions into your game will require some careful planning in the production or even preproduction phases. Many games have successfully followed this approach in recent years. One strikingly good example is *Black and White* by Lionhead Entertainment (developer) and Electronic Arts (publisher). It is a god-game where the user controls a population through a Creature, which is the representation of God on Earth. Creatures built into the game were animals, such as a cow and a tiger. But the development team created extra creatures so they could be bundled with different products, including magazines, web sites, and so on. Then, by purchasing the magazine, you received the extra creature for the game on a CD-ROM. This was a very interesting move because the new content could be used for public relations, benefiting not only the players, but also the sites or magazines that had such an agreement with Electronic Arts.

Another idea is to provide users with content creation tools, so a mod community can be started. Content sharing should not be seen as a potential problem but as an opportunity to increase your user base. Fans will get their friends involved in the game, create new artwork, and so on. A good example of this strategy was clearly shown by *The Sims*. When the development team at Maxis/EA began releasing tools to allow user-created content, the number of sites devoted to the game simply skyrocketed. Being able to create your own character skin, as simple as it might look, was a great feature for many users. In fact, many users that had lost interest in the game got back into it due to the expressive potential that editing tools gave them. The result? *The Sims* stands as a title with one of the longest shelf lives in history. The word-of-mouth mechanism spawned a huge fan base, and today *The Sims* is the biggest selling PC game in history.

Mod-making can also become an interesting business. Many teams have hired personnel directly from the mod community because they were the most talented users of the editing toolset. Others have published compilations of this user-created content in the form of expansion packs, so the game's shelf life is increased, and so on.

Whatever path you choose to follow, make sure your content creation tools are styled and tailored to the end user. Too often, the internal editors used by the development team are released without any adaptation, and users get frustrated by their unintuitiveness and clumsy interfaces. If you plan on releasing content-creation tools, make sure they are suitable for end users. Developers often employ simple editors that are sufficient to get things done if you are familiar with the internal technology the game is running in. Don't forget that by releasing the tool you are creating a new consumer product, and that users are not game developers. Using the editor must be an enjoyable experience, not an uphill battle. Thus, these tools should be designed carefully. Interfaces must be kept simple, a user manual should be almost mandatory, and so on.

Massively multiplayer games are a completely different business when it comes to maintenance (or should I say product development?). These games are actually created in the maintenance phase because we need to keep a living community with ongoing activities, and so on. Because they are pay-per-play titles, keeping new content pouring in is the best (and only) way to make the game profitable.

Finally, the maintenance phase is a great time to organize, archive, and document. Let's face it, many developers forget good coding practices during lengthy crunch times. Too often, code is just forgotten after the game is released. Some maintenance time should go into revising your code, and storing and documenting the reusable modules, so subsequent games can take advantage of those modules and be crafted in less time by a smaller team. After all, there's no deadline pressure on the maintenance phase. You can devote some team members to this task to ensure that the project is closed in the most structured way, that an error-free product is on the market, and that there is a well-documented knowledge base, which can be used in subsequent titles.

In Closing

In Chapter 1, "Chronology of Game Programming," we explored the historical foundations of game programming in order to understand the industry's present state and analyze how games are built today. In this chapter, we explored the foundations of game programming. We analyzed the structure of a game's source code, providing a global taxonomy by which most games can be decomposed. By understanding that taxonomy, you can see the pieces of the puzzle and the dependencies between them. The goal of the rest of the book is to explore each of these pieces in detail, from artificial intelligence to networks. We will delve into the internals of each subsystem so you can use all the techniques that have been discovered for each one of them through the years.

Chapter 3

Data Structures and Algorithms

"The loftier the building, the deeper must the foundation be laid."

Thomas Kempis

Our journey into game programming is going to be long and deep. Before we begin, we must make sure some key concepts are well laid out. We need to take a second to review the game programmer's basic tool set. This chapter is a survey of popular data structures and their access algorithms. We will be basing all our work on these cornerstones throughout the rest of the book. Therefore, it is essential that they be well understood, so we can move on to the game-specific content of the book.

So, consider this chapter a reminder. Read it, and then take a second to review the concepts and parts you feel less familiar with.

Types, Structures, and Classes

The first programming languages only supported operations on a closed set of data types. You could operate integers and floating-point numbers, but that was basically it. The reason for this simplicity was that at the assembly language level, these data types were the only ones available. Even today, anything beyond fundamental data types need to be defined, taken care of, and so on in a software layer. So it is not surprising that in the days when computer speed was a fraction of a megahertz, developers didn't feel the need to operate on anything but ints and floats. In fact, many hardware platforms of yesteryear didn't even support floating-point values, which were implemented in a software layer.

Some developers felt the expressive potential of programming languages was too limited and that creating large software applications was often impossible with such primitive tools. Thus, years went by, and the family of structured programming languages (C, Pascal, and so on) surfaced. In these languages, the concept of user defined data types was introduced as an abstraction to allow developers to encode real-world data easily. If you needed to have a point in space built into your program, you could decide whether to store it in three variables, such as:

```
float x,y,z;
```

Or, by using this new paradigm, you could decide to store it in a user-defined type, which we will call point3D:

```
typedef struct
        {
        float x,y,z;
        } point3D;
```

This new way of working allowed developers to write more compact, easy to follow code. For example, you could access the attributes (each individual element in the type) as follows:

```
        point3D p;
        p.x = 1;
```

Even better, types could be built incrementally, so more complex types use other, less complex types, similar to the layers of an onion. The result was type hierarchies, which were useful for encoding real-world data with complex relationships. Clearly, user-defined types increased the expressive potential of programming languages, and the era of modern software development began.

However, some new problems appeared. Once you had a large type hierarchy, it was very likely that you would have a similarly large block of code full of operations on that data structure. In the previous point3D example, you would need operations to add, subtract, perform both dot and cross product, and so on. If you only had user-defined types, you were condemned to the following:

```
point  pointadd(point,point);
point  pointsubtract(point,point);
float  pointdotproduct(point,point);
point  pointcrossproduct(point,point);
```

As your data structure grew, the accompanying code would also grow. Moreover, you would run into some naming problems, and your code would become a spider web full of #include statements. The size and complexity of your program was again compromised by the language's lack of features.

At this point in time, the second "revolution" in programming language technology took place. Again, the idea was to allow bigger programs with less internal chaos. Because user-defined types were generally considered a good idea, this concept was extended to allow each type to include the source code for its own access operations, so the type became a self-sufficient code and data module. These modules were called *classes*. Additionally, rules governing how classes could relate were established to mimic the real world. Classes could have descendants (inheritance), class members could be renamed so they used standard operators (operator overload), and so on. So, our point data would now become:

```
class  point3D
        {
        private:
        float  x,y,z;

        public:
        point(float  ,  float,  float);
        ~point();
        point  operator+(point);
        point  operator-(point);
        };
```

The advent of object-oriented programming (OOP) really pushed the maximum program size to unknown boundaries. Programs several million lines of code in size are not uncommon these days. Classes have basically become "black boxes," which you can share, recycle, and use with no real knowledge about their internals. By looking at the (hopefully well-documented) class definition, a programmer can effectively use a class much like a driver can use a car with no knowledge of how the engine works. Clearly, OOP benefited developers in two ways: It allowed them to build more structured programs that are easier to maintain, and it improved team-based coding where classes could be exchanged and shared between team members.

A number of improvements have been introduced in recent years, from visual languages to design patterns and the Standard Template Library (STL). Although none of the improvements has had the impact that OOP or user-defined types had, they have provided developers with constant advances that make work easier. For the sake of game development, design patterns and the STL are very useful. At the end of this chapter you will find a section on the STL, whereas the next chapter is completely dedicated to design patterns.

For now, we will focus on reviewing those data structures that are frequently used in game development, so we can reference them in chapters to come. Some of them will seem very simple, but quite likely some of them will also be new to you.

Data Structures

In the following sections, we will cover some of the standard data structures.

Static Arrays

Games rarely need to work with single instances of data. More frequently, you will need to store lists of similar type elements: triangles in a mesh, enemies in a game level, and so forth. Many different structures can be employed to fulfil this task. The simplest of them is the *static array*, which basically allows the developer to store a list of elements that will not change during the program's life cycle. If you need data to vary (for example, add or remove enemies from a dynamic enemy pool), a more involved solution (such as a linked list) might be better suited. But in many situations (such as the vertices in a static mesh mentioned earlier), you just need to store a linear array of data.

This structure has the following general definition:

```
class arrayoftype
        {
        type *data;
        int size;

        arrayoftype(int);
        ~arrayoftype();
        };
```

The constructor would require an initialization such as:

```
arrayoftype::arrayoftype(int psize)
{
size=psize;
data=new type[size];
// subsequent code can be used to access and initialize each element
}
```

The destructor would be as simple as:

```
arrayoftype::~arrayoftype()
{
if (data!=NULL) delete[] data;
}
```

An added benefit of static types comes in search speed. If the element's position in the array can be considered a primary search key (in database programming terms), you get O(1) access time. And there's more: Imagine that you don't have a primary key as the element position. If you can at least guarantee that elements can be ordered by the value of the primary key (for example, alphabetically or in ascending numeric value), you can still get O(log2 # of elements) searches, which is better than the linear cost you are used to. Remember that we need to incur the lowest possible cost in our routines. Linear cost means cost that is linear to the number of processed elements, whereas logarithmic cost means cost is log(number of elements). Because the logarithm function grows more slowly, we will prefer this type of cost over linear cost.

To achieve this, you need to use a simple but effective algorithm, which is called a *binary* or *dychotomic search* depending on the book you read. Here is the core algorithm. For simplicity, I will assume you want to search in a fully ordered passport number list.

```
typedef struct
        {
        int passportid
        char *name;
        } person;

class people
        {
        person *data;
        int size;
        person *seek(int);
        };
```

The seek method returns a pointer to the person if found, or NULL if the person does not exist. Here is the code:

```
person *people::seek(int passid)
{
int top=size-1;
int bottom=0;
// this loop stops when we have narrowed the search to just one element
while (top-bottom>1)
    {
    // compute the midpoint
    int mid=(top+bottom)/2;
    // check which sub-range we want to scan further
    if (passid>=data[mid].passportid) bottom=mid;
    else top=mid;
    }
if (data[bottom].passportid==passid) return (&data[bottom]);
else return NULL;
}
```

Clearly, using static arrays makes sense in many scenarios. Their maintenance is really straightforward, and access functions are efficient. However, sometimes we will need dynamic structures that can insert and delete elements at runtime. Then we will need to revert to some more powerful tools.

Linked Lists

A *linked list* is an extension of the static array. Like the static array, it is designed to store sequences of equal-typed elements. But linked lists have an added benefit: The sequence can grow or shrink dynamically, accommodating a variable number of elements during the structure's life cycle. This is achieved by using dynamic memory for each individual element and chaining each element to the next with pointers. The basic implementation of a linked list follows:

```
typedef struct
        {
        // here the data for the element
        elem *next;
        } elem;

class linkedlist
        {
        elem *first;
        elem *current;
        };
```

Notice how we keep two pointers, one to the first element in the list (which we will not move) and another to the current element, which we will use for searches and scans in the list. Clearly, there is no way of performing a random access to a given position unless you loop through the list until you reach the target element. Thus, the linked list is especially well suited for sequential traversals, but not so much for random access.

Linked lists are superior to arrays because they allow us to resize the data structure as needed. On the other hand, there are two potential issues with this structure. First, it requires some care with memory allocation to make sure leaks do not occur. Second, some access routines (searches and random reads) can be slower than with arrays. In an array we can use direct access to any position. From this direct access, some clever algorithms (such as dychotomic searches) can be implemented on arrays. But in a linked list, we must use pointers to access elements sequentially. Thus, searches are linear and not logarithmic in cost.

Deletions are also a bit more complicated. We would need a pointer to the previous element in order to fix the pointers in the fashion that is depicted in Figure 3.1. This can be solved in search and delete routines by always storing the required pointer to the previous element. This works fine with elements in-between, but requires a specific routine to delete the first element in the list, which does not have a "previous." A different, more popular approach is to use doubly-linked lists.

Figure 3.1   Linked list.

Doubly-Linked Lists

A *doubly-linked list* is a variant of the regular linked list that allows bidirectional scanning by providing, for each element, both a pointer to the next and a pointer to the previous element (see Figure 3.2). This way some routines, such as the deletion routine, are easier to code at a higher memory footprint due to the added pointers. The new data structure could be defined as:

```
typedef struct
        {
        // here the data for the element
        elem *next;
        elem *prev;
        } elem;

class linkedlist
        {
        elem *first;
        elem *current;
        };
```

Doubly-linked lists offer easier insertion and deletion because we can always access both the previous and next elements to perform pointer reassigning. On the other hand, insertion or deletion at either endpoint is a special case because we can't access the next element (in the last case) or the previous one (in the first case).

Figure 3.2   Doubly-linked list.

But what if we want to store a sense of order so we know when each element was inserted?

Queues

A *queue* is a variant of the linked list. The main difference is that insertions to the queue are always performed at the end of the list, and access to the elements is limited to the element at the beginning (see Figure 3.3). This way a software queue resembles a real-world queue, such as a supermarket waiting line. Customers join the line (hopefully) at the end, and only the customer at the beginning is effectively paying the cashier.

```
typedef struct
       {
       // here the data for the element
       elem *next;
       } elem;

class queue
       {
       elem *first;
       elem *last;
       void insertback(elem *);
       elem *getfirst(elem *);
       };
```

Queues are extremely useful for a variety of applications. Generally speaking, queues are used to store lists in chronological order: messages received in a network connection, commands given to a unit in a real time strategy game, and so on. We will insert elements at the end, and extract them in the beginning, thus preserving the order of arrival. This list can be either variable or fixed in size. Fixed-size queues are usually implemented via circular queues and are used to store the N most recent elements. New elements overwrite the oldest ones.

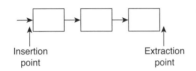

Insertion
point

Extraction
point

Figure 3.3   Queues.

A popular use of circular queues can be found in many 3D games. Imagine that you want to paint the footsteps of your character or bullet marks on the walls. You can't afford to paint lots of these elements because it would clog your rendering engine. So, you decide to paint the last N. Clearly, this is a perfect scenario for circular queues. As the queue gets filled, older elements will be deleted, so only the last footsteps will be painted.

Stacks

A *stack* is another variant of the linked list scheme. This time, though, elements are inserted and popped out at the same end of the structure (see Figure 3.4). This way, a last in, first out (LIFO) behavior is implemented. Stacks thus mimic a pile of paper. The last piece of paper put on top of the list will be the first to be taken out. Here is the code structure for a generic stack:

```
typedef struct
     {
     // here the data for the element
     elem *next;
     } elem;

class stack
     {
     elem *first;
     void push(elem *);
     elem *pop();
     };
```

Stacks are useful in situations where you want to access elements in a geometrically meaningful way: inventories, items dropped to the ground, and so on. Stacks are also used in those cases where newer information makes old information less relevant, as in a cache. The LIFO behavior gives priority to newer elements.

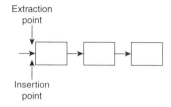

Figure 3.4   Stack.

Deques

When using both a stack and a queue, data structure is sometimes a waste of code, especially considering that both structures are extremely similar (with the exception of the points of insertion and deletion). A popular alternative to having two separate structures is to have a single object that encapsulates both the queue and the stack. This is called a *deque* (double-ended queue), and it allows both push and pop operations to be performed at both endpoints (see Figure 3.5). Queues and stacks are so similar internally, that it makes sense to have a single structure that can handle both behaviors.

The profile for this new data structure is as follows:

```
typedef struct
       {
       // here the data for the element
       elem *next;
       elem *prev;
       } elem;

class deque
       {
       elem *first;
       elem *last;
       void push_front(elem *);
```

```
elem *pop_front();
void push_back(elem *);
elem *pop_back();
};
```

Notice how we have chosen to implement the deque as a doubly-linked list. Although this is the most popular alternative (remember that we need to delete elements from both sides), some clever coding techniques allow deques to be implemented as simple linked lists, with a significant saving in pointers. It is also interesting to remember that being both a first in, first out (FIFO) and LIFO structure, we do not provide any member operation to scan the list or access elements other than the extreme ones. We will never perform random accesses. On the other hand, it is useful to have an extra integer attribute that holds the number of elements currently being held by the deque so we have a size estimate. This is a popular query, which can be implemented easily by initializing the counter to zero at creation time and incrementing its value in each push and decrementing it on each pop.

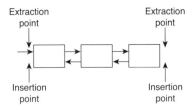

Extraction point   Extraction point

Insertion point   Insertion point

Figure 3.5   Deque.

Tables

Tables are sequential structures that associate data elements with an identifying key. For example, you could have a table where you store people's names, identified by their passport number.

Tables can have many registers (sometimes referred to as rows) and also many fields per register (also referred to as columns). Their main use is in databases, although data-rich games frequently use tables to store anything from weapon types and their characteristics to enemies.

Tables exist in many forms. In the simplest case, a static array can be considered a table where the position of the element acts as the key. In this case, the table is single key (there is only one field that can act as the key), and the key is nonrepetitive (a position can only appear once) and exhaustive (all key values are assigned). This is the optimal case because access time is O(1), and it can be used in some situations. For example, imagine that you are building a role-playing game and need to store weapons and their stats. You could create a table with several columns (for the weight, damage, size, and so on) and use the first one (which will end up as the weapon position in the array) as an identifier. Thus, the long sword could be weapon number 0, the bow number 1, and so forth. Programmers must try to implement tables in such a primitive way when possible to maintain optimal performance.

Unfortunately, most tables are more complex. To begin with, it is hard to find exhaustive keys. For example, you can have a list of customers with their passport numbers, but it is unlikely that all passport identifiers will be occupied. We must divide this problem into two separate contexts, each with a different solution. Will the data be mainly static, and thus insertions and deletions will be nonexistent (or very seldom), or is the table going to involve frequent structural changes?

In static cases, sorting by key and storing data in ascending order in a static array can be a good choice. You can still access data at O(log2 number of elements) by using binary searches. If you need to perform an insertion, you will definitely need to resize the array and make sure the new element keeps the array sorted. Deletions also need array resizing, but overall, both operations can be performed in O(n) cost. Although these operations are rare, the structure is still quite efficient.

Hash Tables

A more involved structure can handle both static and dynamic data as well as nonexhaustive keys. Its downside is more memory overhead and slightly more complex coding. The structure is called a *hash table*, and its main feature offers nearly constant access time for element search, insertion, and deletion.

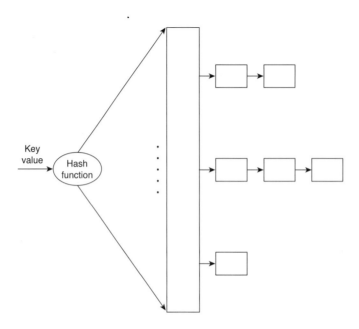

Figure 3.6 Hash table.

A hash table (depicted in Figure 3.6) consists of a data repository that effectively holds the table data, coupled with a function that transforms input keys into pointers to data in the repository. The hashing function "scatters" keys uniformly in the repository space (hence the name), making sure available space is occupied in a homogeneous way. Hashing functions are not magic, however. They provide us with a shortcut to data, but sometimes we will need a bit of processing to reach the element we are looking for. Let's take a look at an example based again on a list of people identified by passport number. We will begin by allocating the following structure:

```
class hash_table
    {
    dlinkedlist data[100];

    void create();
    elem *seek(int key);
    void insert(elem *el);
    void delete(int key);
    dlinkedlist *hash_function(int key);
    };
```

In this example, our hash table will be implemented as an array of doubly-linked lists. The hash function then converts any input key into a pointer at the beginning of one of the lists, where elements are really stored. Here is the source code for the hash function:

```
dlinkedlist *hash_table::hash_function(int key)
{
int pos=(key%100)
return &data[pos]
}
```

Notice how the hash function simply selects the last two digits of the password and uses them to select the linked list where data will be stored. This choice is not, however, trivial. Programmers must select hash functions that scatter data as uniformly as possible, or access time will degrade in those table positions holding more data than others. I have thus assumed that the last two digits in a passport are basically randomly distributed, so using them as a hash function makes sense, whereas selecting the first two digits would probably yield a poorer distribution pattern.

Notice also how hash functions do not really provide direct shortcuts to the element we are looking for. They only point us in the right direction because there might be more than one element in the list. We need to perform a linear search in this (hopefully small) list to find the element we are looking for. Selecting the right array size and hash function is essential to guarantee nearly O(1) access time. If we fail to do so, the table will become saturated, and performance will drop rapidly.

Hash tables are quite popular in mainstream applications that need to perform searches in large data banks. Although memory hungry, they can cut down access times dramatically. For example, imagine that you need to hold about 10 million registers of people by their passport number for a government application. By extending the previous ideas, we could use a larger array (say, 10,000 entries long) and hash with passport modulo 10,000. The average list length would end up being approximately 1,000 units. Now, compare scanning a list of 1,000 units with lists of 10 million. Additionally, you can increase or decrease search speed at will just by scaling up the data structure. Obviously, there is a downside to all this. You must be ready to purchase lots of memory because a larger array of doubly-linked lists clearly needs lots of pointers. Assuming you use 32-bit pointers, a 10,000-unit long array with each entry storing a 1,000 element doubly-linked list occupies for each list:

1,000 elements consisting of two pointers each, plus a variable amount of data (say, 100 bytes): totals 108,000 bytes per list

Then, the whole structure needs 10,000 lists and 10,000 pointers to the first element. The grand total is

10,000 * (108,000 + 4) = 1,080,040,000 = aprox. 1 GB.

Now, a static array holding the entire database, but without the hash table overhead, would occupy 10 million×100 bytes, for a grand total of 1 billion bytes. If you compare both quantities, you can get an approximation of the hash table overhead:

1,080,040,000 / 1,000,000,000 = the hash table needs an extra 8,004 % storing space.

Clearly, data structures holding large records will have less overhead because the size of the pointers will slowly become negligible. On the other hand, lightweight structures are not very suitable for hash tables (in terms of memory footprint, not in terms of speed) because the list pointers can significantly add to the memory use.

Multi-Key Tables

Let's imagine for a second that we need to create a table that we will access by either of two different values efficiently. For example, we might have a table of people that we want to access by passport number or by name (I will assume no two people have the same name).

We could decide which of the two keys is more important, and then prioritize that key, making it a hash table or an ordered list. But what if we really need to access the table using both keys? The best option here is to use two hash tables (one per key) connected to doubly-linked lists that can be traversed horizontally (for the first key) or vertically (for the second). Take a look at Figure 3.7 to better understand the notion of vertical and horizontal in the preceding example.

This way both keys can benefit from the speed gain found in hashing techniques. Note, however, that this choice is not for the faint of heart. Coding the double hash table can be a complex task because each element is part of two lists, and insertions and deletions get a bit more complex. Also, remember that you will be incurring additional memory overhead for the second table because you will need extra pointers and an extra array to handle the new key.

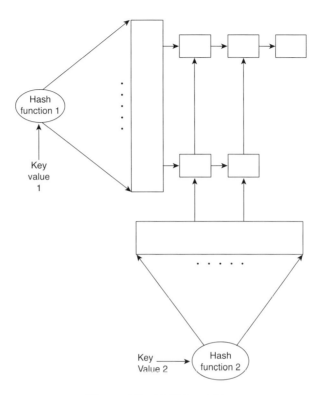

Figure 3.7   Multi-key table.

Trees

A *tree* is a data structure consisting of a series of nodes. Each node holds some relevant information as well as pointers to other nodes in the tree. What makes trees different is the way these node pointers are laid out. Starting from a root node, each node has pointers to nodes that are "descendants" of it. The only restriction is that a given node must only have one direct father (except for the root node, which has none). Thus, a treelike structure appears.

Trees are often approached using a nature-like metaphor: root, branches, leaves, and so on. But this is seldom useful when trying to explain what trees can be used for. It is better to think of a tree as a road that divides itself all the time, where each final destination can only be reached through a single path (due to the single parent condition)—no loops, no confusing crossings. Just think of it as an ever-branching road. Clearly, you will discover that trees are great tools to classify large amounts of information. If you are able to find a classification key, it's all a matter of using the road "divisions" (each node) to ensure that you reach your destination quickly—the faster the road branches (thus, the more descendants for each node), the faster the access. Let's now examine different types of trees and their uses.

Tree Types and Uses

Tree types begin with simple binary trees and run the gamut from N-ary trees to tries.

Binary Trees   A *binary tree* is a data structure where each node has exactly two descendants. This is usually achieved with two pointers called the left and right descendant. Leaf nodes (nodes that do not have descendants) still have two pointers, but they are initialized to NULL values to indicate that no further descendants exist. Data in trees is stored in each node, although some types of trees restrict this in some ways—data is held only at leaves, only at nonleaves, and so on.

The general data structure is

```
typedef struct
      {
      tree *left;
      tree *right;
      // here goes the real data from the node
      (...)
      } tree;
```

Binary trees are widely used in a variety of contexts. Their branching nature makes them ideal as classification devices with logarithmic search time. Each branching divides the search space by a factor of two, granting speedy searches. All we need to do is classify information stored in the tree according to whichever criteria we might need: numeric, spatial, and so on.

As an example, we can implement a *Binary Search Tree* (BST), which is a tree data structure that is used to speed up element searches. A BST is just a regular binary tree with the following added rule:

> For each node in the tree, the key value of all elements in the left subnode must be smaller than the key value of all elements in the right subnode.

This way we can scan the tree quickly, as in a binary search. The added benefit is that the tree is dynamic in nature, so we get O(log2n) access time with dynamic size.

But BSTs can degrade when the tree is unbalanced. Some leaves are much farther from the root than others, so not all branches have the same height.

As shown in Figure 3.8, an unbalanced tree can spoil the access time to make it linear, even if it complies with the BST definition.

So, a new type of binary tree must be introduced. This tree is called an *AVL-tree* (AVL are the initials of the discoverers of the data structure). An AVL tree is a BST with the additional restriction that for every node in the tree, the depth (in levels) of the left subtree must differ at most by one unit from the depth of the right subtree. Take a look at Figure 3.8 for an example. AVL trees keep the tree balanced, ensuring optimal access time. But efficiency comes at a price. Insertions and deletions into the tree must be done carefully, rebalancing the tree in the process to ensure that the new tree is still an AVL. This rebalancing is achieved by a recursive series of branch shuffles.

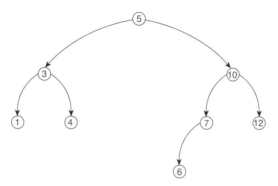

Figure 3.8   AVL tree.

We have seen how a binary tree can be a very good structure to use for classifying items. But that classification does not necessarily need to be based on a scalar or alphanumeric value. A binary tree can be best described as a spatial sorter. Once fed with spatially relevant data such as level geometry, it can effectively classify it, sort it, and so on, according to different criteria: which triangles are closest to the player, which convex cells are there, and so on.

We will call this specific tree a *Binary Space Partition* (BSP) tree. BSPs are very popular in game development. For example, the *Quake* engine is built using them, as are all of id Software's titles since *Doom*.

But many other games use them frequently because they provide a very good spatial sorting behavior. Here the idea is to use each node to recursively split the level geometry in half by using a splitting plane. If the planes are chosen properly, the resulting data structure will help us ask questions such as which triangle is closest/farthest, how many convex areas are there in this geometry, and so on. BSP trees will be covered in detail in Chapter 13, "Indoors Rendering."

N-ary Trees   Binary trees are used to classify data. But sometimes more branches will lead to better classification power. Here is where N-ary trees can be useful. Complex problems are hard to model, even with a binary tree. N-ary trees can use fixed or variable branching factors. In a fixed branching tree, every node in the tree has the same number of descendants. Quadtrees and octrees have branching factors of 4 and 8 as you will soon see. These trees are easier to code at the cost of reduced flexibility. In a variable branching tree, such as a trie, each node can have a different number of descendants. This is harder to code because we need descendant lists instead of fixed pointers, but it provides an additional degree of flexibility in some cases. A trie used as a dictionary can have a branching factor between 1 and 26 depending on the node.

Quadtrees and Octrees   *Quadtrees* and *octrees* are the natural extension of BSP trees. They are fixed-branching, four- and eight-connected trees, respectively. A quadtree is useful in 2D scenarios, whereas an octree is designed to work on 3D data sets. Quadtrees are used in many areas of game programming. In the next chapter, we will see how they can help us perform fast spatial queries, whereas Chapter 14, "Outdoors Algorithms," deals with uses of quadtrees for terrain rendering.

The construction scheme for both is identical, but I will focus on a quadtree now for the sake of simplicity.

A quadtree is built by dividing the incoming 2D data set into four quadrants by using two centered, axis-aligned cutting planes. All four quadrants are thus identical in size. Geometry that crosses quadrant boundaries can either be divided or stored in the quadrant where its major part exists, thus creating different quadtree variants. What should be noted, though, is that not all four quadrants will contain the same amount of data—only in a perfectly homogeneous scenario would this be the case. Thus, quadtrees apply the subdivision method recursively, building tree nodes in the process until a threshold is met. Thresholds are usually expressed in the form "each leaf node can contain N elements at most," but can take alternative approaches. You can see a graphic representation of a quadtree along with its resulting tree structure in Figure 3.9.

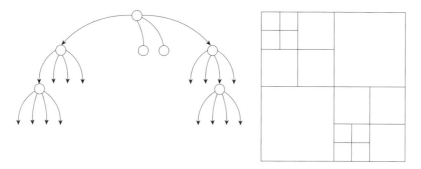

Figure 3.9   Quadtree, octree.

Octrees are the 3D counterpart to quadtrees. Instead of dividing each node into four subnodes (usually dubbed front-left, front-right, back-left, back-right), octrees use three axis-aligned and centered planes to create eight octants.

Quadtrees and octrees are powerful tools for visibility computation. They can be used both in indoors and outdoors scenarios to quickly determine visible regions of the game world. So, we will leave more in-depth explanations for Chapters 13 and 14, where we will explore some of their properties and implementation details.

Tries   A *trie* is an N-ary tree where each node can have a variable number of descendants. Each node represents a character or digit in a sequence, so each unique path from the tree root to one leaf node represents a unique key value. It is a very specific data structure whose main use is the fast classification and validation of data, which can be represented as character sequences, ranging from VISA numbers to a word dictionary. For example, a trie that stores the words "cat," "cow," "coalition," "chamber," and "chameleon" can be seen in Figure 3.10.

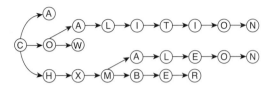

Figure 3.10   Trie.

Tries offer very fast access time, which is sustained as the structure gets larger and larger. Because the branching factor is very high, we can ensure rapid convergence. For a word N characters long, only N levels are visited; each one branching to between 1 and 26 descendants. Thus, cost ranges from an extremely degenerate case of O(number of letters) for a trie storing only one word to O(log26 number of letters) for a trie that stores all possible letter combinations. For numeric tries, O(log10 number of digits) is the cost of a full trie.

As for insertions and deletions, they are just variants of the core search routine. To delete a sequence, we must search for it; if we reach its end node (meaning the word is effectively in the trie), we must backtrack, deleting all the ascendant nodes until one of them has a descendant other than the one we are deleting. This way we ensure that we do not delete any other sequence as a side effect. You can see this in action in Figure 3.11. Insertions are similar. We begin by searching the sequence. In the process, we will reach a node where no possible advance can be made. We have identified part of our word, but the rest is simply not there. All we have to do is create a descendant subtree that contains the required characters to complete the new sequence. All in all, it seems obvious that both methods come at a worst-case cost of O(number of characters) after the initial search has been completed.

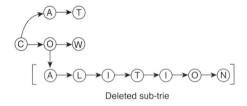

Deleted sub-trie

Figure 3.11   Deletion in a trie.

Tree Traversal Operations

Given the branching nature of trees, traversal cannot be performed in a sequential manner as in a list or table. We need some specific traversal routines that help us access data held by the tree in an intuitive and efficient way. These operations are the addition and subtraction equivalents for trees.

The most usual operation we will perform is the *ordered traversal*, which is a recursive scan of the whole tree using classification criteria. There are three classical traversal algorithms: pre-order, in-order, and post-order. They differ in the order in which they visit a node and its left and its right descendants.

In pre-order traversals, we first visit the node itself, and afterward we recursively scan the left and right subtrees using pre-order traversal. Graphically speaking, it involves scanning the tree visiting left subtrees prior to right ones and outputting the nodes as we "see" them in the first place.

In-order traversal visits the left subtree, then the node itself, and then the right subtree. It is equivalent to scanning a tree in the usual fashion (first left subtrees, then right) and outputting the nodes only after all the left subtree has been outputted.

The last traversal is the post-order, which is simply visiting the left and right subtrees, and only when these traversals—each one recursive in nature—have been performed, output the node itself. In practical terms it means visit in the usual way and output the node only if both subtrees have been fully outputted before. Take a look at Figure 3.12 to better understand each traversal method in a real example.

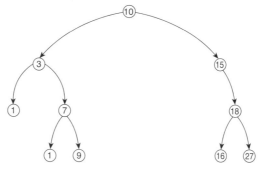

Preorder: 10, 3, 1, 7, 5, 9, 15, 18, 16, 21
In order: 1, 3, 5, 7, 9, 10, 15, 16, 18, 21
Post order: 1, 5, 9, 7, 3, 16, 21, 18, 15, 10

Figure 3.12   Pre-order, in-order, and post-order.

Priority Queues

A *priority queue* is an extension of the queue model that incorporates a sense of priority. When newer elements are inserted, they can "pass" in front of those with lesser priority. Thus, if a top priority element is inserted in a very long queue, all the other elements will be displaced by it.

Priority queues are great for representing commands. You can use them to give orders to troops so they prioritize them, and so on.

They are also very useful in sorting algorithms. In fact, one of the fastest algorithms uses a priority queue implementation called a *heap* to achieve near-optimal O(n*log n) results. The algorithm, dubbed *heapsort*, basically introduces the elements in the queue one by one, and then extracts them. As each insertion reshuffles the queue using the priority, the elements are extracted in order.

Priority queues can be implemented in a variety of ways. As a first but not very efficient solution, you could choose to implement them as a standard queue (enriching each element with priority information). Then, the `insert()` routine should be rewritten, so the elements inserted at the back are effectively pushed forward to the position their priority assigns them to. This approach would yield a not so stellar O(n) performance for each insertion.

A better alternative is to use a heap (see Figure 3.13), which is a priority queue implemented as a static array with some clever access routines. To understand heap structures, we must first learn a bit about ordered binary trees. These data structures are defined so that the descendants of each node have inferior value (or priority) than the node itself. The tree is complete, meaning there are no leaves with only one descendant (except for the ones at the end of the tree). Then, the tree is used to sort elements, so high value elements lie closer to the top and, within a specific level, leftmost nodes have higher priority than rightmost nodes. Thus, if a high-priority element is inserted into the tree, a series of level swaps will be performed so the new element is "promoted," and previously inserted elements are pushed to lower levels of the tree. The new element will reach its destination level in a O(log2 number of elements) time, because the logarithm is the measure of the number of levels in the tree. Then, some minor rehashing inside the level may be needed to ensure intralevel ordering is kept as well.

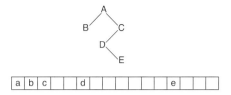

Figure 3.13   Heap.

A heap is nothing but a binary ordered tree implemented in an array.

The first position of the array is the root, and subsequent positions represent the levels of the tree from root to leaves, and from leftmost to rightmost node. This representation has an advantage: Given an array location (and hence a tree node), we can compute the position of the ascendants and the descendants with a simple formula. If you think about it for a second (and maybe do a couple drawings), you will discover that given a node at position n in the array:

➤ The ascendant is at position $n/2$, truncating if needed.

➤ The left descendant lies at the position $2*n$.

➤ The right descendant lies at the position $(2*n)+1$.

These equations make access more efficient and ensure that a heap can insert and remove elements quickly. The only downside is that the priority queue that results from the heap structure will always have a fixed length for the static nature of the array. This is rarely a problem, because most situations requiring a priority queue can actually restrict the maximum number of elements to be queued at any given time.

Graphs

A *graph* is a data structure composed of a series of nodes and a series of connections between them. We can navigate through the node list not by using a sequence, but simply by advancing through the connections of each subsequent node. These connections are formally called *transitions* because they allow us to move from one state to another.

Graphs are a very extensive subject on their own, defining a whole area of knowledge called Discrete Mathematics or Graph Theory. They provide very intuitive ways of representing relational data, such as those in the following list:

➤ Locations on a map with roads and traveling distances

➤ State machines with conditions to change from one state to another

➤ People with relationships between them (friendship, and so on)

➤ Board game configurations with possible moves

Anything that involves a group of entities and relationships between them can effectively be represented as a graph. But there is more to graphs than representing data: Powerful analysis algorithms have been developed, which scan graphs to calculate valuable results, such as:

➤ What is the shortest route (and how long will it take) from city A to B?

➤ What is the chance of a state machine reaching a given state?

➤ Given two people in a group, do they have any friends in common?

➤ In a chess game, what is the best move to achieve victory?

Graphs are so broad that many different classification criteria exist. To begin with, graphs can be directed or nondirected. In a directed graph, a transition between two nodes specifies which is the target and which is the destination, so each transition can only be traversed in one of two ways. A transition in a nondirected graph can be traversed in both ways equally. A road map, for example, would generally be nondirected, whereas a street map is often directed because some streets are one-way only. Another classification that is sometimes handy distinguishes between cyclic and acyclic graphs. A cyclic graph allows you to visit the same node twice by using the available transitions and their directionality. In an acyclic graph, you can only visit the same node once. Because a nondirected graph is always cyclic, this adjective is usually reserved for directed graphs. All street maps are cyclic (it might take some time, but you can return to your starting point in any journey). As an example of noncyclic graphs, think of a river with transitions emanating at the top of different mountains until the river reaches the sea. Take a look at Figure 3.14 for graph examples.

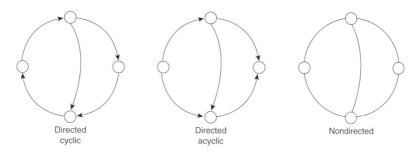

Figure 3.14   Graph examples.

The river will also exemplify the last classification. Some graphs allow you to reach a given node through different paths, others don't. For example, a river can have an island that water must surround. Obviously, we can traverse the island by both sides. Thus, this graph, although directed and acyclic, would allow us to reach a node through different paths. On the contrary, many other graphs (all trees, some road maps, and so on) are purely branching in nature, so each node can be reached through exactly one path.

By using all the preceding classifications, we can see that most of the structures we have seen so far are in fact instances of graphs. For example, an acyclic graph consisting of a single chain of nodes with no repetitions is a linked list. If we make it directed, we can easily identify a stack or queue. Moreover, a directed, acyclic graph with no repetitions is a N-ary tree, and so on.

Interest in graphs is spread across many science disciplines, and it is impossible to cover them all here. Thus, we will concentrate on their application to game development and provide some reading in Appendix E, "Further Reading," for those interested in the subject.

Graphs are great to use to model spatial information. Each node can represent a location on a map, and transitions represent available paths between locations. This simple model can be used in many types of games. In a graphics adventure such as the old LucasArts classics, this is the main data structure holding the map of the world. You can even overload each location with diverse information such as enemies, music to be played, items to pick up, and so on. You would also implement transitions, not by using logical conditions, but as hotspots on the screen the user must click in order to advance.

Another use of graphs also has to do with spatial information, but in a way related to AI programming. In a game such as *Unreal*, graphs can be used to model the level and thus guide the AI. *Unreal* levels consist of a series of rooms connected by portals. Clearly, we have our nodes and transitions well defined once again. This time, we will overload the transition with information about the distance between the two nodes or rooms. Then, an AI routine can easily use this information as a navigational map to chase the player. All it has to do is implement a shortest route algorithm between its current position and the player's position. The most popular algorithm for this problem is called A* and basically builds the graph at runtime, searching for the shortest path (using the transition information) from an initial state to the end state. The result is a sequence of moves (in our case, of rooms we must visit) in order to reach our destination optimally. The same algorithm can be used to perform pathfinding in a real-strategy game, with soldiers avoiding obstacles to reach their destination. Because A* is one of the cornerstones of AI programming, we will explore it in detail in Chapter 8, "Tactical AI."

In addition, graphs are also useful to represent behavior in artificial intelligence. One of the main techniques to represent what characters do and think, which is called *state machines*, is nothing but a graph with nodes representing actions the characters can be engaged in and transitions as changes in activity for the player. This is a very simple formalism used by countless action games. State machines can then exploit the power of graph analysis algorithms.

The Standard Template Library

Having a deep knowledge of all the fundamental data structures and algorithms is key to becoming a successful game programmer. However, coding these structures each time you need them is prone to introduce errors, and thus is a risky process. Let's face it, most game programmers could not write a linked list from scratch and get the code right on the first attempt.

Two solutions have been proposed. Some companies have developed in-house code bases that encapsulate many fundamental and sophisticated classes. These classes are built through the years, and thus are stable, well-tested frameworks from which a game can be derived. An alternative is to use a ready, standard set of classes that provide good performance and are rock solid. This is precisely what the Standard Template Library (STL) is all about.

The STL was introduced in the 1990s as a collection of classes that made OOP easier. It includes lists, queues, hash tables, and many other exotic structures and their access methods. You can trust the STL's code to be error-free because it is used daily by thousands of programmers worldwide. Any error gets fixed quickly, so you can trust the code base to be stable. Moreover, the STL is very efficient. The fastest access algorithms are built into the system, so you can trust the library. In addition, the STL provides flexibility. All classes are built using templates, so you get all the benefits of generic programming. You get generic lists that you can adapt to any element, so the code size also diminishes.

For those not familiar with generic programming, it is a C++ mechanism that allows a class to be parameterized. You can define a generic list, which accepts as a parameter its base type, so the same list can hold a series of integers or a series of complex structures. Another advantage of the STL is coherence. Most data structures are accessed in a similar way, which makes programming more abstract because you don't need to know all the implementation details of the different classes. The access method is usually implemented via iterators, which provide a convenient way to scan the structures.

Use of the STL spread rapidly in the mainstream application development segment. Databases, word processors, and so on take advantage of it frequently. In game development, however, it suffered the "Not Coded Here" syndrome. Developers are rarely enthusiastic about using anyone's code but their own, so the loss of fine-grained control that the STL implies was not very welcome in the beginning. But this reminds us of the old days when C++ was rejected because it was slow, or even earlier, when anything not-assembly was considered a sin. Game developers naturally care a lot about performance and control, and thus introducing any technology takes some time. Luckily, more and more game developers today are embracing the STL as a core technology, and we see less and less developer time being devoted to coding the ever-present linked list or binary tree.

To make life even easier, today the STL is built into many standard compilers such as Microsoft's Visual C++ or Borland's C. Besides, many free implementations of the STL exist (made by companies like Hewlett-Packard or Silicon Graphics).

Now I will provide an overview of the STL structures and philosophy. For the rest of the book, I will combine the STL with non-STL code, so you can gain complete understanding of the different alternatives available.

Containers

The STL includes many container classes, which are where user data is generally stored. These containers are all templates, so you can adapt them to any type of data. The containers provided by the STL are vector, list, deque, set, multiset, map, multimap, hash_set, hash_multiset, hash_map, and hash_multimap.

Vector

A *vector* is a sequence that allows random access to elements: O(1) insertion and deletion of elements at the end of the vector and O(number of elements) insertion and removal of any other element. Vectors can be dynamically resized, and memory management is automatic, so you don't have to call `malloc`. Here is a simple integer vector example:

```
vector<int> v(3);
v[0]=0;
v[1]=1;
v[2]=2;
v.insert(v.begin(), 5);
```

This code produces a vector such as:

```
v[0]=5;
v[1]=0;
v[2]=1;
v[3]=2;
```

Note how the `insert` routine effectively resizes the vector, hiding all memory management details from the user. Vectors have dozens of access functions, which perform tasks such as sorting, reversing order, searching data, and so on.

List

An STL *list* is a doubly-linked list, so it supports bidirectional traversal and constant-time insertion and removal (that is, once we are at the insertion point). Here is a simple list in action:

```
list<int> l;
l.push_back(31);
l.push_front(47);
l.insert(l.begin(),35);
```

In Figure 3.15, you can see a diagram of the list and its contents after this sequence is executed.

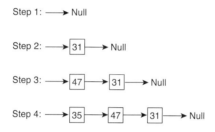

Figure 3.15   STL list example.

Deque

A *deque* is useful for implementing both queues and stacks. It provides constant-time insertion and removal from both the beginning and end as well as linear time insertion and removal for elements in-between. A deque used as a stack will insert and remove elements from the same end of the structure (be it the beginning or the end), whereas a deque used as a queue will perform both operations on opposite ends of the sequence.

Here are two code samples. The first uses a deque to implement a stack, the second a queue:

```
deque<int> s;
s.push_back(1);
s.push_back(2);
s.push_back(3);
```

```
s.push_back(4);
s.push_back(5);
while (!s.empty())
        {
        printf("%d\n",s.back());
        s.pop_back();
        }
```

This code sequence produces the following output:

```
5
4
3
2
1
```

The following code is a queue example. Notice how we only need to make minimal changes to the preceding code:

```
deque<int> q;
q.push_back(1);
q.push_back(2);
q.push_back(3);
q.push_back(4);
q.push_back(5);
while (!q.empty())
        {
        printf("%d\n",q.front());
        q.pop_front();
        }
```

The output will reflect the FIFO behavior we expect from a queue:

```
1
2
3
4
5
```

Sets and Multisets

Sets and *multisets* are sorted, associative containers. These data structures are basically sequential in nature, so they hold a series of similarly typed data. We can have an associative container of integers, character strings, and so on. The main difference between sequential structures (lists, vectors, deques) and sets is that sequences are optimized for access (insertion, removal, and so on), whereas sets are optimized for logical operations. In a set, you can perform a query like, "Which names on set A are also on set B?" efficiently. This query is usually performed by keeping the elements ordered, so inserting elements in the set cannot be performed in a random way.

Both sets and multisets are simple in nature. This means that the element they contain is also the key value for a search or logical comparison. You can have a set of strings, but you cannot have a set of structures each with a string as key. More complex containers are required for that.

The difference between a set and a multiset is simply that sets only allow an element to appear once in the set, whereas multisets allow different elements in the same set to be identical.

Sets and multisets are usually accessed with the functions `set_union`, `set_intersection`, `set_difference`, and `set_includes`. The first three functions are really straightforward:

- ➤ `union`   Returns a set with the elements that are in any of the incoming sets

- ➤ `intersection`   Returns a set with the elements that are in both incoming sets

- ➤ `difference`   Returns a set with the elements that are in set A but not in set B

The function includes is a search method that scans the incoming set to try to find a specific element.

Map and Multimap

A *map/multimap* is a generalization of sets especially designed to model relationships between pairs. A map contains a set of key values and a set of generic data values, which the key values are coupled with in a one-to-one relationship. As an example, here is an STL map:

```
struct ltstr
{
        bool operator()(const char *s1, const char *s2) const
        {
        return strcmp(s1,s2)<0;
        }
};

map <const char *,int, ltstr> ages;

ages[Daniel]=45;
ages[Alex]=12;
ages[Cecilia]=32;
```

Here we are storing a group of people along with their associated ages. As with regular sets, we can perform logic operations and searches on maps, which are optimized for this purpose. We can also traverse the structure using iterators to list the elements it contains.

Hash_set, Hash_multiset, Hash_map, and Hash_multimap

Sets and maps are implemented in a way optimal for logical operations and ordered traversal. Elements in the structure are permanently kept in ascending order so most access operations are logarithmic in cost. But for random access to data (by key value), using hash tables can provide a speed boost. In many cases a hash table provides quasi-constant access time to data held within. Thus, a hashed variant of all associative containers is provided by the STL.

Although different implementations of the STL might offer slightly different behaviors, hashed versions of sets and maps are generally more efficient if you plan to access the data in a random way, directly by seeking by key value. Under this access mode, a hash table provides faster access than a linear structure. But if you plan to list the elements and thus traverse the ordered structure, the regular sets and maps are recommended because they provide sequential access. This consideration is especially important for larger structures, where a small speed improvement might in the end provide a significant time savings.

Again, the difference between a map and a multimap is simply that maps need each element to be unique (in key value). Multimaps are less restrictive and allow multiple identical keys to coexist.

Iterators

An STL *iterator* is a generalization of a pointer. Iterators provide a clean, memory-safe method of traversing STL data structures. For example, if you need to print all the elements in a vector, you can do it by using an iterator:

```
vector<int> v(3);
v[0]=0;
v[1]=1;
v[2]=2;
vector<int>::iterator pos=v.begin();
while (pos!=v.end())
        {
        printf("%s",(*pos));
        pos.next();
        }
```

Iterators have the added advantage over pointers of being type generic. An STL iterator can be used on most of the STL's data structures, and most STL algorithms (sorting, searching, and so on) are designed to work with iterators. Also, memory access using iterators is protected, so you can't move past the end of a list and so on, further helping to reduce errors in code.

A Note on Efficiency

Many programmers do not trust the STL because they think it is slow or inefficient. The reason they think this way is that the STL's feature set is quite impressive, and it is hard to believe that those features have been coded as efficiently as a game programmer would code them. Most programmers tend to think that a specific, well-tailored piece of code should perform better than any standard library call. But this is not true, or at least not totally. The STL is a community effort such as Linux, and thus the code is constantly in a process of improvement. As new, faster ways to code appear, they are quickly implemented into the library. It is true, however, that for specific purposes, a dedicated game programmer could effectively come up with a more efficient implementation. But forget

continues

continued

about coding for a second, and think in terms of product development cycles. A programmer constructing an extremely efficient list manager might outperform the STL's lists by 10 percent, but a programmer using the STL will have a list up and running in 10 minutes, even before the other programmer has typed a single line of code. The evolution of game programming tools is a progression toward higher abstraction tools (at the cost of minimal speed decreases). We could still code in pure assembly, and quite likely our code would be faster and tighter, but it would take ages for anything decent to surface, be debugged, and so on. It simply does not make sense to try to code the fastest code in the world anymore. It is better to try to come up with the fastest implementation given a fixed time frame, and the STL can definitely help you out with that task.

In Closing

Data structures and algorithms most likely constitute the largest field in computer science. As such, there are many places you can go to look for information. A few of those places are listed in Appendix E. But there are some web-based information sources that have proven priceless through the years. At the National Institute of Standards and Technology (NIST), you can access an online data structures and algorithms database that provides information concerning not only the structures mentioned in this chapter but thousands more. It is your one-stop-shop for knowledge in this area. The NIST web site is at www.nist.gov/dads.

Chapter 4

Design Patterns

KEY TOPICS

- Design Patterns Defined
- Some Useful Programming Patterns
- Usability Patterns
- In Closing

"Always design a thing by considering it in its next larger context — a chair in a room, a room in a house, a house in an environment, an environment in a city plan."

Eliel Saarinen, "Time," July 2, 1956

Object-oriented programming (OOP) was a significant advance over classic structured coding. Bigger programs could be handled because code organization was greatly improved. But programs kept growing, becoming too complex and hard to manage. Like structured programming before it, OOP was quickly surpassed.

A series of new techniques have been proposed to increase project complexity once again and keep programs organized. Tools like the Standard Template Library (STL) have been a huge leap forward, because the programmer can now trust a series of components to do part of the job for him. These components are context insensitive and can be used on anything from a spreadsheet to a 3D game. Thus, the coding team can concentrate on the part of the code that actually defines the application functionality by using STL as building blocks.

In recent years, a new technique has surfaced, which is somewhat similar to STL in the sense that it allows you to use predefined components. But its scope and ambition is much broader. Complete sections of your program, not only the base classes, can be substituted with prebuilt components, thus saving lots of man-hours and headaches.

Design Patterns Defined

Design patterns (DPs) are proven solutions to well-established software engineering problems. As computer science has evolved, some problems have become classic and tend to appear frequently in many different contexts. As the years have gone by, different solutions have been proposed, and some of them have finally been accepted as optimal for their efficiency, elegance, and robustness.

A DP is one of these solutions. Specifically, a DP is a complete description of the problem and its respective solution both in terms of macro level design and implementation, so a programmer can read the pattern and solve the problem by using the optimal solution. Obviously, many man-hours can be saved this way. But there is more to a DP than coding faster. By using a well-known DP, a complete section of the application's code (often comprising many classes) is substituted with the recommended implementation of the pattern, thus becoming a black box that we can trust, and to a certain extent, forget about.

So, DPs are an entity of higher abstraction than simple classes or even the STL. They are complete subsystems, sometimes composed of several classes ready and tuned for a specific use. It all boils down to having an eye for detecting these classic problems in your code and being able to solve them accordingly.

DPs are often presented in listings, so the application analyst can browse and search for a pattern for whichever problem he or she might be facing. Some patterns are of very general use, whereas others are more restrictive. Some of them are even designed for common problems regarding computer game coding, and these are the ones we will be emphasizing for the rest of this chapter. However, let's not forget that games are just software applications, and sometimes they are not that different from other applications like spreadsheets or drawing programs.

There are many types of DPs. The two that are most useful to game developers are *programming patterns*, which describe specific coding problems and their standard solutions, and *usability patterns*, which deal with interface design, human-computer interaction, and related concepts. Now we will review some of the most popular patterns in both classes, so you can take advantage of them when coding games.

Some Useful Programming Patterns

Programming patterns include a number of immediately useful solutions, which we will now review one by one. What follows is a listing of popular patterns, with examples taken from typical game development scenarios.

Singleton

A *singleton* is a global object for which only one instance exists in the whole application. Most applications, and definitely all games, need global objects that must be visible from many different classes and scopes. A texture manager, the joystick controller object, and even the player class are all singletons. We need to have them visible at all times, and we only want to store one of these in memory. Traditionally, this has been solved in two ways, neither of which is especially elegant. The first one involves passing the said object as a parameter to all calls requiring access to it. This is inefficient, because an extra parameter must be pushed to the stack every time and makes code harder to read and follow. The second alternative is to define these objects in a source file and reference them using the extern mechanism. This way the compiler simply accepts that symbol, and the linker takes care of establishing the binding with the real object that resides in a different source file. This is a somewhat better technique, but as code size grows, our source files get cluttered with lots of extern definitions, degrading readability and elegance. Moreover, this solution is dangerous from a functional standpoint. As anyone familiar with OOP knows, code components need to have maximum cohesion and minimum bindings to other components. Cohesion means a class should encapsulate all functionality regarding a specific problem or data structure. Binding implies that a class should have little or no dependencies on other classes, so it becomes an independent and self-sufficient reusable component. This is rarely possible; many classes use other classes and so on. But externs generate lots of bindings, and in the end, your class diagram will begin to look like a spider web. Code will be impossible to separate from the rest of the application.

Thus, the solution to the singleton problem is different from those explained earlier. It starts by declaring a class that has only one public method, which will be used to request an instance of the singleton. All instances actually point at the same structure, so this request call must create the singleton for the first call and just return pointers to it in subsequent calls. Thus, the constructor is a protected member, and all outside accesses to the class are done by the instance request call.

Here is the code for a sample singleton:

```
class Singleton {
public:
    static Singleton* Instance();
protected:
    Singleton();
private:
    static Singleton* _instance;
};

Singleton* Singleton::_instance = 0;

Singleton* Singleton::Instance () {
    if (_instance == 0)
    {
    instance = new Singleton;
    }
return _instance;
}
```

Any class requiring access to the singleton will just create one singleton variable (which will be different in each case). But all these variables will end up pointing at the same, unique object in memory. Check out the singleton class hierarchy in Figure 4.1.

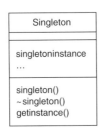

Figure 4.1   Class hierarchy for the singleton design pattern.

Strategy

Sometimes you will need to create objects whose behavior can be changed dynamically. Take a soldier, for example. He might have an update routine that recalculates all his AI. Imagine that his AI can be one of four types: an AI routine to fight, one to escape, one to stay idle, and one to follow a trajectory with his squad mates. Now, it would be great from a simplicity and elegance standpoint to have a single `recalc_AI` function that could handle any of these strategies internally. A quick and dirty solution would be to store a state variable and use it to drive a switch construct that selects the proper routine according to the desired behavior. The code would be something like this:

```
void recalc_AI()
{
switch (state)
    {
    case FIGHT: recalc_fight(); break;
    case ESCAPE: recalc_escape(); break;
    case IDLE: recalc_idle(); break;
    case PATROL: recalc_patrol(); break;
    }
}
```

But this is not very elegant, especially if there are a number of strategies to implement. Another solution is to subclass the object, so each one of the derived objects implements one of the algorithms. This solution is simply too complex in practical terms. Here is where the strategy pattern kicks in. Its goal is to separate the class definition from one (or several) of its member algorithms, so these algorithms can be interchanged at runtime. As a result, our soldier would have a single global algorithm (the `recalc_AI` call), which could be swapped dynamically in an elegant way.

The implementation of the strategy pattern involves two classes. First, there is the strategy class, which provides the strategic algorithm. This is a pure abstract class, from which specific strategies are derived as subclasses. Second, there is the context class, which defines where the strategy should be applied and has a member that executes the selected strategy and swaps strategies when needed. Here is the source code for such a system. The soldier class dynamically changes strategies:

```
class soldier
{
public:
    soldier(strategy *);
    void recalc_AI();
    void change_strategy(strategy *);
```

```
private:
    point pos;
    float yaw;
    strategy* _thestrategy;
};


soldier::soldier(strategy *stra)
{
thestrategy=stra;
}

void soldier::recalc_AI()
{
thestrategy->recalcstrategy(pos,yaw);
}


void soldier::changestrategy(strategy *stra)
{
thestrategy=stra;
}
```

And here is the strategy class along with two derived classes:

```
class strategy
{
public:
    virtual int recalc_strategy(point,float) = 0;
protected:
    strategy();
};



class fightstrategy : public strategy
{
public:
    strategy();
```

```
    virtual int recalcstrategy(point, float);
};

class idlestrategy: public strategy
{
public:
    strategy();
    virtual int recalcstrategy(point, float);
};
```

Here is a usage example:

```
soldier* soldier1= new soldier(new idlestrategy);

soldier1.recalc_AI();

soldier1.changestrategy(new fightstrategy);

soldier1.recalc_AI();
```

Notice how we have increased both the readability and performance of the system by following this DP. Interfaces are much simpler, and the switch/subclassing has been avoided. Figure 4.2 details what a class structure for this pattern might look like.

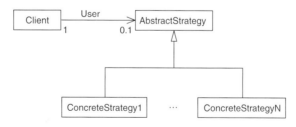

Figure 4.2   Class hierarchy for a strategy design pattern.

Factory

Modern applications need to create and dispose of objects continually. Whether objects are text blocks in a word processor or enemies in a hack-and-slash game, a significant portion of your program is surely devoted to creating them on demand and destroying them at the end of their life cycle. As many programmers work on the same code and applications grow, this creation-destruction code spreads through many files, often causing problems due to inconsistencies in the protocol. The factory pattern centralizes the object creation and destruction, thus providing a universal, rock-solid method for handling objects.

Factories usually come in two flavors: abstract and regular factories. Abstract factories are used whenever we need the product to be an abstract class, and hence we must derive specific products by means of inheritance. This is useful, because we only have a single call, which returns the abstract product. By creating product derivatives, our class can accommodate a variety of situations. Regular factories, on the other hand, need one method per type of product they want to build, because there is no inheritance.

For the abstract factory type, the best example would be a central object creator for a game engine—one object that centralizes the creation of texture maps, meshes, and so on. Here is the source code for such an example:

```
class Product {};

class Texture : public Product {};
class Mesh : public Product {};
class Item : public Product {};

typedef int ProductId;

#define TEXTURE 0
#define MESH 1
#define ITEM 2

class AbstractFactory {
public:
    Product*Create(ProductId);
};

Product* AbstractFactory::Create (ProductId id)
{
switch (id)
    {
```

```
    case TEXTURE return new Texture; break;
    case MESH return new Mesh; break;
    case ITEM return new Item; break;
    }
}
```

And a simple calling example would be

```
AbstractFactory AF;
Texture *t=AF.Create(TEXTURE);
```

Now, here is a variant without using the abstract class. We somehow lose the elegance of the single create method but avoid using virtual classes:

```
class Texture {};
class Mesh {};
class Item {};

class Factory
    {
    public:
    Texture *CreateTexture();
    Mesh *CreateMesh();
    Item *CreateItem();
    };



Texture* Factory::CreateTexture ()
{
return new texture;
}



Mesh* Factory::CreateMesh()
{
return new Mesh;
}
```

```
Item* Factory::CreateItem()
{
return new item;
}
```

In this case, an example using the factory would look something like this:

```
Factory F;
Texture *t=F.CreateTexture();
```

Figure 4.3 illustrates abstract and concrete factories and their products.

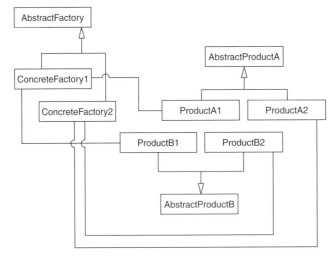

Figure 4.3   Abstract and concrete factories and their products.

Spatial Index

As games grow in complexity, the need for fast 3D tests increases as well. Gone are the days of simple objects with few triangles. Today we are processing several million triangles per second, and too often even the simplest test can become a bottleneck if applied to the complete data set.

Thus, a spatial index is defined as a DP that allows the application programmer to perform queries on large 3D environments, such as game levels, efficiently.

Some of the queries handled by a spatial index are

➤ Is there any primitive closer than X units?

➤ How many primitives are closer than Y units?

Using a naïve approach, we can easily derive algorithms with 0 (number of primitives) cost to solve the preceding problems. The spatial index, however, offers almost constant cost, meaning that tests like the previous ones require an amount of computation that is independent of the input data set. That is the main characteristic of a spatial index: It indexes space so that we can perform queries without examining the whole set.

Spatial indexes can be implemented using different data structures, from the very simple to the very complex. Some solutions will be faster, often taking a higher memory toll in return. Depending on the specifics of your program, you will need to choose the implementation that best suits your needs. But from an API standpoint, a spatial index can be seen as a black box that speeds up geometric tests regardless of how it is implemented internally.

Spatial Index as a List

The simplest (and slowest) spatial index is a regular linked list. In order to compute any of the queries, we must scan the complete list, thus having 0 (number of elements) access time. But lists are a decent option in some circumstances. For example, a list could be an option in those applications that work with small (less than 20, for example) data sets. A classic example would be to store enemies in one game level (as long as there are not many enemies). In this case, more involved solutions simply do not pay off, because the performance will be more or less similar (see Figure 4.4).

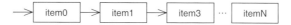

Figure 4.4   Traversal cost makes list-based spatial indexes suited only for small data sets.

Spatial Index as a Regular Grid

The second implementation of the spatial index pattern involves using a regular grid (explained in the previous chapter) that divides the space into buckets of the same size.

Then, each bucket holds a linked list of the elements located there. Bucket size can be determined at load time to ensure a good balance between performance (the smaller the bucket, the better) and memory (the smaller the bucket, the higher the memory footprint). Take a look at Figure 4.5 for a visual representation of such a grid.

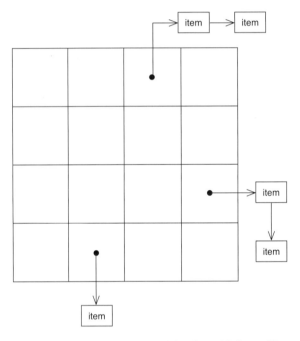

Figure 4.5   A diagram showing the grid spatial index with lists of items in each cell.

Spatial indexing with regular grids really makes a difference in all geometric tests: We only need to find out the position we will be scanning from (the location of the player, for example). Then, we transform that 3D position into cell coordinates and scan the associated list (and maybe those of the neighboring buckets). All in all, in dense scenarios, this can be orders of magnitude faster than using just a list.

Imagine for example a spatial index that holds 1000 primitives (for example, trees), which are evenly spaced in a map that is 1×1 Km. We can store them in a regular grid 100 meters in size. We will thus create a 10×10 grid. To test for a collision with one of the primitives, we will just convert the player position into cell position (this can be easily done using integer divides). Then, once the cell is located, we simply scan the list of that cell and the nine neighboring cells to make sure we haven't hit anyone. Because there are 1000 primitives and 100 buckets, we can assume each bucket holds a

10-element list on average. Thus, scanning 10 buckets (the one we are standing in and the nine neighbors) involves 100 tests in a worst-case scenario. Now compare that to the 1000 tests we would need if we weren't using the spatial index.

Even better, the index can be adjusted. Now imagine that we have refined our scale, and each bucket is now 50 meters across. We would have a 20×20 grid, for a grand total of 400 buckets. In this case, each bucket would hold 2.5 primitives on average, and the collision test would just need 25 tests in total. Obviously, there is a downside to all this magic. This new version takes up four times more memory than the previous version.

The more important downside to all this is that many cells will be useless. The structure is regular, and thus it does not adapt well to the irregularities in the distribution.

Spatial Index as a Quadtree/Octree

Spatial indexes can also be implemented using quadtrees (or octrees if you need to handle real 3D data). In this case, we would split the quadtree until the current node is not holding data beyond a fixed threshold. We can say, for example, that no leaf node should have more than 10 items, and propagate the subdivision of the tree until we reach that goal. The construction of the data structure is adaptive at the core, adjusting to the layout of the data.

Then, for the specific tests, we would traverse the tree using the distance criteria to prune as we advance. For example, here is the pseudocode for a collision detection test with a threshold distance of five meters. I assume the node data structure has four pointers to the four descendant nodes, labeled respectively topleft, topright, bottomleft, and bottomright:

```
checkcollision (point p)

if (topleft node is not empty)
    if (closest point from topleft node is closer than 5 meters to p)
        checkcollision in that node
if (topright node is not empty)
    if (closest point from topright node is closer than 5 meters to p)
    checkcollision in that node
if (bottomleft node is not empty)
    if (closest point from bottomleft node is closer than 5 meters to p)
        checkcollision in that node
```

```
if (bottomright node is not empty)
     if (closest point from bottomright node is closer than 5 meters to p)
          checkcollision in that node
if (all child nodes are empty)
     // we are in a leaf
     scan the list of objects corresponding to this leaf
```

Quadtrees (depicted in Figure 4.6) will usually be slower than grids, because they need to traverse the data structure more thoroughly. On the other hand, memory use is much lower, making them an interesting choice under some circumstances. Keep in mind, however, that quadtrees built this way are not very suitable for dynamic geometry. If we are storing moving objects, they might change the quadtree cell they are stored in, and rebuilding a quadtree on the fly to accommodate this kind of change is not trivial. We need to remove the object that has left the node, or maybe collapse that node completely, and finally insert it in its new location (maybe resplitting as we do so).

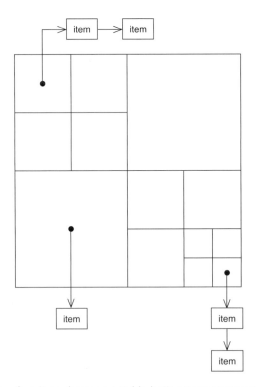

Figure 4.6 Quadtrees/octrees provide better memory management than grids at higher coding complexity.

Composite

Many types of applications, and games in particular, need to hold heterogeneous collections of data together for different reasons. A game level can have sublevels (which in turn can have sublevels), potions, enemies (which can be composed, for example, as in a horse and rider approach), objects, and so on. The overall data structure can be best described as a part-whole hierarchy with each element being either a primitive or a composite, quite likely of different types. Having all data in a single structure makes traversal more intuitive, especially when we couple the composite with a spatial index that allows local queries such as "Which potions are in this room?" Thus, it would be great if programming languages offered some constructs that made the implementation of these complex collections easier. But most programming languages only support homogeneous arrays, so a higher-abstraction solution is needed. This is what the composite DP is all about: creating part-whole heterogeneous hierarchies where we can access primitives and composite objects using a standard interface. This way a single interface will make traversal easier, and each object will retain its specific features and internal structure.

In terms of implementation, the best way to represent a composite is to write a list of elements. The element class will be defined as pure virtual, which means we cannot create objects of this class directly, but need to derive other classes through inheritance. These derived classes will inherit all the attributes and methods of the pure virtual class but will also use extra attributes to encode class-specific information.

As an example, let's take a look at the source code required to implement the level-wide data structure we mentioned earlier: a structure that can hold sublevels, each one with potions and objects. The class `Level` represents the whole level, and then we use the class `LevelItem` to describe primitive entities inside that level: potions, objects the user can grab, and so on.

```
class Level {
public:
    virtual ~Level();

    const char* Name() { return _name; }

    virtual float LifePoints();
    virtual int NumEnemies();
```

```
        virtual void Add(LevelItem*);
        virtual void Remove(LevelItem*);
        virtual Iterator<LevelItem*>* CreateIterator();
protected:
        LevelItem(const char*);
private:
        const char* _name;
};

class Potion: public LevelItem {
public:
        Potion(const char*);
        virtual ~Potion ();

        virtual float LifePoints();
};

class CompositeItem : public LevelItem {
public:
        virtual ~CompositeItem();

        virtual float LifePoints();
        virtual int NumEnemies();

        virtual void Add(LevelItem*);
        virtual void Remove(LevelItem*);
        virtual Iterator<LevelItem*>* CreateIterator();

protected:
        CompositeItem(const char*);
private:
        List<LevelItem*> _items;
};

float CompositeItem::LifePoints() {
        Iterator<LevelItem*>* i = CreateIterator();
        float total = 0;

        for (i->First(); !i->IsDone(); i->Next()) {
```

```
            total += i->CurrentItem()->LifePoints();
        }
        delete i;
        return total;
    }


    int CompositeItem::NumEnemies() {
        Iterator<LevelItem*>* i = CreateIterator();
        int total = 0;

        for (i->First(); !i->IsDone(); i->Next()) {
            total += i->CurrentItem()->NumEnemies();
        }
        delete i;
        return total;
    }


    class Enemy : public CompositeItem{
    public:
        Enemy(const char*);
        virtual ~Enemy();

        virtual float LifePoints();
        virtual int NumEnemies();
    };


    class SubLevel: public CompositeItem{
    public:
        SubLevel(const char*);
        virtual ~SubLevel();

        virtual float LifePoints();
        virtual int NumEnemies();
    };


    void LordOfTheRings ()
    {
    Level* MiddleEarth=new Level("Middle Earth");
    SubLevel* TheShire= new SubLevel("TheShire");
```

```
SubLevel* Moria= new SubLevel("Mines of Moria");
MiddleEarth->Add(TheShire);
MiddleEarth->Add(Moria);

Enemy *Nazgul=new Enemy("Nazgul");
Enemy *NazgulRider=new Enemy("NazgulRider");
Enemy *NazgulSteed=new Enemy("NazgulSteed");
Nazgul->Add(NazgulRider);
Nazgul->Add(NazgulSteed);
TheShire->Add(Nazgul);

Enemy *Balrog=new Enemy("Balrog");
Moria->Add(Balrog);

Potion *Lembas=new Potion("Lembas");
TheShire->Add(Lembas);
cout << "The number of monsters in Middle Earth is " <<
MiddleEarth->NumEnemies() << endl;
cout << "The life points for the monsters are " << MiddleEarth-
>LifePoints() << endl;
}
```

The preceding code creates a hierarchy based on *The Lord of the Rings*. As a result, we create two sublevels (Moria and The Shire) and then a host of creatures and potions in each zone, showing how composites can handle nonhomogeneous data structures. Figure 4.7 complements this code with a drawing of the composite pattern data structure.

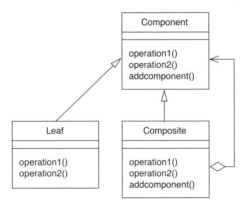

Figure 4.7 The composite design pattern.

Flyweight

The last pattern we will review is the flyweight, which is extremely useful when we need to have large collections of objects that are fundamentally the same except for a few parameters. In this case, we do not want to overpopulate our memory with lots of objects that are mostly identical, but instead we want to use system resources efficiently while keeping a uniform access interface. A simple and very game-oriented example is the units in a real-time strategy game. All infantry soldiers are virtually the same except for two parameters: the position and the life level. But the AI routines, graphics handling code, texture and geometry data, and most other parameters like movement speed and weapons are the same regardless of the instance you examine.

Then, the flyweight pattern suggests dividing the object into two separate classes. First, we need to create the actual flyweight, which is the core object and is shared among all instances. Flyweights are managed through a `FlyweightFactory` that creates and stores them in a memory pool. The flyweight contains all the intrinsic elements of the object; that is, all information that is independent of the object's context and is thus sharable. Second, we will need external objects that will use the flyweights, passing the extrinsic (thus, state dependent) information as a parameter. These concrete objects contain state information, such as the position and life level of our strategy game soldiers.

Let's take a look at how we would code such an example using the flyweight DP:

```
class InfantrySoldier: public AbstractFlyweight
    {
    float speed;
    float turnspeed;
    (...)
    public:
        void Paint(ExtrinsicSoldierInfo *);
        void RecalcAI(ExtrinsicSoldierInfo *);
    };

class InfantrySoldierInstance
    {
    ExtrinsicSoldierInfo info;
    public:
        void Paint();
        void RecalcAI();
```

```
    };

void InfantrySoldierInstance::Paint()
{
FlyweightFactory *FF=new FlyweightFactory;
InfantrySoldier *IS=FF->GetFlyweight(INFANTRY_SOLDIER);
IS->Paint(info);
}

void InfantrySoldierInstance::RecalcAI()
{
FlyweightFactory *FF=new FlyweightFactory;
InfantrySoldier *IS=FF->GetFlyweight(INFANTRY_SOLDIER);
IS->Recalc(info);
}
```

Notice how the InfantrySoldierInstance class is lightened as all the stateless soldier data structures and algorithms are moved to the InfantrySoldier class. All we
would need to add would be a FlyweightFactory object, which would be an object
factory and a singleton. The FlyweightFactory class has a method that retrieves a
flyweight, passing the name of the flyweight (a symbolic constant) as a parameter.
Notice how the returned flyweight will not be created on a case-by-case basis, but
reused over many calls by using the following source code:

```
class FlyweightFactory
    {
    AbstractFlyweight *flyweight;
    int NumFlyweights;
    public:
    AbstractFlyweight * GetFlyWeight(int);
    };


AbstractFlyweight *FlyweightFactory::GetFlyWeight(int key)
{
if (flyweight[key] exists) return flyweight[key];
flyweight[key]=new flyweight;
return flyweight[key];
}
```

Thus, we can keep all our infantry soldiers in memory by translating most of their behavior to the flyweight and externalizing all state-dependent functionality to a higher class abstraction level. Flyweights are pictured in Figure 4.8.

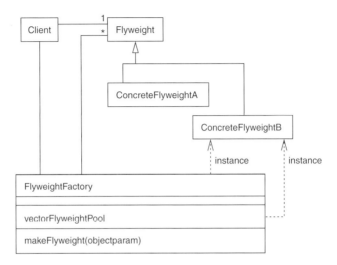

Figure 4.8   Class hierarchy for the flyweight design pattern.

Usability Patterns

In recent years, the concept of DPs has surpassed the boundaries of software architecture and is being used in many other areas of application design and development. Web sites, GUIs, and so on can all be described in terms of DPs that are used frequently and have been researched (and hopefully solved satisfactorily). In this section, I will provide some hints on usability DPs that for some reason or another can be useful for game developers.

Shield

A shield is a protective layer that prevents the user from accidentally activating a feature or function that causes undesirable side effects. For example, a button that causes the game to shut down would constitute an undesirable side effect. When designing these kinds of situations, the shield forces the user to confirm his decision, so two mistakes are required in order to activate the said option by error. A classic example of shields is the confirmation messages to leave the game. But some shields also involve clever screen trickery. Think of a real-time strategy game where the user can choose to disband one unit, thus losing it forever. This is a sensitive option, because choosing it by mistake will have a deep impact on the player. Thus, sometimes games require the player to perform two clicks of a button to choose an option. This way if the player wants to disband the unit, he must select a more complex click sequence, ensuring he is not activating the option by mistake.

State

States are visual cues of the user's current configuration. An example would be the changing mouse cursor in old Sierra adventures. The left mouse button performed an action (moving, talking, and so on), whereas the right button was used to cycle through the available actions. The mouse cursor depicted the current state—a walking character for the move option, an open mouth to engage in dialogue, and so on.

States are incredibly popular. From "lock on" indicators in a combat flight simulator to robes worn by a role-playing game character, states are a handy and elegant way to inform the player of the current configuration.

A potential issue with states is preventing ambiguities. The number of states for a specific option must be small, and their symbolic representations must be clearly distinguishable. Also, state representations must be simple to identify, especially for those states that change often.

Automatic Mode Cancellation

The automatic mode cancellation (AMC) pattern can be used in games that have modes/automata, like a real-time strategy game, for example. To move one unit, a player must first click the unit, then click the Move button on the GUI, and then click the destination. But what happens if the user clicks somewhere in the game's scenario before clicking the Move button on the GUI? Logically, we will cancel the current mode and start over. This is what AMC is all about—detecting actions that do not fit the current mode and using them to cancel the current sequence of operations.

Other known uses of AMC are found in many games where an action requires two key presses/mouse button presses. Imagine a soccer game where you can control the force of each pass and shoot by pressing the Shoot key twice. The first time you press the

Shoot key, a progress bar begins to increase on the GUI. By pressing the key again at the right moment, the shoot is performed using that force. The same principle is found in many golf games and some space shooters. But what if the player does not press the required key the second time? Quite likely, that means the first attempt was a mistake, or he simply has changed his mind and does not want to shoot. From a usability standpoint, we will cancel the shoot so the game is more playable.

Magnetism

Magnetism is a very powerful paradigm to use when we need the user to be precise. For example, consider a first-person shooter where the player needs to aim at enemies from far away in combat. At least in "easy" mode, it makes sense to code an auto-aim, so that if the enemy is located more or less in front of the player, it takes care of the precise aiming. This is what magnetism is about: making some positions dominate, so the user can have more fun with less effort. But sometimes magnetism can get in the way of realism. An advanced player will want to aim manually, so magnetism should always be an option, not a must.

Another interesting use of magnetism is found in strategy games or, generally speaking, games where we must be able to pick units or positions on a map. In a strategy game, we need our mouse cursor to gravitate around units so it is easier to select them. Imagine that you have one unit selected and are in "combat" mode, so you must click on the position of the map where the unit should move in order to engage in a fight. Because it doesn't make sense to fight against a rock or a piece of land, you can code the GUI so when the user clicks, it automatically detects the closest unit to the cursor and sends the player unit there. This way we can prevent the inexactitudes in user control that make the game less fun.

Focus

The focus pattern is useful when we need the user to concentrate on a specific piece of information so the rest becomes momentarily irrelevant. It has been used extensively in games in many visual reincarnations. One of the most popular focus examples is the deactivation of some menu options by graying them out. This is found in many Windows applications. The programmer does not want us to get lost in a sea of possibilities, many of which are actually not useful. Thus, the ones that make no sense are deactivated.

This pattern is used extensively in games, especially in strategy and RPG titles. For example, many sports titles involving teams allow us to specify tactics for each player. While we are working on a specific player, the rest of the team is blurred, thereby reducing the amount of information we must be aware of.

Focusing can be depicted visually in a variety of ways, from graying out to effectively blurring the irrelevant information.

Progress

Progress is one of the most widely used usability patterns. Its main application is displaying quantitative information about a process with a beginning and an end, so the user knows how long the process is and exactly where he is currently.

The obvious example is progress bars such as the ones used to depict level loading. Not providing such a cue makes the player nervous, because he does not know if the game is actually doing something or is simply malfunctioning. But there are other uses of the progress pattern. A good example is life meters. The player character in *Diablo* had two meters, one for health and one for mana, which was useful to perform spells. *Diablo* is a good example of how to integrate the progress inside the game aesthetics. The progress bar was depicted as two flasks, one red and one blue. Other games propose more extreme approaches. A good example is *Wolfenstein*, which depicted the life level using the face of our character with increasing damage levels. There is a potential risk with these artistic representations: Too often they will not convey the distance from our current state to the end of the process as accurately as a numeric/graphic bar would. We play *Wolfenstein* and see our character with a scar and a nosebleed. But do we know how many hits he can sustain, or how far he is from full health? It is hard to tell. Therefore, progress bars should be carefully designed so aesthetics do not destroy the usability pattern.

In Closing

The DP philosophy can greatly improve your coding practices. Reusing proven software components is the best way to create stable and elegant code. However, this chapter has only scratched the surface. Make sure you check out Appendix E, "Further Reading," to learn more about DPs.

Chapter 5

User Input

KEY TOPICS

- The Keyboard
- Mouse
- Joysticks
- Hardware Abstraction
- Force Feedback
- In Closing

"If it keeps up, man will atrophy all his limbs but the push-button finger."

Frank Lloyd Wright

A smooth user interaction model is key to any good game. Without adequate user input mechanisms, gameplay becomes obstructed and frustration occurs. In this chapter, we will explore the basics of user input control. Sadly, there will be few general rules. User interaction takes place at a relatively low abstraction level, and implementations tend to be quite hardware dependent. Where possible, general techniques will be exposed. But most of this chapter is devoted to the specific input methods available for popular platforms on the PC, such as the Win32 API and Microsoft's DirectInput.

The Keyboard

Keyboards are the main input device for PC-based games, but are also available for mobile phones, some consoles, and palm devices. That makes them, in all probability, the most widely available input device. Unfortunately, such a popular input device is not very well suited for games. Keyboard mappings take time to learn, and the general idea of a keyboard is altogether impractical for small children.

Being a multifunction peripheral that can be used to type documents and to play games, it is not surprising that keyboards can be read using a variety of methods, depending on the specific requirements of the application. Some methods retrieve full strings, others work on a key-by-key basis, and so on. But for gaming purposes, two types of routines are relevant. First, there are the synchronous routines, which wait until a key is pressed and then report it to the application. Second, there are asynchronous routines, which return immediately after being called, and give the application information about which keys were pressed, if any.

Synchronous read modes are used to type information, such as the character name in a role-playing game (RPG). They work by polling the controller until new key input messages arrive. But they are not very well suited for real gameplay. The game code must continually check to see whether keys were pressed, and whatever the response, keep drawing, executing the AI, and so on. So, asynchronous controllers are the way to go. They provide fast tests to check the keyboard state efficiently.

Asynchronous routines can also belong to two different families. Some of them are designed to test the state of individual keys, so the programmer passes the key code as a parameter and gets the state as a result. Others, like the ones exposed by DirectInput, retrieve the whole keyboard state in a single call, so the programmer can then access the data structure and check for the state of each key without further hardware checks. The second type of routine is generally more efficient because there is less overhead involved.

As an example, we will focus on a single-key asynchronous call for the PC platform. The call is Windows specific and is part of the Win32 API. The syntax is

```
short GetAsyncKeyState(int keycode);
```

This call receives a key code and returns a short value, which encodes different state information. The key code we pass as a parameter can either be a capitalized character, such as "K", or an extended key code, which is used to read special characters. By using extended key codes, we can read specific keys, such as Delete, the function keys, Tabs, and so on. Table 5.1 provides a list of the main special key codes for this call.

Table 5.1   Keycodes for the `GetAsyncKeyState` call

Keycode	Description
VK_SHIFT VK_RSHIFT, VK, LSHIFT	Either of the two Shift keys
VK_MENU	Either of the Alt keys
VK_CTRL VK_RCTRL, VK_LCTRL	Any of the Ctrl keys
VK_UP, VK_DOWN, VK_LEFT, VK_RIGHT	The cursor keys
VK_F1...VK_F12	The function keys
VK_ESCAPE	The Esc key
VK_SPACE	The Spacebar
VK_RETURN	The Enter/Return key
VK_HOME, VK_END, VK_PRIOR, VK_NEXT	The numeric keypad keys
VK_BACK	The Backspace key
VK_TAB	The Tab key
VK_INSERT, VK_DELETE	The Insert and Delete keys

The return value encodes the state of the key passed as a parameter. The most significant bit is activated if the key is currently pressed, whereas the least significant bit is activated if this key was activated the last time `GetAsyncKeyState` was called. Here is an example of how to check whether the left Shift key is pressed:

```
If (GetAsyncKeyState(VK_LSHIFT))
     {
     // whatever
     }
```

Notice that, due to the nature of the call, we can check multiple keys. The next example shows how to test for the left Shift AND Return combination:

```
If ((GetAsyncKeyState(VK_LSHIFT)) &&
(GetAsyncKeyState(VK_RETURN)))
     {
     // whatever
     }
```

As you can see, each key test requires a system call, which can be troublesome for those systems checking a lot of different keys. Now, let's compare this call with a whole keyboard check, which can be performed by using the call:

```
bool GetKeyboardState(PBYTE  *lpKeyState);
```

Here the result only encodes if the function succeeded, and the real meat is returned as an array passed as a reference. Then, successive checks such as the following perform the individual test, which is nothing but a simple array lookup:

```
if (keystate[VK_RSHIFT])
      {
      // right shift was pressed
      }
```

Again, for games that check many keys (such as a flight simulator), this option can be better than repeated calls to `GetAsyncKeyState`. The programmer only needs to be aware that an initial call to `GetKeyboardState` is required to load the array.

Another possible pitfall to watch out for is that this second mode does not immediately check the keys when you perform the test. Keys are checked at the call to `GetKeyboardState`. If there is a significant delay between this test and the array lookup, undesirable side effects might occur because the array will contain "old" key values.

Keyboard with DirectInput

DirectInput provides fast asynchronous access to key states. A single call can retrieve the state of the whole keyboard, so subsequent tests are just table lookups. The operation is thus very similar to the `GetKeyboardState` Win32 call. But before we delve into keyboard reading code, we need to discuss how DirectInput works.

DirectInput encapsulates keyboards, joysticks, mice, and any other exotic input peripheral under a common interface called a device. The operation is really straight-forward. We first need to boot DirectInput. This implies creating a DirectInput object, from which all other objects dealing with input processing can be derived. The DirectInput object can thus be used to create devices, which are the logical interfaces to peripherals. Once a device has been created, we need to specify several parameters, such as the format of the data we want to interchange with the device, and the cooperative level, which tells DirectInput if the device is to be shared among different applications or if we need it exclusively.

DirectInput devices can then be polled asynchronously. We query the state of the device, not waiting for a specific event like a key or button press. This means DirectInput will take a snapshot of the current state of the device and return it to the application so it can be processed. As a summary, here is a list of the steps involved in setting up a keyboard DirectInput:

1. Create the DirectInput object.

2. Create the keyboard device.

3. Set the data format for reading it.

4. Set the cooperative level you will use with the operating system.

5. Read data as needed.

Let's now move on to a specific example, beginning with the DirectInput code needed to boot the API. The code in this section has been tested in both DirectX8 and DirectX9. DirectInput is almost identical in both versions.

```
LPDIRECTINPUT8 g_pDI=NULL;

HRESULT hr=DirectInput8Create(GetModuleHandle(NULL),DIRECTINPUT_VERSION,

IID_IDirectInput8,(VOID**)&g_pDI,NULL)))
```

In the preceding code, the first parameter is used to send the instance handle to the application that is creating the DirectInput object. Then, we need to pass the DirectInput version we are requesting. The macro DIRECTINPUT_VERSION is a handy way to pass the current version number. Next, we need to pass the unique interface identifier for the object we are requesting. We use IID_IDirectInput8 to request a DirectInput object, but we can use other parameters to define ANSI or Unicode versions of the interface. We then pass the pointer so we can receive the already initialized object, and the last parameter is used to perform Component Object Model (COM) aggregation. You probably won't want to aggregate your DirectInput object to anything else, so leave this as NULL.

Now we have a DirectInput object ready for use. It is now time for the real keyboard code. We will first request the device and set some parameters that define how we will communicate with it. Then, we will examine the source code used to read data from a keyboard.

The first step is to actually request a device from the DirectInput object. This is achieved with the line:

```
HRESULT hr =g_pDI->CreateDevice(GUID_SysKeyboard, &g_pKeyboard, NULL);
```

The call must receive the Global Unique Identifier (GUID) for the desired device. DirectInput is built on top of the COM, an object-oriented programming model. In COM, GUIDs are used to identify specific objects or interfaces. Internally, GUIDs are just 128-bit structures, but they are used to represent functions, objects, and generally any DirectX construct. In this case, classic GUIDs for the different devices are

➤ GUID_SysKeyboard: The default system keyboard.

➤ GUID_SysMouse: The default system mouse.

Additional GUIDs can be assigned to joysticks. However, these GUIDs should not be written directly, but as the result of a call to DirectInput8::EnumDevices. We will be covering joysticks in the next section. For our keyboard, GUID_SysKeyboard will do the job. The second parameter is just the pointer to the newly created device, and the last parameter is again reserved for aggregation and must thus be set to NULL.

Now, we must tell the keyboard how we want to exchange data. This is achieved with the call to SetDataFormat, as shown here:

```
HRESULT hr = g_pKeyboard->SetDataFormat( &c_dfDIKeyboard );
```

The call must receive a parameter of type LPCDIDATAFORMAT, which is a structure defined as:

```
typedef struct DIDATAFORMAT {
    DWORD dwSize;
    DWORD dwObjSize;
    DWORD dwFlags;
    DWORD dwDataSize;
    DWORD dwNumObjs;
    LPDIOBJECTDATAFORMAT rgodf;
} DIDATAFORMAT, *LPDIDATAFORMAT;

typedef const DIDATAFORMAT *LPCDIDATAFORMAT;
```

This structure controls the number of objects we will be requesting, the format of each one, and so on. Because it is a complex structure to fill, DirectInput already comes with several predefined data formats that we can use directly. For a keyboard, the format `c_dfDiKeyboard` tells DirectInput we will be requesting the full keyboard, stored in an array of 256 bytes.

In addition, we need to tell DirectInput about the cooperative level we will be using with this device. This is achieved by using the line:

```
HRESULT hr=g_pKeyboard->SetCooperativeLevel(hWnd,
DISCL_FOREGROUND| DISCL_EXCLUSIVE);
```

Here we pass the window handle as the first parameter, and the second parameter is the OR of a series of flags that control the cooperative level. In this case, we are telling DirectInput that we want exclusive access and that this access should only be valid if the application is in the foreground. As our application moves to the background, the device is automatically unacquired.

Additionally, we need to acquire the keyboard, so we can begin querying its state. The following line will do that for us:

```
g_pKeyboard->Acquire();
```

And now we are ready to begin using the keyboard. Here is the code snippet that declares both DirectInput and the keyboard, and makes sure the device is ready. Error checking has been omitted for clarity:

```
HRESULT hr;
hr = DirectInput8Create( GetModuleHandle(NULL),
DIRECTINPUT_VERSION,
                          IID_IDirectInput8, (VOID**)&g_pDI, NULL );

hr = g_pDI->CreateDevice( GUID_SysKeyboard, &g_pKeyboard, NULL );
hr = g_pKeyboard->SetDataFormat( &c_dfDIKeyboard );
hr = g_pKeyboard->SetCooperativeLevel( hDlg, dwCoopFlags );
hr = g_pKeyboard->Acquire();
```

Reading the keyboard is even easier than preparing it. All we have to do is prepare a 256-byte array and pass it to DirectInput with the keyboard acquired to query its state:

```
BYTE     diks[256];   // DirectInput keyboard state buffer
ZeroMemory( diks, sizeof(diks) );
hr = g_pKeyboard->GetDeviceState( sizeof(diks), diks );
```

Notice how we clear the buffer and then pass it to DirectInput. As with GetAsyncKeyState, specific key codes must be used after the read to query for each key. In this case, all keys are represented by symbolic constants, such as:

```
DIK_RETURN          The return key
DIK_SPACE           The space key
DIK_A … DIK_Z       The alphabetic keys
DIK_F1 … DIK_F10  The function keys
```

Now, to query a specific key, we must test for the most significant bit of the corresponding array position. If that position is set to one, the key is currently being pressed. Thus, to check whether the Return key is activated, the following code can be used:

```
bool return_pressed=(buffer[DIK_RETURN] & 0x80)!=0);
```

As usual, we can read combinations, so we can check whether several keys are pressed simultaneously. Because there is only one DirectInput read at the very beginning, these are just array lookups.

Reading the keyboard is really straightforward. But we must be careful with acquiring and unacquiring the device, which can make our input controller malfunction. Sometimes, especially in some cooperative level modes, we can lose contact with the keyboard momentarily. This is called unacquiring the device. The most popular reason for this is that our application moved to the background, thus losing the keyboard access in favor of another application, which is now in the foreground. Some other events might make us lose track of our device as well. If this happens, we will discover it in the next GetDeviceState call, which will fail. We must then reacquire the keyboard so we can continue querying its state. This is achieved as follows:

```
BYTE    diks[256];    // DirectInput keyboard state buffer
ZeroMemory( diks, sizeof(diks) );
hr = g_pKeyboard->GetDeviceState( sizeof(diks), diks );
if( FAILED(hr) )
        {
        hr = g_pKeyboard->Acquire();
        while( hr == DIERR_INPUTLOST || hr== DIERR_OTHERAPPHASPRIO)
        hr = g_pKeyboard->Acquire();
        }
```

Notice how we detect the error and keep calling Acquire until we regain access to the device.

Once we have finished with our application, it is time to release all DirectInput objects peacefully. Releasing the keyboard is a two-step process. First, we unacquire the device, and then release its data structures. Second, we must delete the main DirectInput object. Overall, the destruction sequence is achieved by using the following code:

```
if( g_pKeyboard ) g_pKeyboard->Unacquire();
SAFE_RELEASE( g_pKeyboard );
SAFE_RELEASE( g_pDI );
```

Notice that we are using the SAFE_RELEASE macros provided with DirectX to ensure that all data structures and allocated memory are deleted.

Mouse

Since their inception in the late 1960s as a CAD input device, mice have been adapted for many uses including computer games. They are especially popular in PC games, but game consoles do not usually support them. Unlike a keyboard or joystick, the mouse not only generates button or key presses, but 2D positions as well. This provides a wider range of input choices at the cost of a higher learning curve for the player.

Mice can be used in a variety of scenarios, from unit picking in a real-time strategy title to the popular mouselook found in most first-person shooters. In all cases, the operation of the mouse can be divided into transmitting positional information (thanks to the internal mouse sensors) and sending button press and release messages.

Let's examine how a mouse operates under DirectInput. The source code is very similar to the keyboard request because DirectInput treats all devices the same. This is beneficial for the programmer because most inner details are hidden. Let's assume we have the main DirectInput object up and running, and start with the device creation pass:

```
LPDIRECTINPUTDEVICE g_pMouse;
HRESULT                 hr;

hr = g_pDI->CreateDevice(GUID_SysMouse, &g_pMouse, NULL);
```

As you can see, it is extremely similar to requesting a keyboard; the only difference being the GUID we pass to request the desired device. Then, the data format is set as follows:

```
hr = g_pMouse->SetDataFormat(&c_dfDIMouse);
```

In this case, the c_dfDIMouse parameter tells DirectInput we will be passing a DIMOUSESTATE structure to IDirectInputDevice::GetDeviceState. This structure has the following signature:

```
typedef struct DIMOUSESTATE {
    LONG lX;
    LONG lY;
    LONG lZ;
```

```
       BYTE rgbButtons[4];
} DIMOUSESTATE, *LPDIMOUSESTATE;
```

This structure returns the X and Y positions, and an optional Z axis, which is usually assigned to a wheel. Then, the button array works like the keyboard array. Buttons are pressed if the high-order bit is set. A variant of this structure is the DIMOUSESTATE2, set by the parameter c_dfDIMouse2. The only difference is that the latter supports eight buttons instead of the four supported by DIMOUSESTATE. These are especially useful in specific mice used for CAD systems, for example.

After the data format has been set, we need to set the cooperative level. No surprises here, as the code is exactly identical to the keyboard version:

```
hr = g_pMouse->SetCooperativeLevel(hWnd,
                DISCL_EXCLUSIVE | DISCL_FOREGROUND);
```

In addition, we need to acquire the ready-to-use device with the line:

```
g_pMouse->Acquire();
```

Here is the full source code in review:

```
LPDIRECTINPUTDEVICE g_pMouse;
HRESULT hr = g_pDI->CreateDevice(GUID_SysMouse, &g_pMouse, NULL);
hr = g_pMouse->SetDataFormat(&c_dfDIMouse);
hr = g_pMouse->SetCooperativeLevel(hWnd,
                DISCL_EXCLUSIVE | DISCL_FOREGROUND);
g_pMouse->Acquire();
```

Reading from this mouse is achieved with the GetDeviceState call, which will return a LPDIMOUSESTATE structure. The source code would be:

```
DIMOUSESTATE dims;          // DirectInput mouse state structure

ZeroMemory( &dims, sizeof(dims) );
hr = g_pMouse->GetDeviceState( sizeof(DIMOUSESTATE), &dims );
if( FAILED(hr) )
{
```

```
                  hr = g_pMouse->Acquire();
while( hr == DIERR_INPUTLOST ||  hr == DIERR_OTHERAPPHASPRIO ||
hr == DIERR_NOTACQUIRED)
hr = g_pMouse->Acquire();
        }
```

Notice how I have added the unacquiring prevention code to avoid losing track of our mouse due to unexpected events. Other than that, the code is very similar to reading a keyboard. To access the mouse attributes, all we have to do is this:

```
int MouseX = dims.lX;
int MouseY = dims.lY;
bool lbutton = (dims.rgbButtons[0] & 0x80)!=0);
```

Usually, button 0 is assigned to the left mouse button, button 1 is assigned to the right one, and button 2 is assigned to the middle button (if available). Regarding positions, remember that a mouse is a relative pointing device. When first acquired, the mouse's position is reset to (0,0). Then, each new read will return the displacement from the last one. Thus, if we move the mouse vertically, we will see displacements in the Y direction. But when we stop the movement, the read mouse value will go back to (0,0). Remember, the mouse does not work with positions but instead works with displacements. Last, but not least, the mouse is usually configured so negative X points to the left, and positive Y points away from our body as we are sitting at a table.

Additionally, remember to release the mouse as soon as you have finished using it. The code is again very similar to the keyboard release code:

```
if( g_pMouse ) g_pMouse->Unacquire();
SAFE_RELEASE( g_pMouse );
SAFE_RELEASE( g_pDI );
```

Mouselook

A popular use of the mouse is to implement the classic mouselook used in many first-person shooters. The mouselook is easy to code once you understand how a mouse operates. All we have to do is use the keys to change our position, and use the mouse to reorient our viewpoint. I will explain the effect fully, so we can combine what we have learned about keyboards and mice.

The game must have at least four degrees of freedom. We must have a position consisting of an X and Z value, and then a yaw and pitch angle. Y values are often added to the mix so we can climb different heights, but roll is generally not needed. We will use the following mapping:

- ➤ Mouse: Mouselook
- ➤ Left arrow: Strafe left
- ➤ Right arrow: Strafe right
- ➤ Up arrow: Move forward
- ➤ Down arrow: Move back

Let's first focus on the keyboard and forget about the orientation for a second. Assuming a standard DirectInput keyboard, we would need the following code to implement the desired behavior:

```
int strafe= (buffer[DIK_RIGHT] & 0x80)!=0) - (buffer[DIK_LEFT] &
0x80)!=0);
int fwd= (buffer[DIK_UP] & 0x80)!=0) - (buffer[DIK_DOWN] &
0x80)!=0);
```

Notice how we have elegantly encapsulated the cursor control. By subtracting opposite directions, we get two numbers, `strafe` and `fwd`, in the range –1..1. These numbers are then used to drive our position update routine:

```
pos.x += fwd*FWDSPEED*elapsed*cos(yaw) +
strafe*STRAFESPEED*elapsed*cos(yaw+3.1416/2);
pos.z += fwd*FWDSPEED*elapsed*sin(yaw) +
strafe*STRAFESPEED*elapsed*sin(yaw+3.1416/2);
```

The `fwd` and `strafe` variables control how each member is multiplied—by –1, 0, or 1—to perform the desired effect. Now, let's take care of pitch and yaw through the mouse:

```
yaw+= YAWSPEED*elapsed*dims.lX;
pitch+= PITCHSPEED* elapsed*dims.lY;
```

So now we have our new pos.x, pos.z, yaw, and pitch player structure updated. Obviously, we need to keep two devices alive, and we need to define all constants in caps to set the desired speed. Notice how each constant is multiplied by an elapsed time factor, which stores the time it took to render the last frame. This way we ensure device-independent performance. For completeness, here is the source code required to compute all specific camera parameters ready to be plugged into an OpenGL or DirectX pipeline:

```
point  campos(pos.x,pos.y,pos.z);
point  camlookat(pos.x+cos(yaw)*cos(pitch),pos.y+sin(pitch),
pos.z+sin(yaw)*cos(pitch));
```

The `lookat` coordinate computation is just a spherical mapping using the pitch and yaw. Depending on how your axes are laid out, a sign might change or you might need to add a constant angle like Pi to the pitch values.

Joysticks

The joystick was introduced in the 1970s as a way to represent positional data easily. The first models were restricted to binary tests: The joystick returned a 0 or 1 to represent whether it was being activated or not. Thus, most joysticks allowed nine positional values: one for the joystick being centered and eight for N, S, E, W, SW, SE, NW, and NE. Usually, the joystick position was mapped to an integer value, with an extra bit used to represent the button press. Most joysticks from eight-bit computers were like this.

As software development houses created better simulations, joysticks began to improve as well. Continuous-output joysticks appeared to satisfy the flight simulation community, but because they offered better control, they became mainstream. Today, all joysticks map the sticks' inclination to a continuous range of values, so we can control our characters precisely.

Controlling a joystick is slightly more complex than working with a keyboard or a mouse. Joysticks come in a variety of shapes and configurations, so the detection and data retrieval process is a bit more involved. Some gamepads have two controllers, whereas others have a stick and a point-of-view (POV). In addition, the number of buttons varies from model to model, making the process of detecting a joystick nontrivial.

In DirectInput, we must ask the API to enumerate the device so it autodetects the joystick so we can use it. For this example, I will assume we already have the DirectInput object ready. The first step is to ask DirectInput to enumerate any joystick it is detecting. This is achieved by using the call:

```
HRESULT hr = g_pDI->EnumDevices( DI8DEVCLASS_GAMECTRL,
                    EnumJoysticksCallback,
                    NULL, DIEDFL_ATTACHEDONLY ) ) )
```

The first parameter tells DirectInput which kind of device we want to detect. It can be a mouse (DI8DEVCLASS_POINTER) or a keyboard (DI8DEVCLASS_KEYBOARD). In this case, we request a game controller, which is valid for both gamepads and joysticks of all kinds. Now comes the tricky part: DirectInput detects all candidate devices. Imagine that we have two joysticks (for example, in a two-player game). DirectInput would need to return two devices. Thus, instead of doing some parameter magic to allow this, DirectInput works with callbacks. A callback is a user-defined function that gets called from inside the execution of a system call. In this case, we provide the EnumJoysticksCallback, a function we write that will get triggered once for each detected joystick. The internals of that function will have to retrieve GUIDs, allocate the device objects, and so on. This is a bit more complicated than returning a list of pointers, but on the other hand, it allows greater flexibility. We will examine our callback in a second. Let's first complete the call profile by stating that the third parameter is a user-defined parameter to be passed to the callback (usually NULL), whereas the last parameter is the enumeration flags. DIEDFL_ATTACHEDONLY is used to state that we only want to detect those devices that are properly attached and installed, the same way DIEDFL_FORCEFEEDBACK is used to restrict the enumeration to force feedback joysticks. Here is the source code for the EnumJoysticksCallback function:

```
BOOL CALLBACK EnumJoysticksCallback( const DIDEVICEINSTANCE*
pdidInstance, VOID* pContext )
{
HRESULT hr;
```

```
hr = g_pDI->CreateDevice( pdidInstance->guidInstance,
&g_pJoystick, NULL );
if( FAILED(hr) ) return DIENUM_CONTINUE;
return DIENUM_STOP;
}
```

Notice how the callback is receiving the device instance, so we only have to create the device using that instance. This is a relatively simple example, where we return to the application as soon as we have found one joystick. If the user had two joysticks attached to the computer, this code would only enumerate the first one. A variant could be used to store each and every joystick in a linked list, so the user can then select the joystick he actually wants to use from a drop-down list.

After the joystick has been enumerated, we can set the data format and cooperative level. No news here—just a rehash of the code required for keyboards and mice:

```
HRESULT hr = g_pJoystick->SetDataFormat( &c_dfDIJoystick );
HRESULT hr = g_pJoystick->SetCooperativeLevel( hWnd,
DISCL_EXCLUSIVE |
                                        DISCL_FOREGROUND );
```

An extra piece of code must be used to set the output range for the joystick. Because it is a device with analog axes, what will be the range of output values? Will it be −1..1 or −1000..1000? We need to make sure the behavior of the joystick is initialized properly. In our case, we will make the joystick respond with a value from −100..100, much like a percentage. To do so, we need to use a second callback. But first we need the following call, which requests the objects associated with the joystick:

```
g_pJoystick->EnumObjects(EnumObjectsCallback, (VOID*)hWnd,
DIDFT_ALL);
```

Objects can be axes, buttons, POVs, and so on. Then, the call will respond via the provided callback. Here is the source code for that callback, which performs the axis initialization:

```
BOOL CALLBACK EnumObjectsCallback( const DIDEVICEOBJECTINSTANCE*
pdidoi,
                                  VOID* pContext )
{
```

```
HWND hDlg = (HWND)pContext;

if( pdidoi->dwType & DIDFT_AXIS )
    {
    DIPROPRANGE diprg;
    diprg.diph.dwSize       = sizeof(DIPROPRANGE);
    diprg.diph.dwHeaderSize = sizeof(DIPROPHEADER);
    diprg.diph.dwHow        = DIPH_BYID;
    diprg.diph.dwObj        = pdidoi->dwType; // Specify the
enumerated axis
    diprg.lMin              = -100;
    diprg.lMax              = +100;
  if( FAILED( g_pJoystick->SetProperty( DIPROP_RANGE, &diprg.diph
) ) )
            return DIENUM_STOP;
    }
}
```

As with the earlier callback, this routine is called once for each object. Then, the if sentence checks whether the returned object is actually an axis, and if so, uses the SetProperty call to specify its response range. The SetProperty call can be used for more exotic functions, such as calibrating the joystick. The first parameter supports many other symbolic constants that can be used for this purpose.

Fortunately, reading from the joystick is not as complex as initializing it. Here the source code is not much different from keyboards or mice. The only difference is that we need to call Poll() before actually reading from the joystick. Joysticks are polled devices, meaning they do not generate interrupts, and thus need to be polled prior to retrieving their state. Other than that, the code is straightforward:

```
hr = g_pJoystick->Poll();
if( FAILED(hr) )
    {
    hr = g_pJoystick->Acquire();
    while( hr == DIERR_INPUTLOST  || hr== DIERR_OTHERAPPHASPRIO)
        hr = g_pJoystick->Acquire();
        return S_OK;
    }
```

```
DIJOYSTATE js;
hr = g_pJoystick->GetDeviceState( sizeof(DIJOYSTATE), &js ));
```

This code returns a DIJOYSTATE structure with all the joystick state information. The profile of the call is as follows:

```
typedef struct DIJOYSTATE {
    LONG lX;
    LONG lY;
    LONG lZ;
    LONG lRx;
    LONG lRy;
    LONG lRz;
    LONG rglSlider[2];
    DWORD rgdwPOV[4];
    BYTE rgbButtons[32];
} DIJOYSTATE, *LPDIJOYSTATE;
```

This structure should suffice for most uses. However, there is a more involved structure with lots of extra parameters available under the DIJOYSTATE2 name. All you have to do is change the SetDataFormat call accordingly:

```
HRESULT hr = g_pJoystick->SetDataFormat( &c_dfDIJoystick2 );
```

Response Curves

We have seen how analog joysticks map the controller position to a continuous range of values so we can detect subtle variations. This behavior can become our best ally or a nightmare depending on how we handle it.

For example, imagine a game like *Mario*, where there is no speed control: Mario is simply running left, running right, or standing still. So how do we implement that using an analog controller? We must discretize the output range so we only get three possible values:

-1 for running left

0   for standing still

1   for running right

Assuming that the analog output is in the range -100..100, we need to define a transfer function that maps a number in the range -100..100 to a number in the range -1..1. Choosing that transfer function—often called *response curve*—accurately is key to keeping good communication with the player. Imagine that we do something like this:

-1   for values [-100..-1]

0   for value 0

1   for values [1..100]

This means the slightest variation or decentering from the controller will trigger a movement, making the game unplayable. For these kinds of response curves (which convert the analog range to a discrete one), we must supply enough dynamic range so that each value will be mapped correctly. For example, a much better solution would be

-1   for values [-100..-25]

0   for values [-24..24]

1   for values [25..100]

This way minimal decalibrations will not trigger the joystick by mistake. This response curve can be seen in Figure 5.1.

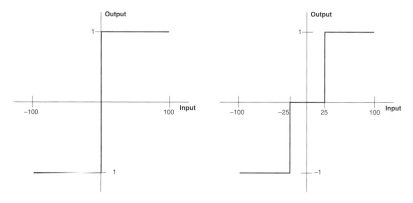

Figure 5.1   Response curve without (left) and with (right) dead zone.

Most games use analog control these days. The analog controller returns a value in a continuous range, and we use that value to implement various degrees of influence (be it speed, turning, etc.) in our game world. An airplane will dive faster if we pull the controller completely, the car will accelerate more aggressively, and so on. However, analog control also needs a response curve. Without a response curve, a car will keep turning if the controller is just minimally decalibrated. Although this is most likely a controller problem, our code must deal with it so the player enjoys a seamless playing experience.

As you might have guessed, we begin by neutralizing the zone around the center of the controller to prevent movements due to bad calibration. But will the neutralization speed map linearly to the controller's position (as in Figure 5.2, left), or will it use a curve (such as the one on the right in Figure 5.2)? Using curves such as parabolas will be useful to implement inertia effects, where the player needs to control the amount of inclination carefully. It makes games a bit harder to master because small errors in the control yield large variations in the effect.

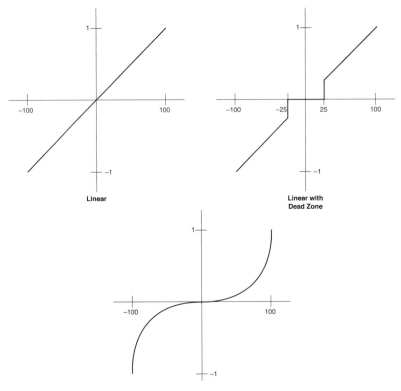

Figure 5.2 Types of response curves.

Hardware Abstraction

Games that run on platforms that support a variety of input controllers offer the richest gaming experience. This is the case not only with the PC (which uses a keyboard, a mouse, and joysticks), but also with most game consoles via exotic peripherals. In recent years, we have used standard controllers, aircraft-style joysticks, snowboards, dance pads of all sorts, and even a fishing rod!

There are two paths a developer might follow when coding for such a platform. Some games will choose to use one (and only one) of the existing controllers. This is the case in most strategy games, which for gameplay reasons are usually coded with a PC mouse in mind. On the other hand, some other games will let the user choose the input method he or she wants to employ. Action games for the PC can often be played with a keyboard, joystick, gamepad, and sometimes even a mouse. Although good for the player, it comes at the cost of complicating the input handling code significantly; and this is exactly where hardware abstraction becomes an issue.

By hardware abstraction, I mean coding your game with a "virtual" controller in mind, so any controller that conforms to that abstract profile can be fitted into the code with zero impact on the game engine. All you need to do is write a generic controller handler (usually, a pure abstract class) from which specific controllers are derived via inheritance. Then, at runtime, only the kind of controller selected by the player is created, providing a seamless and elegant way of integrating different controllers. Figure 5.3 shows how this class structure would work out.

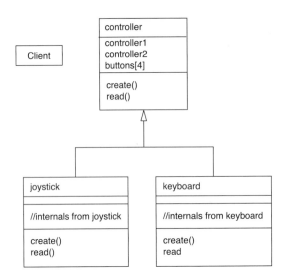

Figure 5.3 A possible class structure to implement device abstraction.

Notice how, for the sake of clarity, I have created a global controller that closely resembles that of a game console. It has two directional controllers and four buttons. These inputs can then be mapped to a keyboard (using keys for the different options), an analog joystick, or a digital joystick. The only item we need to watch out for is the different sensitivity found in keys and sticks. A key can either be pressed or released, thus requiring only a binary value, whereas a joystick will probably map to a continuous set. Thus, some discretization code will be required to offer a standard output.

An even better alternative if you are using DirectInput is to take advantage of action mapping, which allows your device to return not specific state values but game-oriented values. We can assign device events to game events, so the input controller will receive values that are somehow device independent. For example, we can have a joystick and assign a movement on the X axis to the "advance left" action. We can then assign a specific key to the same event, so the input control code becomes independent of the device. We can change the device, and as the control is receiving abstract messages, everything will still work.

Action mapping is not hard to get working under DirectInput, although the code is too lengthy to be detailed here. The first step is defining the actions in our game:

```
enum GAME_ACTIONS {
```

```
WALK,
WALK_LEFT,
WALK_RIGHT,
JUMP
QUIT
};
```

Then, we must provide an action map that relates axis and buttons or keys to the different actions:

```
DIACTION g_adiaActionMap[] =
{
// Joystick input mappings
{ WALK, DIAXIS_FIGHTINGH_LATERAL, 0, ACTION_NAMES[WALK], },
{ JUMP, DIBUTTON_FIGHTINGH_JUMP, 0, ACTION_NAMES[JUMP], },

// Keyboard input mappings
{ WALK_LEFT, DIKEYBOARD_LEFT, 0, ACTION_NAMES[WALK_LEFT], },
{ WALK_RIGHT, DIKEYBOARD_RIGHT, 0, ACTION_NAMES[WALK_RIGHT], },
{ JUMP, DIKEYBOARD_J, 0, ACTION_NAMES[JUMP], },
{ QUIT, DIKEYBOARD_Q, DIA_APPFIXED, ACTION_NAMES[QUIT], },

// Mouse input mappings
{ WALK, DIMOUSE_XAXIS, 0, ACTION_NAMES[WALK], },
{ JUMP, DIMOUSE_BUTTON0, 0, ACTION_NAMES[JUMP], },
};
```

The initialization of the input system would be quite similar to the previous example. All we would need to do is enumerate all input devices supported by the action map. This would be achieved with a call to EnumerateDevicesBySemantics, which would receive the action map and require a callback where all possible devices would be returned. The callback would then have to build the action map for that specific device. Once that is cleared, subsequent read calls would return device-specific data, as in the following example:

```
hr = pdidDevice->Poll();
hr = pdidDevice->GetDeviceData( sizeof(DIDEVICEOBJECTDATA),
                                rgdod, &dwItems, 0 );
for( DWORD j=0; j<dwItems; j++ )
```

```
    {
    UINT_PTR dwAction = rgdod[j].uAppData;
    switch( dwAction )
        {
        case WALK:
            (...)
        }
    }
```

Notice that `GetDeviceData` returns a list of actions, so we can process several buttons or keys in the same loop.

Force Feedback

Many input controllers come with some sort of force feedback these days, from rumble gamepads on game consoles to full force feedback joysticks. This technique is just another layer in our pursuit of immersion and realism.

Force feedback hardware simulates vibration and other force-based effects by incorporating one or more motors that can be configured via programming. These motors vary the position or resistance of the game controller, and by programming fast movement sequences, the illusion of vibration and force are achieved. The number of motors and kind of controller determine the quality of the effect. On the lower end of the spectrum, all gamepads—since the original PlayStation controller—support some kind of force feedback, usually different kinds of vibration much like a cell phone. Joysticks can perform much more sophisticated routines. For example, it is possible to program the joystick to draw a circle with the stick, as well as many other interesting effects.

Programming force feedback devices involves three steps. First, we need a way to create or describe the desired effect in terms of how it affects the controller's position, strength, and so on. Some tools are available for this purpose. Second, the effect must be loaded to the input API. Third, we need a way to reproduce the effect at runtime, either by manually triggering it or by assigning it to a specific event like a timer or specific button press. Sadly, these three steps are largely platform dependent, because developing applications that support force feedback depends greatly on the API. For the remainder of this section, we will focus on Microsoft's DirectInput solution to provide a complete example of how these devices work.

DirectInput allows the creation of force feedback effects both from an external content-creation tool or by using a specific set of commands from within our application. The easiest way is to use the creation tool, called the Force Editor (see Figure 5.4). The editor has a look and feel similar to an audio application, but it works with force curves instead of sound. We can select different kinds of waveforms (square, sawtooth, sine, and so on) and modulate them, so the resulting effect is believable. We can even prototype the effect from the editor, getting a preview of how the end product will feel. When we are happy with the results, we can save them to .ffe files, which will then be read by DirectInput.

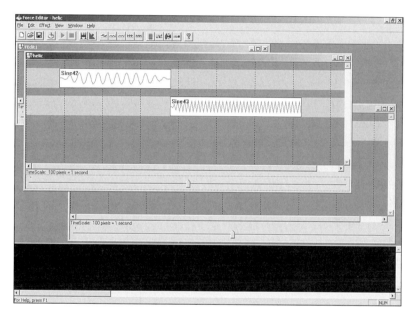

Figure 5.4 Microsoft's Force Editor, built into the DirectX SDK.

From the application's point of view, differences start at the device enumeration phase. We need to query for force feedback compatible devices only, as follows:

```
HRESULT hr = q_pDI->EnumDevices( 0, EnumFFDevicesCallback, 0,
  DIEDFL_ATTACHEDONLY | DIEDFL_FORCEFEEDBACK );
```

No changes to the `EnumDevicesCallback` function are required. A force feedback joystick is, as far as devices go, just a plain joystick that can be read as usual. The next relevant step is reading the effects from a .ffe file. One such file can contain several effects, so we will use an `Enum` call with a `Callback` function to retrieve those effects. Here is the `Enum` call:

```
HRESULT hr = g_pFFDevice->EnumEffectsInFile( strFileName,
                            EnumAndCreateEffectsCallback,
                            NULL, DIEF_MODIFYIFNEEDED );
```

Let's now examine the code for the callback. For simplicity, I will assume the .ffe file only contains one effect; so after retrieving it, no further calls will be pursued. Here is a suggested implementation of the routine, which stores the effect in persistent structure for later access. As usual, error checking is deleted for clarity:

```
LPDIRECTINPUTEFFECT pDIEffect;

BOOL CALLBACK EnumAndCreateEffectsCallback( LPCDIFILEEFFECT
pDIFileEffect, VOID* pvRef )
{
HRESULT hr = g_pFFDevice->CreateEffect( pDIFileEffect->GuidEffect,
     pDIFileEffect->lpDiEffect,
     &pDIEffect, NULL );
return DIENUM_STOP;
}
```

Then, all we have to do is trigger the effect as needed. This is a two-step process. First, we need to stop any previous forces, so both effects do not conflict. Second, we trigger the new effect. Here is a simple example—first, the stop for any other effects:

```
HRESULT hr = g_pFFDevice->SendForceFeedbackCommand( DISFFC_STOPALL );
```

second, the execution of the effect:

```
HRESULT hr = pDIEffect->Start(1, 0);
```

The first parameter is the number of repetitions we want for the effect, and the second parameter is a flags parameter. Passing `INFINITE` as the first parameter causes the effect to loop forever, such as the engine vibration for a helicopter. These kinds of effects must be manually stopped with a call to:

```
pDIEffect->Stop();
```

The force feedback API from DirectInput is very comprehensive. But we have only scratched the surface. For example, we can mix effects dynamically or even create them procedurally without using the Force Editor. With time and lots of experimentation, many interesting uses can be devised.

In Closing

Input is a vast subject, requiring many techniques. But unfortunately, no broad standards are available. Although we have focused on specific techniques for the PC, most ideas are valid for other platforms as well. Ideas like device abstraction, mouselooks, or response curves are universal and are also used on other platforms.

Chapter 6

Fundamental AI Technologies

"I not only use all the brains that I have, but all that I can borrow."

Woodrow Wilson

An interesting artificial intelligence is a major component of any successful game. AI makes games challenging and addictive, and thus generates a large portion of the gameplay value. AI is a deeply evolved science with more than 50 years of history. This means very well-known methods exist to cover a broad range of scenarios and goals, whether it's commanding an army in *Age of Empires* or piloting a tie fighter in a *Star Wars* game.

In this chapter, we will study how game AI is just a specific application of general concepts from classic AI. This means most traditional AI techniques will be perfectly valid for in-game use. On the other hand, our craft will require some specific tricks and twists, such as added attention to performance and a focus on aesthetically pleasing results. In the next two chapters, we will survey game AI techniques in some detail. We will use this first chapter as an introduction to general-purpose AI techniques, so we can devote the next two chapters to action and strategic game AI, respectively. In Chapter 9, "Scripting," we will do a survey of techniques for one of the most powerful paradigms for coding any AI system. These four chapters, taken as a whole, should provide a clear and thorough understanding of the state of the industry.

Context

So, what is AI anyway? What are the goals and conditions that differentiate a good AI system from a bad one? Essentially, bad AI design often starts by setting the wrong goals.

One definition of AI might be something like "AI is the computer simulation of intelligent behavior." This would be valid except for the fact that we really don't know for sure what intelligence is. Does "intelligence" mean "behavior that exhibits great ability to adapt and solve complex problems," or is it "behavior that is close to that of humans"? History shows us again and again that humans are not always brilliant, yet there is a quality to their behavior that makes them intelligent. As you will learn in this chapter, some games make the mistake of trying to follow the first definition, and by doing so, produce results that are completely unrealistic. Take, for example, one of the classic AI problems—finding a route from point A to point B that avoids obstacles.

Many algorithms exist to solve this problem with varying degrees of success. They analyze the map and trace a path connecting the two endpoints and avoid any obstacles in-between. Some of them, however, go too far, ensuring that the path between A and B is optimal—that is, the shortest possible path. This is the case in the popular A* algorithm, which we will cover in Chapter 8, "Tactical AI." According to the first definition, A* is clearly a very intelligent algorithm. In fact, it is so intelligent that it can algorithmically build optimal paths between two endpoints, even if we have to cross many miles and obstacles in the process. But it's completely unrealistic when compared to the behavior of a human being. Humans do not trace optimal paths, and they often make mistakes traversing very complex labyrinths (see Figure 6.1).

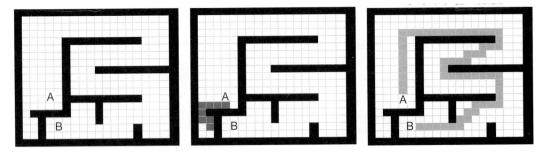

Figure 6.1   Comparison between A* and a human path finder. Left: initial problem. Middle: human. Notice how we try to approach the target, and if there's no path available, often bail out. Right: A* knows the solution beforehand so it traces a highly unrealistic but correct path through the top-right area.

A human going from A to B would follow the solid trajectory (assuming he didn't know the path beforehand), and A* would find the optimal, dotted solution. So, a game using this method might be quite smart, but not very realistic. And this is of extreme importance because concentrating on having a "smart" AI but not a "human" AI can sometimes yield poor gameplay, and that's a capital sin in game AI development. In other words, many times we will be able to create perfect AIs that will be frustrating for the human player. Thus, we will need to keep a reasonable degree of imperfection built into the AI design.

On the other hand, we do not want to create dumb AIs just for the sake of realism. Games are about challenges, and these require smart enemies, which, to an extent, are hard to beat. A good example is a real-time strategy game. The computer creates a strategy for the CPU-controlled army using a variety of techniques. But soldiers on the AI-controlled side are very shallow in terms of the spontaneity and improvisational value of their performance. They are more like robots designed to carry out a master plan. This must be so or the game would be too easy and become boring.

So clearly, game AI is a balance between generating behavior that is both highly evolved and sophisticated, and behavior that is more or less human (in the nonoptimal sense of the word). Several techniques can be used to ensure that our AIs are not just "problem solving robots" but lifelike entities that provide just the right amount of complexity to be challenging and engaging, but not more than that.

Structure of an AI System

Let's begin our journey by taking a virtual microscope and looking inside a single AI entity. It can be a *Quake* enemy, an *Age of Empires* army, or the creature from *Black & White*. Understanding the major building blocks will later help you structure and code your systems efficiently.

Fundamentally, AI systems come in two flavors. The first and most common is the agent, which is a virtual character in the game world. These are usually enemies, but can also be nonplaying characters, sidekicks, or even an animated cow in a field. For these kinds of entities, a biological structure must be followed, so we can somehow model their behavior realistically. Thus, these AI systems are structured in a way similar to our brain. It is easy to identify four elements or rules:

➤ A sensor or input system

➤ A working memory

➤ A reasoning/analysis core

➤ An action/output system

Some AIs are simpler than that and override some components. But this global framework covers most of the entities that exist. By changing the nature of each component, different approaches can be implemented.

The second type of AI entity is abstract controllers. Take a strategy game, for example. Who provides the tactical reasoning? Each unit might very well be modeled using the preceding rules, but clearly, a strategy game needs an additional entity that acts like the master controller of the CPU side of the battle. This is not an embodied character but a collection of routines that provide the necessary group dynamics to the overall system. Abstract controllers have a structure quite similar to the one explained earlier, but each subsystem works on a higher level than an individual.

Let's briefly discuss each element of the structure.

Sensing the World

All AIs need to be aware of their surroundings so they can use that information in the reasoning/analysis phase. What is sensed and how largely depends on the type of game you are creating. To understand this, let's compare the individual-level AI for a game like *Quake* to the abstract controller from *Age of Empires*.

In *Quake*, an individual enemy needs to know:

➤ Where is the player and where is he looking?

➤ What is the geometry of the surroundings?

➤ Sometimes, which weapons am I using and which is he using?

So the model of the world is relatively straightforward. In such a game, the visual system is a gross simplification of the human one. We assume we are seeing the player if he's within a certain range, and we use simple algorithms to test for collisions with the game world. The sensory phase is essential to gathering information that will drive all subsequent analysis.

Now let's take a look at the sensory data used by the master controller in a strategy game, such as *Age of Empires*:

➤ What is the balance of power in each subarea of the map?

➤ How much of each type of resource do I have?

➤ What is the breakdown of unit types: infantry, cavalry, and so on?

➤ What is my status in terms of the technology tree?

➤ What is the geometry of the game world?

Notice that these are not simple tests. For example, we need to know the geometry of the whole game world to ensure that the path finding works as expected for all units. In fact, the vast majority of the AI time in such a game is spent in resolving path-finding computations. The rest of the tests are not much easier. Computing the balance of power so we know where the enemy is and his spatial distribution is a complex problem. It is so complex that we will only recompute the solution once every N frames to maintain decent performance.

In many scenarios, sensing the game world is the slowest part of the AI. Analyzing maps and extracting valuable information from raw data is a time-consuming process.

Memory

Storing AI data is often complex because the concepts being stored are not straightfor-ward. In an individual level AI, this will be less of a problem. We can store points and orientations and use numeric values to depict the "state" the AI is in. If the character is walking, the state equals one; if he's running, the state equals two; and so on. Now, how do we store more abstract information, such as the balance of power from the previous paragraph? And how about a path? How do we store a path so the character has a mini-map in memory and remembers how to go from A to B? Some of these data structures are nontrivial, and we will often end up with case-by-case solutions, especially when coding a master controller.

Analysis/Reasoning Core

The analysis/reasoning core is what people often think about when they talk about AI. It is the part that actually uses the sensory data and the memory to analyze the current configuration and make a decision. Popular methods for such tasks are finite state machines and rule systems, both of which are dealt with in this chapter. Making a decision can be slow or fast depending on the number of alternatives and the sensory data to evaluate. Chess playing is a slow process, whereas moving a character in *Quake* is really straightforward. Obviously, a character in *Quake* has a limited range of options (usually, moving in four directions, jumping and shooting), whereas 20 to 50 moves can be made on a chessboard, given an initial configuration.

Luckily, many games require only simple decision-making processes involving a few choices, and great results often come at a relatively low price. As you will soon see, a lot of games praised for their great AI have been built with relatively simple algorithms.

Action/Output System

Intelligence, no matter how sophisticated, must permeate actions and responses, so we realize something's going on inside the creature's virtual brain. Thus, it is essential to couple our AI routines with clever action subroutines, so we get the feeling of real intelligence. In fact, many games exaggerate this action system much like in a theater play, so the character's intentions are obvious and personality is conveyed. By doing so, the degree of intelligence sensed by the player can be much higher than the actual complexity of the core AI routines. As an example, recall the *Super Mario Bros* game. All types of crazy creatures filled the game world, from turtles to lizards and many other creatures. If you separate logic from the actual actions, you'll discover that these AIs were all very similar. They were either simple enemy chasing AIs or choreographed AIs. But by creating "signature" movements for each one of them, personality and perceived intelligence was enhanced.

Specific Technologies

In the rest of this chapter, we will explore the four main AI constructs most commonly used in game programming: state machines, rule systems, state-space searches, and genetic algorithms.

Finite State Machines

The first AI technology we are going to explore is that of finite state machines (FSMs). Depending on which books you read, the same technology is also called deterministic finite automata (DFA) or simply state machines or automata.

So let's get formal for a second so as to provide a good definition of FSMs. An FSM is a formalism consisting of two sets:

> ➤ A set of states that represent the scenarios or configurations the AI can be immersed in.

> ➤ A set of transitions that are conditions that connect two states in a directed way.

Essentially, an FSM depicts the entity's brain as a group of possible actions (the states) and ways to change from one action to the other. If you say something like the following, you will have created a state machine:

1. A dog is HUNGRY.

2. If you give him a bone, he will not be hungry anymore.

3. He'll be QUIET after eating the bone.

4. And he'll become hungry after four hours of being quiet.

Sentences 1 and 3 represent states, and sentences 2 and 4 represent transitions. However, written descriptions are not very well suited for FSMs. When the number of states and transitions grows, we need a better way to represent information. So, state machine graphs are drawn, using circles for the states and lines for the transitions between states. The initial state is represented with an incoming transition from nowhere, so it can be easily identified.

FSMs are the most popular technique used to create game AIs. The state machine can become the brain of your virtual entity, describing different actions using states and linking those with transitions in a meaningful way. Lots of action games have been using FSMs since the dawn of time (which by the way happened in the late 1970s, more or less). They are intuitive to understand, easy to code, perform well, and can represent a broad range of behaviors.

An Example

Because FSMs are such an important tool, let's look at a complete example, starting with the AI idea, creating the FSM needed to model it, and putting it down in code. This way we will see how each part fits together in an intuitive workflow.

AI Specification   The first task you need to undertake is to specify the behavior of your AI. It is very important to be thorough in this phase because fixing an AI halfway through the process is sometimes problematic.

Thus, it is a good idea to write down the primitive behaviors you need your AI to perform. We will then represent these graphically to lay them down into actual running code. As an interesting example, I have chosen the AI of a patrolling guard that carries a contact weapon, like a medieval soldier. Here is the specs list for our AI, in no specific order:

➤ The enemy is in an outdoors area with no obstacles.

➤ He has a predefined set of waypoints he patrols in a cyclical way.

➤ The enemy activates when you get inside his viewing cone.

➤ If he sees you, he chases you around.

➤ He carries a sword.

➤ If in close contact, he will remain stopped, hitting you with the sword.

Graphical Layout   One of the greatest mistakes in FSM creation is to actually begin by writing code. As the state machine grows, it will become impossible to keep in mind a complete picture of all states and transitions, and most likely, we will end up with clumsy AI that does not actually do what it was intended to. Whatever you are designing, the time required to draw a simple diagram will always pay off in the long run.

You can save the diagram along with the rest of the project documentation for later use, thus making it easier to recycle AIs. It will also help you visualize the behavior in an intuitive way. FSMs are really easy to code when using a diagram as a starting point, but hard to get right without one.

Thus, Figure 6.2 presents the diagram I have chosen for the AI I have just described. The first two states are used to implement the patrolling behavior. The first state follows the current waypoint, and the second is a very simple state that keeps rotating once we have reached a waypoint until we are aligned with the next one. This way our guard will stand still while turning corners, which is a very natural thing to do. Humans do not actually walk in curves like a car would do.

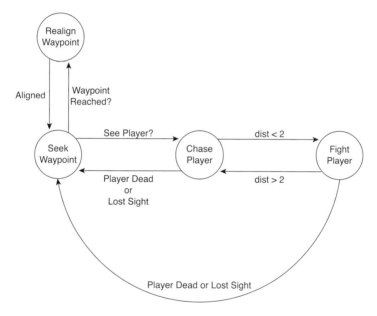

Figure 6.2   Graphical representation of the soldier state machine.

Notice how we have a second subsystem that is triggered from the SEEK_WAYPOINT state and allows us to chase the player once he enters our view cone. The chase and attack subsystem is composed of two states: one chases the player around, and the second is used when we contact him to perform our combat routine. Both states can be abandoned if we lose sight of the player, thus returning to our regular patrol.

Laying Down Some Code   When you reach the coding point, your creativity will have done all the work for you. Coding FSMs is almost an automatic process. If the specs and graph are done right, writing the FSM is very simple.

Essentially, you need to enumerate your states, reserving 0 for the initial state and positive integers for the others. So, if your FSM has N states, your last state will take the number N-1 as its identifier. In C or C++, I recommend using #define statements to create meaningful state names, which make code much more readable. You can do something like this:

```
#define SEEK_WAYPOINT 0
#define ROTATE_WAYPOINT 1
(...)
```

Then, an integer variable will be used to represent the state the AI is at, and thus drive a switch construct:

```
int state;

switch (state)
      {
      case 0:
            {
            // code for this specific state
            break;
            }
(...)
      case N-1:
            {
            // code for this specific state
            break;
            }
      }
```

This way each of the cases in the switch controls a specific state and evaluates the possibility of changing states due to a specific transition in the automata being selected. Now we need to work out the code inside each of those cases. Here we can use another trick to make life easier. Each state's activities should be divided into three thematic areas:

➤ The name of the state

➤ The default actions to be carried out in that state

➤ The calculations to perform in order to evaluate outgoing transitions

We can then lay out the code into each of the cases easily regardless of the specifics of each state. Let's look at an example:

```
case [NAME OF STATE]:
     [DEFAULT ACTIONS]
            [CONDITION EVALUATION]
     if (TRANSITION)
           state=destination state;
     (...)
     break;
```

I recommend that all your cases share this same layout because it will help you code faster and find potential bugs efficiently. With these guidelines in mind, and provided you can code your basic tests (distances, angles, and so on), coding FSMs becomes pretty much a mechanical task. All the creativity was completed in the AI design and formalization phase.

Now, let's look at the code of our chaser enemy. I have implemented him using a class called `patrol`:

```
#include "point.h"

#define SEEK_WAYPOINT 0
#define ROTATE_WAYPOINT 1
#define CHASE_ENEMY 2
#define FIGHT_ENEMY 3

class patrol
      {
      int state;
      int nextwaypoint;
      point *waypoints;
      point position;
```

```
    float yaw;

    public:
          void create(point, point *,int);
          void recalc();
    };
```

The `create` method would create a patrolling enemy at the position passed as first
parameter, load the `waypoint` vector with the incoming data from parameters two and
three, and reset the `nextwaypoint` controller to the first point in the list. Then, it
would put the automata in the state of `SEEK_WAYPOINT`. The real meat comes in the
`recalc` function, which can be browsed in the following listing. Some routines have
been simplified for the sake of brevity and clarity:

```
void patrol::recalc()
{
switch (state)
      {
      case SEEK_WAYPOINT:
            {
            break;
            }
      case ROTATE_WAYPOINT:
            {
            break;
            }

      }

}
```

For completeness, here is the very useful `compute_rotation()` routine, which is
used by the preceding code. The routine receives a position and yaw (from the patrol),
and a position (the waypoint or enemy we are following), and returns the yaw increment we should be applying in order to chase the target. It detects which side it stands
in, and so on:

```
float compute_rotation(point pos, float yaw, point target)
{
point forward=pos+point(cos(yaw),0,sin(yaw));
point up=pos+point(0,1,0);
plane pl(pos,forward,up);
bool left=(pl.evalpoint(target)>0);
if left return -0.1;
else return 0.1;
}
```

I have provided this as an example of where the CPU cycles are actually spent in an FSM—in these small tests that often require floating-point and trigonometric operations. Always double-check your tests for performance. It is essential that you guarantee that the state machine is as efficient as can be. The next chapter provides a great deal of information on computing these tests.

Parallel Automata

Sometimes, especially when modeling complex behaviors, a classic FSM will begin to grow quickly, becoming cluttered and unmanageable. Even worse, we will sometimes need to add some additional behavior and will discover how our FSM's size almost doubles in each step. FSMs are a great tool, but scaling them up is not always a trivial task. Thus, some extensions to this model exist that allow greater control over complex AI systems. Using parallel automata is one of the most popular approaches because it allows us to increase the complexity while limiting the size of the automata.

The core idea of parallel automata is to divide our complex behavior into different subsystems or layers, pretending that the entity being modeled has several brains. By doing so, each sub-brain is assigned a simpler automata, and thus the overall structure is easier to design and understand. I will now provide a complete example of what a parallel automata can look like. As a starting point, I will use a variation of our patrolling enemy from the previous section, adding a gun to his behavior. I will also add simple collision detection. Thus, his behavior consists of patrolling an area and, as he senses you, chasing you around the level, trying to shoot you down. Clearly, he's a pretty complete case study.

Now, let's try to model this character by assuming he has several brains; each one assigned to a type of action. In our case, we will need only two: one will manage loco-motion, and the other will take care of the gun. Let's forget the gun for a second and focus on character movement. Essentially, this enemy can be modeled with a relatively straightforward FSM, which you can see in Figure 6.3. It is very similar to the preceding example except for the collision detection and additional logic required—not to seek contact, but to shoot from the right distance.

The resulting automata has four states. Now, let's add the gun handling control (see Figure 6.4). If you think about it, we only need to keep shooting if the player is directly in front of our virtual creature, which seems simple enough. An FSM that only performs this task would require just two states—an initial state that would detect the condition and a second state where the enemy is effectively shooting. Although we will add a third state to reload the gun, the automata is still quite simple.

But what would happen if, instead of using the parallel automata paradigm, we chose to merge the automatas into a large-size, unique automata? We would discover that whenever we merge the two automata, the size of the overall FSM triples. Why? Because from each state of the first automata we need to be able to shoot or not, depending on the player's position. Clearly, we need the combination of all the states of the first automata with the states of the second. The resulting automata (shown in Figure 6.5) is overly complex and significantly harder to understand.

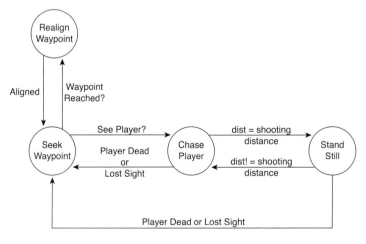

Figure 6.3 Automata for locomotion.

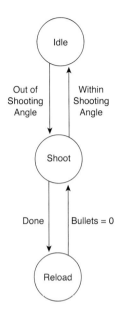

Figure 6.4   Automata controlling the gun.

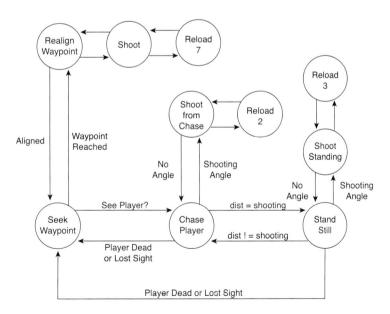

Figure 6.5   Combined automata. Notice how we need to split some states in two so we can return to the calling state when we are done.

So, let's try a different approach. Think of this enemy as if it were a warplane with two crew members: a pilot who controls the direction, speed, and so on, and a gunner who is in charge of shooting down targets. It's not one brain and one FSM, it's two brains acting in parallel. Using this approach, we would depict the behavior of the overall system by drawing both automata side by side and would code them in the following manner:

```
int state1;
int state2:

switch (state1)
        {
        case 0:
                ...
                break;
        (...)
        case N-1:
                ...
                break;
        }

switch (state2)
        {
        case 0:
                ...
                break;
        (...)
        case M-1:
                ...
                break;
        }
```

N and M are the number of states of each automata, respectively. Our design will be more elegant, our code will be shorter, and the performance penalty will be virtually zero.

Parallel automata are great to use to model those systems where we have simultaneous but largely independent behaviors going on—locomotion and attack in this case.

Independent is the key term here. Be careful with parallel automata where the state of one state machine affects the state of the other. For example, imagine that our soldier stops when shooting, so if the second automata's state equals "shooting," we need to change the state of the first one as well. These interconnections are tricky because they can yield deadlock situations and often break the elegance of a parallel automata's design. Keep automata independent as much as you can, and you will be safe.

However, some great AIs and interesting behaviors are directly based in interconnected parallel automata, where state machines share information, and the overall behavior is greater than the sum of its parts. Let's take a look at that technique next.

Synchronized FSMs

Another addition to our FSM bag of tricks is implementing inter-automata communications, so several of our AIs can work together and, to a certain extent, cooperate. By doing so we can have enemies that attack in squads. While one of them advances, the other provides coverage, and the third one calls for help. Such an approach became very popular with the game *Half-Life*, which was considered a quantum leap in action AI, basically because of the team-based AI.

Notice, however, that synchronizing AIs is no silver bullet. The method we will use is not well suited for a full-blown strategic game with complete faction-based AIs involving dozens of entities. Rule systems (explained in the next section) are much better suited for that purpose. Synchronizing AIs via FSMs is just a way to increase the expressive potential of our AI, so we can have small teams working in parallel.

At the core, synchronizing AIs involves a shared memory area where all automata can write to and read data from. I'll use a bulletin board metaphor. Whenever an AI wants to say something to the rest, it posts it in the shared memory area, so others can browse the information; and if it is relevant to them, they take it into consideration in their decision-making process. There are two common approaches to this task. One is to use a message passing architecture, which involves sending messages to those AIs we want to synchronize to. If an AI needs to keep in sync with several others, many messages will need to be sent. The alternative and preferred method is to use a bulletin board architecture, where we don't send dedicated messages, but instead post our sync messages on a shared space that is checked frequently by all AIs. This space is the bulletin board. By using it, we can avoid having to send many messages back and forth.

Thus, we chose bulletin boards instead of a message passing architecture because message passing would slow performance down in systems involving many agents in parallel. With a bulletin board, all we have to do is post the information to the board. Then, it's up to the other AIs (and their internal state) to read that information or simply ignore it. Message passing would need queues, loops to ensure we send the message to everyone, and so on, which is really a big pain for such a simple system.

Let's make a synchronized AI for a squad of three soldiers, designed to attack an enemy in a coordinated manner. I will override their navigation behavior and focus on the actual combat operation. As one of the three establishes contact with the player, he will designate himself as the attacker. The role of the attacker AI is to wait until a second AI, called the cover, begins providing cover fire. Then, the attacker will take advantage of the cover fire to advance toward the player and try to shoot him down. A third AI, dubbed the grenade, will remain in the back behind some protection, throwing grenades. If any soldier gets killed, the remaining soldiers will shift in the chain of command to cover the position. Thus, if the attacker is shot down, the cover will become the attacker, and the grenade will become the cover. This AI does not look very different from those found in many *Half-Life* situations. Figure 6.6 shows the three state machines, not taking communications and sync into consideration for a second.

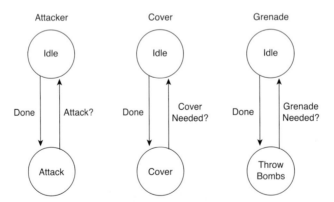

Figure 6.6   The three automata with no synchronization.

Now, we will implement the synchronization mechanism using a shared memory that will store the following data:

```
bool fighting;      // set by the first automata that contacts the enemy
bool attacker_alive; // true if attacker is alive
```

```
bool cover_alive;     // true if cover is alive
bool grenade_alive;   // true if grenade is alive
```

Our state machine code will need two operations: a shared memory read, which will always be part of the transition test, and a shared memory write, which will be performed from a state's own code. For example, the code used to detect the enemy would look something like this:

```
if (enemy sighted)
          if (fighting=false)
                  fighting=true
                  attacker_alive=true;
```

The role played by shared memory writes and reads is obvious. Figure 6.7 presents the full automata for the AI system.

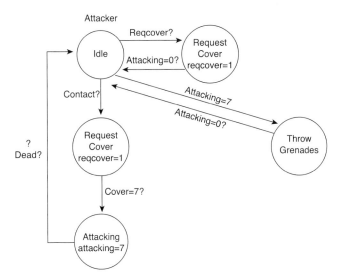

Figure 6.7   Fully synchronized automata using a shared memory zone.

Notice how we have merged all three automata into one large state machine. This is a wise move because this way we can instantiate it three times (making sure the shared memory zone is common between them) and have the three soldiers actually be interchangeable. There is no longer one specific attacker, cover, or grenade, but three soldiers that can play different roles depending on which one spots the enemy first.

Nondeterministic Automata

Classic FSMs are deterministic in a mathematical sense of the word. This means that given a state and the values of all the boundary conditions, we can predict which of the outgoing transitions will be executed (if any). In practical terms, this means that the behavior of our AI entity will be totally predictable, which is generally not a good thing. A corollary of this same principle is that given a state, one transition at most can be valid. It is unacceptable by the mathematical model that two transitions might be available at a given time.

This predictability gives the developer tight control, but is not always desirable. Take, for example, an enemy AI. By playing the game repeatedly, the human opponent would discover the underlying strategy, and thus the gameplay would be destroyed. In these circumstances, a limited degree of randomness can be added to the mix to ensure that the AI will never become predictable, so it will remain challenging even after hours of play. A traditional FSM is not well suited for this.

We can model these situations by relaxing our mathematical model to allow several transitions to be simultaneously valid. This kind of automata is usually called Nondeterministic Finite Automata (NDFA).

Here, a state might have several outgoing transitions, which we can activate or not in a controlled random manner. Take, for example, our classic soldier. We can modify his automata by introducing limited randomness, as shown in Figure 6.8. For example, whenever he reaches a waypoint and feels like it, he can stop for a cigarette. Also, if he is patrolling and sees the player, he can choose between chasing him or shooting him down. This degree of limited randomness is very useful in games where many AIs are using the same state machine. If we do not add a certain jitter degree, the overall impression can become too robotic and repetitive.

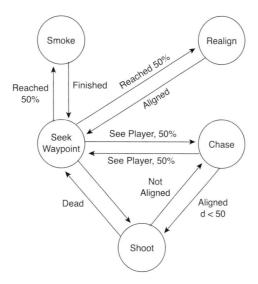

Figure 6.8 Nondeterministic automata for the soldier.

The soldier has a certain degree of "virtual freedom," so he can choose different action courses randomly. This will make his AI less predictable and more engaging. Nondeterminism is especially important for those AI entities that appear in groups, so we can reduce the homogeneous, boring look of the different automata performing the same task.

Rule Systems

Finite state machines are a very convenient tool for designing AIs. They can model different behaviors elegantly. But some phenomena are not easy to describe in terms of states and transitions. For example, imagine the following specs for a virtual dog:

➤ If there's a bone nearby and I'm hungry, I'll eat it.

➤ If I'm hungry (but there is no bone around), I will wander.

➤ If I'm not hungry, but I'm sleepy, I will sleep.

➤ If I'm not hungry and not sleepy, I'll bark and walk.

We have four statements that we might feel inclined to model using an FSM. But if we did so, we would get something like what is shown in Figure 6.9.

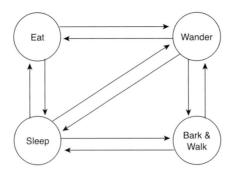

Figure 6.9   Simplified automata for a dog, showcasing how we need all possible transitions.

Clearly, each statement implies one state of the machine, and each state can transition to any of the others. Something is not quite right here, but we can't tell what it is.

The key idea is that FSMs are well suited for behaviors that are

➤ Local in nature (while we are in a certain state, only a few outcomes are possible).

➤ Sequential in nature (we carry out tasks after other tasks depending on certain conditions).

The virtual dog just described is not local. If you analyze it, all states can yield any other state, so the model is not local at all. Also, there are no visible sequences. All the dog actually does is act according to some priorities or rules. Luckily, there is one way to model this kind of prioritized, global behavior. It is called a rule system (RS), and it allows us to model many behaviors that are tricky to model using FSMs.

At the core of an RS, there is a set of rules that drive our AI's behavior. Each rule has the form:

Condition → Action

The condition is also known as the left-hand side (LHS) of the rule, whereas the action is the right-hand side (RHS) of the rule. Thus, we specify the circumstances that activate the rule as well as which actions to carry out if the rule is active. In the previous dog example, a more formal specification of the system would be

(Hungry) && (Bone nearby) → Eat it

(Hungry) & (No bone nearby) → Wander

> If (not hungry) & (Sleepy) $\rightarrow$ Sleep
>
> If (not hungry) & (Not sleepy) $\rightarrow$ Bark and walk

Notice how we enumerated the rules and separated the condition from the actions in a more or less formal way.

The execution of an RS is really straightforward. We test the LHS of each expression (the conditions) in order, and then execute the RHS (the action) of the first rule that is activated. This way, RSs imply a sense of priority. A rule closer to the top will have precedence over a rule closer to the bottom of the rule list.

RSs, as opposed to FSMs, provide a global model of behavior. At each execution cycle, all rules are tested, so there are no implied sequences. This makes them better suited for some AIs. Specifically, RSs provide a better tool when we need to model behavior that is based on guidelines. We model directions as rules, placing the more important ones closer to the top of the list, so they are priority executed. Let's look at a more involved example, so I can provide more advice on RSs. Imagine that we need to create the AI for a soldier in a large squadron. The rule system could be

> If in contact with an enemy $\rightarrow$ combat
>
> If an enemy is closer than 10 meters and I'm stronger than him $\rightarrow$ chase him
>
> If an enemy is closer than 10 meters $\rightarrow$ escape him
>
> If we have a command from our leader pending $\rightarrow$ execute it
>
> If a friendly soldier is fighting and I have a ranged weapon $\rightarrow$ shoot at the enemy
>
> Stay still

Again, just six rules are sufficient to model a relatively complex system. Now, notice how the clever placement of the rules has allowed some elegant design. If the soldier is in the middle of combat with an enemy but is given an order by the leader, he will ignore the order until he kills the enemy. Why? Because the combat rule is higher on the priority list than the "follow order" rule. Hence lies the beauty of RSs. Not only can we model behaviors, but we can also model behavior layering or how we process the concept of relevance.

Notice the condition in rule 3. It should really say:

> If an enemy is closer than 10 meters and I'm not stronger than him

But we have skipped the second condition. If we have reached the third rule, it is because the second rule was computed as false, so we know for sure we can just evaluate the first member only, saving some execution cycles along the way.

In addition, notice how the last rule does not have a condition but is more a "default action." It is relatively normal to have a last rule that is always true. This can be written in a variety of ways, such as:

> Stay still
>
> 1 → stay still
>
> TRUE → stay still

Whichever option you choose, the goal is always the same—express the default action to be carried out if no rule can be applied.

Implementation

Once designed, RSs are very easy to actually code. There are different strategies that make coding rules almost as automatic as writing FSMs. I will now evaluate two different alternatives. One is very well suited for hard-coded RSs, which control actions. The other is a tactical RS, which would be useful in the context of a scripting language in a strategy game, for example.

Decision Trees   Let's start by coding an RS for action games. One of the easiest methods is to code your system using a decision tree. We will use the example from the previous section and lay out the code for the soldier's RS.

The decision tree associated with this system would be

```
if (contact with an enemy) combat
else
        {
        if (closer than 10 meters)
                {
```

```
                    if (stronger than him) chase him
                    else

                              escape him

                    }

        else

                    {
                    if (command from our leader pending) execute it
                    else

                              {
                              if (friendly soldier is fighting and
                                   I have a ranged weapon)
                                        shoot at the enemy
                              else

                                        stay still

                              }

                    }

        }
```

Decision trees are a direct mapping of our rule set, in priority order, to an "if" tree. They are very easy to construct and, for simple systems such as this one, provide an excellent elegance versus cost ratio. Basically, we nest `If-then-else` sentences, using the rules as the conditions of each `if`. The first rule is the condition in the outer level `if` clause. Then, the `if` following the `else` contains the second rule, and so on. Actions are assigned to the corresponding `if`, so the action from the first `if` is whatever action we must carry out if the first rule proves to be valid.

Symbolic Rule Systems   Another implementation of the RS is by means of a scripting language, which symbolically represents the rules. The rules are written according to some specs, parsed from external files, and executed in real time. The best example of such behavior in action is the RSs present in most real-time strategy games, which control the tactical level of the gameplay. Here is an example taken from the *Age of Empires* rule language:

```
(defrule
        (resource-found wood)
        (building-type-count-total lumber-camp < 5)
        (dropsite-min-distance wood > 5)
        (can-build lumber-camp)
```

```
=>
        (build lumber-camp)
)
```

This rule states that if we found wood, the number of lumber camps in our army is less than five, the newfound wood source is farther than five units, and if we have resources to build an additional lumber camp, then we should build one. Both tests and actions are highly symbolic and will require converting them to actual code. You will learn how to parse such an RS in Chapter 9.

However, it's not parsing the rules that should worry us: A simple parser will do the job. The real issue with symbolic RSs is that instead of having to test five rules, we might need to check 50. Tactical reasoning needs lots of rules, and thus the rule evaluation function can become an issue. We will need to optimize the code carefully, and make sure the rule evaluation tests can actually be computed in our AI tick time.

Another tricky problem is coping with variable-duration AI tests. RSs explore rules sequentially until one of them is proven true (or until no more rules are available). Clearly, if the first rule is true, our AI code will be executed in very little time. On the other hand, if no rule is valid, we would need a very significant processing time to reach the final rule. A variable AI processing time generates a variable frame rate, which is by no means a good thing.

Clearly, we need a structured way to lay out RSs, which makes execution time more or less independent of the path taken. One of the best approaches is the Rete algorithm, proposed by C.L. Forgy in 1982.[1] The algorithm greatly improves the efficiency of forward-chaining RSs (the systems where we test conditions sequentially) by limiting the effort required to reevaluate the RS after a first iteration has been run. It exploits two facts:

➤ The activation of a rule usually changes just a few facts.

➤ The same facts and patterns usually appear in the LHS of many rules.

---

1   C.L. Forgy. "Rete: A fast algorithm for the many patterns/many objects match problem," *Artificial Intelligence*, 19(1)(1982): 17-37.

Rete works by keeping a directed acyclic graph that represents the facts in memory. New facts are added to the graph as they are activated by rules. We can also delete facts and modify existing ones (for example, if the number of soldiers in our camp increases from 20 to 21). Each node in the graph represents a pattern (a unique comparison in the LHS of a rule). Then, by tracing paths from the root to the leaves, complete LHSs of rules are extracted.

Here is a very simple example of a Rete built from the rules:

```
(defrule
    (slow(x))
    (has_ranged_weapon(x))
    (stronger_than_me(x))
=>
    (evade(x))
)
(defrule
    (slow(x))
    (weak(x))
=>
    (attack(x))
)
```

The associated algorithm is shown in Figure 6.10.

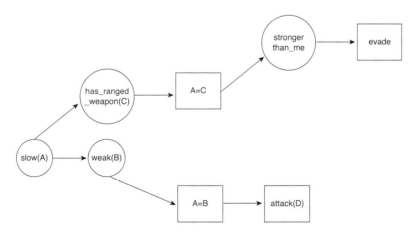

Figure 6.10 Rete algorithm, starting point. Circles are predicates, squares indicate restrictions we must satisfy, rectangles are the RHS of rules. At runtime, the tree is explored so we can cache partial results from one test to the next.

Notice how we have repeated facts that are in fact shared by the two rules. In Rete, we usually merge those, so we eliminate the fact redundancy. We can also eliminate operators that are repeated, so we cache parts of the LHS that are repeated in many rules.

Now, imagine we add a new rule, such as:

```
(defrule
    (slow(x))
    (has_ranged_weapon(x))
    (weaker_than_me(x))
=>
    (attack(x))
)
```

The final Rete for the preceding example is shown in Figure 6.11.

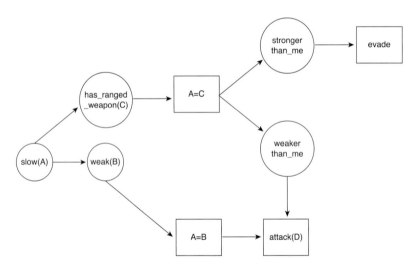

Figure 6.11   Rete after insertions.

The number of elements in the Rete is no longer linear to the number of rules. In fact, as the number of rules grows, the chances of patterns in the LHS being repeated increases. Thus, extra rules will come at little cost for the Rete. Coding the graph function is definitely not for the faint of heart, so I suggest you take a look at Appendix E, "Further Reading," for more details in implementing the algorithm. In the long run, the Rete algorithm guarantees that execution time will be more or less independent from the number of rules because we're not really testing rules anymore but checking for changes in our fact database. In fact, Rete is widely considered to be the fastest pattern-matching algorithm in the world and is used by many popular production RSs, such as CLIPS and Jess.

User-Defined Facts   The RSs we have seen so far only test for conditions and perform actions. Often, a third construct is added to increase the expressive potential of the RS so it can model more problems accurately. User-defined facts are added, so one rule can set a flag, and another rule can test whether the flag has a certain value. This is very useful because it allows the AI programmer to somehow implement the concept of memory or state in the otherwise stateless world of rules.

Imagine that we are working on a strategy game and are coding the RS that controls resource gathering, as in the earlier wood example. We have written a rule for the lumber camp construction that is not very different from the previous one. For increased realism, we want to show the player the process of building the lumber camp. Specifically, once the "build camp" rule is triggered, we want one AI entity to move to the building spot, and then perform a series of animations that show the building process. Obviously, this is a sequence of actions that must be performed in a specific order, and we already know that RSs are not very well suited for this task.

We could achieve this result by writing the following rules, which would do the job:

```
(defrule
        (constructor-available)
        (need-to-build lumber-camp)
        (I-am-in lumber-camp)
=>
        (construct lumber-camp)
)

(defrule
        (constructor-available)
        (need-to-build lumber-camp)
=>
        (move-to lumber-camp)
)
```

```
(defrule
        (resource-found wood)
        (building-type-count-total lumber-camp < 5)
        (dropsite-min-distance wood > 5)
        (can-build lumber-camp)
=>
        (build lumber-camp)
)
```

Now, try to think of the amount of extra facts we would need to add to our system to cover all the possibilities. *Age of Empires* can build dozens of structures, and each one would require specific rules for it. Clearly, that's not the way to go, but some of its philosophy is definitely valid. If you think about it, you will realize that all we have to do is add a construct that allows us to set a value in a memory position, so subsequent rules can read it back as part of their condition evaluation code. Instead of hard coding all the new facts, we would provide an open interface so the user can define them as needed. This is what user-defined facts are all about—allowing the user to implement sequences and store intermediate values, which are read back when needed. The case of the lumber camp constructor can be easily solved with the following rules:

```
(defrule
        (constructor-available)
        (check-fact-value lumber-camp-construction-step  equals 1)
=>
        (build-structure lumber-camp)
)

(defrule
        (constructor-available)
        (check-fact-value lumber-camp-construction-step  equals 0)
        (distance-to lumber-camp less-than 5
=>
        (set-fact lumber-camp-construction-step 1)
)


(defrule
```

```
        (constructor-available)
        (check-fact-value lumber-camp-construction-step   equals 0)
=>
        (move-to lumber-camp)
)

(defrule
        (resource-found wood)
        (building-type-count-total lumber-camp < 5)
        (dropsite-min-distance wood > 5)
        (can-build lumber-camp)
=>
        (build lumber-camp)
        (set-fact lumber-camp-construction-step 0)
)
```

We only need to add the `set-fact` and `check-fact` value constructs. Some systems (*Age of Empires*, for example) do not allow user-defined facts to be identified by character strings but by numbers. We have a certain number of facts whose identifiers are integers. But the added parsing complexity of implementing a symbol table that allows the user-defined facts to be assigned character strings pays off in the long run because readability is increased and rules are easier to debug. In the end, the symbol table is converted to integers as well, so performance does not vary.

Notice how the process of building the lumber camp is in fact a sequence, much like what we would code in a state machine. In fact, user-defined facts make RSs engulf state machines in terms of expressive power. Everything we can do with a state machine can now be done with an RS with user facts. The opposite is not always true because RSs have a sense of priority that is hard to express with a state machine.

Thus, user-defined facts provide a best-of-both worlds solution. Complex behaviors can be prioritized and layered using the RS, but each one might involve sequences of actions, much like a state machine would. Most RSs used in commercial game engines use this approach to increase the flexibility of the system at a very low coding and computational cost.

Planning and Problem Solving

FSMs and rule sets are very useful paradigms to model simple behavior. If our problem can be expressed in terms of sequences and phases, FSMs are clearly the way to go. RSs, on the other hand, are better suited for priority lists or tasks that should be performed concurrently. Clearly, these tools are at the core of any action AI programmer's toolbox. However, both approaches are limited when it comes to modeling other, more complex behaviors. How can we teach a computer how to play chess? Chess is definitely not played in terms of steps, so FSMs won't help much. It definitely doesn't look like the kind of problem we can tackle with rules either. The nature of chess is predicting moves, analyzing the possible outcomes of a certain sequence of operations, and trying to outperform the analysis power of the opponent. Clearly, some problems are simply too hard for the kind of solutions we have proposed so far. Some phenomena require real-world analysis, reasoning, and thinking. Chess is a good example, but there are many others. As a quick sampler, consider the following list:

> ➤ Solve a puzzle

> ➤ Decide the weakest spot in a battlefield to attack the enemy

> ➤ Select the best route to attack N ground targets in a flight simulator

> ➤ Trace a path from A to B with obstacles in between

All these problems have some characteristics in common, which make them hard to model with our existing toolset. These problems require the following:

> ➤ Thinking in more complex terms than numbers. We need to understand the importance of a chess piece or the meaning of a battlefield layout.

> ➤ Planning long-term strategies, well beyond the current AI cycle. We need to create a projection of the future and trace a strategy to reach our final goal.

Clearly, we need to add some additional tools to our battle chest, tools that help us build plans, solve problems, and create tactics. These tools will not replace our FSMs or RSs but complement them.

State-Space Search

If I had to choose between FSMs and RSs, I would say chess is somehow similar to a state machine. It has board configurations that resemble the machine's states, and it has moves that resemble state transitions. But the structural complexity of chess is not easy to describe by means of FSMs. The key difference is that any state machine representing chess would have to be dynamic, not static. We would start from the current configuration of the board and propagate some moves into the future to choose the movement sequence that we think suits us best. A state machine, on the other hand, is completely built beforehand, so all states are designed before we even turn the AI on. Problems like solving a puzzle can also be expressed this way, using an initial state or configuration and a series of potential moves from which we will select the best one according to some strategies. The kind of problems based on exploring candidate transitions and analyzing their suitability for reaching our goals is globally called state-space search problems. We search the state-space to find ways to move from the initial conditions to our goals.

State-space search is a very powerful paradigm that can be used to create strategies and plans. We propagate each possible move into the future and evaluate its consequences. This family of algorithms is well suited for everything from playing chess to finding the exit to a maze. It all boils down to representing the game as a tree with possible configurations as nodes in the tree and moves as branches between moves. Given an initial state and a target state, we can use a variety of methods to find the best route (and thus, move sequence) to go from one to the other. Figure 6.12 shows the classic state-space for the game of tic-tac-toe.

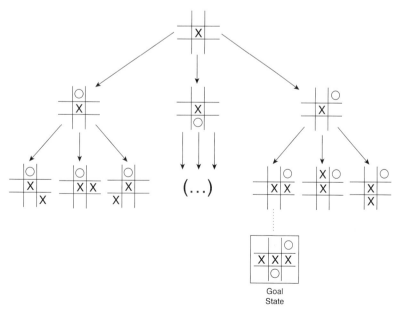

Figure 6.12 State-space tree for tic-tac-toe (subset).

Many exploration algorithms exist for state-space problems. Some of them are blind search methods, meaning they use brute force to explore all possible moves. An example is depth-first search. We select candidates recursively using a single path until we reach an end state from which no further moves can be performed. Then, if the end state is not a goal, we start all over again using the next candidate. Blind search methods always work, but sometimes their cost can make them impractical. Take chess again, for example. Doing a depth-first search for such a game can take forever because the game does not necessarily have to end in a finite amount of time. So, other algorithms have been devised through the years. These algorithms use information about the problem to select not just any candidate, but one that looks like a promising option. These algorithms are said to be heuristic based, which means they use extra information that usually improves results. A good example is a problem-solving algorithm called A*. A* examines the current state and then explores future states, prioritizing those that look like better candidates. It is widely used for path finding. In this scenario, A* needs to have some extra information about the domain of the problem we are trying to solve. Then, it can find very good solutions without exploring all opportunities. In fact, for many problems, A* is an optimal algorithm, meaning it is capable of finding the optimal way to move between two locations. It's all a matter of using information about the problem we are solving. You can find a complete discussion of A* and other path finding algorithms in the next several chapters.

We also need to be aware that some problems are just too big, even for heuristic-based approaches. Chess, again, is a good example. Put simply, there is no computer in the world (and there won't be at least for a few years) that can hold the complete chess movement state space. The number of board configurations is of astronomic proportions (just think about it: the board has 64 squares, there are 16 pieces, each one different. Get a calculator and do the math). Besides, most configurations can be connected in cycles. We can move a queen to a position, only to move it back to the original state. Thus, trying to explore the whole tree is just plain impossible. What most good programs do is analyze the tree with limited depth, trying to forecast the next N moves and select the best strategy for that movement sequence. By concatenating this sequentially, a good game should hopefully emerge.

Biology-Inspired AI

All the core AI technologies we have explored so far are clearly rooted in computer science and mathematics concepts. The graphs, rules, or trees we have been using are not biological concepts but computational structures. Essentially, we have simulated human behavior, but we have used nonhuman tools.

Thus, you could be inclined to generalize this and believe that all AI works the same way, that all simulations take place in the computer's mind-set. Although this is partly true, other techniques exist that are rooted not in computer science but in biology and neurology. We can try to simulate not only the intelligence that emerges from cognitive processes, but also the cognitive processes.

The main issue with this biological approach is that today we are just beginning to scratch the surface of how the brain really works. Our cognitive processes are just being explored, and so far, their complexity has not yet been tamed. Thus, all biology-inspired models suffer from a certain sense of instability. But once these limitations are well understood, some of the methods are mature enough to offer promising results in specific areas.

Genetic Programming

A very popular biology-inspired approach is genetic programming, inspired by genetic theory as developed by Mendel and evolution theory as developed by Charles Darwin (both in the nineteenth century). For those of you who are not familiar with these theories, I'll provide a short explanation in the next two paragraphs.

The core idea behind genetic theory is that all living beings are defined by a molecular construct called genetic code (which was latter discovered to consist of DNA strings). DNA encodes the features of each individual. Different species (such as birds and mammals) have different DNA structures, and individuals from a single species share their DNA layouts. But individuals from the same species have minimal variations in some values in their DNA. These variations yield slightly different individuals, with differences in gender, external appearance, and so forth. Then, each generation can create a new generation whose DNA code will consist of a combination of the parent's respective DNA code, plus a minor degree of mutations.

Based on genetic theory, Charles Darwin developed his theory of evolution. This theory essentially states that living beings in an ecosystem survive or expire depending on the suitability or fitness of their DNA to the said environment. The fittest survive, and the less well suited will simply disappear. Imagine a cold environment and a population of bears. Logically, those with better temperature insulation will live longer and will create a second generation that will, statistically, share their temperature protection scheme (be it thicker hair, stronger skin, and so on). Thus, nature is somehow biased toward better individuals. Every few generations, small mutations will appear, causing some of the DNA elements to change. Most bears will resemble their parents (using a normal distribution), but a small part of the Nth generation bears will have different eyes, longer legs, or even better temperature shielding. These bears, being better suited to their environment, will survive better, statistically breed more and fitter descendants, and so forth. If you extend this process, which is merely statistical, over several thousand generations, these micro changes will have paid off, and the species that will have survived the process will be very well adapted (within the obvious limits of biology) to the environment. Today, evolutionary theory is accepted and proven, despite some annoying questions as to how and why seahorses and other funny-looking animals ever came to be.

The genetic and evolutionary theories work very well as a whole. The complete genetic theory deals with both the creation of a uniform population and the evolution of its individuals according to the rules of survival and improvement in the ecosystem. Interestingly, this process is well suited for numerical simulation. We can generate synthetic individuals and make them evolve using a computer simulation of these evolutionary principles. This way we can evolve virtual creatures and ecosystems in reasonable amounts of time, far from the millions of years it takes nature to select the fittest.

Additionally, genetic programming can be used in game AI. Although FSMs and RSs are the workhorses of any AI programmer, these novel techniques are beginning to find their way into computer games in very specific applications. So let's now explore genetic algorithms in some detail to understand their potential applications. I will pro-pose two examples. In the first example, we will use DNA codes to generate similar, yet varied, individuals. Then, we will explore how a Darwinian selection process can help us tune our game AI.

Generating Populations

The first component we will study is the core genetic simulator, which will allow us to create individuals according to a virtual DNA. The DNA will be represented as an array of values; each one being one parameter of the species to model. So, if we are to genetically derive human pedestrians to act as part of the scenario in a game set in a city (think *GTA3*, *Midtown Madness*, but also *The Sims*, and so on), we could have a DNA string such as this:

Gender: (Male, Female)

Race: (Caucasian, African American, Latino, Oriental)

HairStyle: (No hair, Ponytail, Short hair, Long hair)

DressStyle: (Formal, Jeans and T-shirt, Hawaiian, Military)

Height: (Petite, Small, Medium, Tall, Huge)

Speed: (1…5 meters/second)

Resolution: (1: The character wanders with no apparent goal;
5: The character follows a planned route)

The linear combination of these seven parameters can generate a variety of individuals; each with its own DNA. Given the number of parameters and the possible choices for each individual, we could have approximately 30,000 different specimens. It would then be the task of a sophisticated graphics animation engine to render the different variations.

Here are two specimens from our DNA sequence:

Specimen 1: (Male, Caucasian, No hair, Hawaiian, Medium, 5, 2)

Specimen 2: (Female, Latino, Ponytail, Hawaiian, Petite, 3, 4)

Using genetic combinations, we can derive many descendants from this couple. Genetically speaking, about 200 possible descendants can be generated (not including mutations). Here's how:

➤ Because parents are one male and one female, statistically speaking, we can generate both males and females with the same probability.

➤ Descendants will be either Caucasian or Latino (we are not taking race hybrids into consideration for the sake of simplicity).

➤ Descendants will either have no hair or end up with a ponytail. This does not make much sense biologically speaking, but it is indeed what our DNA encoded.

➤ Regarding clothing habits, clearly all descendants will wear Hawaiian attire.

➤ Assuming size is a linear measure, descendants will range from petite to medium with equal probability, yielding three possible combinations (petite, small, medium).

➤ The same applies to the speed, which will be in the range of 3 to 5 (3 different values).

➤ The resolution will range from 2 to 4, adding 3 possible results for the final gene.

Thus, the equation is the linear combination of all these variations:

```
2*2*2*1*3*3*3 = 216
```

The result is the number of possible descendants from that pair of source genetic codes.

From this simple example, one of the main uses of genetic programming becomes evident. It is a great tool to create variations for groups, whether it's orcs, pedestrians, or lemmings. Genetic programming adds a degree of statistical variance that makes results more interesting. Moreover, genetic programming is not limited to living beings. How about using DNA codes for a cityscape, so each house is a variation of the standard genetic code of a core house? You could even have different neighborhoods with distinctive looks and qualities by creating a unique DNA structure and then modeling each neighborhood in terms of specific values for each gene. Then, you could create transitional zones between two neighborhoods by mating the DNA from each zone, weighted by the distance to the zone itself. Thus, we could seamlessly blend a Victorian downtown with a residential area. Once you get into the computer's realm, the possibilities are endless. Genetic programming can help us overcome uniform and boring games.

Evolutionary Computation

Now it is time to implement Darwin's theory of natural selection. This is slightly trickier than simple genetic computation because we need to test individuals against their ecosystem and somehow measure their performance or fitness. This way the better suited will survive, and the remainder will simply perish (actually, they will become NULL pointers). By iterating this selection process, better-suited generations will statistically dominate in the long run. Here is the general layout of any Darwinian system:

1. Generate the first N individuals with random DNA codes.

2. Perform fitness testing on them.

3. Select the top percent.

4. Generate N descendants that are

    a. Linear combinations of the parents' DNA

    b. Mutations

5. Go to step 2 until you have reached your desired number of generations.

Let's explore each step in detail. We will skip step 1 because it's the traditional genetic computation we have just explored.

Fitness Testing   The fitness test determines which specimens are interesting (and thus deserve new generations) and which ones are simply not worth it. Thus, it is an essential component to ensure proper evolution and improvement. There are two ways of performing the test: automatic and supervised. In an automatic scenario, we define a function that can be computed automatically and will be applied to all individuals with no user interaction. An assisted system needs user supervision to select the cream of each crop. To better understand each system's potential and shortcomings, imagine that we are genetically deriving opponents for a Formula-1 racing game. We have defined their DNA as:

MaxSpeed   (speed in a straight area of the course)

MinSpeed   (speed in a curve)

`MetersBeforeBrake`   (how many meters before a curve does the driver brake)

`BrakeAmount`   (how much does it brake to enter the curve)

`PositionCurve`   (how does it attack the curve: by the inner side or outer side)

`MinDistance`   (minimum distance to any other car to avoid collision)

`AttackAngle`   (angle of attack when entering a curve)

`AccelMoment`   (% of the curve passed when the driver accelerates again)

Obviously, we do not know beforehand which combination of the preceding parameters yields the best driver. Even more interesting, there might be different parameter combinations (and thus different driving styles) that yield top results. So, we build an evolutionary tester and run a number of generations to breed a good selection of drivers. As mentioned earlier, we need a significant number of generations to achieve interesting results. So, we run the system for 50 generations with 50 drivers being born in each one. In each run, we select the top 10 drivers as generators for the next iteration.

Clearly, having to examine 2,500 drivers is a time-consuming task. Besides, as generations advance, the differences in driving will diminish as they converge to create stable, almost perfect driving styles. So, a human supervisor can have a hard time selecting the best specimens.

In these situations, we can define an automatic fitness function, and thus perform the whole evolutionary loop as a batch process. For our driver selector, the fitness function can be a weighted sum of:

The time per lap (lowest=best)

The status of the car (less impacts=best)

Now, assuming we run this as a batch process, and each driver gets a two-minute time slice to run a lap around the circuit and thus generate input for the fitness function, we will need about three days (using a single computer) to reach our final selection. Although significant, this time will ensure that we have top AI opponents using a vastly automatic process. The main programming task is defining the DNA we are going to use and determining the fitness function.

A different strategy of performing the fitness test is to make specimens compete with one another in a tournament. We pair them randomly and test which one of them performs better. Then, the losing specimen is discarded, and the winning one advances to the next round. This can be a very useful technique to select specimens that are combat or competition oriented. For example, you can test *Quake* bots this way by making them fight each other in an empty level, and the one that achieves more frags in a given time is selected. But be careful with this approach. Imagine that two very good contestants are matched in the first round. Even if one of them wins in the end, this does not necessarily mean that the other one should be discarded. This kind of phenomena happens in many sports competitions (the Wimbledon tennis tournament and the Soccer World Cup are good examples). Sometimes, very good teams or players get coupled early on in the competition, which forces some quite good contestants to be discarded too early.

However, in some instances, it will be hard to define a feasible, automatic fitness test. Sometimes the selection criteria will be nonnumeric, or quite simply, hard to put into numbers. Let's go back for a second to our crowd genetic simulator. Imagine you choose to iterate a crowd in an evolutionary way. Your goal is to create visually interesting combinations. You parameterize your virtual pedestrians using a variety of values and simply need to generate a few people that are visually attractive.

One classic method is to let a supervisor select couples and then genetically derive descendants from them. This same method is used to procedurally generate textures in some packages based on the user's desired style. Then, it is hard, if not impossible, to automate what a person might find attractive or ugly. It is much better to create a system that can be evolved interactively, so the user can perform the Darwinian selection. The process can actually be done very quickly. We can select the best-looking pedestrian out of a population of 20 in one minute. This means we can derive 60 generations in an hour, which is more than enough.

When coding this kind of supervised system, there are two guidelines that should be strictly observed:

> ➤ The system must evolve in a relatively small number of iterations.

> ➤ The time required to evaluate and select individuals from one iteration must be brief.

These two conditions try to guarantee the rapid convergence of the evolution, so we can reach interesting results in a short time.

Mating, Mutations, and Plateaus   Once we have selected the best individuals, it is time to generate descendants as linear combinations of the parents' DNA strings. This process is really straightforward and, if the parents were among the cream of the crop, they will generate a better iteration. But it is very important to introduce some kind of mutation to the process. Assign a random gene value to a small portion of the newborn population to test that solution as well. The reason why we must act this way might not be trivial. Evolutionary computation is just a process of local optimization. Each generation is, on average, slightly better than the last one, and in the long run, this leads to perfect specimens. In fact, evolutionary computation is nothing but a special case of what's usually called a hill-climbing approach. Each step of the algorithm produces an improvement based on local characteristics, much like a hill climber. When climbing a hill, provided you always advance in the steepest direction, you should reach the top. But we all know a hill-climbing method only guarantees that we will reach a local maxima because we can reach a plateau from which we can no longer climb (and is not necessarily the top of the mountain). That's why mutations are essential. They guarantee that we can always generate a different individual who can by chance find a different way to evolve and reach better fitness values that the current generation cannot.

In Closing

Artificial intelligence is a deep, involved subject, and game developers are now beginning to harness its real power. In this chapter, we have explored the main techniques that are currently being used in production by game developers worldwide. Other techniques, such as fuzzy logic, Bayesian networks, and neural networks, show great potential as well and will progressively be incorporated into our arsenal in the future. It is now time to move on and apply these methods in different scenarios, from a fast-paced, frantic action game to a slow-paced, strategic title.

Chapter 7

Action-Oriented AI

"Action may not always bring happiness; but there is no happiness without action."

Benjamin Disraeli

Now that we have a global understanding of the building blocks of any AI system, it is time to delve into the details of how AI is built into video games. Because this is a lengthy subject, with different techniques used for different gameplay styles, I have divided the information into three separate chapters. Most game AI techniques might not be very complex, but there are many twists and interesting ideas to which we will have to devote some space.

In this chapter, I will provide an overview of AI methods used in fast-paced action games. We will review general techniques, and then do a case-by-case analysis on fighting games, racing simulators, and so on, providing insider information on many popular algorithms.

The next chapter will deal with the subject of tactical AI, which finds its main use in strategy games. We will learn to build plans, analyze enemy configurations, and trace maneuvers that would marvel most real-world generals.

We will end our journey through artificial intelligence techniques with a chapter on scripting, which is one of the most powerful paradigms for coding AIs. By separating the AI code from the main game engine, scripting provides a robust and flexible way of creating large AI systems. In fact, most professional AIs today are built via some sort of scripting engine. So we will analyze the different scripting techniques in detail.

Let's begin with the basics. We need to create little creatures that chase us and shoot, so let's get to work.

On Action Games

For this book, I will define action as intelligent activity that involves changes of behavior at a fast speed. Examples of action are all locomotion behaviors (a character that runs in *Mario*), simple aggression or defense (enemies shooting or ducking in *Quake*), and so on. Notice how action is put in a contraposition to tactical reasoning, which is in turn described as the analysis process used to create a plan that will then guide the actions of an intelligent character. So, action deals with immediate activity, and tactics plan that activity.

Action is thus driven by relatively simple tests. We will need to compute distances to targets, angular separations, and so on. Action is also quite fast-paced. Action games have higher rhythms than tactic/strategic games.

Choreographed AIs

In its simplest form, an action AI system can be implemented as a preprogrammed action sequence that is executed repeatedly. This form of AI is used in industrial robots and can be applied to simple games as well. An elevator in *Quake*, for example, is just executing a very simple movement sequence. These systems are merely state machines with no optional transitions—just a series of states the automata loops through endlessly.

But we can use the same technique for quite interesting AI entities, well beyond elevators and robot arms. A security guard in an adventure game, for example, can be programmed to walk up and down the alleys in a prison, maybe performing some specific actions. Ships in top-down arcade scrollers sometimes exhibit quite beautiful choreographies, often involving tens of ships. Gameplay in these games emerges from analyzing movement patterns and detecting the pitfall that allows us to avoid the guard, shoot down enemy ships, and so on.

Choreographed AI systems usually employ a very simple scripting engine to represent movement sequences. Figure 7.1 shows a diagram of such a system. Note that we are not talking about a full-blown AI system built with a scripting engine. We are starting with very simple and deterministic behaviors that are stored in files, as in the following example:

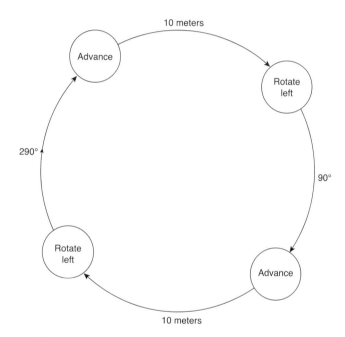

Figure 7.1   Sequencer for a choreographed AI system.

```
set animation "walk"
go to 0 10 0
set animation "rotate"
rotate 180
set animation "walk"
go to 0 0 0
set animation "rotate"
rotate 180
```

The preceding example could very well be an animation for a security guard in a prison. He just walks up and down an alley, executing different animation cycles. Most coin-operated machines from the 70s and 80s used variations of this approach, shared (among other classics) by the LOGO programming language and the *BigTrak* vehicle toy sold by Milton Bradley.

The main design decision you must make when coding any choreographed AI system is selecting the range of commands the AI will respond to, or in other words, the instruction set for your programming language. I recommend you take a second to carefully think about the level of abstraction you will use with your AI system. Should any movement be decomposed into a series of straight lines, or should more complex tasks like spirals and circles be directly built into the language? Clearly, setting the right abstraction level will allow us to create more interesting scripts with less work. Unfortunately, this is a context-sensitive decision. Designing the scripting language largely depends on the kind of game (and AI) you are trying to craft. Once the level is set, decide on the instructions and parameters you will be implementing. Again, try to think in terms of what gives you the most expressive potential for the game.

Implementation

The first choreographed AIs stored sequences that were hard-coded into the game's assembly source. But as time passed and sequencing languages became more and more powerful, small scripting languages were evolved, so content creators could work on more complex sequences easily.

Today, implementing a choreographed AI system is, fundamentally, implementing a very simple script language. You need a parser that reads the script into main memory. Then, a run-time interpreter processes the file and executes its instructions, affecting game engine internals such as enemy positions and orientations. We will discuss script languages in detail in Chapter 9, "Scripting," so I suggest you refer to it when trying to code a choreographed AI system.

Object Tracking

One of the first problems we must deal with in any action AI system is maintaining eye contact with a target, whether it's moving or static. This is used everywhere in action-oriented games, from rotating a static shooting device (like the turrets in *Star Wars'* trenches) to aiming at an enemy we are chasing or evading, or basic navigation (to track a waypoint we must reach).

Eye contact can be formulated as, given an orientation (both position and orientation angles) and a point in space, computing the best rotation to align the orientation with the point. It can be solved in a variety of ways, which I'll cover one by one in the following sections.

Eye Contact: 2D Hemiplane Test

If we are in a 2D world, we can solve the eye contact problem easily with very little math. Let's first take a look at the variables involved in our system. I will assume we are in a top-down view, overseeing the X,Z plane.

```
point mypos;              // position of the AI
float myyaw;              // yaw angle in radians. I assume
                          top-down view

point hispos;             // position of the moving target
```

The first step is to compute whether `hispos` effectively lies to the left or right of the line formed by `mypos` and `myyaw`. Using parametric equations, we know the line can be represented as:

```
X = mypos.x + cos(myyaw) * t
Z = mypos.z + sin(myyaw) * t
```

where *t* is the parameter we must vary to find points that lie on the line. Solving for *t*, we get the implicit version of the preceding equation, which is as follows:

```
(X - mypos.x)/cos(myyaw) = (Z - mypos.z)/sin(myyaw)
```

By making this into a function, we know the points on the line are

```
F(X,Z)= (X - mypos.x)/cos(myyaw)  - (Z - mypos.z)/sin(myyaw)  = 0
```

If we have a point in space and test it against our newly created function, we will have

```
F(X,Z)  > 0
```
(it lies to one side of the line)

```
F(X,Z)  = 0
```
(it lies exactly on the line)

```
F(X,Z)  < 0
```
(it lies to the opposite side)

This test, which is illustrated in Figure 7.2, requires:

➤ 3 subtractions

➤ 2 divisions

➤ 1 comparison (to extract the result)

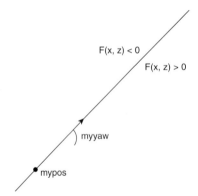

Figure 7.2 Hemispace test.

We can speed the routine up if we need to do batches of tests (against several targets) by calculating the expensive trigonometric functions only once, and storing them as the inverse so we can save the expensive divides. The formula will be

```
F(X,Z)= (X - mypos.x)*(1/cos(myyaw))  - (Z - mypos.z)*(1/sin(myyaw))
```

If we do these optimizations, the overall performance of the test will be (for N computations):

3*N subtractions

2*N multiplies

2 trigonometric evaluations

2 divisions (for the invert)

N comparisons (for the result)

which is fairly efficient. For sufficiently large batches, the cost of divisions and trigonometric evaluations (which can be tabulated anyway) will be negligible, yielding a cost
of three subtractions and two multiplies.

For completeness, here is the C code for the preceding test:

```
int whichside(point pos, float yaw, point hispos)
// returns -1 for left, 0 for aligned, and 1 for right
{
float c=cos(yaw);
float s=sin(yaw);
if (c==0) c=0.001;
if (s==0) s=0.001;
float func=(pos.x-hispos.x)/c - (pos.z-hispos.z)/s;
if (func>0) return 1;
if (func==0) return 0;
if (func<0) return -1;
}
```

3D Version: Semispaces

To compute a 3D version of the tracking code, we need to work with the pitch and
yaw angles to ensure that both our elevation and targeting are okay. Think of a turret
in the *Star Wars* Death Star sequence. The turret can rotate around the vertical axis
(yaw) and also aim up and down (changing its pitch). For this first version, we will
work with the equations of a unit sphere, as denoted by:

```
x = cos(pitch) cos(yaw)
y = sin(pitch)
z = cos(pitch) sin(yaw)
```

Clearly, the best option in this case is to use two planes to detect both the left-right and the above-below test. One plane will divide the world into two halves vertically. This plane is built as follows:

```
point pos=playerpos;
point fwd(cos(yaw),0,sin(yaw));
fwd=fwd+playerpos;
point up(0,1,0);
up=up+playerpos;
plane vertplane(pos, fwd, up);
```

Notice how we are defining the plane by three passing points. Thus, the plane is vertical, and its normal is pointing to the left side of the world, as seen from the local player position.

The second plane is built with the pitch and divides the world into those points above and below the current aiming position. Here is the code:

```
point pos=playerpos;
point fwd(cos(pitch)*cos(yaw), sin(pitch), cos(pitch) sin(yaw));
fwd=fwd+playerpos;
point left(cos(yaw+PI/2),0,sin(yaw+PI/2));
left=left+playerpos;
plane horzplane(pos,fwd,left);
```

In this case, the normal points up. Then, all we need to do to keep eye space with a point in 3D space is compute the quadrant it's located at and react accordingly:

```
if (vertplane.eval(target)>0) yaw-=0.01;
else yaw+=0.01;

if (horzplane.eval(target)>0) pitch-=0.01;
else pitch+=0.01;
```

Notice that the signs largely depend on how you define pitch and yaw to be aligned. Take a look at Figure 7.3 for a visual explanation of the preceding algorithm.

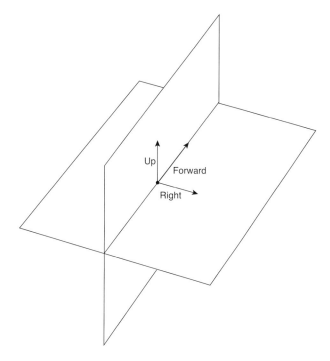

Figure 7.3   Semispace test, 3D version.

Chasing

Now that we know how to aim at a target, we will use that knowledge to implement a chase behavior. To be honest, chasing is easy once you know how to keep eye contact, so this section should be pretty straightforward.

In its simplest form, chasing involves moving forward while keeping eye contact with the target. Thus, we will keep aligned with the target and advance toward it. If by some unknown reason we lose sight of the target (because the target moved, for example), we will correct our orientation and keep moving.

Chase 2D: Constant Speed

The source code for a constant-speed, 2D chaser follows. Notice how we follow the guideline in the previous section, and just try to re-aim while moving forward. More sophisticated, variable-speed methods can be devised for specific purposes.

```
void chase(point mypos, float myyaw, point hispos)
{
reaim(mypos,myyaw,hispos);

mypos.x = mypos.x + cos(myyaw) * speed;
mypos.z = mypos.z + sin(myyaw) * speed;
}
```

The success of this approach largely depends on the relationship between our speed, the target's speed, and our turning ability. If we can turn quickly, we can assume that we will be effectively facing the target much of the time, so we will perform a pretty optimal chase. But we will need our speed to be higher than the target's speed to ensure we make contact. A faster target will thus be unreachable. On the other hand, a much slower target might also escape our pursuit, especially if our maneuverability is restricted. To understand this, think of a fighter jet trying to chase a helicopter. Quite likely, the jet will have a hard time trying to stay aligned with the helicopter.

Predictive Chasing

One alternative to ensure a better chase is to use predictive techniques. Here we will not aim at the target directly, but try to anticipate his movements and guess his intentions. In much the same way as a good chess player can use intuition to discover what his opponent is trying to do, a chaser can use some clever interpolation to anticipate his opponent's moves.

This idea is really straightforward. Keep track of the position history of the opponent and use that information to create a "predicted position" some time in the future. Then, aim at that position. In Figure 7.4, you can see how a predictive chaser can outperform an opponent, even if their respective speeds and maneuverability are the same. The predictive chaser will make more informed decisions, which will ultimately make him succeed.

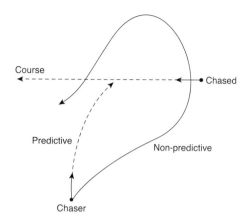

Figure 7.4 Predictive chasing, where the dotted line shows the predictive course.

Predictive chasing is performed as a preprocess to the chase routine just explained. Instead of aiming and advancing, we will use a three-step approach, which involves:

1. Calculating a projected position

2. Aiming at that position

3. Advancing

Calculating the projected position can be implemented with a number of interpolation techniques. We could, for example, take the last two position samples from the enemy and use a straight line as the interpolator. The code for this approach would look something like this:

```
void chase(point mypos, float myyaw, point hispos,point prevpos)
{
point vec=hispos-prevpos;     // vec is the 1-frame position difference
vec=vec*N;                    // we project N frames into the
                              future
point futurepos=hispos+vec;   // and build the future projection

reaim(mypos,myyaw,futurepos);
```

```
mypos.x = mypos.x + cos(myyaw) * speed;
mypos.z = mypos.z + sin(myyaw) * speed;
}
```

Just these three simple lines allow our chaser to perform better. By varying the value of N (which depends on the relationships of speeds and our chaser's turning ability), we can find the perfect match.

An added value of the preceding code is that it will correctly treat the degenerate case of a target that holds still. It will predict that the target will remain unchanged.

We can implement variants of the preceding code using better interpolators. Instead of using the last two points in the trajectory, we could use N points for better results. By using N points, we can derive an N-1 interpolation polynomial. Obviously, as we increase the degree of the polynomial, the fitness to the trajectory will improve, and we will be able to make longer-lived predictions. But we will soon see that this improvement comes at a price. Computing higher-order polynomials has a computational cost that you might not be willing to pay.

One of the best ways to compute interpolation polynomials is to use the method of finite differences. These are a set of equations that define the Nth degree polynomial (thus, passing through N+1 values). For a quadratic polynomial, the equation has the form:

```
P(x) = a0 + a1*(X-x0) + a2*(X-x0)*(X-x1)
```

where:

```
a0 = y1
a1 = (y1 - y0) / (x1-x0)
a2 = (((y2 - y1) / (x2-x1)) - ((y1-y0) / (x1-x0))) / (x2-x0)
```

You can guess the pattern that generates the Nth degree equation by examining the way each extra parameter—a0, a1, and a2—value is generated.

Evasion

Once we know how to chase targets around, it is easy to learn to evade. Essentially, evading is the opposite of chasing. Instead of trying to decrease the distance to the target, we will try to maximize it. Thus, an evasion algorithm will be very similar to a chasing algorithm except for some sign changes. Here it is in detail:

```
void evade(point mypos, float myyaw, point hispos)
{
reaim(mypos,myyaw,hispos); negated

mypos.x = mypos.x + cos(myyaw) * speed;
mypos.z = mypos.z + sin(myyaw) * speed;
}
```

Patrolling

Another interesting behavior in any action AI system is patrolling. Policemen, dogs, and many other in-game characters patrol a predefined area, sometimes engaging in combat when an enemy is discovered.

To implement a patrolling behavior, we have to store a set of waypoints that will determine the path followed by the AI. These waypoints can be followed in two configurations: cyclic and ping-pong. Given waypoints W1…W5, here are the visit sequences for both schemes:

> Cyclic: W1 W2 W3 W4 W5 W1 W2 W3 W4 W5 …
>
> Ping-pong: W1 W2 W3 W4 W5 W4 W3 W2 W1 W2 …

I recommend using the cyclic approach because ping-pong trajectories can be expressed as cycles (explicitly adding the way-back), whereas the opposite is not true. Following a waypoint is not very different from a chase behavior. It is just a chase where we follow a sequence of targets. The easiest way to implement this is through a minimal, two-state finite-state machine. The first state is used to advance toward the next waypoint (represented internally by an integer). Then, as we approach closer to a predefined threshold, we move to the second state. This is a nonpersistent state, where the integer used to represent the next waypoint is updated. We then go back to the first state, follow the waypoint, and so on.

Patrol behaviors (depicted in Figure 7.5) can often be enhanced by adding a third state, which implements a chase behavior. This is usually triggered by using a view cone for the AI, testing whether the player actually entered the cone (and was thus discovered by the AI). Games such as *Commandos: Behind Enemy Lines* made good use of this technique.

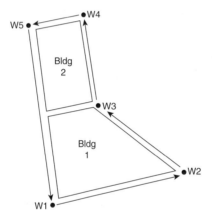

Figure 7.5 A patrolling AI, surrounding two buildings.

Hiding and Taking Cover

Sometimes we will need our AIs to run for cover or remain unnoticed by the player. For example, maybe they want to catch the player by surprise, or maybe the AI is controlling a soldier under heavy player fire. Whatever the case, knowing how (and where) to seek cover is always an interesting twist for the AI. Many game reviews praise this behavior as highly sophisticated, and players enjoy seeing it in action because it offers an extra challenge.

Taking cover is usually a matter of two actions performed sequentially. First, a good hiding spot must be located in the game level. Second, we must move there quickly. This second phase is nothing but a chase routine, very similar to those explained earlier in this chapter; so we will focus on detecting good hiding spots. To do so, we will need three data items:

➤ The position and orientation of the player

➤ Our position and orientation

➤ The geometry of the level

The geometry of the level must be stored in such a way that it allows proximity queries on objects that can actually become hiding spots. A good structure, for example, is having the world separated into terrain data with objects laid on top. Then, the objects must be laid out using quadtrees, spatial indices, or any other technique, so we can quickly compute which objects lie closest to certain map locations.

The actual algorithm involves finding the closest object to the AI's location and computing a hiding position for that object. The algorithm works as follows. We start by using the scene graph to select the closest object to the AI. This step largely depends on how the world is laid out. Once we have selected the object, we shoot one ray from the player's position to the barycenter of the object. We propagate the ray beyond that point, computing a point along the ray that's actually behind the object (from the player's standpoint). As shown in Figure 7.6, that's a good hiding spot. Keep in mind that hiding in places can be sped up if we can guarantee convex hiding spots.

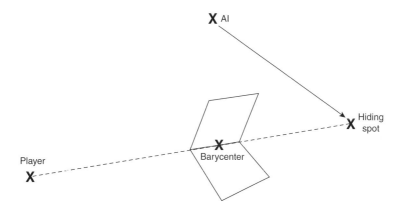

Figure 7.6   Geometry of playing hide-and-seek with the player.

AIs that implement hiding behaviors can easily be enhanced to work with the player's view cone. This is very useful for shooters. As shooters, we remain hidden while the view cone is focused on us. As soon as the player is looking somewhere else, we know we can leave our hiding spot and attack him. Games such as *Medal of Honor* have made great use of this technique, with German soldiers staying under cover until the right opportunity arises.

Shooting

We know how to chase the player, evade him, and keep an eye on his position. We have even predicted his future actions. So, now it's time to work on the mechanics of shooting. We need to learn when is it a good idea to shoot at the player in different contexts. We also need to know whether we are handling a machine gun, a sniper rifle, or a catapult. As you will soon see, each one requires slightly different approaches to the problem of targeting.

Before starting, I need to give some personal words of warning. The same way I enjoyed movies like *Star Wars*, *Alien*, and *Saving Private Ryan*, I think games with a fighting/shooting element should be recognized as enjoyable experiences. I don't have any moral problem with that, and I think any healthy person can differentiate between the fictitious violence shown by games/movies/books and real violence. On the other hand, I'd recommend that people play many different games, not all of them with a combat/violence component, just as I'd go to see different types of movies. That said, the following sections deal with the specifics of shooting, so they necessarily focus on the algorithms required to target and shoot down enemies.

Infinite-Speed Targeting

The first approach we will explore is shooting with a weapon that has infinite speed, or in practical terms, very high speed compared to the speed of the target. This can be the case of a laser gun, which would advance at light speed, for example. Then, we can assume the time it takes for the projectile to reach the target is virtually zero. Thus, the selection of the shooting moment is really easy. All you have to do is make sure you are well aligned with the target at the moment of shooting. As the velocity is very high, we will have a sure hit because the target will have very little time to move and avoid the collision with the bullet. Clearly, it is not a good idea to abuse infinite-speed weapons because they can unbalance your game. If you build these weapons into the game, make sure you balance them well in terms of gameplay. For example, the firing rate can be very low, the ammunition limited, or the weapon might be really hard to get.

Real-World Targeting

What happens with a real-world firing device? Even a real gun shoots projectiles at a limited speed (approximately 300-600 meters per second). This means shooting a fast moving target is harder than shooting one that stands still. Thus, most weapons must be modeled as finite-speed devices, where some careful planning is used. I will explain two popular approaches.

Version A: The Still Shooter

The still shooter targets the enemy and only shoots whenever the enemy is standing still for a certain period of time. The reason is simple. If the bullet takes one second to hit the target, and the target has been standing still for a certain period of time, it is a good hypothesis to assume the target will stand still for another second, thus making it a good moment to attempt shooting.

An enhancement to this algorithm is to watch the target for specific actions that indicate restrictions in his ability to move. For example, if the target is standing still, he might begin walking in any given moment, thus making it an unsafe target. But what happens if he sits down or if he is tying one of his shoes? Clearly, we have a better aim here because we know for sure he won't be going anywhere in the next few seconds. This would be the kind of reasoning that would drive a sniper-style AI. He looks for very safe shoots that hit the target most of the time. By shooting only when a safe hit is granted, the shooter ensures one kill while not giving away his position easily. The disadvantage is that maybe the shooter will have very few opportunities to actually shoot, so it is a good idea to make him less restrictive. The way to do this is to introduce errors in his processing. He might sense time incorrectly, confuse animations, and so on. So sometimes he will shoot when he's not supposed to. When done carefully, this can accurately model fatigue and morale, affecting the ability of the sniper to stay focused.

As a summary, here is the algorithm in detail:

```
Global variables:
Timestill              time since the enemy began standing still
StandingStill          1 if standing still, 0 otherwise

When it begins standing still
```

```
        StandingStill=1
        Timestill=now
```

```
If StandingStill and more than X seconds have elapsed since
Timestill
        Shoot
```

Version B: The Tracker

The tracker AI also tries to model the behavior of a sniper. In this case, he will shoot moving targets, not just those who are standing still. Shooting a moving target is really hard. We need to combine the shooting behavior with a target tracking routine, and there is a predictive component going on as well. If the gun has a finite speed, we need to target not the current position, but the position where the target will be when the bullet hits him.

The idea is simple: Compute the distance from the sniper to the target, use the projectile velocity to compute how long it will take for the projectile to reach the target, and predict where the target will be in the future, exactly when the projectile arrives. This way you can aim at that spot and get a safer shoot, especially in distant or fast-moving targets. The algorithm in full is depicted in Figure 7.7.

```
float d=distance (sniper, target)
float time=d/bulletspeed
point pos=predictposition(target,time)
if aiming at pos shoot()
else target at pos;
```

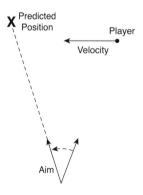

Figure 7.7 Predictive shooter.

Whether predictive or still shooters, we have focused so far on single-shot firing devices, where each shot is considered an individual AI decision. But other weapons, such as machine guns, offer the possibility of shooting bursts of bullets at high frequency but with reduced precision. The AI logic for such weapons is a completely different subject, and thus deserves its own separate discussion.

Machine Guns

Machine guns offer fast firing rates at the cost of inferior precision. Shots cause the cannon to shake due to recoil, making it hard to aim accurately. Thus, their main use is found not in targeting people, but areas. The machine gun is aimed in the right direction, and short bursts are fired to hit anyone in the area.

The first type of gun we will examine is the fixed machine gun. This kind of behavior is exhibited by gunners in bunkers, trenches, and so on. Some classic guns would be the MG-42 used by the German army in World War II, the M60 used in Vietnam, and so on. Here are some stats from the former:

> MG-42 (with lightweight tripod)
>
> > Firing rate: 25 rounds per second
> >
> > Range: 1000 meters
> >
> > Muzzle velocity: 820 meters per second
> >
> > Weight: 11.6 Kg
>
> MG-42 (with Lafette tripod)
>
> > Firing rate: 25 rounds per second
> >
> > Range: 1000 meters
> >
> > Muzzle velocity: 820 meters per second
> >
> > Weight: 31.1 Kg

From these statistics, several lessons can be extracted. First, these guns hardly ever moved, but instead kept on targeting and shooting down enemies from a fixed position. Second, these guns did not have a lot of autonomy, the standard feed type for the MG-42 was a 50/250 metal belt. Thus, a burst could not last longer than 10 seconds, followed by a pause to change the metal belt. These guns were thus used for performing short firing bursts. Their algorithm is relatively straightforward. By default, the soldier stands still, waiting for new enemies to arrive. Then, as they begin to get closer, the gunner must rotate the gun to face the enemy. Rotation must somehow be penalized for slower models. When the angular difference between the gunner and the enemy is smaller than a certain threshold, the gunner will hold down the trigger while trying to refine his aiming. Keep in mind each shot introduces some distortion to the aiming due to recoil, so the gunner must re-aim every time. As a result, fixed gunners do not usually aim carefully; they aim at an area. Thus, these gunners are especially useful when we need to stop a wave composed of many soldiers. By pure chance, some bullets shot by the gunner will reach their target.

A common mistake is to forget about feed sizes. Many World War II games display machine guns that seem to have infinite ammunition.

Let's now examine the problem of a moving character carrying a light machine gun, such as an AK-47 or an M-16. As a rule of thumb, only movie characters use moving machine guns to shoot long bursts. Recoil makes it impossible to aim, especially if standing up. So, ammunition is wasted because most projectiles will be lost. Besides, these guns do not have long cartridges, so ammunition must be used with care. Here are some stats from the World War II Thompson submachine gun, aka the "Tommy gun":

> Thompson
>
> > Firing rate: 10–12 rounds per second
> >
> > Range: 50 meters
> >
> > Muzzle velocity: approximately 400 meters per second
> >
> > Weight: 5 Kg

The gun came with 30 bullet cartridges, and a soldier in World War II usually carried three such magazines. As you can see, ammunition was still more of an issue than with heavy, fixed machine guns. Thus, the most common practice is to treat these assault guns as rifles with very high firing rates. Bullets are shot one by one or in very short bursts. The only situation where a moving gunner can effectively waste ammo is in a fantasy setting, such as space ship games. Here we can forget about realism and make the tie fighter or other ship of your choice shoot long firing bursts.

Putting It All Together

We have seen the basic routines to move a character, chase other people, and shoot different weapons. But these are all individual tasks, which must somehow be combined. To do so, I will now examine two techniques that allow us to blend these simple behaviors into a rich, engaging AI system: parallel automata and AI synchronization. The techniques we have seen so far will thus behave like bricks in a *LEGO* game, each serving a specific function or task.

Parallel Automata

The first way to blend different actions together is to use a parallel automata. In this case, the first automata would control locomotion (chasing, evading, patrolling, hiding), whereas a second automata would evaluate the firing opportunities. The algorithm for this solution would be best implemented via state machines (thus, two state variables would be required). You can see this in the following example:

```
class enemy
      {
      int locomstate,gunstate;
      void recalc();
      };


void enemy::recalc()
{
switch (locomstate)
      {
      state IDLE:
      state WALKING:
      }
switch (gunstate)
      {
      state IDLE:
      state WALKING:
      }
}
```

We have thus divided the problem in two. Now, the locomotion AI is in charge of tasks such as reaching waypoints, collision detection, seeking cover as needed, and so on. Then, the gunner AI takes care of targeting and shooting down enemies.

AI Synchronization

Another way of combining simple behaviors into complex systems is to make use of AI synchronization. This is generally considered an advanced topic, but adding it to our toolbox of action AI techniques can greatly increase the expressive potential of the overall system—the same way a group of ants looks more intelligent to the observer than an individual ant. Groups of enemies that coordinate, implement tactics, and work as a team are one of the most impressive features of any AI system. This technique was made popular by *Half-Life*, where enemy soldiers would call for help, cover each other, and operate as a squad realistically.

Implementing enemy synchronization is just a matter of using a shared memory pool, which is visible to all entities and can be written and read by the AIs. Then, the rule systems or finite-state machines must be enhanced to take advantage of this shared memory.

At the simplest level, our shared memory pool can be something like this:

```
typedef struct
        {
        bool flags[64];
        } sharedmemory;
```

We need this structure to be visible from all automata, so we can add sentences like this:

```
if (sharedmemory[3]) state=(…)
```

As an example, imagine a game that takes place in a prison. The center of the prison is dominated by a large tower with a powerful light cannon, which continually scans the ground at night to prevent inmates from escaping. A simple AI controls the light. Then, there are a few patrol AIs that walk around the complex, and if the player enters their view cone, they chase him and kill him. Now, imagine that the watchtower AI uses a shared memory location to indicate whether the player is actually inside the light cone. If this is so, another memory location stores his position. Then, patrol AIs are implemented just like we discussed earlier, but with an exception. They read the said memory location, and if the player is detected, they run to the location specified by the watchtower. This very simple synchronization, illustrated in Figure 7.8, can yield a significant improvement in the gameplay. The player can voluntarily enter the light cone to be detected, then run away, so guards are sent to an area of the camp while he escapes somewhere else.

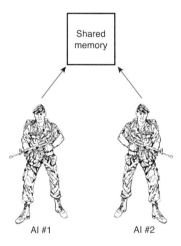

Figure 7.8   Two AIs use the shared memory to communicate.

More complex synchronization mechanisms can be devised. A soldier can confront the player, and if the player is carrying a more powerful weapon, the soldier can run for cover. Once hidden, he can raise a signal so other AIs can come to help him. Add some radio messages as sound effects, and you have a very credible AI behavior.

Synchronization becomes more complex if we try to model larger groups involved in more sophisticated interactions. If we need to create lifelike behaviors involving dozens of entities, we better use artificial life techniques. These techniques use specific tools to convey the illusion of living entities acting in groups, such as troops, schools of fish, or birds in the sky.

In Closing

As a conclusion, I will provide some AI coding hints for a variety of action-based genres.

Platform Games

The first genre we will address is that of platform/jump'n'run games such as *Mario* or *Jak and Daxter*. In these games, AI is all about variety, having lots of enemies to keep the game fresh and new. On the other hand, these AIs are not very complex because encounters with AI enemies are quite short and simple. From the moment we see the baddie in such a game to the moment either he or we are dead, only a few seconds pass.

Platform game enemies can be easily coded using finite-state machines. In the simplest incarnation, they can be sequential/choreographed AIs that perform deterministic moves. Turtles in the first *Mario* game, for example, walked up and down map areas and killed on contact. Many old-school classics were built with this idea in mind.

One step higher in the complexity scale, we can implement chasers that get activated whenever the player is within a certain range. This represents the vast majority of AIs found in platformers, often hidden in great aesthetics that largely increase the believability of the character. Sometimes, these chasers will have the ability to shoot, which is implemented with parallel automata. One controls locomotion and the other just shoots whenever we are within angular reach.

Another interesting AI type is the turret, be it an actual turret that shoots, a poisonous plant that spits, or anything in between. A turret is just a fixed entity that rotates, and when aiming at the player, shoots at him. This behavior can be implemented with the eye contact approach explained at the beginning of the chapter.

Whichever AI type you choose, platform games require AIs to perform sequences that show off their personalities. The basic behavior will be one of the behaviors we have seen so far. But usually, we will code an AI system with some extra states, so the character somehow has a personality that is engaging to the player. I will provide two examples here.

In *Jak and Daxter: The Precursor Legacy*, there are gorillas that chase the player and kill on contact. They are triggered by distance. A gorilla stands still until we approach to within 10 meters. Then, he just walks toward us, and whenever he makes contact, tries to hit us. But this is just a plain chase behavior, which would make the game too linear and boring if that is all the gorilla did. Besides, we need a way to beat the gorillas—maybe a weak spot that makes them winnable. Thus, the gorilla expands his behavior to incorporate a short routine that involves hitting his chest with both fists, the same way real gorillas do. As a result, the gorilla chases us around, and whenever he's tired or a certain amount of time has elapsed, he stops, does the chest-hitting routine, and starts over. This makes sense because the gorilla is showing off his personality with this move. But this is also useful because we know we can attack the gorilla whenever he is hitting his chest. That's his weak spot. Many enemies in *Jak and Daxter* work the same way. They have a basic behavior that is not very different from the behaviors explained in this chapter and some special moves that convey their personalities to the player.

Another, more involved type of enemy is the end-of-level bosses. I'm thinking about usually large enemies that perform complex AI routines. Despite their spectacular size, these AIs are in fact not much different than your everyday chaser or patrolling grunt. The main difference is usually their ability to carry out complex, long-spanning chore-ographies. Although these routines can become an issue from a design standpoint, their implementation is nearly identical to that of the cases we have analyzed so far. As an example, consider the killing plant from *Jak and Daxter: The Precursor Legacy*. This is a large creature, about 5 meters tall, that tries to kill our hero by hitting him with its head. The flower is fixed to the ground, so it's not easy to avoid it. To make things more interesting, every now and then the flower will spawn several small spiders, which will become chasers. So you have to avoid the flower and keep an eye on the spiders while killing them. Then, the carnivorous flower will fall asleep every so often, so we can climb on it and hit it. By following this strategy repeatedly, we can finally beat it. Take a look at the summary presented in Figure 7.9.

As engaging and well designed as this may sound, all this complexity does not really affect our implementation. The boss is just a sequential automata that has a special ability of generating new creatures, but overall the implementation is really straightforward.

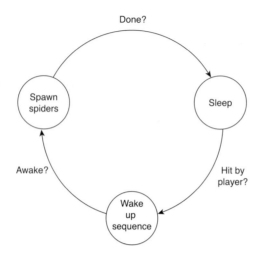

Figure 7.9 A classic boss from *Jak and Daxter: The Precursor Legacy*.

Shooters

We will now focus on shooters like *Half-Life* or *Goldeneye*. These games are a bit more complex than platformers because the illusion of realistic combat must be conveyed. The core behavior engine is usually built around finite state machines (FSMs): simple sequential algorithms that convey the attack and defend sequences. Also, the comment about aesthetics-driven AI in the previous section is also valid here. We need the character to convey his personality in the game.

Most shooters these days allow enemies to think in terms of the scenario and its map. Enemies can follow us around the game level, understand context-sensitive ideas like taking cover, and so on. Thus, we need a logical way to lay out the scenario. A popular approach is to use a graph structure with graph nodes for every room/zone and transitions for gates, doors, or openings between two rooms. This way you can take advantage of the graph exploration algorithm explained in the next chapter. We can use Dijkstra's algorithm to compute paths, we can use crash and turn (also in the next chapter) to ensure that we avoid simple objects such as columns, and so on.

Another interesting trend, which was started by *Half-Life*, is group behavior for games—being chased by the whole army and so on. Group dynamics are easily integrated into a game engine, and the result is really impressive. Clearly, it's one of those features in which what you get is much more than what you actually ordered.

Fighting Games

The algorithms used to code fighting games vary greatly from one case to another. From quasi-random action selection in older titles to today's sophisticated AIs and learning features, fighting AI has evolved spectacularly.

As an example, we could implement a state machine with seven states: attack, stand, retreat, advance, block, duck, and jump. When connected in a meaningful way, these states should create a rather realistic fighting behavior. All we need to do is compute the distance to the player and the move he's performing and decide which behavior to trigger. Adding a timer to the mix ensures the character does not stay in the same state forever.

If you want something more sophisticated, we can build a predictive AI, where the enemy learns to detect action sequences as he fights us. Here, the enemy would learn our favorite moves and adapt to them. The idea is quite straightforward: Keep a list with the chronological sequence of the last N player movements. This can be a circular queue, for example. Then, using standard statistics, compute the degree of independence from the events in the queue. For example, if the player is performing a kick and then a punch, we need to compute whether these two events are correlated. Thus, we compute the number of times they appear in sequence versus the number of times a kick is not followed by a punch. Tabulating these correlations, we can learn about the player's fighting patterns and adapt to them. For example, the next time he begins the kick sequence, we will know beforehand whether or not he's likely to punch afterward, so we can take appropriate countermeasures.

The finite-state machine plus correlations approach is very powerful. It is just a problem of adding states to the machine so we have more and more flexibility. If we need to create several fighters, each with its own style, all we need to do is slightly change the states or the correlation-finding routine to change the fighter's personality. Don't be overly optimistic, though, most games implement character personality at the purely aesthetic level, giving each character specific moves, a certain attitude in the animation, and so on.

So far, our fighter is highly reactive. He knows how to respond to attacks efficiently by learning our behavior patterns. It would be great, especially for higher-difficulty enemies, to make him proactive as well, making him capable of performing sophisticated tactics. To do so, the ideal technique would be to use space-state search. The idea would be to build a graph (not a very big one, indeed) with all the movement possibilities, chained in sequences. Then, by doing a limited depth search (say, three or four levels), we can get the movement sequence that better suits our needs according to a heuristic. Then, the heuristic would be used to implement the personality. Although this looks like a good idea, executing the state search in real time at 60 frames per second (fps) can be an issue.

Thus, a simpler approach is to use a tabulated representation. We start with a table with simple attack moves and their associated damage. Then, every time we do a new attack combination, we store the damage performed and the distance at which we triggered it. For example, we can store:

> Distance = 3 meters, high kick, jump, punch, Damage = 5

Then, we can use this list afterward, accessing it by distance and selecting the attack that maximizes damage. It's all just very simple pattern matching both for the attack and defense, but it produces the right look and feel.

Racing Titles

Racing games are easily implemented by means of rule-based systems. Generally speaking, most racing games are just track followers with additional rules to handle actions like advancing on a slower vehicle, blocking the way of another vehicle that tries to advance, and so on. A general framework of the rule set would be (starting with the higher priority rules):

> If we are behind another vehicle and moving faster → advance
>
> If we are in front of another vehicle and moving slower → block his way
>
> Else → follow the track

The advance behavior can be implemented as a state machine or, even simpler, using field theory to model the repulsion that makes a car advance on another by passing it from the side. Here the cars would just be particles attracted to the center of the track, and each car we happen to find standing in our way would be repulsive particles.

The track follow is often coded using a prerecorded trajectory that traverses the track optimally. A plug-in is used to analyze the track and generate the ideal trajectory. Then, at runtime the drivers just try to follow that race pattern, using the higher-priority rules as needed.

Chapter 8

Tactical AI

KEY TOPICS

- Tactical Thinking
  Explained

- Military Analysis:
  Influence Maps

- Representing Tactics

- In Closing

*"We are not retreating—we are advancing in another
direction."*

General Douglas Mac Arthur

Now we know how action-oriented AI can be built into any
game. We have seen simple methods to convey the illusion
of intelligent behavior, from chasing a spaceship to choosing
an attack move in a fighting game. However, these behaviors
can hardly qualify as "intelligent thinking." They more
closely resemble the behavior of a robot. They are simple
sequential tests, which, despite looking intelligent as a
whole, are not very far from conventional programming.

Now we will move one step higher on the reasoning scale as
we advance into the realm of tactical AI. In this chapter, we
won't bother with the behavior itself, but instead will worry
more about analyzing and making the right decisions in
complex scenarios. We will learn to create intelligent
paths through game worlds, to sense and analyze combat
strategies, and to synthesize general solutions to complex
problems. We will learn to make informed decisions or,
even better, to think.

Tactical Thinking Explained

A formal definition of tactic is the sequence of operations
designed to achieve a goal. Thus, a tactic consists of three
elements:

- ➤ An initial state

- ➤ A goal state

- ➤ The plan to move from one state to the other

Human brains are very well suited for tactic creation. Consciousness informs us of our current state, the goals are set by our internal needs, and our brains create (and modify on the fly) pretty good plans. Machines, on the other hand, are not designed for tactics. They are much better at numerical computations than they are at these kinds of cognitive processes. Proof of this difference is the speed at which a good sorting algorithm was evolved (about 30 years ago). Playing chess, which involves tactics, has only recently been completely mastered, and even today the methods are quite brute force, radically different from what a brain would do.

Machine tactics are complex for a variety of reasons. As an example, take a bird's eye view of a battlefield, as seen in popular games such as *Age of Empires*. It is no problem for a computer to perform a variety of tests, such as computing distances between enemies, making sure they do not overlap, and so on. But a question like "Who is winning the battle?" is a completely different business. Computers do not know what "winning" means. It's a highly sophisticated concept and definitely not the kind of idea you can represent easily with ones and zeros. Any human being flying over a battlefield would recognize at first sight which side is actually winning, but computers have a hard time coping with this kind of query. Thus, we must begin by creating specific data structures that allow us to ask meaningful questions about the status of the system, so we can build plans based on that status.

Another problem derived from machine tactics is making the actual plan. Machines are good at computing plans, but creating one that actually looks human is very complex. As you will soon see, many tactical algorithms have an undesirable side effect. They are too perfect, and thus can frustrate the player in the long run. Besides, they can kill realism in a game. Players will detect an unnatural behavior pattern, and the sense of immersion will be destroyed.

We will now study several classic problems, which we can broadly classify into three large groups: learning to move intelligently in a scenario (path finding), learning to analyze the scenario (its geometry, enemies, and so on), and learning to create a meaningful plan in terms of selecting the right actions to achieve our goals.

Path Finding

In the previous chapter, we learned how to chase a moving target. We assumed no obstacles were around, and by doing so, calculations were greatly simplified. Now, let's make things more interesting by assuming there are a few existing obstacles. The more obstacles, the more we need to plan the sequence of moves we will use to reach our destination. In fact, as path finding complexity increases, we will reach a point where most animals, man included, would get lost and be unable to succeed in finding an adequate path through the obstacles. Just think about how easy it is to get lost in a city you don't know. Clearly, some analysis beyond basic animal capabilities is required, and that is what this section is all about—finding paths between two endpoints in a world full of obstacles.

This problem has been studied thoroughly in both academia and in the games industry, and many good solutions exist. It belongs to the search field of AI: Given initial and end states (represented by the two endpoints), find a sequence of transitions (movements) that allows us to go from one state to the other efficiently. Some of the proposed algorithms will even be optimal, computing the perfect path between two endpoints. But these solutions will often look too perfect and unnatural, because a living entity rarely uses the optimal solution. So let's start with the simplest approaches and refine them to more involved solutions.

Path finding algorithms can be divided in two broad categories: *local* and *global*. Local approaches try to find a path to a destination by analyzing the surroundings of the current position only. We know in which direction we want to go, and we try to perform the best move by studying our local neighborhood. Global algorithms, on the other hand, analyze the area as a whole and trace the best path using all the information, not only the surroundings. As a side effect, local algorithms are computed online on a frame-by-frame basis, whereas global approaches are usually precomputed in a single shot and then executed.

A person visiting a city for the first time would use a local path finding algorithm, trying to determine from his surroundings which is the way to a certain location. Now, give that same visitor a map, and he will be using a global algorithm. He will be able to study the path as a whole and trace an efficient path beforehand. Keep this distinction in mind as you choose which path finding approach you implement. Are your AI entities well informed about the structure of the game world (and can we assume they have a map), or should they use more trial-and-error, which is realistic but nonoptimal? Strategy games have usually chosen global algorithms (such as the popular A*, which we will study later in its own section), whereas action games tend to prefer local approaches.

Crash and Turn

The first algorithm we will explore is a local method that quite closely resembles what a simple animal would try to do. Let's start at point A and try to find a way to point B. Logically, we would try to move in a straight line as long as we can. Once we reach an obstacle, we would choose one of the two sides (left or right) and try to go around it using the left- or right-hand rule—follow the object parallel to its sides until we have open line of sight of the destination again, and thus can return to the straight line of advance. The algorithm can thus be formalized as follows:

```
while we have not reached our destination
    if we can advance in a straight line to the destination point,
do so
    else
        select one direction (left or right) using one of several
heuristics
        advance in the said direction keeping your left/right hand
touching the obstacle's wall
        when you can advance in a straight line towards the target
again, do so
    end if
end while
```

We can see this algorithm in action in Figure 8.1.

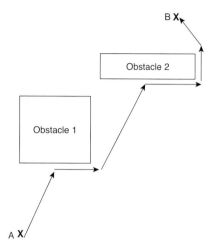

Figure 8.1   The crash and turn path finding algorithm.

All we need to define is which heuristic we will use to decide which side we will use to go around the obstacle. Two possibilities are

➤ Choosing the side that deviates less from the initial trajectory

➤ Choosing a random side (sounds crazy, but works surprisingly well)

Crash and turn always finds a way from origin to destination if we can guarantee that obstacles are all convex and not connected (two connected convex obstacles could form a concave one). The path is seldom optimal, but will look fine, especially if you are modeling wandering behaviors that do not need to be efficient in the first place. The algorithm is quite lightweight and thus can be implemented with very low CPU impact. As you can imagine, the algorithm has some problems dealing with concave obstacles. We will get stuck in C-shaped areas in an infinite loop, because we won't be able get around the obstacle once we get inside. This situation is clearly depicted in Figure 8.2

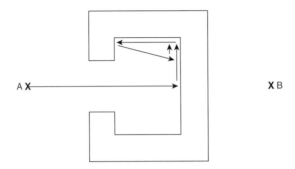

Figure 8.2   Stuck trajectory in crash and turn.

There are some improvements to the original algorithm, but none of them solves the problem completely. In fact, the problem arises from the fact that the algorithm computes the best path based on partial data, and that always incorporates errors into the solution.

Dijkstra's Algorithm

This algorithm, named after its inventor, E. W. Dijkstra, finds optimal paths in those cases where we can describe the geometry of the game world as a set of vertices with weighted connections between them being used to express distances. Take, for example, a level from a first-person shooter as shown in Figure 8.3. To the right you can see the same level represented in terms of vertices (rooms) and edges that are labeled with the distance from one room to another. This kind of data structure, often called a *weighted graph*, is what Dijkstra's algorithm starts with, so it shouldn't be surprising that this algorithm has been very popular in first-person shooter AI programming. Dijkstra's algorithm is also called a "single source, shortest paths" algorithm, because it does not compute the path between two endpoints, but rather the optimal paths from one source node to all other nodes. The algorithm is very compact and elegant, but quite complex. We will now review it thoroughly, so you can fully understand this cornerstone of path finding programming.

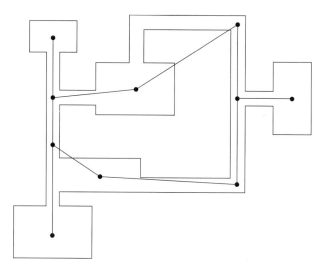

Figure 8.3   Top-down view of a game level and associated graph.

The explanation for Dijkstra's algorithm starts with a graph G=(V,E), with V vertices and E edges, and a node s, which is the source. It also has a weight matrix W, which is used to store the weights of the different edges. Starting from the source, we explore the graph using the edges, choosing the lightest weight ones first. For the first step, only the edges from the source can be expanded. But as we move forward, other nodes will have been visited already, and the newly expanded edge will be the one from all the vertices in the visited set that offers the lowest cost.

Every time we visit a new node, we store an estimate of the distance between that node and the source. For the first iteration, the estimate is just the weight of the edge we have expanded. Later, as new edges are added to the visited nodes list, the distance can always be broken down into two components: the weight of the edge we just expanded and the best distance estimate of an already visited node. Sometimes, the expansion process will find a way to reach an already visited node using an alternative, lower-cost route. Then, we will override the old path and store the new way of reaching the node. This progressive optimization behavior is called *node relaxation*, and it plays a crucial role in the implementation of Dijkstra's algorithm.

Let's now focus on the algorithm. To begin with, we use two sets. One set contains the nodes that have not been visited (the Pending set), and the other holds the nodes that have already been explored (the Visited set). For efficiency reasons, the Pending set is usually implemented as a priority queue. Additionally, we need two numeric arrays. One array stores the best distance estimate to each node, and the other stores, for each node, its predecessor in the expansion process. If we expand node five, and then we expand node nine, the predecessor of nine is five. The first step of the algorithm initializes this data structure, so we can later loop and compute the shortest paths. The initialization is pretty straightforward, as shown in this subroutine:

```
initialise_single_source( graph g, vertex s)
for each vertex v in Vertices( g )
    distance[v]=infinity;
    previous[v]=0;
end for
distance[s]=0;
```

The second step consists of the relaxation routine. In graph theory, relaxation is the process of iteratively updating a value by looking at its immediate neighbors. In this case, we are updating the cost of the path.

Thus, Dijkstra's relaxation routine works by comparing the cost of the already computed path to a vertex with a newer variant. If the new path is less costly, we will substitute the old path for the new one and update the distance and previous lists accordingly. To keep the main algorithm clean and elegant, here is a subroutine that computes the relaxation step given two nodes and a weight matrix:

```
relax(vertex u, vertex v, weights w)
if (distance[v] > distance[u] + w(u,v))
    distance[v]=distance[u]+w(u,v);
    previous[v]=u;
end if
```

The w structure stores the weights of all edges in the graph. It is nothing but a 2D array of integers or floats. The value stored at w[i][j] is the weight of the edge from vertex i to vertex j. For unconnected vertices, w[i][j] equals infinity.

Here is the complete source code for Dijkstra's algorithm in all its glory, making reference to both the initialization and relaxation functions previously provided. Notice how we pass the graph, the weight matrix that specifies the lengths of the edges, and the source vertex that starts the whole process:

```
dijkstra(graph g, weights w, vertex s)
initialize_single_source(G,s);
Visited=empty set;
Pending=set of all vertexes;
while Pending is not an empty set
    u=Extract-Min(Pending);
    Visited=Visited + u;
    for each vertex v which is a neighbour of u
        relax(u,v,w);
        end for
end while
```

We start by resetting the distance and previous vectors. Then, we put all vertices in the Pending set and empty the Visited set. We must extract vertices from Pending to convert them to Visited, updating their paths in the process. For each iteration we extract the vertex from the Visited set that has the least distance to the source. This is done using the distance array. Remember that Pending is a priority queue sorted by distance. Thus, in the first iteration, the source (distance=0) will be extracted from the Pending queue and converted to Visited. Now, we take each edge from the extracted vertex u and explore all neighbors. Here we call the relax function, which makes sure the distance for these nodes is updated accordingly. For this first iteration, all neighbors of the source had distance set to infinity. Thus, after the relaxation, their distances will be set to the weight of the edge that connects them to the source.

Then, for an arbitrary iteration, the behavior of the loop is not very different. Pending contains those nodes we have not yet visited and is sorted by the values of the distance. We then extract the least distance node and perform the relaxation on those vertices that neighbor the extracted node. These neighboring nodes can be either not-yet-expanded or already expanded nodes for which a better path was discovered. Iterating this process until all nodes have been converted from Pending to Visited, we will have the single-source shortest paths stored in the distance and previous arrays. Distance contains the measure of the distance from the source to all nodes, and backtracking from each node in the previous array until we reach the source, we can discover the sequence of vertices used in creating these optimal length paths.

Dijkstra's algorithm is a remarkable piece of software engineering. It is used in everything from automated road planners to network traffic analyzers. However, it has a potential drawback: It is designed to compute optimal paths between one source and all possible endpoints. Now, imagine a game like *Age of Empires*, where you actually need to move a unit between two specified locations. Dijkstra's algorithm is not a good choice in this case, because it computes paths to all possible destinations. Dijkstra's algorithm is the best choice when we need to analyze paths to different locations. But if we only need to trace a route, we need a more efficient method. Luckily it exists and is explained in detail in the next section.

A*

A* (pronounced A-star) is one of the most popular and powerful problem-solving (and hence, path finding) algorithms. It is a global space-search algorithm that can be used to find solutions to many problems, path finding being just one of them. It has been used in many real-time strategy games and is probably the most popular path finding algorithm. We will thus devote some space to study it carefully. Before we do so, I'd like to examine some simpler algorithms such as depth or breadth first, so we get a better understanding of the problem and can visualize what A* does more easily.

Let's begin by realizing that for the sake of path finding, states will be used to represent locations the traveler can be in, and transitions will represent unitary movements in any direction. Remember our good old checkerboard? Think about path finding in the same way. We have checkers that represent each portion of the map, and we can move one checker in any direction. So how many positions do we need to represent or, in other words, how many states do we need if we can only move on a checkerboard? A checkerboard consists of eight squares by eight squares, for a grand total of 64 possibilities. Games like *Age of Empires* are not very different: They use grids that also represent map locations. For *Age of Empires*, maps between 64×64 and 256×256 were common. A 64×64 grid yields 4,096 possible locations, whereas a 256×256 grid yields the infamous, 65,536 (two raised to the sixteenth power).

The original algorithms devised to explore such structures were exhaustive: They explored all possibilities, selecting the best one between them. The depth-first algorithm, for example, gave priority to exploring full paths, so nodes were expanded until we reached the endpoint. A score was computed for that path, and then the process was repeated until all paths were computed. The name depth-first indicated that the algorithm would always advance, reaching deeper into the graph before exploring other alternatives. A different algorithm, called breadth-first, followed the opposite approach, advancing level-by-level and exploring all nodes on the same level before moving deeper.

That worked well for games such as tic-tac-toe, where the number of steps is small. But what happens when you try to apply the same philosophy to something like chess? There's a huge number of states to explore, so this kind of analysis is very risky both in terms of memory and CPU use. What about finding a path? In a 256×256 map (which can be used to represent a simple, 256×256 meter map with a resolution of down to one meter), we would need to examine 65,000 locations, even though some of them are obviously not very good candidates.

Are we really going to use regular state-space searches, where we will basically need to examine all those options one by one—in real-time? To make the response even more obvious, think not only about how many locations but also about how many different paths we need to test for. How many paths exist between two endpoints in a playing field consisting of more than 65,000 locations? Obviously, brute force is not a good idea in this situation, at least not if you want to compute this in real-time for dozens of units moving simultaneously. We need an algorithm that somehow understands the difference between a good path and a bad path, and only examines the best candidates, forgetting about the rest of the alternatives. Only then can we have an algorithm whose CPU usage is acceptable for real-time use. That's the main advantage of A*. It is a general problem-solving algorithm that evaluates alternatives from best to worst using additional information about the problem, and thus guarantees fast convergence to the best solution.

At the core of the algorithm lies a node expansion policy that analyzes nodes in search of the complete path. This expansion prioritizes those nodes that look like promising candidates. Because this is a hard-to-code condition, heuristics are used to rate nodes, and thus select the ones that look like better options.

Assuming we model the path finding problem correctly, A* will always return optimal paths, no matter which endpoints we choose. Besides, the algorithm is quite efficient: Its only potential issue is its memory footprint. As with Dijkstra's approach, A* is a short but complex algorithm. Thus, I will provide an explanation first, and then an example of its implementation.

A* starts with a base node, a destination node, and a set of movement rules. In a four-connected game world, the rules are move up, down, left, and right. The algorithm is basically a tree expansion method. At every step, we compute possible movements until all movements have been tried, or we reach our destination. Obviously, for any mid-sized map this could require many states, with most of them being arranged in loops. Thus, we need a way to expand the tree in an informed way, so we can find the solution without needing to explore all combinations. This is what sets A* apart from the competition: It quickly converges to find the best way, saving lots of CPU cycles. To do so, it uses a heuristic—a metric of how good each node is, so better looking paths are explored first.

Let's summarize what we have discussed so far. Starting with the base node, expand nodes using the valid moves. Then, each expanded node is assigned a "score," which rates its suitability to be part of the solution. We then iterate this process, expanding best-rated nodes first until these paths prove invalid (because we reach a dead-end and can no longer expand), or one of these paths reaches the target. Because we will have tried the best-rated paths first, the first path that actually reaches the target will indeed be the optimal path.

Now, we need to devote some space to the rating process. Because it is a general-purpose problem-solving algorithm, A* uses a very abstract way of rating states. The overall score for a state is described as:

```
f(node) = g(node) + h(node)
```

where f(node) is the total score we assign to a node. This cost is broken down into two components, which we will learn to compute in the next few pages. For now, suffice it to say that g(node) is the portion that takes the past decisions into consideration and estimates the cost of the path we have already traversed in moves to reach the current state. The h(node) is the heuristic part that estimates the future. Thus, it should give an approximation of the number of moves we still need to make to reach our destination from the current position.

This way we prioritize nodes, not only considering how close they are to the destination but also in terms of the number of steps already taken. In practical terms, this means we can have a node with a very low h value (thus, close to the target), but also a very high g value, meaning we took many steps to reach it. Then, another, younger node (low g value, high h value) can be prioritized before the other one because it obtains a lower overall score. Thus, we estimate it is a better candidate. Figure 8.4 provides a visual representation of the A* algorithm.

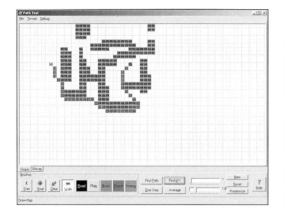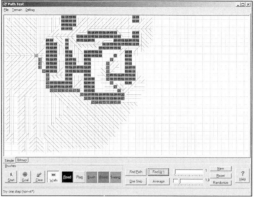

Figure 8.4   The A* algorithm. Left: chosen path. Right: nodes required to compute it.

Notice how this method is valid for many problems, whether it's playing tic-tac-toe, building a puzzle, or computing paths. We add a component that accounts for our past behavior and estimate our future as well. For path finding problems, computing g is not really a problem; it's just the number of steps taken to reach the node. If we think in terms of a tree, it's the level in the tree. The heuristic part, on the other hand, is more complex. How do we estimate the remainder of the path without effectively examining it? For path finding, the main approach is to estimate remaining distance as the Manhattan distance between our current location and the destination. Remember that the Manhattan distance is the sum of the differentials in X and Z, as in the expression:

```
Manhattan(p1,p2) = abs(p2.x-p1.x) + abs(p2.z-p1.z)
```

If you try to visualize it, the Manhattan distance is the number of steps we would need to make if we were unobstructed. Thus, it is an optimistic heuristic. It always underestimates the effort required to reach our goal. This is an essential characteristic. If we can guarantee our heuristic is always underestimating (or giving the exact estimation) of the path ahead, A* always produces optimal paths. This is because it will try to find the path that more closely resembles (in terms of score) the estimate. Think about it for a second: A target node has a score of $(N,0)$, which means N is the number of steps we needed to take, and 0 is the estimation of what remains. Using an estimate that is always optimistic forces us to reach the path with a minimal N value for the end node, which is what we are looking for. By the way, the Manhattan distance heuristic is a good choice for four-connected game worlds.

If your world is eight-connected, Manhattan would not always be optimistic, so I'd recommend the classic Euclidean distance equation defined here instead:

```
distance = sqrt( (p1.x-p2.x)2 + (p1.z-p2.z)2)
```

The downside is the added cost of squaring and computing square roots, but convergence to the optimal solution always requires optimistic heuristics.

We have seen how and why A* works. Now, let's propose a complete A* algorithm. Here is the pseudocode:

```
priorityqueue Open
list Closed

s.g = 0  // s is the start node
s.h = GoalDistEstimate( s )
s.f = s.g + s.h
s.parent = null
push s on Open
while Open is not empty
    pop node n from Open  // n has the lowest f
    if n is a goal node
        construct path
        return success
    for each successor n' of n
        newg = n.g + cost(n,n')
        if n' is in Open or Closed, and n'.g < = newg
            skip
        n'.parent = n
        n'.g = newg
        n'.h = GoalDistEstimate( n' )
        n'.f = n'.g + n'.h
        if n' is in Closed
            remove it from Closed
        if n' is not yet in Open
            push n' on Open
    push n onto Closed
return failure
```

Notice how we use two data structures: `Open` is a priority queue that stores nodes we have visited, sorted by f-value. Thus, we can always extract the best-rated node. Then, we start by placing the start node in `Open`. We expand nodes in the `while` loop until no more nodes exist (that means we have explored the whole tree and did not find a solution, so we return `failure`). Then, at each step, we pop the best candidate from `Open`. We compute all successors from this node and rate them, storing them in `Open` as well. If the new rating is better than the previous one for the same node, notice how we overwrite the old value with the new one. This is useful when we have already visited one node, but a newer path yields a better score. As nodes are visited and expanded, we place them in `Closed`. We iterate this process until we have reached a goal or until no more nodes are in `Open`, meaning there is no solution.

A* is a powerful algorithm. But it does not come without a host of problems of its own. First, it precomputes the whole path before even performing the first step. This makes it unusable for scenarios with dynamic geometry, such as collisions between soldiers, and so on. Second, A* always produces optimal results. This might seem like an advantage instead of a problem, but paths computed using A* sometimes look too perfect, and we need to modify the algorithm to add a degree of believability to the results. Third, A* computes the whole path in a single process. So how can we blend that with fog-of-war techniques? Many times we won't be seeing the whole path at once, so precomputing it using A* will simply be wrong. Our walking character will effectively see inside the fog-of-war to construct the path, which is cheating. Fourth, A* can create memory use problems. In any decent-sized map with obstacles, A* will explore lots of states to compute the best option. It is true that the end result will be optimal, but it will have claimed a high price in the process. A* is a memory-hungry algorithm, and considering its main use is found in strategy games where we need to move many units at once, this can become a pretty serious issue. Some variants have been proposed to deal with these issues. Two of the most popular variants are explained in the following sections. However, A* is currently the most widely used path finding algorithm: It is robust, it can handle both convex and concave geometry, and it is very well suited to games.

Region-Based A*

One problem with the A* algorithm is that if many obstacles block our advance, we need to expand a lot of nodes to reach our destination. This results in a very high memory footprint and low performance. We need to store lots of states. Two solutions have been proposed to deal with this problem. One solution involves tracing the path at a higher-abstraction level. The other involves tracing the path progressively, not expanding the whole state space at once. Region-based A* is explained in this section, and the next section describes Iterative-Deepening A* (IDA*).

Regular A* decomposes paths in terms of primitive operations. In a four-connected scenario, we can move up, down, left, and right. Obviously, using such a low-level operator has a downside. Any reasonably sized path will be composed of many actions, and that means the search space will grow quickly. Now, A* does not necessarily need to use such primitives. We could implement A* using a different, higher-abstraction level space representation. For example, we could divide our game world into regions (be it rooms, zones in a map, and so on) and implement an edge or state transition whenever we move from one room to the other.

Using a region-based A* algorithm is especially useful when coupled with convex map regions. If a region is convex, we can move between two endpoints without finding any obstacles in our way. This is the basis of Jordan's curve theorem. We can paint a line, and if the region is indeed convex, the line will cross it exactly twice. This means path finding inside the region can be handled in the simplest form—no obstacles to worry about, just walk in a straight line between the entry and exit point. The same idea can be extended to support convex obstacles in convex rooms as well. Imagine a square room full of columns. We can use A* to navigate the complete scenario and crash and turn (which works fine on convex obstacles) for intra-room navigation. This is an especially interesting result. If you think about it for a second, most obstacles in an indoors environment are either convex or can easily be considered convex by means of a convex hull/bounding box computation preprocess. Then, we would have the global correctness of A* while using a low-cost, low-memory footprint such as crash and turn for local analysis. The overall solution would also be faster to compute, because A* would converge faster in a smaller state space.

Interactive-Deepening A*

Another alternative to reduce space requirements in A* is to compute the whole path in small pieces, so we do not examine the whole search tree at once. This is the core concept behind IDA*, a very popular variant to the basic A* algorithm.

In IDA*, a path is cut off when its total cost f(n) exceeds a maximum cost threshold. IDA* starts with a threshold equal to f(start node), which by the way is equal to h(start node) because g(start node) = 0. Then, branches are expanded until either a solution is found that scores below the cutoff cost or no solution is found. In this case, the cutoff is increased by one, and another search is triggered. The main advantage of IDA* over A* is that memory usage is significantly reduced. A* takes O(b^d), where b is the tree's branching factor and d is the number of levels in the tree. IDA* is just O(d) due to its iterative deepening nature.

A Note on Human Path Finding

To get some perspective on path finding algorithms, let's stop and think about how humans trace paths in the real world. We tend to rely on very different methods than those used by machines. As mentioned earlier, tracing a path with or without a map really does make a difference—the difference from a local to a global algorithm. When using the global approach, our methods would not be very different from A*. But how do we trace paths in unexplored areas? Drop a tourist in the center of a city, give him a compass, and he'll find a way to a certain monument (provided we tell him in which direction to aim). How can he, and people in general, do that?

To begin with, people use a hybrid local-global algorithm. It is local whenever we are exploring new ground. But we have the ability to build pretty good mental maps on the fly. When we walk through an unfamiliar neighborhood, we automatically store information about the places we see, so we can recognize them later. Thus, if we return to the same location (say, because we reached a dead end), we will be using a global path finding method. We have all the information about the area, and thus use it to our advantage.

Formally, the main path planning routine is fundamentally a depth-first, trial-and-error algorithm, assisted by the maps we make in our mind. We try to advance in the direction the goal seems to be, and if we reach a dead end, we back up using the map and try a different strategy. Different people use slightly different strategies, but the overall algorithm stays the same. The pseudocode for such an algorithm would be something like this:

```
while not there yet,
    detect the direction where the target is at
    choose from the unexplored available paths the one that seems
```

```
to move in the right direction
    explore the path, storing the features of the areas we visit
in an internal map
    if we reach a dead-end, back-up to the latest junction,
marking everything as already tried (and failed)
    go to step 3
end while
```

With quite a bit of precision, the algorithm we use enables us to find our way around in places we've never visited before. And I might add, it works remarkably well as long as we have the ability to remember places we just visited. As you can see, the algorithm does not look very hard to implement. But how do you store relevant information for later use as a map? What is relevant? How do we store map data? Humans are light years ahead of computers when it comes to representing and working with symbolic information. We can remember locations, sounds, and people, and build accurate maps based on them. We can handle types and amounts of information that a computer, as of today, cannot deal with well. Notice, however, that the human path finding algorithm is essentially local, and thus does not guarantee an optimal path will be found. As we repeat the same journey or simply wander around the neighborhood, we will gather more information for our map, thus making path finding less local and more of a global strategy. However, even with the imperfections of the map making, the algorithm is light years away from its philosophy from the mathematical perfection of an algorithm like A*.

On the other hand, there is a clear reason for using algorithms such as A*. Most games using path finding need it for military simulations, where the AI must be solid and compelling. Keep in mind that games are not about realism: They are about having a good time, and no one wants soldiers to get stuck trying to find a way to the front-line—no matter how realistic that might be. After all, people do get lost in cities all the time, but programmers don't want that to happen in the middle of a game.

However, it is likely that the near future will bring more humanlike path finding to games, where behavior is not so much based in tactics but in conveying the complexity of real creatures.

Group Dynamics

We will now move higher on the abstraction scale to study how we can emulate the movement patterns of groups of entities, whether it's a highly unorganized herd of mammals or a Roman cohort performing complex formations. We will not use the synchronization ideas from the previous chapter, because they do not scale well. Synchronizing two soldiers is qualitatively different from trying to move a wedge of 500 cavalrymen, so a whole different approach must be devised. We will start with a classic animal behavior algorithm and then move on to formations in the next section.

Boids

One of the best examples of synthetic group behavior can be found in the boids algorithm introduced by Craig W. Reynolds in the 1990s. The algorithm was initially designed for creating movie special effects and was used in movies like Disney's *The Lion King*. The boids algorithm became a cornerstone in real-time group dynamics and was a huge influence in many movies, such as *Starship Troopers*. As years went by, the boids algorithm slowly found its way into computer games, from simple flocking birds in *Unreal* to complete group dynamics for large-scale strategy games. You can see many types of boids-driven behaviors in Figure 8.5.

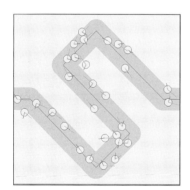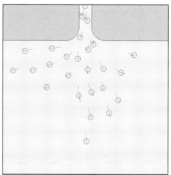

Figure 8.5   Different types of boid-like algorithms: follow the leader, enter through a door, follow a path.

The boids algorithm allows the real-time simulation of flocks, herds, schools, and generally speaking, any creature that acts as part of a group with hardly any room for individuality. Interestingly enough, the boids algorithm can efficiently simulate traffic jams on a highway, pedestrian behaviors, and many other human activities as well as simple animal behavior.

The core hypothesis of the boids system is that the behavior of a group of individuals is largely governed by a relatively small set of simple rules. Birds, goats, and even human beings are not extremely intelligent when it comes to working in groups. Thus, Reynolds believed that the apparent complexity must simply arise from relatively straightforward mechanisms. After some research, he found that flocking behavior could easily be modeled with as few as three rules:

➤ Separation: Each member of the group will try to prevent having another member closer than a set threshold, thus avoiding a collision within the flock. If a member invades the area of influence of another member, they must both correct their orientation to try and separate.

➤ Alignment: All members of a group will try to aim in the same direction, much like a herd of sheep would do. It simply makes no sense for each member to be facing in a completely different direction.

➤ Cohesion: All members of the same group should try to stay close to the group's center of gravity or barycenter. By doing so, the flock stays together, except for those circumstances when the separation rule needs to be enforced.

The combination of these three rules (depicted in Figure 8.6) can effectively simulate any flock. The system is really simple to code. Notice that a boid does not even have an internal state variable. Each computed frame starts from scratch, so it makes no sense for the bots to have a working memory. On the other hand, some changes need to be made in order to increase the boids system's expressive potential. For example, one of the members of the formation must be a scripted AI (or even the player). We need someone to generate the influence field so the others will conform to this behavior. Another interesting issue is the handling of a more complex system. To analyze this, we need to fully understand how boids works, and even better, why.

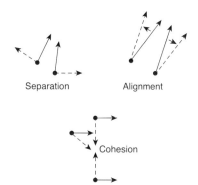

Figure 8.6 The three rules of boids.

To better understand boids, you need to think about them as analogies to fields or zones of influence. Imagine that each boid is actually a charged particle. It is repelled by a strong (but quickly diminishing) field, so it never collides with another particle of the same sign, and it has an attractive force toward the center of gravity (in the boids case, the center of the flock). Thus, we can rewrite most of the boids algorithm in terms of attractions and repulsions. Even more complex and involved simulations can be created by just adding layers and layers of information to the core boids algorithm. Imagine, for example, two types of birds, pigeons, and hawks. Hawks try to catch pigeons, which in turn try to escape as soon as they see an incoming hawk. We can simulate this behavior by just adding a fourth rule to the core boids system. It is a special-case separation rule, which affects much higher distances than the traditional separation rule explained in the original formulation. If you have followed this example, you will see how this hawk and pigeon approach allows us to elegantly incorporate obstacle handling in our boids code. Obstacles can be modeled as an extra type of entity, so other entities just feel a strong repulsive force toward them. Notice how a group of birds will effectively avoid the collision using the obstacle information. On the other hand, once the obstacle has been avoided, the third rule (cohesion) will play a key role, ensuring that everyone is working diligently to reestablish the formation.

Let's now adapt these methods to groups of humans, quite likely in the context of military strategy.

Formation-Based Movement

Moving in formation is a bit more involved than acting on an individual basis or acting like a flock of birds. Any error in our alignment or speed will generate unwanted collisions with other members of our unit and quite likely will end up breaking up the group. Several approaches can be used to implement formation-based navigation.

In one approach, you can totally discard the individual component and make the whole squadron act as a single soldier. The AI is assigned to the squadron, so each soldier is just placed wherever needed. For example, imagine that we need to control a squadron consisting of 60 men in 6 ranks, 10 men per rank. We represent the squadron by its barycenter and yaw vector. Thus, here is the rendering code needed to paint each soldier individually:

```
#define SPACING 2
for (int xi=0;xi<COLUMNS;xi++)
    {
    for (int zi=0;zi<RANKS;zi++)
        {
        point pos(xi-(COLUMNS/2),0,zi-(RANKS/2));
        pos=pos*SPACING;
        pos.rotatey(yaw);
        pos.translate(barycenter);
        }
    }
```

This approach has a limitation, however: We cannot assign individual behaviors. For example, our troops will fight in perfect formation and will not avoid obstacles on an individual level. The whole troop will change its trajectory to avoid a tree, for example. Thus, more powerful ways of dealing with group dynamics must be devised.

Adapting the ideas from the boids algorithm, we can represent group dynamics for humans by means of a summation of potential fields. Here, we will resolve locomotion as the addition of several fields of influence, such as:

➤ One field (repulsive) that keeps us separated from nearby units

➤ One field (attractive) that keeps us near the position we are supposed to occupy in the formation

➤ One field (repulsive) that is used for collision detection with obstacles

By adding the influence of these three fields, you can achieve very realistic formation-based movement. A column might break to avoid an obstacle, only to merge again on the opposite side. Formations can perform rotations, and so on. The main pitfall of such an approach is that obstacle geometry must be kept simple, so we can generate potential fields efficiently. Concave objects will definitely not be modeled. Another issue comes from computing the repulsion with obstacles and enemy units. Here we will need an efficient data representation to ensure we can compute these fields without having to resort to N×N tests. A spatial index can definitely help us in this respect.

Military Analysis: Influence Maps

An *influence map* (IM) is a data structure that allows us to perform queries useful to tactical analysis. Once built, an IM can tell the AI system about the balance of power, frontlines, flanks, and so on with very simple queries. The data structure is dynamic in nature, so it responds well to changes in the conditions. Entities can be added, others suppressed due to dying, and some others might move, and the IM will still be valid. All that needs to be done is to recompute the structure every few seconds to ensure the analysis is based on current conditions.

An IM is a 2D array of numeric values. Integers, floats, and so on can all be used. The map is very similar to a field in physics. The values held at each 2D position represent the influence of a certain variable. As a very simple example, imagine two armies. Each soldier on a side will have a value of –1, whereas soldiers on the opposite side will have a value of 1. Then, cells in the array holding one soldier will have the soldier's value, whereas the remaining cells will simply be interpolated, so there is a smooth gradation in neighboring cells. IMs are thus rather easy to build and can provide useful information to the tactician if analyzed well. The trick is that once abstract information has been mapped to a 2D array, obtaining information is a matter of image analysis, which is a well-known, deeply researched science.

For example, analyzing the map and searching for zero-valued points will give us the exact location of the frontline between the two armies, the point at which both armies are equidistant. Searching the point on the map that is a local maxima will give us unit locations; and selecting between these, the point whose neighbors are more distant (in value) to the central point will give us the more isolated enemy unit, which is more suitable for targeting.

Once the basics of IMs have been explained, we will explore implementation details for the data structure as well as a collection of IM analysis routines.

Data Structure

IMs are usually just 2D arrays (see Figure 8.7 for an example) with size depending on the size of the scenario. Choosing the right size is essential: Bigger maps take longer to compute, whereas smaller maps can lose some detail. In some circumstances, hierarchical maps can be used in a way similar to mip-maps; each map being half the size of its ancestor.

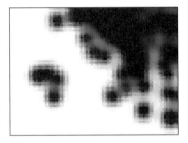

Figure 8.7   Influence maps. Dark colors represent the influence of one army, white represents the other.

The cell value can be any numeric value or a list of numeric values. IMs are not limited to mapping a single value. One of their main uses is analyzing several parameters in parallel, so all of them can then be used to create a plan. For example, here is the declaration of an IM holding the balance of power and information relative to the speed of the units as a 2D map:

```
typedef struct
    {
    float speed;
    float value;
    } cell;
```

```
class influencemap
    {
    cell **data;
    int sizex,sizez;
    };
```

The structure is rather simple. Only the dynamic nature of the 2D array can be a problem for less advanced programmers. Then, a routine to update the structure is needed. In a simple scenario, the routine would be something like this:

```
for (ix=0;ix<sizex;ix++)
    for (iz=0;iz<sizez;iz++)
        for each primitive
            compute the influence of the primitive on the cell
(ix,iz)
```

This is a three-times nested loop, which is not very good in terms of efficiency.

Some Useful Tests

This section provides a listing of useful tests for IMs. These tests provide the 2D analysis routine and the "tactical meaning" of the analysis for the AI engine.

- ➤ **Balance of Power.** Using the balance of power test, we compute the summation of the whole IM. If the value is greater than zero, the side represented by positive values is winning. If the value is smaller, the other side wins. This test should be applied to an IM where each cell holds the value of each unit. This value can be as simple as the life level plus the damage value, or some more complex computation.

- ➤ **Frontline Location.** In an IM map, such as the one previously mentioned, locate the zeros. If you want the frontline as a strict distance metric from opposite units, consider only locations with +1 and −1 and forget each unit's life level. If you use the life level, a strong unit displaces the frontline toward the enemy.

- ➤ **Breakability of Enemy Forces.** Use an IM as the one previously mentioned. Then, detect the two largest (or smallest) values on the enemy side of the field. Trace a line between those two points and compare the values along the line with the values at both tips. If the line's values differ by more than a given threshold, the enemy is basically divided, so you can charge the weakest spot to divide and conquer.

➤ **Weakest Enemy.** The weakest enemy is the minimum (or maximum) value on the enemy field that is surrounded by smaller values. If the enemy is assigned negative values, we must look for a point on the map that is minimal regarding its neighbors, but which itself is the least negative minimum. This implies a unit of least value.

➤ **Detecting Charges.** To detect whether the enemy is charging toward us, we store the map at regular intervals (say, every second). Then, a progressive drop in value in a point near our units (assuming the enemy is negatively valued) means that enemies are approaching. The faster the drop, the faster they move. Similarly, the opposite implies if they are retreating.

➤ **Safe Routes.** To detect whether a moving unit will enter an enemy zone, we must make sure each and every cell the unit visits has the same sign as the unit. This means the unit will be closer to its own army than to any enemy.

Many more tests can be implemented using simple math on the IM. All that's needed is some imagination of how to express tactically relevant tests in terms of simple additions and so on.

Representing Tactics

Most real-time strategy games are built around a two-layered AI system. From a low-level perspective, individual units are controlled by simple rule systems or state machines, which control their behavior, simple interactions with the environment, and so on. But how about tactics? How do armies get built, and how do they command troops on the battlefield? Most times, a higher-abstraction, complex rule system is used, which becomes an expert system that holds a significant body of knowledge regarding the art of war. In this section we will explore this tactical layer.

For our simple AI example, we will use classic rules in the form:

```
FACT -> ACTION
```

Our fact list will need to store all those items we need to test for. A similar system was used in Microsoft's *Age of Kings*. Here are, for example, two rules that control the frequency of the computer attacks:

```
(defrule
.(game-time > 1100)
=>
.(attack-now)
.(enable-timer 7 1100)
.(disable-self)
.(chat-local-to-self "first attack")
)

(defrule
.(timer-triggered 7)
.(defend-soldier-count >= 12)
=>
.(attack-now)
.(disable-timer 7)
.(enable-timer 7 1400)
.(chat-local-to-self "other attacks")
)
```

The first rule is triggered after 1,100 seconds have elapsed (approximately 20 minutes into the gameplay) and once every 23 minutes from that initial wave. Notice how timers are used to control the timing of these second-wave attacks, and how subsequent attacks are only started if 12 or more soldiers are available to defend our positions.

Also notice the fact that action language is highly symbolic. We need to implement each and every call in our programming language so AI programmers can work from a comfortable, high-abstraction level.

Imagine that we need to create a rule system for a Roman army battle that starts with the configuration shown in figure 8.8. I'll first provide some brief background information on the Roman army on the battlefield. In Roman battles, troops were deployed on a frontline with less-trained infantry in the first ranks and more experienced soldiers behind them. Some artillery and archer support were also available. The cavalry was kept to a minimum and was located at the wings to perform flanking moves around enemy troops. As the battle started, the first ranks of infantry (the lesser-trained soldiers) advanced while archers and ballistae rained projectiles on the enemy. As the distance between the first ranks of the infantry to the enemy reached a threshold, soldiers threw their spears or pila toward the enemy and kept advancing until the final clash actually took place. At that moment, the highly experienced legionnaires from the second wave started to advance toward the enemy as well. Then, after a short battle, the lesser-trained infantry would retreat through the gaps in the formations, and the experienced legionnaires would appear from the back, engaging in close combat with the enemy. At this point, the cavalry from the wings would charge until the battle was resolved.

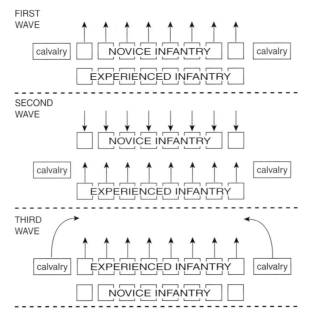

Figure 8.8 Roman army disposition on the battlefield.

Now, let's build a rule system for such a battle. We will begin with some general rules that start the confrontation and follow the syntax from the *Age of Kings* AI system for simplicity:

```
(defrule
.(true)
```

```
=>
.(shoot-catapults)
.(shoot-arrows)
.(disable-self)
)

(defrule
.(true)
=>
.(enable-timer 1 30)
.(disable-self)
)
```

These first two rules start the battle. The first rule states that both arrows and catapults must continue to shoot throughout the battle. The second rule is just used to delay the advance of the first wave by 30 seconds. We set a timer so it triggers after 30 seconds, signaling the start of the infantry advance. Notice how we use the fact true whenever we want to express a rule that is always available for execution. Also notice how we need a construct like disable-self to manually delete a rule, so it is not inspected in further execution loops:

```
(defrule
.(timer-triggered 1)
=>
.(attack-first-wave)
.(disable-timer 1)
.(disable-self)
)

(defrule
.(first-wave-distance < 100)
.(have-pilum)
=>
.(throw-pilum)
)

(defrule
.(first-wave-distance < 20)
=>
```

```
.(engage-combat)
)

(defrule
.(first-wave-distance < 20)
=>
.(attack-second-wave)
.(disable-self)
)
```

These four rules implement the advance, pilum-throwing, and engagement in combat of the first wave. The last two rules allow us to begin fighting (rule 3, which can be activated repeatedly) and to notify the second wave that we are requesting their help (rule four, which is disabled right after its first activation). Now, these rules should provide you with a practical example of how tactical AIs are designed.

But this example only shows part of the picture. After all, a choreographed battle has a defined sequential pattern, and rule systems are great when parallel behaviors are to be modeled. Now, imagine the power of such a system where rules apply not to the army as a whole, but to specific squadrons. Each squad would evaluate the expert system, and complex behaviors would emerge from apparent simplicity.

Here is when a choice must be made or a balance must be found. Will we implement our tactic as rules and hence as a reactive, highly emergent system, or will we choose to sequence actions as in the preceding Roman example? Sequential systems are all about memorizing the CPU's actions and learning how to defeat them. Emergent gameplay is somehow harder to master because it requires skill more than memory.

In Closing

Tactic AI is a huge field that goes on forever. We have focused on three areas: path finding (individual and group-based), tactic analysis, and tactical representation. But many subjects are left for the reader to explore: learning, adaptation, and a great deal of real-world military tactics.

Chapter 9

Scripting

"Life is like a B-picture script. It is that corny. If I had my life story offered to me to film, I'd turn it down."

Kirk Douglas

So far we have discussed how hard-coded AI systems can deal with many scenarios efficiently, from action to strategy and everything in between. Some games will work fine with small AI systems, whereas others will require tons of code to implement the AI feature set. However, as the AI grows in complexity, keeping it hard-coded will eventually become a problem. Hard-coded AIs are efficient, but are often limited in terms of flexibility. The internals of the AI are built into the game's source, so adding or changing anything requires recompiling the full source code, making the process tiring and troublesome. This is especially important in large-sized games, where many different AI types exist. Imagine a role-playing game with dozens of characters, each with his or her own personality, behavior patterns, and dialogs. Hard coding these AIs can create a bottleneck, can introduce bugs in the game's source code, and is overall a risky decision.

Under these circumstances, it would be great to externalize the AI so it could be run from separate modules that were "satellites" to the core engine. These satellite modules would be written in a specific programming language (often different from the one used in the main engine) and would run in a "safe" environment, so a faulty AI module would not cause problems for the main application. If these conditions were met, the AI modules could be coded by different people, such as AI designers, content production people, and so on rather than those coding the main engine. As a result, the benefits would not be limited to flexibility. These satellite modules would be useful for team management and program security issues as well.

Each of these satellite modules that externally implement AI (or, more generally, game-play-related) routines in a specific language is called a *script*, and the global technique, *scripting*, is what this chapter is all about.

Scripting is a very popular method used these days where large teams work on even larger games. It streamlines the creation of the AI and logic content by placing that responsibility in the hands of people different from those actually coding the engine. It also allows for more creative AI design. Often, a dedicated AI programmer using a scripting language will come up with new ideas, and because the language will allow him to test them immediately, he will create more compelling and believable characters. It all boils down to selecting the right feature set for the scripting language so that it combines a powerful set of primitive calls with the ease of use your content team will demand.

Obviously, scripting languages will incur a significant performance hit, more so than a compiled, binary implementation done in a language such as C++. Here your mileage may vary greatly depending on your choice of language, because some scripts perform much better than others. Notice, however, that focusing on performance is actually missing the point concerning why scripting makes sense in the first place. A scripting language has more to do with extensibility and flexibility than it does with efficiency. But some of the more modern script engines, such as Lua, offer a small memory footprint and very good performance, so you get a "best of both worlds" solution.

There are many different approaches to using scripting languages. You can code your own, use an embedded language, or even communicate with the engine using a network connection. Although the goals are more or less identical, each approach has its advantages and disadvantages. For the rest of this chapter, we will analyze each approach in detail, so you can make an informed decision in your next game project.

Building a Scripting Language

The first technique we will explore is building a scripting language from scratch. This used to be common some years ago, when each team had to devote many hours to get a flexible scripting language to work. But recent advances in programming languages have made this technique less and less popular, as newer and better methods have appeared through the years. Today, you can have a top-class scripting engine up and running in just a few hours, with little or no trouble at all. However, for completeness, let me give you some idea of how creating your own programming language might work. I will deliberately only provide some hints, because programming language creation is a very in-depth subject to which you can devote many years (and several books as thick as this one). Check out Appendix E, "Further Reading," at the end of the book for some suggested reading on compilers, parsers, and other tools.

Generally speaking, creating a programming language involves a three-step process. The first step entails defining the programming language syntax. This can be done on paper, because it is basically a matter of deciding which features you need and which syntax those features will be exposed through. The second step involves the creation of a program loader, which takes a file written in the said programming language and loads it into memory for execution. In this step, we must check for syntactic validity and take the appropriate steps to ensure efficient execution. The third and final step is the execution of the program itself. Depending on the coding strategy, this can range from just executing a binary module written in machine code to interpreting a high-level language such as BASIC, to something in between like Java.

Whichever route you choose, the complexity of the task will largely depend on the syntax of the language of choice. As an example, we will now focus on two popular choices: a simple language that we will use to code a symbolic rule system and a full-blown structured language similar to BASIC or C.

Parsing Simple Languages

In this section, I will describe the process of creating the parser and execution module for a simple language. I have chosen a language that is to be used to specify rule systems via scripting. The language is very similar to that used in the *Age of Empires* series. It is composed of a list of rules, and each rule is made up of a condition and an action, so the run-time engine selects the first one (in order) whose condition is active and executes the associated action.

Following the preceding scheme, we will begin by deciding the syntax of our programming language: which constructs will be supported, the keywords, and so on. There are dozens of different approaches to this problem. But for this example, we will use the following syntax:

```
defrule
        condition1
        condition2
        ...
=>
        action1
        action2
        ...
```

Each rule can have multiple conditions (which are ANDed) and multiple actions (which are run sequentially). As an example, let's define a very simple scripting language that we will use as a case study. We will build the parser manually because the syntax is very simple. Each condition, for example, can be defined by the simple grammar:

```
condition -> [float_function] [operator] float | [boolean_function]
float_function -> DISTANCE | ANGLE | LIFE
operator -> GREATER | SMALLER | EQUAL
boolean_function -> LEFT | RIGHT
```

So we can query the Euclidean distance, angular distance, and life level of the enemy. We can also test whether he is to our left or to the right. As you may already have guessed, this rule system is designed for controlling an action AI such as a ship.

The actions we can perform can be defined as:

```
action ->   [float_action] float | [unary_action]
float_action -> ROTATE | ADVANCE
unary_action -> SHOOT
```

Thus, here is a complete rule system built using these rules to demonstrate the expressive potential of the language:

```
defrule
        distance  smaller  5
        left
=>
        rotate  0.01
        advance  0.1

defrule
        distance  smaller  5
        right
=>
        rotate  -0.01
        advance  0.1

defrule
        angle  <  0.25
=>
        shoot

defrule
        left
=>
        rotate  -0.01
        advance  0.1

defrule
        right
=>
        rotate  0.01
        advance  0.1
```

Because rules are executed in order, the previous example enacts a ship that tries to shoot down the player while avoiding collisions. The first two rules detect whether the player is too close and evades the player (rotating in the opposite direction, in radians). The next rule detects whether we can actually shoot down the player because he's at a small angular distance, whereas the last two rules implement a chasing behavior.

These kinds of languages are really easy to load because their syntax is very regular. For each rule, you just have to parse the conditions, and depending on its value, parse the right parameter list. Then we repeat the process for each action. Thus, we will start by defining the data structure we will use to hold the rules. For our case, this can be defined as

```
typedef struct
        {
        int opcode;
        int operation;
        float param;
        } fact;

typedef struct
        {
        list<fact> condition;
        list<fact> action;
        } rule;
```

Thus, the whole virtual machine would be

```
class vmachine
        {
        int pc;
        int numrules;
        rule *program;

        public:
                void load(char *); // Loads from the provided file name
                void run();
        };
```

The first phase (language definition) is complete. Now it is time to implement the loader and parser, so we can initialize the data structures while checking for the validity of the script. Because the language is very regular in its structure, the loader is not a big issue. Here is a portion of its code, which begins by computing the number of rules by counting the number of defrule apparitions in the source file:

```
void load(char *filename)
{
(…)
for (i=0;i<numrules;i++)
        {
        while (convert_to_opcode(readtoken(file))!=THEN)
                {
                fact f;
                // read a condition
                char *stropcode=readtoken(file);
                f.opcode=convert_to_opcode(stropcode);
                switch (f.opcode)
                        {
                        case ANGLE:
                                char *operation=readtoken(file);
                                f.operation(convert_to_opcode(operation);
                                // GREATER, etc
                                f.param=atoi(readtoken(file));
                                rules[i].condition.push_back(f);
                                break;
                        (…)
                }
        // rule conditions ok… move on to actions
        while (!file.eof() &&
(convert_to_opcode(readtoken(file))!=DEFRULE))
                {
                fact f;
                // read an action
                char *stropcode=readtoken(file);
                f.opcode=convert_to_opcode(stropcode);
                switch (f.opcode)
                        {
                        case ROTATE:
                                f.param=atoi(readtoken(file));
                                rules[i].action.push_back(f);
                                break;
```

(...)
```
            }
        }
```

We only need to provide a routine to parse tokens (strings or numeric values separated by spaces or newline). Notice how we have assumed there is a define for each opcode, which we use to access its symbolic value. In our case, the define list would be

```
#define LEFT 0
#define RIGHT 1
#define ADVANCE 2
#define ROTATE 3
#define SHOOT 4
#define ANGLE 5
#define DISTANCE 6
#define DEFRULE 7
#define THEN 8
#define GREATER 9
#define SMALLER 10
#define EQUAL 11

#define WRONG_OPCODE -1
```

Notice how we reserve an additional opcode to process parsing errors. By following this convention, the final code to the convert_to_opcode routine would just be

```
int convert_to_opcode(char *opcode)
{
if (!strcmp(opcode),"left") return LEFT;
(...)
if (!strcmp(opcode),"=>") return THEN;
return WRONG_OPCODE;
}
```

In this example, our language is case sensitive like C. By changing the strcmp call, you can implement case-insensitive languages as well.

Once we have defined the language syntax and have coded a loader, it is time to move on to the execution module of our virtual machine. Again, because this is a relatively simple language, it is very helpful. We just have to scan the list of sentences and take the appropriate actions for each one of them. Here is the source code for part of the vmachine::run operation:

```
void vmachine::run()
{
rule *ru;
bool end=false;
pc=0;

while ((!end) && (!valid(rule[pc]))
        {
        pc++;
        }
if (valid(rule[pc].condition))
        {
        run_action(rule[pc]);
        }
}
```

Notice that we really scan the rules searching for the first one that has a valid condition. If we fail to find such a rule, we simply return. Otherwise, we call the action execution subroutine, which will take care of executing each and every action assigned to that rule. The real meat of the algorithm lies in the routine that evaluates whether a rule is valid and the routine that executes the actions. Here is part of the source code of the first routine:

```
bool valid (rule r)
{
list<fact>::iterator pos=r.condition.begin();
while (pos!=r.condition.end())
        {
        switch (pos->opcode)
                {
                case ANGLE:
                        // compute angle... this is internal game code
                        angle=...
                        if ((pos->operation==GREATER) && (angle<pos->param))
```

```
                                return false;
                    if ((pos->operation==SMALLER) && (angle>pos->param))
                            return false;
                    if ((pos->operation==EQUAL) && (angle!=pos->param))
                            return false;
                    break;
            case DISTANCE:
                    (...)
                    break;
            }

        pos.next();
        }
return true;
}
```

Basically, we test all the facts in the condition. As we AND them, all of them must be valid for the rule to be valid. Thus, the moment one of them is not valid, we reject the rule totally and return `false`. If we happen to reach the end of the fact list and all of the facts are true, the whole rule is true, and we must validate it.

Now, here is the action execution:

```
void run_action(rule r)
{
list<fact>::iterator pos=r.action.begin();
while (pos!=r.action.end())
        {
        switch (pos->opcode)
                {
                case ROTATE:
                        yaw+=pos->param;
                        break;
                case ADVANCE:
                        playerpos.x+=pos->param*cos(yaw);
                        playerpos.z+=pos->param*sin(yaw);
                        break;
                    (...)
```

```
            }
        }
    }
```

Notice how in this case we do not test but instead execute actions sequentially, as if the routine were a regular computer program.

We have seen how to parse and execute a simple programming language in the form of a symbolic rule system. From here, we can add many constructs to enhance the expressive potential. *Age of Empires* had well over 100 facts, so both action and conditions could be based in sophisticated routines. In an extreme case, you could end up with a very involved programming language. It all depends on your knowledge of parsing techniques and the time spent polishing the language. Efficiency, on the other hand, is quite good, especially if each sentence has strong semantics (its execution is complex and takes many clock cycles). In a language such as the one outlined earlier (and pictured in Figure 9.1), each sentence has an implicit performance hit for the loop and switch constructs. But the rule execution is just binary code. Clearly, the impact of the parsing and switch constructs will be noticeable if each rule has very light-weight binary code that takes almost no time to execute. Now, in a language where each instruction takes a lot of binary code to execute, the overhead of the loop and switch will be negligible, and performance on your scripting language will be almost identical to that of native code.

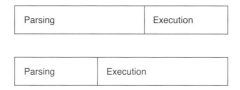

Figure 9.1   Weak (top) versus strong (bottom) semantics.

Parsing Structured Languages

It is possible to code parsers for more complex languages following the ideas outlined earlier. But coding a language such as C from scratch would definitely be a challenging task. There are hundreds of constructs, function calls, and symbols to account for.

That's why specific tools, such as lexical scanners, were designed many years ago to help in the creation of programming languages. Lexical scanners are used to detect whether a token (character string in a programming language) is valid or not.

The most popular example of these analyzers is called Lex. Basically, you use Lex to generate a beefed-up version of our `convert_to_token` routine. Lex receives a formal definition of the lexicon for the language and is able to generate C code that decodes and accepts valid tokens only. To declare this lexicon, you must use Lex's convention. For example, here is a portion of the lexicon for the C programming language:

```
"break"        { count(); return(BREAK); }
"case"         { count(); return(CASE); }
"char"         { count(); return(CHAR); }
"const"        { count(); return(CONST); }
"continue"     { count(); return(CONTINUE); }
"default"      { count(); return(DEFAULT); }
"do"           { count(); return(DO); }
"double"       { count(); return(DOUBLE); }
"else"         { count(); return(ELSE); }
"enum"         { count(); return(ENUM); }
"extern"       { count(); return(EXTERN); }
(...)
"*"            { count(); return('*'); }
"/"            { count(); return('/'); }
"%"            { count(); return('%'); }
"<"            { count(); return('<'); }
">"            { count(); return('>'); }
"^"            { count(); return('^'); }
"|"            { count(); return('|'); }
"?"            { count(); return('?'); }
```

Once Lex has detected the lexical constructs, it is time to move higher in the abstraction scale and detect full language constructs such as an `if-then-else` loop. To achieve this, the syntax of the language must be described in mathematical terms. An `if` sequence, for example, can be described in a variety of alternative ways, such as:

1. [if] (LOGICAL_EXPRESSION) SENTENCE

2. [if] (LOGICAL_EXPRESSION)

```
{

SENTENCE_LIST

}
```

3. [if] (LOGICAL_EXPRESSION)

   ```
   {

   SENTENCE_LIST

   }
   ```

   else

   ```
        SENTENCE
   ```

4. [if] (LOGICAL_EXPRESSION) SENTENCE

   else

   ```
   {

   SENTENCE_LIST

   }
   ```

5. [if] (LOGICAL_EXPRESSION)

   ```
   {

   SENTENCE_LIST

   }
   ```

   else

   ```
       {

       SENTENCE_LIST

   }
   ```

Formally speaking, this sequence can be described using a mathematical construct called Context-Free Grammars (CFGs). CFGs allow us to declare languages by using a substitution rule. For example, here is the rule for the IF construct in the C language:

```
if_statement
        : IF '(' expression ')' statement
        | IF '(' expression ')' statement ELSE statement
        ;
```

Each lowercase token is another rule we can apply. For a simpler example, here is a CFG for evaluating numeric expressions:

Expression

> : NUMBER
>
> | expression opcode expression
>
> | (expression)
>
> ;

opcode

> : '+'
>
> | '-'
>
> | '*'
>
> | '/'
>
> ;

Thus, we can apply the two rules recursively to obtain the syntactic tree shown in Figure 9.2.

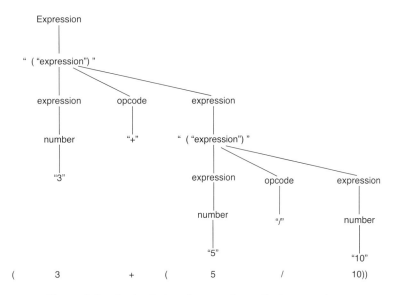

Figure 9.2   Syntactic tree for a mathematical expression.

Once we have specified our programming language by means of its grammar, we need a program that actually parses the input file, and once it has been converted to tokens, checks for syntactic correctness. The most popular of such applications is called Yet Another Compiler Compiler (Yacc). Yacc takes a grammar file as input and generates the C code required to parse the grammar. Then, it's up to the application developer to decide what to do with this syntax checker. We could decide to convert the input file to a different format, such as a bytecode used in the Java programming language. Alternatively, we could decide to execute the program as it's being checked for validity. We would then use an interpreter, such as BASIC. In addition, we could choose a middle-of-the-road solution and convert the input file to an intermediate representation, such as an assembly-like syntax, which is faster to execute in an interpreter-like fashion. This is usually referred to as a just-in-time (JIT) compiler.

For computer game scripting, Yacc is commonly used as an interpreter or as a JIT compiler. It does not make much sense to actually output any bytecode, because we really want to run the script.

Embedded Languages

In the preceding section, you got an idea of how to create a new programming language from scratch using simple tools. But most projects would do with a regular, C-like language, and quite likely developers do not see much added value in coding the language themselves. It would be great to have off-the-shelf languages designed specifically with scripting in mind. Embedded languages are exactly that—programming languages designed specifically to be called from a host application, much like the way plug-ins work. Thus, they provide both the internals of the programming language and an API to communicate back and forth with the host application. This way you can start with a full-featured language instead of having to code your own, which is time-consuming, and most of the time, does not make a difference in the final product.

Embedded languages exist in two fundamental flavors. Some are specifically designed to be embedded, such as Python or Lua. And others are just regular programming languages that can be embedded by using special tools. The Java Native Interface (JNI), for example, allows Java code to be executed from a C/C++ application. We will now explore one of each kind in detail. Let's begin with Lua, which is one of the most popular embedded languages.

Learning Lua

Lua is a lightweight programming language developed at the Pontifical Catholic University of Rio de Janeiro in Brazil. It follows a BASIC-like syntax with dynamic typing and can be compiled into efficient bytecodes, which can then be run from either a command-line interpreter or, more often, from a C application. Lua is very popular among game studios because it includes a great feature set while providing a low learning curve. It was used in games such as *Grim Fandango*, *Escape from Monkey Island*, *Baldur's Gate*, and *Impossible Creatures*.

We will now explore Lua programming and integration with your game code. For the rest of this section, it is recommended that you download the latest version of Lua, which can be found at www.lua.org.

Just make sure you download the precompiled binaries for your platform of choice, or the source code, should you want to build the language for a different platform. You only need the `include` and library files as well as the associated DLLs. Make sure you also grab a copy of the reference manual so you can learn all about Lua.

Programming

In this section, I will try to provide you with a brief overview of Lua as a programming language. Coding Lua scripts is really straightforward if you are fluent in high-level languages. The syntax is not very different from BASIC or C. You can code loops, `if-then-else` sequences, define and call your own functions, and so on. There are some specific syntax rules, but overall you should feel right at home using the language. Take a look at this example:

```
function calculate(a,b)
    local temp
    temp=a+b
    return temp
end

c=calculate(1,2)
if c==0 then
    result="zero"
elseif c<0 then
    result="negative"
else
    result="positive"
end
print("the result is: ",result)
```

The example adds two numbers using a subroutine and prints whether the value of the result is positive, negative, or zero. The syntax is really straightforward and can be learned in a matter of hours, not days. But Lua scripts are nothing but a curiosity if we do not embed them into actual binary code. The possibility of exchanging data back and forth between the two languages is where Lua's power really exists.

Integration

From the host application's standpoint, a Lua script is just a regular function you can call. You can pass parameters and retrieve results, and the function can have an internal state so subsequent calls to it store previous values. The main difference is that the function is an interpreted script, so it runs in a safe environment, can be modified without affecting the core code, and so on.

As an example, let's see how we can call a Lua script from C++, with no parameters or results involved. The code is really straightforward. We initialize Lua, make the call, and shut down the language interpreter:

```
lua_State *ls=lua_open(100);

int result=lua_dofile(ls,"d:/lua/bin/work/hello.lua");
lua_close(ls);
```

The first line is used to initialize both the Lua stack (which we will use in a second to send data back and forth with the script) and the lua_State variable, which is the main Lua object. Stack size should be at least 100, with larger values for scripts with lots of variables or recursive behavior. This stack is associated with the lua_State object, which is required by all calls to the Lua C API. Once Lua is up and running, the second line is used to execute a Lua script by simply passing the file name. Notice that the file can either be a pure Lua script or precompiled for higher speed. The function call should return 0 if everything goes well, and a host of error codes otherwise. It is interesting to note that Lua scripts can be run either from a file, as shown in the preceding code, or from a user-defined string using the interface:

```
lua_dostring(lua_State *, const char *);
```

Whichever the case, lua_close should be called as soon as we are done with Lua to shut down all data structures in memory.

However, running Lua scripts is useless if you can't exchange data with them. Lua is great for AI scripting; thus, we will need the results of the AI processing or any other behavior we choose to implement. Communicating with Lua is made possible by a stack where we can push parameters from the C/C++ side, so Lua can retrieve them. Once the Lua script is finished, it can dump its results to the same stack, so we can read them back from C++ code.

In the following example, we will pass an integer to a Lua script, and it will return a different string for each number. To begin with, here is the C++ code to interface with Lua:

```
lua_State *ls=lua_open(100);

lua_pushnumber(ls,3);
lua_setglobal(ls,"index");

int res=lua_dofile(ls,"d:/lua/bin/work/hw.lua");

int i=lua_gettop(ls);
const char *s=lua_tostring(ls,i);

lua_close(ls);
```

The first line is again the Lua initialization sequence. We then pass the integer 3 to the stack. To do so, we first push it to the stack, and then we use the `setglobal` call to assign the value at the top of the stack (the integer 3) to the variable we pass as a parameter—in this case, `index`. After these two calls, Lua knows it must assign the value 3 to the variable index. Then, we call the script, which we will examine in a second. For now, let's look at the different interfaces to send data to Lua:

```
lua_pushnumber(lua_State *, double);
lua_pushstring(lua_State *, const char *);
```

Once we are done, it is time to retrieve the results from the execution of the Lua script. To do so, we first call `lua_gettop`, which returns the position index of the element at the top of the stack. If the stack only holds one element, it will have the index 1, and so on. Then, we can directly retrieve the stack element value by passing its index to the `lua_tostring` call. We can directly use `tostring` because we know the element we are trying to retrieve is a string. But here are other options:

```
double lua_tonumber(lua_State *, int);
const char *lua_tostring(lua_State *, int);
int lua_strlen(lua_State *, int);
```

From the Lua side, the code associated with this example (the `hw.lua` script) is also really simple. Here it is:

```
if index==1 then
        do
        return "Hello world 1"
        end
end

if index==2 then
        do
        return "Hello world 2"
        end
end

if index==3 then
        do
        return "Hello world 3"
        end
end

if index==4 then
        do
        return "Hello world 4"
        end
end

if index==5 then
        do
        return "Hello world 5"
        end
end
```

Notice how we do not set an index to any value at the beginning of the script. The variable will already have a value set by the C++ code. We can thus use it as if it was already initialized. Then, to send a result value to the calling application, we just need to use the return function, which, in this case, returns a different string for each `if-then` block. These strings will then be read back from the stack by the C++ application.

A corollary to the preceding example is how do we return more than one result from a Lua script? The return call is clearly limited to single variables, and many times we will need to return more complex data structures. To do so, we only need to read Lua variables back using the getglobal call. The getglobal call receives the name of the Lua variable to retrieve and pushes it to the top of the stack so we can read it back. Here is a very simple example:

```
lua_State *ls=lua_open(100);
float x=5;
float y=6;
lua_pushnumber(ls, x);
lua_setglobal(ls,"xvalue");
lua_pushnumber(ls, y);
lua_setglobal(ls,"yvalue");

int res=lua_dofile(ls,"addition.lua");

lua_getglobal(ls,"xvalue");
int i=lua_gettop(ls);
x=lua_tonumber(ls,i);

lua_getglobal(ls,"yvalue");
i=lua_gettop(ls);
y=lua_tonumber(ls,i);

lua_close(ls);
```

Notice how getglobal pushes the variable id to the top of the stack. Then, a gettop - tonumber sequence must be used to retrieve its value. Here is the very simple addition.lua script:

```
xvalue=xvalue+1
yvalue=yvalue+1
```

The retrieved value must be incremented.

User-Defined Functions

Lua is an extensible language. If we provide a function in our game code, we can make it callable from Lua. This is a great way to customize the base language so newer, more powerful constructs are supported. Games like *Baldur's Gate* ran on highly customized versions of Lua, taking advantage of all core constructs such as if-then-else and for loops, but adding new routines as needed. Let's look at a complete example on how to add a new routine to Lua.

To begin with, we must implement the C function, which must conform to some Lua coding standards. The function will receive all its arguments coming from Lua by using a lua_State structure and will send back its results by pushing them in the same state used to retrieve arguments. The number of arguments is passed on the top of the stack. Then, stack positions from 1 to the number of args store the arguments. Once we have the arguments ready, we can carry out whichever task the routine has been designed for. Just remember to push the results to the stack when finished. Also, inform Lua of the number of results to expect using the standard return C call. Take a look at this function, which returns the life level and gender of a given character, assuming we have indexed them by a serial number in a large character array:

```
static int lifelevel (lua_State *L)
{
int nargs=lua_gettop(L);
int characterid=lua_isnumber(L,1);

// here we access the game's data structures
int result=character_array[characterid].life;
lua_pushnumber(L,result);
int result2=character_array[characterid].gender;
lua_pushnumber(L,result2);

// the next line tells Lua there were two results
return 2;
}
```

This is just a very simple function to expose the binding mechanism. But the philosophy is obvious: Define C functions that grant the Lua script visibility of in-game symbols and values. Now it is time to register the function so it is callable from Lua. This is achieved by using a single line:

```
lua_register(L, "lifelevel", lifelevel);
```

And that's all really. Just make sure you register the new function before you actually execute any Lua code that tries to use it, or the program will fail. Thus, the correct sequence would be as follows:

```
lua_open
lua_register
(...) pass arguments
lua_dofile
(...) retrieve results
```

Remember, Lua pushes values in direct order. Thus, a Lua call like the following expects the C side to first retrieve id1, and then id2 from the stack:

```
Life, gender = lifelevel(id1,id2)
```

As far as results go, notice how Lua supports multiple assigns. In this case, we must first push Life, and then Gender, when creating the results from the C side.

Real-World Lua Coding

I'd like to complete this section with a brief overview of what a real-world Lua-based script might look like. Lua is an interpreted language. This has the benefit of the scripts running in a safe environment, and because each script is a separate entity, Lua is able to build large AI systems consisting of thousands of scripts. Unsurprisingly, Lua was used in *Baldur's Gate*, one of the games with the largest AI in history. On the other hand, a binary, hard-coded approach would have been better in terms of efficiency, but would not have scaled well. Imagine the whole nonplayer character cast from *Baldur's Gate* in C++ code. So, the idea is to choose the best of both worlds. Enrich Lua with some C++ side functions, which are precisely those that require higher performance: complex geometrical tests, database accesses, and so on. Then, expose them through an API to Lua so programmers can use these new calls. This way your Lua code will be more elegant and performance will increase.

Another interesting idea is to use Lua as an action selector for a state-machine-based language. Code a state machine in C++, which does not really have transitions, but just a switch construct with lots of behaviors. Then, build some C++ queries visible from

Lua that allow you to perform action selection, thus, setting the state for the C++ state machine. The Lua code could look like this:

```
if EnemyCloserThan(Myself, 10) then
        Attack()
else
        Stay()
end
```

Here `EnemyCloserThan` would be a query receiving a numerical character id and a threshold distance. The `Myself` string is a Lua variable that has been loaded as an argument from C. The C caller pushes the enemy identifier so it can perform its own tests. Notice how `Attack` and `Stay` are two behaviors, which we are selecting with the script. `Attack` involves path finding and seeking contact with the enemy, and `Stay` is just an idle behavior. The C++ code has the behavior implementation details, which are executed efficiently, but the task of selecting the right action for each moment is left to Lua. As a more involved example, we can have a behavior collection consisting of many different behaviors, and by changing the Lua script, recode the personality of the AI. This way we would only have a single enemy class, because behaviors are similar at all times. Then, Lua would customize each state machine and make sure the AI is rich and varied.

Java Scripting

Lua is a very popular choice for game scripting. We will now focus on an alternative option, which is to use the Java programming language as an embedded script interpreter. With Java, you get a multiplatform, object-oriented language, which has more libraries and built-in routines than you will need in your whole life. Overall, the option is not so different from Lua as you would expect. Both are embedded languages that can exchange information with the host and both support user-provided routines on the host side to be called from the script. So, in the end, differences are more related to specific language features and not so much about the design philosophy. Java will probably be more powerful than Lua, but is that extra power really needed for game AI? As usual, there are lots of opinions about this, and most times it all boils down to personal preferences.

The main difference between Lua and Java is that the former was designed to be embedded, whereas the latter is multipurpose. Thus, a specific tool set is required to make Java embeddable. We will not worry much about Java here. There are tons of books on programming in Java, and the specifics have little to do with actual game programming. We will just cover the basics of embedded Java, focusing on how to connect a Java module to an application, which is achieved with the Java Native Interface (JNI).

Java Native Interface

The JNI is a specific set of calls within the Java programming language that makes integrating Java and classic compiled languages such as C or C++ easier. The mechanism is bidirectional. From one side, a Java program can call a C/C++ routine, and thus extend its functionality. This is especially useful when the Java code needs to access platform-specific functionality. It is also interesting if you need to access legacy code that is already written in a compiler language or, even better, if you need to perform time-critical tasks that are more efficient in a low-level language.

On the other end of the spectrum (the end we will be more interested in), a C/C++ program can access methods written in Java using the Invocation API. Under this model, we have a C/C++ program, which we want to extend using Java. We can examine Java objects, call methods, or even embed the whole Java Virtual Machine in our game code for full flexibility and efficiency. Clearly, this is what we will be interested in as far as scripting goes—providing a clean method for scripts written in Java to be called from our C++ code.

Let's begin with a very simple example: a C program that calls a Java routine via JNI. The Java code is just a `hello, world` application, but we will use it to understand the JNI boot sequence and overall operation. Here is the code from the C side:

```
#define USER_CLASSPATH "." // where Prog.class is

void main()
{
JNIEnv *env;
JavaVM *jvm;
JDK1_1InitArgs vm_args;
char classpath[1024];
```

```
vm_args.version = 0x00010001;
JNI_GetDefaultJavaVMInitArgs(&vm_args);

// append where our .class files are to the classpath
sprintf(classpath, "%s;%s",vm_args.classpath, USER_CLASSPATH);
vm_args.classpath = classpath;

// create the java VM
jint res = JNI_CreateJavaVM(&jvm,&env,&vm_args);
if (res < 0)
        {
        // can't create the VM
          exit(1);
        }

jclass cls=env->FindClass("Prog");
if (cls == 0)
        {
        // can't find the class we are calling
          exit(1);
      }
jmethodID mid=env->GetStaticMethodID(cls,"main",
"([Ljava/lang/String;)V");
if (mid == 0)
        {
          // can't find Prog.main
          exit(1);
        }

env->CallStaticVoidMethod(cls, mid, args);
jvm->DestroyJavaVM();
}
```

Now, here is the content of Prog.java, which is the module called from the previous
C++ code:

```
public class Prog {
  public static void main(String[] args) {
```

```
System.out.println("Hello World %d\n",args[1]);
  }
}
```

The operation is pretty similar to Lua. We first create the virtual machine. But we need to be very careful with the CLASSPATH, or the virtual machine will not boot. Then, the FindClass and find GetStaticMethodID are used to retrieve the class compiled Java file and the method within the file we want to call. In our case, we are just trying to call the main function. Then, all we have to do is execute the JNI call. We pass the class and method identifiers and a number of arguments that will be retrieved by the Java module.

As with Lua also, all you have to do from here is establish an interfacing method that passes arguments and retrieves results from the C/C++ side. To pass arguments, the following code can be used:

```
jstring jstr = env->NewStringUTF(" argument");
args = env->NewObjectArray(1, env->FindClass("java/lang/String"), jstr);
env->CallStaticVoidMethod(cls, mid, args);
```

Notice how we declare a UTF8 string, which is the kind of string used internally by the Java Virtual Machine. Then, we need to put it in an array, because the standard command-line argument mechanism calls for arrays. Additionally, we use the created array in the CallStaticVoidMethod array, so the standard argument passing mechanism can retrieve the arguments from the Java side. Notice that CallStaticVoidMethod was used as the method we were calling and is of type static void. Other variants exist to adapt to all the possible return values. For example, if we need to retrieve a floating-point value from C as a result of a computation performed in Java, the method would be

```
jfloat jf=env->CallFloatMethod(cls,mid,args);
```

So we get the return value in the jf variable. Also note that the method we used to locate the Prog.main routine can be changed to adapt to any routine you need to execute. This way you can have a Java file that is just a library of useful routines, which get triggered from C.

Socket-Based Scripting

Most projects will work well if you choose one of the scripting methods just explained. Whether it's a custom-built language, something like Lua, or the JNI, we have covered a lot of ground that should help you in most scenarios. For improved flexibility, we have even taken a look at how a dynamically linked library scripting system might work.

However, there is an additional technique that can be useful when extreme flexibility and safety are required. We could choose to code our application's scripts using a DLL. But a DLL can contain malicious code that can make our application misbehave or even crash. Besides, DLLs (or whatever equivalent mechanism you end up using) are highly platform specific.

So, we will try to come up with a new solution that provides:

➤ A separate running environment for the script, so it can be safely shut down if necessary

➤ A platform-independent infrastructure

The solution is to implement your scripting modules by means of sockets. Sockets (explained in detail in Chapter 10, "Network Programming") are the standard mechanism to implement network connections using the TCP/IP protocol. They can be imagined as bidirectional queues. Both peers in a communication stream can write data to one end of the socket, and the other computer will then be able to retrieve it by reading from the opposite end.

As you might have already guessed, one end of the socket will belong to the main game module, and the other end will be at the script module. Because they will be two separate applications, a faulty script module will not necessarily affect the game. On the other hand, socket programming is largely standard. Sockets are supported by PCs, UNIX/Linux boxes, and Macintosh computers, and will probably be supported in Internet-ready game consoles. They can be coded from C, C++, Java, and a host of other programming languages.

But sockets have two unexpected benefits. First, the script module can be a compiled binary, which means performance will be better than in other scripting strategies (DLLs excluded). Second, the script does not need to be physically on the same machine as the main game code. Scripts are executed through Internet connections, which can be handy in certain scenarios.

Notice, however, that these benefits come at a cost. The scripting language will have to be your programming language of choice (C, C++, and so on). Custom routines can certainly be added to make life easier for script writers, but overall you get less control of the syntax (as opposed to a custom-built language). In addition, socket communications are not very well suited for time-critical tasks. Admittedly, networks are getting better all the time, but some projects will find sockets too limiting in terms of performance— not for the script itself, but for the time required to pass arguments (and return results). Another issue you must be aware of is that sockets can be tricky to maintain if lots of scripts must be handled. In the extreme case, your game can begin to resemble a massively multiplayer title with scripts instead of gamers.

Let's examine the creation of a socket-based script system. The first step is to decide the taxonomy of the callable module. Clearly, we want maximum efficiency, so we will keep the module loaded in memory instead of executing it every time. Besides, by making it persistent, we can make modules that keep their own state variables and use them from one iteration to another.

Thus, modules will by started by the parent, and once booted, will enter an infinite loop that will remain until told by the caller to shut down. While on the loop, they will watch the socket for requests, process them, and optionally return any results to the calling process. Here is the coding idea for such a module:

```
// open socket to main game module
while (!end)
      {
      // read opcode from socket
      switch (opcode)
            {
            case QUIT:
                  end=true;
                  break;
            // opcode specific operations go here
            }
      }
// close socket
```

This algorithm is quite efficient both in terms of speed and CPU use. Concerning speed, keeping the module loaded and the socket open ensures that communication overhead is kept to a minimum. But keeping many scripts in memory can cause some problems, especially if they are CPU hungry. That's why we keep the socket open and read from it at the beginning of each iteration. As you will learn in Chapter 10, most sockets are usually blocking. This means that reading from an empty socket causes the process to halt until new data arrives. Thus, the "read socket" call somehow acts like a semaphore. It pauses the script process until a command arrives (so CPU use is virtually zero). Once a new request arrives, the process is resumed, the request is dealt with in one of the switch opcode-handling routines, results are returned using the same socket, and the process is put to sleep again until new commands are received. The complete process is showcased in Figure 9.3.

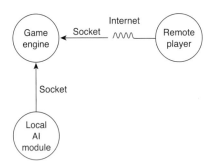

Figure 9.3   Socket-based scripting transparently integrates the network into the game engine.

Notice, however, that the problems we had with Java scripting are still present here. For example, it is hard for the script to access data structures or algorithms stored on the core game engine. When we were using JNI, we saw how making a call from the script to native C/C++ code was a little complex and had associated overhead. With sockets, the situation gets even worse. The script is simply designed to receive parameters through the socket, perform local calculations, and return a result.

There are two solutions to this problem. The first one is the poor man's solution: sending commands through the pipeline to the host application using a predefined protocol. This can work with simple use cases, but when lots of commands are present, will quickly become unmanageable. A more elegant solution to this is using the Remote Procedure Call (RPC) mechanism to ensure that we can make calls to our code from the script module. RPC allows developers to register functions at compile time so they are visible by both peers. A routine implemented in the core game engine can be exposed to the script and the other way around. This makes compilation a bit more complex because we need to use tools like RPCGen, but the benefit is obvious.

In Closing

Not so long ago, games were a single, monolithic entity. With scripting, you can now decompose your code into smaller components that interact with each other. We have seen how this technique can be used to prevent errors, isolate portions of the code that might endanger the whole application, or separate engine code from all the code that is effectively written by the content development team.

The scripting alternatives and languages we have explored should help you increase the expressive potential of your AI subsystem. Coupled with the techniques we have covered in the previous chapters, you should now be ready to create solid, compelling behaviors.

Chapter 10

Network Programming

"...it is important to realize that any lock can be picked with a big enough hammer."

Sun System & Network Admin manual

Playing against human opponents is more rewarding than playing against a machine or, even worse, playing alone. Games such as football, chess, and hundreds of others teach us how competing against an opponent creates addiction—a desire to play repeatedly, well beyond the shorter entertainment value of automatic opponents.

Ever since the first multiplayer games appeared, their popularity has been steadily increasing. Although today it seems clear that both single-player and multiplayer games will exist in the future, it is in the multiplayer arena where some of the most interesting innovations are taking place.

In this chapter, we will explore the techniques required to create multiplayer games. From the foundations of Internet protocols to game-specific optimization techniques, we will try to cover lots of ground that will allow you to create compelling online gameplay experiences. The first few pages of this chapter will provide a thorough overview of the fundamentals of network programming. Once we are able to create reliable client-server systems, we will deal with networked game issues.

How the Internet Really Works

The Internet is a packet-switched, fault-tolerant network. Packet switching means that information is broken down into small packets (usually a few bytes or kilobytes in size) and sent from point A to point B by traversing a weblike server structure (which we commonly call cyberspace). By saying the Internet is fault-tolerant, we mean that packets are sent using paths that adapt to network circumstances, errors, server malfunctions, and so on. If a server goes down, packets will use alternative paths to reach their destination. As a corollary of both these principles, a large block of information sent between two communicating peers does not necessarily need to follow a unique route. Some packets might use different paths to take advantage of the network's status.

Packet-switched networks differ from circuit-based networks. In circuit-based networks, we "own" a private communication circuit from the origin to the destination, which we access exclusively. In a circuit system, we have a path from the origin to the destination, and we simply transfer all the information as a single block. A classic example of such systems is the "traditional" (nondigital) telephone system.

It is very intuitive to picture the Internet as a large factory. On one end of the communication pipeline, a machine breaks data into smaller pieces, so it can be transferred efficiently. These packets of information are then numbered and sent through a vast network of Internet servers, sometimes using separate routes. Once these packages reach their destination (probably not in the correct order), a second factory looks at the serial numbers and puts the data back together in a meaningful way.

Clearly, there are two tasks taking place at very high speeds. First, data is fragmented and reassembled. Second, individual packets are routed through the Internet. These two tasks are performed by two protocols working in parallel. Transmission Control Protocol (TCP) is the data separator and assembler, and Internet Protocol (IP) takes care of the routing. So now you know what TCP/IP is about: dividing data into blocks so it's easier to transfer and then routing it efficiently.

In network programming jargon, TCP is said to be a connection-oriented protocol. In other words, the protocol keeps a permanent connection open between two (or more) peers. Notice how this does not necessarily imply a dedicated, fixed communication channel. Because IP performs *dynamic* routing, some data might follow different courses in order to reach its destination. But TCP works on top of IP, providing a logical end-to-end connection that can be used at any time.

TCP/IP is recommended for "traditional" networking. Connection-based protocols guarantee FIFO operation (data arrives in the right order) and ensure that all data sent from one end of the TCP stream will reach its destination. A variety of mechanisms allow the receiver to detect lost packets, re-request them, and thus make sure all the data is received (in the right order). However, there is a downside: Connection-based protocols are slow. They need to wait for several packets to arrive to rebuild the initial sequence, and they check for lost packets. As a result, they provide secure transmission at the cost of reduced performance.

Another protocol exists that can be used to replace the TCP in TCP/IP. It's a very light-weight protocol that sacrifices some of the "slower" features for the sake of speed. It is the User Datagram Protocol (UDP), and because it does not require an active connection, it is said to be a connectionless protocol. UDP allows us to send fixed-size packages of information between two endpoints. These packages might or might not reach their destination (although they almost always do). Additionally, they might not arrive in sequential order. A package might be routed through a faster server path, thus passing other packages emitted before it. But UDP offers very good performance. Table 10.1 lists the differences between TCP and UDP.

Table 10.1   Differences Between TCP and UDP

TCP	UDP
Keeps connection	Does not keep connection
Variable-size packets	Fixed-size packets
Guarantees reception	Does not guarantee reception
FIFO	Not necessarily FIFO
Slow	Fast

However, it would be wrong to think of UDP as "good" and TCP as "bad" per se. The protocol you choose depends on what you are trying to code. If you need to code a strategy game where lags are acceptable but each move is essential for the sake of the game, TCP is still the way to go. It is a slower protocol, but the pacing of your game will be able to handle that well. If you need to code something like a first-person shooter running at 60 fps on today's networks, TCP will most likely be too slow for you, and UDP's packet loss will be a minor inconvenience.

For the remainder of this chapter, we will discuss both protocols in detail, showing examples of both in use and exposing potential pitfalls, so you can make an informed decision about which one to use.

The Programmer's Perspective: Sockets

As you know, the Internet is a very complex system, consisting of millions of servers speaking quite elaborate languages. Luckily, most of the Internet's complexity is hidden from the programmer by some cleverly designed APIs. You don't have to deal with TCP, UDP, or IP directly, nor are they separate tools. You don't even have to break the information into pieces manually. From a programmer's viewpoint, accessing the Internet is pretty much like accessing a file: You can "open" a site, read from it, write to it, and so on. All this elegance is achieved through an abstraction layer that makes network programming a breeze. This abstraction layer is called the *socket interface* and was introduced in the 1980s at the University of California, Berkeley.

A socket is simply an input/output device (such as a file, a modem, and so on) that opens a communication pipeline between two sites. To transfer information, both sites must keep a socket open (and aimed at the other). We will soon discover that establishing the communication channel can sometimes be a tricky process that requires some specific programming. But once the socket is working, sending data back and forth is as simple as writing it to the socket. Every byte written at one of the socket's endpoints will automatically appear at the other end. Sockets can either operate in TCP or UDP mode. In both modes, they automatically route information between both sites. For TCP, the typical partition/reassembly routines are performed as well as packet numbering and reordering. So, data is recovered at the destination endpoint in the same sequence as it was sent, much like in a FIFO queue. The socket internally reassembles the data so we don't have to bother with transmission issues. The UDP socket interface is more lightweight, but offers greater speed and flexibility.

Data transfer using the Internet is not very different from traditional file input/output (I/O). Establishing the communication is, on the other hand, a bit more complicated. To understand this complexity, we need to classify networked applications into two broad groups called *clients* and *servers*.

A client application (such as a web browser) is typically an endpoint of the communications network. It always works in connection to a server and consumes data transferred from the server to the client. Sometimes clients send data back to the server (commands, and so on), but the main *raison d'être* of a client is reading data provided by the server. Generally speaking, a client is connected to one (and only one) server, which acts as the data provider.

Servers, on the other hand, can be connected to many different clients simultaneously. Think of a web server such as Yahoo! and the multitude of connections it is simultaneously serving. In a more game-related scenario, think of the game server in a massively multiplayer game. Individual players use clients to retrieve data about the game world and to update the game server with their current position and status.

Clearly, communications on the client's side are very simple. One socket connects us to our game server, so data transfer takes place using a well-established route. Establishing such a connection is also pretty simple. Game servers, on the other hand, have a harder time keeping up with all the incoming connections. A new player might join the game at any time, or another player might abandon it, either because he quits the game, or because there was a network problem. In these server-side scenarios, communications get more complicated, and some careful code planning is required.

Clients and servers can both be connection-oriented (thus coded with TCP) or connectionless (coded with UDP). In the following section, we will take a look at both TCP and UDP clients, and then move on to the server side.

Clients

We will start by creating a minimal TCP client, and then we will tackle a minimal UDP client.

A Minimal TCP Client

Let's take a close look at the client's perspective in any networked application. The client's perspective fundamentally involves one socket that we will use to explicitly connect to a game server whose address is known beforehand. Because we are using TCP for this first example, our communication protocol will thus consist of four fundamental operations:

➤ Connecting to the game server

➤ Writing data to the server

➤ Reading data from the server

➤ Closing the connection when the game is over

Connection

Establishing a connection is a very simple process for a network client. All we need to do is retrieve the required connection information (IP address, port) and then execute the connect call using that information. A step-by-step analysis of the connection process follows:

```
int sock = socket(AF_INET, SOCK_STREAM,IPPROTO_TCP);
```

This first line creates a socket. As in typical UNIX file system programming, a socket is identified by a file descriptor, which is a nonnegative integer. The first parameter to the socket call specifies that we want the socket to use the Internet (other values such as AF_UNIX are used to perform communications that take place inside a single computer). The second parameter specifies that we want stream-based communications, which fundamentally means we want TCP to keep packets in sequence. Other values would be SOCK_DGRAM for datagram-based communications (more on this later) or SOCK_RAW, which is a low-level interface that dumps data as it is received by the socket, with no reordering or sequencing. The third parameter indicates we effectively request TCP as the transport protocol. Other values would be IPPROTO_UDP, which would initialize the socket in UDP mode.

Once the socket is available, we need to make it target the server. Remember that we are using TCP, so we need a stable connection between the client and the server. This is a relatively complex process because we traditionally like to work with DNS addresses such as:

```
gameserver.myprovider.com
```

But computers need these addresses to be converted to numeric IP addresses. This conversion process is performed by the *name server*. So, the first step in the connection is to perform this translation, which is achieved by using the following code, where host is a character string containing the server's DNS address:

```
struct hostent *H=gethostbyname(host);
```

This call connects to the name server and retrieves addressing information for the DNS address passed as the parameter. The hostent structure returned by this call consists of the following members:

```
struct hostent
    {
    char * h_name;
    char **h_aliases;
    int h_addrtype;
    int h_length;
    char **h_addr_list;
    };
```

The first member contains the official DNS address of the host. The second parameter is a list of null-terminated strings containing all the aliases (alternate DNS addresses) to the host. The third parameter contains a symbolic constant to identify which type of address we are using. Currently, it always holds the AF_INET constant. The h_length parameter contains the length of the address in bytes. The addr_list contains a list of IP addresses for the host.

Additionally, a #define statement is used to define the member h_addr. This points to the first address in the h_addr_list. It is a convenient addition because the first IP address in the list is the one we will be using later in the process.

So, `gethostbyname` allows us to retrieve address data for the specified server using the name server. Once we know the IP address, all we need to do is complete our connection using the socket and connection data. This is achieved by using another structure called `sockaddr_in`. Here is the required source code:

```
struct sockaddr_in adr;

adr.sin_family=AF_INET;
adr.sin_port = htons(port);
adr.sin_addr.s_addr=*((unsigned long *) H->h_addr);
ZeroMemory(adr.sin_zero,8);
```

This seems to be getting more complex, but it really isn't. Think of `sockaddr_in` as the address information on a postcard. The `sin_family` member must indicate that we want an Internet connection. The `sin_port` attribute must contain the port we need to open at the destination server. Notice that we use the `htons` call (Host-To-Network) to ensure that the port number is in network format. Remember that different computer architectures encode numbers in different ways (big-endian, little-endian, and so on), so making sure we encode these network-related numbers as a neutral format is a must.

Once the port has been initialized, we load the `s_addr` attribute with the IP address, which we obtained from the `h_addr` attribute of the `hostent` structure. In addition, we use the `ZeroMemory` call because we must clear the `sin_zero` attribute.

Now we have a new structure that holds all the connection data. All we have to do is effectively connect our socket to the server using it. This task is performed by using the following line:

```
int error=connect(sock,(struct sockaddr *) &adr,sizeof(adr));
```

Here the `connect` call will attempt to connect the socket to the specified host. A return value of 0 will indicate success. Errors are indicated by –1, and the standard `errno` reporting mechanism is set to indicate the error cause.

Once the `connect` call has been executed, we have an active line of communication with the other endpoint. Let's take a second to review the following encapsulated, fully functional client-side connection method, which tries to connect and returns the socket descriptor:

```
int ConnectTCP(char *host,int port)
{
int sock= socket(AF_INET, SOCK_STREAM,IPPROTO_TCP);
struct hostent *H=gethostbyname(host);

struct sockaddr_in adr;

adr.sin_family=AF_INET;
adr.sin_port = htons(port);
adr.sin_addr.s_addr=*((unsigned long *) H->h_addr);
ZeroMemory(adr.sin_zero,8);

int error=connect(sock,(struct sockaddr *) &adr,sizeof(adr));
if (error==0) return sock;
else return error;
}
```

Data Transfer

Once your communication pipeline is open, transferring data is just a matter of reading and writing from the socket as if it were a regular file descriptor. For example, the following line reads from an open socket:

```
int result=recv(sock,buffer,size,0);
```

Here we are attempting to read "size" bytes from the socket and then store them on the buffer. Notice that this buffer must have assigned memory to accommodate the incoming data. The ending parameters are flags that allow us to maintain sophisticated control over the socket.

By default, sockets have a blocking nature. This is the source of many problems and fundamentally means a recv call will only return when the socket effectively holds as much data as we have requested (or if the other peer closes the connection). So, if we try to receive 256 bytes, but the socket only holds 128, the recv call will remain blocked until more data can be read. This can result in deadlocks and annoying situations, so we will need to add a bit more code to ensure that we handle this situation properly. This code will create nonblocking sockets, which will not block regardless of whether or not data is available. We will cover nonblocking sockets in the section "Preventing Socket Blocks" later in this chapter, because they are an advanced subject.

But for our simple client, the preceding code should suffice.

Once we know how to read from a socket, we can implement the following code, which performs the opposite operation, writing data so that the other peer can read it:

```
int result=send(sock,buffer,strlen(buffer),0);
```

Notice that the syntax is very similar. A word on `result` values must be provided, though. Both the `recv` and `send` calls return an integer value, which tells us how many bytes of data were actually sent or received. In a `send` command, this could be due to a network malfunction. Because data is sent sequentially, sending less than the whole message means that we will need a second call to `send` to make sure the remaining data makes it through the network.

With a `recv` call, receiving less data than we are supposed to usually means that either the emitter closed the socket or we have implemented some nonblocking policy that allows us to receive shorter than expected messages. Remember that sockets should block if the amount of data available is less than expected.

Closing Sockets

After all the data has been transferred, it is time to close the socket. On a low-level, this involves making sure the other endpoint has received all the data, and then effectively shutting down the communication port. This is performed by using a very simple command:

```
close(sock);
```

A Minimal UDP Client

Working with UDP is much easier than with TCP. As mentioned earlier, the downside is reduced reliability. But from our simplified look at the world of networking, all we need to know is that there is no connection establishment or shutdown, so all the networking takes place directly in the data transfer sequences. We will still need to create a socket, but other than that, it is pretty accurate to say that UDP really consists of two calls. Let's first create a UDP socket, which can easily be achieved through the following line of code:

```
int sock= socket(AF_INET, SOCK_DGRAM,IPPROTO_UDP);
```

Notice that we request a datagram socket and specify UDP as the desired transport protocol.

Once this initial step is performed, we can directly send and receive data with our datagram socket. Notice that each data transfer call must explicitly specify the destination of the datagram because we don't have a "live" connection. Thus, our regular send primitive won't be of much use here. We will revert to its datagram counterpart:

```
Int sendto(int socket, char *msg, int msglength, int flags,
sockaddr *to, int tolen);
```

Again, we initially specify the socket, message, message length, and flags. All these parameters are identical to a regular send call. Additionally, we must specify a sockaddr structure and its length, as in a connect call. As an example, here is the source code to send a message in datagram mode:

```
Void SendUDP(char *msg, char *host, int port,int socket)
{
struct hostent *H=gethostbyname(host);

struct sockaddr_in adr;

adr.sin_family=AF_INET;
adr.sin_port = htons(port);
adr.sin_addr.s_addr=*((unsigned long *) H->h_addr);
ZeroMemory(adr.sin_zero,8);

Sendto(socket,msg,strlen(msg),0, (struct sockaddr *)
&adr,sizeof(adr));
}
```

Notice that we are accessing the name server for each send call, which is inefficient. Alternatively, we could store the sockaddr structure and reuse it for each call. Even better, we can use a variant of UDP called connected UDP, which maintains UDP's non-sequential, nonguaranteed performance while storing a connection to a server. To work with connected UDP, we will follow these simple steps:

1. Create a datagram socket with UDP as the protocol.

2. Use a `connect` call to specify the destination server.

3. Use regular `send` calls instead of `sendto`.

Connected UDP is the protocol of choice for UDP applications working with a permanent, stable server (such as a game server). The `sendto` call provides greater flexibility because we can send messages to different servers easily. But for a one-to-one scenario, connected UDP has a lower overhead and thus offers better performance.

Receiving data from a UDP socket is performed through the `recvfrom` call:

```
int recvfrom(int socket, char *buffer, int buflen, int flags,
sockaddr *from, int fromlen);
```

Again, we need extra parameters to retrieve information about our peer. Because we are working in connectionless mode, we need the `from` parameter to tell us where the message comes from. Server programming under UDP is simpler than with TCP precisely for this reason. We can have a single socket serving many connectionless peers.

As a summary of simple clients, Table 10.2 shows you the call sequence for our minimal TCP, connectionless UDP, and connected UDP clients.

Table 10.2 Call sequences for TCP, connectionless UDP, and connected UDP for a simple client protocol.

TCP Client	Connectionless UDP	Connected UDP
socket	socket	socket
connect		connect
send—recv	sendto—recvfrom	send—recv
close		close

A Simple TCP Server

Now that we know how to connect to a server and exchange information with it, we are ready to take a look at the other end of the wire. Be warned, though, coding servers is a very involved process.

To begin with, servers must be able to exchange information with many peers at once. This can be achieved either by sequentially scanning the open sockets (in a nonblocking manner or we might get in trouble) or by writing a concurrent server that runs several processes in parallel, each with its own socket and peer.

To start our discussion of servers, we will focus on a single-peer server. This should suffice for two-player games and will serve as a foundation from which we will move on to more involved solutions.

In a two-player scenario, we don't need to worry about several sockets at once because we are in a one-to-one situation. But this is not a symmetrical relationship. The client and the server play different roles and thus need different system calls.

As a first step, the server must create its own socket and put it in a "listening" mode. Under this mode, the socket is left open on a specific port, so it awaits incoming connection requests from the client. As new connections arrive, a brief setup sequence takes place and data transfer can begin. So, let's focus on the initialization of our TCP server. As usual, it all begins with the creation of a socket. This process is identical to the client side and is performed by using the line:

```
int sock= socket(AF_INET, SOCK_STREAM,IPPROTO_TCP);
```

Now, we must create a relationship between this socket and an IP address/port pair. This way we state that the socket will be looking for connection requests arriving through that entry point. You might ask why we should specify an IP address to listen to if we know which server we are at. The answer lies in the nature of Internet servers. An Internet server might be known by different IP addresses (aliases to the base IP). So, we need to specify whether we want the socket to respond to only one of those addresses. However, most servers will want to respond to requests arriving at any of the IP addresses the server is identified by, so a special command will allow us to specify all of the addresses at once. Overall, this binding between socket and IP/port pair is performed by the bind call, whose prototype is as follows:

```
int bind(int socket, sockaddr *s,int saddrlen);
```

We will use the sockaddr (sockaddr_in in the case of Internet servers) to specify the IP/port pair. Here is the exact initialization code for such a call:

```
struct sockaddr_in adr;

adr.sin_family=AF_INET;
adr.sin_port = htons(port);
adr.sin_addr.s_addr=INADDR_ANY;
ZeroMemory(adr.sin_zero,8);

bind(socket, (struct sockaddr *) &adr, sizeof(adr));
```

Notice the use of the INADDR_ANY wild card to specify that we want to respond using any of the aliases the server is known by. Alternatively, we could manually specify an IP address for the socket to respond to exclusively. That IP address could easily be taken from the gethostbyname() return value. Upon completion, bind() will return an integer value, which will be zero if the call was successful and −1 otherwise. Popular errors include the socket being undefined or already bound, or the IP/port pair being already in use by another service.

By now your server is up and running, and the OS knows which address and port it is bound to. Thus, it is now time to enter passive mode or, in other words, put the server to sleep while waiting for connections. This is performed by using the call listen(), which makes the server wait for an incoming connection:

```
int listen(int socket, int queuelen);
```

As usual, the first parameter is the socket to work with. The second parameter allows programmers to specify the length of the connection queue. The TCP/IP stack will queue up to queuelen connections while the server is handling another request. As you will soon see, a server can be busy taking care of one entrant connection. To prevent other connections from being lost while this process takes place, you can save them in a queue for later use. Traditionally, `queuelen` has a maximum size of five, allowing six connections to be "on hold" while the server handles one peer.

There is only one call ahead of us in the process of starting our server. This call effectively puts the server on hold until a new connection takes place. The call is

```
int accept(int socket, sockaddr *addr, int *addrlen);
```

`Accept` remains blocked until a new connection takes place. Its parameters are the socket we are listening from and a `sockaddr`/length pair that will hold the data from the client, mainly its IP and DNS addresses. As a result of the `accept()` call, we will receive either –1 if there was an error, or a nonnegative socket descriptor. This new socket is activated and ready to transfer data with the client, whereas the initial socket remains untouched so we can keep accepting connections.

After `accept`, we are ready to begin working with our client in a `recv-send` manner. As a summary of the client-server relationship, see Figure 10.1. Notice that the server must be in `accept()` state to be able to receive connections. Obviously, this means that the server-side boot process must already have taken place.

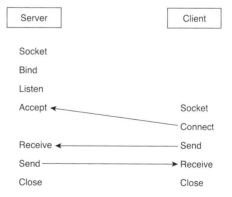

Figure 10.1   Client-server protocol call by call.

Multiclient Servers

We have now seen how a TCP server is initialized and performs data transfer with a single client. Although this suffices for a very simple, two-player game, real-world game servers need to cope with more complex scenarios. At least eight players should be supported, and many massively multiplayer games can handle thousands in parallel. But our server can only carry out one task at a time. If, after `accept()`, we decide to take care of the client, we will lose the ability to handle any more incoming connections.

Clearly, we need a way of keeping an eye on the incoming connection queue while we perform data transfers with the already connected players. At least two ways exist to perform this task. We could take a concurrent approach and create several processes running in parallel from our core server, each one taking care of different tasks. Under this assumption, we would have N+1 processes (where N is the number of connected users). N processes would handle one connected socket each while the extra process would be the one running the server, and thus permanently waiting for new connections at an `accept()` call. Alternatively, we could take an iterative approach, and by making sure we don't get blocked at any connected socket, check all the communication endpoints into a loop. The following sections describe these two approaches.

Concurrent, Connection-Oriented Servers

In this section, we will focus on concurrent (thus, multiprocess) TCP servers. The strategy we will use is to spawn a child process for each accepted connection, so the parent can always keep waiting for new connections.

For those not familiar with multiprocess programming, it usually revolves around the `fork()` UNIX system call. This is a parameterless call that, upon execution, duplicates the execution environment, so there are two copies of the program in execution. `Fork()` returns an integer that has the peculiarity of being different for the two newly created processes. The child process will receive a 0, whereas the parent will receive a nonnegative integer that is the process identifier of the child process. `Fork()` is available only in UNIX and Linux operating systems, which are the operating systems on which many servers are built. For Windows-based servers, a similar technique would use the `CreateThread` call.

As a sample of the fork() call's behavior, take a look at the apparently innocent code that follows:

```
#include <stdio.h>

void main()
{
printf("I am a simple program\n");
int id=fork();
printf("My id is: %d\n",id);
}
```

This program produces the following output:

```
I am a simple program
My id is: 0
My id is: 37
```

Intrigued? Well, remember that fork() divides the program in two. So, the first printf() is executed once, and the second printf() is executed by the two programs, producing a different output in each one. Now that we know how the fork() call operates, the following algorithm should be easy to understand:

Master 1: Create a socket, and bind it to the IP and port

Master 2: Put it in passive mode with listen

Master 3: Wait for a new connection with accept

Master 4: When a new connection arrives, fork, creating Slave

Master 5: Go to step 3

Slave 1: Enter a send-recv loop with the new connection

Slave 2: Once the connection terminates, exit

So we have a master process that is permanently blocked in the accept call, spawning child processes to handle the connected users. You can see this method in action in Figure 10.2. We need to make sure the number of processes remains in control (for example, limited to the number of players), but other than that, the algorithm is relatively straightforward. Here is the commented source code for the preceding example:

```
// create a TCP socket
int sock= socket(AF_INET, SOCK_STREAM,IPPROTO_TCP);

// fill the address info to accept connections on any IP on port
"port"
struct sockaddr_in adr;

adr.sin_family=AF_INET;
adr.sin_port = htons(port);
adr.sin_addr.s_addr=INADDR_ANY;
ZeroMemory(adr.sin_zero,8);

// bind socket to address
bind(sock, (struct sockaddr *) &adr, sizeof(adr));

// put the socket in passive mode, and reserve 2 additional
connection slots
listen(sock,2);

// loop infinitely for new connections
while (1)
    {
    struct sockaddr_in connectionaddr;
    int caddrsize;
    // we have a new connection
    int newsock=accept(sock,&connectionaddr, &caddrsize);

    // spawn a child process
    switch (fork())
        {
        case 0:        // child, I handle the connection
            communicate(newsock,connectionaddr);
            exit(0);
        case -1:
            // error in fork
            exit(-1);
        default:
            close (newsock);
```

```
        break;
    }
}
```

Some error handling code as well as the `communicate()` function have been eliminated for the sake of clarity. Notice how the parent must close the `newsock` socket
descriptor because `fork` duplicates variables, which means we have an open descriptor
that we are not going to use. If we do not close sockets handled by the child process,
we might run out of descriptors.

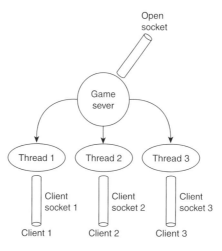

Figure 10.2   Concurrent, connection-oriented server with three clients and an open
socket awaiting connections.

Iterative, Connection-Oriented Servers

Now, imagine that we want to implement the same behavior without using the `fork()`
call, so the whole server is run in a single process. This is easy for just two peers: Put
the server in `accept` mode and wait until a new connection arrives. But how can we
do this with many users? As soon as the first user is accepted and we are exchanging
messages with him, we can no longer execute an `accept` call because it would stop
the whole server while we wait for a new connection that can or cannot take place.
Thus, we need a way to keep a socket open for incoming connection requests while we
continue working with already connected clients. This is achieved with the `select`
call, which allows us to check many sockets at once. The syntax follows:

```
int select(int nfds, fd_set *read, fd_set *write, fd_set *except,
struct timeval *timeout);
```

The call returns the number of sockets for which activity was detected. Then, the parameters are used to pass the sockets we want to check. To do so, the socket's API provides a structure called `fd_set`, which represents a set of sockets. The name `fd_set`, incidentally, comes from "file descriptor set," because in UNIX systems (where sockets were first devised), a socket is similar to a regular file descriptor. So, we can add sockets to an `fd_set`, delete them, and check for activity on such a set with the `select` call. Thus, the following three parameters for `select` are a set with those sockets we want to read from, a second set with sockets to write to, and a third, generally unused set with exceptions. The last parameter is just a timeout so `select` does not wait forever. Because the syntax is pretty obscure, here is a full `select()` example:

```
int msgsock;
char buf[1024];
fd_set ready;
int sock;
int maxsocks;

listen(sock, 5);            // 5 positions in the queue
FD_ZERO(&ready);
FD_SET(sock, &ready);
maxsocks=sock;
while (1)                   // server loops forever
    {
    struct timeval to;
    to.tv_sec = 5;
    to.tv_usec = 0;
    select(maxsocks, &ready, 0, 0, &to);

        if (FD_ISSET(sock, &ready))
        {
        msgsock = accept(sock, (struct sockaddr *)0, (int *)0);
        bzero(buf, sizeof(buf));
        read(msgsock, buf, 1024);
        printf("-->%s\n", buf);
        close(msgsock);
```

```
    maxsocks++;
    }
  }
```

I'll comment on the code a bit. Basically, we want to check those sockets we have already been connected through while keeping an eye on the initial socket, so we detect new connections. To do so, after `listen()`, we initialize an empty set of socket descriptors. We clear the array with `FD_ZERO`, which is just a macro. Then, we initialize the entry occupied by our own socket to specify that it's the only socket available, and we are awaiting connections through it. After we do this, we enter the infinite loop where we call `select`, passing the maximum number of sockets to be tested. We also pass the `ready` array so the call fills it with data referring to those sockets that have data available. Obviously, here we can find two situations: data available in the base socket, which means we have a new incoming connection that must be accepted, or data in another socket, which is already communicating with us. If we're receiving a connection request, the entry corresponding to the initial socket will be activated. Then, we check for that event with the `FD_ISSET` call and, if needed, accept the incoming connection and read the string the other peer is sending out. This way we are effectively handling many clients with just one initial socket and opening new ones as needed using `select`. A complex communication protocol should then be implemented on top of this skeleton, but this simple example should suffice to understand how `select` works.

UDP Servers

TCP servers are complex, especially when several clients are to be handled. UDP, on the other hand, provides a much easier communications mechanism. The downside is reduced reliability and security, but for fast-action games, UDP is the way to go. As you already know, UDP does not maintain a fixed connection, so each packet must come identified with its source. We read packets with `recvfrom` and send them back with `sendto`. Using the same `sockaddr` structure for both calls guarantees perfect echoing, thus, returning the packet to its originator. Here is a simple echo example:

```
void do_echo(int sockfd)
{
struct sockaddr *pcli_addr;
```

```
char mesg[MAXMESG];
while (1)
    {
    int n = recvfrom(sockfd, mesg, MAXMESG, 0, pcli_addr,
&clilen);
    nosent = sendto(sockfd, mesg, n, 0, pcli_addr, clilen);
    }

}
```

The socket has already been opened and bound to an address. Then, we loop, reading packages and sending them back to the client. This is a connectionless, stateless server. It does not store any state information, but just acts like a data relay.

Preventing Socket Blocks

Sockets are delicate by nature. They are designed for a network that never fails, transfers data at infinite speeds, and thus always works under ideal conditions. However, this is the real world, and therefore some extra code must be employed to ensure that our sockets respond well to the hazards of everyday use.

One potentially big issue is that of not having enough data to read. Imagine a client-server system where messages can be of variable size and where you read data with recv calls. As a parameter, you pass the amount of data you want to read back from a call, but how are you supposed to know how much data there is without looking at the socket in the first place?

You could play it safe by reading data on a byte level: one byte at each call. However, that strategy would be slow and could potentially backfire on you. If no data is available, the socket would still block.

At least two different methods can cope with this situation. The first tries to take "sneak peeks" at sockets before actually reading any data from them, ensuring that we read as much as is available. The second allows us to directly request any number of bytes from the socket while making sure it does not block due to insufficient data.

In the first method, we will use the flags provided by the recv() call. These flags can have the following values:

- ➤ 0   Default value, no special behavior.

- ➤ MSG_OOB   Used to handle Out-Of-Band data. OOB data is data marked as urgent by the sender. To send OOBs, the sender must specify MSG_OOB in the send call. Then, when the receiver uses the MSG_OOB flag on the recv call, the OOB data is retrieved as an individual element, outside of the sequence stream.

- ➤ MSG_PEEK   Used to peek at the socket without reading data from it. A recv call with MSG_PEEK correctly returns the number of bytes available for a subsequent recv call, but does not remove them from the incoming queue.

Clearly, MSG_PEEK can be very useful to us. A code sequence like the following correctly ensures that we only read as much data as the socket effectively holds:

```
#define BUFFERSIZE 256
Char *buffer=new char[BUFFERSIZE] ;

int available=recv(sock,buffer,BUFFERSIZE,MSG_PEEK) ;
recv(sock,buffer,available,0);
```

This way we can prevent the blocking nature of sockets.

Another strategy is to convert our regular socket into a nonblocking socket. Nonblocking sockets do not get locked if there is not enough data in the incoming pipeline. They just return the call and inform us of this circumstance. To create a nonblocking socket, we first need to open it, and once the communications channel is set, modify its characteristics with the powerful fcntl() call. Here is a simple UNIX example that converts a socket passed as an argument to nonblocking:

```
void setnonblocking(int sock)
{

int opts = fcntl(sock,F_GETFL);
if (opts < 0)
    {
    perror("fcntl(F_GETFL)");
```

```
    exit(EXIT_FAILURE);
    }
opts = (opts | O_NONBLOCK);
if (fcntl(sock,F_SETFL,opts) < 0)
    {
    perror("fcntl(F_SETFL)");
    exit(EXIT_FAILURE);
    }
return;
}
```

Designing Client-Server Games

We have mastered the basics of network and socket programming, so let's put on a designer's hat for a second and try to relate all this knowledge to a real game. Fundamentally, all the preceding sections expose the tools we have access to. Thinking about the goals for a moment will provide some perspective and focus. In this section, I will focus on a small area game (8 to 16 players), whereas the next section deals with massively multiplayer game design issues.

In a small area game, all players are running a game client, and one player (usually the one with the fastest computer and Internet connection) runs the server as well. This is the main reason that these games must maintain reduced user groups. A larger user base would make the server too resource consuming, and running a client and server on the same machine would become unfeasible.

In Figure 10.3, the architecture for this kind of system implies that the user running the server starts a new game, putting the server in an accept() call. This is usually performed through a "game lobby." At this point in time, the other users join the game, so the server can effectively stop accepting any further calls. Once the multiplayer game begins, no one can join until the server enters the lobby again.

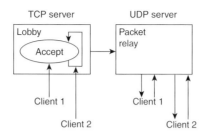

Figure 10.3   UDP acts like a data relay, whereas TCP maintains
session control and manages the game lobby.

This allows the game server to easily blend inside the main game engine, using the following algorithm:

Server, step 1: Create socket, and bind to IP and port.

Server, step 2: Listen, and wait in an `accept` call. Open "game lobby" and show
IP/port.

Server, step 3: Now the server is awaiting connections. Two threads/processes are
required: an interface thread running the game menu interaction
and another running the `accept` call so the system does not lock.

Client, steps 1 to N: Open socket, and connect to the game server.

Server, step 4: Update screen for each accepted connection. Implement the
desired connection policy (connectionless iterative, connection-
oriented concurrent).

Server, steps N+1: At this point, all the clients are connected to the server. When
the game menu interaction thread indicates a player has started
the game, you can effectively close the main server socket,
interrupt the `accept` call, and start the game with the connection sockets. The game server thus shuts down and accepts no
further connections.

This method allows us to simplify our game code. The game server only works at boot
time, and afterward it is all a data transfer issue. But there are some potential pitfalls
we must be aware of.

What happens when a player loses his connection? The server will realize this either by the socket closing or simply by not receiving data over a long period of time. As soon as we detect this inconvenience, we must create a new socket, put it in `accept` mode, and wait for the lost user to (hopefully) resurface.

Massively Multiplayer Games

A massively multiplayer game (MMG) is a dream come true for devoted network programmers. The techniques, problems, and solutions found in their design and programming are as complex as network programming can get: lots of connections, lots of data transfer, and very restrictive time constraints. Add the ever-present lag to the equation and, well, you get the picture.

To begin with, I'll describe MMGs as those games that serve a large community, using a single machine (or more) as dedicated game servers. The players run clients that update the servers with player state information, whereas the servers basically broadcast information to the playing community. MMGs are hard to code, not because they are an inherently complex problem, but because of their sheer size: Coding an eight-player game with a dedicated game server is not complex "per se." The problems arise when you try to cover thousands of players. So, all we need to do is work on techniques that allow us to "tame the size" of the problem. Let's explore a few of these methods.

Data Extrapolation

Unfortunately, networks are sometimes slower than we would like them to be. We code our client-server systems assuming that the network is an infinitely fast and reliable highway, but this is seldom the case. Lags occur, and many times gameplay gets interrupted as we wait for the next position update from the other end of the wire. Under these circumstances, we must take every possible step to try to minimize the lag's impact on the gameplay, so the player can enjoy our game despite the network's problems. In a slow-paced game, speed will seldom be the problem. However, if you are playing a fast-action game, the last thing you expect is your opponent to freeze due to a network malfunction. Clearly, we need to put some math to work to ensure that we "smooth out" these network irregularities.

The technique that we will use tries to determine the value of any player state charac-teristic at the present time, even when we haven't had a recent update. It works for any continuous value, so I will demonstrate its use with the most common parameter in any networked game: a player's position. For simplicity, I will assume we are in a 2D world with a player's position expressed using an x,z pair of floating-point values.

Under these circumstances, all we have to do is store the last N position updates (I will demonstrate with N=3) as well as a time stamp (provided by `timeGetTime()`) for each one of them. As you already know, three values can be interpolated with a quad-ratic polynomial. If our positions are labeled P0, P1, and P2 (P2 being the most recent) and time stamps are respectively T0, T1, and T2, we can create a function:

```
P(T)
```

which gives us a position given a time stamp. To create the polynomial, we must only remember:

```
P(T) = aT^2 + bT + c
```

By substituting P0, P1, and P2 and T0, T1, and T2 in the preceding equation we get:

```
P0x = ax T0^2 + bxT0 + cx
P1x = ax T1^2 + bxT1 + cx
P2x = ax T2^2 + bxT2 + cx
```

Remember that P0.x, P1.x, P2.x, T0, T1, and T2 are well known, so the only unknown values are ax, bx, and cx. This system can easily be solved by triangulation. Once solved for x and z, we have two polynomials:

```
Px(T) = axT^2 + bxT + c
Pz(T) = azT^2 + bzT + c
```

These polynomials compute, given a certain value for T, a pair x,z that corresponds to that time stamp. If T represents one of the initial values (T0, T1, T2), obviously the polynomial will return P0, P1, and P2, respectively (because we used them to compute the polynomial). But because we have chosen a parabolic curve (a polynomial of grade 2), values in between P0, P1, and P2 will be smoothly interpolated, so we will get an approximation of the value of a smooth trajectory going from P0 to P1 and P2.

A more interesting property of polynomials tells us that they are continuous functions, meaning that values located close in parameter space (T, in this case) have similar return values (x,z pairs). Thus, if we extrapolate (which means we choose a value *close* but *beyond* P2), the value returned by the polynomial will still be valid (as shown in Figure 10.4) as an approximation of the trajectory in the vicinity of P2. In other words, a car performing a curve at time stamp T will very likely follow a smooth trajectory for a while, and thus we can assume the polynomial will be an accurate approximation.

As a result, we can trust this polynomial to accurately represent the future behavior of the position (assuming we don't get too far from T2 in time).

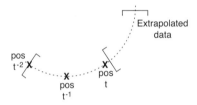

Figure 10.4   Extrapolating data to cover network lags.

So, every time a new position update arrives, we must discard the oldest update and rebuild the interpolation polynomials. Thus, we will use the interpolator to evaluate the position of the networked player until we receive a new update, and so on. If lag grows, we might perceive a "jump" in position when a new sampling point arrives (because we are moving from a very distant predicted position to a very close one). However, in real-world, moderate-lag scenarios, the preceding technique should help to significantly smooth out a player's trajectories.

Hierarchical Messaging

Imagine a game where lots of network packets are continually being sent between players. Not all players have the same level of connection. Some players are playing on high-speed DSL or cable, whereas others are still using an analog modem. As traffic intensity increases, the modem user will begin feeling an information overload, and his playing experience will degrade. Hierarchical messaging is a technique designed to ensure that everyone gets the best information on a heterogeneous configuration.

At the core of the method lies the notion that messages have different importance levels. For example, an enemy position update is more relevant than the configuration of his arms with regard to the animation system. Messages should be classified and assigned relevance levels. Then, as a new player enters the game, a network test should provide us with information on the user's expected bandwidth—how much data he can exchange per second. Then, we will decide which messages are sent to him depending on that bandwidth to ensure he gets the most important messages, but maybe loses some secondary information.

Take, for example, a first-person shooter. Messages could be (in descending order of relevance):

➤ Position updates

➤ Shooting

➤ Weapon changes

➤ Mesh configuration/animation

Each "level" of transmission must be quantified in bytes per second, and then the right set of messages will be determined. Thus, in a first-person-shooter, maybe one player is just seeing positions and ignoring the rest of the information. But because he has the most relevant information, the game is still playable on a low-end machine.

Spatial Subdivision

Spatial subdivision is designed specifically for massively multiplayer games. It uses spatial indexing to ensure that only relevant packets are transmitted and, by doing so, it can decrease the overall traffic by orders of magnitude.

Imagine a squad-based game, where a player can join teams of up to four players in a quest—something like *Diablo*, for example. Obviously, we will need to send the position updates quite frequently, because the game is pretty high-paced. This is not much of a problem, because we are only dealing with four players. However, try to imagine what goes on inside a game such as *Everquest*—thousands of players roaming a huge game world, many of them located at days of distance (in gameplay terms) from other gamers. Under these circumstances, does it really make sense to update everyone about our current state? We might be consuming the bandwidth of a gamer at the other end of the game world with useless information.

Now, imagine that players are stored in a spatial index data structure, usually held on the game servers managed by the publisher. Every time we want to broadcast new data regarding a player, we start by querying the spatial index about which players are located within a certain distance from the first one. Then, we only send the data to those players, saving lots of bandwidth. Let's stop and review an example. Think of an *Everquest* type of game with 100,000 players in a game world that is 100×100 kilometers across.

The first alternative is to use standard broadcasts, where each packet is sent to everyone. Using very simple math, you will see that this requires sending $100,000^2$ packets of information if we want to update all players.

Now, imagine that we divide the game world into a grid 100×100 meters. Each grid section contains the players specific to that grid. Assuming that their distribution is homogeneous, we would have 10 players per grid cell. Now, let's assume we only send the update to those players located in the current cell or in any of the nine neighboring cells. That means an update must be sent to 100 players (10 cells, 10 players per cell). Thus, the grand total of packets required to update everyone is just 10,000,000, which is 1,000 times less than if we did not use spatial subdivision. The only hidden cost is the data structure, but we can definitely afford that for a game server, which usually comes with lots of RAM.

Send State Changes Only

If you are willing to accept some restrictions, you can greatly reduce your game's bandwidth by sending only state change information, not the actual in-game data stream. To understand how this method works and which restrictions we need to apply, think of a game like *Diablo* or *Dungeon Siege*, where two peers connected in a network are playing in cooperative multiplayer fashion. They explore the game world and solve quests. There are lots of monsters (each with its own logic routines) onscreen and lots of items to choose.

In a game like this, you can choose between two networked approaches. Using one approach, you can run the game logic engine on only one of the two machines and propagate results to the other machine, which would receive all game logic information through the network and use it to drive the presentation layer. The second PC would thus only have the graphics engine and not much else, becoming a "game terminal." But the problem is ensuring that the network will be able to pump the data at the right speed, so the other player sees exactly the same game world, and the experience is seamless. This can be achieved on a local area network (LAN), but the Internet is a whole different business.

Thus, we need an alternative. Basically, we keep two world simulators working in sync on both PCs. Both simulators must be 100 percent deterministic for this to work, meaning they must not depend on any outside events or random numbers. Only by ensuring this can we stop sending all game world update messages (monster positions, and so on) and focus on transmitting just player positions. This is a very popular approach, which requires checking for world syncing every now and then to make sure both game worlds don't diverge and end up being two completely different representations of the same level.

If you are following such an approach, we can move one step further, changing the explicit information in our messages by using state change messages. Currently, you are sending a player position update for every logic tick, which is a waste of bandwidth. If the player is on a deterministic system (obviously, with the chaos inherent to gamer interaction), we can send only state changes and save much of this bandwidth. Instead of saying "the player is here" all the time, you only need to send "the player pressed the advance key" when a state change condition takes place. Do not forget that our player is, at the core, a finite-state machine. The player will continue performing the same action (such as walking or fighting) for many clock cycles. Sending only the state change lets you forget about all this continuous messaging, making your bandwidth requirements drop sharply.

Just remember the restrictions imposed by this method: Both game worlds must be kept in sync. This will force some changes in your code, like the random number processing, for example. You can still have random numbers as long as both PCs have the same ones. Generating the same sequence in both PCs might seem like a crazy idea, but it's one of the essential tasks to ensure proper synchronization. To keep both random number generators in sync, all you have to do is have a random number table precomputed in memory (the same one for both machines, obviously) and use it instead of actually computing numbers. This change will have the desirable side effect of a significant performance gain, because random number generators are traditionally very slow, and tabulating them is a classic optimization trick as well.

Working with Server Clusters

No serious MMG can be managed with a single server. As player count increases, we reach a point when we need to move to a cluster, so more users can be accommodated. This opens the door to a whole new area of programming, which deals with how to lay out the players on the servers, how to communicate with them efficiently, and so on. This is a relatively new science, but some interesting methods have already arisen. I will now comment on those, explaining the methods behind some popular solutions.

To begin with, multiple servers are used to reduce the number of players that each server must handle. This might seem obvious, but most problems come from not understanding this key fact. We need each server to handle less players. So, we need:

➤ Less players connected directly to the server

➤ Tests for one player inside one server to be resolved in the same server

The second item in the list is the key fact. Imagine that we have 100 users, and we split them randomly into two groups of 50. Because we split them randomly, chances are that checking the collision of a player will require us to look at other players on his server, and on the other server as well, totally killing performance. We will still need to check with all the players in the game world.

The solution, obviously, is to map our spatial subdivision engine to the server level. Each server will handle players located in a continuous part of the game world, thus ensuring that most tests can be solved locally. For example, we can divide the game world in half. Then, when we need to send a player update to the rest of the players, we test which other players are close to the original player. This is performed by the game server, hopefully on a local basis. All players needing the update will lie on the same machine as the original player. Once we have the list of those players that actually need to know that the original player has moved, we send the message to them only.

Notice how we have improved performance in two ways. At the server level, only half of the gamers were tested. The rest of them lie on another server and did not even notice the player in the example moved. We optimized network bandwidth as well, sending the update only to those players within a certain range of the player.

Now, let's generalize this to N servers in a large game world. We can divide the scenario in a gridlike fashion and assign grid quadrants to individual servers, so all players within that region are handled internally, and CPU and bandwidth are kept to a minimum. If the developer wants to add new regions to the game world, all we need to do is add extra servers to the cluster. Obviously, this approach will mostly have server-user traffic, but server-server communications will be important as well. How do we notify a server that a player has crossed the grid boundaries and must thus be relocated to the neighboring grid cell? To help visualize this, think in terms of vertical (server-user) and horizontal (server-server) messages. Vertical messages will be most frequent, whereas horizontal messages will carry control information and be less frequent.

Dynamic Servers and the Braveheart Syndrome

Sometimes the clustered approach explained in the preceding section will fail to do its work. Basically, we have divided the game world spatially, assuming that means a homogeneous player division as well. Each cell region has approximately the same number of players. But what happens if a large number of gamers are, at a point in time, located in the same grid cell? Imagine a "hotspot" region to which many players converge for some game-related reason. Obviously, that server will sustain more workload than the rest. Imagine the "launchpad" area, where most gamers in a MMG appear when they first enter a game. It's an overpopulated area, which will make our servers stall.

The first option would be to study these cases carefully and further divide the game world, much like in a quadtree, around these regions. But this implies that these hotspot regions are fixed, which doesn't really have to be the case. Imagine that one day there's an extra quest proposed by the game developers, and that quest increases traffic in a certain portion of the game world. How can we ensure that the gaming experience will not degrade that day? And how can we get things back to normal after the activity is over, and the traffic level is reduced? This is often referred to as the Braveheart syndrome: how to prevent a situation in which lots of gamers move to a small portion of the map and then leave it, much like in a battle like those portrayed in the *Braveheart* movie. This phenomenon is depicted in Figure 10.5.

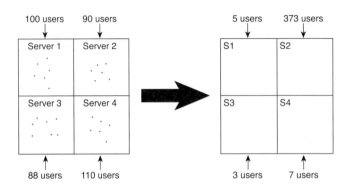

Figure 10.5 The Braveheart syndrome. Left: servers with homogeneous load. Right: players concentrate on a specific spot, bringing the system down.

Obviously, the solution is to allow dynamic server reallocation, so servers can be assigned to specific regions in real time with no user-perceived performance loss. When lots of players converge to a specific region, the server array must reconfigure itself automatically, subdividing the affected regions further so the overall number of players per server stays under control. This is a very involved solution, implemented (among others) by games such as *Asheron's Call*. It is also offered by many MMG creation packages, like the *Game Grid* by Butterfly.net.

Two ways of dealing with the Braveheart problem come to mind. One approach would be to resize server zones to try to guarantee that all servers are equally loaded at all times. The idea is that if a zone gets overcrowded, this implies that other zones are emptying, and thus we can expand those zones so they assume part of the load from the crowded zone.

Another approach would be to have hot-swappable servers that are basically ready and waiting for spikes. If a spike occurs, the whole game world stays the same. Only the affected server will call for help, dividing itself in two and passing part of the population to the hot-swappable server. This passing can cause some annoyances as the players are moved from one server to the other, but assuming the spike is progressive (players enter the zone one by one), we can gradually move them to the new server so performance loss is not detected. This second idea has an added benefit: If we implement hot-swappable servers, we can grow the game world dynamically without big changes in the design. We just add more servers and assign them to specific game zones, and we are all set.

In Closing

Networked games are one of the areas of game programming that is growing faster than others. The advent of the massively multiplayer titles has taken the world by storm, and all analysts forecast that this growth will continue for at least the next few years. After all, playing against (or with) other humans is always more rewarding than confronting an AI-controlled character. We feel challenged, we get more addicted, and we have more fun.

Chapter 11

2D Game Programming

KEY TOPICS

- On Older Hardware
- Data Structures for 2D Games
- Mapping Matrices
- 2D Game Algorithms
- Special Effects
- In Closing

"PICTURE: A representation in two dimensions of something wearisome in three."

Ambrose Bierce, *The Devil's Dictionary*

The first generation of video games were all two dimensional. The internal representation of the game world had only two axes at most (usually up-down or left-right). Some games, such as *Diablo*, tried to give the illusion of depth by using isometric perspective, but it was all make-believe.

Two-dimensional games are mostly gone from high-end platforms such as PCs and consoles. However, there are many other uses of two-dimensional technologies, which still remain today. Handhelds, game-capable telephones, and even interactive television are only some of the scenarios where 2D is still the way to go. Moreover, the strict limitations imposed by the 2D programming rules are a good exercise for any modern game programmer. Many of the optimizations and techniques found in 2D titles are still used in higher-end platforms today.

On Older Hardware

In the age of 2D games, computers were limited by slow CPUs and small memory sizes. The Sinclair ZX Spectrum, for example, used a Zilog Z80 8-bit processor running at 4.77 MHz and included 48KB of RAM. In the console arena, the original Nintendo Entertainment System (NES) ran on a 6502 chip. So, game programming was really a case of creating detailed, rich environments on very restrictive platforms. As an example, a typical 640×480 image taken from a digital camera is, by today's imaging standards, pretty low resolution. But stored in 24-bits of color, that image would take approximately 900KB—about 20 times the amount of memory available on a classic 8-bit computer.

In fact, reversing this equation, you would discover that the 48KB available on these little machines can barely hold a 128×128 image using 24 bits per pixel for the color. And that's assuming we could use all the memory for the bitmap, forgetting about the operating system (OS) and main program code!

The size of the memory is only one of the problems of coding for 8-bit machines. You might assume that those 48KB of RAM would be arranged in an intuitive fashion, such as a linear array you could freely allocate. But no, old-school memory mapping was more complex. Memory was usually fragmented into sections reserved for specific purposes. Part of the addressing space was taken by the OS, part was dedicated to interrupt vectors (which held the machine code for low-level routines such as keypresses and hardware timers), and part was dedicated to devices such as the color palette, and so on. Coding for one such platform involved knowing the memory map very well, so the programmer understood what could be placed where.

This might sound like history for many programmers, but it is more recent than you think. The IBM PC was coded this way for ages until Windows 95 (and hence DirectX) came along. In the following listing, you can see a traditional memory map of a PC-compatible machine, with the interrupt vectors (IV), interrupt service routines (ISRs), and frame buffer at address A0000H.

```
   1 Mb     = 0x10000:0000
 1 Mb-1     = 0xFFFF:000F    End System BIOS area
 896 Kb       0xE000:0000    Start System BIOS area
 896 Kb-1  = 0xDFFF:000F    End Expansion card BIOS area
 768 Kb       0xC000:0000    Start Expansion card BIOS area
 768 Kb-1  = 0xBFFF:000F    End Video RAM
 640 Kb       0xA000:0000    Start Video RAM
 640 Kb-1  = 0x9FFF:000F    End DOS RAM
   0 Kb       0x0000:0000    Start DOS RAM
```

As a final note on memory, it is important to understand that many systems did not have "secondary storage," such as a hard drive where you can store data and swap it in at runtime. In a modern game, only the data for the current level is usually held in memory; every time a player advances one level, old data is flushed out to leave room for the new data. Many old machines did not have file systems. Data and code were interleaved in an integrated whole, and programmers had to be careful that coding mistakes did not access data zones. These machines came with a program loader that basically dumped data from physical media (tapes, cartridges, and so on) to main memory.

Notable exceptions to this rule were game consoles, which did not need to load memory because the cartridge was the memory, and the IBM PC, which had a reasonable file system thanks to DOS.

Today, it is hard to understand what it means to code for some of the older hardware. CPU speed is now measured in gigahertz, but some of the older machines barely reached the megahertz scale. However, there is more to programming than raw speed. Do you want to code a game like *Asteroids*, with its simple yet elegant physics and inertia? If you try that as an exercise, you will surely need trigonometric functions such as the sine and cosine. They govern the direction (given the yaw angle and the speed) using the popular equation:

```
X=x+speed*cos(yaw)
Z=z+speed*sin(yaw)
```

Mathematical signs and whichever axis you call X or Z can vary depending on the convention you follow. But the heart of the equation should be familiar to you. Now, let's stop and consider that simple but devilish equation. You can see that we need two trigonometric evaluations, two multiplies, two additions, and two variable assigns. Simple enough, isn't it? But the situation is far from ideal, especially in 8-bit computers. To begin with, imagine that you don't have that fancy floating-point unit that performs sin and cos for you. Getting headaches? Well, I can hear the advanced readers telling me to revert to lookup tables instead. But wait, there's more. Imagine that you don't have floating-point instructions such as the multiply and the addition. To make matters worse, also imagine that you don't have floating-point numbers, but instead have 8-bit integer values only. Does this sound like mission impossible? Well, that's the world game programmers lived in for about 15 years, and some of them on simpler platforms still code under these restrictions today.

In this chapter we will first cover the data structures that made these games possible. We will then move on to classic algorithms, and wrap up with a summary of popular 2D-age special effects. As a whole, this should provide a good overview of 2D game programming algorithms.

Data Structures for 2D Games

We have seen how hardware was the main limiting factor for game development. Clearly, coding *Quake* on 48KB sounds like a nice challenge. But 2D games use simpler and smaller data structures, and less-involved routines than more advanced 3D titles. We will now study these constituent elements of classic 2D games. Defining the structure to three key elements here is essential:

➤ A way to encode the character graphics

➤ A way to encode background images

➤ A way to store the game map

Sprite-Based Characters

Let's take a look back in time to see how characters were represented in the early days of the animation industry. In the days of Walt Disney, each frame of each character was painted on cellophane sheets with transparent areas where the character would "see through." To produce the illusion of animation, drawings were layered and movement was simulated by swapping the frames from each animation. This technique became known as *cel animation*, from the cellophane sheets used in it.

Analogous to cellophane sheets, 2D games store each character in a rectangular, bitmapped graphic, so it can be drawn quickly onscreen. Additional information allows the game code to detect transparent areas, so our characters blend seamlessly with the backgrounds. Then, specific hardware and software is used to render these layers to the screen. Each of these bitmaps (with its associated transparency information) is called a *sprite*. The name comes from the early days of 2D games. Because most games involved ghosts, sprites, and knights, graphics adopted the name.

Sprites can be stored in a variety of ways depending on the hardware. A cell phone can have a black-and-white, 200×150 pixel display, whereas some newer sprite games on the PC can run at 800×600, 24-bit color with alpha effects. Again, memory and CPU performance are the limiting factors. The former would occupy 30,000 bits (black and white requires one bit per pixel only), which is about 4KB. The latter option would be in excess of 1MB. Next, I will explore some formats that have been popular through the years.

A first format stores the sprites in black and white (or any two given colors), and restricts sprite sizes to multiples of eight. Some cell phones, as well as 8-bit machines like the Spectrum, support this format. It is very convenient because each pixel in the sprite can be stored in one bit, and keeping sizes in multiples of eight makes the sprites easier to store in bytes. The Spectrum, for example, used 8×8, two-color sprites. The foreground and background colors are selected from a 16-color palette, so each of them requires 4 bits, for an extra byte total. Overall, this format uses 9 bytes per sprite only. Because the frame buffer is 256×176 pixels, or 32×23 sprites, the whole frame buffer occupies approximately 6KB (if the sprites are "flattened out" so we have a picture of the screen). For increased efficiency, many 8-bit machines do not have a frame buffer, but can work with a tile table and a buffer holding only sprite identifiers. This is the case with the NES (more on its architecture can be found in Chapter 1, "Chronology of Game Programming"). Assuming the same resolution as a Spectrum and one byte for each sprite, this representation system only requires 736 bytes (plus the sprite memory). Whichever method you choose, the low memory footprint comes at a cost. Each 8×8 square can only hold two colors, significantly degrading the visual richness.

A more involved option can be used if you are working on a display adapter that supports a palette of 16 colors, directly mappable to each pixel (so you can display more than two colors per sprite). Under these circumstances, each pixel can be coded to 4 bits, and every two pixels take one byte. Thus, in this case, the restriction is that sprite size needs to be a power of 2 (8, 16, 32, 64…). An 8×8 sprite will then require as much as 32 bytes. Again, a 256×176 display would take up 23KB, around four times more space than the preceding case. But we can represent much richer scenes.

Building on this last approach, we can encode sprites supporting up to 256 colors per pixel. These colors usually come from a fixed palette or a palette freely defined by the user. This is the case with the popular 320×200 PC format, where each palette entry can encode a 24-bit RGB triplet. Given these restrictions, our 8×8 sprite takes exactly

64 bytes, a display with the resolution of a Spectrum display would take 46KB, and a PC frame buffer running at 320×200 takes exactly 64,000 bytes. Add the space needed for the palette table (256 colors of 24 bits each, 768 bytes total), and the whole will fit perfectly in the 64KB found in one memory segment of our beloved PCs.

Moving up in the color scale we can encode high-color sprites (16 bits per pixel). Here, two options are available. First, you can choose to encode using 5-5-5-1 (five bytes for red, green, and blue, plus one for alpha). Second, you can encode using 6-5-5 and encode the transparency color as one of the color combinations that you are not really using, as in a chroma key approach.

In an ideal world, you could use true-color sprites, either in 24 or 32 bits if you want to work with alpha blending. Quite likely, 8 bits for alpha will be way too much, but this has the advantage that each pixel can be transferred in one double word (32 bits), which is convenient. However, by the time you begin working with true-color sprites, your hardware platform will most likely support 3D graphics. So that's the reason why 2D games using true color are much less popular than their 8-bit counterparts.

Now, we need to talk about transparency. Our sprites need to blend seamlessly with the background, so we need a way to encode the parts of the sprite that should leave the background unaffected. Several approaches have been used to achieve this effect.

One popular alternative is to use a separate 1-bit mask to encode transparent zones. This mask is used in the transfer process to ensure the blend is performed properly. In Figure 11.1, the mask is multiplied by the background, leaving in black the area that will later be occupied by the sprite. Then, by adding the sprite to the background directly, the blending is achieved.

Figure 11.1   Mask and sprite.

This approach is simple to code, but the mask takes a significant amount of memory, especially in animated sprites. For a 32×32, 256-color sprite (which itself takes 1KB), we would need 128 extra bytes for the mask. There is an alternative to this technique: reserving one color entry in our palette as the "transparent" color and storing only those pixels that encode nontransparent colors. In a 256-color palette, the loss of one color would be reasonable. But on a lower-color platform, such as a 16-color palette, losing one color for the sake of transparency might be unacceptable; thus, the masking approach would be preferred.

To produce the illusion of animation, sprites need to be layered on the screen quickly. At least 25 screen updates per second are required, but numbers in excess of 50 are not uncommon. This operation of layering sprites onscreen is called *blitting*. The name comes from the word "blit," which is a contraction of "block image transfer." Some platforms, such as early game consoles, employed specific hardware to perform these blits. Blitting engines were usually modified memory copy routines, because 2D screens are usually mapped into linear memory arrays.

Mapping Matrices

Many 2D games were able to present large, varied game worlds on very limited machines. The trick was to use compression techniques to make data fit on the very small memory chips. As an example, let's analyze how much memory a top-down game such as *The Legend of Zelda* required. To support the argument, I'll assume the game level occupies 5×5 television screens across, and that every screen is 256×200 pixels, palletized to 16 colors. If you do the math, you'll discover that a bitmap with those dimensions would take up 1.25MB of space, clearly more than a Nintendo console had at that time. There must be a trick somewhere, and that trick is called *mapping*.

Mapping is a compression technique that will allow us to create good-looking game worlds at a fraction of the memory footprint. We will lose some visual variety in the process, but our dream game will fit on our target platform. Mapping is an extremely popular technique. It was used in thousands of games for classic consoles and arcades, and is still used today, even in some 3D games. The key idea is to divide our game world into a set of tiles or basic primitives. Each tile will represent a rectangular pattern, which we will combine with other tiles to represent the level. So, if our game world must represent grass, stone, snow, and sand, we will use four tiles, and then map them as if we were putting tiles on the floor.

The compression comes from the fact that, if we repeat the same pattern frequently, we will only have it once in memory. To prove this, let's assume we represent our initial game with a tile set. We will use 256 different tiles (more than enough to provide richness to the game world). Each tile will be 8×8 pixels.

So, each tile occupies

```
8×8 = 64 = 32 bytes (we are using 16 colors only)
```

The whole tile set will require

```
32×256 = 8KB
```

We will call this structure the tile table (more on tile tables in the next section). We will then need a second data structure, called the mapping matrix. This structure stores the layout information: how the tiles should be arranged in game level. From the sprite size, we know the size of our mapping matrix will be

```
256×5/8=160
200×5/8=125
```

Because each entry will be a byte-sized value so we can index the 256 possible tiles, the whole table will require

```
160×125 = 20000 bytes
```

So, our compressed map will take up around 19.5KB, with 8 extra kilobytes dedicated to the tile list. On the whole, that is 27.5KB, down from 1.25MB. That means dividing by a factor of 50 approximately. Clearly, there is a big gain to mapping, and that's the reason mapping was extremely popular in the '80s. Games such as *Mario Bros*, *Zelda*, *1942*, and many others use variants of the mapped scheme.

Tile Tables

We have seen how to encode character graphics. We have also explored how to store a game map based on a mapping matrix. It is time to talk about the background graphics or tiles. Thus, the data structure we will now cover is the tile table (TT). Put simply, it is a list of background images that can be tiled and combined using a mapping matrix to create a complete game map. Some platforms, such as the NES, had this structure defined in the hardware's specifications. Others, like PCs, allowed the developer to specify its own. Whatever the case, the TT is used to store unique tiles that will later be mapped to the screen. There are a number of decisions involved in creating an efficient TT.

Format of the Tiles

First and foremost, we need to know the format of the tiles we will be storing. This is a really important choice, because different formats dramatically affect the table's size. Traditionally, tile sizes used to be powers of 2, as this allowed some optimization in the blitting routines used to transfer them to the screen. Instead of transferring bytes, we can use words or even 32-bit values for increased efficiency.

We also need to decide whether all tiles will be the same size or if they will differ. Classic games used equal-sized tiles for easier screen rendering. But if we consider a real-time strategy game that uses an isometric view where buildings are all different sizes, wouldn't it be wiser to allow for different tile sizes?

In addition, we must decide the color format of the tiles. In the old days, tiles were paletized, so each pixel was encoded in one byte that indexed the color palette. However, more recent games have used high-color modes (16 bits encoding RGB in 6-5-5) or even true color (24 bits encoding RGB as 8-8-8). Clearly, the more colors the better. But keep in mind that more colors means more memory, more bus usage, and thus less performance.

However, there is an equation that will give us the memory size of a single tile, as a function of several parameters. Keep this in mind when designing your game so your graphics fit in memory:

> Size = bits per pixel * wide * tall

Number of Tiles

The number of tiles held in the TT will be as important as their format. On one hand, more tiles means nicer graphics. On the other hand, memory use will increase dramatically in more ways than you think.

Imagine that our game needs to hold 256 different tiles. The TT will encode them in positions 0 to 255. Thus, each position in the mapping matrix will need to index that table using an unsigned, 8-bit number. However, imagine that our artist raises the bar to 300 tiles. The TT will grow accordingly, but the mapping matrix will also undergo some changes. We cannot encode 300 values in a byte. We have two options:

➤ Use 9 bits, which allow 512 values, but require some rather obfuscated code to access.

➤ Use a 16-bit value, which will take up double the memory but give us simple access.

An alternative to allow this in platforms that have some sort of file system is to ensure that only 256 tiles are used per level, so each level has a different TT. This way we can preserve the variety without the memory hit. But some platforms require the full program (including data) to be in main memory at the same time, so there is no way to select the TT.

2D Game Algorithms

We have reviewed the constituent elements of traditional 2D games. We will now move on to specific game techniques, reviewing the algorithms behind popular classics such as *Zelda* and *Mario Bros*. All the algorithms use the same data structures we discussed previously: tile tables, sprites, and mapping matrices.

Screen-Based Games

The simplest mapped game is the screen-based game, in which the player confronts a series of screens. When he exits one screen through its edge, the graphics are substituted by those in the next screen, and so forth. There is no continuity or transition between screens. The classic *Boulder Dash* would be a good example of this technique.

In these games, each screen is represented using a different mapping matrix, which represents the screen layout of the different elements. So, for a 320×240 screen using 32×32 tiles, we would store the screen in a 10×8 matrix of bytes. Notice that 240 does not allow for an exact number of tiles to be rendered vertically onscreen (we can fit 7.5 tiles). So, we take the integer excess to ensure the whole screen is mapped.

Then, the rendering routine is very straightforward. Its code would look something like this:

```
#define tile_wide 32
#define tile_high 32
#define screen_wide 320
#define screen_high 240

int xtiles=screen_wide/tile_wide;
int ytiles=screen_high/tile_high;

for (yi=0;yi<ytiles;yi++)
      {
      for (xi=0;xi<xtiles;xi++)
            {
            int screex=xi*tile_wide;
            int screey=yi*tile_high;
            int tileid=mapping_matrix [yi][xi];
            blit(tile_table[tileid],screenx,screeny);
            }
      }
```

An interesting variant of the preceding code generalizes the mapping matrix to a 3D matrix indexed by room identifier, x value and y value. This way a single data structure can hold the whole game map. To use this approach, we would need a line such as this in our code:

```
int tileid=mapping_matrix [roomid][yi][xi];
```

Two- and Four-Way Scrollers

Screen-based games divide the gameplay into chunks that must be dealt with individually. That makes rendering easier, at the cost of breaking the entertainment each time screens are changed. It would be much better, in terms of gameplay, if the action was a continuum, with no screen swapping at all. This is the goal of scrolling games: to create a larger-than-screen gameworld that we can continually explore from a sliding camera. Classics like *1942* (2-way top-down scrolling), *Super Mario Bros* (2-way side-scrolling), and *Zelda* (4-way top-down scrolling) are all part of this large family. Games such as *Diablo* or the Commodore classic *Head over Heels* used isometric perspectives, but the approach is virtually the same.

Scrolling games are a bit more complex than screen-based games. The game world is larger than the player's screen, so we need to process only those areas that are visible to the player. Besides, the screen mapping of a scrolling world depends on the player's position, making our code significantly harder.

The initial problem we will be dealing with will be selecting the "window" or portion of the game world that will be visible. For consistency, I will use the same constants we used in the preceding section:

```
#define tile_wide 32
#define tile_high 32
#define screen_wide 320
#define screen_high 240
```

Clearly, the number of onscreen tiles is

```
int xtiles=(screen_wide/tile_wide)+1;
int ytiles=(screen_high/tile_high)+1;
```

Notice how we added one in each direction to account for the last tile showing, which will probably be cut.

Then, we need to know which cell in the mapping matrix the player is standing on. This way, assuming the player is in the middle of the screen, we can deduct the window coordinates. Specifically, assuming the player is at

```
Int playerx;
int playery;
```

his cell position will be

```
tileplayerx= Playerx/tile_wide
tileplayery= Playery/tile_high
```

And we must paint the following tile intervals:

```
X: ( tileplayerx - xtiles/2 .... tileplayerx + xtiles/2)
Y: ( tileplayery - ytiles/2 .... tileplayery + ytiles/2)
```

Now we know which tiles in the mapping matrix are visible and should be painted. We must now calculate where in screen space those tiles should be painted. Again, this is relatively straightforward. In a screen-based game, we would project at

```
int screenx=xi*tile_wide;
int screeny=yi*tile_high;
```

which means we are painting the screen as if it was a checkerboard. Now, the checkerboard is larger than the screen, and it slides according to the player's position. Thus, the new transform will be

```
int screenx=xi*tile_wide - playerx;
int screeny=yi*tile_high - playery;
```

There is a caveat to this though. If we implement the previous transform "as is," we are translating by the player's position, which would mean the player is located in the coordinates 0,0 in screen space. This is not usually the case, as players in scrollers are usually placed in the center of the screen. Clearly, the player's coordinates are

```
Screenplayerx=screenx/2
Screenplayery=screeny/2
```

So, the final, correct world-to-screen transform must be

```
int screenx=xi*tile_wide - playerx-screenplayerx;
int screeny=yi*tile_high - playery-screenplayery;
```

And the complete rendering loop must be

```
#define tile_wide 32
#define tile_high 32
#define screen_wide 320
#define screen_high 240
```

```
int beginx= tileplayerx - xtiles/2;
int beginy= tileplayery - ytiles/2;
int endx= tileplayerx + xtiles/2;
int endy= tileplayery + ytiles/2;

tileplayerx= Playerx/tile_wide
tileplayery= Playery/tile_high

int xtiles=screen_wide/tile_wide;
int ytiles=screen_high/tile_high;

for (yi=beginy;yi<endy;yi++)
    {
    for (xi=beginx;xi<endx;xi++)
            {
            int screenx=xi*tile_wide - playerx-screenplayerx;
            int screeny=yi*tile_high - playery-screenplayery;
            int tileid=mapping_matrix [yi][xi];
            blit(tile_table[tileid],screenx,screeny);
            }
    }
```

Notice how I was careful not to impose any restriction on which axis does the scrolling effect. Thus, the preceding code will handle both 2- and 4-way scrollers equally well. If you want to do 2-way only scrolling, you will need to deactivate the superfluous code from the general case explained earlier.

Multilayered Engines

Basic scrollers have been very successful through the years. So successful that a number of variants have been developed for specific scenarios to overcome restrictions imposed by the basic code. We will now see some of them, starting with multilayered engines.

Imagine that we are doing a top-down game that takes place outdoors, in forests and fields. Our art team has created a number of ground tiles to provide variation. The team has also created some great looking trees; so overall, the scenario looks natural and non-repetitive. Clearly, if all the trees can be painted on all the terrains, we will need a large number of combinatory tiles in order to reach the desired variety. For five terrain types and 10 trees, we will be occupying 50 tiles in our precious, limited memory.

This is one of the use cases for multilayered engines, which allow us to encode the mapping in layers of tiles, so we can combine different tiles (such as terrain and trees from the previous paragraph) at a lesser cost. This is a popular method, which can be used if

➤ We need to combine tiles.

➤ We need to move objects over the background.

➤ We want to give the illusion of depth.

Multilayered engines use several mapping matrices to encode the game map. One matrix represents the background, another matrix the trees, and so on. Then, matrices are painted in a parallel fashion, such as:

```
for (yi=beginy;yi<endy;yi++)
        {
        for (xi=beginx;xi<endx;xi++)
                {
                int screenx=xi*tile_wide - playerx-screenplayerx;
                int screeny=yi*tile_high - playery-screenplayery;
                for (layeri=0;layeri<numlayers;layeri++)
                        {
                        int tileid=mapping_matrix [layeri] [yi] [xi];
                        blit(tile_table[tileid],screenx,screeny);
                        }
                }
        }
```

Notice how I assumed that layers are ordered back-to-front in ascending order: 0 is the background, and larger numbers are closer to the viewer.

Also notice in the preceding code that although the first layer (numbered 0) will usually completely cover the screen, those layers in the foreground will mostly be empty. In other words, there will only be a few trees or clouds. So, front layers will need some optimization to ensure we can handle empty tiles efficiently.

The best way to achieve this is to reserve one tile (usually, the first one) as the "empty space" indicator. So, the preceding code can easily be changed into the following code, which will handle empty space, ensuring that we don't waste time painting empty tiles:

```
for (yi=beginy;yi<endy;yi++)
      {
     for (xi=beginx;xi<endx;xi++)
             {
             int screenx=xi*tile_wide - playerx-screenplayerx;
             int screeny=yi*tile_high - playery-screenplayery;
             for (layeri=0;layeri<numlayers;layeri++)
                    {
                    int tileid=mapping_matrix
[layeri][yi][xi];
                    if (tileid>0)
blit(tile_table[tileid],screenx,screeny);
                    }
      }
```

Parallax Scrollers

We have seen how multilayered engines can reduce our memory footprint in some scenarios, but this is only one of their properties. With some extra code, we can convert our plain scroller to a semi-3D approach, which adds a sense of depth and perspective at no extra cost. This is what parallax scrollers are all about.

Parallax is the optical phenomenon described as the apparent displacement of a distant object (with respect to a more distant background) when viewed from two different positions. In other words, if you are driving a car on a highway and you see a fence along the side with mountains on the horizon, the fence seems to move much faster than the mountains. This is due to the fact that perceived object size decreases with the distance to the viewer squared. Thus, apparent movement speeds from distant (but large) objects are smaller than speeds from foreground objects.

Now, imagine that each layer in our tile engine represents one of *x* possible depth values: Layer 0 will represent the mountains, layer 1 the fence, and layer 2 the foreground. If we move the different layers at decreasing speeds (depending on their depth), we could somehow fool the eye and achieve a sense of depth similar to that found in 3D viewing. This technique is what we usually refer to as parallax scrolling: storing depth-layered tiles and moving them at different speeds to convey a sense of depth.

For easier coding, layer 0 is usually the farthest one, so we can paint back-to-front, increasing the movement speed. Then, we only have to move each layer at a different speed so the parallax effect becomes visible. Because we are really not moving the background but instead are moving the player in front of it, one of the easiest ways to code this is by storing several player positions, depending on the layer. The position from layer 0 (mountains) will advance at a set speed, the position from the next layer (fence) will advance faster, and so on. In practical terms, this will make the layers move at different speeds on the screen, and thus create the illusion of depth. Here is a parallax loop in full:

```
if (pressed the right cursor)
    for (layeri=0;layeri<numlayers;layeri++) playerx+=1*(layeri+1);

for (layeri=0;layeri<numlayers;layeri++)
      {
      for (yi=beginy;yi<endy;yi++)
            {
            for (xi=beginx;xi<endx;xi++)
                  {
                  int screenx=xi*tile_wide - playerx[layeri]-
screenplayerx;
                  int screeny=yi*tile_high - playery[layeri]-
screenplayery;
                  int tileid=mapping_matrix [layeri] [yi] [xi];
                  if (tileid>0)
blit(tile_table[tileid],screenx,screeny);
                  }
      }
```

Notice that, as parallax scrollers slide layers on top of others, we choose to make the outer loop cycle through each layer. This way we render the entire first layer before moving on to the next one, making sure order is preserved.

Isometric Engines

Parallax scrollers attempted to convey the illusion of a third dimension by simulating depth. But there is another way to simulate a 3D scenario. It was discovered by architects and industrial designers centuries ago. Using isometric perspective, we can create a convincing 3D effect on a 2D piece of paper, or if we want, in a computer game. The technique was extremely popular in the 1980s, with games such as *Knight Lore* and *Head over Heels* leading the way. It is still in use today, and games such as *Diablo* and many real-time strategy titles are living proof.

Isometric perspective consists of representing an object or game level sideways and from a raised viewpoint, as if it was rotated 45°. It is a parallel perspective, meaning that lines do not converge as in conic perspective projection. Thus, isometric perspective does not suffer from distortion and keeps the object's real proportions and relationships.

Isometric games are coded in a very similar way to regular games. They still use a mapping matrix, a Style Table, and so on. The only changes are that tiles are defined as rhomboids not rectangles, and the screen projection routine is somewhat more complex.

To begin with, tiles for an isometric title are rhomboids, leaving the outer area blank for easy tiling with neighboring tiles. Thus, rendering these tiles requires keeping a transparency mask active at all times. Another characteristic is that these tiles tend to be wider than they are high. The reason for this is that isometric perspective only looks convincing when the viewer is not very high above the ground. Thus, a regular square tile will be converted to a rhomboid with 3×1/6×1 width-height aspect ratio. Several examples using different width-height ratios are shown in Figure 11.2.

Figure 11.2   Isometric tile examples.

Isometric tile rendering must be performed with a different projection routine. We project diagonally on the screen, along the two mapping matrix axes. Here is the source code for the full rendering loop:

```
int i,j;
for (i=LIM;i>-LIM;i--)
        {
        for (j=-LIM;j<LIM;j++)
                {
                int sx=MAXSCREENX/2+(i*TILEWIDE/2)+(j*TILEWIDE/2)-
(TILEWIDE/2);
                int sy=MAXSCREENY/2-(i*TILEHIGH/2)+(j*TILEHIGH/2)-
(TILEHIGH/2);
                sx=sx-lx+ly;
                sy=sy+(lx/3)+(ly/3);

                int orgx=0;
                int orgy=TILEHIGH*(world[px+i][py+j]);
                int tx1=orgx;
                int tx2=orgx+TILEWIDE;
                int ty1=orgy;
                int ty2=orgy+TILEHIGH;

                if ((sx<MAXSCREENX) && (sy<MAXSCREENY) &&
                    (sx+TILEWIDE>0) && (sy+TILEHIGH>0))
                        {
                tiles.render(tx1,ty1,tx2,ty2,sx,sy);
                        }
```

To begin with, we loop from −LIM (a fixed constant) to LIM, so we make sure enough tiles are actually painted to cover the screen. The specific value for LIM will depend on the tile size and screen resolution. In this case, we are working at 640×480, and tiles are 150 pixels wide and 50 pixels high. Thus, we need to loop from −7 to 7 to ensure full screen coverage.

Then, sx and sy are assigned the screen coordinate for the tile being rendered. The equation is simpler than it looks. Let's look at sx first. An increase in the iterator i (used to iterate in X sense of the mapping matrix) causes the next tile to shift TILEWIDE/2 pixels. Tiles are overlapped, and we need to displace by half of the tile width for each X increment. Variations in j (used to loop in Y) produce the same effect. Then, the other two parameters are used to recenter the matrix to the middle of the screen. Now, let's look at sy. A change in X (which is controlled by the iterator i) reduces the *Y* value by a factor of TILEHIGH/2. Think about it: As the matrix is painted sideways, advancing in positive *Y* places tiles closer to the top of the screen, thus decreasing their *Y* value. What happens if we increase the *Y* (by changing the j iterator)? We will then be placing the tile closer to the bottom of the screen, thus adding TILEHIGH/2 for each iteration in j. For additional clarification, see Figure 11.3.

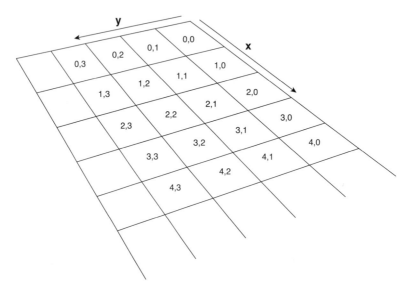

Figure 11.3   Isometric.

Page-Swap Scrollers

Another variant of the classic scrolling algorithm can be used in those games where we want to offer a scrolling playing field without being restricted to a closed set of tiles. Imagine a level that offers the gameplay smoothness of a scroller, but where every single piece of art is indeed unique. Games such as *Baldur's Gate* or the *Monkey Island* saga come to mind as classic examples of page-swap scrolling.

The starting point is to work on the level map as a single image, and then divide it into sectors, much like checkers on a checkerboard. Then, we use the player's position to determine which sectors should be loaded into main memory. The rest are stored on secondary media (hard drive, CD, etc.), but will be swapped into main memory as needed. It is all a matter of ensuring that our disk bandwidth is good enough so that the player does not notice the loading going on in the background. The smaller the rectangle, the less noticeable it will be. The mapper thus resembles a cache memory:

keeping frequently used data within fast reach and swapping it to ensure that we always maintain optimal performance.

There is a specific data structure that can be very helpful when coding this kind of game. It allows us to represent the visible data window and thus pan through a large game map comfortably. The structure is a 2D array, where each node represents one tile of the larger map. The array has a size we will have specified, depending on the preceding parameters, as well as memory constraints. Here is the sample source code:

```
class tile *tileptr;

class pagescroller
        {
        tileptr **matrix;
        int sizex,sizey;
        int cornerx,cornery;
};
```

Notice that we store the matrix itself but also need two attributes that help us map the window to the game world. cornerx and cornery tell us where the upper-left corner of the matrix should be placed in the whole map.

Also notice that the double pointer is just used to declare a dynamic-size 2D matrix of pointers to sectors. We use pointers so we can shift the whole matrix just by doing some pointer assigns, not really copying data, which would be too slow. For example, here is the routine used to shift the whole matrix as we advance to higher *X* values:

```
for (int iy=0;iy<sizey-1;iy++)
        {
        aux=matrix[iy][0];  // the first element is really thrown away
for (int ix=0;ix<sizex-1;ix++)
        {
                matrix[iy][ix]=matrix[iy][ix+1];
                }
        matrix[iy][sizex-1]=aux;
        Fill matrix[iy][sizex-1] with new data from the sector
appearing in high X
        }
```

It is good to note how we wrap the deleted column around so it appears on the opposite end and is reassigned the newly loaded data. This way we avoid having to call `delete` and `new`, which is always costly.

Some techniques that can improve the performance of these scrollers have to do with the format of the graphics also. If your game runs at a very high resolution, the screen updates will need to take place more frequently, because the user will pan through a bigger data set. Similarly, using more colors can reduce performance. Files will become larger and loading times will increase. The last factor we need to keep in mind is the velocity of the player. Clearly, a walking character will traverse the game world at a slower pace than a jet fighter, simplifying the loading routines. Fast players in page-swap scrollers require lots of reloading.

Special Effects

In the early years of 2D gaming, titles were simple sprite renderers with little or no visual enhancements. These were the years of very restrictive hardware, where every call to `PutPixel` was counted in clock cycles. As years passed and hardware evolved, programmers began implementing special effects (sometimes referred to as eye candy), so games looked better than the competition. In this section, I will provide a list of common effects that have become classic through the years. They are all very easy to code and will greatly enhance any 2D game.

Palette Effects

Most graphics displays from the old days were palletized, offering between 16 and 256 colors. Those systems didn't have very good access time to the frame buffer (or did not have a frame buffer), so sometimes effects had to be coded without directly accessing the screen memory. The most popular of those effects were implemented by manipulating, not the screen itself, but the hardware color palette that controlled how colors were displayed onscreen. A palette was usually composed of 256 entries; each consisting of three bytes (red, green, and blue). So altering the palette was much faster than having to write to the frame buffer.

A good example of this family of effects can be found in the popular fade-in and fade-out routines present in many games. To ease the transitions, these games progressively illuminated (or switched off) the screen, so colors appeared smoothly. This would be a really simple effect in a true-color game. Take a look at the following fade-out routine, which works on a fictitious true-color screen. Each pixel represents an RGB triplet in byte format, thus representing the full 24-bit spectrum:

```
for (ix=0;ix<SCREENX;ix++)
      {
      for (iy=0;iy<SCREENX;iy++)
            {
            color col=screenarray[ix][iy];
            if (col.r>0) col.r--;
            if (col.g>0) col.g--;
            if (col.b>0) col.b--;
            screenarray[ix][iy]=col;
            }
      }
```

Notice that this loop is computationally expensive. It depends on the screen resolution; and even on a low-resolution setting like 320×200 pixels, it would take 64,000 loop iterations to achieve the effect. Now, assume the screen is palletized, and each pixel is represented by a single byte that points to a hardware palette. Again, the palette will be composed of RGB byte triplets. Then, we could save some precious clock cycles by using an alternative loop such as this one:

```
for (ip=0;ip<NUMCOLORS;ip++)
      {
      color col=palette[ip];
      if (col.r>0) col.r--;
      if (col.g>0) col.g--;
      if (col.b>0) col.b--;
      palette[ip]=col;
      }
```

This loop is much faster and does not depend on the screen resolution. Because the palette is implemented in hardware, changing it will immediately affect all the pixels on screen regardless of how many pixels are affected. Here is the full source code of a fade-out routine written in C++, using the PC-VGA graphics architecture as a starting point:

```
void GetPaletteEntry(unsigned char id, unsigned char &r, unsigned
char &g, unsigned char &b)
{
outp(0x03C7,id);
r=inp(0x03C9);
g=inp(0x03C9);
b=inp(0x03C9);
}

void SetPaletteEntry(unsigned char id, unsigned char r, unsigned
char g, unsigned char b)
{
outp(0x03C8,id);
inp(0x03C9,r);
inp(0x03C9,g);
inp(0x03C9,b);
}


void FadeOut()
{
unsigned char r,g,b;

for (int isteps=0;isteps<64;isteps++)
        {
        WaitVSync();
        for (int ipal=0;ipal<256;ipal++)
                {
                GetPaletteEntry(ipal,r,g,b);
                if (r>0) r--;
                if (g>0) g--;
                if (b>0) b--;
                SetPaletteEntry(ipal,r,g,b);
                }
        }
}
```

Notice how the VGA frame buffer was accessed by reading and writing to specific ports. Port 0×3C7 was used to request a palette read, and port 0×3C8 was used for palette writes. These routines, which I have presented here in C++, were usually hard-coded in assembly language for improved performance. In addition, I call the routine `WaitVSync` to make sure we change palette colors only when the screen is not being accessed by the electron beam. Failing to do so would result in flicker. Finally, the outer loop runs for 64 iterations because 64 was the maximum value of R, G, and B values in the VGA palette.

A fade-in routine could be implemented in a similar way. We only need a persistent palette in main memory, and the routine will increment the hardware palette progressively until it matches the persistent version. Here is the full source code:

```
void FadeIn()
{
unsigned char r,g,b;

for (int isteps=0;isteps<64;isteps++)
    {
    WaitVSync();
    for (int ipal=0;ipal<256;ipal++)
        {
        GetPaletteEntry(ipal,r,g,b);
        if (r<palette[ipal].r) r++;
        if (g<palette[ipal].g) g++;
        if (b<palette[ipal].b) b++;
        SetPaletteEntry(ipal,r,g,b);
        }
    }
}
```

We have seen how some clever palette handling can implement fade-ins and fade-outs. But there is much more we can achieve using palettes. Now, I will focus on one of the most popular effects used in countless games, technology demos, and so on in the 1980s. The effect is generally called a *palette rotation* and can be used in many scenarios, from drawing flowing water to creating animated textures.

The trick is to realize that, if we change some palette entries, we can produce color changes in sprites that look like real animation. I will begin with a simple palette effect and afterward show a general-case palette rotation trick. Imagine that we want to produce a semaphore with a red and green light. In order to render the right color, depending on the state of the semaphore, we could simply paint a colored sprite on top of the semaphore graphic, which represents either a green walking character or a red stop sign. But we can achieve the same effect with only one sprite and some clever palette tricks. To better understand this technique, take a look at Figure 11.4. Here, we reserve four palette entries for the semaphore sprite. The first color (labeled 1) will be used for the semaphore and will be a yellow hue. The second (2) will be the background color for the semaphore, generally black. The third color will be used to render the green walking character, and the fourth color will be used for the red stop sign. Instead of repainting the screen with sprites, we only paint the semaphore once, and then manipulate palette entries 3 and 4 to modify the semaphore. To make the semaphore appear in the green state, we put green as the third palette color and leave the fourth color black. Inversely, turning the traffic light red only requires putting red as the fourth color, leaving the third one black.

Figure 11.4   Traffic light.

We have saved precious clock cycles, because we only need to render the semaphore light. But there is a downside to all this. We are manipulating palette entries 3 and 4, which will need to be reserved for this traffic light. If we have two semaphores, we will need more palette entries, or the semaphores will be in sync because they will share the palette.

Now, let's extend this core idea to a more complex situation. Let's imagine that we want to paint a river with animated water. I am not thinking about real-time, reflective water. All we need is some animated water such as the kind found in many 8-bit games. We will use the same technique as we did for the semaphore, but extend it a bit. For example, let's reserve six palette entries, which we will use to store different hues of water color. Initially, the entry labeled 1 will contain very deep blue, and entry number 6 will hold a light blue color. Then, if we rotate the colors in these six palette entries, all sprites using those colors will keep on changing. If we draw them carefully, water animation will seem to appear. It is all a matter of artistic talent: being able to imagine how a sprite will evolve as we rotate its colors. In Figure 11.5, you can see a larger-than-life version of the sprite I will be using. You can also see a waterfall as rendered using this technique. Although these effects look simplistic in today's cutting edge graphics cards, some of these concepts might prove useful even today, because they provide a simple, cheap way of cheating the eye and conveying a sense of motion.

Figure 11.5 Water sprite.

Palette rotation tricks were used for water, lava, fire, neon glows, and countless other tricks. Once you master the core technique, it is really easy to adapt it to many situations. Surely, the next time you play an old-school game you will discover many of its incarnations.

Stippling Effects

Another interesting technique you can use in 2D games is *stippling*. A stipple is just a simple patterned texture that combines one color (generally black or grey) with the transparency index. This way, rendering a stipple on top of another sprite covers it in part, creating a rather convincing illusion of shadow. All you have to do is

1. Render the background

2. Using the transparency index, render the stipple

3. Render the character

If you follow these simple steps, the shadow of the character will effectively look as if it is blended with the background: Some areas will look darker than others, and so on. Stippling looks especially good in high resolutions. The pattern is almost indistinguishable, and the blending becomes smoother.

There are many other uses for stippling. For example, you can implement varying-density fog by using several stippling patterns (with different densities). To achieve this, you will need to reverse the rendering order, so you actually do the following:

1. Render the background.

2. Render the character.

3. Using the transparency index, render the stipple.

This way the character will also be immersed in the fog.

Another interesting use of stippling is to illuminate parts of the scene, for example, the trail of an explosion or a torch in the ground. Here, the stippling pattern must be colored as the light source (yellow, orange). By painting the stipple, the background will seem to illuminate, with more light at the center of the stippling pattern.

In addition, stippling has been broadly used in fog-of-war techniques. These techniques are used in real-time strategy games, where only the part of the map where the player has actually explored is shown, and the rest is covered in fog—the closer the area, the less dense the fog. Stippling patterns have been used in games such as *Warcraft* and *Age of Empires* for the PC to implement fog-of-war. As a summary, you can see a variety of stippling effects in Figure 11.6.

Figure 11.6 Stipples.

Glenzing

Stippling is nothing but a poor man's transparency. But we can do more to simulate transparency effects, whether it's a shadow, light, or fog-of-war. The technique we will be using is called *glenzing*, and it allows us to really mix colors as if we were painting a partially transparent object. In the end, it all boils down to some palette handling tricks, but the results will be quite convincing, usually better than those achieved by simple stippling.

Basically, glenzing converts a color interpolation, such as the ones required to compute semitransparent objects, into a palette value interpolation. If you wanted to paint a semitransparent object on top of another, opaque object, you would mix both objects' colors according to an opacity index. The resulting color would be

```
Color=Color_transparent*opacity + Color_opaque*(1-opacity)
```

Now, we simply cannot do that in a palletized world. But we can do something similar. Imagine that we lay out our palette so that for each semitransparent object, we have some extra palette positions that are reserved for transparency effects. If the transparent object is blue, and the background is red, we will make sure we have a position with some sort of magenta to be used when both objects collide.

Several glenzing methods exist. The most popular substitutes the sprite or triangle-rendering core with one that looks up the current frame buffer value and increments it by the new fragment's palette value. The code would be

```
set the palette
paint the base object
paint the semi-transparent object
      for each pixel, read the frame-buffer value
      add the second object's palette value
      write the pixel back
```

Then, we must make sure the palette is cleverly laid out to guarantee that proper transparency colors are generated.

Fire

Fire can be simulated using a variety of techniques. It can be an animated sprite painted by hand, so it loops properly. Or, it can use some kind of 2D particle system (see Chapter 19, "Particle Systems," for more on particle systems). But in the 2D era, the word "fire" didn't really refer to the previous options. Fire was extensively used in menus, special effects, and so on using a cellular automata on the frame buffer. As you might already know, a cellular automata is an automata consisting of a number of cells running in parallel whose behavior is governed by neighboring cells. They have been used to simulate life, and in the '80s, they were the best way to create fire.

Essentially, the effect consists of defining an area that will work as the fire emitter. This could be the bottom of the screen, some text, a drawing, and so on. Then, each frame pixel belonging to the emitter is initialized to the pure white fire color. This made each pixel in the emitter glow and flicker. All that was needed were some flames, which is what the cellular automata did. Let's consider each pixel as a cell in our automata, continuously executing the following algorithm (assume we are working on pixel (x,y)):

```
color(x,y) = (color (x,y+1) + color (x+1,y+1) + color (x-1,y+1))/3
```

This rather minimal routine simply computes a pixel's new color as the average of the colors of the three pixels below it. This makes fire rise above the emitter, and because the emitter's colors are somewhat random, the averages inherit this randomness and produce a somewhat chaotic living effect.

Fire was usually mapped on palletized modes. The palette was occupied entirely or in part with a gradient of colors suitable for fire, from whites to reds and oranges. Thus, averaging colors was really a process of averaging color indices. Here is a full example of a fire effect that is emitted by the bottom of the screen (y=SCREENY-1) and climbs vertically. I assume a 256-color palette, with the first entry being used for pure white colors, which fade to yellow, orange, red, and finally black as we traverse the palette.

```
// generate new sparks
for (int i=0;i<SCREENX/2;i++)
        {
        int x=rand()%SCREENX;
        int col=rand()%25;
        PutPixel(x,SCREENY-1,col);
        }

// recompute fire
for (int ix=0;ix<SCREENX;ix++)
        {
        for (int iy=0;iy<SCREENY;iy++)
```

```
                    {
                    unsigned char col=(GetPixel(ix-1,iy+1) +
GetPixel(ix,iy+1) + GetPixel(ix+1,iy+1)) / 3;
                    PutPixel (ix,iy,col);
                    }
          }
```

As you might have guessed, fire was an expensive effect, because it needed the whole screen to be recalculated at each frame. Sometimes the effect was confined to a specific area to avoid recalculating the whole screen and keep the focus on the fire-accessible area only.

In Closing

Looking back at the techniques that made 2D games so popular, you cannot help but feel a sense of respect for the professionals that crafted them and admiration for those who still use these ideas today. Platforms were much harder to code back then.

On the other hand, this difficulty is what made coding so much fun: having to be creative to get a faster fade-in routine or simulate more colors than you actually had. It was all about challenges and creative people trying to confront them.

Chapter 12

3D Pipeline Overview

KEY TOPICS

- A First Look
- Fundamental Data Types
- Geometry Formats
- A Generic Graphics Pipeline
- In Closing

"Show me how you do that trick... the one that makes me scream" – she said

The Cure

The advent of powerful consumer-level 3D accelerators has increased the expressive potential of games at the cost of higher development complexity. Graphics engines have evolved from simple sprite painting routines to real-time geometry processors; their complexity spiraling up to rival high-end CAD systems and military simulations.

In this new scenario, getting the graphics code right is probably the biggest challenge any development team will face. Developers must be able to create the illusion of immersion and reality at interactive frame rates. The complexity (and hence, the beauty) of the problem comes from the fact that each game poses new challenges and requires specific techniques. But some global coding ideas can be shared between most 3D games, making the design and coding of graphics subsystems feasible and cost-manageable.

We can imagine any 3D engine as a sequence of operations performed on incoming geometry, from the moment it's loaded from secondary storage to the moment part of it is displayed on screen. This process resembles a pipeline consisting of different segments: Geometry is pumped in through one end. Then, each pipe segment has a unique filter that is applied to the incoming stream (eliminating unseen data, illuminating it, and so on). After a number of stages, the surviving geometry exits through the opposite end of the pipeline, where it is displayed onscreen. It is thus common to refer to this process as the 3D graphics pipeline and to the data as the geometry stream.

This chapter provides a first look at the design and coding of 3D pipelines. We will analyze the global data structures and algorithms required to deliver the geometry stream to the 3D hardware efficiently. We will present a global pipeline framework, which we can use to build a wide range of simple games.

More elaborate titles will require using more advanced algorithms that deal with very specific problems: rendering organic geometry, indoor scenarios, and so on. We will explore those subjects in subsequent chapters. By using all this information combined, you should have a deep understanding of how commercial graphics engines are designed and coded.

A First Look

If you want to design and code 3D game engines, it is essential that you fully understand one fundamental truth that determines the way games are written. This theorem states: "No matter how powerful the target platform is, you will always need more."

Game development is an innovative craft. Each game version must be better than the last one. Thus, you will always need more memory than you actually have, require better sound cards, and as far as this chapter is concerned, employ more and better graphics. If you can draw six million triangles per second, you will want to draw nine million, and so forth. In fact, games are one of the main reasons that keep computer hardware evolving so quickly. If you think about it, most of the standard applications do not have very restrictive hardware requirements.

But we need to restrain our ambition. Blue-sky thinking works great as a design tool, but as we try to put our design into actual running code, we need to be realistic and learn to discard the most extreme concepts. The hardware progression is sadly limited, and frequently, we will have ideas whose time will not have arrived yet. So writing games is a craft that involves prioritizing and selecting, and being able to transform your wild design ideas into working code that can be executed on the target platform at an interactive frame rate.

Fundamental Data Types

3D pipelines are built on top of a number of basic data types, which are common regardless of the API in use. In the following sections, a concise list is provided, which should provide some "common ground" for the rest of the book.

Vertices

Vertices are usually stored in XYZ coordinates in a sequential manner. The most frequent format uses the float type, which provides enough precision for most uses. Some applications will require using doubles for special calculations, but most of today's graphic processing units (GPUs) will only use floats as their internal format.

Vertices are of little use individually. But in a serial way, they can be used to explicitly enumerate the vertices of a 3D object. A list of vertices can be interpreted, taking them in triplets as a sequence of triangles composing a 3D solid mesh. So the representation would be something like this:

Triangle 0, 1st vertex

Triangle 0, 2nd vertex

Triangle 0, 3rd vertex

Triangle 1, 1st vertex

Triangle 1, 2nd vertex

Triangle 1, 3rd vertex

(…)

Triangle N-1, 1st vertex

Triangle N-1, 2nd vertex

Triangle N-1, 3rd vertex

A variant of this method can be used for primitives with triangles that share vertices between their faces. Take a cube from (-1,-1,-1) to (1,1,1), for example. As you already know, a cube consists of 8 vertices and 6 faces, totaling 12 triangles. Using our initial approach, we would code this cube by enumerating the 3 vertices of each one of the 12 faces. This would yield a list of 36 entries. Because each vertex is 3 floats, and a float is 4 bytes, we have a total memory footprint for the cube of 36×3×4 = 432 bytes.

Indexed Primitives

Now, let's follow a different approach. We are repeating the same vertices many times in the list using this initial representation. A single vertex can appear as many as six times because it belongs to different triangles (see Figure 12.1). To avoid this repetition, let's put the vertices in a list (with no repetition), and then use a second list to express the topology of the faces. We will then have two lists: The first one will contain exactly eight vertices (remember, no repetition). The second one will be a list of the face loops required to build the cube. For each triangle, we will write down not the vertices themselves, but the position on the first list where they can be found.

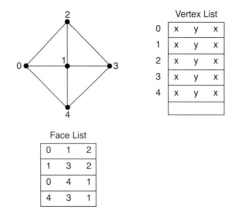

Figure 12.1 A sample mesh with its vertex and face lists.

This second list is called the *index list* because it provides you with the indices of the vertices for each face. If we are coding a cube, the index list will be 36 elements long (12 faces, each with 3 vertices). Each element will be a 16-bit unsigned integer value. Now we are ready to do some math and compare the results of the classic versus indexed coding. For this new variant, we will have

8 vertices, taking up 8×3×4 bytes = 96 bytes total

36 short integers, taking up 36×2 = 72 bytes total

So, the whole cube will take up 96 + 72 = 168 bytes, which is roughly 40 percent of what it would require using the classic method. These results can be extrapolated to higher complexity meshes, with triangle indexing cutting the memory footprint in half, approximately.

Triangle indexing is a very good technique to use to reduce memory footprint for your games. Most 3D packages can directly export indexed primitives, which you can plug into your engine. Indexing is essential for economizing memory in memory-limited platforms (read: all of them), but is also relevant to your engine's performance. Do not forget that data transfer through the bus has a cost, which depends on the amount of data. Thus, sending half the data is approximately twice as fast. Moreover, this technique has an additional advantage: Most graphics cards and applications have internal support for indexed primitives, so it all becomes a cradle-to-the-grave solution. All phases in the pipeline can work with this efficient strategy, yielding an overall improvement on the performance and the memory use at zero CPU cost.

They say every rose has its thorn, so it shouldn't surprise us that this technique has a potential problem. As you will soon see, texture coordinates and materials, which are essential to convey a sense of realism, are applied to vertices on a triangle basis. Imagine a vertex shared by two faces that have different material identifiers and texture coordinates depending on the triangle you are looking at. Handling these situations in an indexed list is an additional burden. You need to reenter the vertex in the vertex list as many times as the different "impersonations" it appears under. If it's shared between four triangles, each one with different texture coordinates and materials, that vertex must appear as many as four times in your vertex list.

Quantization

Vertex indexing can reduce the memory hit in 3D meshes at no cost. There is no CPU overhead involved, nor does the data suffer any loss of quality in the process. Now we will explore a different technique aimed in the same direction. This time we will be using a *lossy* technique (meaning some quality will be lost along the way). Under the right circumstances, we will be able to minimize the loss and achieve additional gain, keeping a very good quality. The method is *data quantization*.

The core idea behind quantization is very simple: Keep the data compressed in memory, and uncompress it whenever you need to use it. In fact, quantization is really the name of the compression scheme, but the overall compress-in-memory philosophy could be implemented with other compression schemes as well. The reason it's called quantization is because this specific compression technique is very fast, so it can be used in real-time applications. Decompressing a different format (say, ZIP files) would definitely have a significant processing time, which makes it less attractive to game developers.

Quantizing can be defined as storing values in lower precision data types, thus saving precious space in the process. You can downsample a double to a float, and you will be taking up half the memory space. You will have lost bits of precision along the way, but in many cases, that extra precision conveyed little or no information anyway, so the results look almost identical. However, quantizing does not usually involve doubles and floats. Those types have good precision and usually can fit any value perfectly. Quantizing has more to do with coding floats into unsigned shorts (16 bits) or even unsigned bytes (8 bits).

For example, imagine that you want to store the geometry for a human being. You have modeled him in a 3D package and centered his feet in the origin. Thus, you can expect him to be bound by a box 2 meters high, 80 centimeters wide, and maybe 50 centimeters deep. In other words, the vertex coordinates you will be storing are (assuming you model in meters):

X (wide): -0.40 .. 0.40

Y (tall):   0.. 2

Z (deep): -0.25 .. 0.25

Then, if you store each vertex coordinate in a floating-point value, chances are you will be using IEEE 754-compliant floats (IEEE is the Institute of Electrical and Electronics Engineers, and 754 is the name of the standard). Under this standard, a floating-point value is encoded in a 32-bit sequence consisting of:

1 bit for the sign (s)

8 bits for the exponent (e)

23 bits for the mantissa (m)

As a result of this coding scheme, the range of the float type is, as specified in the standard:

```
+- (3.4E-38 to 3.4E+38)
```

which means you can represent incredibly small and very large numbers on both the positive and negative ends of the spectrum. But we don't need to encode a huge number. We are only trying to encode numbers in a 2-meter range at most. So, do we really need to occupy that much storage space?

Let's try a different way. Take a smaller precision data type (shorts or bytes usually) and encode the floating-point coordinates into that data type. For example, to encode numbers in the range from MINVALUE to MAXVALUE, we could do the following:

```
Compressed_value=Compressed_type_size*(original_value-
minvalue)/(maxvalue-minvalue)
```

This would map the float value range limited by MIN and MAX linearly to the compressed type. For example, to encode the Y value of our human model into unsigned shorts (16 bits), we would do the following, because an unsigned short is in the range of 0 to 65535 ($2^{16} - 1$):

```
Compressed_value=65536*(original_value-0)/(2-0)
```

Using this approach, we would divide by two the memory requirements for our geometry, but would lose some precision in the process. If we do the math, we will see that the loss of precision is relatively small. Generally speaking, the precision of a quantization will be

```
Precision = (MAXVALUE-MINVALUE)/Compressed_type_size
```

which in this case yields a precision of:

```
Precision = 2/65535= 0,00003
```

This is about three hundredths of a millimeter. We can even compress this into a byte, yielding the following:

```
Compressed_value=255×(original_value-0)/(2-0)
Precision = 2/256 = 0,007 meters
```

So the maximum error we can incur when compressing is about 7 millimeters, which is quite likely acceptable for many uses.

The decompression routine (sometimes called "reconstruction") is again relatively simple and follows the equation:

```
Reconstructed_value=Precision*compressed_value+Min_value
```

There are several strategies for both compression and reconstruction that have slightly different results and side effects. The one I recommend using is called the *TC method* (because it *truncates* and then *centers*). Scale to the desired value (in the following example, a byte) and truncate the floating point to an integer. Then, to decode, decompress by adding 0.5 to make each decompressed value stay in the middle of its interval:

```
unsigned char encodeTC (float input)
{
float value = (input-input_min)/(input_max-input_min);
unsigned char = (int)(value * 255);
return result;
}

float decodeTC(int encoded)
{
float value= (float)(encoded + 0.5f)/255;
return value* (input_max - input_min) + input_min;
}
```

Color

3D games mainly use the RGB (or RGBA) color space. For simple applications and demos, using floating-point values is again the format of choice. Using floats is handy if you need to work with software illumination algorithms or need to do color interpolation. Usually, floats are restricted to the range from 0 to 1 in each of the three components, with black being (0,0,0) and white being (1,1,1). The other color spaces, such as Hue-Saturation-Brightness, Cyan-Magenta-Yellow, and so on are mostly useful when working in printed media or to perform image-processing algorithms. So, they are used in games only on very few occasions.

Coding colors in float values is somehow an excess. If you remember the explanation about quantization, the same ideas can be applied here: We have way too much range and precision, which we are not taking advantage of. Also, with RGB screens working in 24-bit modes, it doesn't make much sense to deliver color values to the GPU in anything but bytes. Any additional bits of information will be discarded, so the extra precision provided by floats will not make any difference in the final output. Additionally, colors coded as bytes are internally supported by most APIs and GPUs, so no decompression/reconstruction is required. Again, we have a winning strategy with no undesired side effects.

In some special cases, you will work with BGR (and consequently, BGRA) formats. This is a regular RGB stream where you must swap the red and blue bytes before displaying. BGR colors are used for historical reasons in some applications and texture formats—one being the very popular *Targa* texture format. Always keep this in mind if you don't want inaccurate colors onscreen. As a helper, some APIs, like OpenGL, support these new formats internally as well, so no manual swapping is really required.

In addition, some applications do not use color but instead use luminance values. For example, you might want to store only the grayscale value of the color so you can use it for static lighting. By doing so, you are losing the chromatic information, but you can save even more memory. However, you will need to decompress in a full RGB triplet if your API of choice cannot use luminance data directly.

Alpha

Alpha encodes transparency and can be associated with the color value to obtain a 32-bit RGBA value. The transparency value can either be used per vertex or per pixel by embedding it into texture maps. In both cases, the rule to follow is that the lower the value, the less opacity: Zero alpha would be completely invisible. Alphas closer to 1 (in floats) or 255 (in bytes) designate opaque items that will not let the light pass through them.

Using alpha values embedded into texture maps should be kept to a minimum because they will make your textures grow by one fourth. If you need to do a map with constant alpha (such as a glass window, for example), you can save precious memory by using a regular RGB map and specifying alpha per vertex instead. If you think about it, you will find similar strategies to ensure that you only use alpha in a texture map whenever it's absolutely necessary.

Texture Mapping

Texture mapping is used to increase the visual appeal of a scene by simulating the appearance of different materials, such as stone, metal, and so on, using pictures that are then mapped to the geometry. Thus, two separate issues must be dealt with. First, we must specify which texture map we will use for each primitive. Second, we need to know how the texture will wrap around it.

Textures are specified by using numerical identifiers. So each of your texture maps is assigned at load time a unique identifier that you must use in order to make it current. These texture maps are assigned per face, so every triangle has a single texture map that covers it fully. An interesting side effect is that a single vertex can indeed have more than one texture. Imagine a vertex that is shared between two faces, each having different materials. The vertex will have a different texture identifier (and probably texturing coordinates) depending on the face you are looking at.

Sometimes we will be able to layer several textures in the same primitive to simulate a combination of them. For example, we could have a base brick texture and a second map layered on top to create dirt. This technique (called *multitexturing* or *multipass rendering*) will be explored in Chapter 17, "Shading." It is one of the most powerful tools used to create great looking results.

Now you know how textures are specified. However, the same texture can be applied in a variety of ways to the geometry, as shown in Figure 12.2. Let's stop for a second to understand how textures are mapped onto triangles. Essentially, we need to specify where in the texture map each triangle vertex will be located, so by stretching the texture according to these texturing coordinates, it is applied to the triangle. Each vertex is assigned a pair of coordinates that index the texture map's surface fully. These coordinates, which are commonly referred to as (U,V), map that vertex to a virtual texture space. By defining three (U,V) pairs (one per vertex), you can define the mapping of a triangle. Texture mapping coordinates are usually stored as floats in the range (0,1). This makes them ideal candidates for quantization and compression.

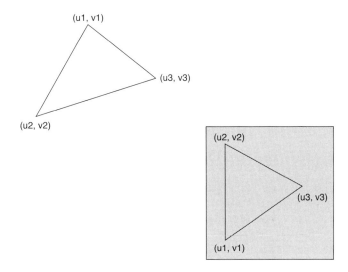

Figure 12.2 Texture mapping explained.

In most cases, you will want to specify texture coordinates manually, taking them from a 3D modeling package. But some special effects will require these coordinates to be evaluated on the fly. One such example is environment mapping, which is a technique that allows you to create the illusion of reflection by applying the texture not directly to the surface but as a "reflection map." In these situations, coordinates might be manually computed by your game engine or, in most cases, by the API. We will see more of these advanced uses when we talk about shading techniques in Chapter 17.

Geometry Formats

Once all the fundamental data types have been laid out, it is time to move one notch higher in the abstraction scale and concentrate on how we will deliver the geometry stream to the graphics subsystem. It is essential to understand the different geometry packing methods because performance will largely depend on them. The same engine can achieve x2 performance, just by packing the geometry in an optimal way. Additionally, understanding geometry formats will yield lower memory footprints, which is a must for most games.

As mentioned earlier, our geometry stream will consist of five data types: vertices, normals, texture coordinates, colors, and optionally, indices to them to avoid repetition. Generally, I'll describe the geometry formats in an encoded way, similar to that used in chemistry. As a first example, the following format means three floats per vertex, two floats per texture coordinate, three floats per normal, and three floats per color:

```
V3f T2f N3f C3f
```

This takes up 132 bytes per triangle, which is quite a lot. You can choose to pre-illuminate vertices, and thus skip the normal information. This eliminates the option of dynamic lighting, but saves lots of space: A V3f T2f N0 C3f format takes 96 bytes per triangle.

Other options allow us to reduce memory footprint even more. We can quantize the different data values until we reach this aggressive configuration, which takes only 18 bytes per vertex:

```
V3b T2b N0 C1b
```

Notice how vertices and texture coordinates have been quantized, normals have been skipped completely, and we have stored the color information in bytes, using the luminance channel only.

Also notice how indexing can significantly reduce these memory footprints due to vertex sharing. An indexed mesh usually takes between 40 and 60 percent of the space used by the original data set, so it always pays off in terms of performance and memory usage.

A Generic Graphics Pipeline

The first part of the chapter dealt in detail with the data types and structures we will be using in our graphics engines. Now it is time to move on and describe the algorithms we will need to render the data efficiently. This is a vast subject, and we will be discussing it in the following three chapters as well. So, I will begin by describing a global framework for a graphics pipeline, from which any specific graphics engine can be built by refining the desired components.

Generally speaking, we can decompose any 3D pipeline in four stages:

- ➤ Visibility determination
    - ➤ Clipping
    - ➤ Culling
    - ➤ Occlusion testing
- ➤ Resolution determination
    - ➤ LOD analysis
- ➤ Transform, lighting
- ➤ Rasterization

By combining these processes, we can make sure we paint the desired scenario at a frame rate suitable for real-time games. By refining the design of each component (and the relationships between them), we can achieve a broad result spectrum.

Clipping

Clipping is the process of eliminating unseen geometry by testing it against a clipping volume, such as the screen. If the test fails, we can discard that geometry because we will know for sure it will not be seen. Obviously, the clipping test must be faster than drawing the primitives in order for clipping to provide a significant speedup. If it took us longer to decide whether to paint or not to paint the primitive, clipping would be an unneeded burden.

There are several ways to do clipping for games, depending on how early in the pipeline you perform the test. In general, it is important to clip geometry as soon as we can in the graphics pipeline, so we can reduce data transfer to the GPU, and ultimately, the rasterization of unseen primitives.

Clipping can provide a very significant speedup to any graphics engine. But exact results vary between different clipping methods (and engine types). For example, a game like *Tekken*, where most of the geometry is visible all the time, will not benefit from clipping. As a corollary, games with small, spatially localized data sets will not be able to eliminate lots of geometry in a clipping pass. This would apply to fighting games, but also to many other genres.

Let's look at a more favorable case to see the real benefit of clipping. Consider a 3D game that takes place in the XZ plane, such as most first-person shooters (FPS), driving simulators, and so on. Here, we are surrounded by geometry that extends in all directions in a more or less homogeneous way. This is the ideal scenario for a clipping algorithm: large, homogeneous levels that we can traverse freely. The reason is simple: In this case, lots of geometry will be outside the clipping volume behind our back or to the sides.

For example, imagine that you want to clip against your camera to discard unseen primitives. The camera has a horizontal aperture of 60°, which would be pretty much standard. Taking an average case, we would be seeing 60/360 of our full level, so only one of every six primitives would be processed. This means that we can concentrate on 17 percent of the geometry and discard the remaining 83 percent of the data. Clearly, clipping makes a big difference in this case. All games with large levels, such as role playing games (RPGs), FPSs, real-time strategy (RTS) games, space simulators, driving games, and so on, will yield equally interesting results.

Now that we know clipping can provide a very significant performance boost to our engine, let's explore how clipping can be implemented.

Triangle Clipping

We will start by clipping each and every triangle prior to rasterizing it, and thus discard those that lie completely outside of the clipping frustum. Again, this only makes sense if the triangle clipping is significantly faster than the rasterization process. However, even if this is the case, the triangle-level test will not provide very good results. But let's discuss it for a second because it will provide some useful concepts for more advanced methods.

You should know that almost all current graphics accelerators provide triangle-level clipping tests for the frame buffer. This means that you can safely send all your geometry to the graphics chip, where nonvisible fragments will be discarded. Thus, only visible portions will take up processing time in the rasterization engine.

You might think that you will get great performance with no coding because the hardware clipper will get rid of unseen triangles. Unfortunately, great performance rarely comes for free. Hardware clipping your triangles is a good idea, but you will need some code to ensure top performance. The reason is simple: In order to decide whether to paint or not paint a triangle, you must send it to the graphics chip, where it will be tested. This means your triangle (whether it's seen or not) will travel through the data bus, which is slow.

However, clipping geometry at the triangle level requires sending it through the bus to the graphics card, which is where the clipping is performed. In other words, using triangle-level clipping forces us to send lots of invisible triangles to the card, just to be clipped there. Clearly, we are not using the bus very efficiently. This is where object-level clipping can help.

Object Clipping

As mentioned earlier, triangle clipping is limited by the bus speed. So, we will need a new method that allows us to clip the geometry before it is sent to the graphics card. Additionally, this method must work on a higher abstraction level than triangles. Software testing each triangle is too slow for rich, real-time games that display millions of triangles per second.

The preferred approach is, obviously, to work on an object level. Rejecting a complete object, which is possible in the thousands of triangles, with a simple test will provide the speed boost we are aiming for. Essentially, we will decompose our scene into a list of objects and test each one as if it were a fundamental primitive for clipping. As you will soon see, some easy tests can tell us if a whole object is completely invisible so we can discard it. For those objects that lie completely or partially within the clipping volume, hardware triangle clipping will automatically be used.

This approach is not limited to objects in the "game logic" sense of the word. We can cut any large geometry block into spatially localized chunks and consider them as objects for our clipping routines. This is especially helpful for level geometry processing. We can cut the complete area into rooms, including walls and ceilings, and reject nonvisible data very quickly.

The core idea behind object clipping is simple: For each object, compute a simpler volume that can quickly be clipped. This volume will represent the boundary of the object. Thus, performing the test on the volume will provide an easy rejection test.

Sometimes, the bounding volume will be visible but the object won't, yielding a "false positive." But the benefits clearly outperform the added cost of these false positives.

So why don't we use the actual geometry for the clipping test? The answer is that regardless of the clipping strategy you used, you would end up with a computational cost that would depend (in terms of cost) on the geometry complexity. For instance, testing a 1,000-triangle object would be faster than testing a 10,000-triangle object, and that's an unpleasant side effect.

Bounding volumes provide us with constant-cost clipping methods, so we can keep a stable frame rate regardless of the object's inner complexity. Many bounding objects can be used, but spheres and boxes are by far the most common. Let's study their properties and tests in detail.

Bounding Spheres

A bounding sphere is defined by its center and radius. Given the six clipping planes mentioned earlier, rejecting a sphere is very easy. Let's start with a single plane, represented by the equation:

```
Ax + By + Cz + D = 0
```

where A,B,C are the normalized components of the plane normal, and D is defined using A,B,C and a point in the plane.

For a sphere with its center in SC and radius SR, the following test:

```
A · SCx + B · Scy + C · SCz + D < -SR
```

returns true if (and only if) the sphere lies completely in the hemispace opposite the plane normal, and false otherwise. You can see a graphic representation of this in Figure 12.3.

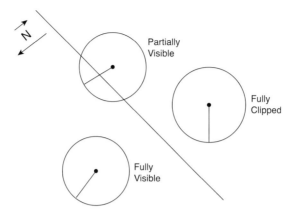

Figure 12.3 Clipping spheres against a plane.

Notice how this test requires only three multiplies, four additions, and one compare. Interestingly, this test is a logical extension of the point versus plane test, which for a point *P* would be:

```
A · Px + B · Py + C · Pz + D < 0
```

This would return true if (and only if) point *P* was in the hemispace opposite the plane normal.

Returning to our main argument, we can use the sphere versus plane test to implement a very efficient sphere versus view frustum. Here I will use the view frustum notation we used in preceding sections. The pseudocode would be:

```
For each clipping plane
      If the sphere is outside the plane return false
End for
Return true
```

In a strict C implementation, the preceding code would translate into:

```
for (i=0;i<6;i++)
        {
        if (fr[i][0]*sc.x+fr[i][1]*sc.y+fr[i][2]*sc.z+fr[i][3]<=-sr)
                return false;
        }
return true;
```

The first conclusion reached from the preceding analysis is that testing against a sphere is inexpensive. In fact, the cost is the same as testing a point. This makes spheres a good idea for tests that have to be performed frequently.

A second advantage of using spheres is rotation invariance. Imagine that you have a spaceship you need to clip against the view frustum. The bounding sphere will remain the same regardless of the orientation of the ship; rotating the object will not affect the bounding volume. This is another handy property of spheres.

Spheres are not, however, perfect. For example, they tend not to fit the geometry well, yielding lots of false positives. Imagine a pencil-shaped object, as shown in Figure 12.4. In this case, using a bounding sphere will create a false impression of size, which will translate into lots of false positives in our clipping routines. Generally speaking, spheres work better with geometry that occupies the space in a more or less homogeneous fashion—objects that occupy all directions of space similarly.

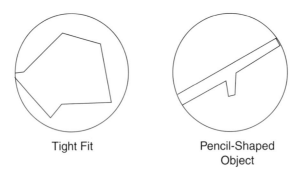

Tight Fit

Pencil-Shaped
Object

Figure 12.4 Pencil-shaped object.

Bounding Boxes

As an alternative to spheres, we can use boxes to clip our geometry. Boxes generally provide a tighter fit, so less false positives will happen. In contrast, the clipping test is more complex than with spheres, and we don't have rotational invariance. So clearly, choosing between spheres and boxes is not a black-and-white scenario.

Boxes can either be axis aligned or generic. An axis-aligned bounding box (AABB) is a box whose faces are parallel to the X,Y,Z axes. They are the simplest form of box, and thus the easiest to compute. To compute an AABB for a set of points, the following algorithm must be applied.

From all the points,

> Select the minimum *X* value found in any of them
>
> Select the minimum *Y* value found in any of them
>
> Select the minimum *Z* value found in any of them
>
> Select the maximum *X* value found in any of them
>
> Select the maximum *Y* value found in any of them
>
> Select the maximum *Z* value found in any of them

The AABB is defined by two points: one that will store the minimum values and another one for the maxima.

The visibility test is significantly harder than for spheres. We need to test whether any vertex is inside the frustum while keeping in mind that a box with all vertices outside the frustum can still be visible if it totally encloses it. Here is one of the possible tests for such a routine:

```
bool CubeInFrustum( float x, float y, float z, float sizex, float
sizey, float sizez )
{
int p;

for( p = 0; p < 6; p++ )
    {
    if( frustum[p][0] * (x - sizex/2) + frustum[p][1] * (y -
sizey/2) + frustum[p][2] * (z - sizez/2) + frustum[p][3] > 0 )
        continue;
    if( frustum[p][0] * (x + sizex/2) + frustum[p][1] * (y -
sizey/2) + frustum[p][2] * (z - sizez/2) + frustum[p][3] > 0 )
        continue;
    if( frustum[p][0] * (x - sizex/2) + frustum[p][1] * (y +
sizey/2) + frustum[p][2] * (z - sizez/2) + frustum[p][3] > 0 )
        continue;
    if( frustum[p][0] * (x + sizex/2) + frustum[p][1] * (y +
sizey/2) + frustum[p][2] * (z - sizez/2) + frustum[p][3] > 0 )
        continue;
```

```
    if( frustum[p][0] * (x - sizex/2) + frustum[p][1] * (y -
sizey/2) + frustum[p][2] * (z + sizez/2) + frustum[p][3] > 0 )
        continue;
    if( frustum[p][0] * (x + sizex/2) + frustum[p][1] * (y -
sizey/2) + frustum[p][2] * (z + sizez/2) + frustum[p][3] > 0 )
        continue;
    if( frustum[p][0] * (x - sizex/2) + frustum[p][1] * (y +
sizey/2) + frustum[p][2] * (z + sizez/2) + frustum[p][3] > 0 )
        continue;
    if( frustum[p][0] * (x + sizex/2) + frustum[p][1] * (y +
sizey/2) + frustum[p][2] * (z + sizez/2) + frustum[p][3] > 0 )
        continue;
    return false;
    }
return true;
}
```

In the preceding code, x, y, z is the center of a box of sizes: `sizex`, `sizey`, `sizez`. Notice how the frustum still contains the six clipping planes given the current camera position.

Culling

Culling allows us to eliminate geometry depending on its orientation. A well-executed culling pass can statistically eliminate about one half of the processed triangles. As an added benefit, the culling pass can be connected to a clipping stage, providing the combined benefit of both stages.

To better understand culling, we must first discuss the nature of 3D objects. Compare both sides of Figure 12.5, which represent two 3D entities. In the right figure, you can see a large number of triangles laid out in a chaotic, unorganized way. On the left is a 3D model of a house. Clearly, when we talk about a 3D object we are referring to the figure on the left. But what are the characteristics of these objects?

 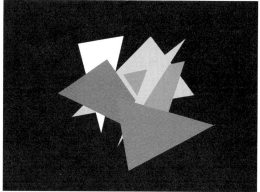

Figure 12.5   House mesh versus polygon soup.

Primarily, a properly defined 3D object uses its triangles to fully divide the space in two: a volume enclosed by the object (which we will call inside) and the remaining area (the outside). This is what we will call the boundary representation (B-rep) of an object. As a corollary of this property, both subspaces (inside and outside) are mutually disconnected: The object has no openings or holes that allow us to look inside. We can have a passing hole that allows us to cross the object, but we will never see the inside of the object. You can see examples of B-reps and non-B-reps in Figure 12.6.

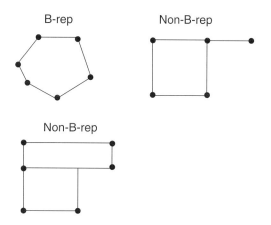

Figure 12.6   B-rep versus non-B-rep geometries.

Another important property of a well-formed object is that the vertices of each triangle are defined in counterclockwise order (as seen from the outer side of the object).

Applying the polygon winding rule, this means that face normals should point outward. When doing a simple cross product, we can automatically generate per face normals.

Having defined these fundamental properties, we can now move on and enumerate the following theorem: Given an arbitrary 3D well-formed object, the faces whose normals are pointing away from the viewpoint will be occluded by other faces, and thus can be culled away.

The simplest (and most frequently used) form of culling takes place inside the GPU. As triangles are received, their winding order is used to determine the direction of the normal. Essentially, the order in which we pass the vertices defines the orientation (and hence the normal) of the triangle. This direction is used to discard back-facing primitives. Notice how the GPU can perform triangle culling even if we do not provide the normals of the triangles: The order of the vertices is enough. The reason is simple: Some methods use per triangle normals, others use per vertex (for example, Phong shading). Thus, the algorithm for rejecting primitives has to be independent of the normal format.

After reading the preceding section on clipping, you should expect a section on object-level culling, so we can work with higher abstraction on the pipeline. But object-level culling is by far less popular than object-level clipping. There are several reasons for this:

> ➤ The benefit of culling is 50 percent; the benefit of clipping is about 80 percent.

> ➤ Object culling is significantly harder to do.

> ➤ If your geometry is prepacked in linear structures (vertex arrays or buffers), you don't want to reorder it because of the culling.

Object Culling

The basis of object-level culling involves rejecting back-facing primitives at a higher abstraction level. To do this, we will need to classify different triangles in an object according to their orientation. This can either be done at load time or as a preprocess. The result of this process will be a series of clusters of similarly aligned primitives. Then, the rendering loop will process only those clusters that are properly aligned with the viewer.

Several methods have been designed to create these clusters; all of them trying to do a partition of the normal value space. Because normals are unit vectors, their longitude and latitude are used. To prevent distortions at the poles, one popular method uses a cube as an intermediate primitive. Each face of the cube is divided into subfaces like a checkerboard, and then vectors are computed from the center of the cube to the edge of each square. Each square represents a range in the longitude–latitude normal space. We only need to sort our triangles into these clusters, and then paint only the clusters that can potentially face the viewer. You can see this approach in action in Figure 12.7.

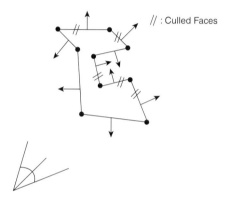

Figure 12.7   Object culling.

Occlusion Testing

Clipping and culling can dramatically reduce the scene's triangle complexity. But some redundant triangles can still survive those tests. If we do not implement additional measures, all triangles lying in the view frustum facing the viewer will be considered valid. But what if two visible, camera-facing primitives overlap each other? You can see this situation depicted in Figure 12.8. In this case, the pipeline will process both, consider them valid, and paint them using the Z-buffer to properly order them. Evidently, only one of them will be seen (the one closest to the viewer, sometimes referred to as the *occluder*). So we will need to process both, and only in the fragment rasterization stage decide which one will stay on the Z-buffer and get painted. We will have committed one of the deadly performance sins: overdraw.

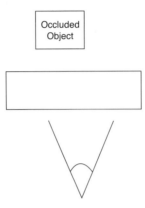

Figure 12.8 Occlusion.

The best way to picture overdraw is to think of an FPS that takes place indoors in a maze full of twisting corridors. In these types of games, our line of sight is usually limited to a few meters. There's always one corner or gate to ensure we don't see what we are not supposed to. In graphics jargon, these scenarios are "densely occluded." Now, imagine that we do not perform some kind of occlusion testing on the depicted situation. Clearly, performance from the viewpoints marked as *A* would be poor, whereas performance on *B* would be very good. To avoid this situation, FPS designers try to ensure that approximately the same number of triangles are visible onscreen at any given time. And having a good occlusion policy is fundamental to reaching this goal.

Many occlusion prevention policies largely depend on the kind of game you are building. Many of the tests (such as Potentially Visible Set [PVS] culling, portal rendering, and so on) are designed to work in indoor scenarios, and some of them (the lesser part) are designed for the great outdoors. So, we will leave those for the following chapters and concentrate on universal policies.

Some hardware has built-in occlusion testing options. This is the case in some Hewlett Packard cards as well as NVIDIA's cards starting with the GeForce3 onward. ATIs from the 8500 upward can also perform occlusion testing, which can be handled by both DirectX and OpenGL. Take a look at Chapter 13, "Indoors Rendering," for a complete tutorial on enabling hardware occlusion.

Using the hardware is an extremely powerful and flexible way of performing occlusion tests and is growing quickly in popularity. Essentially, it works on an object level and allows you to discard large blocks of geometry with a single query. The interface is relatively straightforward: Each object must be completely surrounded by a bounding object, which can be an AABB, a sphere, a generic bounding box, a convex hull, and so on. In fact, any geometry that completely encloses the object can be used. We must then run the occlusion query by sending the bounding object down the graphics pipeline. This object will not be painted, but instead will be tested against the Z-buffer only. As a return from the test, we will retrieve a value that will tell us:

- ➤ If the object actually modified the Z-buffer
- ➤ If it did so, how many pixels were modified

So, we now have a trivial occlusion rejection query. Draw the geometry front to back (so large occluders are painted first), and then paint the geometry testing for each object if its bounding volume (BV) will alter the Z-buffer. If the BV will not affect the results (because it is fully behind other objects), we can reject the object and skip to the next one. Needless to say, the speedup achieved by hardware occlusion culling techniques can be huge, especially in dense scenes with lots of occluders.

As usual, this test can yield false positives. There is a minimal chance that the BV will be visible, but the object will not. However, being able to reject most occluded objects with a single test is such an advance that false positives are definitely a minor issue.

Resolution Determination

When I think about realism in a computer game, I always think of Yosemite National Park in California—huge mountains and thousands of trees in a richness and variety that makes any visitor feel tiny in comparison. I don't think we will be reaching that level of complexity in some time. So, it's a perfect example to show how resolution and level-of-detail (LOD) techniques work.

Let's imagine for a second that you actually tried to do a game set in Yosemite with the tools we have seen so far. You do some aggressive clipping, which, because your camera has an aperture of 60°, reduces complexity to one-sixth of the total triangles. Then, some serious culling chops that in half to reach one-twelfth. Also, you have a dream-like occlusion calculator. Let's daydream for a second and imagine that after the three stages, you have reduced the visible triangle counts to about one-fiftieth.

Now, how many triangles does Yosemite have? I know it might sound absurd, but follow me through this exercise because it will be a true eye-opener. Let's assume you do a 20km×20km square terrain patch, with terrain sampled every meter. If you do the math, you will see we are talking about a 400 million triangle map. Not bad, but let's not stop there. Now comes the fun part: trees. Trees are hard to get right. From my experience, a high-quality, realistic tree should be in the 25,000 triangle range (yes, each one). Assuming one tree for every 20 meters, that yields 1 million trees for the whole park, or even better, 25 billion triangles per frame. At a very reasonable 30 frames per second, the triangle throughput of our engine is…well, you get the idea, right?

We can reduce that by 50 using conventional techniques. We could even reduce it by 500, and still the cost would be prohibitive. At the core of the problem there's a brute-force approach that has resulted in this exponential growth scheme. Assuming the trees are about 50 meters high and remembering that objects have a perceived size that is inversely related to the distance, squared, we will reach the conclusion that our magnificent tree, seen from one kilometer away, is almost invisible. So, it didn't really make any sense to use 25,000 triangles for it, right? These kinds of tactics are what resolution determination is all about. Clipping, culling, and occlusion tests determine what we are seeing. Resolution tests determine how we see it.

Our Yosemite game is an example of the ideal scenario for multiresolution strategies: an outdoor game with little or no occlusion and a very high triangle count. At the core of such a system lies the concept of priority: We can assign more triangles to items in the front, using lower quality models for those in the back. The human visual system tends to focus on larger, closer objects (especially if they are moving). If done right, we can make the player think the whole scenario is as detailed as the closer elements, and thus create the illusion of a larger level.

Many multiresolution strategies exist, depending on the scenario. Some methods are better suited for outdoors landscapes, whereas others are designed to work on individual objects. But generally speaking, all consist of two components. First, a resolution-selection heuristic that allows us to assign relative importance to onscreen objects; and second, a rendering algorithm that handles the desired resolution.

Focusing on the heuristic that sets the resolution level, we could begin by computing the distance from the object to the viewer and use that as a resolution indicator. As the object moves away from the viewer, its resolution can change accordingly. But this method is far from perfect. Imagine that you are looking at the San Francisco Bay, with the Golden Gate Bridge looming near the horizon. The bridge might be very far away, but it's huge, so reducing its resolution can have undesirable side effects.

Thus, a more involved heuristic is required. This time, we project the bounding box of the object onscreen and calculate the area of the projected polygon. An object's importance has to do with perceived size, not with distance: A small onscreen object can be painted at a lower level of detail than a huge object. Thus, we can use this projected area as the selection criteria for the multiresolution algorithm. With this strategy, a case like the Golden Gate Bridge, mentioned earlier, will be treated correctly. If we are looking at the bridge from a distance and a car is crossing the bridge, we will assign a much lower detail level to the car than we will to the bridge, even if they are more or less at the same distance from the viewer.

Once the selection criteria have been evaluated, it is then time to apply the painting policy. Here the criteria largely depend on the kind of primitive we are painting because different primitives employ completely different rendering strategies. Terrain renderers, for example, use very specific techniques such as Continuous Level Of Detail (CLOD), Real-time Optimally Adapting Meshes (ROAM), or GeoMipMapping. Because these are involved subjects, Chapter 14, "Outdoors Algorithms," has been devoted to outdoors renderers. However, primitives broadly conform to two different families of solutions. We can choose either a discrete approach, where we simply select the best-suited model from a catalog of varying quality models, or we can use a continuous method, where we can derive a model with the right triangle count on the fly. The first method will obviously be memory intensive, whereas the second will have a lower memory footprint but a higher CPU hit due to the inherent calculations. Let's examine both in detail.

Discrete Level of Detail Policies

Using the discrete approach, we would have a table with different models (anything from two to five is common) of varying quality. These models can easily be computed using standard 3D packages, because all of them offer excellent triangle-reduction options. Models are stored in an array, top-quality first. Each model must be assigned an associated numeric value that represents the upper limit that the model is designed for (either in distance or screen area). Then, in the painting routine, we only have to compute the chosen metric and scan the list to see which model suits us best.

This first technique can be seen in hundreds of games, especially those with large viewing distances where the size of the displayed items can vary a lot. The characteristic is a more or less noticeable popping that happens whenever there is a change in the displayed model.

Some simple techniques exist that eliminate the popping and provide the continuous look without the CPU cost. One of the most popular techniques is alpha-blended LODs. The idea is to start with the classic discrete approach as explained in the previous paragraph. Then, additional code is added to ensure no popping is visible. The new code is designed to ensure a smooth transition between models by alpha-blending them.

The idea is simple and can be seen in Figure 12.9. Instead of storing only the distance at which models are swapped, we store a pair of values that represent the beginning and the end of the transition. As we move inside that range, the two models are blended accordingly, so only model A is shown at one end of the range, and model B is shown at the opposite end. Carefully selecting the blending function ensures a smooth, almost unnoticeable transition.

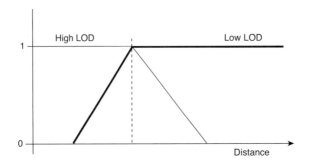

Figure 12.9 Alpha-blended LODs.

Alpha-blended LODs have the advantage of building upon the simple, well-analyzed technique of discrete LODs. Thus, they are simple to code and provide excellent results. The only downside is that painting two objects during the transition has a significant GPU overhead. But this technique is gaining ground rapidly, surpassing in popularity the mesh reduction algorithms.

Continuous Level of Detail Policies

To avoid the popping completely, we can implement a continuous method, which can decrease the triangle count on the fly and thus generate the right model for each distance. There are many different approaches to reach this goal; all of them involve a good deal of math and computational geometry. To begin with, we will need to store more information about the object to perform the triangle reduction tests at an interactive frame rate that includes edge information, neighboring data, and so on.

To better understand continuous LOD strategies, we will now explore one of the most popular methods in some detail. This method (called *Edge Collapsing*) involves detecting edges that carry little information and eliminating them by joining the two end vertices into one. By doing this to a solid model, we are eliminating two triangles, two edges, and one vertex. By performing this operation sequentially, we can reduce our model's triangle count to whatever fits us best.

Collapsible edges should be selected from those that carry the least information. Thus, because an edge can be shared between two (and only two) triangles, we are looking for those edges where the support planes from their neighboring triangles are almost coplanar, or at least the angle between those planes is smaller than a threshold. Once the desired edge is found, two different collapse operations can be performed.

You could collapse one vertex into the other, as shown in Figure 12.10. Again, the vertex that will be destroyed in the process is the one whose neighboring faces are more coplanar (thus conveying less information). Another strategy is to collapse the edge to a new vertex (thus both old vertices are destroyed) located along the edge. This second strategy can yield better results at a higher computational cost.

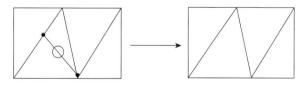

Figure 12.10   Edge collapse.

This process is not trivial when you want to eliminate more than one triangle. Either you do N loops, eliminating one edge at each iteration (which is costly), or you do a composite loop where you take away many triangles at once (which is hard to code).

However, there is a significant CPU hit involved in this process. A way to lower the computational cost is to use temporal coherence. Perform the edge collapse only once every few frames, using a metric. Every time you do the math, you store the distance (or screen area) of the object, and before you perform the calculation again, you make sure there has been a significant difference between the previous metric value and the current value. The pseudocode for this strategy would be

```
// global variable
float distance, area;

// rendering loop
newdist = compute distance to object
newarea = compute screen area of object
if ( abs(newdist-distance)>DISTANCETHRESHOLD ||
abs(newarea-area)>AREATHRESHOLD)
    {
    perform edge collapse
    distance=newdist
    area = newarea
    }
paint object
```

This temporal coherence technique can greatly speed up your code because the costly edge-collapse routine will only be calculated when it is necessary.

Whichever option you use, real-time triangle reduction policies are sometimes described as a total solution and a panacea. On one hand, this is partly true, because they allow us to get rid of the popping and have the exact triangle count that we need. But an objective analysis will also reveal some interesting drawbacks. First, there is a significant CPU hit in any reduction strategy: Edge collapsing is a pretty involved process if you want to get rid of many polygons at once. Second, there are texturing issues involved: What happens if the two vertices shared by the edge are made of two different materials? There are many caveats similar to this one, which limit the scope in which we can use the strategy.

Transform and Lighting

Before being displayed onscreen, the geometry stream passes through transform and lighting stages. These stages are hardware accelerated in current accelerators (GeForces, Radeons), but some older hardware performed these routines in the software driver.

The transform stage is used to perform geometric transformation to the incoming data stream. This includes the familiar rotation, scaling, and translation, but also many other transforms. In its more general definition, a transform can be described as a 4×4 matrix, which left-multiplies incoming vertices to get transformed vertices back. This stage also handles the projection of transformed vertices to screen-coordinates, using projection matrices. By doing so, 3D coordinates are converted into 2D coordinates, which are then rendered to the screen.

The lighting stage implements lighting models to increase the realism of the scene. Most current APIs and GPUs offer hardware lighting, so we can define light sources and surface properties, and have illumination applied at a zero CPU hit. Unfortunately, only per-vertex, local models of illumination can be applied directly in today's hardware, so no real-time ray tracing or radiosity is performed on the hardware automatically.

Sometimes, per-vertex local lighting will not be enough for your game. You might want a more involved global illumination look (such as radiosity in *Quake II*) or special effects that must be computed per pixel. Then, you might decide to override the hardware lighting model and use your own lighting policy. Unsurprisingly, per-vertex techniques are losing ground as better hardware lighting is introduced (especially programmable pipelines with vertex and pixel shaders). However, many games still use these approaches. One of the most popular is lightmapping, which stores the lighting information in low-resolution textures that are then painted on top of the base textures using multitexture techniques. Lightmapping allows per-pixel quality at a reasonable cost, and when coupled with a radiosity preprocessor, yields strikingly good results. Light mapping is fully explained in Chapter 17.

Rasterization

Rasterization is the process by which our geometry is converted to pixel sequences on a CRT monitor. Since the advent of the first consumer accelerators, this process is performed fully in hardware, so the only task left to the programmer is the delivery of geometry to the GPU. This is very good news because rasterizing triangles is extremely time-consuming when done in software. Today, there are even several ways to perform this task, each one suited to different scenarios—thus having specific advantages and disadvantages.

As a first, introductory option, geometry can be delivered in an immediate mode. Under this mode, you will be sending the primitives (points, lines, triangles) individually down the bus, one by one. It is the easiest to code, but as usual offers the worst performance. The reason is that sending data in many little packets results in bus fragmentation. Because the bus is a shared resource between many devices in your computer, it is not a good policy. However, a complete example of a triangle delivered in immediate mode in OpenGL is provided:

```
glBegin(GL_TRIANGLES);
glColor3f(1,1,1);
glVertex3f(-1,0,0);
glVertex3f(1,0,0);
glVertex3f(0,1,0);
glEnd();
```

The preceding code would paint a white triangle on the screen. Notice how you are using six commands, and how each vertex and color is specified separately.

Next in the performance scale are packed primitives, which are available in both OpenGL and DirectX under different names. In OpenGL, we call them *vertex arrays*, whereas DirectX refers to the same concept as *vertex buffers*. These primitives allow us to pack all the data in one or more arrays, and then use a single call (or very few calls) to deliver the whole structure to the hardware. Because the arrays can be sent in a single burst to the hardware, and there are fewer API calls, performance is greatly increased.

The most basic form of array uses one array per type of data. Thus, to deliver a mesh with vertex, color, and texture information to the hardware, you would need three separate arrays. After all the arrays have been loaded and exposed to the graphics hardware, a single call transfers them and does the rendering. Keep in mind that vertex arrays store their data in system memory, so you are accessing the bus every time you want to draw the desired object. As an improvement, arrays can use the indexing policy explored at the beginning of this chapter. This way the amount of data delivered to the hardware is smaller, and the performance gain is bigger.

One alternate strategy is to use interleaved arrays, in which all the information is encoded in a single array, interleaving the different types of information. So, if you need to send vertex, color, and texture information, your geometry stream would look something like this:

```
V[0].x V[0].y V[0].y C[0].r C[0].g C[0].b T[0].u T[0].v (...)
```

Using interleaved arrays, you can reduce the number of calls required to deliver the geometry. There might be a performance increase, but overall, this strategy would be quite similar to regular vertex arrays. The most popular use of interleaved arrays is the implementation of vertex buffers in Direct3D.

All the techniques we have explored so far share a common principle: Geometry is delivered to the hardware from system memory on a frame-by-frame basis. Although this is appropriate in many situations, remember that bus bandwidth is usually the bottleneck, so we must avoid using it as much as we can. Imagine, for example, a car racing game, where you need to display several cars that look the same. Wouldn't it be a good idea to be able to send the car once through the bus, and then paint it several times without having to resend it? This functionality, which I will refer to generally as *server-side techniques*, is available in modern hardware, offering much improved performance over regular vertex arrays and obviously immediate mode.

Server-side techniques allow us to deliver the geometry to the GPU, and store it there for a period of time. Then, each time we need to render it, we only send the render call, not the geometry, which is living in GPU memory space. This way we are rendering at the top speed the GPU can offer and are not being limited by bus bandwidth.

This technique must be handled with care, though. GPU memory is limited, so its use should be kept under strict control. However, if we master this technique, we will achieve a performance gain, sometimes doubling regular performance.

Server-side techniques must be supported by your graphics hardware. ATI Radeon and anything beyond GeForce2 support different rendering primitives that work from GPU memory. But most of the older hardware doesn't, so you will need to implement this as an option (or be restrictive in your hardware requirements). Additionally, different vendors and APIs expose this functionality in different ways.

As an example, we can use Compiled Vertex Arrays (CVAs), which offer functionality that is similar to cache memory. Using CVAs, we can deliver geometry to the hardware and leave it there if we are going to need it again soon. Thus, subsequent calls get the geometry from the GPU, not main memory. This technique is very useful in instance-based scenarios, such as the car racing game mentioned earlier. You specify the primitive once, and from that moment on, it is "cached" on the GPU. As an extreme case, imagine the Yosemite resolution example mentioned in a previous section. In these cases, it makes no sense to have all trees modeled individually. Rather, you would do a few different instances, and by combining them randomly, get the overall feeling of a forest. Then, using CVAs can greatly speed up the rendering of the trees because many of them would really be the same core geometry primitive.

Extending this concept, we could think of GPU memory as a fast cache, which we can freely access and manage. We could write models to it, delete them, and send them down the rendering pipeline efficiently. The main advantage to CVAs would be complete control over the memory, which would become similar in functionality to system memory. This new primitive is available on newer cards (GeForce2 GTS and later, ATI Radeon) and on both OpenGL (as an extension) and DirectX 8. The sad news is that cards implement this functionality under proprietary standards, so you need to code differently depending on the hardware you are running. Under OpenGL, NVIDIA cards expose this as the `Vertex_Array_Range` (VAR) extension, whereas ATI uses `Vertex_Array_Objects`. Although both are essentially the same, coding is card specific, which is a burden on the programmer. Under DirectX 8, all these functions and alternatives are encapsulated in the `VertexBuffer` interface for easier access. All we need to do is mark the vertex buffer as write-only, so the API knows it can be delivered and cached in the graphics card for efficient rendering.

Having complete access to GPU memory offers the programmer top flexibility and performance. Models that are used frequently or that require instancing can be stored in GPU memory and will be rendered without bus speed constraints.

There are, however, limitations to these techniques. Primarily, they are designed for static data only. If you need to display an animated character, it makes no sense to store it persistently in GPU memory. The same applies to procedural geometry, or simply geometry that goes through a triangle reduction routine on a frame-by-frame basis. GPU memory is slow to access, so performance with dynamic geometry is comparatively low.

In Closing

In this chapter, we explored the building blocks of a generic, basic graphics engine. Starting with geometry formats and delivery methods, we then moved on to clipping, culling, and occlusion testing, which provide different ways to quickly determine the visible part of any given scene. We saw how LOD techniques can be used to reach a playable frame rate in the target platform. We also explored transform and rasterization stages to make sure we are sending data to the hardware in the most efficient manner.

Using these techniques, you could build many basic games or even some that are not so basic. Professional, high-end games are, however, a different business. There's more to them than a few general techniques that can be applied regardless of the nature of the game we are working on. To craft something unique and technologically advanced, we will need to understand the nature of our design; and by restricting its scope to a specific genre or gaming perspective, we will unleash better and faster tools that will allow us to reach state-of-the-art game programming.

Chapter 13

Indoors Rendering

"His house was perfect, whether you wanted food, or sleep, or work, or story-telling, or singing, or just sitting and thinking, best, or a pleasant mixture of them all."

J. R. R. Tolkien, *The Fellowship of the Ring*

Indoors rendering has been a popular technique for game development ever since Wolfenstein 3D by id Software was released. Games taking place inside buildings have become widespread; their visual appeal increasing with each new hardware iteration or engine release. In this chapter, we will explore the building blocks for any indoors engine. Three popular approaches— Binary Space Partitions (BSPs), portal rendering, and octree rendering—will be explored in full, and some specialized solutions will be covered thereafter. As you will soon discover, indoors games often require quite complex techniques.

General Analysis

In the previous chapter, you saw how any good 3D pipeline can be divided into clipping, culling, occluding, and computing the right level of detail (LOD). This structure can be adapted to any game genre, so different genres emphasize certain components to reach the desired performance. Let's now analyze clipping, culling, occlusions, and LODs to understand how indoors games work and why they have been (and still are) so popular.

To begin with, we must understand that the clipping phase is usually independent from the game genre. Cameras always cover more or less the same angle, so the amount of clipped geometry can be considered stable. A camera covering 90° will statistically clip around three-quarters of the global geometry of the level. Culling follows a pretty similar pattern: It is usually performed by the hardware, and we can expect about one-half of the geometry to be back-facing, and thus not painted. Combining both clipping and culling, we reach the conclusion that approximately one-eighth of the incoming geometry effectively survives this two-pass sequence and can be considered to be both onscreen and front-facing.

In an ideal world, this one-eighth would be sufficient to display the desired geometry, but this is not usually the case. Game graphics are about richness and complexity; therefore, we will often need more than we can afford. Thus, we need to use the LOD and occlusion phases to reduce the triangle count even more. Now, is level-of-detail relevant to an indoors game, where view distances are bounded? Clearly not much, because we will rarely see geometry from very far away. Thus, by elimination, occlusion culling must be the way to go, because we have lots of walls that are perfect occluders.

We can now formally define an indoors rendering algorithm as one software piece that optimizes the rendering pipeline by quickly determining occlusions (in addition to clipping and culling) in the level geometry, thus allowing interactive rendering. This clearly draws a distinction with outdoors rendering methods (explained in the next chapter), which will in turn emphasize LOD processing because view distances will be large. This characterization does not imply that an indoors algorithm does not use LODs: some of them do, some don't. But it's the occlusion component that will dominate. In addition, both indoors and outdoors algorithms will have similar approaches with regard to clipping and culling, which are genre independent and provide the same speed-up factors in both cases.

Occluder-Based Algorithms

Occlusion testing is not an easy task. Generally speaking, it is a O(number of triangles^2) problem, because we need to test each triangle in the view frustum against each other to see whether they are occluding themselves. Clearly, some clever approaches are required to compute this at interactive frame rates. The first approach we will explore works by reducing the number of potential occluders to a small set of very promising candidates. Because closer triangles will statistically cover more area on the screen than distant ones, we only need to test for occlusions between very close geometry (which we will call occluders) and distant objects (occluded objects). This can decrease our initial cost to almost O (number of triangles). If you couple this with the fact that we know an upper bound to the view distance, we can further decrease the cost by assuming any triangle located away from this bound is effectively occluded, without really testing it. Here you can see the pseudocode of this raw occlusion algorithm:

```
from the current viewpoint…
select a set of potential occluders (close, large triangles)
for each triangle in the scene
    if it is closer than the viewing distance
        test for occlusion with any of the occluders
        if passes the test -> paint it
        end if
    end if
end for
```

This algorithm can also take advantage of the clipping and culling steps. Obviously, an occluder must be visible and thus not be clipped away, and must not be culled. Back-facing triangles will never cover geometry, because they are not even painted.

The implementation details for such an algorithm are relatively straightforward. For each frame, perform software clipping and culling. Then, sort the remaining triangles by Z distance and take the first N entries of the list. Because the sorting process is relatively expensive, we can just perform it every few frames. If you think about it, the results will not change if the viewer did not move between two successive frames. Thus, we store the player's position and orientation, and only recompute the solution if the change in position or orientation exceeds a fixed threshold. This philosophy, called *frame-coherence*, can yield significant improvements, especially in costly routines. The overall structure of a frame-coherent loop would be

```
if  orientation or position changed more than X
    recompute solution
    store new position
    store new orientation
end if
```

Then, in the painting phase, we take triangles and test for inclusion inside the pyramid formed by the viewpoint and the occluder. The problem with such an approach is that a per triangle test is costly, and thus we will probably end up with a CPU-bound application. The CPU is the bottleneck here, sorting and testing for inclusion. Better methods need to be employed: methods in which we do not need to perform the full occlusion detection test at runtime, because part of the solution is precomputed beforehand. These are the methods used in most commercial games.

Binary Space Partition Algorithms

One of the classic approaches to compute indoors rendering at interactive frame rates involves using a BSP data structure. Variants of this approach have been used in the *Doom* and *Quake* series as well as in dozens of other games. *Doom* used a 2D BSP, whereas newer versions have moved to 3D data structures and added a host of optimizations and improvements.

A BSP is just a binary tree data structure that allows us to classify geometric data (in our case, triangles) spatially. As you will soon see, its main advantage is viewpoint-independent triangle ordering. We can query the BSP from a given waypoint, and it will return to us the list of triangles it's storing, ordered by Z-value. With some enhancements, a BSP can also be customized to help with occlusions. Unfortunately, BSPs are traditionally considered hard to explain, so we will need some in-depth analysis to understand how to harness their power.

Construction

The construction of a BSP begins with an unordered set of triangles, which we want to classify. The usual starting point is the whole geometry data set of a game level, for example. The algorithm is recursive and can be outlined as follows:

1. Begin with the complete set.

2. Select the triangle that best divides the set in half.

3. Compute the support plane of the said triangle.

4. Store the selected triangle and its support plane in the current node.

5. Divide the remaining triangles depending on which side of the selected plane each one stays.

6. If any of the two sublists is not empty, create a new node and go to step 2.

This is rather obscure, so let's try to shed some light on the whole construction process. I will use a 2D drawing to illustrate, so instead of 3D triangles (which are quite hard to picture on a flat page), you will see 2D lines. But the process is the same. Think of this drawing (see Figure 13.1) as a top-down view of a *Quake* level; each line depicting one wall.

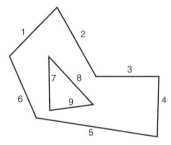

Figure 13.1   Game level, top-down view.

The process would begin by splitting the set in half using 8 as a base (see Figure 13.2).

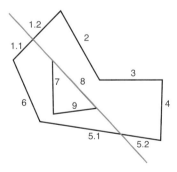

Figure 13.2   Figure 13.1 is split using 8 as a base. The front contains 1.2, 2, 3, 4, 5.2, whereas the back contains 1.1, 6, 7, 9, 5.1.

Then it would split the front using 3 (see Figure 13.3).

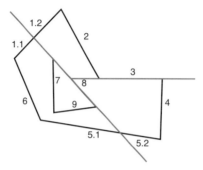

Figure 13.3 After this second split, the front contains 4 and 5.2, and the back contains 2 and 1.2.

The two remaining nodes can be split trivially: Given a node with two primitives (4 and 5.2, for example), one will always be the root, and the other will be one of the two children. In this case, we choose 4 as a root, and thus 5.2 is in the front node. In the second case, 1.2 is the root, and 2 is in front of it.

Thus we have the first subtree. The map is shown in Figure 13.4.

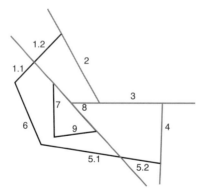

Figure 13.4 State of the map after the front subtree has been completely processed.

The tree is shown in Figure 13.5.

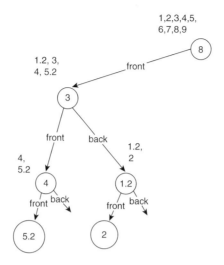

Figure 13.5 BSP tree with the front subtree processed.

Working similarly with the front node from the root, we get the tree shown in Figure 13.6.

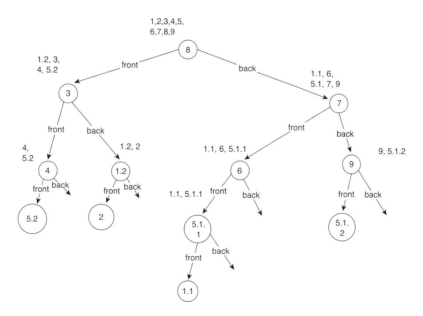

Figure 13.6 Full BSP tree after completely scanning the map.

Figure 13.7 illustrates what the map looks like now.

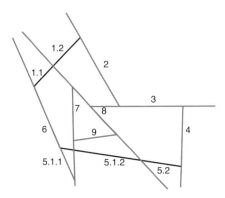

Figure 13.7   Resulting map after BSP construction, showcasing the partition planes.

BSPs just take geometrical sets and divide them recursively using support planes. In the end, each node of the BSP holds exactly one triangle, which was used to split the data set at that point. There are just two questions we need to solve in order to code the algorithm. First, we need to define the criteria of selection for the splitting plane. Second, we need to decide what to do when a triangle is divided into two halves by the splitting plane.

Choosing the ideal splitting plane can be achieved in a variety of ways. One option is to divide the set using the triangle whose support plane is closest to the center of the set, trying to make sure both subtrees have the same amount of geometry, which results in a balanced BSP tree. But such criteria can often generate lots of vertex splits, and thus the geometric data set will quickly grow, increasing our memory footprint. An alternative method consists of selecting, from the triangles located approximately in the middle (close to the center), the triangle whose support plane generates less vertex splits.

> **NOTE**
>
> Let's clarify what "center" means here. One option would be to use the mathematical barycenter, expressed as the average value of all points comprising the set. Thus, for a set V, the barycenter would be as follows:
>
> `Barycenter= (Σ(V`$_{[i]}$`))/i`

Although mathematically correct, this might not suit our needs completely. Because this is a subtle concept, I will provide an example. Imagine an object with vertices distributed unevenly. Think, for example, of a lollypop: Its barycenter will be displaced toward the center of the candy ball, just because that area has more vertices. Although this is correct (both sets resulting from the plane split will be equally sized in terms of number of primitives), we might run into trouble because cells created by the BSP will not be of equal size. In some games, AI developers will prefer to sacrifice tree balance in order to keep equal-sized cells. If this is your situation (your AI programmer will tell you so), a better choice for a center will be the midpoint of the bounding box of the incoming data set. This way you ensure that the set is divided in half not by number of primitives, but by its spatial allocation.

Whichever division plane you choose, the main problem with the implementation of a BSP is deciding what to do if, when splitting the geometry set, one triangle effectively crosses the support plane. The usual strategy is to split the triangle, which in general generates three new triangles—one on one side of the support plane and two on the opposite side. Triangle splitting makes coding BSPs a bit more complex. The code is not that hard, but it's pretty unstable, and thus many special cases must be covered carefully. The following listing, one of the longest in the book, is the complete triangle split routine, commented. I think it is of great value because it's a pretty involved routine that hasn't been published in many books. The main idea of this implementation is to evaluate the three points in the triangle against the plane, compute the addition of these values, and use that to drive a switch construct. This way we narrow down the different cases quickly (there are 27 variants, many of them symmetrical) to achieve good performance.

```
int triangle::split(plane pl,triangle *tris1,int &num1,triangle
*tris2,int &num2)
{
int v1= pl.testpoint(p1);              // -1, 0 or 1 depending on
which side we are in
int v2= pl.testpoint(p2);
int v3= pl.testpoint(p3);

int val=v1+v2+v3;

switch (val)
    {
```

```
   case 3:
      // triangle completely in positive side
      tris1[0]=(*this);
      num1=1;
      num2=0;
      return 1;
   case -3:
      // triangle completely in negative side
      tris2[0]=(*this);
      num1=0;
      num2=1;
      return 1;
   case -2:
      // triangle with two vtx on the plane and the other on
negative side
      // no need to divide it
      tris2[0]=(*this);
      num1=0;
      num2=1;
      return 1;
   case 2:
      // triangle with two vtx on the plane and the other on
positive side
      // no need to divide it
      tris1[0]=(*this);
      num1=1;
      num2=0;
      return 1;
   case 0:
      // triangle in plane or triangle with one vertex in plane and
      // other two in opposite sides. The latter requires a divide.
      if (v1 || v2 || v3) // two vertices on opposite sides... divide
         {
         point pivot, positive, negative;
         if (v1==0)
```

```
              {
              pivot=p1;
              if (v2>0) { positive=p2; negative=p3; }
              else { positive=p3; negative=p2; }
              }
          if (v2==0)
              {
              pivot=p2;
              if (v1>0) { positive=p1; negative=p3; }
              else { positive=p3; negative=p1; }
              }
          if (v3==0)
              {
              pivot=p3;
              if (v1>0) { positive=p1; negative=p2; }
              else { positive=p2; negative=p1; }
              }
          // here positive, pivot and negative are ready
          point i;
          pl.testline(positive,negative,i);
          tris1[0].create(positive,i,pivot);
          num1=1;
          tris2[0].create(negative,pivot,i);
          num2=1;
          return 2;
          }
      else // triangle is inside plane... assign to positive node
          {
          tris1[0]=(*this);
          num1=1;
          num2=0;
          return 1;
          }
      break;
   case -1:
      // can be: two vtx on plane and one on negative side, one vertex
      // on positive and two vertices on negative. Latter
requires a divide
```

```
    if (v1*v2*v3==0) // one of them was zero: we're on the first case
        {
        tris2[0]=(*this);
        num1=0;
        num2=1;
        return 1;
        }
    // one vertex on positive, two on negative. Split
    point positive,negative1,negative2;
    if (v1==1) { positive=p1; negative1=p2; negative2=p3;}
    if (v2==1) { positive=p2; negative1=p1; negative2=p3;}
    if (v3==1) { positive=p3; negative1=p1; negative2=p2;}
    point v1=negative1-positive;
    point v2=negative2-positive;
    point i1,i2;
    pl.testline(negative1,positive,i1);
    pl.testline(negative2,positive,i2);
    tris1[0].create(positive,i1,i2);
    num1=1;
    tris2[0].create(negative2,i2,i1);
    tris2[1].create(negative2,i1,negative1);
    num2=2;
    return 3;
case 1:
    // can be: two vtx on plane and one on positive side, one
vertex
    // on negative and two vertices on positive.Latter requires
a divide
    if (v1*v2*v3==0) // one of them was zero: we're on the first case
        {
        tris1[0]=(*this);
        num1=1;
        num2=0;
        return 1;
        }
    // one vertex on negative, two on positive. Split
    point positive1,positive2,negative;
```

```
            if (v1==-1) { negative=p1; positive1=p2; positive2=p3;}
            if (v2==-1) { negative=p2; positive1=p1; positive2=p3;}
            if (v3==-1) { negative=p3; positive1=p1; positive2=p2;}
            point v1=positive1-negative;
            point v2=positive2-negative;
            point i1,i2;
            pl.testline(positive1,negative,i1);
            pl.testline(positive2,negative,i2);

            tris1[0].create(positive1,i1,i2);
            tris1[1].create(positive1,i2,positive2);
            num1=2;

            tris2[0].create(negative,i2,i1);
            num2=1;
            return 3;
        }
}
```

It's a very lengthy routine. But if you examine it carefully, you will discover that the execution paths rarely run more than a few instructions.

Once we have the triangle splitting routine, we need the overall definition of the BSP tree:

```
class bsp;

class bsp
    {
    bsp *leftnode;
    bsp *rightnode;
    plane supportplane;
    triangle tri;

    public:
        void create(list<triangle>);
    };
```

Then, creating the BSP is just a routine:

```
select best support plane
for each triangle in the input set
    split it
    arrange the resulting triangles in a front and back list

if front list is not empty
    call create with this front list
if back list is not empty
    call create with this back list
```

View-Dependent Sorting

You have now seen how to build a BSP data structure. It is a complex, counterintuitive process with no apparent goal. From the building algorithm, it is hard to imagine how useful BSP trees can really be. As a first glimpse toward its benefits, consider the following algorithm:

```
begin with a viewpoint, and at the root node of the tree
test if we are "in front" or "behind" the plane
if we are in front:
    scan the back node
    paint the triangle which divides the set
    scan the front node
else
    scan the front node
    paint the triangle which divides the set
    scan the back node
```

If we execute this algorithm recursively on the BSP in the previous section, using the viewpoint as specified in the figure, the order in which the triangles will be painted is shown in Figure 13.8.

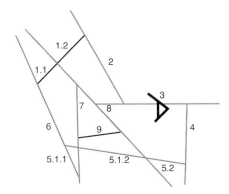

Figure 13.8   BSP example for view-dependent sorting. Triangles are painted
(back to front) as follows: 6, 5.1.1, 1.1, 5.1.2, 9, 8, 1.2, 2, 3, 4, 5.2.

Note how the list enumerates all the triangles in the set in Z-order from back to front while keeping a linear cost. The capability of ordering triangles back to front was an immediate benefit from BSPs, because it eliminated the need for a Z-buffer at a time when Z-buffers were implemented in software at a very high computational cost. If you want to understand why a BSP can order in linear time, consider this explanation: We basically scan the tree, and we keep selecting the most distant nodes from the available ones. So, each node we paint will be a bit closer to the viewpoint than the already painted ones, but not closer than any other.

Clearly, the complex construction algorithm was worth it. However, Z-ordering is less important today than in the 1980s when BSPs were introduced. We have 3D accelerators that come with built-in hardware Z-buffers, right? Well, not really. By reversing the algorithm just explained, we can achieve front-to-back order as well, and that's a blessing for a modern video card. Video cards usually perform a set of operations on each pixel:

```
Test if the pixel's Z-value affects the Z-buffer
If it doesn't, reject the pixel and move on to the next
If it does,
Compute texture mapping
Compute interpolated colors
Compute lighting
Mix these to generate a single pixel color
Paint the pixel
Update the Z-buffer
```

Quite clearly, the "accept pixel" path is much longer than the "reject pixel" path. Pixels that are rejected by the Z-buffer early in the process take less time from the GPU. Painting back-to-front in such an architecture actually hurts performance. Each new triangle will cover old triangles, so there will be lots of "pixel accept" paths. If you reverse the order, large, close triangles enter the Z-buffer first and make sure many subsequent calls fail due to early Z-rejection. As a result, most modern 3D accelerators experience a noticeable performance increase if you paint primitives front-to-back, and this is something a BSP can definitely help you with.

Hierarchical Clipping

BSPs can easily be extended to accelerate clipping computations, which allow us to eliminate the geometry that effectively lies outside of the view frustum. The key concept here is really simple: As part of the construction process, compute a bounding volume for each tree node. Clearly, successive levels in the BSP will have smaller bounding volumes because the partition condition of the tree guarantees that each node will consist of a spatially tighter triangle set. Besides, if the planes effectively divide sets in half, we can ensure that this bounding box hierarchy will divide box sizes in half approximately, with each new iteration.

Now it is just a matter of using these bounding boxes as part of the traversal algorithm, which is explained in the next section. The required modification works as follows:

```
begin with a viewpoint, and at the root node of the tree
if the current node's bounding box is visible
test if we are "in front" or "behind" the plane
if we are in front:
   scan the back
   paint the triangle which divides the set
   scan the front node
else
   scan the front node
   paint the triangle which divides the set
   scan the back node
end if
end if
```

Notice how this algorithm can prune large sections of the BSP tree very early in the rendering pipeline. As we traverse the tree, the moment one bounding box lies outside the frustum, we can reject not only that node but the complete subtree that is derived from it. Remember, boxes will be stacked hierarchically, so if an Nth level box is outside the frustum, any further box, which will be inside the initial box, will be outside as well. So, you can expect this improvement to greatly effect the overall performance of an indoors renderer. Remember, we are talking about game levels where the geometry surrounds the player, so there are lots of opportunities for clipping geometry that's behind him. Additionally, you can enhance the "is visible" test with a Z-rejection step. If you know the upper bound of the visibility range (distance at which geometry can be seen), any bounding box located further than that can definitely be pruned along with its complete subtree. If you review the code, you will see that our clipping processor has a huge impact, consuming very little CPU time in the process—just a few box-in-frustum tests.

Occlusion Detection

BSPs can also be used to compute occlusion detection. But for this technique to work, it requires some additional preprocessing because a regular BSP is not well suited for these tests. A new type of BSP, called the *leafy-BSP*, needs to be introduced at this point. Leafy-BSPs are at the core of *Quake*'s rendering pipeline, which is the program that made them quite popular for game developers. They have the property of automatically dividing the incoming data set in an array of convex cells, which will prove very useful.

A leafy-BSP is a regular BSP where all the geometry has been propagated to the leaves. In a regular BSP, data is stored in internal nodes in the form of triangles that divide the triangle sets. So, leaf nodes really only store the last triangle that survived the plane division approach. Now we will need to transform this BSP to leafy form by "shaking" the tree from the root so all triangles in internal nodes are propagated to the leaves. You can see the leafy process applied to our classic BSP tree in Figure 13.9.

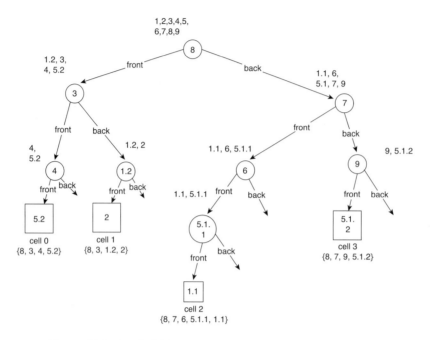

Figure 13.9 Leafy-BSP, showing the contents of each leaf node.

Once we have propagated the data, we can forget about the tree for a second and store the triangle list of each node in a list of numbered cells. The list for our previous example, along with its geometrical representation in the game level, is shown in Figure 13.10.

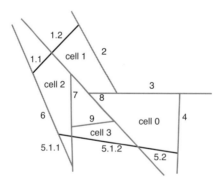

Figure 13.10 Leafy-BSP with cells.

Notice how each cell represents a contiguous spatial zone in our initial triangle set. Moreover, we can demonstrate that each of those cells is really a convex zone of the map, which will be very handy. The walls of the cells can either be areas occupied by level geometry or openings between cells. We will detect these openings at this point and store them along with the cells they belong to. Each opening should belong to exactly two cells.

If you analyze the process we have just gone through, you will see that we have just found an automatic algorithm to convert any triangle set into a list of convex cells and gates that connect them. The hard part is well behind us, and it is now time to take advantage of this new data structure the same way we took advantage of the classic BSP.

We will first precompute cell-to-cell visibility. Starting with one cell, we need to detect the set of cells that can be seen standing from the first one. To do so, we will use the gates (usually called portals) associated with that cell. We send rays from points in the portal toward the other portals in the level, and test whether any of them effectively reach their destination. If a single ray travels from portal A to portal B, it means the rooms connected to that portal are mutually visible. Note how visibility is a symmetrical property. This algorithm was introduced by Seth Teller and is called *portal stabbing*. As you will learn in the next section, there is a slightly different approach called *portal rendering*, which somehow has the same starting point.

Additionally, we will store the visibility information in a data structure called a Potentially Visible Set (PVS). A PVS is just a matrix of bits. If position X,Y has a value of true, then room X sees room Y. Thus, the PVS stores a summary of all the visibility processing. This is the real meat we will be using in the rendering loop.

Rendering

Now that we have analyzed how to perform clipping, view-independent sorting, culling, and occlusion determination using a BSP, let's examine a complete rendering algorithm that combines all these features in a general solution. The algorithm that follows is not very different from the one used in *Quake III: Arena*.

We start by using the BSP to quickly determine the cell the player is standing in. We traverse the BSP and use the splitting plane to narrow down and finally reach the cell. Then, we use the PVS to determine which cells are visible from the one we are standing in. All we need to do is scan the bit masks in the PVS. Notice how, at this stage, we have already computed occlusions, which was the hardest of all computations before leafy-BSPs were introduced. Then, we need to render all the potentially visible cells.

We paint front-to-back (which helps the Z-buffer reject unseen fragments as soon as possible and is thus more efficient than back-to-front), sort the cells by distance, use their bounding box to clip them to the screen, and send them to the graphics hardware.

Overall, we have taken occlusions, clipping, and culling (which will be performed on the hardware) into consideration, with almost zero visibility computations in the real-time loop. All we need to compute is the room the player is standing in and the view frustum culling of the visible cells. Besides, we know which cell the player is staying at, so we can use that information for AI, collision detection, and so on. The combination of clipping, culling, and a leafy-BSP approach for occlusion determination provides a complete rendering framework that tames the visibility problem's complexity.

Portal Rendering

BSP algorithms are a very efficient way of computing visibility in occluded environments. But they are not the only way of achieving interactive frame rates with indoors data sets. A completely different approach, called portal rendering, has been evolving through the years, offering a similar performance with a different approach. A variant of this algorithm was used in the *Unreal* engine and has gained widespread acceptance since then. Like BSPs, it allows programmers to paint only what is effectively seen. Unlike BSPs, the world hierarchy is not automatically computed, and visibility is computed in real time, not preprocessed.

I will begin by describing the data structure used to perform the portal visibility checking, and then move on to the algorithms. Portal rendering is based on the concept that the game world is divided into cells or rooms connected by doors or portals. Thus, our game world is really a list of rooms; each one connected to other rooms by a number of portals. It is a very human and logical way of laying out the game level. If you think about it, you will see that the data structure that more closely resembles this one is the nondirected graph (see Figure 13.11). Each room is considered a graph node, and each portal is represented by an edge between two rooms or graph nodes. The only difference with regular graphs is that two rooms can be directly connected with more than one portal (imagine two rooms with two windows separating them). Thus, our graph must allow two connected nodes to have any number of edges between them.

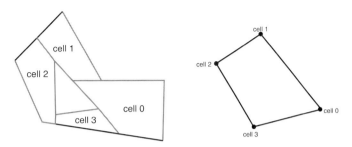

Figure 13.11   Map and graph.

Each room will hold its geometrical data and a tight bounding volume (a convex hull is a good choice) to test whether the player is effectively inside the room. Some portal implementations, especially the older ones, need the rooms to be convex. Later versions of the technique remove this restriction and handle concave rooms as well. Whichever you choose, keep in mind you need a bounding volume that can perform a precise player-in-room test. Thus, concave rooms will require a more complex point inclusion test. Check out Chapter 22, "Geometrical Algorithms," for more information on geometric tests.

Once the room structure is defined, we need to specify a list of portals emanating from it. For each portal, we will need links to both rooms connected by it and the geometry of the polygon that describes the portal shape. Portal polygons can be concave or convex, although some implementations impose some restrictions on their shape. Some use four-sided portals only, others force them to be all convex, and so on. By using the portals along with the associated rooms, we need to be able to traverse the game level much like a walking character would do, moving through the rooms using the doors that connect them. This is the core of any portal rendering algorithm.

The data structures that support the portal rendering algorithm are usually created by hand in the content development phase. The world editing tool must allow designers to cut geometry into pieces, place portals, and so on. In this respect, portal rendering is a bit more complex than BSP handling, where the world hierarchy is created automatically. However, this complexity will result in many advantages in the long run.

It is now time to move on to the painting algorithm. Portal systems do not store pre-computed visibility tables like some BSPs do. They resolve visibility queries at runtime using the portals to cull away unseen geometry. We begin by using the bounding volumes of the different rooms (either individually or using some hierarchy) to detect the room the camera is standing in. This room will be the starting point of the rendering algorithm. Then, we paint the room geometry, locate any visible portals, and move on to the rooms connected to them. For this second-level of rooms, we clip geometry through the portals, test whether there is any second-level portal that can still be seen, and so on. We will recursively explore the game level as long as new portals are still visible. When no more portals can be seen, the rendering routine will return (see Figure 13.12).

 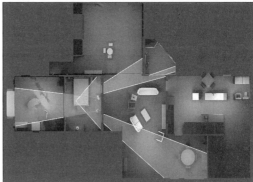

Figure 13.12   Recursive portal rendering.

The main difficulty in portal rendering is learning how to use portals as clipping volumes. We need to detect which triangles are seen through them, what part of a portal is visible through another portal, and so on. The main tool for the job will be a variant of the view frustum, which we will call the *portal frustum*—a frustum that emanates at the camera position and passes through the portal's vertices. This type of frustum can be used to test for inclusion of triangles inside the portal and only paint those that are effectively inside. But wait, there's more. We can intersect two portal frustums to compute the part of a second-level portal that is visible through a first-level portal. Frustum-based computations are the meat of any good portal rendering system. They are the core routines that make the algorithm complex and also determine the final performance of the technique.

Now, let's take a look at different strategies regarding frustums that have been used throughout the years. I will start with a perfect, general-case frustum analyzer and then present optimized, more restrictive options.

In a general case, a portal can have any number of vertices and be both convex and concave. Intersecting two such portals is thus a case of 2D shape intersection. We start by projecting both portals to 2D window coordinates. This way the test only needs to handle the X and Y coordinates, simplifying some math. Then, to compute the test, we start with the first vertex of portal P1 and follow the sequence of vertices used in the portal definition. For each vertex, we do a point-in polygon with P2. Clearly, those points that are part of P2 will be part of the intersection. But there's more: Imagine an edge composed by two subsequent vertices. The first vertex on the sequence is not in P2, but the second vertex is. This case represents an edge that crossed P2's boundaries. Thus, we need to compute the intersection between that segment and P2, and store the intersection point in the result as well. In addition, we need to test the opposite case. If a point is outside P2 but the previous point in sequence was inside, we need to compute the intersection again and store that point. If you do this until you have cycled P1, the resulting list will contain the new portal (or nothing if there was no intersection). Here is the pseudocode for the algorithm in full:

```
portal intersect(portal p1, portal p2)
{
list<points> result;
bool previnside=false;

if p2.contains(p1.vertices[p1.numvertices-1])
    {
    previnside=true;
    }
for (i=0;i<p1.numvertices;i++)
    {
    curinside= p2.contains(p1.vertices[i]);
    if (curinside)
    result.push_back(p1.vertices[i]);
    if ((previnside && !curinside) || (!previnside && curinside))
        {
        int aux=i-1;
        if (aux<0) aux+=p1.numvertices;
        point inter=compute_intersection(p1.vertices[aux],
p1.vertices[i], p2);
        result.push_back(inter);
```

```
        }
    previnside=curinside;
    }
portal presult(result);
return presult;
}
```

Notice how we take special measures to guarantee that we cycle through the array. Thus, we begin by initializing the previous value to that of the last vertex to check the segment formed by the last and the first vertex.

However, this is not a fast routine. Each call is linear to the number of vertices in P2, and the intersection test is not much better. Remember that this must be recomputed per frame, so we might not reach the desired performance with such a complex test. Thus, faster alternatives must be devised.

A popular choice was proposed by Luebke and Georges. Using their method, we don't use the portal, but instead use the screen-aligned 2D bounding box of the portal, making the portal intersection routine very straightforward. Intersecting screen-aligned boxes is just a matter of selecting the right X and Y values through very simple tests, and thus the routine is significantly sped up. The downside is precision. The resulting bounding box will be bigger than the portal it contains; and some tests that should return a negative value will return a positive value, as if a fragment or triangle were actually visible.

However, in modern-day hardware, rendering some extra triangles comes at no additional cost, so we should not worry about this. Remember, most geometry data structures are usually grouped together (like all triangles in a room, for example). A vertex buffer or vertex arrays in OpenGL will be prebuilt for each room. So, the effort of classifying triangles one by one will clearly not pay off in the long run, and a gross visibility test such as the one we have just proposed will be perfect.

Optical Effects Using Portals

One of the main advantages of portal rendering is that optical effects such as reflections and translucency can be elegantly implemented on top of the core algorithm. This was first showcased in games such as Epic's *Unreal*. All you have to do is enrich the portal data structure, so a portal can be much more than a simple door. It can be a mirror, a glass surface, and many other surreal effects you can think of.

Take reflections, for example. Any optics manual will tell you that looking at a mirror is, in practical terms, equivalent to looking at the same room from a virtual position that is the specular reflection of your position through the mirror. That is, if you look at a mirror at a 45° angle from five meters away, the scene you will see in the mirror is exactly the same scene a viewer located five meters away inside the mirror would see. Feeling like Alice in Wonderland? Check out Figure 13.13 for a visual explanation.

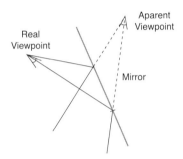

Figure 13.13 Mirrors on portals.

So, implementing a reflection is only a matter of having a special kind of portal that connects a room with itself while inverting the viewing matrices in the process. A general portal structure that incorporates this optical phenomenon would be as follows:

```
class portal
    {
    point *vertices;
    int numvertices;
    int type;
    roomid room1,room2;
    };
```

where `type` would store the type of portal—that is, regular, reflective, or translucent. Remember that both room identifiers for reflective portals would be the same, because a mirror does not really connect two rooms. Then, the portal propagation code would be something like this:

```
switch (type)
    {
    case REGULAR:
        {
        // Paint destination room of the portal
        break;
        }
    case REFLECTIVE:
        {
        // calculate the virtual camera using the support plane of
the portal
        // invert viewing matrices
        // Paint destination room of the portal
        // paint portal using alpha blend if you need a "stained
glass" effect
        break;
        }
    case TRANSLUCENT:
        {
        // Paint destination room of the portal
        // paint portal using alpha blend if you need a "stained
glass" effect
        break;
        }
    }
```

The amount of code needed to implement these great looking effects is minimal, keeping the overall elegance of the portal approach.

Hierarchical Occlusion Maps

You have seen how both BSP and portal implementations try to compute indoors environments by means of quickly computing the occlusion portion. Clipping and culling are usually added to the mix easily, but it's the occlusion part that causes most trouble. Let's now review another approach. Like portal rendering, this technique is designed to compute occlusions at runtime. The main advantage of this new technique, called hierarchical occlusions maps (HOM), is that no preprocessing is actually needed.

Occlusions can be computed from geometry that comes directly from your modeling package of choice. Another advantage is that HOM can handle static and dynamic geometry seamlessly, making it a bit more powerful (but also more complex) than portal rendering.

HOM was introduced in 1998 by Zhang. It is based on a hierarchy of occlusion maps, each one half the size of the previous one. We start with a full-resolution black-and-white rendering of our scene and compute a series of mipmaps, blending every 2×2 pixel into one. Obviously, this makes the algorithm easier to code if you start with a power-of-two sized image. This series of bitmaps is the hierarchical occlusion map. The occlusion map does not represent the whole scene, only a set of good occluders chosen with a method similar to the one explained in the first section of this chapter: large, close objects that are aligned to the screen.

Then, at runtime, we paint object-by-object, probably assisted by some hierarchical representation such as an octree or quadtree. For each object or node, we need to compute the screen-aligned bounding rectangle. This rectangle will enclose the whole object and be used in the occlusion processing part. Then, we select the HOM level in which the pixel size is approximately the size of the rectangle. If the HOM pixels are all white, there's a full overlap, so the object is either in front of the occluders or behind them. If the HOM is pure black, the object must be painted because no occlusion took place. If the HOM is gray, it means the current resolution cannot determine clearly whether we are occluded or not, so we will need to examine higher-resolution HOMs to discover whether we are in a white area after all.

For those objects in white zones, we need to test for Z-values and thus discover whether they are in front or behind the occluders. This is achieved with a depth estimation buffer (DEB), which is just a software Z-buffer constructed from the occluders. The DEB takes the bounding box of each occluder and stores in the pixels covered by it the farthest Z-value. Notice that we use farthest, not closest as in a regular Z-buffer. Because the DEB has a lower resolution than a regular Z-buffer, each pixel must provide a conservative estimation of the Z-value for all objects contained within its boundaries. Selecting the farthest Z-value performs that task.

The overall algorithm for the HOM is as follows. During preprocessing, preselect a good database of occluders. Objects smaller than a certain threshold, narrow, or with high polygon counts are discarded. Redundant objects are rejected as well. Any decoration on top of a wall should be discarded, and so on. In the end, the best occluders are probably room walls and large pillars. An alternative is to not use real scene geometry, but instead use placeholder objects that are manually located to act as good occluders.

Then, at runtime, we select the N closest occluders from the database. Remember that occluders need to be visible, so performing a clipping test as well will be worthwhile. We then build the HOM based on these objects. The high-resolution version is created with render-to-texture capabilities. To create the low-resolution copies, we can compute them on software, or even better, using lower resolution textures and bilinear minification filters. As we traverse our scene graph, we test visible nodes against the HOM. If they lie in a black zone, we need to paint them. If they are in a white zone, we perform the Z-test with the DEB and decide whether we should discard them or not based on the results. Objects in gray areas require further refining in the HOM before moving on to the DEB phase. In the end, a well-built HOM can cull away between 40 and 60 percent of all incoming geometry.

Hybrid Approaches

Pure BSPs, portals, and octrees are just general-purpose, academic solutions. Real-world games have specific requirements and often combine these approaches along with other clever ideas to create unique, high-quality solutions. In this section, I will show you some of the hybrid algorithms used by some high-end games today.

Portal-Octree Hybrid

Some games show very detailed and dense indoors environments. Think of a game that takes place in a large castle with rooms full of objects: lamps, tables, chairs, and treasure chests galore. The overall environment gives a sense of density and richness to the player. Also, the design of the game calls for a highly interactive world. We need to be able to push objects, grab items, and drop them wherever we want to. Can we handle this kind of environment with the techniques explained earlier? Although all methods will definitely support such a scenario, performance will not be very good. BSPs, for example, will tend to grow indefinitely, because the triangle count will be extremely high. Even worse, using a BSP will also impose the restriction of geometry being static. How does that fit with our interactivity requirements for the game world?

Portal methods look a bit more promising at the beginning, until you realize that each room is actually composed of a high number of triangles, thus making it slow to test for triangle visibility. You could choose to test for the room walls only, but you need some fast way to test for the visibility of room contents as well.

A better solution to this problem is to use a nested portal-octree system, which combines portal visibility for the rooms and hierarchical culling using an octree for the room contents. Thus, the level is laid out in a series of rooms connected by portals, as in a regular portal renderer. Rooms include the geometry for the room walls only, but not for the contents. Each room must hold a small octree with the contents arranged in it. This octree will only be a few levels deep, but will allow us to test for object visibility hierarchically.

Another benefit of this technique is that the octree must not really hold the object data, but instances to it. By doing so, we can have a room full of chairs with just one chair model, thus reducing the memory footprint. In this type of scenario, level-of-detail policies for the room contents could be easily integrated with the core algorithms, thus creating a complete solution. A global visibility algorithm would be implemented using portals, and octrees would deal with the room contents. This approach also allows objects to be moved around with just a small cost for redoing the affected octree. In addition, level-of-detail processing can be used to ensure that triangles are spent where they can affect the results, not on distant, background objects.

Quadtree-BSP Hybrid

A quadtree-BSP hybrid approach can be used in games where large areas need to be explored, especially if very precise collision detection needs to be used. Here the idea is to divide the game world into a quadtree, stopping the creation process when leaves reach a certain number of triangles or a predefined size. We could start with a level that is one kilometer in size and subdivide until a cell is either below 500 triangles or 10 meters in size. Then, each leaf node would store the geometry in a BSP tree data structure. The implementation details are definitely nontrivial, but the resulting structure has a number of advantages.

Quadtrees converge faster than BSPs do. A quadtree divides the input data by four in each level, whereas BSPs only divide in half. A quadtree would thus be faster in determining the area the player is in. A pure quadtree is not very helpful for collision detection. BSPs, on the other hand, can be configured to speed up this process signifi-cantly. (Take a look at Chapter 22 for information on computing collisions with a BSP.) Thus, blending the two structures gives us the best of both worlds. The quadtree allows us to detect where we are quickly, and then a BSP helps us refine our location to the triangle level to perform collision detection efficiently.

Hardware-Assisted Occlusion Tests

Some modern video cards (GeForce3 and later, and most ATI recent boards) support specific calls to make occlusion detection easier by computing it on the hardware. Although these calls will never be a substitute for our occlusion code completely, they are a nice addition because code complexity is largely reduced. Let's examine how hardware-assisted occlusion detection works, and then reformulate some of our algorithms to take advantage of them.

Generally speaking, all video cards perform early Z-rejection these days. Z-buffer is checked for as early as possible, so subsequent passes (texturing, color interpolation, and so on) can be skipped for those fragments where the Z test fails. However, we still need to send the data to the video card, thus spending time on the bus transforming vertices, projecting, and so on. For hardware occlusion detection to really make a difference, we would need calls that would work on an object level and have the ability to reject many triangles at once, thus saving lots of effort. This is exactly what modern cards provide—tests that can be used on full objects. The idea is quite simple. First, we need to activate the occlusion query mode. Second, we send whatever geometry we want to test occlusions for. This geometry will not be painted, but only checked against the Z-buffer using speedy routines. Third, the call will tell us if the said primi-tive actually altered any pixels of the Z-buffer. It will even tell us how many pixels were updated, so we get a measure of relevance for the object. Now, we could use this approach for each triangle on an object, but then we wouldn't benefit much. In fact, performance would degrade due to more vertices being sent.

The real benefit from occlusion queries comes from using them with bounding objects, such as boxes or spheres. A bounding box is just 12 triangles, and by sending them and testing for occlusions, we can effectively avoid sending thousands. Complete objects can be rejected this way. So, here is the full algorithm:

```
for each object
   activate occlusion query
   send bounding box
   deactivate occlusion query
   if pixels were modified by the test
      render object
   end if
end for
```

We can further improve this approach by sending data front-to-back, and thus maximize occlusions. Closer objects will be painted earlier, and thus many primitives will be fully covered by them. Additionally, we can implement our occlusion tests in a hierarchical manner. If the bounding box of a set of objects is rejected, all bounding boxes from descendant nodes (such as in a quadtree) will be rejected as well, and thus we can prune the tree data structure. This last approach can be elegantly integrated with a clipping pass, resulting in a global visibility algorithm that performs all tests efficiently. Here is the pseudocode for such an algorithm:

```
Paint (node *n)

Sort the four subnodes using their distance to the viewer
for each subnode (in distance order)
   if subnode is not empty
      if subnode is not clipped
         activate occlusion query
         paint bounding box
         if pixels were modified
            paint object
         end if
      end if
   end if
end for
```

When using occlusion queries, not all bounding volumes will offer the same performance. Spheres should be avoided because painting the bounding volume while performing the occlusion query pass will be costly. There are a lot of faces and vertices in a sphere. Boxes, on the other hand, offer tighter packing and require much less rendering effort.

For the sake of completeness, let's look at two working examples of hardware occlusion queries that could be implemented in OpenGL using a proprietary NVIDIA extension and in DirectX 9. Here is an implementation for a GeForce board using OpenGL:

```
Gluint queries[N];
GLuint pixelCount;
glGenOcclusionQueriesNV(N, queries);
for (i = 0; i < N; i++)      {
    glBeginOcclusionQueryNV(queries[i]);
    // render bounding box for ith geometry
    glEndOcclusionQueryNV();
    }
for (i = 0; i < N; i++)
    {
    glGetOcclusionQueryuivNV(queries[i], GL_PIXEL_COUNT_NV,
&pixelCount);
    if (pixelCount > MAX_COUNT)
    // render ith geometry
    }
```

The same functionality comes built-in directly in DirectX 9. To access occlusion queries, we must create an IDirect3DQuery9 object with the call

```
CreateQuery(D3DQUERYTYPE Type,IDirect3DQuery9** ppQuery);
```

Here is a complete example:

```
IDirect3DQuery9 *myQuery;
g_pd3dDevice->CreateQuery(D3DQUERYTYPE_OCCLUSION, &myQuery);
myQuery->Issue(D3DISSUE_BEGIN);

// paint the object to test occlusions for

myQuery->Issue(D3DISSUE_END);

DWORD pixels;
```

```
while (myQuery->GetData((void *)&pixels, sizeof(DWORD),
D3DGETDATA_FLUSH) == S_FALSE);

if (pixels>MAX_COUNT)    {
    // render the object
    }
```

The philosophy behind the code is very similar to the OpenGL version. We send an occlusion query and render the object we want to test visibility for. Notice that occlusion queries are asynchronous (as in OpenGL, by the way). This means that GetData might be executed prior to the occlusion test actually returning any results, and hence the while loop. In the end, the GetData call returns the number of painted pixels, so we can use that information to paint geometry or not.

Now, some advice on hardware-assisted occlusion queries must be provided to ensure that you get good performance. Although the technique looks very powerful on paper, only careful planning will allow you to get a significant performance boost. Remember that rasterizing the occlusion query objects will take up some fill rate, so use these wisely. Make sure culling is on, and turn off any textures, lighting, and so on. You need your occlusion queries to be as fast as possible. You don't want to speed up rasterization at the cost of wasting fill rate in the query. This issue is less important with hierarchical occlusion queries. Build a bounding box hierarchy, and prune it with an occlusion query so large parts of the scene are culled away. Eliminating several objects with one test will definitely pay off the effort of rendering the occlusion query object.

Another interesting idea is to use occlusion queries with geometry you actually would render anyway. A good example here is multipass rendering. If we need to render the same object two or more times, we can activate the occlusion query for the first pass, and only if it returns a no occlusion result, render subsequent passes. This way we are not throwing away our precious fill rate because we would be rendering the object anyway. Another good idea is to substitute objects by lower triangle count approximations: Convex hulls can be a useful primitive in this situation.

In Closing

Hardware-assisted occlusion queries are revolutionizing the way indoors rendering algorithms are coded, now that clipping, culling, and occlusions have been mastered. But there's plenty of room for innovation. Whether it's better indoors lighting, movable geometry pieces such as tables and chairs, or dense environments, there will always be room for improvements.

Chapter 14

Outdoors Algorithms

"It's a dangerous business going out your front door."

J. R. R. Tolkien, *The Fellowship of the Ring*

In the previous chapter, we explored indoors rendering algorithms in detail and learned all about dungeons, castles, and houses. Now we will move out of the building and into the great outdoors. We will focus on hills, trees, and valleys, where we can see for miles away. Rendering outdoors scenarios is a completely different business than indoors rendering. Luckily, some robust methods have been devised through the years, which ensure that we can render virtually any outdoors scene with reasonable performance. Let's study these popular algorithms in detail.

Overview

In any indoors renderer, we can take advantage of clipping and culling to detect the portion of the game world that effectively lies inside the viewing frustum. Then, an occlusion-detection policy must be implemented to minimize overdraw, and thus ensure optimal performance. Occlusion tests can be performed because the visibility range (sometimes called Z-distance) is bounded. Outdoors renderers are a bit different. Like indoors algorithms, they can take advantage of clipping and culling. This way a significant part of the game world's geometry can simply be eliminated because it does not lie within the viewing frustum.

But what about occlusions? Well, truth be told, there are frequent occlusions in nature: a hill covering parts of the scene, trees acting as natural occluders, and so on. But even with that level of occlusion, the triangle counts for any outdoors scene are generally beyond the hardware's capabilities. Imagine that you are on top of a mountain looking downhill onto a huge plain. How many triangles do you need to render that scene? There are some nearby objects (stones, for example) that can be modeled using just a few triangles, but what about the distant horizon located at least 10 miles away? Will you still model each stone and crack of the ground, even if it's unnoticeable from where you are standing?

Clearly, outdoors algorithms are all about level-of-detail (LOD) strategies—being able to reallocate triangles so more relevant items (in terms of screen size) get a better resolution than distant or smaller items. This relationship is summarized in Table 14.1, which I use to explain the difference between indoors and outdoors rendering.

Table 14.1 Characterization of Outdoors Versus Indoors Rendering Algorithms

Algorithm	Clipping	Culling	Occlusions	LOD
Indoors	Yes	Yes	Yes	Optional
Outdoors	Yes	Yes	Optional	Yes

For the remaining sections of this chapter, I will define outdoors algorithms as those algorithms that work with large viewing distances and focus on LOD strategies instead of occlusion testing algorithms.

This is not to say that occlusions will be secondary or even irrelevant. Most outdoors algorithms have a significant degree of occlusion. But because outdoors data sets are generally larger than their indoors counterparts, sometimes computing occlusions will be too complex, and thus will be discarded altogether. Some outdoors approaches incorporate occlusions into the equation; others focus on the LOD policies only. The last algorithm in this chapter is an example of an outdoors renderer that handles occlusions elegantly.

Data Structures for Outdoors Rendering

We will begin our journey by examining the different ways commonly used to store the outdoors rendering data. We must begin by distinguishing the different elements. The data used to represent terrain is what will concern us most. We have already explored ways to deal with regular objects that you can use to store objects laid on top of the land—like a building, for example. You can find more on that in Chapter 12, "3D Pipeline Overview." Some interesting approaches to this problem that are well suited for outdoors scenarios (namely, a continuous LOD policy called *progressive meshes*) are discussed in Chapter 22, "Geometrical Algorithms." If you need information on trees and vegetation, look no further than Chapter 20, "Organic Rendering."

We will now focus on storing land masses, which is an interesting and difficult problem in its own right. First, we will need to store large data sets. Second, we will need some kind of LOD policy to make sure we don't spend lots of triangles painting very distant areas. Third, this policy must be smooth enough so we can progressively approach a new terrain region and switch from the low-res version to the high-res version imperceptibly. This makes terrain rendering algorithms somewhat more specialized and complex than most of their indoors counterparts.

Heightfields

The easiest way to store terrain is to use a grayscale bitmap that encodes the height of each sampled point at regular distances. Traditionally, dark values (thus, closer to zero) represent low height areas, and white values encode peaks. But because bitmaps have a fixed size and color precision, you need to define the real scale of the map in X, Y, and Z so it can be expanded to its actual size. For example, a 256×256 bitmap with 256 levels of gray can be converted into a landmass of 1×1 kms and 512 meters of height variation by supplying a scale factor of (4,4,2).

Heightfields are the starting point for many terrain renderers. They can be handled directly and converted to quadtrees, and they provide a simple yet elegant way of specifying the look of the terrain. You can even create these bitmaps with most paint programs or with specific tools such as Bryce, which creates very realistic terrain maps using fractal models. Once created, heightfields can be stored in memory either directly as an array of height values or in uncompressed form, with each value expanded to its corresponding 3D point. The first option is usually preferred because the memory footprint is really low, and expansion is not that costly anyway. Additionally, painting a heightfield is usually achieved through triangle strips, indexed primitives, or a combination of both. A landmass is really just a grid with the Y values shifted vertically, and grids are very well suited for strips and indices (see Figure 14.1).

Figure 14.1 Terrain and underlying heightfield.

The downside of the simplicity and elegance of heightfields is that they are limited to 2D and half maps. Obviously, for a fixed X,Z pair there is only one pixel value on the heightfield, so it is impossible to implement an arch or an overhang using this representation. These elements must be handled in a second layer added on top of the base terrain. Additionally, heightfields are not especially well suited for LOD modeling. Thus, they are frequently used only in the first stage, deriving a better-suited structure from them. Most popular algorithms, such as the geomipmapping and Real-time Optimally Adapting Meshes (ROAM), use heightfields as a starting point. However, other data structures such as quadtrees and binary triangle trees are used when it comes to LOD processing.

Quadtrees

Another way of storing terrain is to use a quadtree data structure. Quadtrees are 4-ary trees that subdivide each node into four subnodes that correspond to the four sub-quadrants of the initial node. Thus, for a terrain mass lying in the X, Z plane, the quadtree would refine each node by computing its midpoint in X and Z and creating four subnodes that correspond to the (low X, low Z), (low X, high Z), (high X, low Z), and (high X, high Z). Figure 14.2 will help you to better picture this splitting.

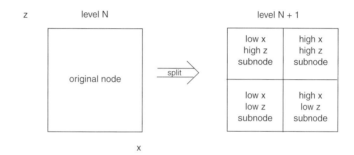

Figure 14.2   Node splitting on a quadtree.

Quadtrees are popular for terrain representation because they provide a twofold adaptive method. The construction of the quadtree can be adaptive in itself. Starting with a heightfield, you can build a quadtree that expands nodes only when more detail is needed. The resulting quadtree will be a 4-ary, fully unbalanced tree, meaning that some branches will dig deeper than others. The metric for the detail level can then be of very different natures. A popular approach is to analyze the contents of the node (be it a single quad or the whole terrain landmass) and somehow estimate the detail as the variance between the real data and a quad that took its place. For each X,Z pair, we retrieve the Y from the original data set and compare it to an estimated Y, which is the bilinear interpolation of the four corner values. If we average these variances, we will obtain a global value. Larger results imply more detail (and thus a greater need to refine the quadtree), whereas smaller, even zero, values mean areas that have less detail and can thus be simplified more.

But that's only one of the two adaptive mechanisms provided by a quadtree. The second mechanism operates at runtime. The renderer can choose to traverse the quadtree, selecting the maximum depth using a heuristic based upon the distance to the player and the detail in the mesh. Adding the proper continuity mechanisms to ensure the whole mesh stays well sown allows us to select a coarser representation for distant elements (for example, mountain peaks located miles away from the viewer) while ensuring maximum detail on nearby items.

This double adaptiveness provides lots of room to design clever algorithms that take advantage of the two adaptive behaviors of the quadtree.

Binary Triangle Trees

A *binary triangle tree* (BTT) is a special case of binary tree that takes most of its design philosophy from quadtrees. Like quadtrees, it is an adaptive data structure that grows where more detail is present while keeping a coarser representation in less-detailed areas. Unlike quadtrees, the core geometrical primitive for a BTT is, as the name implies, the triangle. Quadtrees work with square or rectangular terrain areas, whereas BTTs start with a triangular terrain patch. In order to work with a square data set, we must use two BTTs that are connected.

Because the core primitive is different from a regular quadtree, the division criteria for the BTT are different from that of quadtrees as well. Quadtrees are divided in four by the orthogonal axis at the center of the current region. A BTT triangle node is divided in two by creating two new triangles, which share an edge that splits the hypotenuse of the initial triangle in half (see Figure 14.3).

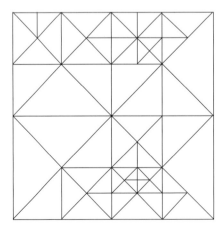

Figure 14.3   Top-down view on a terrain patch scanned using a BTT.

BTTs are popular for terrain rendering because they provide an adaptive level of detail, and each node has fewer descendants and neighbors than quadtrees. This makes them easier to keep well connected in continuous LOD algorithms. The ROAM algorithm explained in a later section in this chapter takes advantage of this fact and uses a BTT to implement a continuous level-of-detail (CLOD) policy efficiently.

Geomipmapping

Mipmapping (explained in detail in Chapter 18, "Texture Mapping") is a texture mapping technique aimed at improving the visual quality of distant, textured primitives. In a distant triangle, the screen area of the triangle (in pixels) will be smaller than the size of the texture. This means each pixel gets to be textured by several texels, and as the triangle moves even slightly, flicker appears. Texture mipmapping works by precomputing a series of scaled-down texture maps ($1/2$, $1/4$, and so on) called *mipmaps*. Mipmaps are prefiltered so they average texel value correctly. Then, when texturing, the triangle is textured using the mipmap that most closely resembles its screen size. This way flicker is reduced, and even distant triangles get proper texturing.

Based on the same concept, Willem de Boer devised the geomipmapping algorithm (www.flipcode.com/tutorials/geomipmaps.pdf), which implements a CLOD terrain system by using mipmaps computed not on textures, but on the terrain geometry (hence the name). All we need to do is select the right geometrical representation depending on the distance to the viewer, and make sure the seams where two different representations meet merge smoothly without visible artifacts.

The concept behind geomipmapping can be adapted to any terrain data structure. However, because it is a texture-like approach, the easiest way to use it is to start from a heightfield representation. Incidentally, heightfields can be represented using grayscale images, so the similarities with texture maps are still present. We then need to compute the geometry mipmaps. To do so, we can scale down the heightfield bitmaps using image processing software or simply compute them at runtime. Just remember that mipmaps are computed sequentially by dividing the last texture map's size by a factor of two, combining each of the four texels of the initial map into a single, averaged value. Again, building geometry mipmaps is no different than working on textures.

Remember that your terrain size must be a power of two for this method to work (because of the subdivision step). Specifically, terrain size must be in the form $2n+1$ because we need an extra vertex to make sure we get a power-of-two number of quads. See Figure 14.4, which shows this in a 4×4 mesh, using 5×5 vertices.

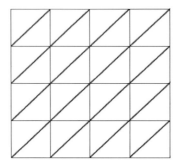

Figure 14.4 To create a 4×4 triangle mesh (which actually holds 32 triangles), we need a 5×5 vertex mesh.

The first step in the rendering process is to effectively load the data structures in memory. For geomipmapping, terrain data is organized in a quadtree; each leaf node contains what's called a *terrain block*. Terrain blocks are pieces of terrain consisting of several triangles each. In his initial formulation, de Boer suggests using a 4×4 mesh (consisting of 32 triangles). To build the quadtree, you start with the whole terrain data set. The root node stores its 3D bounding box, and then each of the four descendants contains one of the four subquadrants of the data set. Each subsequent node will contain the bounding box of the incoming set and pass four pointers to its descendants until a node is exactly composed of a single terrain block. A 257×257 terrain map will require exactly six levels (measuring 256, 128, 64, 32, 16, 8, and 4 triangles across each). Organizing the data in a quadtree will help us perform fast hierarchical clipping. We will depth-traverse the tree, and as soon as the bounding box from one node is rejected as totally invisible, the whole subtree will be rejected, hence speeding up the calculations significantly.

Notice how, up to this point, we have not performed any LOD. All we have done is arrange the source data in a quadtree, which will indeed speed up clipping, but that's about it. In fact, we could stop here and implement the preceding algorithm. Using hardware culling, it would be a good way of selecting only those triangles effectively onscreen. Besides, the block layout allows for packed primitives such as strips and indexed triangle lists to be used, delivering quite good performance.

But there is no LOD policy yet, so distant triangles would probably eat away all our CPU cycles, effectively killing performance. This is where geomipmaps enter the scene to speed up the rendering process. The idea is straightforward: As we reach the leaves of the quadtree, we decide which resolution to use for that terrain block. We need to store not only the high-resolution terrain, but mipmapped versions as well. The decision criteria, as usual, depend on the quantity of detail in the block and the distance to the viewer. We begin by computing the error of a geometry block, expressed as the maximal distance (in screen space) from a mipmap's position to the real position of the actual geometry. We call this an error because it is a measure of how much deviation actually exists between the real value (taken from the mesh) and the value we are using for rendering purposes.

Thus, we take all the vertices in a block and compute the distances from the mipmapped vertices to the real geometry. When projected to the screen, these return pixel amounts, which take into consideration detail (the more detail, the more error) and distance (the more distance, the less error). Then, we work with a fixed threshold (values of about 5 pixels are frequent) and select the first mipmap level so error is bounded. Thus, distant geometry blocks will be heavily simplified, and closer blocks will not. An interesting side effect of such an approach is that top-down cameras will usually end up rendering lower resolution meshes, because the screen-space error will be virtually none.

Using geomipmapping, we must deal with two potential issues in order to convey a good sense of realism. First, we must deal with the geometry gaps that occur whenever two blocks of different resolution are adjacent. This breaks the continuity of the terrain. Second, we must ensure that a change in detail in a certain area is virtually imperceptible, so the player does not realize the LOD work that is taking place. Let's examine each problem and the way to deal with it.

We will start by dealing with geometry cracks and gaps, which occur whenever two blocks with different mipmaps are adjacent. This is a common problem that is shared by most terrain algorithms, not just mipmapping, so the solution we will propose is valid for other algorithms as well. A good overview of different approaches can be found in de Boer's original paper. The best solution proposed is to alter the connectivity of the higher detail mesh so it blends with the lower detail mesh seamlessly. Basically, we have a high detail mesh and a lower detail mesh (see Figure 14.5, left). Then, all we have to do is reconstruct the high-res mesh so it connects cleanly with the low-res mesh. By skipping one in each of the two vertices of the high-res mesh, we can ensure that both meshes connect properly with no gaps. This implies that some vertices in the high-res meshes will remain unused, but the result will be unnoticeable.

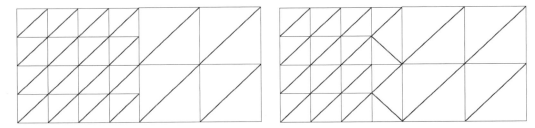

Figure 14.5 Left: Connected, unsown mesh. Right: Skip one of every two vertices in the high-res mesh and reconstruct the face loops to weld terrain blocks together.

Let's now discuss how to avoid sudden pops that take place whenever we change the resolution level of a terrain block. A powerful technique for this problem is called *geomorphing* and involves smoothing the transition from one mipmap to the next by linear interpolation. The key idea is simple: Popping is caused whenever we change the resolution suddenly, so new vertices appear (each with its own shading), and overall we see an abrupt change in appearance. Geomorphing works by ensuring that no single frame actually changes the appearance more than a fixed threshold. Whenever we want to increase the detail level, we start by using the high-detail mesh but with its new vertices aligned with the plane of the low-res mesh. Thus, we change a low-res mesh by using a high-res mesh, but the Y of each point in the terrain is still the same for both resolutions. We then take these interpolated Y values and progressively shift them to their final position as the camera approaches. This way detail does not appear suddenly but "pops in" slowly, ensuring continuity and eliminating pops completely.

ROAM

ROAM is one of the most powerful outdoors approaches devised to date. The algorithm was designed by a team working at the Lawrence Livermore National Laboratory, led by Mark Duchaineau. It became popular in games such as *Tread Marks* by Seumas McNally and has been used in many others since then. The algorithm combines a powerful representation of the terrain with a dynamic LOD rendering approach that changes the resolution of the terrain as we move around. What follows is a thorough description of the ROAM algorithm. However, I must provide a word of warning. ROAM, like BSPs, is a very complex algorithm. I suggest you take the following sections one step at a time, making a drawing along the way to ensure you understand it. For more information, I recommend that you review the original paper, which provides many implementation details, and the Gamasutra article by Bryan Turner. Both are referenced in Appendix E, "Further Reading." Having these papers at hand will prove very useful if you are serious about ROAM.

ROAM is a two-pass algorithm that allows very fast terrain rendering. ROAM does not have a geometric representation of the terrain beforehand: It builds the mesh along the way, using precomputed measures of detail to know where it should refine further. On the first pass, terrain data is scanned into a bintree, and a view-independent error metric is computed. This metric will allow us to detect zones in which more detail is needed. Then a second pass constructs a second bintree, which performs the actual mesh construction and rendering.

Pass One: Construct the Variance Tree

In the first phase, we will build a representation of the detail in the terrain. To do so, we need to establish a metric for detail. Several metrics are proposed in the original paper, and others were devised later. One of the most popular error metrics is called the *variance*, which was introduced in the game *Tread Marks*, and is defined inductively. For a leaf node (a bintree that is one pixel across), we define the variance as the difference in height between the interpolated hypotenuse and the real value of the heightmap for that point. Thus, we compute the hypotenuse midpoint and compare that to the real value of the terrain (see Figure 14.6).

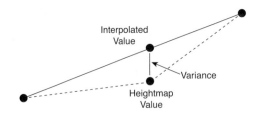

Figure 14.6   Variance in ROAM for a leaf node.

For any node in the tree that is not a leaf, the variance is the maximal variance of any descendant from that node. Thus, we need to explore the terrain fully until we reach the base nodes, each representing just one pixel from our heightmap. We compute basic variances at these nodes, and then propagate them to build nested variances in the backtracking phase. The variance of the root node will be the maximal variance of any of the triangles that are derived from it. Here is the algorithm to compute the variance:

```
int CalcVariance(tri)
{
int RealHeight = the map height at the middle of the hypotenuse
int AvgHeight = the average of the real heights at the two ends
of the hypot
int v = abs( RealHeight - AvgHeight )
if tri->LeftChild is valid
    {
    v = max( v, CalcVariance(tri->LeftChild) )
    }
if tri->RightChild is valid
    {
    v = max( v, CalcVariance(tri->RightChild) )
    }
return v
}
```

As you can see, we need a data structure for the nested variances. The logical structure would be a binary tree, so we can reproduce the nested behavior of variances. This tree is often mapped to a static array for faster access in the rendering phase because we will need to access this structure frequently.

Thus, the first phase of any ROAM implementation basically builds the nested variance data structure, which provides us with useful information for the mesh reconstruction and rendering phase.

Pass Two: Mesh Reconstruction

Once the variance tree is built, we can take advantage of it to build the mesh for rendering. To do so, we build a BTT of geometry, and then expand it more or less using the variance hints.

The BTT is just a regular tree that is used to store triangles. The root node represents a large triangular area of the terrain, and each descendant covers a subset of that initial zone. Because it is a triangular shaped tree, some magic will be needed to support quadrilateral zones (usually two trees joined at the root). Each node of the triangle tree approximates a zone of the terrain by storing only its corner values. If the vertices inside the zone are not coplanar to these corners, we can use the variance tree to determine how much detail still exists inside that subzone, and thus make a decision to supersample it further. You can see this construct along with a complete BTT in Figure 14.7.

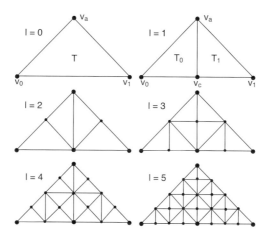

Figure 14.7   BTT, shown from the top down.

The key idea of the BTT construction is to use the view-independent error metric, coupled with a view-dependent component to decide how deep we must propagate into the tree while building the mesh in the process. As with geomipmaps, we set a maximum threshold and recurse until a node generates an error smaller than the threshold. But we know beforehand that this process will indeed introduce gaps and cracks because neighboring triangles need not be of the same resolution level. Thus, sometimes their edges simply will not match. Geomipmapping solves this issue by welding patches of different resolution together. ROAM works in a different direction. Whenever we encounter a discontinuity, we oversample neighboring patches to make sure they are sown together properly. To do so, we need to label each side of a triangle and use some rules that guarantee the continuity of the mesh.

We will call the hypotenuse of the triangle the base and call the other two sides the left and right sides, depending on the orientation of the triangle. The same terminology applies to neighbors. Thus, we can talk about the base neighbor (which is along the hypotenuse) and so on (see Figure 14.8). If you analyze several bintrees, you will discover that neighbors from a triangle can only exist in specific configurations. For example, the base neighbor will either be from the same level as the original node or from the next coarser level. Left and right nodes, on the other hand, can either be located at the same level or one level finer at most.

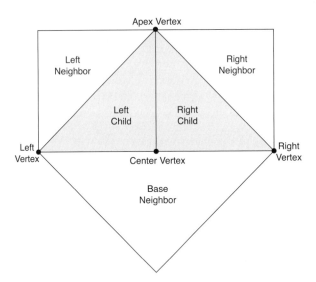

Figure 14.8 Triangles and their labels.

From this fact, we can derive three rules of splitting that govern when and how we can recurse further into the tree. The first rule applies to those nodes that are part of a diamond (thus, connected to a base neighbor of the same level). In these cases, we must split the node and the base neighbor to avoid creating cracks. Both nodes will split in sync, and continuity will be preserved. A second case happens when a node is at the edge of the mesh. This is the trivial case because we can keep splitting even if we cause side effects. The third case deals with nodes that are not part of a diamond. In this case, we must first-force split the base neighbor before we split our current node, and thus preserve continuity. Here is a summary of these rules:

➤ If part of a diamond, split the node and the base neighbor.

➤ If at the edge of a mesh, split as needed.

➤ If not part of a diamond, force-split the base neighbor before splitting the current node.

So fundamentally, the run-time algorithm is as follows: Traverse the bintree and couple the view-independent variance with a view-dependent component (usually, the distance to the viewer) so a view-dependent metric of error is returned. We then want to recurse until the error level for that node is lower than a fixed threshold. We must follow the three splitting rules as explained in the previous paragraph to ensure we create a continuous mesh. For an example of the splitting at work, take a look at Figure 14.9.

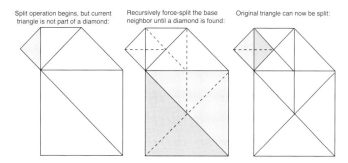

Figure 14.9   Left: Split begins; we are not part of a diamond, so if we split the shaded triangle, continuity will be lost. Center: We recursively split (using the rules) the base neighbor so we gain the vertex, which we will use to (right) split the current node.

Notice that the mesh will be quite conservative. Because of rules 1 and 3, we will sometimes be forced to split a node further than required, so its resolution will be higher. This is because the node might have a highly detailed neighbor, and because we need to recurse the neighbor further, we also end up recursing the node more than is needed. Notice, however, that the opposite is not true: The mesh will never be coarser than the fixed threshold.

Nodes pending a split operation are usually arranged in a priority queue, called the *split queue*. This is sorted by priority, which is generally the view-dependent error. Then, we start at the base triangulation of the bintree (the root, which covers the whole terrain with a single triangle) and trigger the following greedy algorithm:

```
T = base triangulation
while T is too inaccurate
        identify highest priority node from T (node with biggest
error)
        force-split using the rules
        update queue:
                remove the node that has just been split
                add the new nodes resulting from the split
end while
```

So we store nodes where the algorithm is standing currently. We compute the incurred error of the triangulation as the biggest error in the nodes, and if the overall error is too large, we select the node with the highest priority (biggest error) and force split it using the splitting rules previously explained. We then remove the offending node, substitute it with those nodes arising from the split, and start over. If we implement the splitting rules correctly, this generates an optimal, continuous mesh with error levels below the fixed bound.

This is the simplest type of ROAM and is usually referred to as *split-only ROAM*. It computes a continuous mesh for a terrain heightfield, but it comes with a host of problems that must be addressed to reach reasonable performance. ROAM is a hard algorithm because its base implementation is not fast enough for more or less anything.

Optimizations

As you have seen, ROAM is a CPU-intensive algorithm. In fact, its performance is seldom limited by the sheer number of triangles to render, but by the binary triangle tree construction and traversal. Experience shows that, in most cases, a split-only ROAM will not be fast enough to render large, detailed pieces of terrain. We will now cover some optimization techniques that will multiply the performance of any split-only ROAM implementation.

The first change to the ROAM engine is to divide the terrain into sectors so the bintree does not cover the whole map. Rather, we would have a 2D matrix of bintrees, each covering parts of the terrain. This makes trees less deep and also simplifies tessellation. ROAM is still too expensive to be computed per frame, and besides, doing so is a complete waste of resources.

Imagine that the player is standing still facing the landscape. Do we really need to recompute the tessellation per frame? Obviously not, and that's why ROAM is usually implemented on a frame-coherent basis. The terrain is only recomputed every few frames, usually using an interleaved bintree policy as well. We do not recompute each bintree each frame, but rather cycle through the different trees frame by frame (or even every number of frames). So if we have an $N \times M$ array of bintrees, we compute a bintree's tessellation once every $N \times M$ frames. This greatly reduces the CPU hit of the tessellation. A similar approach is to make ROAM retessellation dependent on the player's change of position and orientation. We can force a recalc if and only if the player has moved more than X meters from the last recalc position or has rotated more than Y degrees. If coupled with the sector-by-sector approach outlined earlier, this should definitely put an end to most of our performance concerns. Take a look at a ROAM algorithm in action in Figure 14.10.

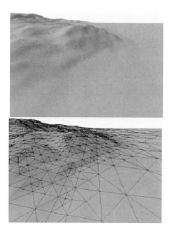
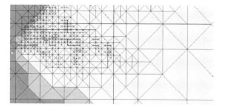

Figure 14.10   ROAM at work. Left: Camera view of the level with the mesh (above) and the wire frame views (below). Right: The same frame, seen from a top-down camera. Notice how the blending of the view-dependent and the view-independent components preserves detail.

Another completely different line of thought is to work on frustum culling. Remember that we are working with a BTT, so there's some interesting issues that arise from the frustum cull phase. The most popular technique is to label each node in the bintree with six flags, one for each half space delimiting the frustum. This effectively means storing a Boolean for each one of the six clipping planes to determine if the triangle is completely inside or if it's either partially or totally outside. Then, a global IN, OUT, and DON'T-KNOW (for triangles part-in, part-out) label is assigned to the node. Because the tree is hierarchical, we can update this information easily on a frame-to-frame basis. A node IN means all subnodes—until we reach the leaves—that are all IN, for example, and the opposite is also true for OUT nodes. Because we recalc the culling information, only some portions of the tree will have changed, and we will devote our efforts to those. Suddenly, a node that was IN or OUT (and required no further analysis) will turn to DON'T-KNOW because it will be partly inside, partly outside. We then need to scan only that subtree to keep the information current. Then, for painting purposes, all we need to do is render those nodes that are IN or DON'T-KNOW and prune OUT nodes directly.

Another improvement to the core ROAM algorithm is to stripify triangles as we retessellate. This is obviously not for the faint of heart, because real-time stripification is a complex problem. In the original paper, a suboptimal incremental tristripper tries to create strips as nodes are split. Results show splits between four and five vertices on average, which also helps reduce the amount of data sent over the bus.

Chunked LODs

The algorithm discussed in this section was proposed by Thatcher Ulrich of Oddworld Inhabitants at SIGGRAPH 2002. Its main focus is allowing massive terrain data sets to be displayed in real time. As an example, the classic demo of chunked LODs involves a *Puget Sound* data set that covers 160×160 km. The triangle data takes 512MB, and the textures require 3GB uncompressed (60MB in JPEG). Thus, the algorithm is very well suited for huge terrain data sets, such as the data sets found in flight simulators.

The algorithm starts with a huge data set, usually coming from a satellite picture. Then, it builds a quadtree so the root node contains a very low-resolution mesh from the original data set, and each descendant node refines the area covered by its parent in four quadrants, adding detail to the base geometry in each one of them. Leaf nodes then contain chunks of geometry that cover a very small area on the map, but provide very good quality.

A number of approaches can be used to implement this strategy. One possibility is to start at the leaves and build the quadtree bottom up. We start by dividing our picture into chunks of fixed sizes using a geometric progression. The base picture should be a power of two for this to work easily. For example, if the map is 4096×4096, we can start by doing chunks of 32×32 pixels. This means we will need a seven-layer quadtree. We then recurse by building the parent to each cluster of four chunks. Because we want this new cluster to have more or less the same geometric complexity as any one of its four descendants, we must apply a triangle reduction algorithm to the mesh. Overall, we will end up with chunks that are all about 32×32 triangles. Leaf nodes will represent small areas on our map, and as we move closer to the root, the area covered by the chunk will be much higher. So, any given level from our quadtree will cover the whole map. The only difference is the resolution at which we cover it. Take a look at Figure 14.11 to see the level of detail and huge data sets processed by a chunked LOD algorithm.

Figure 14.11 Chunked LOD demo by Thatcher Ulrich. If you look closely at the wire frame version, you will notice the skirts used to weld different resolution zones together.

Quadtree construction is usually performed as a preprocess. We start from a high-resolution reference mesh, creating lower resolution meshes by using mesh simplification algorithms. We then store these meshes hierarchically in the nodes of the quadtree: lower resolution, global meshes at the root, and then we refine them into higher resolution (and lower scope) meshes as we move toward the leaf nodes of the quadtree. For each node, we store a measure of its error with regard to the real data set. We compute the maximum geometric deviation of a chunk from the portion of the underlying mesh. Logically, nodes closer to the root will have higher error values, with errors converging to zero as we move toward the leaves. Then, at runtime, we set a screen-space maximum error threshold and use the nodes' error metrics to compute a conservative LOD error level. If a node has error level delta, the screen-space error is computed by:

```
Rho= delta/D*K
```

where D is the distance from the viewpoint to the closest point in the bounding volume, and K is a perspective scaling factor that corrects the fact that the viewport is using perspective projection. The following equation is used:

```
K=viewportwidth/(2*tan(horizontalfov/2))
```

Rendering the chunk quadtree is then pretty straightforward. The quadtree is traversed, using it to perform hierarchical clipping. Then, at each node we can choose between expanding it (thus, accessing higher detail data located closer to the leaves) or staying where we are, and use the current node's data to render it. The decision depends on the screen-space error metric, which determines if the region and the distance require further refinement or if we are fine with the current resolution. Thus, a view-dependent approach is used.

The problem with chunked LOD approaches is, as with ROAM and quadtrees, the appearance of pops and cracks. Pops are solved by geomorphing, which was explained in the "Geomipmapping" section. Remember that geomorphing involves transitioning from one base node to its children (and thus expanding data into a finer version), gradually. We start by placing the finer representation triangles along the planes used by the coarse version; we then interpolate those positions linearly with their final, fine detail version. This way detail in the terrain grows slowly, and popping is eliminated.

As for the cracks in the terrain, they can easily be solved by stitching terrain chunks together with additional mesh strips. Ulrich suggests sowing adjacent meshes by using vertical ribbons that join together the two meshes. This is the simplest of the possible approaches, and given the resolution at which we are working, results are fine. The ribbon will be limited in screen size due to our error metric bound, becoming virtually invisible.

An alternative is to use a skirt that surrounds each chunk. The skirt is simply a strip of triangles that vertically extends around the perimeter of the chunk. Its size is determined by the maximum error bound. With reasonable bounds (about five pixels typically), the skirt is unnoticeable, and assuming our texturing function is computed from X,Z values, texturing will work as expected. Skirts have an additional advantage over ribbons in that we do not really need to sew chunks together, so the algorithm is much simpler. We just place chunks beside each other, and use skirts to fill the gaps (see Figure 14.12).

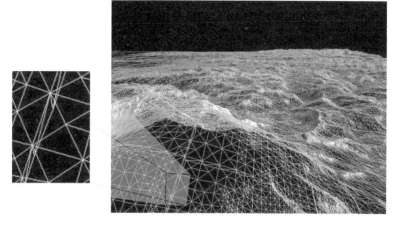

Figure 14.12   Zooming in to reveal one of the skirts used to weld regions together.

A note on texturing: Texturing a chunk LOD approach is done in a very similar way to regular geometry processing. Textures are derived from an initial, high-resolution map (usually satellite pictures). Then, we build a texture quadtree similar in philosophy to the geometry quadtree. The root represents the lowest resolution texture, and each level toward the leaves expands the map, covering a smaller region with higher resolution. This way, at runtime, the criteria used to expand the geometry quadtree are recycled for the texture quadtree. Because texturing data sets are usually in the hundreds of megabytes, it is common to use two threads and load new texture portions in the background while we keep rendering frames to the graphics subsystem. All we need to do for this paging scheme to work is to be aware of the amount of memory available for texturing. As we move closer to the terrain, and new maps are paged in, we will be able to discard other maps (usually closer to the root of the tree). So the overall memory footprint for textures will stay consistent throughout the execution cycle.

A GPU-Centric Approach

All the algorithms we have reviewed so far share one feature in common: They all implement some kind of CLOD policy. This means that these algorithms require expensive computations, usually performed on the CPU, to generate the multi-resolution mesh. Simple performance tests show algorithms like ROAM tend to be bounded not by the raw rendering speed, but by the CPU horsepower, which needs to recompute the terrain mesh frequently.

In a time when CPUs are mostly devoted to AI and physics, occupying them with terrain rendering can be dangerous because it can take away precious resources needed for other areas. Besides, remember that today's GPUs have huge processing power, not just to render triangles, but to perform tests on them as well. In fact, in many cases, the GPU is underutilized because it is not fed with data properly by the application stage.

Thus, I want to complete this chapter by proposing a radically different approach to terrain rendering, one where the CPU is basically idle, and all the processing takes place on the GPU. This might sound a bit aggressive, but the experience will be clarifying, at least in perspective. Our research shows such an algorithm can not only compete with traditional CPU-based approaches, but can surpass them in many cases as well.

The premise of the algorithm is simple: The CPU must be idle at all times, and no data will use the bus for rendering purposes. Thus, terrain geometry will be stored directly on the GPU in a method suitable for quick rendering. The format we have selected is blocks of 17×17 vertices, totaling 512 triangles each. These blocks will be stripped and indexed to maximize performance. By using degenerate triangles, we can merge the different strips in one sector into one large strip. Thus, each terrain block consists of a single strip connecting 289 unique vertices. Assuming the index buffer is shared among all terrain blocks, we only need to store the vertices. A couple lines of math show that such a block, stored in float-type variables, takes only 3KB. A complete terrain data set of 257×257 vertices takes 700KB of GPU memory.

Then, geometry blocks will be stored in the GPU and simply painted as needed. Bus overhead will thus be virtually nonexistent. The CPU will then just preprocess culling and occlusion information, and dispatch the rendering of blocks. Thus, we will begin by dividing the terrain map using a quadtree data structure, where leaf nodes are the terrain blocks. This quadtree will be in user memory, and we will use it to make decisions on what blocks need to be rendered. This way we can quickly detect the block the player is standing on and perform hierarchical clipping tests using the quadtree.

We can easily integrate culling into the algorithm. For each terrain block, we compute the average of all the per-vertex normals of the vertices in the block. Because terrain is more or less continuous, normals are more or less grouped. Thus, on a second pass, we compute the cone that, having the average normal as its axis, can contain all of the remaining normals. We call this the clustered normal cone (CNC) (see Figure 14.13). We can then use the CNC to perform clustered backface culling as explained in Chapter 12. For each block, we test the visibility of the CNC and, if the cone is not visible, the whole terrain block is ignored. Notice how testing for visibility with a cone has exactly the same cost as regular culling between vectors. For two vectors, we would cull away the primitive if the dot product between the normal and the view vector was negative. For a cone, all we need to do is the dot product between the view vector and the averaged normal. Then, if the result is below the cone's aperture, we can reject the whole terrain block.

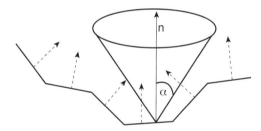

Figure 14.13   The CNC, which holds information about the normals of a terrain block.

Clustered backface culling is performed on software. For a sector that is going to be totally culled away, one test (that's a dot product and a comparison) will eliminate the need to do further culling tests on each triangle.

As a final enhancement, we can use our terrain blocks to precompute visibility and thus perform occlusion culling. The idea is again pretty straightforward: In a preprocess, we compute the Potentially Visible Set (PVS) for each node and store it. Thus, at render time, we use the following global algorithm:

```
using the quadtree, find the block the player is on
for each block in its pvs
    if it can't be culled via clustered culling
        if it can't be clipped
            paint the block
        end if
    end if
end for
```

To precompute the PVS, we compute a bounding column (BC) for each terrain block. A BC is a volume that contains the whole terrain block but extends to infinity in the negative Y direction. Thus, the terrain will be simplified to a voxel-like approach. Once we have computed the BC, it is easy to use regular ray tracing using the boxes to pre-compute interblock visibility. Fire rays from points at the top of each bounding column toward surrounding cells, trying to detect if they reach them or are intersected by other geometry. An alternative method for a platform supporting occlusion queries is to use them on the BC geometry to detect whether a block is visible.

Now, let's examine the results. Notice that this algorithm does not use a CLOD policy. But it performs similarly to ROAM using the same data set. The main difference is the way time is spent in the application. In ROAM, we encountered a 10–20 percent CPU load time, whereas the GPU-centric approach used only 0.01 percent. Additionally, the full version with clustered culling and occlusions outperformed ROAM by a factor of two, and occlusion detection can be very useful for other tasks like handling occlusions for other elements (houses, characters, and so on), AI, and so on.

As an alternative, we have created tests on a variant that does use LODs in a way similar to the chunked LOD/skirts method explained earlier in this chapter. We store terrain blocks at four resolutions (17×17, 9×9, 5×5, 3×3 vertices) and at runtime select which one we will use, depending on the distance to the viewer and an onscreen error metric. Unsurprisingly, performance does not improve: It simply changes the cost structure. The GPU reduces its workload (which wasn't really an issue), but the CPU begins to slow the application down. The only reason why implementing LOD in the core algorithm makes sense is really to make it work on cards that are fill-rate limited. On these cards, adding LODs might improve performance even more. In this case, the algorithm would be

```
using the quadtree, find the block the player is on
for each block in its pvs
    if it can't be culled via clustered culling
        if it can't be clipped
            select the LOD level for the block
            paint the block
        end if
    end if
end for
```

This section is really meant to be an eye-opener for game developers. Sometimes we forget that there's more than one way to solve a problem, and this terrain rendering approach is a very good example.

Outdoors Scene Graphs

The first outdoors games were just plain terrain renderers—simple flight simulators with coarse meshes. The advent of faster graphics cards has allowed for greater realism, and today, we can do much more than render vast areas of land. Cities, forests, and rivers can all be displayed to convey the sense of size and fullness players have learned to expect. But rendering realistic outdoor environments does not come without a host of challenges and restrictions that you should be aware of. In this section, we will explore them, exposing some well-known approaches to some of these problems.

To begin with, outdoors scenarios are significantly bigger than indoors-only levels. Often spanning several square kilometers, the amount of geometry required to fill these levels is simply huge. How many triangles does a forest have? Well, recall that we did the math a couple of chapters ago and reached the conclusion that Yosemite National Park is about 25 billion triangles. Assuming approximately 100 bytes per triangle, which is reasonable, we get 2.5 trillion bytes, or 2.5 terabytes. That's quite a challenge in terms of fill rate, bus speed, and memory footprint.

There are three obvious conclusions to this analysis. First, we will need to use instance-based engines, so we don't store each geometry piece individually but as an instance that we will repeat many times. Storing unique geometry would require a huge amount of storage space. Second, some kind of LOD analysis will be required to maintain a decent performance level. Third, a fast routine to discard an object (based on its size and distance) will be required.

A popular approach is to combine a primitive table with some clever spatial indexing and LODs to ensure that we can display a realistic, full environment at interactive frame rates. To begin with, we will have a primitive list, which is nothing but an array holding the fundamental building blocks of our scenario, similar to the old-school sprite tables used to hold tiles in a side scroller. This table will store each unique geometrical entity in our game world. For a forest, for example, we will need several types of trees as well as some stones and plants. Clearly, we won't store each tree, but just a few, which, once combined, will provide enough variation for the game. From my experience, 10 to 15 good quality trees are all you need to create a good-looking forest.

Each object should then come with LOD support, so we can vary its triangle rate depending on distance. Discrete LODs, probably with alpha-blending, are the most popular technique. Other, more sophisticated methods such as progressive meshes can be used as well, but we need to be aware of some potential pitfalls. Remember that a progressive mesh recomputes the representation as a combination of vertex splits and edge collapses dynamically. The key is to reuse the solution for several frames, so we are not recomputing the object model in each frame. So how can we do that in an instance-based game world? Quite possibly, the same tree will appear at varying distances within a single frame, making us recompute it too frequently and slowing down the application.

Once we have our primitive list, equipped with LODs, we need to decide how to access spatial information. For large scenarios, it is fundamental to allow fast queries such as "Which objects are in our view frustum?" and so on. We simply cannot afford to traverse the instance list object by object. Imagine a large game level, spanning many miles. We will then store the map in a spatial index. I recommend using a regular grid with each bucket holding a list of <primitiveid, position> pairs. By using a spatial index, we can quickly scan only that portion of the map surrounding the player, not the whole thing. The choice of a gridlike approach offers great performance at the cost of some extra memory footprint. But it surely pays off at render time. Other approaches such as quadtrees work equally well, but they are designed for static geometry only. A grid can easily be tailored so items can continually move around without degrading performance.

The spatial index should then be used for two different purposes. Using a frustum test, we will need to know which objects lie within the viewing frustum, and process only those. Here I recommend using not the four lateral planes, but the far Z plane as well. This way we can incorporate Z clipping elegantly. Add some fog so objects do not pop in too abruptly, and you are all set. Then, the second purpose of the spatial index is to aid in computing collision detection. Here we can restrict the search to the cell the player is staying in and the nine neighboring cells. Only objects located in these cells will be checked, so our collision detection can be considered effectively as independent of the level size.

There is a downside to all these great features, and that is memory footprint. A grid spatial index will eat some of your precious resources, so make sure you select the cell size carefully to control memory usage. Indexing a 1×1 km with a cell size of 10 meters (great for speedy collision detection) involves slicing it into 10,000 cells. Even if each cell is just a `<primitiveid, position>` pair (assuming only one object per cell), the resulting structure will only be a couple of megabytes in size.

In Closing

Outdoors algorithms are extremely different from their indoors counterparts. The focus is no longer on occlusion, but on detail handling, and this makes a huge difference in their design. Indoors algorithms are well understood today, whereas terrain (and especially scene graphs) rendering for outdoors algorithms is still being researched. Currently, most effort goes into occlusion detection for outdoors games. For example, how can we detect that a hill is actually occluding part of the action, and thus save precious triangles? This is no easy question. The amount of data makes this a very interesting question. A quick and easy solution, assuming your hardware supports occlusion culling, is to render the terrain front-to-back before rendering any other objects such as houses and characters. We can then use the Z information from the terrain to drive an occlusion query phase. But this is not a perfect solution. Thus, many teams are working to incorporate concepts such as PVS and view distances into outdoors scene graphs. The complexity of the problem definitely makes for an exciting challenge!

Chapter 15

Character Animation

"As a director, I wouldn't like me as an actor. As an actor, I wouldn't like me as a director."

Robert Redford

We have seen many different techniques to effectively display compelling scenarios in real time. These game worlds are the perfect setting for our adventures. But who will the player be? Who will his enemies be? And his friends? In traditional drama theory, characters are used to make us feel emotions. We are attracted to or repulsed by them, and thus get attached to the story. Computer games and video games are no different. Characters play a key role in the gameplay. Whether they are purely decorative, used as narrative elements, or are part of the action, characters make us feel involved in the game.

Analysis

Some problems in computer science have well-established, solid solutions. The intricacies of such problems are completely understood, and optimal algorithms have been found. As anyone familiar with algorithm theory knows, sorting a list of N numbers needs at most $N*\log(N)$ comparisons, and no algorithm can perform better than that (in a worst-case scenario). Sorting algorithms is thus a great example of these "silver bullets." But most problems are a bit more complicated, and each solution has some downsides, so evaluating and selecting the right option is far from trivial. Character animation is one of these tricky problems. Many different approaches have been devised through the years, but all of them have potential pitfalls. Generally, we will be able to choose between CPU-intensive methods (which use little memory) or memory-hungry methods (which in turn use little CPU resources). In this chapter, I will expose many different methods, trying to make evident the advantages and shortcomings of each technique. This way you will be able to select the algorithm that best suits your needs.

Explicit Versus Implicit Methods

A first distinction divides animation algorithms into two broad categories: explicit and implicit methods. Explicit methods store the sequence of animated vertices from our geometry every few frames, like snapshots from a movie. Once stored, a variety of techniques can be used to reconvert the original data, ensuring smooth animation. As a characterization, explicit animation methods are easy to code and understand, and often involve very simple math. On the other hand, storing animated vertices is memory intensive. Many poses are needed to convey the true sense of motion, and that means storing lots of data. A typical MD3 file (the popular explicit animation format used by *Quake 3*) is about 10MB, and that is only for one character. See Figure 15.1 for an example of an animation loop created using one of the explicit methods explained in this chapter.

Figure 15.1   Explicit animation. We store the full mesh animated for each frame.

On the other end of the spectrum, we have implicit animation systems. These methods do not store the animation data, but instead store a higher level description of the motion. Skeletal animation systems, for example, store the configuration (in terms of its rotation angles) for each joint, like the elbow, knee, and so on in our virtual character. Then, in real time, this description is mapped to an unanimated character mesh, so the animation is computed. This computation usually involves complex math with trigonometry and matrices. Thus, these methods are all fairly intensive for the CPU.

On the other hand, memory footprint is minimal. Implicit methods only need small data structures to convey the description of the motion. You can see skeletal animation depicted in Figure 15.2.

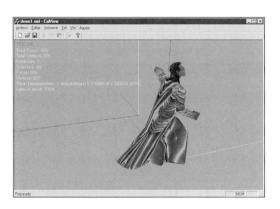 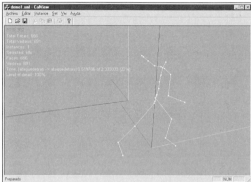

Figure 15.2   Left: animated character; right: skeleton that generates the animation.

Explicit methods were very popular in older 3D games because the hardware did not have CPU power to spare. Those games did not use many animation cycles anyway, so the relatively high memory footprint was fairly acceptable. More recently, explicit methods have successfully been used in games depicting groups of people, because animating them using implicit (hence, CPU-intensive) methods would be prohibitive. On the other hand, implicit animation is becoming more and more popular. It is the way to go as character animation becomes more detailed, triangle counts skyrocket, and games try to provide a broad variety of interactions. In these scenarios, you simply can't have all the animations precomputed. It would be memory suicide.

An added advantage of implicit methods is that they can be adapted to the scenario. Imagine a character who walks in an outdoors scenario full of hills and slopes. If explicit animation is used, all the possible animation cycles must be preprocessed. Thus, if the character can walk on different sloped terrain, you need to have cycles readily computed for each one. With an implicit method, it is easier to modify the animation on the fly so the feet adapt to the irregular ground. Using inverse kinematics, the animation can be recomputed, so the terminal elements (hands, feet, and so on) are in specific configurations. The same applies to characters grabbing objects, dropping them, climbing, or any other situation in which the character interacts with external elements.

Explicit Animation Techniques

We will begin by reviewing explicit animation techniques. Although they are being substituted by the more powerful implicit paradigm lately, there are still many applications for explicit methods. Some games will need to render lots of characters onscreen, and the CPU hit imposed by implicit methods will be prohibitive. Other games will need simple animations attached to characters, and using an implicit solution might be a bit too much effort for the results needed. Whichever the case, we will review three classic approaches to explicit animation.

Frame Animation

The simplest way of animating a character can be derived from traditional animation techniques. In old-school animation, the frames of a character in an animated movie were drawn on cellophane sheets, so there were as many sheets as poses or frames we should depict. Frame animation works similarly: It involves storing each frame in the animation sampled at whichever rate we will be displaying it (usually 25 frames per second or more). We will thus store many copies of the same mesh, one per frame. Then, at runtime, we will just paint the mesh that depicts the current state of the character. By synchronizing this with a timer or an input controller, the illusion of animation can be achieved.

So, what do we need to store for each frame? Clearly, we need to store vertex coordinates. But it does not really make much sense to store mapping coordinates as well, because texture mapping will very likely be constant throughout the animation cycles. We only need one copy of this data for the whole animation. In the end, you will discover we only really need the vertices for each position and probably the shading information: vertex colors, normals for lighting, and so on. This greatly reduces the memory footprint. Even better, if our character is defined by means of an indexed list of faces, the index list only needs to be stored once.

Even with all these optimizations, frame animation is memory hungry. This brute-force approach can only be recommended for very specific situations involving very few frames and small triangle counts.

Frame animation can also have another potential downside. In-game frame rates are never completely stable. Oscillations in geometry complexity, number of onscreen characters, or many other situations can make our ideal frame rate go up or down. As you saw in the opening chapters, we need to implement some measures to ensure that the in-game action does not vary in speed as well. We don't want our characters to walk faster or slower depending on the circumstances.

The solution comes from using a real-time clock and using the timing to compute real-time positions for all in-game elements. The problem with frame animation is that we have the mesh evaluated at discrete points in time. We can choose the closest available evaluation to the current point in time, but we will always see the jitter in animation speed.

To keep animation running at a smooth rate, we will need to accurately compute in-between frames, so we can display a good approximation of the animation with arbitrary precision. To do this, we will use interpolation techniques, which use mathematical functions to compute the desired value. Interpolation is extensively used in the next section, so read on for more information.

Keyframe Animation

A more involved technique can help us reduce our memory needs while keeping the same simplicity and elegance as regular frame animation. To better understand this variant, we first need to discuss how animation is created in content-creation packages such as 3ds max, Maya, or Lightwave. Animators usually create a motion by defining a number of "key frames," or well-known positions that determine the complete motion in their package of choice. For a 50-frame sequence, this might involve setting keyframes at frame 0, 15, 30, and 45. The character will then loop through the sequence, using keyframes and interpolation to derive all the remaining frames. This is a timesaver for the artists because they can determine a complex motion using just a few directions. A two-second cycle (which would total 50 frames) can often be described within 5 to 10 keyframes.

Taking advantage of this property is the core of keyframe animation. We will only store these keyframes as specified in the modeling package. This is clearly a memory savings from traditional frame animation. The animation engine will take care of computing any in-between frame at runtime. As shown in Figure 15.3, if we are requesting the frame at 0.67, we need to blend the two closest keyframes (the one at 0.5 and the one at 0.9). You might think the interpolator is an added CPU cost to the algorithm, but this is actually untrue. Any frame animator would end up using interpolation as well, and thus, the CPU cost of frame and keyframe animation is essentially the same.

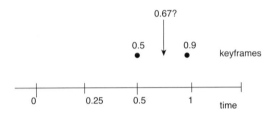

Figure 15.3   Interpolation is required to render a frame in-between two keyframes, such as frame 0.67 in the figure.

There are several variants of the keyframe animation scheme, and each differs fundamentally in the interpolator used. As a first (and most popular) option, we can choose to compute the required frames using linear interpolation, which will interpolate each value (X, Y, and Z) using a straight line between an initial and an end value. Linear interpolation can be computed easily using the following equation:

```
Interpolator=(timevalue-lastkeyframe)/ (nextkeyframe-lastkeyframe);
Interpolated value=lastvalue*(1-Interpolator) +
nextvalue*Interpolator
```

In the equation, `lastkeyframe` and `lastvalue` store the time and value of the last keyframe (to the left), and `nextkeyframe` and `nextvalue` store the time and value for the next keyframe (to the right). Remember to perform this same computation for X, Y, and Z. Here is the complete code to interpolate two 3D points:

```
point interpolate(point p1,long time1,point p2,long time2,long
currenttime)
{
float alpha=(currenttime-time1)/(time2-time1);
float alphainv=1-alpha;
point res;
res.x=p1.x*alphainv + p2.x*alpha;
```

```
res.y=p1.y*alphainv + p2.y*alpha;
res.z=p1.z*alphainv + p2.z*alpha;
return res;
}
```

Linear interpolation ensures smooth movement at a very low CPU cost. In the preceding example, we get a cost of six additions/subtractions, six multiplies, and one divide per vertex. If we are just using frame animation (time2-time1) equals one, we save one subtraction and one expensive divide. On the other hand, linear interpolation can sometimes yield poor results. Most animation packages use more powerful interpolators (Bézier, Hermite, and so on), so when we see the results with just linear interpolation applied, some motions tend to look robotic and unnatural.

One solution to raise the quality is to make sure your keyframes are not too far apart, thus reducing the blockiness of the motion. A popular mathematical lemma states that any continuous curve can be reduced to a straight line if the interval is small enough, and this is what we will try to exploit here. Trial and error in this situation is the best choice because fast motions (such as fighting moves) will require higher sampling rates than slower, paused motions. Note, however, that more keyframes implies a higher memory cost.

Thus, a better solution is to automatically extract keyframes from a high-resolution animation sequence, so the chosen keyframes ensure that a fixed quality threshold is maintained, and blockiness is minimized. The coding idea is pretty straightforward: Store the animation at a high sampling rate (such as 25 fps), and then use an analyzer to find out which frames can be discarded with little or no effect on the results. This can be achieved in an iterative manner, discarding the least significant frame at each step until we reach a limit error level. By doing this, we can ensure that our resulting animation is well suited for real-time display, keeping the best possible quality. Be warned though: The problem of deciding on just the perfect set of frames to achieve optimal results is an inherently complex problem, so any solution you implement will be computationally expensive.

For those working on high-powered platforms, we can solve all these problems by using a more powerful interpolator, hopefully the same one used by your animation package of choice. This way you can store fewer frames and ensure one-to-one correspondence between what your artists animate and what the engine renders.

As an example of this approach, one of the most popular interpolators utilizes a cubic curve, which smoothly interpolates using the beginning and endpoints as well as the beginning and ending normals. Techniques such as Hermite polynomials or even Bézier curves can be used to do the math.

Tagged Interpolation

Both frame and keyframe animation methods are easy to code, but come with a host of problems for the programmer. Memory footprint, as we have seen, can become a serious issue, especially if we try to animate high triangle counts or need to store lots of keyframes.

Still, there are other, more subtle problems. Imagine that you are creating a character for an action title. The character must perform a variety of animations, so the game is visually rich. For example, he must be able to stand still, walk, and run (both forward and backward). He also needs to jump, crouch, and shoot three different weapons. A first, superficial analysis reveals we will be using 10 different animation cycles:

➤ Stand still

➤ Walk forward

➤ Walk backward

➤ Run forward

➤ Run backward

➤ Jump

➤ Crouch

➤ Shoot first weapon

➤ Shoot second weapon

➤ Shoot third weapon

Everything looks fine until the lead designer comes along and suggests allowing the player to shoot while moving for increased realism. This might look like an innocent suggestion to the untrained eye, but if you do the math, you will discover you don't need 10 cycles anymore but 28. You have seven "poses" (stand, walk forward, walk back, run forward, run back, jump, and crouch) and four "actions" (do nothing, and shoot each of the three different weapons). Notice the combinatorial pattern? That's the root of an annoying problem with keyframe approaches.

➤ Stand; do nothing

➤ Walk forward; shoot weapon 1

➤ Walk backward; shoot weapon 2

➤ Run forward; shoot weapon 3

➤ Run backward

➤ Jump

➤ Crouch

In the *Quake II* game engine, this problem could be easily spotted during multiplayer games. To save the then scarce animation resources, these combinatorial cycles simply were not available. So, an enemy running toward us while shooting would correctly render the "shoot" pose while keeping both legs still as in an idle animation. This was sometimes dubbed "player skating" because players seemed to glide over the map.

For *Quake III*, the team at id Software found a satisfactory solution, which they called *tagged animation*, and implemented in the MD3 animation system. The key idea is to think of each character as if it were divided into several body parts, much like action figures. For *Quake III*, characters were usually divided into a "head" block, a "torso" block (from the neck to the belt level), and a "legs" block (from the belt downward). Then, each of these body parts had its own animation cycles, so combinatorial actions could be achieved by stacking cycles from each body part. In this case, our head part would remain unanimated. Animation cycles for the torso and the legs are as follows.

Legs:

➤ Stand still

➤ Walk forward

➤ Walk backward

- Run forward

- Run backward

- Jump

- Crouch

Torso:

- Stand still

- Shoot first weapon

- Shoot second weapon

- Shoot third weapon

Once the animation cycles have been identified, it is time to link the body pieces together, so the whole looks like a complete character. To do so, the designer must manually specify a pivot point in each body part, so each part basically knows where it should be attached. These pivots (which are nothing but coordinate systems essentially) are called *tags*, and hence the name of the animation system. In typical *Quake III* terminology, we have three body parts (head, torso, and legs), and four tags. The first tag (`tag_floor`) is used to indicate the ground level, so the character stands well on the terrain. This tag is usually attached to the legs. A second tag (`tag_legs`) specifies the joint between the legs and torso. A third tag (`tag_head`) provides the binding between the torso and head. The fourth tag (`tag_weapon`) is usually placed inside the right hand, so the character can hold interchangeable weapons realistically. You can see a tagged animation character with body parts highlighted in Figure 15.4.

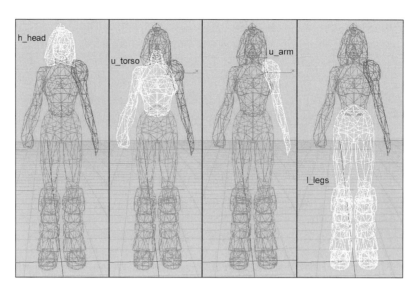

Figure 15.4   A character ready for tagged animation. In this case, the body has been divided into head, torso, legs, and arm, so the arm can be animated as well.

Notice that tags specify where each body part should be placed (both in terms of rotations and translation). But how do we ensure continuity between legs and torso (or torso and head)? Ideally, we should stitch both body parts together to ensure a perfect joint between them by sewing continuous triangles together. However, the *Quake III* animation system chose the easiest solution. No sewing is performed, so the two body parts are not really integrated: They are just put one beside the other like two bricks. To prevent players from noticing this, the body parts interpenetrate each other slightly, so the whole character always stays together. Artist tricks such as wide belts and clever textures help convey the sense of continuity.

Tagged systems can be extended to achieve quite sophisticated effects. Imagine that you need to bind characters to vehicles, whether it's a horse for a medieval role-playing game (RPG) or a motorbike in a racing game. All you have to do is tag your vehicle so your animation engine knows where to place each element. Need to do a system where your character can be heavily customized with weapons, a helmet, and shoulder pads? Tags are the way to go whenever flexibility and expandability are needed. Tags are also very convenient. You can add props to your character dynamically. In the end, a character like a flying dragon that carries a rider holding a sword, which in turn has an apple stuck to the tip, can be achieved with a tagged-animation system. In fact, the paradigm is so well thought-out that some implicit animation systems use tags to handle props for characters.

Tagged systems offer a significantly lower memory footprint than regular keyframed systems, especially for those cases where we need to perform different actions with different body parts simultaneously. Obviously, memory footprint will still grow linearly to the number of vertices as you add cycles to your animation. CPU use, on the other hand, will remain more or less stable and similar to that of regular keyframe animation, because we are just interpolating keyframes and placing geometry blocks in space. If the graphics hardware supports hardware transforms, the placement of each body part comes at almost no cost to the CPU.

However, tagged animation systems have some limitations that we must be aware of. First, animation is still bound explicitly to the character. So, if we need to represent a lot of different characters using the same animation cycles (say, nonplaying characters in a role-playing title), we will need many copies of those cycles, and sooner or later we will run out of memory. It would be great to share animation loops between different characters so two characters would only use one walk cycle.

Second, a tagged animation engine will not provide us with environment adaptation: Following the slopes in the ground, reaching out for objects realistically, and so on, are nearly impossible to do with the methods we have seen so far. Even if we have a large collection of animation cycles, our range of actions will be limited to what has been canned previously.

Third, there is a limit to body part division. Imagine that you want to do a sword fighting game, where you need to have a wide range of motions. Your animation programmer proposes doing a tagged system, using more tags to ensure that no combinatorial cycles are ever needed. Specifically, he proposes the following list:

➤ Head

➤ Torso (from neck to belt, no arms)

➤ Left arm

➤ Right arm

- ➤ Left leg

- ➤ Right leg

This may look good at first glance, but notice how many motions require synchronizing many body parts. Holding a weapon, for example, will involve both arms and the torso. Walking will involve both legs, and if the upper body is actionless, both arms and the torso. All these relationships will need to be coded into the system, so our animation engine will require a significant layer of glue code to ensure that body hierarchies are well kept. Compare that to the classic MD3 file where there are just two body parts to take care of (the head is usually not animated). The animation logic layer is still there, but it is simpler to manage.

So clearly, tagged animation is a case for the "too much of a good thing can be bad" discussion. In the right measure, it can greatly improve upon a keyframe approach, often reducing the memory footprint by half or even better. But dividing our body into more parts than is strictly required will make things worse: The control layer will grow out of control. When programmers fall into this "overdivision" syndrome with a tagged system, it is usually a sign that they really need to get a skeletal animation system instead. They are just trying to force the tagged system to behave like a skeletal system at a fraction of the cost, and that's generally not a good idea.

Implementing a tagged animation system is almost as straightforward as implementing a regular, single-mesh keyframe interpolator. We only need to store animation pointers for each body part, so we can keep track of which animation and frame each mesh is playing. Then, we need to be able to render the whole hierarchy, using the pivot points. To do so, most systems use a geometric object that hints at the pivot's location and orientation. In most *Quake*-based modelers, a triangle is used, so the first point in the triangle is used as the pivot's location, and then two vectors from that point to the other two define the coordinate axes. By computing the cross product between these two vectors, an "up" vector is returned.

At runtime, the pivot's position and orientation are usually stored in a quaternion, a mathematical operator that encapsulates locations and orientations elegantly. A quaternion is the generalization of a complex number, consisting of four floating-point values. Quaternions are explained in the next chapter as a way of implementing camera interpolators in games like *Tomb Raider*. Generally speaking, they are the way to go whenever you need to smoothly blend between successive interpolations. Read the next chapter, especially the section referring to the spherical linear interpolation, for a thorough description on how a quaternion can be used to compute the pivot point at runtime. Once we have the pivot point in place, all we need to do is use the transform stacks to apply the right rotations and translations to the vertices.

Implicit Animation Overview

Now that we have mastered explicit techniques and learned to exploit their benefits, we will move on to implicit animation. Be warned though: Implicit systems are significantly more complex than explicit systems, so you better make sure your matrix knowledge is up-to-date. You will surely need it. On the other hand, implicit engines are much more powerful and offer sophisticated controls for the animation programmer. Perfect environment adaptation, very low memory hit, and higher triangle counts are just a few of its benefits.

As stated in the opening section, implicit animation stores a description of the movement and evaluates it on the fly, effectively animating vertices in real time. To do this, it requires different data structures than those used in explicit animation.

To begin with, we need to know about the character topology. Usually, a skeletal structure is stored, specifying the rigid bones that drive that character's movement as well as the relationship between bones and vertices. We need to know which vertices each bone should influence in order to animate them properly. We will also need to know which bones are connected by joints, so we know how to inherit movement. Moving the knee should affect the foot, for example.

Additionally, we will need an animation file that stores the animated cycle in implicit form. Usually this file will consist of a series of snapshots that sample not the geometry, but the joint configuration. By knowing the bone structure and the rotations of each joint at a given time, we can apply the pose to the geometry and thus animate it.

Two general paradigms exist for implicit animation: forward (or direct) kinematics (FK) and inverse (or reverse) kinematics (IK).

In FK, we will start from a root node (usually, the pelvis) and propagate the skeleton downward, inheriting motions as we advance. The upper arm should inherit the chest, the lower arm both the upper arm and chest, and finally the hand. FK is coded by stacking series of transformation matrices as we enter each body part. It is the method of choice for motion-capture data or for coding general, broad moves.

IK works the other way around: It starts at the terminal element (the hand, for example) and computes the joints as it moves higher in the animation skeleton. Thus, IK allows us to locate an element in space, and then calculate the needed configuration of its ancestor joints. We can begin by saying "the hand must be here," and automatically compute where the elbow and shoulder should be. IK is very useful for adaptive and physically correct animation. Characters can adapt their footsteps to irregular ground or reach out to grab an object realistically. But this sophistication comes at a cost: IK is computationally more expensive than FK.

IK is not, however, a miracle solution. IK alone allows us to position hands and feet on the ground, but this has nothing to do with realistic walking or running. A new technique has emerged that blends both techniques for better results. The core idea of this hybrid approach is to use FK (possibly coupled with motion capture) for overall movement, and blend the results with IK for terminal joints and its direct ancestors. This way we can combine the perfection and realism of a canned walk cycle while getting realistic knee and feet adaptation to the ground.

Some systems use physically based animation for increased realism. Under this technique, movement is computed as the consequence of physical processes. Each body part has a weight and inertia. As the result of the physical simulation, joint configurations are computed, and the character is finally animated using FK.

Implicit animation has many advantages (and a few disadvantages) over explicit systems. On the plus side, memory use is greatly reduced. Implicit systems only store joint configurations, which is orders of magnitude cheaper than storing the complete mesh at each keyframe. Moreover, implicit systems can implement many advanced effects such as physically correct animation, adaptation to rough terrain, or realistic intercharacter interactions, to name a few. Last, but not least, an implicit animation system can share animation data between different characters. If you have 10 different in-game characters that share a common walk cycle, you only need to store the animated joint list once, because the vertices are computed on the fly.

The main disadvantage of an implicit animation system is the coding complexity and computational cost. Programming a skeletal animation system is significantly harder than storing explicit animation data. Because matrix math is involved, if you decide to implement IK or a physically correct system, the equations are not trivial. As a direct consequence of this, your animation subsystem will consume more CPU cycles. Depending on the application and target platform, this computational cost might be prohibitive, and explicit systems might be the way to go.

Forward Kinematics

FK is the easiest way of implementing implicit animation. In its simplest conception, we start at some base node (usually the pelvis) and propagate transforms to the descendants. Each joint has its own local coordinate system, which we will use to propagate transforms in a hierarchical manner. The pelvis will only have its own transform, whereas the femur will stack both the pelvis and the local transform, and so on until we reach our toes. You can see the hierarchical nature of FK pictured in Figure 15.5.

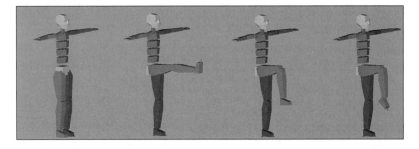

Figure 15.5   Left-to-right, sequence of FK animation, starting from the pelvis and moving downward to the right foot.

FK requires three components: the skeleton, the base mesh, and the animation cycles. To begin with, the skeleton defines the hierarchy of body parts that constitute one complete character. A simple skeleton can consist of about 18 bones:

Hand	Upper leg for both legs
Lower arm	Pelvis
Upper arm for each of the two arms	Three bones for the chest
Foot	Neck
Lower leg	Head

But more bones can be added as needed: Fingers and facial muscles can all be simulated using extra bones. As an example, we will review bone-based facial animation at the end of this chapter.

The second element of an FK animation system is the mesh, which is affected by the underlying bones. Skeletal systems usually employ single-skinned meshes, so continuity is preserved. Additionally, they can choose to let each vertex in the mesh be influenced by one and only one bone in the skeleton or to allow for multibone influences for smoother animation. This is sometimes not very relevant in highly rigid body parts like a finger, but a chest, or even more so, a face, will definitely show improved quality by using multibone influences. Old titles, like the original *Tomb Raider*, did not use a single-skinned mesh, but instead used a list of separate body parts: Head, arms, legs, and so on were all divided. This way identifying vertex-bone relationships became trivial. Each object was coupled with one bone and only one bone. But this technique was quickly abandoned because gaps appeared as the animation was applied, and the body did not hold together sometimes.

Skeletons and meshes are usually stored in a reference pose, which involves horizontal arms to each side of the body, palms-down, and legs straight vertically. We will assume this pose does not have any joint rotation component. Then, animation cycles simply store joint rotations. Most joints are monoaxial (like the elbow, for example), whereas others are biaxial (a shoulder can yaw and pitch, but cannot roll). A third group allows the three degrees of freedom, like the neck or wrist.

At runtime, we carry out a two-step process. We first reconstruct the matrices for each body part. To do so, we begin at the base node (pelvis) and follow the skeletal hierarchy, stacking each joint's transforms. Again, this can be achieved easily both with regular matrices or quaternions (see Chapter 16, "Cinematography"). If you choose matrices, be aware that gimbal lock may arise, especially in joints that can rotate over more than one axis. If this is the case, switch to quaternions instead.

Once we have recomputed the condensed matrix for each joint, we need to apply matrices to vertices. This process is the most time-consuming, and the one we need to optimize carefully to reach optimal performance. After all, it's nothing more than matrix-vector multiplies.

Logically, skeletal animation has a much lower memory footprint than frame-based methods. We only need to store each joint's orientation, and the run-time engine will take care of reconstructing the mesh.

Math of Skeletal Animation

Let's now assume we have a character mesh where each vertex is influenced by one or more bones. We will also assume each bone has three degrees of freedom (roll, pitch, and yaw). This can be optimized easily later on for joints with less degrees of freedom. Additionally, bones are laid out in a hierarchy, so we can access ascendants and descendants easily.

The algorithm works as follows: We first process the skeleton and compute the actual transform for each vertex. To do so, we begin at the root, which is assigned the transform specified by its roll, pitch, and yaw. Then, we move into the skeleton, chaining transforms along the way. A first degree descendant of the base node will have the base transform and the descendant's own transform applied. The process is recursed until all bones have been processed in a treelike fashion. Let's examine the specifics.

We start at the base bone. Then, we perform a nested loop. The outer loop scans the bones that are direct descendants from the one we called the routine with. If we start with the pelvis, we will probably have three bones to scan: the lower back, the right femur, and the left femur. We then need to scan each vertex in the mesh and compute whether the bone we are examining actually influences that vertex. This is performed by a weight function. The weight function usually comes from your modeling package of choice as a series of values that determine which bones influence which vertices and how. But if you don't have such a function, you can cook your own. All you need to do is compute weights based on the distance from the vertex to the bone (a line segment). Computing segment-point distances is not very hard. Store the segment in parametric equation form, such as:

```
X= X1 + (X2-X1)*t
Y= Y1 + (Y2-Y1)*t
Z= Z1 + (Z2-Z1)*t
```

Thus the segment is defined with t-values in the 0..1 range. Then, solve the point-line test, computing not the actual point, but the t-value assigned to it. Three cases are possible:

> `T<0`   X1 is the least-distance point
>
> `0<=T<=1` The computed point is the least distance
>
> `T>1`   X2 is the least-distance point

Then, the weight function can take the form

```
Weight = k/distanceⁿ
```

with k determining the scale of the function, and n controlling the falloff speed. For human-sized characters, values of 1 and 4, respectively, do the job remarkably well.

Back to our main algorithm, we now have two loops. The outer loops bones, and the inner iterates vertices and computes bone-vertex weights. Then, if the weight is below a threshold, we can forget about it and leave the vertex unaffected by that bone. If, on the contrary, we detect a significant weight, it is time to transform the vertex.

To do so, we need to first translate it with regard to the bone's pivot point. Because rotations are centered around the origin, we need to make sure the bone is properly centered before the math can actually start. We can then stack the transform, either in quaternion or matrix form. At this stage, we actually apply the transform from the bone to the vertex. This involves both the point versus matrix/quaternion multiply and scaling the processed vertex by the bone weight. Remember that other bones further along the hierarchy can affect this vertex as well, so we need to accumulate results from each analyzed bone. In addition, we can undo the translate transform so the bone and vertices are referenced to world coordinates again.

This is a recursive algorithm. If the current bone has any descendants, we must call the same routine, so more transforms are weighted in and incorporated into the solution. In the end, once terminal nodes are reached, the whole mesh will have been affected by different bones. Here is the complete pseudocode for this routine:

```
deform   (bone root, mesh originaldata, mesh processeddata)

for each children of root
    for each vertex in the original mesh
        compute weight from bone to vertex
        if weight > threshold
            translate vertex by negated bone pivot (place pivot at origin)
            multiply vertex by joint rotations
            scale the resulting point by the bone weight
            translate by bone pivot
            increment the definitive value of such vertex by this solution
        end if
    end for
    if this bone has children
        deform (children of this node, original mesh,processed mesh)
    end if
end for
```

Now, the ideal way to perform this on a single-skinned continuous mesh is to store vertices indexed (so less processing is needed) and then paint them using a call to DrawPrimitiveIndexed (Direct3D) or DrawElements (OpenGL). DirectX programmers will have the advantage of internal support for quaternions, but overall the algorithm is not very complex.

However, this is a poor solution in terms of performance. Several stages can be improved by thinking a bit. For example, it makes no sense to compute vertex weights on a per frame basis for all bones and vertices. It is just a waste of resources. In the end, the weight is a number in the 0..1 range, which can be easily quantized to a byte. Assuming V vertices and B bones, we could store the weights as a $V \times B$ matrix. As an example, such a matrix for a character consisting of 1,000 vertices and 20 bones (a reasonable amount by any of today's standards: notice I said 1,000 vertices, not 1,000 triangles) would occupy around 19KB, which is fairly reasonable. Remember that the weight computation is pretty intensive because there are segment-point tests. Preprocessing all that information looks like a pretty good idea, because we can turn it into a simple table lookup.

Hardware-Assisted Skeletal Animation

Another interesting idea is to rearrange your code so you actually store matrices as you go instead of vertex coordinates. This way you can actually cache results for bones that did not change from one frame to the next, and so on. The source code would use an array of matrix lists, so we can store which matrices affect which vertices. It would look something like this:

```
deform   (bone root, mesh originaldata, mesh processeddata)

for each children of root
    for each vertex in the original mesh
        compute weight from bone to vertex
        if weight > threshold
            translate vertex by negated bone pivot (place pivot at
origin)
            multiply vertex by joint rotations
            translate by bone pivot
            add the condensed matrix to the list of matrices for the
vertex
        end if
    end for
    if this bone has children
        deform (children of this node, original mesh,processed
mesh)
    end if
end for
```

The main advantage of this technique is twofold. First, we can cache partial bone structures and their matrices for parts of the body that did not actually change. Second, we can take advantage of better animation support in later versions of Direct3D (version 7 and later). In Direct3D 9, for example, we can use the SetTransform interface to, in the end, stack matrices on a per vertex basis. The code is as follows:

```
for (vert=0;vert<numvertex;vert++)
    {
    // I assume four matrices per vertex
    d3ddev->SetTransform(D3DTS_WORLDMATRIX(0),matrixarray[vert][0]);
    d3ddev->SetTransform(D3DTS_WORLDMATRIX(1),matrixarray[vert][1]);
    d3ddev->SetTransform(D3DTS_WORLDMATRIX(2),matrixarray[vert][2]);
    d3ddev->SetTransform(D3DTS_WORLDMATRIX(3),matrixarray[vert][3]);

d3ddev.DrawPrimitive(D3DPT_TRIANGLELIST,FVF_VERTEX,vertex[vert],3,0);
    }
```

And vertex weights are passed as part of the Flexible-Vertex-Format (FVF). A final improvement over this approach is to implement all the animation pipeline in a vertex shader. If we follow the previous approach and accumulate the matrices required for each vertex, we can animate on the hardware by passing the mesh in base position and the matrices on a per vertex basis. In the Cg programming language, for example, we can do so with a very simple shader. We receive vertices along with four matrices, which are multiplied and weighted to compute the final sum. Here is the source code for such an approach:

```
struct inputs
    {
    float4 position        : POSITION;
    float4 weights         : BLENDWEIGHT;
    float4 normal          : NORMAL;
    float4 matrixIndices   : TESSFACTOR;
    float4 numBones        : SPECULAR;
    };

struct outputs
    {
    float4 hPosition       : POSITION;
    float4 color           : COLOR0;
    };

outputs main(inputs IN, uniform float4x4 modelViewProj,
    uniform float3x4 boneMatrices[30], uniform float4 color,
    uniform float4 lightPos)
```

```
{
outputs OUT;

float4 index = IN.matrixIndices;
float4 weight = IN.weights;

float4 position;
float3 normal;

for (float i = 0; i < IN.numBones.x; i += 1)
    {
    // transform the offset by bone i
    position = position + weight.x *
float4(mul(boneMatrices[index.x], IN.position).xyz, 1.0);

    // transform normal by bone i
    normal = normal + weight.x *
mul((float3x3)boneMatrices[index.x], IN.normal.xyz).xyz;

    // shift over the index/weight variables, this moves the index and
    // weight for the current bone into the .x component of the
    // index and weight variables
    index = index.yzwx;
    weight = weight.yzwx;
    }

normal = normalize(normal);

OUT.hPosition = mul(modelViewProj, position);
OUT.color = dot(normal, lightPos.xyz) * color;

return OUT;
}
```

Given the CPU hit of any skeletal animation approach, this new hardware-skinning approach will likely become a de facto standard because we get skeletal animation at a very low cost. All the heavy weight lifting is performed on the GPU.

Prop Handling

One typical enhancement to our base animation system is the addition of props, which can range from weapons to clothes, or even vehicles. This feature adds richness to the game and has been key to the success of many popular titles. Luckily, accessories are relatively easy to program. All that is needed are some minor changes and a bit of math, and our characters will be able to carry (or be carried by) almost anything.

To begin with, we will need to add prop tags to our character. Basically, we need to know where each accessory attaches. The method I recommend is essentially the same used in the *Quake III* MD3 format, adding symbolic objects with no geometry value other than they help us store the orientation of the prop throughout the animation cycle. Then, we will consider the prop as a rigid object attached to the prop tag. This can easily be achieved by translating and rotating the prop to the attachment point.

The translation-rotation code can be implemented using two different strategies. If you are working on a frame-by-frame basis, the best choice is to use matrix math. On the other hand, if you are working with temporally distant keyframes, a more powerful operator such as quaternions will be a better match. For matrices, I suggest you build basis matrices for the orientation and use those to transform the prop to its definitive location. The approach is very similar to the one we used for skeletal animation:

1. Translate the pivot point to the origin.

2. Multiply by the basis matrix.

3. Translate to the final position.

And basis matrices are built easily from the tag's geometry. Assuming your tag is a triangle (which is what *Quake* used), you can extract two vectors from the triangle's sides: Segments *AB* and *AC* (see Figure 15.6) define them. Then, a cross product between them will give you the third vector. Storing them in column form will give you the basis:

Right.x	Up.x	Front.x	Pos.x
Right.y	Up.y	Front.y	Pos.y
Right.z	Up.z	Front.z	Pos.z
0	0	0	1

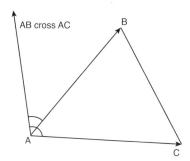

Figure 15.6   Building a base to place props with.

This matrix represents a transform, which, when fed with points in the form (x,y,z,1), will convert them to the coordinate system defined by the basis. In other words, if we transform each vertex in the prop using this matrix, the transformed vertices will be placed (and oriented) the way our marker depicts. Life could be easy and fun all the time, but not usually. Problems occur when no one expects them, and prop handling is a good example. To expose its problems, imagine that the sampling rate for the prop marker is lower than the rate at which you will be displaying animations. Or even worse, imagine that you want to use interpolation to smooth the animation and improve the results.

In both cases, your animation system would basically need to render something like frame number 3.765, which is definitely not 3, and not quite 4 either. We have seen how we can use interpolation to approximate the position of the vertices at any given point in time, integer or fractional. So how do we apply this to prop handling?

Quite clearly, our problem consists of generating a new transform basis for frame number 3.765. Unfortunately, this is easier said than done. How can we interpolate a matrix, or even worse, an orthonormal matrix? Remember that we need all column vectors to be normalized to have a modulus of 1. This is the normalization part of the equation. We also need the orthogonal part. The three vectors (up, front, right) must be perpendicular to each other, which effectively means the determinant must be 1.

At this point, I will make use of our initial assumption. Our sampling rate is high, so orientation differences from one frame to the next will be relatively small. As a result, we can safely do a direct interpolation of the basis matrices. This would be a deadly sin to a strict mathematician, but consider this:

➤ The bottom row (0 0 0 1) does not really affect the interpolation because it remains the same.

➤ The rightmost column represents the position, which can definitely be interpolated safely.

➤ The orientation 3×3 submatrix undergoes a minimal change if frames are close in time.

This process will introduce some artifacts because the interpolated matrix is not a transform basis in the strict sense. But the error incurred will be unnoticeable.

A more robust alternative would be to interpolate the two matrices and renormalize the three vectors (up, front, right) that make the 3×3 orientation submatrix. By doing this, we make sure we comply with the normalization condition of the basis. We can even interpolate front and right only, and recompute the up vector doing a cross product. This would increase the computational cost but help comply with the orthogonal condition.

A Note on Vehicles

Vehicles can greatly enhance the player's experience. From bikes to horses and seven-headed dragons, riding vehicles is as good as gameplay gets. Vehicles can be implemented as if the character was a prop to the vehicle. We will place markers in the exact positions where the character will be placed. All we need to do is make sure character and vehicle blend well together using good animation cycles. If we are using IK, we can even make sure the hands of the character really hold the car's steering wheel for increased realism. Additional markers will help us with this. Again, we will need both position and orientation to make sure the character's hands not only stay on the wheel, but are also properly aligned with it.

Limb Slicing

Limb slicing (or being able to cut away pieces of an animated character in real time) can be easily added to any skeletal animation system. The problem can be divided into two tasks: Cutting away the geometry (and filling any possible holes) and animating it.

Cutting away a character's arm and leg can easily be performed by deciding on the bone we will be cutting and deleting all triangles that are influenced by it or any descendant above a threshold weight. Consider that we want to cut an arm away at the shoulder, for example. We scan all the vertices and compute the bone weight from the upper arm. Those vertices with weights above a threshold will be marked. Then, the same process is applied recursively to all bones below the selected one in the hierarchy. Notice that I said "above a threshold," not "above zero." Some relatively distant vertices (for example, part of the chest) might be affected by the bone, even if it's still distant. Thus, it is good practice to be conservative and set a threshold at which the cutting will begin. Here's the pseudocode for such an algorithm:

```
void amputate (bone root, mesh originaldata)
{
for each children of root
   for each vertex in the original mesh
      compute weight from bone to vertex
      if weight > amputation threshold
         mark vertex as deleted
      end if
   end for
   if this bone has children
      amputate (children of this node, original mesh,processed
mesh)
   end if
end for
}
```

Once this step has been performed, we will have our original mesh with some vertices marked as deleted. All we need to do is actually update the mesh structure deleting the vertices. Then, we will have a mesh with a hole where the arm should begin. We now need to retriangulate that zone so the whole mesh is completed. To do so, we can follow a number of strategies. We can, for example, take the pivot point of the amputated bone as a reference and do a star triangulation so the mesh is closed again. To detect which vertices we should triangulate to, we take those affected by the bone with a weight below the amputation threshold and above a slightly inferior limit. Clearly, these are vertices close to the amputation zone. Any triangulation algorithm can be used on this small data set to actually reconstruct the mesh.

As for animation, there is no significant change. Matrices and bones will still be valid; the only change being the deletion of several vertices in the mesh. Overall, the same algorithm can be used.

Facial Animation

Most of a character's emotion and personality are conveyed through his face: Anger, fear, and disenchantment are really hard to simulate if facial gestures are not available. Many of today's games and most games from the future will incorporate some kind of real-time facial animation. The first step is lip-synching, or the ability to move the mouth and lips so the character looks like he's actually pronouncing each word. On top of that, you can build a whole facial emotion system. Taking this to the extreme, facial animation could be integrated with a full-body animation system, so characters could express themselves through body and facial gestures. This kind of approach yields elegantly to a level-of-detail based policy. Facial expressions are only required for up-close characters because the nuances of emotion are lost at larger distances. Thus, you could code a system that performed full-body animation, and as characters moved closer to the camera, introduce facial animation and emotions as well.

There are two schools of facial animation. The first one is characterized by animating the vertices directly. Computational cost is reduced, but memory footprints can grow, especially if a highly detailed face is to be animated. The second trend is to animate facial muscles using a skeletal system. The skeleton of the character simply extends to his face, so we can animate areas of the face hierarchically. This second method is CPU-intensive because many bones are required. For a character in the Sony game *The Getaway*, as many as 35 bones were used for the face alone.

Vertex-based facial animation is popular for simple games. Vertices are clustered according to face muscles, and displacement functions are applied to convey personality. Coding such a solution is not very hard, and with some care, emotions can be layered to create complex expressions. One of the best examples of this philosophy is the facial animation demo by Ken Perlin, which can be seen in Figure 15.7 and is available from his web site at `http://mrl.nyu.edu/~perlin/facedemo`.

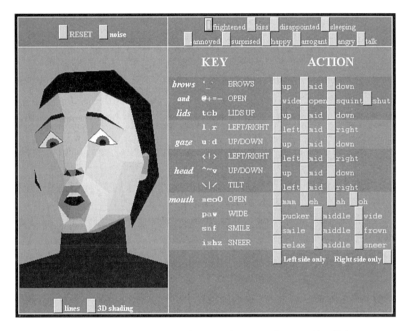

Figure 15.7   Ken Perlin's facial animation demo with all the controls to set parameters to expressions.

Vertex-based systems do not scale well. As the number of expressions increases, especially if you add lip-synching to the mix, the amount of expressions to model becomes unfeasible, both in terms of man-hours and memory footprint. In these scenarios, using a skeletal animation system will yield much better results. Representation is extremely compact, and results are equally impressive.

Skeletal animation, on the other hand, animates vertices using a bone hierarchy. For a face, the hierarchical component of skeletal systems will not be very useful, because these kinds of relationships do not really occur in faces. However, another characteristic of skeletal animation will indeed be very useful: the ability to influence a single vertex by more than one bone, so a vertex in the cheek gets influence from the jaw, eyes, and so on. Additionally, skeletal animation systems are great for performing selective blends—mixing a face for the brows with a different expression for the rest of the face, for example. It's all a matter of selecting which bones from which expression will be mixed.

Whichever method you choose, it is fundamental to understand the structure of the face in order to achieve realistic results. In this respect, I recommend taking a look at the Facial Action Coding System proposed by Ekman and Friesen in the late 1970s. This system tries to describe facial expressions objectively, using scientific criteria. It starts by analyzing expressions in terms of the muscles used to generate them. All facial muscles affecting the look of the face were analyzed, and a thorough listing of their effect on the face was built. The list had 46 entries, which appeared by moving one single muscle or muscle group. You can then combine different muscles and their states to convey a composite expression: a different muscle configuration for the eyes, jaw, brows, and so on.

To perform lip-synching, your software must be able to animate the mouth area to simulate the different phonemes, or sounds in the language the character is speaking. Each language has a different number of phonemes; English has approximately 35. Because that is such a large number (just imagine the amount of work needed to create the array of animated faces), sometimes phonemes that are pronounced similarly are simplified, so less work needs to be done. This was discovered a long time ago by Disney animators, who simplified the whole phoneme set to just 12 canonical mouth positions. Then, a facial animation system such as face morphs or skeletal animation can be used to perform the actual animation. One of the problems with such an approach is that pronunciation has a high emotional component. The same word said whispering or yelling at someone will look radically different.

However, facial animation using bones looks like the way to go for the industry—similar to the way skeletal animation replaced frame-based methods progressively in the past. All that is needed are better bone layout strategies that help convey the wide range of expressions and emotions of a human face. Obviously, most bones will control either the eyes (or brows) or the mouth, because these are the main expressive elements in a face. But it's the precise layout that still needs to be mastered.

Inverse Kinematics

IK works from the terminal nodes and solves the transforms for the whole hierarchy, so the terminal has a certain position and orientation. It is used widely in movies, and it is slowly finding its way into games. Grabbing objects, keeping feet on the ground realistically, and character-to-character interaction are just some of the uses of IK.

From a programming standpoint, IK starts with some restrictions (usually, a terminal location and orientation) and tries to find solutions depending on the skeleton geometry. To find such solutions, some approaches use analytic methods, computing solutions from problem-specific equations. These methods, when possible to use, are the fastest at the cost of lower generality. Then, for complex configurations, iterative processes are used, much like in numerical analysis where an exact solution is found by progressive refinement, such as in the popular hill-climbing, problem-solving method. We will now take a look at two examples, one using an analytic solver and another using Cyclic Coordinate Descent (CCD), which is one of the most popular iterative algorithms.

Analytic IK

Analytic IK solutions are found by describing the animation system we want to model in terms of equations and solving them. For simple systems, this can be computed in real time and add a greater sense of control to the player. For example, a custom analytic solver could be designed to animate the shoulder-elbow-wrist system in an RPG, so we can make the character grab objects or open doors realistically. If we know the constraints beforehand, and the number of joints is small, analytic IK is the way to go.

Take a single bone that can rotate around a single axis, for example. Given a rotation angle R1 and a bone length L1, the endpoint of the bone is

```
Px = L1*cos(R1)
Py = L1*sin(R1)
Pz = 0
```

Notice I assumed that the bone rotates in the X,Y plane and is centered at the origin. Now, imagine that we concatenate that bone to a second one in a chain.

The second bone is expressed in terms of length L2 and rotation R2 (see Figure 15.8). The equation for the endpoint of the second bone in terms of L1 L2 and R1 R2 is

```
Px = L1*cos(R1) + L2*cos(R1+R2)
Py = L1*sin(R1) + L2*sin(R1+R2)
```

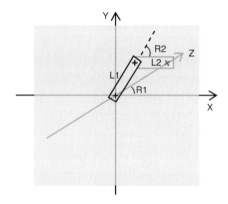

Figure 15.8 Two-bone chain as used for analytic IK.

This gives us positions based on bone configurations, which is what we have been calling FK so far. It is now time to inverse these equations and represent R1 and R2 (the real parameters, because L1 and L2 can be considered constants) in terms of a predefined *Px,Py* pair. Thus, the equation must give us the joint orientations required to reach one endpoint in particular. Now, we will need some algebra to get this working. To begin with, we will use the following identities:

```
cos(a+b) = cos(a)*cos(b) - sin(a)*sin(b)
sin(a+b) = cos(a)*sin(b) + sin(a)*cos(b)
```

Coupling these with our FK equations and squaring both FK equations and then adding them, we reach the following:

```
PX2 + PX2 = L12 + L22 + 2L1L2cos(R2)
```

which can be trivially solved into:

$$R2 = \arccos \frac{Px2 + Py2 - L12 - L22}{2L1L2}$$

And substituting we get:

$$R1 = \arctan \frac{-(L_2 \sin(R_2))P_x + (L_1 + L_2 \cos(R_2))P_y}{(L_2 \sin(R_2))P_y + (L_1 + L_2 \cos(R_2))P_x}$$

This is the analytical solution to our IK problem, assuming it's happening in 2D. Similar approaches can be used for 3D, or we can simply rotate the bones so they lie in one of the coordinate planes.

Now, you need to notice several relevant ideas. First, notice how the equations introduce the concept of reachability. Take a look at the way we compute R2. It's an arc-cosine. Thus, it is assuming the argument is in the range between –1 and 1. So what happens if this isn't so? Obviously, the equations would have no solution, and the geometric interpretation would be that the point Px,Py is just too far.

Second, notice how reachability does not imply the use of restrictions. Imagine that this two-link system is indeed the upper and lower parts of an arm. Maybe the proposed solution will imply bending it in ways we humans simply cannot do. Pure IK does not handle that. We would need additional equations to take care of restrictions. In the case of a human elbow (which would be controlled by R2), we would add:

```
R2>0
R2<Pi
```

to represent the fact that an elbow can actually only bend approximately 180 degrees.

The third interesting fact about all this is that sometimes more than one solution will appear. In our case, I guess it's fairly clear that two solutions are always possible, as shown in Figure 15.9.

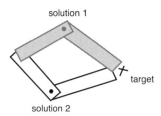

Figure 15.9 Different solutions are often frequent in inverse kinematics.

Analytic solutions are used frequently in games, because they are easy to solve and can handle many game-specific problems. Need a character to reach out with a hand? The preceding code is perfectly well suited for this, because the arm-hand is not very relevant, and we need to focus on the shoulder and elbow. Need a character to place his feet on the ground? You can adapt the preceding equations easily, maybe adding a third restriction that represents the angle at which the foot must stand on the ground, probably derived from the slope. But what about general IK solvers? There are numerical methods available that can solve more or less anything by using iterative processes. By using them, more complex systems with many restrictions can be analyzed. One of the most popular algorithms is the CCD. Let's take a look at it.

Cyclic Coordinate Descent

CCD (introduced in 1993 by Chris Welman) works by analyzing joints one by one in a progressive refinement philosophy. It starts with the last joint in the chain (the hand, for example) and tries to rotate it to orientate it toward the target. Then, it moves one link up, and so on. Let's take a look at the example in Figure 15.10.

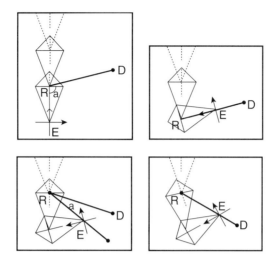

Figure 15.10   CCD.

We start at the last link in the chain. If the target was effectively within reach, that would mean we would need to rotate that bone to aim at the goal. Thus, we compute that hypothetical rotation. This is easy, especially if you've read the chapter on action AI. It is like a starship rotating to face an enemy. We create two vectors: one from the last joint position to the endpoint of the last bone (the effector) and another from the same last joint to the target we are trying to reach. Now we can compute the angle between these two vectors by computing the dot product of their unit vectors. Notice that we have the angle between two vectors, but we need to make sure we rotate in the appropriate direction to make the shortest path possible. Again, we can use our AI knowledge by performing a cross product between the two vectors to obtain a third, perpendicular vector. Then, we use the sign of the Z coordinate of the newly computed vector. This sign determines the direction at which we must rotate, and the arc-cosine of the dot product will give you the angle.

Now we can move up one link and repeat the angle rotation process. In the end, this is a progressive refinement algorithm that will eventually leave the last bone's endpoint close enough to the target, or bail out. But remember that this is just a computational algorithm. The results are not meant to be shown to the user because the process of reaching out to the target by CCD does not necessarily look very human. What we would actually do is use the angles computed as results of the CCD process to drive a quaternion or matrix interpolator, which would create the animation. Thus, CCD is a preprocess we perform the moment we decide we must reach out for something.

Here is the pseudocode for the CCD system I have just outlined. I'll assume we are starting at the final bone in the system.

```
While distance from effector to target > threshold and
numloops<max
        Take current bone
        Build vector V1 from bone pivot to effector
        Build vector V2 from bone pivot to target
        Get the angle between V1 and V2
        Get the rotation direction
        Apply a differential rotation to the current bone
        If it is the base node then the new current bone is the
last bone in the chain
        Else the new current bone is the previous one in the chain
End while
```

Blending Forward and Inverse Kinematics

Sometimes neither FK nor IK will do the job for us. FK will give us high-quality animation, especially when coupled with motion capture. But the cycles will be canned, and thus behaviors like reaching out or placing feet on the ground properly will be impossible. On the other hand, IK can help us in these situations, but solving a full body animation using IK will often yield unnatural animation. A human body is full of micromovements and nuances that IK will fail to simulate, and there is a great deal of physics involved as well. IK cannot compete with the quality of motion-capture data, and motion capture cannot provide us with the adaptiveness of IK.

Clearly, the solution is to blend both mechanisms. After all, techniques are just that: techniques. Our goal is not IK or FK per se, but the creation of realistic character movement. Thus, we want high-quality characters that can interact with their environment realistically. This problem was also encountered by the movie industry some years ago, and specific methods were devised to take advantage of the best of both worlds. One interesting technique that I'd like to take a second to explain involves mixing FK and IK on a bone-by-bone basis, making bones closer to the root more FK-oriented and bones closer to the terminals more geared toward IK. After all, both methods output the same kind of data, usually in the form of quaternions.

Take a human arm, for example, and imagine that we want the character to shake hands with another character of variable height realistically. If you think about it, this usually involves raising your shoulder more or less and changing the orientation of the elbow. Now, imagine that we have a very good FK animated character with its arm motionless. All we have to do to take advantage of this cycle and still create the IK handshake is to make joints closer to the hand more influenced by IK and less by FK. The shoulder would have most of its control under FK with a little IK thrown in. The elbow would mix the two solutions in equal parts, whereas the wrist would almost totally be controlled by IK.

To compute this, we can use CCD on top of an FK animation, making joints more stiff as we reach higher in the hierarchy. The chest, for example, will be immovable; the shoulder will have a rotation factor that is half of what the elbow has; and so on. This way IK will be weighted with FK, and both animation systems can coexist on the same platform. Such an approach was used in *The Lord of the Rings* movies, because FK provided very good overall movements (such as walking and fighting). But IK was required in the terminals to ensure good interaction with the environment.

In Closing

Character animation is a lengthy subject, and we have only scratched the surface. Subjects like motion blending or full-body IK animation are left for the reader's research. Animation is an evolving subject, and new techniques are being devised constantly. Today, the tide seems to be moving away from keyframed animation, and FK and IK are becoming more widely used. Physically based characters that keep self-balance and implement correct joint rotation restrictions are beginning to surface for real-time games. After all, the CPU is free from most rendering tasks, and that benefits animation engines. On the other end of the spectrum, many hardware-assisted animation algorithms are surfacing. Right now, shader-based multibone skinning has become a reality, and some demos show the incredible potential of this scheme. But there's much more. A few books the size of this one are available, devoted entirely to character animation. Luckily, some of them are listed in Appendix E, "Further Reading."

Chapter 16

Cinematography

"Movies should start with an earthquake, and keep on growing in action."

Cecil B De Mille

Old-school games were little more than a few sprites painted onscreen with some bleeps pumping through the speakers. But as technology has evolved and our craft has become more sophisticated, attention to detail has increased as well. Today, games involve millions of polygons, visual and audio effects not so different from those used in movies, and strong cinematographic production values. Placing the camera and illuminating the scene is extremely important from a narrative standpoint. It helps convey the story, but also can act as a gameplay improvement. How many interesting games have been spoiled due to bad camera angles?

This chapter tries to shed some light on the world of interactive cinematography. More than a structured chapter, it is an unordered collection of techniques that can be used to control cameras and lighting in a variety of games. Most of these algorithms will not be very complex. Some trigonometry and algebra should suffice. But these simple techniques will in the end make a difference, enabling you to create games that truly showcase a movielike experience to the player.

First-Person Shooters

The first camera approach we will explore is the first-person camera used in many first-person shooter titles, such as *Quake*. It is a camera defined by at least four degrees of freedom (*X,Y,Z* and yaw), with pitch sometimes added to the mix. As far as control goes, the camera uses the left and right cursor to rotate, and up and down are used to advance or move backward in the direction we are facing. A side movement called *strafing* is sometimes present, allowing us to advance sideways. Strafing is useful in dangerous corners.

The math for such a camera is not very complex. To begin with, here is the code (using an abstract input controller) for the left and right cursors:

```
yaw+=ROTSPEED*elapsed*(input.right-input.left);
```

In this line of code, `input.left` and `input.right` return 1 if the specified cursor is pressed, and 0 otherwise. The parenthetical expression will return –1 if we are pressing left, 0 if both (or none) are pressed, and 1 if right is pressed. The result of this parenthetical expression will act as a modifier to the first part of the expression. Basic physics tells us that

```
Velocity=Space/Time
```

Then, solving for Space we get

```
Space=Velocity*Time
```

which is fundamentally what we are doing here (albeit in an angular fashion)— multiplying a constant `ROTSPEED` (which will determine how fast our character can turn) by the elapsed time; that is, the time it takes to complete a full game loop. By using this formula, we get nice, device-independent rotation speeds. The character will rotate at the same speed on different computers.

Now we need the code that handles the up and down cursors. It follows the same strategy:

```
int dz=(input.up-input.down);
playerpos.x= SPEED*elapsed*dz*cos(yaw);
playerpos.z= SPEED*elapsed*dz*sin(yaw);
```

In the preceding code, *dz* is just the same idea we used before to control which keys are pressed. The meat lies in the next two lines. As we did earlier, we'll use `SPEED*elapsed` to obtain device independence. To understand the next section (`dz*cos(yaw)`), a small diagram and some trigonometry is required. See Figure 16.1.

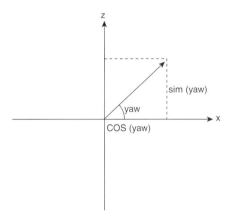

Figure 16.1   Trigonometrical sphere, FPS camera.

Remember that the cosine and sine functions relate the angle in a right triangle to the length of its sides. In our case, we have the angle (the yaw), and we need to compute the length of the side contiguous to it (which will become the increment in *x*) and opposite to it (which will be *z*). We assume the hypotenuse to be 1 and scale by `SPEED*elapsed*dz` to reach the end result.

Strafing is just a variant of the advance controller just shown. The trick is that a strafe move is performed by advancing sideways—that is, with a 90° increment with respect to regular movement. Here is the source code:

```
int dstrafe=(input.straferight-input.strafeleft);
playerpos.x= STRAFESPEED*elapsed*dstrafe*cos(yaw+3.1416/2);
playerpos.z= STRAFESPEED*elapsed*dstrafe*sin(yaw+3.1416/2);
```

Handling Inertia

Most first-person shooters (FPSs) implement inertia on their camera controllers for increased realism. Our character accelerates progressively and also stops moving in an inertial fashion. This makes movement smoother at almost no coding cost. To add inertia, we just have to remember a few physics equations, such as this one:

```
acceleration=velocity/time
```

Solving for velocity, we get

```
velocity=acceleration*time
```

Consider how a car works: You do not actually set the speed of the vehicle but instead use the pedals to add acceleration (or braking) to it. So we really need to implement our controller in terms of acceleration, not velocity directly. Our yaw controller would thus be

```
yawvel+=ROTACCEL*elapsed*(input.right-input.left);
if (yawvel>ROTSPEED) yawvel=ROTSPEED;
if (yawvel<-ROTSPEED) yawvel=-ROTSPEED;
if (input.right-input.left==0) yawvel=yawvel*BRAKINGFACTOR;
yaw+=yawvel*elapsed*(input.right-input.left);
```

The first line is just the acceleration version of our initial controller. Then, we use two lines to limit the velocity, so we cannot rotate faster than our initial #define. The fourth line is probably the most cryptic of them all. To understand it, notice that the if condition is activated if neither left nor right are pressed. In this case, we need to slow down the rotation progressively. We achieve this result by multiplying the current speed by a braking factor (0.85, for example). The last line only updates the yaw according to the calculated rotation velocity.

Almost identical code can handle forward and backward movement:

```
dz=(input.up-input.down);
vel+=ACCEL*elapsed*dz;
if (vel>SPEED) vel=SPEED;
if (vel<-SPEED) vel=-SPEED;
```

```
if (dz==0) vel=vel*BRAKINGFACTOR;
playerpos.x+=vel*elapsed*dz*cos(yaw);
playerpos.z+=vel*elapsed*dz*sin(yaw);
```

Now that we have seen how to implement cameras for FPSs, it is time to render them. In most graphics APIs, like OpenGL and DirectX, we have macro routines that place the camera, given a camera position and a look-at point. We will use these primitives because they provide a convenient way to specify this kind of camera.

Specifying the camera location is trivial. Now, to specify the look-at point, we will use some trigonometry again. If you understood the sin and cos used to advance according to the yaw angle, the following should become obvious:

```
lookat.x=playerpos.x+cos(yaw);
lookat.z=playerpos.x+sin(yaw);
```

Intuitively, the look-at point is placed in the same direction we are aiming; thus, using the same increments to compute it is very convenient. Assuming that convention, we can specify our FPS camera in OpenGL with the following piece of code:

```
glMatrixMode(GL_PROJECTION);
glLoadIdentity();
gluPerspective(fovy,aspect,nearplane,farplane);

glMatrixMode(GL_MODELVIEW);
glLoadIdentity();
gluLookAt(playerpos.x,playerpos.y,playerpos.z,lookat.x,lookat.y,
lookat.z,0,1,0);
```

The line that actually places the camera is the last two lines, but I provided the full camera setup code for completeness. Remember that the `gluPerspective` call sets optical parameters such as field of view, aspect ratio, and so on, whereas the `gluLookAt` places the camera by means of nine parameters grouped in triplets. The first triplet is the camera position, the second is the look-at point, and the third is a vector pointing up, which we will need for more sophisticated camera models.

Camera setting is very similar under DirectX. The syntax here is

```
D3DXMATRIX matView;
D3DXMatrixLookAtLH(&matView,&D3DXVECTOR3(playerpos.x,playerpos.y,
playerpos.z),&D3DXVECTOR3(lookat.x,lookat.y,lookat.z),
&D3DXVECTOR3(0,1,0));
g_pd3dDevice->SetTransform( D3DTS_VIEW, &matView );

D3DXMATRIX matProj;
D3DXMatrixPerspectiveFovLH( &matProj, fovy, aspect, near, far);
g_pd3dDevice->SetTransform( D3DTS_PROJECTION, &matProj );
```

assuming `playerpos` and the look-at point have all been computed using the algorithms we just explored.

Flight Simulators and Quaternions

Placing your virtual camera inside an airplane cockpit (or a spaceship, for instance) is a bit different from what we have seen so far. It is a first-person camera, but we need to account for six degrees of freedom (three for position, and one each for the roll, pitch, and yaw angles). Besides, most airplanes can perform loops, which imply that the camera is effectively upside down. We must be careful, however. If you take a look at the following equations for the sphere and analyze them, you will discover they are not what we are looking for.

```
x = r cos(v pi) cos(u 2 pi)
y = r sin(v pi)
z = r cos(v pi) sin(u 2 pi)
```

Here *u* would represent yaw, whereas *v* would represent pitch (forget roll for a second). Now, imagine that we are climbing vertically using such equations to represent movement. The airplane then tries to rotate using the yaw angle to perform any kind of acrobatic move, and unexpectedly, the yaw becomes a roll, and we just roll around the north pole of the parameter sphere.

The problem with the roll, pitch, and yaw representation (sometimes called the Euler angle representation) is that often axes get all mixed up, and combining rotations does not work as expected. This is called the *gimbal lock problem*. The solution is to use a whole different representation altogether. The representation was devised in the 18th Century by Hamilton and is called *quaternions*. Quaternions are a powerful mathematical operator that can be used for anything involving orientations, from a flight simulator camera to implementing scripted camera paths. Because it's one of the core techniques used by many games today, I will provide a short tutorial on quaternions.

A quaternion is a mathematical construct that consists of four real numbers. These numbers represent an extension of a complex number. Remember that complex numbers have a real and an imaginary part. Quaternions have one real and three imaginary parts, so their representation is as follows:

```
Q = w + xi + yj + zk
```

In this representation, (x,y,z) is the vector, and w is the scalar. The vector is not related to regular 3D vectors, so forget about that representation for a second. Quaternions can alternatively be expressed in this form:

```
Q = [w,v]
```

So, we place the scalar followed by the vector components.

Popular Operations

Let's now review how popular operations are implemented using quaternions. Here is the list:

➤ Addition: `q + q' = [w + w', v + v']`

➤ Multiplication: `qq' = [ww' - v · v', v * v' + wvv +w'v]`

where · denotes vector dot product and * denotes vector cross product.

➤ Conjugate: `q* = [w, -v]`

➤ Norm: $N(q) = w^2 + x^2 + y^2 + z^2$

➤ Inverse: $q^{-1} = q* / N(q)$

➤ Unit quaternion: q is a unit quaternion if $N(q) = 1$ and then $q^{-1} = q*$

➤ Identity: [1, (0, 0, 0)] (when involving multiplication) and [0, (0, 0, 0)] (when involving addition)

➤ Rotation of a vector v by a unit quaternion q: $v' = q*v*q^{-1}$ (where v = [0, v])

Quaternions can be converted to homogeneous matrices and vice versa. To begin with, here is the operation that computes a matrix based on a quaternion:

$$
\begin{bmatrix}
w^2 + x^2 - y^2 - z^2 & 2xy - 2wz & 2xz + 2wy \\
2xy + 2wz & w^2 - x^2 + y^2 - z^2 & 2yz - 2wx \\
2xz - 2wy & 2yz + 2wx & w^2 - x^2 - y^2 + z^2
\end{bmatrix}
$$

If the quaternion is normalized, we can simplify the preceding transform to the matrix:

$$
\begin{bmatrix}
1 - 2y^2 - 2z^2 & 2xy - 2wz & 2xz + 2wy \\
2xy + 2wz & 1 - 2x^2 - 2z^2 & 2yz - 2wx \\
2xz - 2wy & 2yz + 2wx & 1 - 2x^2 - 2y^2
\end{bmatrix}
$$

The opposite operation can also be performed easily. Here is the transform that computes a quaternion based on a Euler rotation:

q = qyaw qpitch qroll

where

```
qroll  = [cos (y/2), (sin(y/2), 0, 0)]
qpitch = [cos (q/2), (0, sin(q/2), 0)]
qyaw   = [cos(f /2), (0, 0, sin(f /2)]
```

For completeness, here is the source code for a function that converts a quaternion into a matrix:

```
QuatToMatrix(QUAT * quat, float m[4][4])
{
float wx, wy, wz, xx, yy, yz, xy, xz, zz, x2, y2, z2;

// calculate coefficients used for building the matrix
x2 = quat->x + quat->x; y2 = quat->y + quat->y;
```

```
z2 = quat->z + quat->z;
xx = quat->x * x2; xy = quat->x * y2; xz = quat->x * z2;
yy = quat->y * y2; yz = quat->y * z2; zz = quat->z * z2;
wx = quat->w * x2; wy = quat->w * y2; wz = quat->w * z2;

// fill in matrix positions with them
m[0][0] = 1.0 - (yy + zz); m[1][0] = xy - wz;
m[2][0] = xz + wy; m[3][0] = 0.0;
m[0][1] = xy + wz; m[1][1] = 1.0 - (xx + zz);
m[2][1] = yz - wx; m[3][1] = 0.0;
m[0][2] = xz - wy; m[1][2] = yz + wx;
m[2][2] = 1.0 - (xx + yy); m[3][2] = 0.0;
m[0][3] = 0; m[1][3] = 0;
m[2][3] = 0; m[3][3] = 1;
}
```

And the reverse operation that converts a rotation matrix to its corresponding quaternion follows:

```
MatToQuat(float m[4][4], QUAT * quat)
{
float   tr, s, q[4];
int     i, j, k;

int nxt[3] = {1, 2, 0};
// compute the trace of the matrix
tr = m[0][0] + m[1][1] + m[2][2];

// check if the trace is positive or negative
if (tr > 0.0)
    {
    s = sqrt (tr + 1.0);
    quat->w = s / 2.0;
    s = 0.5 / s;
    quat->x = (m[1][2] - m[2][1]) * s;
    quat->y = (m[2][0] - m[0][2]) * s;
    quat->z = (m[0][1] - m[1][0]) * s;
    }
```

```
else
    {

    // trace is negative
    i = 0;
    if (m[1][1] > m[0][0]) i = 1;
    if (m[2][2] > m[i][i]) i = 2;
    j = nxt[i];
    k = nxt[j];

    s = sqrt ((m[i][i] - (m[j][j] + m[k][k])) + 1.0);
    q[i] = s * 0.5;
    if (s != 0.0) s = 0.5 / s;
    q[3] = (m[j][k] - m[k][j]) * s;
    q[j] = (m[i][j] + m[j][i]) * s;
    q[k] = (m[i][k] + m[k][i]) * s;
    quat->x = q[0];
    quat->y = q[1];
    quat->z = q[2];
    quat->w = q[3];
    }
}
```

Additionally, here is the code for a routine that converts from Euler angles (roll, pitch, and yaw) to quaternion:

```
EulerToQuat (float roll, float pitch, float yaw, QUAT * quat)
{
float cr, cp, cy, sr, sp, sy, cpcy, spsy;

// compute all trigonometric values used to compute the quaternion
cr = cos (roll/2);
cp = cos (pitch/2);
cy = cos (yaw/2);

sr = sin (roll/2);
sp = sin (pitch/2);
sy = sin (yaw/2);
```

```
cpcy = cp * cy;
spsy = sp * sy;

// combine values to generate the vector and scalar for the
quaternion
quat->w = cr * cpcy + sr * spsy;
quat->x = sr * cpcy - cr * spsy;
quat->y = cr * sp * cy + sr * cp * sy;
quat->z = cr * cp * sy - sr * sp * cy;
}
```

So how do quaternions solve our gimbal lock problems? Well, basically, we need to follow a four-step routine.

First, we need to encode rotations using quaternions. If our engine internally uses roll, pitch, and yaw, we can transform those to a quaternion as in the code in the previous section. Second, we will encode frame-to-frame orientation variations in a temporary quaternion, which represents the change in orientation from one frame to the other. Third, we will post-multiply the frame-to-frame quaternion with the original one. This results in a new orientation that combines both rotations. Fourth, we convert the quaternion to a matrix and use matrix multiplication as usual to render the object. By doing so, gimbal lock is gone, and our flight simulator is flying.

Quaternions are not internally supported by OpenGL, so we need to create a new class or library for them. DirectX provides a quaternion object along with all the logical operations in the D3DX utility library. The structure is called D3DXQUATERNION and comes with approximately 20 useful operations, such as the Euler angle-quaternion transform, which can be performed with the following code:

```
D3DXQUATERNION*D3DXQuaternionRotationYawPitchRoll(D3DXQUATERNION
*pOut, FLOAT Yaw, FLOAT Pitch, FLOAT Roll);
```

Third-Person Cameras

Now that we have mastered flight simulators (and quaternions, hopefully), we will learn to specify a floating camera that follows the player behind and above his head, much like those in the classic *Tomb Raider* titles. To do so, our first approach involves always placing the camera behind the player and at a certain elevation angle over his position. The camera will be aimed at the player, who will therefore occupy the center of the screen. Using very simple math, here are the equations for this first camera's position and look-at point:

```
camposition.x= playerpos.x - cos(yaw)*cos(pitch)*distance;
camposition.y= playerpos.y + sin(pitch)*distance
camposition.z= playerpos.z - sin(yaw)*cos(pitch)*distance;

camlookat=playerpos;
```

We can implement such a camera by rehashing the OpenGL or DirectX we previously used in this chapter. Notice how we are basically applying a spherical coordinate transform using distance as the radius and pitch and yaw as the sphere mapping parameters. Then, pitch=0 means the camera is at the same height as `playerpos`, and we should limit the camera to a pitch no greater than PI/2 (90°). If we didn't impose such a restriction, the camera would be upside down because we would have surpassed the vertical (90° from ground level). Remember that sphere mapping creates *X,Y,Z* coordinates from radius, longitude, latitude, using an equation such as

```
X=Radius*cos(longitude)*cos(latitude)
Y=Radius*sin(latitude)
Z=Radius*sin(longitude)*cos(latitude)
```

where longitude is a number in the range (0..2*PI), and latitude is in the range (-PI/2.. PI/2). Latitude=0 would, in this equation, yield Y=0, thus representing a point on the equator or the imaginary sphere, or in camera terms, horizontal.

Although it should suffice for simple demos, there are a number of problems involved with this camera model. Our first limitation is having to target the player directly. After all, we are designing an action title, so we not only care about the player, but also about whatever he is currently seeing. Imagine that there is an enemy coming toward the player frontally. If we aim the camera at the player, he will most likely occlude the enemy, so we won't see the enemy until it's too late. Thus, we will improve the preceding code so we do not aim our camera at the player directly but at a point in space located in his viewing direction. In practical terms, this will make the player move vertically to the lower part of the screen, ensuring that we get a clear vision of whatever he's facing (see Figure 16.2). The math for this camera is quite straightforward. We will use the same approach as before, changing the look-at point (and thus shifting the whole sphere):

```
point camlookat=playerpos;
camlookat.x+=fwddistance*cos(yaw);
camlookat.z+=fwddistance*sin(yaw);

camposition.x= camlookat.x - cos(yaw)*cos(pitch)*distance;
camposition.y= camlookat.y + sin(pitch)*distance
camposition.z= camlookat.z - sin(yaw)*cos(pitch)*distance;
```

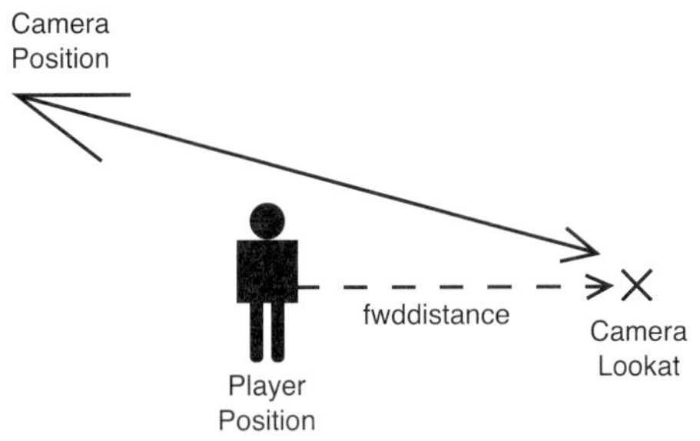

Figure 16.2   Camera parameters for a third-person view ahead of the player.

Now our camera is correct, both in its position and orientation. But this camera model will definitely cause lots of motion sickness. Notice how rotating the player will cause the camera to describe large arcs through the game level: The camera will move too fast. To reduce this effect, an inertial camera must be implemented. Here the idea is to limit the speed of the camera and use the position and look-at values computed previously only as indications of where the camera is moving to, not where the camera really is.

When doing inertial cameras, we need to implement smooth interpolations between different orientations. Doing so in terms of Euler angles will again look wrong. The camera will shake, look unnatural, and lose most of its smoothness. To solve this problem and compute smooth interpolations, we will again use quaternions. Quaternions provide an intuitive, simple mechanism to interpolate orientations. All we need to do is to describe both orientations using quaternions, and then interpolate between them using the Spherical Linear Interpolator (SLERP).

A SLERP interpolates between two quaternions using a sphere (see Figure 16.3), so orientations transition from one to another smoothly.

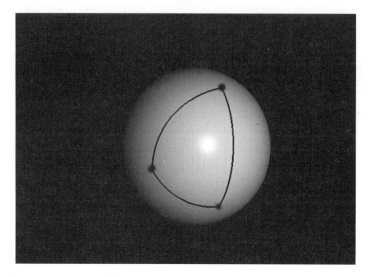

Figure 16.3 Interpolating with SLERP blends orientations that follow the surface of a unit sphere.

Its mathematical definition is

```
SLERP(q0,q1,t)=(q0*sin((1-t)*theta)+q1*sin(t*theta))/sin theta
```

where q0, q1 are the source and destination quaternion, t is the interpolation parameter that is in the range of 0 to 1, and theta is the acute angle between both quaternions. This produces a new quaternion, which is the spherical interpolation of the two. Here is the full source code for the SLERP routine:

```
QuatSlerp(QUAT * from, QUAT * to, float t, QUAT * res)
{
float to1[4];
double omega, cosom, sinom, scale0, scale1;

cosom=from->x*to->x + from->y*to->y + from->z*to->z + from->w*to->w;
```

```
if ( cosom <0.0 )
    {
    cosom = -cosom; to1[0] = - to->x;
    to1[1] = - to->y;
    to1[2] = - to->z;
    to1[3] = - to->w;
    }
else
    {
    to1[0] = to->x;
    to1[1] = to->y;
    to1[2] = to->z;
    to1[3] = to->w;
    }

if ( (1.0 - cosom) > DELTA )
    {
    // standard case (slerp)
    omega = acos(cosom);
    sinom = sin(omega);
    scale0 = sin((1.0 - t) * omega) / sinom;
    scale1 = sin(t * omega) / sinom;
    }
else
    {
    // "from" and "to" quaternions are very close
    //  ... so we can do a linear interpolation
    scale0 = 1.0 - t;
    scale1 = t;
    }
// calculate final values
res->x = scale0 * from->x + scale1 * to1[0];
res->y = scale0 * from->y + scale1 * to1[1];
res->z = scale0 * from->z + scale1 * to1[2];
res->w = scale0 * from->w + scale1 * to1[3];
}
```

The last issue we must deal with when coding a third-person camera is preventing it from colliding with the level geometry. Imagine that your character moves backward, so his back ends up leaning against a wall. If we use any of the algorithms explained in this section, the camera will actually cross the wall, and the sense of realism will be destroyed. Lots of games have suffered from bad camera placement in the past, and to most gamers' surprise, many of them still do today. A camera that crosses room walls sends a really negative message to the player in regard to game quality, so we must address this problem carefully.

The first option is to let the camera cross geometry, but never allow this geometry to occlude what's going on. To solve this issue, geometry between the camera and the player is alpha-blended, so room walls become partially transparent. This is a relatively straightforward effect, but is not very convincing to the player.

A second option is to seek alternative camera positions if we detect we are about to cross level geometry. This is the most common approach, but finding the right spot is not an easy task. We can choose to raise the camera vertically, but by doing so, we lose some perspective on what's coming toward the player. Besides, we can encounter a side problem if the room has a low roof. Another approach involves placing the camera laterally, which can again be tricky if we are at a corner or anywhere with geometry to the sides. An alternative solution involves doing an inverted shot. Instead of shooting from behind the player, we can place the camera in front of him, so we actually see the monsters approaching.

Cinematic Cameras: Camera Styles

Some games have gone well beyond established methods with regard to their camera handling. They have borrowed ideas from the film industry and have thus attempted to implement novel types of cinematic cameras where the action is followed not by one camera, but by a team of cameramen who watch the action and always try to show it from the best angle. I'm referring to games like *Ico* and *The Two Towers*; games in which dedicated algorithms are used to select which of the available cameras is best suited to follow the gameplay at any given time.

To implement these algorithms, we need a little inside information on how real-world cameras work. Cameras are usually described by how they are placed on the set. The most popular types include

- ➤ Fixed cameras
- ➤ Dolly cameras
- ➤ Crane cameras
- ➤ Steadycams

Fixed cameras are the simplest type of camera. They are fixed to the ground using a tripod or stable base, giving filmmakers a fixed viewpoint to the set. But these cameras are not limited to static takes. Sometimes, they can use tilting, panning, or zooming to move around and focus on different items.

Dolly cameras, or dollies, are moving cameras placed on top of wheeled structures so they can be displaced using straight or curved tracks, much like railway lines. They are used when we need to follow the action and want the camera to move as events unfold. The track placement and trajectories must be carefully planned so the track is never visible, and the movement is smooth.

Crane cameras are perched on top of large arms so they can perform wide arcs on the set. Arm sizes between 9 and 30 feet are normal. Crane cameras are usually controlled by one or more operators remotely, so they can displace the arm, but also change the tilt, pan, zoom, and so on of the camera from the ground. For added flexibility, some cranes can be mounted on top of dollies, so the best of both worlds can be combined.

A steadycam is a portable camera that is usually attached to the chest of an operator. To move the camera, the operator must move around the set. Steadycams provide an added degree of flexibility because there are no tracks or crane arms to watch out for. Steadycams also employ sophisticated stabilization mechanisms to ensure smooth, continuous placement regardless of any tremor from the operator. Sometimes steadycams can be used to film in an "over the shoulder" style, made so popular in films like *Saving Private Ryan*, by just deactivating any stabilization mechanism.

As far as filming goes, another factor to keep in mind is the type of shot you are recording, which usually has to do with the distance and scope of the shot—what is seen, what is not seen, and where the camera focuses. Depending on these factors, the following list of popular shots can be compiled.

Dramatic shots focus on the character and his attitude:

➤ An extreme close-up: Cuts over the mouth, focusing on the eyes

➤ A medium close-up: Cuts at the chin

➤ A full close-up: Cuts at the neck

➤ A wide close-up: Cuts at the shoulder

➤ A close shot: Cuts at the chest

➤ A medium close shot: Cuts at the waist

Informational shots include

➤ A medium shot: Cuts at the hips

➤ A medium full shot: Cuts under the knees

➤ A full shot: Shows the entire person

➤ A long shot: Provides a distance perspective

As we create more complex games, it is important that the games industry get used to this terminology (depicted in Figure 16.4). Most games today use long shots, so we can see both the main character and the surrounding scenario. But games such as *GTA3* are beginning to show us what can really be done with a cinematic approach to game development.

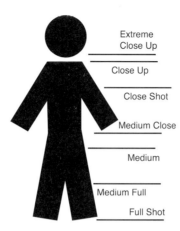

Figure 16.4   Description of different camera shots.

One interesting and luckily easy to code algorithm begins by placing the cameras using your content creation tool of choice, much like a movie director would do. It is essential to the success of this approach to offer different types of cameras, which are then implemented as a pure abstract class from which specific cameras are derived via inheritance. Content creators must have fixed cameras: fixed cameras with pan/tilt dollies so cameras can follow trajectories while focusing on the action, and so on. Notice how computer-simulated dollies are easier to create than their real-world counterparts because there is no fear of the tracks showing in the end result. We can also have vertical, helix-shaped, or any kind of path you can think of.

Then, all you need to do is implement a real-time algorithm that selects the best camera according to a heuristic. The classic choice is to select the camera that is closest to the player, but that's not the only option. We can cut to a very distant, bird's-eye view camera or any other setup. If you choose the "closest to player" criteria, the code is really straightforward. We have a list of cameras, each of one type, but all of them share one property in common: a placement, whether it's a point for fixed cameras or a line or spline for dollies. Thus, the algorithm is just a matter of testing which of the camera placement primitives is closest to the player. Will it be one point, so the player's perspective will use a fixed camera, or will it be a helix, so we can follow him as he climbs a spiral staircase? In the end, it's just point-point or point-line distances and not much else. Here is the structure for such a system:

```
class cinematographer
    {
    camera *cameras;
    int numcameras;
    public:
        void render(point);
    };

class camera
    {
    // each camera will define how it uses the control points
    point *path;
    int numpts;

    public:
        virtual float computedistance(point);
        virtual void render();
    };

class fixedcamera: public camera
    {
    (...)
    };

float fixecamera::computedistance(point playerpos)
{
return playerpos.distance(&path);
}

float dollycamera::computedistance(point playerpos)
{
float mindist=distancepointsegment(playerpos,path[numpts-
1],path[0];
int candidate=numpts-1;
int i;
for (i=0;i<numpts-1;i++)
    {
```

```
    float tmp= distancepointsegment(playerpos,path[i],path[i+1]);
    if (tmp<mindist)
        {
        mindist=tmp;
        candidate=i;
        }
    }
// here i store the segment where shortest distance was found in
a class attribute
bestsegment=candidate;
return playerpos.distance(&cameras);
}

float camera::computedistance(point playerpos)
{
float mindist=cameras[0].distance(playerpos);
int candidate=0;
int i;
for (i=1;i<numcameras-1;i++)
    {
    float tmp= cameras[i].distance (playerpos);
    if (tmp<mindist)
        {
        mindist=tmp;
        candidate=i;
        }
    }
return mindist;
}
```

This kind of approach has been widely used in many brilliant games, especially in the game console arena, where we get the feeling of a virtual cinematographer following the action to always ensure the best viewpoint. Take a look at Figure 16.5 to see how cameras can be included in a level design.

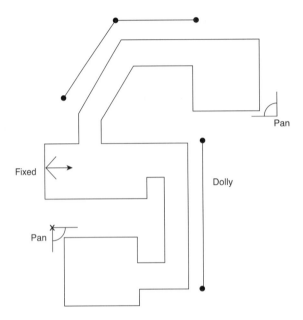

Figure 16.5   A top-down view of the game world, with cameras placed for cinematographic effects.

Cinematic Cameras: Placement Algorithms

We will complete this chapter with an overview of camera placement algorithms for character interaction. Consider this scenario: We have two people speaking, and a third person is approaching them. Which is the ideal location for a camera? Think about it for a second, and you will see it's a nontrivial problem. We must grant visibility to all three characters while keeping the camera as close as we can so no detail is lost. On top of that, we need characters not to occlude each other, so the whole scene is transmitted clearly. Camera placement algorithms have emerged in recent years due to the trend toward greater cinematic values. Many titles are implementing such algorithms already, and many others will surely join them in the near future. I'll provide a survey on how to compute good camera angles, especially when several items (both characters and scenario) must be displayed simultaneously.

The first item to keep in mind is that we will not use full characters but will instead use their bounding volumes for camera computation. Using full characters would be too costly, and as far as results go, the effort would not pay off. Thus, many algorithms will work on spheres or boxes that represent our locations and characters. We then need to compute camera positions and orientation vectors, which help convey the action of the scene. There are some general rules that we will need to implement in order to achieve realistic results. These really boil down to three basic rules:

➤ The camera should show everything relevant to the scene.

➤ The camera should be placed so obstruction between relevant information does not occur.

➤ The camera should be aimed at a point of interest in the scene.

These rules leave lots of room for experimentation. Using the previous example, we can choose the distance where we will place the camera with respect to the characters. If they were in an empty area, we would place the camera as close as possible, so we could see the action with full details. But if the scenario is somehow relevant, we might choose to move back a bit, so some context information is included in the shot. Let's refine each of our choices a bit.

Selecting the Camera Target

We will begin by aiming the camera in the right direction. But what is "the right direction"? This is basically a storytelling concept: Where is the camera supposed to be facing to cover the shot? There's no golden rule, so let's examine some case-by-case situations.

In a general case, we would begin by targeting the player, who is, after all, the screen alter ego of the gamer. Aiming at the chest of the character ensures that he is well located in the center of the screen, and we get some visibility of his surroundings.

But what if a monster is approaching the character? Maybe we should aim somewhere in the line of interest, which is defined by the character's and the monster's position, much like fighting games target the camera at the midpoint between the two fighters. This way the character shifts closer to the edge of the screen, and the monster is placed on the opposite side. Clearly, any good camera placement algorithm must make sure we not only see the main character, but also everything he is seeing.

A more complex case arises from group situations, such as a conversation between several peers or a small battle. Here the point of interest must be placed around the barycenter of the scene to make sure everyone can fit on the screen. It makes no sense to aim at the person currently speaking because this state will change often, and the camera will move back and forth all the time, surely annoying the player. For these cases, a neutral camera placement is preferred.

Generally speaking, cameras should be moved only when needed. Computer graphics possess a higher control level over camera placement than real-world cameramen do. We can shake the camera as fast as we can, converting our game into a virtual roller coaster ride. This can be seen in many computer graphics-based short films. But we need to understand that the camera should be as unobstrusive as possible, enhancing the gameplay instead of destroying it. Camera moving and even switching between different cameras should be kept to a strict minimum.

As an example, imagine a car racing game where the screen follows the action from different ground-based cameras, much like in TV retransmissions. In one camera, the car is seen sideways, advancing toward the right of the screen as it moves along the racecourse. Then, we switch to a different camera, which makes the car advance in a top-down direction on the screen. Obviously, the player will get the feeling that controls have changed, and thus interaction will be degraded. Games are about feeling in control of the gameplay, and switching cameras often destroys that feeling.

Selecting the Relevant Information

We know where we want to aim the camera. Now, how can we ensure that all the interesting information is inside the view cone? This is usually a two-step process that includes 1) understanding what's relevant and what's irrelevant for a given scene and 2) computing an adequate camera frustum so everything fits. The first problem is largely game dependent. We need to tag important elements so we can later use them to place the camera. Generally, the following are considered "relevant" items:

➤ The main character

➤ Other characters in the vicinity

➤ Pickable items closer than a set threshold

➤ Objects relevant to the gameplay, such as an obstacle

Each of these items must come with a bounding volume. For this algorithm, boxes are preferred for their tight-fitting property. We must then consolidate all bounding boxes into one, which represents the bounding box of the relevant information we want to target. Then, all we need is half a page of trigonometry to compute, given the aperture of the camera, the distance required to fit all the information in it. Notice how we must take into consideration the camera optical parameters (aperture, mainly), scenario characteristics (in the form of the bounding box for the relevant information), and camera view directions. Some scenarios will be larger in one dimension with respect to the others, and thus the distance where we place the camera will also depend on which direction we are aiming from. For example, imagine that you are trying to take a picture of a car from the front or sideways. Clearly, the second situation requires more distance because the object you are targeting covers a larger angle in the picture.

Thus, the variables for the analysis are as follows:

- ➤ *B*: The bounding box.
- ➤ *V*: The unit vector that defines the view direction.
- ➤ *P*: The center of attention. Sometimes it will be the center of the box, sometimes it won't.
- ➤ *VP*: The viewpoint we are trying to compute.
- ➤ *F*: The aperture of the camera in radians.

We then need to compute a point along the line that passes through *P* and has direction *V* so that the whole bounding box *B* lies within the angular distance defined by *F*. The algorithm is as follows.

We first create a point along the line emanating from P with *V* as its direction. Call that point *Q*. Then, for each vertex in the bounding box, we compute a vector *QV* from *Q* to the vertex. We compute the angle from *QV* to *V*, and store the bounding box point, which is at maximal angular separation from *V*. This is the point that will define when we are seeing the whole scene, so we only need to work with this point from now on. Let's call this bounding box point *R*.

Now we need a point along *V* that ensures that the point *R* is at an angular separation from *V* of exactly *F*. This is just regular trigonometry. The point is in the form:

```
X = Px - Vx*t
Y = Pz - Vz*t
Z = Pz - Vz*t
```

And the angular test can be easily added: The angle from *V* (the axis) to *QR* must be *F*:

```
V dot RQ = acos(F)
```

which is expanded into

```
Vx*(Qx-X) + Vy*(Qy-Y) + Vz*(Qz-Z) = acos(F)
```

or

```
Vx*Qx - Vx*X + Vy*Qy - Vy*Y + Vz*Qz - Vz*Z = acos(F)
```

Notice how we have four equations and four variables, so we can solve this system easily using any algebraic method. *P*, *V*, *F*, and *Q* are just constants we need to feed into the different equations.

A word of advice: Nobody likes relevant information to lie in an extreme corner of the screen. It is a wise idea to keep a safety zone, so there is a margin between any relevant item and the edge of the screen. This can be easily added to the preceding algorithm by substituting the real aperture of the camera by a value that is decreased in a set percentage, such as 10–15 percent. This way the camera will move back a bit to make sure we get some space around the different objects in our game world.

Selecting View Angles

Placing the camera at the right distance is a relatively straightforward problem. All we need to do is compute some angular math to do the job. Making sure we select a good view direction is quite a bit harder. We need to ensure that all elements are well proportioned, avoiding occlusions between them. If you review the preceding sections, you'll see that by now we have a point of interest we are aiming the camera to and a view distance suitable to show all objects from. That gives us a spherical crust where we can place the camera. Which points in the crust provide a better viewing angle?

From a purely technical standpoint, we can compute the best view direction as the one that generates fewer occlusions in the scene. But there are other issues to consider: If occlusions were the driving force, most scenes would be shot from a crane at a top-down angle. Obviously, we want as few occlusions as possible while keeping a comfortable, not too vertical viewpoint.

Let's begin by working with the occlusion portion and later add features on top of that. To simplify the math, we can select the position that generates fewer occlusions by working with average angular separations (AASs) between objects. The AAS is, given a point, a measure of the divergence of the rays emanating from it and heading toward the different objects in a scene. A purely horizontal viewpoint will have smaller angular separation than a vertical viewpoint, thus recommending vertical over horizontal viewpoints, at least as far as occlusions go.

AAS can be computed in a variety of ways. Because the number of involved elements will usually be small, the algorithm will not imply a significant CPU hit. Here is the pseudocode for such an algorithm:

```
for each object in the scene
    trace a ray from the viewpoint to the object
end for

average=0
for each ray
    select the closest ray (in terms of angular separation)
    average=average+angular separation between them
end for
average=average/number of rays
```

The `select the closest ray` function encapsulates most of the algorithm's complexity. For smaller data sets, brute-force, optimized approaches can be used. If this is not the case, spatial indexing techniques can somehow improve performance.

Now we need to compute the AAS for several points in the scene to discover which one yields better occlusion behavior. Generally speaking, vertical viewpoints have higher AAS values, so we need to compare two camera placements located at the same height for the analysis to provide some meaningful results.

Therefore, we need to modify our AAS value so more horizontal view directions are preferred over higher, vertical shots. One good idea is to use the angle to the ground as a modifier of the computed AAS value. By doing so, you can effectively compute suitable camera locations so the action and gameplay can be followed intuitively.

Agent-Based Approaches

The mathematical approach followed in the previous section is not the only way to deal with camera placement issues. After all, a real-world camera operator is not a machine. He's a human being using his brain and aesthetics criteria to select the best camera placement and orientation. Thus, camera placement looks like a great field in which to apply AI techniques. Many of the ideas discussed in other chapters of the book, such as rule systems, expert systems, or constraint solvers, can all be used to model the decision process used by our virtual cinematographer in order to call the best possible shot.

The camera operator could easily be implemented by means of a rule-driven agent. Rules describe the guidelines of the behavior, and rule priorities are used to select which decision must be taken at each moment. The rule system could look something like this:

```
defrule
(npc-closer-than 25)
(closest-npc equals ENEMY)
=>
(select-camera-destination npc)
(select-camera-origin overhead-from me)


defrule
(true)
=>
(select-camera-destination ahead-from me)
(select-camera-origin overhead-from me)
```

If this rule system is executed just once every few cycles, and results are interpolated using quaternions, we can reach strikingly good results and ease of use as far as the content pipeline is concerned.

In Closing

The winding road is ahead for those researching camera placement. Some work on automatic camera placement has already been done both in academia and the games industry. But it seems we are just scratching the surface. Predictably, this will be a very active field now that games borrow lots of aesthetics and techniques from the movie industry.

Chapter 17

Shading

"I paint objects as I think them, not as I see them."

Pablo Picasso

Real-world objects and scenarios are not only defined by their geometry, shape, and structure. We are also very sensitive to the look and texture, and how light interacts with the different materials. Imagine a beach with no sand texture or a wavy sea that did not reflect sunlight properly. A huge part of an object's essence lies within its shading properties, and that is what this chapter is all about.

In computer graphics, shading is a very broad term used to represent all the processes involved in assigning colors to pixels, which in turn represent geometry. Shading is usually divided into two large areas: *material synthesis* and *illumination*. Material synthesis deals with textures and surface properties, and illumination handles light and shadows. This chapter deals with the illumination component, whereas the next chapter is devoted to texture-based techniques.

Be warned, though: These are lengthy subjects, and hundreds of pages could be devoted to them. Hopefully, these chapters will show you the core routines, and your imagination and personal research will take care of the rest.

Real-World Illumination

Before talking about illumination algorithms for real-time games, let's stop and do an overview of how real lighting works. This will provide us with a solid foundation from which software algorithms can be derived.

Light is both an electromagnetic wave and a stream of particles (called photons), which travel through space and interact with different surfaces. In a vacuum, light travels at exactly 299,792,458 meters per second, or approximately 300 million meters/second. Speed decreases as the medium becomes more resistive to light. Light travels slower in the air, even slower inside water, and so on. As an example, a team from Harvard and Stanford University was able to slow down a light beam to as little as 17 meters per second (that's around 40 miles per hour) by making it cross an ultracold sodium atom gas.

Light emanates from surfaces when their atoms are energized by heat, electricity, or a host of chemical reactions. As atoms receive energy, their electrons use that incoming energy to move from their natural orbit to higher orbits, much like traffic on the fast lane of a highway. Sooner or later, these atoms will fall back to the normal orbit, releasing a packet of energy in the process. This packet is what we commonly call one photon. A photon has a fixed wavelength and frequency depending on the type of orbital change. The frequency determines the light color and also the amount of energy the light beam will transport. On the lower energy side, we have red light with a frequency of 430GHz. On the opposite end is violet light, which has a frequency of 730GHz. Some colors, such as white, are not related to a fixed frequency, but are achieved by the sum of different frequencies in a light beam in an interference pattern. But remember that light occupies a tiny fraction of the wave frequency spectrum. Radio waves have lower energy than any visible light, whereas x-rays and gamma rays transport more energy.

As light travels through space it might hit an object, and part of it might bounce back. When a hit occurs, photons hit the electrons of the object, energize them, and eventually they fall back again, emitting new photons. So really what you see is a secondary light ray that can in fact be of a different frequency (and thus color) than the first one because of the orbital change in the object. The way objects absorb some frequencies and thus generate light in a specific color pattern makes us see the color in objects. Thus, we can see light from a light source or from an object absorbing light selectively. But notice how both cases are internally similar: An object is just a secondary light source.

When light hits an object, the energy beam is divided into three main components. One part is absorbed by the object, usually increasing its energy levels in the form of heat. You feel that component whenever you lie on a sunny beach. A second component bounces off the surface and generates a reflected ray of light. That's what we see in a mirror or any reflective material. A third light beam enters the object (usually changing its speed due to the variation of density between both mediums) and travels through it. This phenomenon is called *refraction* or *transmission*, and the best example is light entering the sea. The change of speed makes the light rays bend, sometimes making us think objects immersed in the medium are broken (like a straw in a glass viewed sideways).

By understanding the preceding explanation you can model most light phenomena in the real world. Shadows, for example, are nothing but the occlusion of light rays by an opaque object, which in turn makes a region (the shadow volume) appear darker. The glitter on the crest of waves is just the reflection of the sunlight and only happens when the wave's orientation allows for a perfect reflection. Even the light concentration phenomena such as a hotspot caused by a lens or the patterns in a swimming pool can be explained. As the rays refract entering the water, they bend. Because many bent rays converge on a small area, it ends up receiving lots of energy, and appears burnt. Unfortunately, the nature of light cannot be directly transported to a computer. As with most atom-level phenomena, the amount of data required for a real-world simulation is prohibitive by today's standards. Computing any scene would require shooting billions of photons and tracing them around the scene to model their behavior accurately. That's what some offline rendering algorithms, such as ray tracing or radiosity, do. They are used in commercial renderers, but take anything from minutes to days to render a single frame.

A Simple Rendering Equation

For the sake of game programming, we will now explore some computational methods that simulate light interaction. We will start with a relatively straightforward algorithm used in many graphics applications and games. Later in this chapter, we will explore more involved solutions like the Bidirectional Reflectance Distribution Function (BRDF). But to begin with, we will use a model that computes lighting in a point as the result of three components:

➤ **Ambient**. Light that scatters in all directions and provides a base lighting to the scene.

➤ **Diffuse**. Light reflected from surfaces in all directions. The amount of reflected light is proportional to the angle of incidence of the light striking the surface. This component is viewpoint independent.

➤ **Specular**. Light reflected on a surface along the mirror direction, which accounts for pure reflection between the object and the light source. Like all mirrors, the intensity is view dependent.

Here is the global lighting equation for such a model:

```
Color = Kₐ*ambientColor + K_d*diffuseColor*(N dot L) +
K_s*specularColor*(R dot V) shininess
```

The equation has three major components, one for ambient, one for diffuse, and one for specular. Let's review each.

Ka, Kd, and *Ks* perform a breakdown of the lighting components. Different materials have different proportions of each one, but when added, these components should be 1. Typical values are K_a=0.2, K_d=0.5, and K_s=0.3, for example.

The three colors (`ambientColor`, `diffuseColor`, and `specularColor`) are RGB triplets specifying the colors of the three components. They can be computed using different criteria. The `ambientColor`, for example, is usually white or some subtle color that has to do with daylight color: pinkish in the evening, and so on. The reason for using white light as ambient is that, generally speaking, we can assume that the scene has many light waves of different wavelengths, so they result in white light when combined. Diffuse and specular color are dependent on the object's color and light source color. The specular component, for example, is usually initialized with the light source color, whereas the diffuse color must take both the surface and light colors into consideration. Intuitively, a white ball illuminated with blue light does not look pure white, nor does it look pure blue. Thus, using the following technique is common:

```
ambientColor = white
diffuseColor = surfaceColor * lightColor
specularColor = lightColor
```

Notice that this is an approximation. Nature does not have an ambient component per se, and multiplying surface and light source colors for diffuse color is somewhat wrong. But results are very good and can be computed in real time.

Now, let's take a look at the rest of the equation. The diffuse component is scaled by (N dot L), where N is the object's normal, and L is the vector from the point being shaded to the light source. Assuming both vectors are normalized, this means diffuse contribution is total whenever the light falls on the object parallel to its normal—thus, in a perfectly vertical way. This configuration is showcased in Figure 17.1.

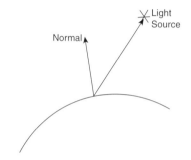

Figure 17.1   Normal and light vector explained.

All light is then bounced back, and the diffuse contribution is maximal. Then, the specular contribution is scaled by (R dot V), where R is the light's reflected vector, and V is the viewing vector. This configuration is showcased in Figure 17.2

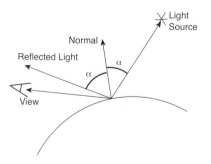

Figure 17.2   Normal, light, reflected light, and view vector illustrated.

Intuitively, light is reflected off the surface as in a mirror, and if we are angularly close to that mirror (that's what R dot V means), we see a hotspot. The only problem is computing R and V. Here are the equations:

```
V = vector from the point being shaded to our position
R = 2*N*(N dot L) - L
```

The formulation for R can take advantage of N dot L, which was already computed for the diffuse component.

Also, note how we add an exponent to the equation. Intuitively, polished objects show smaller, more focused highlights, so the shininess parameter helps us model that.

Here is a generalized equation that adds support for multiple sources and takes attenuation into consideration:

```
Color = Ka*ambientColor + Σ(1/(kc+kL*di+kQdi²))*(Kd*diffuseColori*
(N dot Li) + Ks*specularColori*(Ri dot V)shininess)
```

Notice that a global, light-source independent ambient contribution is added to the sum of the individual contribution of each lamp in the scene. Then, each lamp has a diffuse and specular component. I have added the i subindex to represent those values that must be computed per light, such as colors and reflection vectors.

Now, a note on attenuation factors: In the real world, light is absorbed by the distance squared. This is very well suited for the large distances present in the real world, but gives strange results in computer graphics. So, both OpenGL and DirectX use a slightly different model, where attenuation is a general quadratic equation in the form:

```
attenuation=1/(kc+kL*di+kQdi²)
```

In the equation, d_i is the distance between the point being shaded and the light source. Now all we have to do is tune the k_C, k_L, and k_Q parameters to reach the results we want. A constant attenuation, for example, would be expressed as (k_C!=0, k_L=k_Q=0). On the opposite end, a quadratic equation that mimics the real world would be achieved by (k_C=0, k_L=0, k_Q!=0). And the very popular linear attenuation used by many games is achieved by k_C=0, k_L!=0, k_Q=0.

A word of warning on these kinds of equations: These are ideal models that do not take many factors into consideration. Shadows, for example, need to incorporate the scene geometry into the equation. If a point is in shadow from a light source, its diffuse and specular components would either be eliminated completely (for opaque occluders) or scaled by the opacity value (if the object causing the shadow is semi-transparent). We will talk about shadows later in the chapter in their own section.

Per-Vertex and Per-Pixel Lighting

The first way to generate convincing illumination effects on a computer game is to use per-vertex lighting. This type of lighting is computed at the vertices of the geometry only and interpolated in between. Thus, to illuminate a triangle we would compute a lighting equation at each one of the three vertices. Then, the hardware would use these three values to interpolate the illumination of the entire triangle.

The rendering equation from the previous section is a popular choice because it can be implemented easily. In fact, variants of that equation are used internally by both OpenGL and DirectX renderers.

But per-vertex lighting is only computed as vertices. So what will happen to a large wall represented by only two triangles? Imagine that we place a light source right in the middle of the quad, far away from the four vertices. In the real world, the light source would create a very bright hotspot in the center of the wall, but because we do not have vertices there, per-vertex illumination will look completely wrong (see Figure 17.3). We need to either refine the mesh (which will definitely impact the bus and GPU) or find a better way to shade.

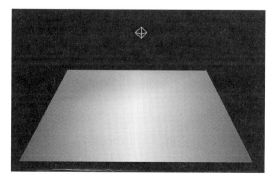 

Figure 17.3   Per-vertex (left) versus per-pixel (right) lighting.

This is where per-pixel shading kicks in. This lighting mode does not compute lighting at the vertices only, but in any pixel in between, so illumination has higher resolution and quality. Techniques such as light mapping (explained in the next section) or fragment shaders (explained in Chapter 21, "Procedural Techniques") are used to compute per-pixel lighting.

But if per-vertex lighting is what you are looking for, there's two options. You can either precompute lighting colors and store them as per-vertex colors, or you can leave this task to OpenGL or DirectX lighting engines. The first approach has the advantage of being faster because no computations are done in the real-time loop (lighting is a costly equation). On the other hand, the specular contribution cannot be precomputed because it is view dependent. The second option takes advantage of current-generation GPUs, which all support hardware lighting and transforms.

You can find complete examples of how lighting works in Appendix B, "OpenGL," and Appendix C, "Direct3D."

Light Mapping

We have seen how per-vertex illumination results can vary in quality depending on the mesh resolution, normal vector placement, and so on. A fine mesh with good smoothing can look great with just hardware, per-vertex lights. But coarse meshes with large triangles (walls, for example) are not well suited for the technique. Adjacent vertices are too far apart, and thus the hardware takes too few samples to convey a realistic sense of lighting. To make things worse, interpolation artifacts frequently occur, especially with moving lights, completely breaking the sense of immersion.

Light mapping is the global name used to describe different techniques that try to simulate pixel-correct illumination values by using textures to encode illumination properties (not only materials). Textures used to store lighting data are called *light maps* and can encode both diffuse and specular characteristics for any light, whatever the shape, color, and orientation. Light mapping became popular through its use in the *Doom/Quake* sagas, and since then has become absolutely fundamental to many games. It provides a relatively easy and effective way of creating realistically lit scenarios (see Figure 17.4).

Figure 17.4 Left: base texture. Middle: additive (specular) light map. Right: result.

To understand light mapping, you must first be fully aware of texture and color arithmetic and blending, so make sure you review these concepts before moving on. We will fundamentally use texture arithmetic to implement lighting equations, so textures are blended together to produce the end result.

Diffuse Light Mapping

The first technique we will explore is diffuse light mapping, which uses light maps to simulate Lambert's equation of diffuse lighting. Essentially, we will try to keep materials unchanged in well-lit areas while making them darker in shady areas. If you think about this in arithmetic terms and review the diffuse portion of the lighting equation from the previous section, you will see that this situation is equivalent to a texture multiplication. The light map will be white $(1,1,1)$ in lit zones and black in dark corners. If we paint the texture and then multiply it by the light map, a convincing diffuse shading effect will be achieved.

Specular Light Mapping

Specular lighting can also be simulated with light maps. Here, we try to "burn" textures due to light being emitted intensely in a certain direction. Specular lighting has a potential downside, though. Remember that the specular component is viewpoint dependent, so a viewer moving around an object should see the highlights move as well. Because we are limiting ourselves to static light mapping now, we cannot simulate this effect accurately. But imagine that the distance from the light to the lit wall is much smaller than the distance from the viewer to the wall. In this case, the dependency of specular highlights with regard to viewer movement would be very small, and therein lies the trick: Specular light mapping can accurately model highlights caused not by distant lamps illuminating highly reflective surfaces (think of a bright light and a metal ball), but by regular lights placed close to surfaces, thus producing the usual color burn. These highlights are almost viewpoint independent and look convincing when rendered with light maps.

In terms of texture arithmetic, a specular light map can be considered a texture addition. We add the light to the base material, so those pixels with high specular components are highlighted. Again, the light map would encode lighting using pure white (or whatever the light color is) for specularly lit areas and black for nonspecular zones. Specular light maps must be used sparingly. The main lighting contribution in any scene is always diffuse, and specular highlights are used only as finishing touches over that base illumination layer.

Global Illumination Using Light Maps

We can combine the diffuse and specular component of light maps to achieve a high-quality result, very similar to the solution proposed in the previous section. Again, it all boils down to texture arithmetic. A global illumination light map engine would use three textures, combined in the following way:

```
Color = Material_Color * Diffuse_light_map + Specular_light_map
```

Implementing Light Mapping: OpenGL

Light maps can be implemented in OpenGL via multipass rendering or by using multi-texture on capable hardware. The multipass option is somewhat slower, but code is probably easier to understand, so let's cover both. For completeness, we will cover the more complex, global illumination solution, which handles diffuse as well as specular lighting.

Multipass Version

We will implement light maps using three passes: The first will render a base object with corresponding material. Then, a second pass will multiply, simulating the diffuse component. A third pass will perform an additive blend to incorporate specular highlights. Let's look at some code, and comment it:

```
// first pass
glBindTexture(GL_TEXTURE_2D,basematerialid);
glDisable(GL_BLEND);
```

```
glDepthFunc(GL_LESS);

// here you would render the geometry
(...)

// second pass: diffuse multiply
glBindTexture(GL_TEXTURE_2D,diffusematerialid);
glEnable(GL_BLEND);
glBlendFunc(GL_DST_COLOR,GL_ZERO);
glDepthFunc(GL_LEQUAL);

// here you would re-send the geometry, only mapping coordinates
would differ
(...)


// third pass: specular additive
glBindTexture(GL_TEXTURE_2D,specularmaterialid);
glEnable(GL_BLEND);
glBlendFunc(GL_ONE,GL_ONE);
glDepthFunc(GL_LEQUAL);

// last geometry submission, only mapping coordinates would differ
(...)
```

It all boils down to setting the right blending mode and sending the geometry as many times as needed.

Implementing Light Mapping: DirectX

In this section, I will expose the code necessary to handle light mapping under DirectX 9. The code is thoroughly commented and is actually quite straightforward. If you are not familiar with texturing stage operations, take a look at the "Texture Arithmetic" section in Chapter 18, "Texture Mapping," for more information. In this first example, we implement diffuse light mapping using only two passes: one for the base texture and a second pass used to modulate it with the lightmap.

```
// This example assumes that d3dDevice is a valid pointer to an
// IDirect3DDevice9 interface.
// lptexBaseTexture is a valid pointer to a texture.
// lptexDiffuseLightMap is a valid pointer to a texture that contains
// RGB diffuse light map data.

// Set the base texture.
d3dDevice->SetTexture(0,lptexBaseTexture );

// Set the base texture operation and args.
d3dDevice->SetTextureStageState(0,D3DTSS_COLOROP,
D3DTOP_SELECTARG1);
// first operator: the base texture
d3dDevice->SetTextureStageState(0,D3DTSS_COLORARG1, D3DTA_TEXTURE );

// Set the diffuse light map.
d3dDevice->SetTexture(1,lptexDiffuseLightMap );

// Set the blend stage. We want to multiply by the previous stage
d3dDevice->SetTextureStageState(1, D3DTSS_COLOROP, D3DTOP_MODULATE );
// first parameter is the light map
d3dDevice->SetTextureStageState(1, D3DTSS_COLORARG1, D3DTA_TEXTURE );
// second parameter is the previous stage
d3dDevice->SetTextureStageState(1, D3DTSS_COLORARG2, D3DTA_CURRENT );
```

Now, a more involved example which handles both specular and diffuse using three stages:

```
// This example assumes that d3dDevice is a valid pointer to an
// IDirect3DDevice9 interface.
// lptexBaseTexture is a valid pointer to a texture.
// lptexDiffuseLightMap is a valid pointer to a texture that contains
// RGB diffuse light map data.

// Set the base texture.
d3dDevice->SetTexture(0,lptexBaseTexture );
```

```
// Set the base texture operation and args.
d3dDevice->SetTextureStageState(0,D3DTSS_COLOROP,
D3DTOP_SELECTARG1);
// first operator: the base texture
d3dDevice->SetTextureStageState(0,D3DTSS_COLORARG1, D3DTA_TEXTURE );

// Set the diffuse light map.
d3dDevice->SetTexture(1,lptexDiffuseLightMap );

// Set the blend stage. We want to multiply by the previous stage
d3dDevice->SetTextureStageState(1, D3DTSS_COLOROP, D3DTOP_MODULATE );
// first parameter is the light map
d3dDevice->SetTextureStageState(1, D3DTSS_COLORARG1, D3DTA_TEXTURE );
// second parameter is the previous stage
d3dDevice->SetTextureStageState(1, D3DTSS_COLORARG2, D3DTA_CURRENT );
// Set the specular light map.
d3dDevice->SetTexture(2,lptexDiffuseLightMap );

// Set the blend stage. We want to add by the previous stage
d3dDevice->SetTextureStageState(2, D3DTSS_COLOROP, D3DTOP_ADD );
// first parameter is the light map
d3dDevice->SetTextureStageState(2, D3DTSS_COLORARG1, D3DTA_TEXTURE );
// second parameter is the previous stage
d3dDevice->SetTextureStageState(2, D3DTSS_COLORARG2, D3DTA_CURRENT );
```

As you can see, neither of them is complex: It is all a matter of knowing the math behind lightmapping and expressing it correctly in your API of choice.

Creating Light Maps

Light maps can be created in a variety of ways. A first, naïve approximation would be to paint them by hand. This can be achieved with any image processing software such as Adobe Photoshop, and depending on the artist's talent, can produce strikingly good results. But it is a time-consuming process, and getting right the subtle interaction of light on surfaces is sometimes easier said than done. Some illumination effects are pretty unpredictable, and an artist might fail to convey the complexity of real-world lighting.

A second alternative is to compute them with the aid of rendering packages. Most rendering packages can help us, with varying degrees of success, in the process of creating light maps. However, most of them will require post-processing because they seldom offer a "cradle-to-grave" light map creation option. Thus, a third and quite popular alternative is to compute these maps with proprietary tools, which perform complete lighting analysis, compute textures, and store them in a suitable format.

Many software packages can help you compute light maps. Commercial renderers can create images seen from light sources, so you can reuse this shadow map. Radiosity processors can analyze lighting in a scene and output the information per vertex, and in some cases, even produce the required light maps. Sometimes, it is even coupled with a radiosity preprocess to ensure that lighting data is true to life.

Light Map Computation: Phong

The first and simplest way of computing light maps is to simply evaluate the diffuse and specular components of lighting by taking lights into consideration, but forgetting about occluders and shadows. The process is relatively straightforward and will lead the way to the more involved solutions exposed in the following sections. To keep things even simpler, let's forget about light map packing for a second and focus on creating the light map for a single quad, lit by several colored light sources.

The first decision to make is the light map size. As you will soon see, this size determines not only the quality of the results, but also the memory footprint of our application. Light maps are usually low resolution because they represent lighting gradients. Thus, when magnified, interpolation does not produce visual artifacts, but instead helps smooth out the lighting. Another issue to watch out for when selecting the right size is that to achieve realistic results, all light maps should be more or less of the same scale: A larger quad will require a larger light map, and so on. Thus, it is useful to think about light maps in terms of world-space size. For example, what sampling frequency do you want to establish in world units? Will one lumel (the equivalent to a pixel on a light map) correspond to one centimeter, 10 centimeters, or half a kilometer?

For our simple example, let's assume our quad is a square 1×1 meter. We will use a 64×64 light map, so lighting will have a resolution of 1.5 centimeters per sample approximately.

Once light map resolution has been set, we need to compute the coordinates of each sampling point, so we can then illuminate it. The sampling point computation for a quad is a simple bilinear interpolation, which divides the quad in a tile as fine as the light map size. Here is the code to compute light map coordinates (in 3D space) for lumel (*lu,lv*):

```
point Create3Dpoint(float lu,float lv)
{
// interpolate along the U axis
point v1=p2-p1;
point v2=p3-p4;
point v1=p1 + v1*(lu/LIGHTMAPSIZEU) ;
point v2=p4 + v2*(lu/LIGHTMAPSIZEU) ;

// interpolate along the V axis
point w1=v2-v1;
point w2=v1+w1*(lv/LIGHTMAPSIZEV);

return w2;
}
```

Now we have a 3D point we want to compute illumination for. But this is the easy part, because we discussed the classic ambient-diffuse-specular illumination equation earlier in the chapter. Now, it is all a matter of looping through the scene lamps, computing their contribution to the lighting of the lumel we are working on. All in all, computing a single light map affected by a number of lights is a $O(n^3)$ process. We need to loop through a bidimensional array of lumels, each one affected by several lights. Keeping in mind that this is just the simplest (and fastest) light map computation process, you will understand why light maps are usually created in a preprocess, often taking several minutes to complete.

In summary, here is the pseudocode for a light map processor that handles a complete scene. For simplicity, I have assumed each light map is stored in a different texture map. We will cover light map packing in the section "Storing Light Maps."

```
for each primitive in the scene
    compute the ideal light map size
    for each position in the light map along the u axis
    for each position in the light map along the v axis
            un-project U,V to 3D coordinates
            initialize the lighting contribution to 0
            for each lamp in the scene
             add the influence of the lamp to the overall contribution
            end for
            store the lighting contribution to the light map
        end for
    end for
    store the light map
end for
```

Notice that, depending on how you compute lighting, you can generate diffuse-only, specular-only, or both specular and diffuse light maps using the preceding algorithm. It all depends on how you implement the lighting equation. However, some effects will not be rendered correctly. Shadows, for example, will not be accounted for. We will need a more involved algorithm to increase the realism.

Light Map Computation: Ray Tracing

We can produce better looking results by introducing ray tracing techniques into the preceding algorithm. The core algorithm will stay the same, but before considering the contribution of a given lamp to a lumel, we will fire a shadow ray from the lumel to the lamp and test for intersections with the rest of the scene. This way we can handle shadows for much increased realism. Notice how we won't be using recursive ray tracing, which is reserved for reflections and transparencies. A single shadow ray from the lumel to the light will tell us if the lumel should be lit by the lamp or if it stays in the shade.

Thus, the main addition to the previous algorithm is both the construction of the shadow ray and the shadow ray-scene intersection test. The construction is very simple: Rays are usually represented by an origin (in our case, the lumel being lit) and a unit direction vector:

```
ray.origin=lumel;
ray.direction=lamp.pos - lumel ;
ray.direction.normalize() ;
```

Now, computing ray-scene intersection tests is a different problem (sadly, a more complex one). Efficient ray-triangle set tests are hard to find. I will expose the simplest test (which is incidentally the slowest one) and also a very efficient test, which will yield near-optimal results.

In a simple scene, the easiest way to compute the intersection between a ray and a triangle set is to examine triangles one by one and triangle-test each one. If any of the triangles effectively intersects the ray, our lumel is in shadows. The ray-triangle test is as follows:

1. Perform a ray-plane test between the ray and the triangle's support plane.

2. If they intersect, compute the intersection point.

3. Using the triangle winding rule, make sure the intersection point is inside the triangle.

You can make an early rejection test by making sure the ray's origin effectively lies in front of each triangle you test (using the triangle's normal). Only visible (nonculled) triangles can actually cause a point in a level to be in shadows.

This algorithm runs at O(number of triangles in the scene). Now, because light map processors are usually run offline, this high cost might not be a problem. But remember to keep an eye on your total computational cost. Ray tracing is an intensive algorithm, and processing times can skyrocket if you are not careful. As a sampler, here is the composite cost of a light map processor using ray tracing with this intersection test:

```
O(number of triangles * lightmap U size * lightmap V size *
( number of lights * number of triangles ))
```

Notice how the cost in the inner parentheses is for the ray tracing pass. Each lumel must shoot a ray to each lamp, and this ray needs to be tested against all level geometry—all in all, $O(n^5)$.

Now, we can use a better ray-triangle intersection test to help reduce processing times. The one we will use takes advantage of visibility computation. By knowing which areas of the level are visible from a given lumel, we can reduce the potential lamp and occluder set. Imagine, for example, that you are working with a portal approach. Then, given a lumel (in 3D coordinates), you can compute which cells are visible from that point. Because we are only considering direct lighting, only lamps in visible cells can potentially illuminate the lumel, so we can begin by eliminating all the others as candidates.

A second improvement appears in the ray-triangle intersection test. For a triangle to shadow the lumel, the triangle must lie in one of the visible cells as well. If a triangle is not in the Potentially Visible Set (PVS) of the lumel, how can it shadow the lumel?

Thus, a better light mapping processing algorithm can be built. Here is the pseudocode for this algorithm:

```
for each primitive in the scene
 compute the ideal light map size
 for each position in the light map along the u axis
  for each position in the light map along the v axis
   un-project U,V to 3D coordinates
   initialize the lighting contribution to 0
   compute the potentially visible cells from the lumel
   for each lamp in the visible set
    compute a shadow ray from lumel to lamp
    for each triangle in the visible set
     test for intersections between ray and triangle
    end for
    if no intersections occurred
     add the lamp influence to the global contribution
    end if
   end for
   store the lighting contribution to the light map
  end for
 end for
 store the light map
end for
```

Note how this new version is much more efficient than using brute-force ray-triangle intersections. In large levels with high triangle (and lamp) counts, the difference between using brute-force ray tracing and this new, accelerated method would be of orders of magnitude, given the intensive nature of ray tracing approaches.

As a final note, you can also speed up the ray-triangle test directly if you can't count on a visibility structure. Many methods have been devised through the years—the most efficient probably being Fujimoto's algorithm. This method, along with intersection tests for spheres and boxes, is explained fully in Chapter 20, "Organic Rendering."

Advanced Light Maps Using Ray Tracing More powerful ray tracing techniques can be used to compute complex light mapping effects. In this section, I will provide a listing of effects and suitable techniques.

Penumbras, for example, can easily be added to the ray tracing pass by using Stochastic (Monte-Carlo) ray tracing. Here we extend the shadow ray to a group of rays, which are directed in a Poisson distribution toward the light source (which in turn needs to become an area light) in a cone. Each ray is then tested with the scene for occlusions. By sampling the whole lighting area, shadows are no longer binary, but can offer subtle gradations (see Figure 17.5). Stochastic ray tracing is significantly slower than the classic algorithm, but results have heightened quality. Also, we can again use visibility techniques to speed up the process. We will only fire several rays toward those lamps that, being visible from the lumel, have an area.

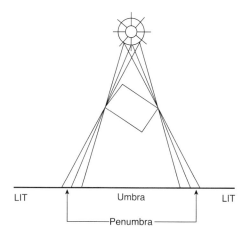

Figure 17.5 Umbras and penumbras.

A variant of ray tracing called *photon mapping* can be used to precompute light concentration phenomena or caustics. Here, a preprocess fires a number of rays from the different light sources (usually, several hundred thousand) and makes them bounce off the different surfaces. Whenever a lumel is hit by a ray, we increase a counter. So at the end of this preprocess, we can see if a lumel received lots of illumination or if it remained in the shade. If we consider semitransparent objects using Snell's law, light concentration phenomena will take place, and thus will be incorporated into the light maps.

But do not overestimate light maps. Because we are computing them as a preprocess, shadows won't animate as lights move, and caustics made by a swimming pool will remain motionless.

Light Map Computation: Radiosity

An alternative to ray tracing, and probably the method that delivers the best results, is using a radiosity processor to compute light maps. Radiosity is a lighting analysis algorithm based in real physics, with each surface element acting as both an absorbent of incoming light and a reflector. Thus, radiosity can accurately compute how light reacts in a scene, where it concentrates, and where shadows appear.

The radiosity algorithm is quite involved. Thus, many companies use commercial software to compute a solution for the problem. If you want to code your own, this section provides you with an overview.

Radiosity tries to compute global lighting in terms of energy transfer between the different surfaces in the scene. It starts by dividing the scene into patches and assigning two values to each: the illumination value (which represents how much light it is receiving from other patches) and the radiative energy (the amount of energy at the patch). As you probably know, there are no light sources in radiosity. A light source is nothing but a patch with radiative energy. Now, we need to compute the energy transfer from each pair of surfaces, which is a $O(n^2)$ problem. We take each patch and compute a factor that depends on the distance, shape, and orientation, and represents how much energy can be transferred from one patch to the other. This factor is known as the *form factor*.

Form factors are laid out in an N×N matrix, which represents all the relationships between patches. Then, to compute the energy transfer, we scan the matrix looking for patches with radiative energy. When we find one, we transfer part of that energy to other patches by means of the form factors, thus executing one step in the illumination process. We then start over, analyzing again which matrix positions still hold radiative energy. In this second wave, we will consider both the initial emitters and the emitters that received energy in the previous step, which became secondary emitters. This process is iterated until the energy transfer is below a threshold, and we can say the solution is stable.

There are a number of issues concerning this approach. The matrix can become large, especially if we want a pixel-accurate solution. A 1,000-triangle level needs a 1,000×1,000 matrix, assuming one triangle needs one patch exactly. That's rarely the case, because we will need more resolution and will subdivide triangles to compute finer results. The solution to this problem comes from progressive refinement, an improvement over the base radiosity algorithm proposed by Cohen, Chen, Wallace, and Greenberg in 1988.

In progressive refinement, we no longer use a radiosity matrix to compute the solution. Instead, we compute the solution surface by surface. We scan the surface list and select the surface with the most radiative energy to contribute to the scene. Then, we "shoot" that energy and propagate it to the scene using form factors. This results in a redistribution of energy in the rest of the patches. We then select the surface with the most radiative energy. The original surface may be on the candidate list, but not with the same amount of energy: That energy was already shot. So, we select the new radiator and iterate the process. The algorithm stops whenever the next biggest radiator has an energy level below a threshold, and thus we can assume its contribution to the final solution is minimal. As you can see, we haven't spoken about matrices at all. All we need to store for progressive refinement to work is the energy level of all surfaces at a given moment. Here's the algorithm:

```
repeat
   select the surface i with highest radiative energy
   store its radiative energy
   calculate form factors from i to all other surfaces j F_ij
   for each surface j
      update illumination based on F_ij and radiosity of i
      update radiative energy based on F_ij and radiosity of I
   end for
   set emission of i to zero
until the radiative energy of the selected surface < threshold
```

Another advantage of progressive refinement is that an observer can very well oversee the solution building process. It would start with a black screen, and as energy is radiated, the scene would be illuminated. This allows for the rapid rejection of scenes whose solution is not looking good and for previewing the results.

Another popular issue concerning radiosity is how form factors are computed. A number of solutions have been proposed, from ray tracing and computing the percentage of rays that reach the destination surface to analytical solutions and texture-based approaches. The formal definition is as follows:

$$F_{ij} = (\cos \theta_I \cos \theta_j) / (pi*r^2) * H_{ij} dA_j$$

In this equation, the cosines represent the angular difference between both patches. To compute them, we just have to:

➤ Compute the vector V that represents the direction from the center of the transmission patch to the center of the receiving patch.

➤ The first cosine is the result of the dot product of the vector V with the normal of the transmission patch.

➤ The second cosine is the result of the dot product of the vector V with the normal of the receiving patch.

➤ Because the result of a dot product is a cosine (assuming normalized vectors), we choose this compact notation.

Then, we divide the result by $Pi*r^2$ to account for distance between patches. Farther patches should have smaller form factors because the probability of light from one reaching the other diminishes. The Pi factor is needed to account for the hemispherical nature of the emitted energy. The transmitting patch shoots out energy in a hemispherical distribution, not in a single direction, and the Pi factor incorporates that into the form factor.

The H function represents the visibility from patch i to patch j. How do we handle occluders? We need the form factor to incorporate any potential occlusions, so two patches with large form factors with a wall in between do not transmit energy to each other. H is just a visibility factor that scales the result from 0 to 1 depending on how much of a patch is visible from the other. The name H comes from the visibility algorithm used by many radiosity processors, which is the hemicube algorithm. Place a hemicube right above the patch in consideration and discretize it. Then, analyze the visibility on a cell-by-cell basis and store the fraction of visible cells in the H parameter. Other popular approaches involve shooting rays using a nonrecursive ray tracing approach and storing the fraction of the rays that actually hit the opposite patch.

The dA_j parameter is used to express the form factor in terms of differential areas. The form factor is defined per infinitesimal area element of the receiving patch, so should we want to compute it for the whole path, we would need to multiply it by the patch's area.

With this explanation of how radiosity works, let's examine how we can build light maps based on radiosity. Basically, we would need a fine representation of the level geometry, where each light map texel represents one sampling point in our radiosity processor. We would start with the level geometry, setting the detail level we want to work with. Will one texel in the light map represent one centimeter or one meter? From this first analysis, light maps of the proper size must be allocated. Then, each texel in each light map can be used to trigger a radiosity processing loop. Prior to that, we need to set which patches will be radiative, so our scene has some lighting information. This is usually embedded in the content creation tools. Then, we must perform the radiosity algorithm. Progressive refinement here is the best option because the radiosity matrix for any decent-size level can become unmanageable. Imagine that your game level consists of 10,000 triangles (not uncommon for *Quake*-style shooters), but due to the light map resolution, that is converted into 2,560,000 patches (on average, each light map being 16×16 texels in size). Because the radiosity matrix is $N{\times}N$, be prepared to handle a $2M{\times}2M$ matrix!

Then, the progressive refinement algorithm would work on a set of textures that encode both the illumination (which is part of the final solution) and the radiative energy, which is what we will try to minimize by iterating the process. Visibility can be computed in many ways, some of them assisted by the use of the engine's own scene graph, whether it's a Binary Space Partition (BSP) or some kind of portal engine. Computing H_{ij} is one of the main bottlenecks in any radiosity processor.

Storing Light Maps

Using only one light map might be fine for small demos, but as soon as you want to illuminate a complete game level the need to store large numbers of light maps arises. After all, each wall and detail has unique lighting properties, so the amount of light maps must be correlated to the amount of geometry in the game level.

But this might become a big issue as texture requirements grow: How many light maps are we going to store? What size will each one be? These and other questions have troubled graphics engine programmers for years, and luckily some clever solutions have been found.

To begin with, light maps are usually very low resolution textures, often just a few pixels across. Sizes of 16×16, for example, are not uncommon. The reason for this resolution comes from texture filtering: The graphics card will interpolate between the different texels anyway, so a small light map can stretch over a relatively large level patch. Sharp shadows and abrupt changes of illumination will only be possible if larger light maps are used. But for the classic radiosity-like rooms with a large diffuse lighting contribution, low-res maps should be perfect.

Another interesting decision is to pack several light maps in a composite, unique global texture that encapsulates them. Think about it for a second: If each light map spans across one or two triangles only, we will end up with hundreds of small textures, and we will need to swap the active texture all the time. Remember that texture swaps are costly. Thus, it is very common to store many light maps in a large map, so we can render them all with a single call. However, this otherwise great idea has a potential downside: finding an algorithm that can automatically pack light maps optimally. Doesn't sound like a big problem, right? Unfortunately, evil lurks from unforeseen corners, and packing light maps on a larger texture might be much harder than you might think. In fact, it's an instance of a classic computational problem called "set packing": placing N objects, each one with a different shape, inside a container to find the distribution that allows better space allocation. This problem is very well known, and studies demonstrate that it is an NP-Hard problem.

NP-Hard problems (such as set packing of the traveling salesman) are problems so complex, no algorithm designed to work in polynomial time can solve them. Thus, we must revert to exponential approaches, which is the "elegant" way to designate brute-force approaches. In our light map example, we would need to test all possible configurations in order to find the optimal one. And, with hundreds if not thousands of light maps, exponential algorithms can take quite a while to compute.

So some heuristic algorithms have been devised. These algorithms are far from optimal, so the solutions won't be perfect. But they run in reasonable times. Now I will explain one of these algorithms, which combines speed with fairly good results.

The idea is pretty simple: Allocate light maps one by one, building a binary tree along the way. We will use the tree to specify occupied and free zones until all light maps have been inserted. Then, for each light map, we use the region of the tree where it can be fitted better. Every time we place a new light map, we split new nodes so the tree expands and keeps track of all light maps. For example, take a look at the progression shown in Figure 17.6, and the end result in Figure 17.7.

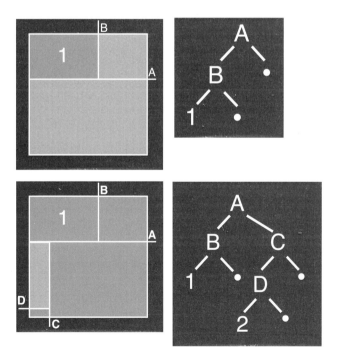

Figure 17.6 Top: first pass, one texture inserted. Bottom: two textures into the package.

And here is the source code for the complete algorithm:

```
class node
{
    node* child[2]
    rectangle rc;
    int imageID;
}

node *node::insert(lightmap img)
{
if we're not a leaf then
    {
    (try inserting into first child)
    newNode = child[0]->insert( img )
    if newNode != NULL return newNode;
    (no room, insert into second)
    return child[1]->Insert( img )
    }
else
    {
    (if there's already a lightmap here, return)
    if imageID != NULL return NULL

    (if we're too small, return)
    if img doesn't fit in pnode->rect return NULL

    (if we're just right, accept)
    if img fits perfectly in pnode->rect
        return pnode

    (otherwise, gotta split this node and create some kids)
    pnode->child[0] = new Node
    pnode->child[1] = new Node

    (decide which way to split)
    dw = rc.width - img.width
    dh = rc.height - img.height
```

```
if dw > dh then
    child[0]->rect = Rectangle(rc.left, rc.top,
    rc.left+width-1, rc.bottom)
    child[1]->rect = Rectangle(rc.left+width, rc.top,
                                        rc.right, rc.bottom)
else
    child[0]->rect = Rectangle(rc.left, rc.top,
    rc.right, rc.top+height-1)
    child[1]->rect = Rectangle(rc.left, rc.top+height,
    rc.right, rc.bottom)

(insert into first child we created)
return Insert( img, pnode->child[0] )
    }
}
```

In Figure 17.7, the results for such an approach occupy space in a very efficient way. Cost is $O(n*\log n)$, because we need n insertions, each one taking logarithmic access time.

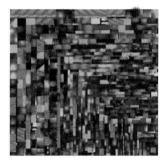

Figure 17.7   Composite light map computed by our simple packing algorithm.

The BRDF

The BRDF is one of the most powerful mathematical paradigms for computing real-world lighting (see Figure 17.8). It is a mathematical function that describes how much light is reflected off surfaces when a light beam makes contact with those surfaces. We will begin by analyzing its parameters, so we can give a complete formulation of the function. To begin with, reflectance depends on the light position and viewer position. As we saw in our simple example at the beginning of the chapter (which is nothing but a special case BRDF), the light position affected the diffuse component as well as the specular component, and the viewer's position affected the specular component.

In our equations, we will represent the light's position using two parameters, θ_i and ϕ_i, which represent the incoming light direction in spherical coordinates. View direction will be represented by θ_o, ϕ_o, which are in spherical coordinates as well and depict the outgoing view direction. Additionally, BRDF is a function of the wavelength of light. We saw this in our photon explanation of light transport mechanisms. Thus, we shall add a parameter called λ, which depends on the wavelength.

Figure 17.8 Teapot lit using a metallic-look BRDF function.

In addition, light interacts differently with different areas of a surface because of its inner details and structure. A tiled floor can have different reflectances for different types of tiles, and a stone can have varying properties depending on the exact mix of its constituents. This characteristic of surfaces, called *positional variance*, is expressed in terms of two parameters, u and v. These parameters represent the position parameterized to texture space, which in the end is where materials are specified. So, combining all this, we get a general BRDF formulation in the form:

$\mathrm{BRDF}_\lambda (\theta_I, \phi_I, \theta_o, \phi_o, u, v)$

Now, this is a very ambitious approach, and BRDFs are complex to compute. So, some simplifications are applied. For example, position dependency is usually skipped, so the BRDF is computed per material. Such a BRDF is said to be position-invariant or shift-invariant, and is expressed by:

$\mathrm{BRDF}_\lambda (\theta_I, \phi_I, \theta_o, \phi_o)$

We have now seen how the BRDF depends on angles that are usually expressed in terms of spherical coordinates. These coordinates are continuous values representing a unit sphere. But for computation purposes, we will discretize the interval and define the notion of *differential solid angles* as the area of a small rectangular region in the unit sphere. It is a powerful concept because it allows us to represent light in terms of energy flow through an area, which is expressed in Watts/m^2. The units for solid angles are steradians.

Let's try to shed some light on the value of a BRDF. For an incoming light direction *wi* (a differential solid angle) and a viewer direction *wo* (solid angle as well), the BRDF has a value related to *Lo* (the amount of light reflected) and *Ei* (the amount of light arrived at the surface). The ratio is

$$BRDF = \frac{L_o}{E_i}$$

Now, let's analyze the denominator. *Ei* represents the amount of light that arrives at the surface from direction *wi*. So how does that relate to the actual light intensity emitted from the original light source? Well, assuming *Li* is the emitted intensity, we must understand that we need to modulate the light intensity with regard to the incident angle, because the incoming light intensity must be projected onto the surface element (vertical light produces more intensity than sideways light, and so on). This projection is similar to the projection that happens with diffuse lighting as explained at the beginning of the chapter and can be simulated by modulating that amount by $\cos\theta_i = N \cdot w_i$. This means $E_i = L_i \cos\theta_i dw_i$. As a result, a BRDF is given by the following computation:

$$BRDF = \frac{L_o}{L_i \cos\theta_i dw_i}$$

And, after a couple pages of algebra, the global BRDF lighting equation is defined as:

$$L_o = \sum_{j=1}^{n} BRDF\ (\theta_i^j, \phi_i^j, \theta_o, \phi_o) L_i^j \cos\theta_i^j$$

with j denoting each light source's contribution. Several lighting models have been devised in terms of their BRDFs, and the Phong equation from earlier in this chapter is just one of them. The Torrance-Sparrow-Cook model, for example, is good for primarily specular surfaces. Other models are designed for rough diffuse surfaces. This is the case in the Oren-Nayar model and the Hapke/Lommel-Seeliger model, which were designed to model the dusty surface of the moon. Other interesting approaches are Minnaert, and on the complex end of the spectrum, He-Torrance-Sillion-Greenberg and Lafortune's Generalized Cosine Lobes, which both try to account for most observed phenomena.

That's all we need to know for now about BRDFs. We will now focus on how to code a BRDF into a real-time application. Remember that BRDFs are four-dimensional functions, and thus storing them into a 4D texture is out of question because of memory restrictions. Some alternative methods have been proposed and implemented successfully. The most popular one decomposes the 4D function as the multiplication of two 2D functions. Then, each 2D function is represented in a cube map (see Chapter 18), and multitexturing is used to perform the function multiply on the hardware. The tricky part is not the rendering. Cube maps have been around for quite a while now, and multitexturing is even older. The separation process is, on the other hand, pretty complex.

The process (called *normalized decomposition*) basically consists of the following separation:

$$BRDF\ (\theta_i, \phi_i, \theta_o, \phi_o) \cong G(\theta_i, \phi_i) \cdot H(\theta_o, \phi_o).$$

where G and H are the functions we will represent as cube maps. To compute them, we start by realizing that our BRDF could be computed (assuming we were to compute the 4D function) with code like this:

```
double deltat = (0.5 * M_PI) / (16-1);
double deltap = (2.0 * M_PI) / 16;
```

```
double theta_i, phi_i;
double theta_o, phi_o;

for ( int h = 0; h < 16; h++ )
for ( int i = 0; i < 16; i++ )
for ( int j = 0; j < 16; j++ )
for ( int k = 0; k < 16; k++ )
   {
   theta_o  = h * deltat;
   phi_o    = i * deltap;
   theta_i  = j * deltat;
   phi_i    = k * deltap;
/* Compute or lookup the brdf value. */
   val  = f( theta_i, phi_i, theta_o, phi_o )
   /* Store it in a 4D array. */
   BRDF[h][i][j][k] = val;
   }
```

This code assumes each value is sampled 16 times. Then, h represents θ_o, i represents ϕ_o, j represents θ_i, and k represents ϕ_i. We need to map this matrix to 2D. To do so, we unroll the 4D matrix into all combinations of parameter pairs. Each row and each column has two parameters fixed, and the other two varying in all possible combinations. The result is a larger matrix; each direction (rows and columns) being $N{\times}N$ in size. An example of such a matrix is shown here, where each parameter (theta and phi) has only two values, 0 and 1:

$$
\begin{array}{c}
\\
\theta_{o0},\phi_{o0} \\
\theta_{o0},\phi_{o1} \\
\theta_{o1},\phi_{o0} \\
\theta_{o1},\phi_{o1}
\end{array}
\begin{array}{cccc}
\theta_{i0},\phi_{i0} & \theta_{i0},\phi_{i1} & \theta_{i1},\phi_{i0} & \theta_{i1},\phi_{i1} \\
\left[\begin{array}{cccc}
F(\theta_{i0},\phi_{i0},\theta_{o0},\phi_{o0}) & F(\theta_{i0},\phi_{i1},\theta_{o0},\phi_{o0}) & F(\theta_{i1},\phi_{i0},\theta_{o0},\phi_{o0}) & F(\theta_{i1},\phi_{i1},\theta_{o0},\phi_{o0}) \\
F(\theta_{i0},\phi_{i0},\theta_{o0},\phi_{o1}) & F(\theta_{i0},\phi_{i1},\theta_{o0},\phi_{o1}) & F(\theta_{i1},\phi_{i0},\theta_{o0},\phi_{o1}) & F(\theta_{i1},\phi_{i1},\theta_{o0},\phi_{o1}) \\
F(\theta_{i0},\phi_{i0},\theta_{o1},\phi_{o0}) & F(\theta_{i0},\phi_{i1},\theta_{o1},\phi_{o0}) & F(\theta_{i1},\phi_{i0},\theta_{o1},\phi_{o0}) & F(\theta_{i1},\phi_{i1},\theta_{o1},\phi_{o0}) \\
F(\theta_{i0},\phi_{i0},\theta_{o1},\phi_{o1}) & F(\theta_{i0},\phi_{i1},\theta_{o1},\phi_{o1}) & F(\theta_{i1},\phi_{i0},\theta_{o1},\phi_{o1}) & F(\theta_{i1},\phi_{i1},\theta_{o1},\phi_{o1})
\end{array} \right]
\end{array}
$$

If you understand the previous explanation of matrix unrolling, the following source code should be pretty easy to understand. Notice how we reindex the matrix positions to keep them mapped in 2D:

```
double deltat = (0.5 * M_PI) / (N-1);
double deltap = (2.0 * M_PI) / N;
```

```
double theta_i, phi_i;
double theta_o, phi_o;

for ( int h = 0; h < N; h++ )
  for ( int i = 0; i < N; i++ )
    for ( int j = 0; j < N; j++ )
      for ( int k = 0; k < N; k++ )
        {
        theta_o  = h * deltat;
        phi_o    = i * deltap;
        theta_i  = j * deltat;
        phi_i    = k * deltap;
        /* Compute or lookup the brdf value. */
        val  = f( theta_i, phi_i, theta_o, phi_o );
        /* Store it in a N² x N² matrix. */
        BRDFMatrix[h*N+i][j*N+k]  = val;
        }
```

It looks like this is getting more and more complex, so let's recapitulate for a second and regain perspective. We started with a 4D BRDF, which I assume we have at hand and can evaluate at any given moment. BRDF data is available from a number of sources. It can be a mathematical expression, tabulated data acquired through a goniometer, and so on. Then, all we do is map this 4D data set to a 2D matrix by using linear combinations of parameters. Why? Because this makes it easier to separate it afterward.

So, we will now perform the last step, which is to compute the separation based in this 2D representation. To do so, a two phase approach should be followed:

1. For each row, compute the norm of all BRDF values in that row.

2. For each column, divide each column value by its corresponding row-norm and compute the mean average of these "normalized" values.

Our 2D matrix is now full of numeric values. The norm we are talking about is the generalization of the Euclidean norm we are familiar with. Euclidean norm, also called the 2-norm, is defined by:

$$(|x_1|^2 + |x_2|^2 + \ldots + |x_n|^2)^{1/2}$$

The norm we will be using here is defined as:

$$(|x1|^n + |x2|^n + \ldots + |xn|^n)^{1/n}$$

This means we take each full row of the 2D matrix and compute its norm, storing all the results in a column vector N of positions. Let's call this vector of norms *nvec*. We then compute a new vector based on the columns. We scan each column and compute the difference in value between the matrix value and the norm corresponding to that column. Then, we store the average of these norm-matrix differences in a second vector, as shown here:

BRDF Matrix

$$
n \times n \quad
\begin{bmatrix}
m_{1,1} & m_{1,2} & \cdots & m_{1,n-1} & m_{1,n} \\
m_{2,1} & m_{2,2} & \cdots & m_{2,n-1} & m_{2,n} \\
\vdots & \vdots & \vdots & \vdots & \vdots \\
m_{n-1,1} & m_{n-1,2} & \cdots & m_{n-1,n-1} & m_{n-1,n} \\
m_{n,1} & m_{n,2} & \cdots & m_{n,n-1} & m_{n,n}
\end{bmatrix}
$$

$$
1 \times n \quad
\begin{bmatrix}
\dfrac{1}{n}\sum_{k=1}^{n}\dfrac{m_{k,1}}{nvec_{k,1}} & \dfrac{1}{n}\sum_{k=1}^{n}\dfrac{m_{k,2}}{nvec_{k,2}} & \cdots & \dfrac{1}{n}\sum_{k=1}^{n}\dfrac{m_{n-1,1}}{nvec_{n-1,1}} & \dfrac{1}{n}\sum_{k=1}^{n}\dfrac{m_{n,1}}{nvec_{n,1}}
\end{bmatrix}
$$

Average Vector

The average vector must be computed per color component. Now, let's identify G and H. If you take a look at the row vector or norm vector, you will see that, due to the unrolling process, each value represents a sampled outgoing direction (θ_o, ϕ_o), which were the two parameters we fixed per row. So, this norm vector (identifying theta and phi as two parameters, and thus returning it to 2D form) is the function $H(\theta_o, \phi_o)$. The average vector or column vector has a similar property: Each column is correlated to an incoming direction, so for each sampled incoming direction (θ_i, ϕ_i) there is a corresponding average value in the average vector. As a result, this average vector can serve as the function $G(\theta_i, \phi_i)$.

As a result of this process, we can store two textures, G and H, which are the decomposition of the BRDF. By multiplying them, the whole BRDF matrix is generated. Remember that these textures (the matrices we have been talking about) are not indexed by position, but by the polar coordinates of the incoming and outgoing light direction. Theta and phi serve that purpose. All we need to do is create a cube map based on this angular shading data. By rendering it with multitexturing and a combine/multiply flag, we can effectively paint implement the BRDF.

Shadows

The lighting models we have discussed so far, both the Phong and BRDF equations, account for scene lighting quite well. But they assume no occlusions ever take place, so shadows are not integrated into the equation. Rendering shadows in real time is a complex problem, and only recent advances in graphics hardware have allowed for general-purpose, robust techniques to appear. In this section, we will explore some of them.

A shadow is a dark region on a surface caused by the occlusion of incident light by another object (the occluder). Shadow extends along a prism with its apex at the light source and its edges along the silhouette of the occluder. In other words, a surface element is in shadow if (and only if) a ray from the element to the light source collides with the occluder prior to reaching the light.

Shadows are a per-pixel phenomena and are thus hard to compute. For some years, only special-case solutions were possible: shadows on a plane, shadows on very simple geometry, and so on. Today, at least two general-purpose algorithms can solve the issue properly.

Shadow Maps

Shadow mapping works by representing shadows by means of a shadow map, a special-case texture that represents the light and shadow information in a scene. The algorithm contains four steps:

1. Render the scene from the light's point of view and direction.

2. Use the light's depth buffer as a texture (shadow map).

3. Projectively texture the shadow map onto the scene.

4. Use "texture color" (comparison result) in fragment shading.

We start by setting the camera at the light source and aiming in the direction we want to compute shadows for. Then, we render the scene and read back the contents of the

Z-buffer, which will become our shadow map. We do not need color, texturing, or lighting information, so all these features can be switched off to ensure that the shadow map is computed quickly. After we have created a texture out of the Z-buffer data, we need to use the shadow map information to render shadows to the scene. To do so, we render the scene again, this time setting the viewpoint at the camera location. Then, we need to merge the color information from this rendering pass with the shadowing information. This is the complex part of the algorithm, because the projection in both cases was computed from different orientations.

To solve this discrepancy in orientations, we use the approach described by Heidrich in his doctoral dissertation, subdividing the second step in two rendering passes. We first render the whole scene from the camera's viewpoint, with all lighting turned off and depth testing enabled. This paints the whole scene as if everything was in shadows. Then, a second pass and some clever alpha testing paints the lit areas, discarding shadowed fragments with the alpha test. The result is the combination of lit and unlit areas we expect. Take a look at Figure 17.9, where you can see both the result and the shadow map used to achieve it.

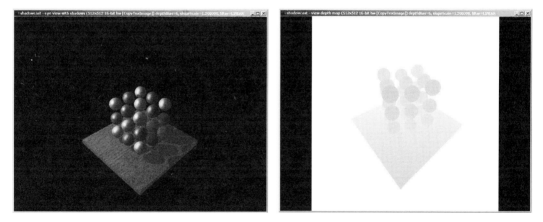

Figure 17.9   Left: resulting image. Right: shadow map that generates it.

In the second pass, we use two-unit multitexturing and register combiners or fragment shaders to implement the alpha testing. We assign the first texture unit to the depth map, which is stored in intensity format (RGBA with all channels storing the same value). The second texture unit is just a 1D linear ramp texture, which we will use to map the Z-values (from the viewpoint) to the [0..1] range. This way we can compare two textures based on their contents and actually perform a Z-comparison.

Obviously, we will need to create some specific projections, because the shadow map was initially created from the light's position. To create this projection matrix, we will rely on automatic texture coordinate generation functions, such as `glTexGen`.

For the first stage, which handles the shadow map, we must set the S, T, and Q texturing coordinates as follows:

$$
\begin{matrix} S \\ T \\ R \\ Q \end{matrix} = \begin{vmatrix} 1/2 & 0 & 0 & 1/2 \\ 0 & 1/2 & 0 & 1/2 \\ 0 & 0 & 0 & 0 \\ 0 & 0 & 0 & 1 \end{vmatrix} \quad * \text{ light projection } * \text{ light modelview}
$$

Note how the R coordinate is not actually required to perform a 2D texture mapping. For the second stage, a similar approach will be used, but because the texture is 1D, only S and Q will be used. The matrix to pass to `glTexGen` is

$$
\begin{matrix} S \\ T \\ R \\ Q \end{matrix} = \begin{vmatrix} 0 & 0 & 1 & 0 \\ 0 & 0 & 0 & 0 \\ 0 & 0 & 0 & 0 \\ 0 & 0 & 0 & 1 \end{vmatrix} * \begin{vmatrix} 1/2 & 0 & 0 & 1/2 \\ 0 & 1/2 & 0 & 1/2 \\ 0 & 0 & 0 & 0 \\ 0 & 0 & 0 & 1 \end{vmatrix} \quad * \text{ light proj } * \text{ light view}
$$

Then, setting `TexGen` is straightforward once we have the matrices. Take the S coordinate, for example. To set it from the resulting matrix, all we have to do is something like this:

```
float p[4];
p[0] = m1[0];
p[1] = m1[4];
p[2] = m1[8];
p[3] = m1[12];
glTexGenfv(GL_S, GL_EYE_PLANE, p);
```

Now we have the matrices and texture maps. All we need to discuss is how we combine them to generate the alpha values. These values will accept or reject fragments depending on their depth. Remember that texture unit 0 holds the depth map, which is stored in all RGB and A channels. Texture unit 1 holds a 1D identity texture. But as we render the vertices, we will assign them texture coordinates based on their Z, so in the end we have two textures that have Z-values in their alpha channel. Thus, we only need to subtract these alphas (Z-values) and bias to 0.5. Thus, this operation assigns a resulting alpha value depending on the Z-comparison, so we can use this new alpha to reject or accept fragments depending on their relative depth. Specifically, fragments with Z-value (seen from the shadow map) larger than the Z-value seen from the viewpoint will be assigned alpha values larger than 0.5.

These fragments will be rejected, and vice versa. Here is the equation we are trying to implement:

```
fragment alpha= alpha(Tex0) + (1 - alpha(Tex1)) - 0.5
```

For completeness, here is the full texture combiner source code needed to perform the required texture arithmetic for this operation:

```
// activate the 0th texture unit
glActiveTextureARB(GL_TEXTURE0_ARB);
// combine textures: ON
glTexEnvi(GL_TEXTURE_ENV, GL_TEXTURE_ENV_MODE, GL_COMBINE_EXT);
// we want to replace the RGB value
glTexEnvi(GL_TEXTURE_ENV, GL_COMBINE_RGB_EXT, GL_REPLACE);
glTexEnvi(GL_TEXTURE_ENV, GL_SOURCE0_RGB_EXT,
GL_PRIMARY_COLOR_EXT);
// by the color of the source fragment
glTexEnvi(GL_TEXTURE_ENV, GL_OPERAND0_RGB_EXT, GL_SRC_COLOR);
// store the texture alpha as well
glTexEnvi(GL_TEXTURE_ENV, GL_COMBINE_ALPHA_EXT, GL_REPLACE);
glTexEnvi(GL_TEXTURE_ENV, GL_SOURCE0_ALPHA_EXT, GL_TEXTURE);
glTexEnvi(GL_TEXTURE_ENV, GL_OPERAND0_ALPHA_EXT, GL_SRC_ALPHA);

// activate the 1th texture unit
glActiveTextureARB(GL_TEXTURE1_ARB);
glTexEnvi(GL_TEXTURE_ENV, GL_TEXTURE_ENV_MODE, GL_COMBINE_EXT);
glTexEnvi(GL_TEXTURE_ENV, GL_COMBINE_RGB_EXT, GL_REPLACE);
// take the color from the previous stage
glTexEnvi(GL_TEXTURE_ENV, GL_SOURCE0_RGB_EXT, GL_PREVIOUS_EXT);
glTexEnvi(GL_TEXTURE_ENV, GL_OPERAND0_RGB_EXT, GL_SRC_COLOR);
// add signed implements the interpolation function
```

```
glTexEnvi(GL_TEXTURE_ENV, GL_COMBINE_ALPHA_EXT,
GL_ADD_SIGNED_EXT);
glTexEnvi(GL_TEXTURE_ENV, GL_SOURCE0_ALPHA_EXT, GL_PREVIOUS_EXT);
glTexEnvi(GL_TEXTURE_ENV, GL_OPERAND0_ALPHA_EXT, GL_SRC_ALPHA);
glTexEnvi(GL_TEXTURE_ENV, GL_SOURCE1_ALPHA_EXT, GL_TEXTURE);
// filtered by the alpha
glTexEnvi(GL_TEXTURE_ENV, GL_OPERAND1_ALPHA_EXT,
GL_ONE_MINUS_SRC_ALPHA);
```

And here is the DirectX equivalent to the preceding code:

```
// Set the base texture.
d3dDevice->SetTexture(0,lptexBaseTexture );

// Set the base texture operation and args.
d3dDevice->SetTextureStageState(0,D3DTSS_COLOROP,
D3DTOP_SELECTARG1);
// first operator: the base texture
d3dDevice->SetTextureStageState(0,D3DTSS_COLORARG1, D3DTA_TEXTURE );

// Set the interpolated texture on top.
d3dDevice->SetTexture(1,lptexSecondTexture);

// Set the blend stage. We want to do a signed add
d3dDevice->SetTextureStageState(1, D3DTSS_COLOROP,
D3DTOP_ADDSIGNED);
// first parameter is the light map
d3dDevice->SetTextureStageState(1, D3DTSS_COLORARG1, D3DTA_TEXTURE );
// second parameter is the previous stage
d3dDevice->SetTextureStageState(1, D3DTSS_COLORARG2, D3DTA_CURRENT );
```

After this pass has been performed and the scene rendered, the results are as follows:

➤ RGB is lit color (lighting is enabled during second pass).

➤ Alpha is the biased difference between both textures.

➤ Unshadowed fragments have an alpha > = 0.5.

➤ Shadowed fragments have an alpha < = 0.5.

So all we have to do is enable alpha testing with a threshold of 0.5 and we're all set:

```
glEnable(GL_ALPHA_TEST);
glAlphaTest(GL_GREATER, 0.5);
```

A couple words of advice about the preceding technique: First, shadow mapping largely depends on the size of the shadow maps. Being a texture-based algorithm, the larger the shadow map, the smoother the shadows. Some games show staircase patterns in their shadows due to shadow maps being too small. On the other hand, this can become a memory issue.

Second, a more subtle piece of advice: Sometimes, your depth map–viewpoint comparisons will generate inaccurate results because of the finite resolution of the shadow map and the Z-buffer. On one hand, remember that our shadow map is 8-bits only. To handle this, I recommend you take a look at the higher color depth textures available under modern hardware. On the other hand, even with the highest resolution, sometimes fragments that are supposed to be lit will appear shadowed. The reason for this is very simple: As you render the shadow map, you are effectively storing the Z-values (up to the Z-buffer resolution) at which the first object was found. Then, in the second pass, when you render the same pixel, minimal Z-buffer differences can cause the fragment to be caught in its own shadow. If the Z-value of the second pass is slightly beyond what was computed on the first pass, the sphere's surface will be "inside" the sphere's surface, and we will consider it shadowed. The solution to this problem is easy. Use calls like `glPolygonOffset` to shift Z-values slightly in the shadow map computation pass so the stored Z-values are a bit on the conservative side. By doing so, we can ensure that a surface will always be "outside" of its shadow.

Stencil Shadows

Shadow mapping quality is a result of shadows based on a texture mapping approach. But we can approach shadows from a wholly different perspective. Imagine that you take the light source and construct a frustum that passes through the light source and through all vertices in the silhouette of the object acting as the occluder. If you examine the shape of the frustum, you will realize it's a volume that designates the area in space covered by shadows. Somehow, we could try to render shadows not based on texture maps, but on the shadow volume they project. This way our solution would be resolution independent: no jaggies, just perfectly straight lines. This approach is implemented via a special hardware device called the *stencil buffer*. So the technique we will now cover is called stencil shadows.

Stencil shadows work by somehow "painting" the shadow volume and using it as information for the renderer. To use this information, the renderer takes advantage of the stencil buffer. So before moving on, it would be a good idea to review what the stencil shadow is and what it can do for us. The stencil buffer is an offscreen buffer that we can select and paint into. The peculiarity is that whenever we paint into the stencil buffer, we create a mask. The shapes we paint there are stored, and then afterward, we can render in "normal" mode and paint only if the stencil buffer is set to a specific value. The first use of the stencil buffer was as a clipping region delimiter. Imagine that you need to render through a strange-shaped window. You would enable the stencil buffer, render the shape of the window, and then render whatever you actually wanted to paint, with stencil testing enabled.

So how can a stencil buffer help us paint realistic shadows? Let's first review the abstract algorithm and later implement it using the stencil buffer. The idea is simple: On the first pass, we render the shadow volume with culling disabled, so both front- and back-facing primitives are rendered. Then, on a per-pixel basis, we shoot a ray from the viewpoint and through the pixel being shaded. If the pixel does eventually reach an object, we must count the number of collisions between the ray and the sides of the shadow volume. Each front-facing intersection adds one to a counter, whereas each back-facing intersection decrements the counter by one. The object is shadowed if the counter retains a positive value before we reach it. Unshadowed objects are defined by counter values equal to zero. Take a look at Figure 17.10, where the shadow volume used for initializing the stencil is clearly shown.

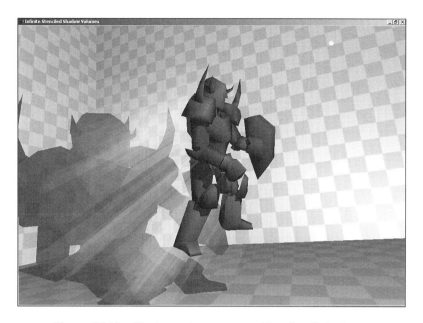

Figure 17.10   Shadow volumes as used for stencil shadows.

Let's now implement the previous algorithm, taking advantage of the stencil buffer. Here is the outline:

```
clear the frame buffer
render the visible scene using ambient light (this renders
everything in shadows)
clear the stencil buffer
for each light source,
    determine objects that may cast shadows in the visible region
of the world.
    for each object
        calculate the silhouette from the light source
        extrude the silhouette from the light to form a shadow volume
        enable writing to the stencil buffer
        render front part of volume, incrementing stencil on z-pass
        render back part of volume, decrementing stencil on z-pass
    end for
```

```
    enable reading from the stencil buffer
    render the scene with lighting on, painting where the stencil
is zero
end for
```

The stencil buffer actually counts intersections for us, and we are allowed to read its contents back. Let's refine some of the main portions of the algorithm so the implementation details become obvious. We first need to render the scene with lights off, so everything is in shadow. Then, we clear the stencil so we can begin pouring the geometry and shadow volume data. In this first code snippet, we clear the stencil buffer, enable stenciling so it always passes, and set the depth test and function:

```
glClear(GL_STENCIL_BUFFER_BIT);
glEnable(GL_STENCIL_TEST);
glStencilFunc(GL_ALWAYS, 0, 0);
glEnable(GL_DEPTH_TEST);
glDepthFunc(GL_LESS);
```

We are only going to draw into the stencil buffer, so we need to disable writes to the color buffer and depth buffer as follows in order to guarantee maximum efficiency:

```
glColorMask(GL_FALSE, GL_FALSE, GL_FALSE, GL_FALSE);
glDepthMask(GL_FALSE);
```

We have reached the point when we have to actually render the shadow volume, increasing or decreasing the intersection count as needed. This might seem complex, but can be achieved with these simple lines of code:

```
glEnable(GL_CULL_FACE);
glCullFace(GL_BACK);
glStencilOp(GL_KEEP, GL_KEEP, GL_INCR);
DrawShadowVolume();
glCullFace(GL_FRONT);
glStencilOp(GL_KEEP, GL_KEEP, GL_DECR);
DrawShadowVolume();
```

We then render the lighting pass, which effectively adds illumination to the scene. This is achieved using the following code:

```
glColorMask(GL_TRUE, GL_TRUE, GL_TRUE, GL_TRUE);
glDepthFunc(GL_EQUAL);
glStencilFunc(GL_EQUAL, 0, 0);
glStencilOp(GL_KEEP, GL_KEEP, GL_KEEP);
glEnable(GL_BLEND);
glBlendFunc(GL_ONE, GL_ONE);
```

The same sequence can be mapped easily to DirectX. DirectX code tends to be a bit longer sometimes, so make sure you refer to the preceding OpenGL sample if you get lost. That said, here is the step-by-step code, rewritten for DirectX 9. We clear the stencil buffer, enable stenciling so it always passes, and set the depth test and function:

```
d3dDevice->SetRenderState(D3DRS_STENCILENABLE, TRUE);
d3dDevice->SetRenderState(D3DRS_STENCILFUNC,D3DCMP_ALWAYS);
d3dDevice->SetRenderState(D3DRS_ZENABLE, TRUE);
d3dDevice->SetRenderState(D3DRS_ZFUNC,D3DCMP_LESS);
```

To write to the stencil buffer we disable color and Z-writing for maximum efficiency, using the lines:

```
d3dDevice->SetRenderState(D3DRS_COLORWRITEENABLE, FALSE);
d3dDevice->SetRenderState(D3DRS_ZWRITEENABLE, FALSE);
```

Again, we have reached the point when our DirectX code needs to actually render the shadow volume, increasing or decreasing the intersection count as needed. Here is the DirectX version of the code:

```
d3dDevice->SetRenderState(D3DRS_CULLMODE, D3DCULL_CW);
d3dDevice->SetRenderState(D3DRS_STENCILFAIL, D3DSTENCILCAPS_KEEP);
d3dDevice->SetRenderState(D3DRS_STENCILZFAIL,
D3DSTENCILCAPS_KEEP);
d3dDevice->SetRenderState(D3DRS_STENCILPASS, D3DSTENCILCAPS_INCR);
DrawShadowVolume();
d3dDevice->SetRenderState(D3DRS_CULLMODE, D3DCULL_CCW);
d3dDevice->SetRenderState(D3DRS_STENCILFAIL, D3DSTENCILCAPS_KEEP);
```

```
d3dDevice->SetRenderState(D3DRS_STENCILZFAIL,
D3DSTENCILCAPS_KEEP);
d3dDevice->SetRenderState(D3DRS_STENCILPASS, D3DSTENCILCAPS_DECR);
DrawShadowVolume();
```

We then need to render the lighting pass, which effectively adds illumination to the scene. This is achieved using the following DirectX code:

```
d3dDevice->SetRenderState(D3DRS_COLORWRITEENABLE, TRUE);
d3dDevice->SetRenderState(D3DRS_ZFUNC,D3DCMP_EQUAL);
d3dDevice->SetRenderState(D3DRS_STENCILFUNC, D3DCMP_EQUAL);
d3dDevice->SetRenderState(D3DRS_STENCILREF, 0);
d3dDevice->SetRenderState(D3DRS_STENCILMASK, 0);
d3dDevice->SetRenderState(D3DRS_STENCILFAIL, D3DSTENCILCAPS_KEEP);
d3dDevice->SetRenderState(D3DRS_STENCILZFAIL,
D3DSTENCILCAPS_KEEP);
d3dDevice->SetRenderState(D3DRS_STENCILPASS, D3DSTENCILCAPS_KEEP);
d3dDevice->SetRenderState(D3DRS_ALPHABLENDENABLE, TRUE);
d3dDevice->SetRenderState(D3DRS_SRCBLEND, D3DBLEND_ONE);
d3dDevice->SetRenderState(D3DRS_DESTBLEND, D3DBLEND_ONE);
```

Notice that we use a depthfunc of GL_LEQUAL, so we're effectively overwriting those fragments already on the Z-buffer.

As with shadow maps, stencil shadows have some issues we must learn to deal with. First and foremost, there's the silhouette extraction process. The classic way to compute it is to store edge connectivity information, so we can detect edges whose neighboring triangles face one in each direction with regard to the viewpoint. These are the edges that make up the silhouette. Currently, much work is being done in computing the extruded shadow volume in a vertex program. Whichever you choose, algorithmic cost is always going to be O(number of triangles). That's why many games and algorithms use lower quality meshes for the silhouette-extrusion process. We are very sensitive to the existence or absence of a shadow, but we are not extremely picky when it comes to its shape. Thus, using a lower resolution mesh will probably do the job equally well.

A second potential problem is handling camera in-shadow scenarios: What happens if our camera is inside the shadow volume? All our cleverly laid out stencil buffer math stops working because the crossings count does not mean what it's supposed to. The rule here is to render the shadow volume as well as the caps so we have a closed object and change the stencil tests to:

```
glCullFace(GL_FRONT);
glStencilOp(GL_KEEP, GL_INCR, GL_KEEP);
DrawShadowVolume();
glCullFace(GL_BACK);
glStencilOp(GL_KEEP, GL_DECR, GL_KEEP);
DrawShadowVolume();
```

Or, if you prefer DirectX, to something like this:

```
d3dDevice->SetRenderState(D3DRS_CULLMODE, D3DCULL_CW);
d3dDevice->SetRenderState(D3DRS_STENCILFAIL, D3DSTENCILCAPS_KEEP);
d3dDevice->SetRenderState(D3DRS_STENCILZFAIL,
D3DSTENCILCAPS_INCR);
d3dDevice->SetRenderState(D3DRS_STENCILPASS, D3DSTENCILCAPS_KEEP);
DrawShadowVolume();
d3dDevice->SetRenderState(D3DRS_CULLMODE, D3DCULL_CCW);
d3dDevice->SetRenderState(D3DRS_STENCILFAIL, D3DSTENCILCAPS_KEEP);
d3dDevice->SetRenderState(D3DRS_STENCILZFAIL,
D3DSTENCILCAPS_DECR);
d3dDevice->SetRenderState(D3DRS_STENCILPASS, D3DSTENCILCAPS_DECR);
DrawShadowVolume();
```

This changes the behavior, so when the depth test fails, we increase/decrease instead of doing so when the test passes. By doing so, we ensure that the rest of the algorithm works as expected. All we need to do is create the caps, which can be done in the same pass where we extrude the shadow volume.

Nonphotorealistic Rendering

Throughout this chapter, we have tried to model the subtle interactions of light with surfaces and materials, and convey a sense of realism. We will now change our mind-set completely. Nonphotorealistic rendering (NPR) tries to create intentionally unrealistic images. Cartoons, oil paintings, and line drawings are simulated using some clever texturing tricks, so a unique, artistic look is achieved. These techniques began as offline processes, but the advent of powerful 3D accelerators and faster algorithms have recently opened the doors to real-time games with NPR looks.

NPR techniques must be explained one by one because there is no general principle. Some of them are postprocesses to the rendered frame, others are part of a modified rendering algorithm, and so on. Here I will provide some samples for different effects to explore the usual strategies. We will explore painterly rendering, which tries to simulate brush strokes; sketchy rendering, which gives a pencil sketch look; and cartoon rendering, which mimics the style of a comic book.

Pencil Rendering

Simulating a pencil drawing can be performed at rendering time by using a two-pass approach. The first pass renders full objects; the second sketches them with pencil-drawn edges. To reach good results, it is very important to acquire good source textures, which we will use to cover the walls. One such texture can be seen in Figure 17.11, along with a frame of *Quake* rendered using sketchy rendering. The picture belongs to the NPR *Quake* project.

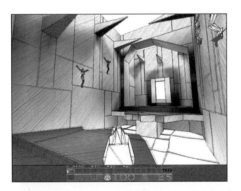

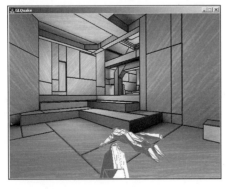

Figure 17.11 Style renderings from the NPR *Quake* project. Top left: pencil. Top right: ink. Bottom: cartoon.

Sketch rendering uses two techniques to convey the feeling of pencil-drawn graphics. First, objects are silhouetted, making sure strokes are not very well defined. Second, surfaces are painted with pencil-drawn textures, which complete the nonrealistic look.

Outlined Drawing

Computing the outline of an object is a somewhat involved process, which can be solved in a variety of ways. If you have edge-triangle adjacency information, you can compute the silhouette of the object by selecting those edges whose two support triangles have different orientations with regard to the viewer. If one of the two support triangles faces the viewer, and the other does not, clearly that edge must be part of the silhouette. This simple algorithm runs in O(number of edges) time. But many games do not store triangle-edge relationships. Thus, simpler algorithms are needed.

A second method uses a two-pass rendering scheme to paint the outline. The whole object is painted with front-facing triangles eliminated with culling. Thus, only back-facing primitives are painted. At this step, we render primitives as thick lines, the thickness depending on the look we want to achieve.

Then, we paint the object once again, culling back-facing triangles away. We use triangles, which will overlay the lines painted in step one, making them disappear. But lines painted in the silhouette will not be deleted because they will extend outside the boundary of the object due to their thickness. Here is the source code in OpenGL for this effect:

```
// First pass: render the geometry
glPolygonMode (GL_BACK, GL_FILL);    // we want to fill with
geometry
glCullFace(GL_BACK);    // don't draw back-facing
RenderTriangles();    // render (1st pass)

// Second pass: silhouette rendering
glPolygonMode(GL_BACK,GL_LINE);    // Draw backfacing as wireframe
glLineWidth(5);    // Set the line width
glCullFace(GL_FRONT);    // Don't Draw Any Front-Facing Polygons
glDepthFunc(GL_LEQUAL);    // Change The Depth Mode
glDisable(GL_TEXTURE_2D);
RenderTriangles();    // render (2nd pass)
```

This method has the downside of painting the object twice in order to get accurate silhouettes. Although many other methods exist, all of them have an incurred penalty cost. As an example, take the method shown by Jason Mitchell et al. at SIGGRAPH 2002. In this paper, the scene is rendered separately to two different render targets: one holds RGB data, whereas the second will hold depth values. Then, an edge detection filter is applied in order to highlight the edges. Computing silhouettes always involves a bit more work, so triangle counts and detail levels should be watched in order to achieve reasonable real-time performance.

Stroked Outlines

Artists often draw outlines not as a single, continuous stroke, but as a series of nonperfect strokes, which, when combined, create the illusion of shape. Even the outlines we have discussed in the previous section are a straight, constant width, so the sense of realism is not very good. We can enhance them by simulating these kinds of stroked outlines.

To do so, all we need to do is follow a three-step algorithm:

```
Detect the silhouette
For each edge in the silhouette
        Project it to 2D space
        Generate N sub-strokes
        whose starting and ending point are along the base stroke
        ...plus some random jitter
        Render these
End for
```

As for the silhouette detection code, we can follow two alternative approaches again. We can compute it if we have the edge adjacency information. If we don't, we can simply project all edges, painting strokes for all of them. Then, in a second pass, we paint the object with a Z-buffer offset that pushes it back slightly (enough so front-facing polygons are behind the strokes in terms of Z-value). By doing so, the strokes of the back-facing polygons will be covered by the object itself, much like in the outline algorithm prior to this one.

Cel Shading

Cel shading implements very simple coloring patterns with two or three shades per color only: one for highlighting, one for regular use, and one for shadows. Painting the triangles in flat color would do quite a good job, but the most popular technique is to use a 1D texture map with coordinates derived from lambert illumination values computed per vertex. First, you generate a 1D texture map, which is just a line. The line should be divided into three discrete portions: one with a lighter shade, one with a midtone, and one for highlights. Because we will be using the same texture map for all the rendering and implement colors as per-vertex modulations, the map should be grayscale.

Second, at rendering time, we need to calculate texture coordinates for each vertex. The process is relatively straightforward. Using the illumination information, you compute the Lambertian diffuse lighting coefficient. Remember that this coefficient comes from the equation:

```
Id= N*L
```

where N is the per-vertex normal and L is the vector from the vertex to the light source. If there is more than one light source, a summation is performed and divided by the number of lights.

In a realistic rendering core, we would use this diffuse intensity to modulate vertex colors. But in cel shading this value is needed to index the 1D texture map. The result is that well-lit areas get the lighter shade, midtones are attached to medium-lit zones, and so on. The main difference with regular texture mapping and lighting is that in cel shading you can see a line that divides the highlights, midtones, and shadows. There is no gradation of colors. Remember that for this technique to work, all vertices must be assigned per-vertex colors, which, by modulating the 1D texture, generate the real mesh colors. So, artists will need to vertex-colorize their meshes before putting them in the rendering engine.

Notice how cel shading uses only one very small texture map. There is no texture swapping, and bus usage is reduced. This usually means you can create higher resolution meshes, which is handy because cartoonlike characters tend to have a high-resolution, curved geometry look.

Painterly Rendering

Another NPR technique is painterly rendering, or directly trying to mimic the look of different painting styles in real time. These techniques are well explored in offline packages such as Photoshop and Fractal Design Painter. In both cases, approaches involve some sort of particle system that runs the stroke simulation. Each stroke is a particle with a life cycle and movement rules, such as follow the color patterns, paint edges, and so on. Generally speaking, all systems start with either a rendered frame (where each particle is just a "color space navigator") or pure geometry. Then, particles are assigned predefined texture maps, which help convey the style of painting we want to mimic.

The downside to all these approaches is that the number of particles and complexity of the simulation makes them hard to port to a real-time environment with conventional techniques. Most implementations do not move beyond 2–3 frames per second, if at all, and require particle numbers in at least the thousands. The main hope here resides in shader-based approaches, which take advantage of vertex and fragment shader capabilities, and are able to offload these computations from the CPU. The same way regular particle systems can be easily implemented into a shader, painterly rendering algorithms will definitely follow their lead.

In Closing

Seen in perspective, this is probably the single longest chapter in this book. And still, there's no way we have covered all the material I initially intended. Many areas like BRDF real-time rendering, dynamic light mapping, BTDFs (the equivalent of a BRDF for transmitted and nonreflected light), and nonphotorealistic rendering are some of today's hottest research topics, so the amount of documentation and bibliography is overwhelming. This chapter is thus little more than an eye-opener. Check out the materials quoted in Appendix E, "Further Reading."

Chapter 18

Texture Mapping

"We are living in a material world, and I am a material girl."

Madonna, Material Girl

Most end users believe top-class games use very detailed geometry to render the lush scenarios and characters seen onscreen. Although sometimes that's actually true, there are other, more powerful weapons in the game developer's toolbox. Geometry has a very high cost, and most of the time the same amount of detail can be supplied not by means of more vertices, but with clever use of materials and textures. Sharp, crisp textures convey lots of information and are, in the end, responsible for most of the believability of the scenarios.

In the previous chapter, we discussed how lighting goes a long way in providing realism to a scene. However, well-lit surfaces are just one part of the equation. We need actual materials, bricks, stones, and mortar. Characters need eyes and skin, and many other details that are usually conveyed with texture mapping techniques. This is what this chapter is all about. However, this chapter should be read along with the previous one because many techniques are common, and others are simply steps in a continuous progression. Both chapters, taken as a whole, will help you understand how we can set the look and feel of our graphics engines.

Types of Textures

Before we delve into specific texture mapping techniques, we must start by classifying textures and their uses. Textures is a very broad topic, and just using the term alone can result in misunderstandings.

Textures can be classified as *explicit* or *procedural*. An explicit texture map consists of a regular bitmap, which we can create with a paint program, scan from a picture, and so on. It is very easy to apply and has almost no CPU cost. We just have to provide the texture coordinates, and the graphics subsystem will take care of the texturing process. On the other hand, a procedural texture is the output of a computer program that computes the texture map. Marble, fire, and many other materials can be decomposed in some primitive equations and functions, which can be implemented as a program. Procedural textures have several benefits over explicit textures. They are resolution independent because we can zoom into the texture and compute the details. Because they are defined by mathematical functions that include some randomness, they are usually not as repetitive as explicit maps. On the other hand, they have a significant performance hit. Whether they are executed on the CPU or on a dedicated shader platform, procedural maps will take up some system resources. This chapter will focus almost exclusively on explicit textures, whereas procedural maps are covered in Chapter 21, "Procedural Techniques."

Another interesting classification can be established between static and dynamic texture maps. The difference between them is that dynamic maps are recomputed in real time, whereas static maps are just created at boot time. Both explicit and procedural textures can be static or dynamic. The most common type of texture map is both static and explicit. Games like *Quake* used a sequence of looping fire bitmaps to create torches, which is a good example of a dynamic and explicit technique. Marble and procedural fire would be adequate examples of static and dynamic procedural maps, respectively.

Dynamic, explicit textures are frequently encoded by storing all the frames in a single, large texture map, and somehow computing the texture coordinates automatically from the current timer value. So, if the texture holds $N \times N$ frames, and the speed (in frames per second) at which we want to animate the map is S, the following pseudocode computes texturing coordinates:

```
current_frame=(S/current_time) % (N*N)

row=current_frame/N
column=current_frame % N
u1=(1/N)*row
u2=(1/N)*(row+1)
v1=(1/N)*column
v2=(1/N)*(column+1)
```

In the preceding code, we are cycling through the texture map, using subimages as the actual texture map. Notice that I assume each image occupies a square zone.

Texture Mapping

Whichever the type, textures can be 1D, 2D, and 3D data sets. 2D maps are the most widely used because they can be represented with bitmaps. 3D textures are also called *volume textures*. They appear in fields like surgery to display 3D medical images and have slowly appeared on game-oriented hardware. They take up huge amounts of memory, and thus their use must be very limited. A 256×256×256 3D image with each texel representing a 256-color value (such as a grayscale image) can take up as much as 16MB. 1D maps have become increasingly popular over time as a way to implement a color translation table. The texture coordinate (in the range 0..1) is used as an index to a 1D table, where different colors are stored. A good example of this technique is cel shading, which produces quite convincing cartoonlike renderings. Cel shading is discussed in Chapter 17, "Shading."

Now, let's go back to our classic 2D texture maps. Because objects are inherently three dimensional, we need a way to precisely specify how the texture map should stretch and wrap the object, so we can place it. This process is called *texture mapping*.

In the 2D case, texture mapping is a function that goes from X,Y,Z to U,V, which are the mapping coordinates. This way it defines the correspondence between vertices on the geometry and texels in the map. For example, the following function is a proper texture mapping function:

```
U = X + Z
V = Y
```

However, things are rarely this simple, and more involved functions must be used. Following is a survey of classic mapping functions.

XYZ mapping

This function is used for 3D textures, especially procedural textures. It directly maps space to texture coordinates, possibly with translations, rotations, and scalings added on top. The general equation is as follows:

```
U = X
V = Y
W = Z
```

A scaled function would look something like this:

```
U = X*sx
V = Y*sy
W = Z*sz
```

Cylindrical Mapping

Another classic texture mapping function involves using a cylinder as the projector. Imagine a cylinder along the Y axis, wrapping the object with the material. That cylinder would be defined by the following parametric equations:

```
X = r cos(u* 2 pi)
Y = u * h
Z = r sin(u* 2 pi)
```

where r and h would determine the cylinder's radii and height, respectively. Now, we can invert the preceding equation to solve for U and V, which are the mapping coordinates. In that case, the resulting equation would be:

```
V = arctan (X/Z)
U = Y/h
```

Notice that this mapping is computed with the cylinder along the Y axis. Euclidean transforms could be applied to ensure that the cylinder lies in an arbitrary axis.

Spherical Mapping

Mapping onto a sphere is somewhat similar to using a cylinder. All we have to do is use the parametric equations of the sphere to construct inverse equations that represent the texture mapping. Assume a sphere defined by the following:

```
x = r sin(v pi) cos(u 2 pi)
y = r sin(v pi) sin(u 2 pi
z = r cos(v pi)
```

Notice how we have used *U* and *V* (in the texture mapping sense) as the parameters for the sphere; both are in the range 0..1. Then, reversing the equation after half a page of algebra you get:

```
u = ( arccos(x/(r sin(v pi))) ) / (2 pi)
v = arccos(z/r) / pi
```

The preceding formula assumes that `arccos` returns a value from 0 to 2Pi. Most software implementations return values in the range 0..Pi, so some changes to the code are needed for correct rendering. Here is the source code for a spherical texture mapping function:

```
#define PI 3.141592654
#define TWOPI 6.283185308

void SphereMap(x,y,z,radius,u,v)
double x,y,z,r,*u,*v;
{
*v = acos(z/radius) / PI;
if (y >= 0) *u = acos(x/(radius * sin(PI*(*v)))) / TWOPI;
else *u = (PI + acos(x/(radius * sin(PI*(*v))))) / TWOPI;
}
```

Notice how spherical mapping causes distortion to appear near the two poles of the sphere. To prevent this phenomenon called *pinching*, we need to preprocess the texture, either by using a commercial image processing software package or by implementing the process ourselves. Simply put, we need to convert the texture from polar to rectangular coordinates. Tools like Photoshop and Paint Shop Pro do this type of processing.

Texture Mapping a Triangle

The methods discussed in the previous sections are used for full objects that more or less conform to the mapping shapes, such as a planet or a banana. Most objects, however, have complex shapes that cannot be easily assigned to a sphere or cylinder. In these cases, we will need a general method that offers triangle-level control over the texturing process. We will need to assign texture coordinates manually, so the maps wrap the object precisely and accurately.

Given a triangle p1, p2, p3 with texture coordinates (u1,v1), (u2,v2), and (u3, v3), deciding the texture coordinates for a point p (in world coordinates) inside the triangle is just a bilinear interpolation. We start by building two vectors from p1 to p2 and from p1 to p3, and construct the point p as the linear combination of these two vectors. Assuming the initial vectors were normalized, the components of the linear combination are the blending coefficients that, once applied to the per-vertex texture coordinates, will give us the U,V coordinates for the point p. See the example in Figure 18.1.

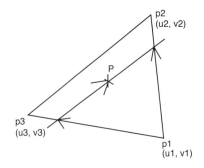

Figure 18.1 Texture mapping triangles.

On the other hand, rasterizers usually texture pixels in 2D after projection, but not full 3D points. Thus, a different mapping approach is followed. We start with the triangle defined not by 3D points, but by 2D, projected coordinates. Then, the triangle is painted one scanline at a time, drawing the horizontal line of pixels and texturing them along the way. Clearly, we need some kind of depth information to distinguish, from a texturing standpoint, two triangles that look the same onscreen but are not the same in 3D (see Figure 18.2). Thus, the 2D triangle coordinates are augmented with additional data that is then used to perform perspective-correct texture mapping, taking depth into consideration. Because these computations are performed on the hardware, they are beyond the duties of a game programmer these days.

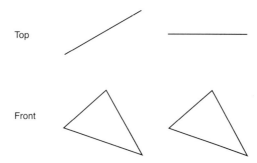

Figure 18.2   Two distinct triangles that share the same projection.

Tiling and Decals

Texture coordinates are theoretically defined in the range 0..1 in both directions, but can be easily extended beyond that. This is very useful for tiling materials, like a brick wall. A quad textured in the u,v range from (0,0) to (10,10) will repeat the same texturing pattern 10 times in each direction. Tiling is supported internally in both OpenGL and DirectX. All you have to do is set the proper texture parameters at load time. Under OpenGL, you need the calls:

```
glTexParameteri(GL_TEXTURE_2D,GL_TEXTURE_WRAP_S,GL_REPEAT);
glTexParameteri(GL_TEXTURE_2D,GL_TEXTURE_WRAP_T,GL_REPEAT);
```

which repeat in both directions. Under DirectX, the same result is achieved by using:

```
IDirect3DDevice9::SetSamplerState(0, D3DSAMP_ADDRESSU,
 D3DTADDRESS_WRAP);
IDirect3DDevice9::SetSamplerState(0, D3DSAMP_ADDRESSU,
 D3DTADDRESS_WRAP);
```

The syntax for OpenGL and DirectX is very similar.

Decals are the exact opposite. Textures do not repeat and are usually employed on top of another tiling material. The classic example is a car with a sticker. The car's texture can be tiling (some kind of metallic material), whereas the sticker will usually be laid out on top of it and be a decal. Under DirectX, we would need to change the last parameter of the `SetSamplerState` call to `D3DTADDRESS_CLAMP`, whereas OpenGL programmers need to change it for `GL_CLAMP`.

Filtering

Texture coordinates are usually described as floating-point values. We have just seen how they can extend beyond the 0..1 range, but for the sake of this section, let's assume they are restricted to 0..1 values. We can multiply the texture coordinate by the size of the texture map to obtain the texel we must apply to a given pixel. For example, a texturing coordinate of (0.75,0.35) applied to a 256×256 map will end up mapped at texel (192, 89.6). The *U* coordinate is an integer value, but notice how the *V* value falls in the middle of two values, or texels.

We could choose to truncate or round that value to the nearest integer, but that would result in an awkward behavior. Textures would flicker with subtle camera motions as pixels "jumped" from one texel to another. That's why most graphics cards support texture filtering, which averages texel values using different filters to obtain the proper appearance.

A card with no filtering, such as the early models and most software rasterizers, is said to use a nearest neighbor policy. It rounds the texel values to the nearest integer. But the most popular texture filter is *bilinear filtering*, which filters both in *U* and *V* directions using the two contiguous values. In the previous case, the *U* value would remain unfiltered because it's already an integer number, whereas the *V* value would be the composite of 60 percent of texel (192,90) and 40 percent of texel (192,89).

A more sophisticated type of filtering is *trilinear filtering*, which is used in mipmapping strategies. Mipmapping is a very important technique that we will discuss in the next section.

Whatever the case, texture filtering is usually available under most programming APIs. In OpenGL, filtering can be set per texture, so each one can have its own filtering options. The required function call is

```
glTexParameteri(GLenum target, GLenum pname ,GLenum param);
```

where `target` must either be `GL_TEXTURE_1D` or `GL_TEXTURE_2D` depending on the texture type. The second parameter, `pname`, specifies which filter we want to modify. OpenGL has a magnification filter, which is used whenever a texel is assigned to an area larger than a pixel, and a minification filter, which is applied to texels of subpixel size. The two symbolic constants are `GL_TEXTURE_MIN_FILTER` and `GL_TEXTURE_MAG_FILTER`. The last parameter (`Glenum param`) is used to specify the value of the selected filter. Available values are `GL_NEAREST` and `GL_LINEAR`, which sets bilinear filtering. Here is the code to set bilinear texture under OpenGL:

```
glTexParameteri(GL_TEXTURE_2D, GL_TEXTURE_MIN_FILTER, GL_LINEAR);
glTexParameteri(GL_TEXTURE_2D, GL_TEXTURE_MAG_FILTER, GL_LINEAR);
```

Under DirectX, the same results can be achieved with texture samplers, which are objects that determine how texture maps are accessed and filtered. Here is the equivalent source code:

```
IDirect3DDevice9::SetSamplerState(0, D3DSAMP_MAGFILTER,
D3DTEXF_LINEAR);
IDirect3DDevice9::SetSamplerState(0, D3DSAMP_MINFILTER,
D3DTEXF_LINEAR);
```

Mipmapping

Sometimes, especially in objects located far away, you will see textures flickering, with small camera movements causing them to look strange. As discussed earlier, texture maps should be filtered, so each pixel is assigned a value that interpolates the nearest texels to the desired value. But what happens when we are very far from the object? The answer is that the projection of a texel is much smaller than the size of a pixel, so blending four values is not enough. In this case, a slight movement in the camera will result in a quick move per-pixel on texture space. This causes the textures placed on distant objects to flicker and produce an annoying effect. Let's visualize this with an example, such as a quad located very far away but parallel to the screen. One pixel has texture coordinates (0.5, 0.5), whereas the next, in no particular direction, is mapped to (0.65, 0.5). The difference in coordinates comes from the fact that being so far away, coordinates are far apart in texture space. Then, assuming the map is 256×256, the first pixel is mapped to texel (128, 128) plus interpolation. The second is mapped to texel (166, 0.5). Clearly, there's an ocean between both samples. Any minimal camera movement will make a huge impact in texture space and result in very noticeable flickering. See Figure 18.3 for two examples.

Figure 18.3 Left image shows an image rendered with texture filtering, whereas the right image shows the same application running with filtering disabled.

The solution for this problem is called *mipmapping*, which is a filtering technique that will make your textures look good regardless of the distance. Mipmapping computes each texture as a sequence of maps—each one half the size than the previous. So, if you begin with a 256×256 texture map, your mipmaps will be 128×128, 64×64, 32×32, 16×16, and so on. These downsampled maps are computed by interpolating texels together, so they provide a smooth detail reduction for faraway polygons. Then, at run-time, the triangle to texture is projected in screen space, and the mipmap whose area matches the triangle's area better is used. This way we can eliminate the flickering (at the cost of extra texture memory usage). Reviewing our previous example, imagine that our quad is assigned to the mipmap that is 8×8 pixels in size. Then, the first pixel, with coordinates (0.5, 0.5), will be mapped to texel (4,4). The second pixel, mapped with (0.65, 0.5) as coordinates, will go to texel (5.2, 4), which is contiguous to the previous texel.

Mipmaps can be computed automatically in both OpenGL and DirectX. Under OpenGL, they are created with the call:

```
gluBuild2Dmipmaps
```

This call's syntax is very similar to that of `glTexImage2D`, the standard call for defining and passing a texture to OpenGL. Then, mipmap selection is an automatic process. Under DirectX, mipmaps are handled via the `GenerateMipSubLevels` call belonging to the `IDirect3Dtexture9` interface. Alternatively, mipmaps can be generated auto-matically at texture creation if we pass the `D3DUSAGE_AUTOGENMIPMAP` constant in the usage parameter of the `CreateTexture` call.

Texture Optimization

Using many quality textures is essential to creating believable, good-looking levels. But textures are costly. A single 256×256 RGB texture map takes as much as 192KB. If you want mipmapping on top of that, your map's memory footprint will double. And, let's face it, you will need dozens of different maps to create each level. Stop for a second and try to estimate how much memory you are going to need to store all your texture maps. A fellow developer once told me he was using between 40 and 100 maps per level, and that was an indoors game! At some point in time (better sooner than later), you will discover you have less memory in your target platform than you actually need. This is especially true in consoles, where memory is a precious resource, but is valid for PC game development as well. PCs have larger memory pools on the graphics subsystem, but buses are slower, and thus reducing memory sizes is of primary impor-tance here as well. You could try to implement a caching policy, which is a good move, but as you will discover in the next section, that does not solve all your problems. Moving textures up and down the bus will then become a performance killer.

Clearly, you need to think very carefully about how much memory you will dedicate to texture maps. In this section, we will first explore several simple ideas that can greatly reduce your texture's footprint. Most of the time, we waste precious bits by storing tex-tures inefficiently. Once you are able to keep memory use to the bare minimum, we will go on to explore real-time texture compression techniques.

The first option you can explore is to reduce color depth in your maps. Most APIs support this feature internally, so you only have to specify this at load time, and the GPU will take care of it. The advantage is clear: smaller maps. The downside is a perceived quality loss, which in most cases will be unnoticeable anyway. One of the most popular reduced-color formats is RGB4 (RGB, four bits per component), which needs 12 bits per pixel (and 16 bits per pixel in RGBA4). This mode works out very well in textures that do not have subtle color gradients, which luckily are the vast majority. The uniform gradient in the left picture is lost in the picture on the right, so this would be a very good example of when this technique should not be used. Subtle color changes do not reduce well. But most textures will yield better results. In Figure 18.4, you can see two maps that look almost exactly the same. One map is encoded using RGB4, and the other is standard RGB. Can you tell the difference? Even if you can, remember that graphics cards perform filtering in RGB space anyway, so they will help even more to make the color reduction unnoticeable. By the way, the RGB4 map is the one on the right.

Figure 18.4 A gradient seen in RGBA8 (left) and RGBA4 (right) formats.

Several reduced-color formats exist, and RGB4 just happens to be very popular. You can, however, use other formats in specific situations. For example, you can store illumination-only textures by using ALPHA4 format (alpha only, four bits per pixel). In the end, the rule of thumb is to examine your API and select the format that gives the right visual appearance using less space. DirectX is the winner here because it provides many exotic formats that are very useful in specific situations.

Taking this color-reduction scheme to the extreme, we can directly use paletized texture maps. These are 8-bit bitmaps where each pixel represents not the RGB value, but the index to a 256-entry table, much like in classic quantization schemes. Palletized maps thus occupy approximately one-third the size of the RGB texture map (plus the space for the palette). Again, deciding when to use palettes is a matter of knowing your textures. Gradients and rich-color maps might degrade significantly, but many maps will look great in 8 bits. Also, 8-bit terrain textures usually look great when applied to some kind of detail textures and lighting. As usual, having both options in your game engine is surely the best policy.

Texture Compression

Once all your options have been considered and tried, you might still need to reduce texture sizes even further. If so, it is then time to implement texture compression. Most likely, your textures will have already shrunk using color-reduction techniques, so compression will be icing on the cake. Using compression when most of your texture space is poorly managed is absurd.

Texture compression takes maps in compressed formats and only decompresses them internally on the GPU for display. Thus, both the file size and the memory footprint are smaller than with uncompressed maps. The disadvantage is that compressed textures have a small performance hit, because the GPU needs extra clock cycles to map the texels to the screen. Several compression schemes exist. Some of them are proprietary, and some are public. Similarly, some provide lossless compression, whereas others degrade the texture quality in the process.

DirectX provides very good support for texture compression, which is elegantly built into the core API. For example, the following line loads a texture map with full properties included:

```
D3DXCreateTextureFromFileEx(pd3dDevice, strPath, D3DX_DEFAULT,
 D3DX_DEFAULT, D3DX_DEFAULT,
 0,  D3DFMT_UNKNOWN, D3DPOOL_MANAGED,
 D3DX_FILTER_TRIANGLE|D3DX_FILTER_MIRROR,
   D3DX_FILTER_TRIANGLE|D3DX_FILTER_MIRROR,
0, NULL, NULL, ppTexture );
```

The beauty of this approach is that on a single call we are setting the texture object we want to load, the source data, the filtering options and mipmapping options, and texture compression, which is autodetected from the file we pass as a parameter. Thus, the programmer does not need to worry about such details. OpenGL developers will have a slightly more involved time because they will need to manually handle compression. This used to be done through the ARB_texture_compression extension, but is now part of the OpenGL core. The main call sequence to this extension is

```
ddsimage = ReadDDSFile("flowers.dds",&ddsbufsize,&numMipmaps);
glBindTexture(GL_TEXTURE_2D, already_compressed_decal_map);
glCompressedTexImage2D(GL_TEXTURE_2D, 0, ddsimage->format,
ddsimage->width, ddsimage->height,        border, image_size,
ddsimage->pixels);
```

which directly downloads a compressed texture in Direct Draw Surface (DDS) format to OpenGL. Remember that because DDS is part of DirectX, we need to do an include if we want to access textures in this format. DDS files for both DirectX and OpenGL can be created using DxTex, a tool included in the DirectX SDK.

Texture Caching and Paging

Despite all color reduction and compression efforts, in many cases you simply will not be able to keep all the textures in video memory. Remember that your video memory is a limited resource, and it must also accommodate the different buffers (two for double buffering, plus Z-buffer, plus stencils, and so on) as well as resident geometry. As a result, most games use more maps than they can fit in the GPU. So clearly, some caching policy must be implemented.

A commonsense rule of thumb is that the set of textures required to render any given frame (sometimes called the working set) must fit in GPU memory completely. Swapping textures should be kept to a minimum (such as your character traveling along the level and discovering a new area with different maps). Swapping on a frame-by-frame basis is a performance nightmare and should be avoided at all costs.

If this rule is followed, we will have textures that spend a number of frames in video memory; and as they become unused, get swapped out to provide room for newer ones. With this in mind, we can build a caching engine.

The engine will have a memory pool consisting of N textures (the value of N depends on the available physical memory). Each cached texture must consist of a structure like this:

```
typedef struct
    {
    texturedata *texdata;
    unsigned long timestamp;
    } cachedtexture;
```

We need the `timestamp` to control when textures were last accessed, so we can implement some kind of swapping policy. So, for each rendered frame, we must update the
`timestamp` attribute for each texture map that's actually used. This has a very low
CPU cost and allows us to keep track of which textures are "fresh" (are being queried
all the time) and which are "getting old."

Whenever we get a texture request, we need to do the following:

```
look if the texture is in the cache
if it is, use it and update the timestamp
else
    // we have a miss
    scan the cache, looking for the oldest texture
    swap-out the selected texture
    swap-in the new one
end if
```

Notice that we are implementing a last-recently used (LRU) policy. This means we
throw away the map that was last used, and use that space to allocate the new map. An
alternative policy, first in, first out (FIFO), ensures that the oldest map in the cache is
discarded, no matter how recently it was used. Because this cache engine will have a
very low performance hit (except for the actual swapping, which will depend on your
bus speed), we can use LRU, which is the best performing algorithm because it generates the least number of misses.

In addition, notice that we need a cache that is at least able to hold the textures
required to render a single frame (plus some extra space to have some margin). Cache
engines cannot do their job on a per-frame basis. The number of misses must be one in
every N frames, with larger N values yielding better performance.

Multipass Techniques

Imagine that you want to paint a large brick wall. You use a tiled brick pattern, which gives the wall a solid look. We have already seen how to achieve this by conventional texture mapping. But a plain brick wall is not very appealing, so you decide to add the ability to represent bullet marks dynamically on the wall as the player shoots a gun at it. To achieve this effect, you initially consider having two texture maps (one of the empty wall and another one of the same wall with a bullet mark), using the appropriate one at the proper time. But this is not practical. What if the user shoots at a different location on the wall, or even worse, shoots several times? Will you end up having N texture maps for what was supposed to be a simple effect?

The solution to this problem (and many others) is to multipass rendering techniques. We can use several layers of texture, which can be blended together, so the composite result looks good while keeping a reasonable memory footprint. With a multipass approach, we would only have a brick texture and a small texture map representing the bullet mark (with no bricks). You can see both maps in Figure 18.5.

Figure 18.5 Bricks and bullets, showing the original map (left), the bullet mark (middle), and the composite image (right).

Then, we would paint a first layer or pass with the brick texture. After the first pass, we would add a second layer with the bullet mark texture in the right spot on the wall. We just need to be careful to blend both maps properly, so the right effect is achieved. Multipass rendering techniques are a great tool to increase the realism of scenes. Here is a list of possible uses:

➤ Decals (bullet marks, tattoos, footsteps, and so on)

➤ Per-pixel diffuse and specular lighting

➤ Translucent objects

➤ Level of detail texturing

Multipass rendering is, on the other hand, slower than the traditional, single-pass approach. We will be sending more geometry to the frame buffer because we will use extra texturing passes to encode special effects, so the application will suffer a significant slowdown.

Coding a multipass rendering algorithm is just a bit more complex than coding a regular rendering algorithm. The key steps for an *N*-pass rendering block are

1. Paint the layer 0 geometry with the layer 0 texture.

2. Prepare the Z-buffer to accept coplanar data.

3. Increase the layer counter.

4. Set the right blending operation for the current layer.

5. Paint the current layer with its texture.

6. If you haven't finished, go to step 3.

As an example, here is the source code to render a quad using a multipass approach in OpenGL:

```
// set first texture
glBindTexture(GL_TEXTURE_2D,layer0id);

// render quad, first pass
glBegin(GL_QUADS);
glColor3f(1,1,1);
glTexCoord(0,0);  glVertex3f(-1,0,-1);
glTexCoord(0,1);  glVertex3f(-1,0,1);
glTexCoord(1,1);  glVertex3f(1,0,1);
glTexCoord(1,0);  glVertex3f(1,0,-1);
```

```
    glEnd();

    // accept co-planar fragments
    glDepthFunc(GL_LEQUAL);

    // set the blending mode
    glEnable(GL_BLEND);
    glBlendFunc(GL_ONE,GL_ONE);

    // set second texture
    glBindTexture(GL_TEXTURE_2D,layer1id);

    // render second pass
    glBegin(GL_QUADS);
    glColor3f(1,1,1);
    glTexCoord(0,0);  glVertex3f(-1,0,-1);
    glTexCoord(0,1);  glVertex3f(-1,0,1);
    glTexCoord(1,1);  glVertex3f(1,0,1);
    glTexCoord(1,0);  glVertex3f(1,0,-1);
    glEnd();

    glDepthFunc(GL_LESS);    // return to normal depth mode
    glDisable(GL_BLEND);     // don't need blending any more
```

The first rendering pass of the preceding code needs no explanation. It just paints a quad with a texture map. But notice that we will be rendering the exact same quad in the second pass, using a different texture this time. That is the reason we need to change the default Z-buffer behavior. By default, a Z-buffer is modified by a fragment if (and only if) the fragment's Z-value is strictly smaller than the Z-value stored in the Z-buffer. To allow a second rendering pass, we must relax this restriction and allow a fragment if its Z-value is smaller or equal to the contents of the Z-buffer.

A second item to watch out for is the blending equation. If we did not use blending, the second quad would overwrite the first quad, and all we would see would be the second texture map. To avoid this, we must use a blending function, which combines the different layers according to a blending equation.

Blending equations are specified in terms of a source and destination fragment. To understand the roles of both, remember that the source fragment is painted to the destination fragment. So, in a two-pass rendering routine such as the preceding one, the source fragment is what we will paint to the frame buffer (thus, the new data will be added to the composition), whereas the destination fragment represents what is already in the frame buffer (usually, data from previous rendering passes).

The blending equation specifies how the source and destination fragment will be combined together in a multipass core. Here is a general view of this equation:

```
destination = destination * destination_factor + source *
source_factor
```

Clearly, all we need to do is provide the multiplication factors so we can compute the output value for that pixel. Multiplication factors are usually not provided directly but as a symbolic constant. Table 18.1 contains symbolic constants.

Table 18.1   Symbolic Constants for OpenGL and DirectX

OpenGL	DirectX
GL_ZERO	D3DBLEND_ZERO
GL_ONE	D3DBLEND_ONE
GL_SRC_ALPHA	D3DBLEND_SRCALPHA
GL_DST_ALPHA	D3DBLEND_DESTALPHA
GL_SRC_COLOR	D3DBLEND_SRCCOLOR
GL_DST_COLOR	D3DBLEND_DSTCOLOR
GL_ONE_MINUS_SRC_ALPHA	D3DBLEND_INVSRCALPHA
GL_ ONE_MINUS_DST_ALPHA	D3DBLEND_INVDESTALPHA
GL_ ONE_MINUS_SRC_COLOR	D3DBLEND_INVSRCCOLOR
GL_ ONE_MINUS_DST_COLOR	D3DBLEND_INVDESTCOLOR

And the blending equation is specified by the following calls:

OpenGL:

```
void glBlendFunc(source_factor, destination_factor);
```

DirectX:

```
pd3dDevice9->SetRenderState(D3DRS_SRCBLEND, source_factor);
pd3dDevice9->SetRenderState(D3DRS_DESTBLEND, destination_factor);
```

Both APIs are absolutely equivalent in this respect, only minor syntactic differences exist. But getting blending modes right takes some practice, so here is a reminder of the most popular combinations of source and destination:

- ➤ `one one`   Additive blending; used to "burn" a surface with a specular highlight; ocean caustics and so on.

- ➤ `src_alpha one_minus_src_alpha`   Filtered blending; useful to create glass surfaces. The source (second pass) alpha will regulate the glass's opacity. It is also useful for diffuse light maps.

Multipass techniques can be extended to any number of passes. You can add dirt, then apply a diffuse lighting effect, and add specular highlights on top of that. But remember that performance will decrease as the number of rendered triangles increases. Additionally, note that painting geometry with blending enabled is frequently slower than without blending, so performance will decrease drastically if you don't control blending use.

Multitexture

Multitexture-capable hardware has been very popular since the age of the 3dfx Voodoo2 card. Multitexture basically enables us to assign N texture coordinates to the same triangle, so we can render more than one texture in a single step. Additionally, we can specify different texture arithmetic functions, so we can control the way the different texture maps are combined.

Multitexturing is at the core of most advanced rendering algorithms, from light mapping to bump mapping. It is accessible from both OpenGL (it used to be an extension, but now is part of the standard) and as part of the core functionality in Direct3D. Let's first review how we can specify multitexture under both APIs. Under OpenGL, multitexture is declared as follows:

```
// layer 0
glActiveTexture (GL_TEXTURE0);
glEnable(GL_TEXTURE_2D);
glBindTexture(GL_TEXTURE_2D,id0);
// here we would set texture combination parameters for layer 0

// layer 1: modulate incoming color+texture
glActiveTexture(GL_TEXTURE1);
glEnable(GL_TEXTURE_2D);
glBindTexture(GL_TEXTURE_2D,id1);
// here we would set texture combination parameters for layer 1


// render geometry
glBegin(GL_TRIANGLES);
glMultiTexCoord2fARB(GL_TEXTURE0_ARB,u0,v0);
glMultiTexCoord2fARB(GL_TEXTURE1_ARB,u1,v1);
glVertex3f(px,py,pz);
(...)
glEnd();
```

We need to initialize each texture unit separately, enabling texture mapping and setting the texture map we want to use with each one. Notice how we reserve some space for the texture combination code. How will both maps be blended together? Obviously, it makes no sense to render both maps with no blending options at all. But because this is the subject of the next section, I prefer to keep the code simple and easy to follow.

Also, notice the changes at the geometry rendering stage. We need to set texturing coordinates for each texture unit separately, so different units can be mapping with different coordinates. Let's now examine how we can specify blending options for texture maps.

Texture Arithmetic and Combination

Some years ago, textures were used to represent materials only: bricks, stones, and wood, which is what textures were designed for. At most, some brave developers encoded lighting information into them, and by multiplying a base and light texture, created fairly convincing indoors scenes. Years went by, and some interesting new effects (namely, environment and bump mapping) were described in terms of mathematical functions on textures. These textures no longer encoded material colors only, but also other properties, such as surface normals, lighting information, and so on.

Loading textures with non-RGB information was never a problem. After all, the different APIs do not perform any kind of checking on the texture's contents. The real issue was combining them using operations other than additions and not much more. A broader range of operations, which included simple algebraic operators as well as other functionality like dot products, and so on were needed.

The first attempt was the GL_COMBINE_EXT extension, which appeared in OpenGL. This extension allowed us to specify blending operations for multitexturing, so multitexturing had an expressive potential similar to regular blending operations. We could interpolate both textures with regard to the per-vertex alpha; we could add, multiply, and so on. For example, the following code (which is rather old and thus still uses the Architecture Review Board conventions in places) combines both textures using the second texture's alpha value as the interpolator:

```
// layer 0
glActiveTexture (GL_TEXTURE0);
glEnable(GL_TEXTURE_2D);
glBindTexture(GL_TEXTURE_2D,id0);
glTexEnvi(GL_TEXTURE_ENV, GL_TEXTURE_ENV_MODE, GL_REPLACE);

// layer 1: modulate incoming color+texture
glActiveTextureARB(GL_TEXTURE1_ARB);
glEnable(GL_TEXTURE_2D);
glBindTexture(GL_TEXTURE_2D,id1);
glTexEnvi(GL_TEXTURE_ENV, GL_TEXTURE_ENV_MODE, GL_COMBINE_EXT);
glTexEnvi(GL_TEXTURE_ENV, GL_COMBINE_RGB_EXT, GL_INTERPOLATE_EXT);
glTexEnvi(GL_TEXTURE_ENV, GL_SOURCE0_RGB_EXT, GL_PREVIOUS_EXT);
glTexEnvi(GL_TEXTURE_ENV, GL_OPERAND0_RGB_EXT, GL_SRC_COLOR);
glTexEnvi(GL_TEXTURE_ENV, GL_SOURCE1_RGB_EXT, GL_TEXTURE);
glTexEnvi(GL_TEXTURE_ENV, GL_OPERAND1_RGB_EXT, GL_SRC_COLOR);
glTexEnvi(GL_TEXTURE_ENV, GL_SOURCE2_RGB_EXT,
GL_PRIMARY_COLOR_EXT);
glTexEnvi(GL_TEXTURE_ENV, GL_OPERAND2_RGB_EXT, GL_SRC_ALPHA);
```

The syntax is rather cryptic. To understand it, you must analyze each line carefully. At the beginning, we are enabling the COMBINE_EXT extension. Then, we are requesting it to do an interpolation. SOURCE0 is then set to the previous value (thus, the color from the other texture unit) and SOURCE1 to the texture's own color. SOURCE2 is used to specify the interpolation factor, which is the alpha value of the texture.

This syntax was very non-intuitive. Thus, a new mechanism, called the *register combiners*, was devised by NVIDIA. The register combiners basically are a set of registers that can take the output of each texturing stage and perform arithmetic operations between them. The main advantage over the combine extension is generality and a slight improvement in ease of use.

Using register combiners usually starts by enabling/disabling them with the calls:

```
glEnable(GL_REGISTER_COMBINERS_NV);
glDisable(GL_REGISTER_COMBINERS_NV);
```

We must then understand how many combiners we have and how they are laid out. The best way to deal with this is to have one of NVIDIA's charts at hand, so you get a global picture of who is connected to whom and how you can arrange data. In the end, the combiner operation is controlled by two calls. The first call controls the inputs to the registers, whereas the second call deals with outputs. Here is the first call:

```
glCombinerInputNV(GLenum stage,
    GLenum portion,
    GLenum variable,
    GLenum input,
    GLenum mapping,
    GLenum componentUsage);
```

Parameters are usually specified as symbolic constants. By specifying different combinations, you can perform different arithmetic operations on texture inputs. You can see each parameter's possibilities in Table 18.2.

Table 18.2 Possible Values for `glCombinerInputNV`

Parameter	Values
`portion` =	`{ GL_RGB, GL_ALPHA }`
`variable` =	`{ GL_VARIABLE_A_NV, GL_VARIABLE_B_NV,` `GL_VARIABLE_C_NV, GL_VARIABLE_D_NV }`

`input` =	`{ GL_ZERO, GL_PRIMARY_COLOR_NV,`
	`GL_SECONDARY_COLOR_NV,`
	`GL_CONSTANT_COLOR0_NV,`
	`GL_CONSTANT_COLOR1_NV, GL_TEXTURE0_ARB,`
	`GL_TEXTURE1_ARB, GL_FOG, GL_SPARE0_NV,`
	`GL_SPARE1_NV }`

`mapping` =	`{ GL_UNSIGNED_IDENTITY_NV,`
	`GL_UNSIGNED_INVERT_NV, GL_EXPAND_NORMAL_NV,`
	`GL_EXPAND_NEGATE_NV, GL_HALF_BIAS_NORMAL_NV,`
	`GL_HALF_BIAS_NEGATE_NV,`
	`GL_SIGNED_IDENTITY_NV, GL_SIGNED_NEGATE_NV }`

`componentUsage` =	`{ GL_RGB, GL_BLUE, GL_ALPHA }`

The second call controls the outputs of the registers. Here is the syntax:

```
glCombinerOutputNV(GLenum stage,
    GLenum portion,
    GLenum abOutput,
    GLenum cdOutput,
    GLenum sumOutput,
    GLenum scale,
    GLenum bias,
    GLboolean abDotProduct,
    GLboolean cdDotProduct,
    GLboolean muxSum);
```

Outputs have a different set of parameters and possible values. They are listed in Table 18.3.

Table 18.3 Possible Values for `glCombinerOutputNV`

Parameter	Value
`portion =`	`{ GL_RGB, GL_ALPHA }`

`abOutput, cdOutput,`
`sumOutput =`
	`{ GL_DISCARD_NV, GL_PRIMARY_COLOR_NV,`
	`GL_SECONDARY_COLOR_NV, GL_TEXTURE0_ARB,`
	`GL_TEXTURE1_ARB, GL_SPARE0_NV, GL_SPARE1_NV }`

`scale =`	`{ GL_NONE, GL_SCALE_BY_TWO_NV,` `GL_SCALE_BY_FOUR_NV, GL_SCALE_BY_ONE_HALF_NV }`
`bias =`	`{ GL_NONE, GL_BIAS_BY_NEGATIVE_ONE_HALF_NV }`

In a way, we can consider register combiners as a precursor of shading languages (specifically, of fragment shaders). Today, most developers are implementing this kind of operation, such as per-pixel lighting, Bidirectional Reflectance Distribution Function (BRDFs), or bump mapping in fragment shaders, which are far more general and standard ways of achieving these results. As such, register combiners will very likely fade out as time passes. Take a look at Chapter 21, "Procedural Techniques," and you will see the difference.

Currently, a simplified combiner version has found its way into DirectX. We can specify how each texture stage is to interact with the others, in a way reminiscent of the register combiner syntax. It all revolves around the call:

```
ID3Ddevice::SetTexture( stage, textureid);
```

and the call:

```
ID3Ddevice:: SetTextureStageState( stage, property, value)
```

The first call sets the texture stage and map to be used there. Then, a series of `SetTextureStageState` calls set the combiner parameters. Again, the DirectX documentation is almost mandatory to take advantage of this functionality. The best way to understand what you are doing is to draw a graph with the texture stages as boxes with lines connecting them, as if the whole system was an electrical circuit. In fact, this is not so different from the real world, because these operations are actually implemented by connecting components and registers to perform the selected arithmetic operations. Take a look at the following code example, and the graph in Figure 18.6, which depicts the relationships between the different stages:

```
// Phase 0: bump mapping using dot3 (explained later)
D3DXVECTOR3 m_vLight;
point p(0.5,1,0.5);
p.normalize();
m_vLight[0]=p.x;
m_vLight[1]=p.y;
m_vLight[2]=p.z;
DWORD dwFactor = VectortoRGBA( &m_vLight, 10.0f );
// we store the factor so we can use it to combine
d3d_device->SetRenderState( D3DRS_TEXTUREFACTOR, dwFactor );
// set texture2 on stage 0
texture2->activate(0);
// operation: dot product
d3d_device->SetTextureStageState(0,D3DTSS_COLOROP,
D3DTOP_DOTPRODUCT3);
// 1st operator the texture (a normal map)
d3d_device->SetTextureStageState(0,D3DTSS_COLORARG1,
D3DTA_TEXTURE);
// 2nd operator: the factor that encodes the light position
d3d_device->SetTextureStageState(0,D3DTSS_COLORARG2,
D3DTA_TFACTOR);
// store results in a temporary register
d3d_device->SetTextureStageState(0,D3DTSS_RESULTARG, D3DTA_TEMP);


// phase 1: enter first texture pass... the previous one was saved
texture1->activate (1);
// pass the 1st parameter, do not perform computations
d3d_device->SetTextureStageState(1,D3DTSS_COLOROP,
D3DTOP_SELECTARG1 );
// 1st parameter: the texture, a grass map
d3d_device->SetTextureStageState(1,D3DTSS_COLORARG1, D3DTA_TEXTURE );
// phase 2: blend with second texture using alpha map stored in
per-vertex alpha
texture2->activate (2);
// this blends the two operators using the per-vertex alpha
d3d_device->SetTextureStageState(2,D3DTSS_COLOROP,
D3DTOP_BLENDDIFFUSEALPHA );
```

```
// 1st argument: current, which means the previous stage
d3d_device->SetTextureStageState(2,D3DTSS_COLORARG1, D3DTA_CURRENT );
// 2nd argument: the new texture, a rocky map
d3d_device->SetTextureStageState(2,D3DTSS_COLORARG2, D3DTA_TEXTURE );
// 2nd pass: modulate using bump map info
d3d_device->SetTextureStageState(3,D3DTSS_COLOROP, D3DTOP_MODULATE );
// get previous stage
d3d_device->SetTextureStageState(3,D3DTSS_COLORARG1,
D3DTA_CURRENT);
// modulate with the temporary register
d3d_device->SetTextureStageState(3,D3DTSS_COLORARG2, D3DTA_TEMP );
// final pass: modulate with per-vertex diffuse light info
d3d_device->SetTextureStageState(4,D3DTSS_COLOROP, D3DTOP_MODULATE );
// 1st parameter: previous stage (combined textures + bump)
d3d_device->SetTextureStageState(4,D3DTSS_COLORARG1, D3DTA_CURRENT );
// 2nd parameter: per-vertex diffuse
d3d_device->SetTextureStageState(4,D3DTSS_COLORARG2, D3DTA_DIFFUSE );
// here we go!
d3d_device->DrawIndexedPrimitiveUP(D3DPT_TRIANGLESTRIP,
```

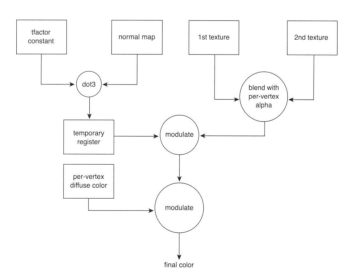

Figure 18.6 Graph of the preceding code: the relationships between the different texture stages.

Notice how we can specify, for each stage, which operation to perform, which inputs to choose from, and where to store the result. Typical operations are adding, modulating, or computing dot3 bump maps. Operators can be textures, results from previous stages, or temporary registers we can use to store intermediate values. A stage writes its result automatically so it can be accessed by the next one using the D3DTA_CURRENT argument. But sometimes we will need to store values for stages other than the immediate next one. A good example is the bump mapping portion in the preceding code: It is generated at phase 0, but it is used at stage 3 only. Thus, we can redirect the output of any stage to a temporary register, so we can retrieve it whenever it is actually needed.

OpenGL has followed a similar path, and today the API has incorporated most of the relevant extension tokens into the glTexEnv core call. Here is a complete example, which starts by setting the env mode to combine, so we can use the texture combiners:

```
glTexEnvf(GL_TEXTURE_ENV,GL_TEXTURE_ENV_MODE,GL_COMBINE);
```

And these lines set the parameters for the combiner. Notice that no extensions are used:

```
glTexEnvf(GL_TEXTURE_ENV,GL_COMBINE_ALPHA,GL_SUBTRACT);
glTexEnvf(GL_TEXTURE_ENV,GL_SOURCE0_ALPHA,GL_TEXTURE);
glTexEnvf(GL_TEXTURE_ENV,GL_OPERAND0_ALPHA,GL_SRC_ALPHA);
glTexEnvf(GL_TEXTURE_ENV,GL_SOURCE1_ALPHA,GL_PREVIOUS);
glTexEnvf(GL_TEXTURE_ENV,GL_OPERAND1_ALPHA,GL_SRC_ALPHA);
```

Now, depending on what we are specifying, we can access different parameters. If the value we are setting is a color value (both RGB or RGBA), Table 18.4 provides the possible values for the third parameter along with the equations that govern its behavior.

Table 18.4   Possible Values and Equations for a Third Parameter

Values	Equations
GL_REPLACE	(a_0)
GL_MODULATE	$(a_0 * a_1)$
GL_ADD	$(a_0 + a_1)$
GL_ADD_SIGNED	$(a_0 + a_1 - 0.5)$
GL_INTERPOLATE	$(a_0 * a_2 + a_1 * (1-a_2))$

GL_SUBTRACT	(a0-a1)
GL_DOT3_RGB	$4*((a0_r-0.5)*(a1_r-0.5) + (a0_g-0.5)*(a1_g-0.5) + (a0_b-0.5)*(a1_b-0.5))$
GL_DOT3_RGBA	$4*((a0_r-0.5)*(a1_r-0.5) + (a0_g-0.5)*(a1_g-0.5) + (a0_b-0.5)*(a1_b-0.5))$

Table 18.5 lists the values for the alpha combiners.

Table 18.5   Possible Values and Equations for the Alpha Combiners

Values	Equations
GL_REPLACE	(a0)
GL_MODULATE	(a0 * a1)
GL_ADD	(a0 + a1)
GL_ADD_SIGNED	(a0 + a1 − 0.5)
GL_INTERPOLATE	(a0*a2 + a1*(1-a2))
GL_SUBTRACT	(a0-a1)

All of the values and equations shown in Tables 18.4 and 18.5 make for a simpler, standard interface to perform texture combinations and arithmetic.

Detail Textures

Some games will require more detailed textures than you are willing to pay for. A flight simulator, for example, might call for very high-resolution texture maps, sampling large terrain data sets with accuracy. If we choose to implement these maps directly, they will definitely result in a prohibitive memory footprint. Thus, some clever techniques must be used to ensure we can combine large textures and resolution with reasonable memory requirements. Detail textures, as you will see, provide a good solution to this problem.

A detail texture is a texture map that encodes the high-frequency information, and thus the detail, in a larger scale texture. Detail textures are very popular in terrain rendering and in many cases where you need to simulate high detail with low-resolution texture maps. The idea is to split the texture information into two channels. A low-frequency layer provides the basic coloring patterns, whereas a high-detail, tiling detail texture provides the grain and finesse players expect. By painting both textures using multitextures, they are blended together to create the desired effect.

Then, as the object moves away from the viewer, we can alpha blend the detail texture, so distant objects show only the base texture. We can even choose between different blending modes. Although a combine or multiply equation is the most popular, additive blends can be used as well for specific effects.

Environment Mapping

Environment mapping is a relatively simple technique that tries to simulate the look of reflective surfaces such as water or metals. Instead of computing the true reflection, which is a costly process, it uses a texture map and some texture coordinate trickery to create a quite convincing reflective effect. Notice, however, that environment mapping does not simulate true reflections. It is just a clever mathematical trick that fools the eye almost completely.

An environment map is just a regular texture map that we use to encode the reflections for a specific object. For example, if we want to display a teapot in the middle of a large room, the environment map encodes the room information, and then we use some techniques to assign mapping coordinates over that texture map. The map is usually projected either in spherical coordinates or by using a cube. Spherical coordinates are easier to create, but the result suffers some distortion at the poles. Cube mapping, on the other hand, suffers no distortion, is supported by new hardware, and opens the door to computing true reflections. All we need to do is generate a dynamic cube map whose six faces encode the reflection information for an object.

As far as implementation goes, environment mapping needs texture coordinates to be computed per frame. If the teapot rotates, we will see different reflections on its surface. Recall from the previous chapter that reflections are largely view dependent, and thus environment mapping is always dynamic. Now, these mapping coordinates are not that hard to compute. For a spherical map, all we have to do is get the per-vertex normal, convert it from XYZ to polar coordinates, and use these coordinates to access the environment map. Luckily, both OpenGL and DirectX support automatic texturing coordinate generation, so all we have to do is ask our API of choice for automatic generation on spheres, planes, or cubes, and it will handle it internally, much faster than a software implementation. In OpenGL, automatic texture generation is controlled by the `glTexGen` call. For a sphere map, the call must be

```
glTexGen(GL_S, GL_TEXTURE_GEN_MODE, GL_SPHERE_MAP);
glTexGen(GL_T, GL_TEXTURE_GEN_MODE, GL_SPHERE_MAP);
glTexGen(GL_Q, GL_TEXTURE_GEN_MODE, GL_SPHERE_MAP);
```

Under DirectX, the same can be achieved by using

```
d3dDevice->SetTextureStageState( 0, D3DTSS_TEXCOORDINDEX,
                                 D3DTSS_TCI_CAMERASPACENORMAL );
```

which sets texture coordinates to be computed from the surface's normal, thus yielding spherical coordinates.

Using environment mapping in only one texture stage and combining it (using texture combiners) with other stages yields extremely realistic results. Metallic surfaces that combine reflectivity with rust, or bump-mapped, reflective water are both possible using these techniques together.

Bump Mapping

Bump mapping simulates high-detail surface irregularities, not by using additional geometry but by perturbing the normals. Because normals are the driving force behind most rendering equations, the shading is locally modified, giving the illusion of bumps, wrinkles, and so on to the viewer.

Bump mapping was introduced by Blinn in the late 1970s and is now an extremely popular technique in offline renderers. Slowly, more and more games are incorporating it as well, as hardware manufacturers keep inventing simpler, more powerful ways to specify bump mapping. In this section, we will review the three most popular methods along with some specific code to generate bump mapping in DirectX.

Emboss Bump Mapping

Embossing an image is a processing operation that enhances edges directionally, giving them a raised look. Emboss bump mapping tries to achieve the same results in real time by using several texturing passes. Specifically, the classic algorithm uses three passes. Here's the complete rundown:

1. Render the object with the bump map in grayscale.

2. Compute new (u,v) coordinates translated in the direction of the light.

3. Render the bump map again, subtracting from the first pass.

4. Render the final shaded texture.

We can reduce this to two steps by encoding the bump map in the alpha channel, so the algorithm is as follows:

1. Render the base texture with the bump map as the alpha channel.

2. Add the negative version of the bump map.

As you may have guessed, the blending between the RGB and the alpha channel must be a multiply, so we implement Lambert's equation for diffuse lighting. The following DirectX 9 example uses this approach:

```
m_pd3dDev->SetTexture( 0, m_pEmbossTexture );
m_pd3dDev->SetTextureStageState( 0, D3DTSS_TEXCOORDINDEX, 0 );
m_pd3dDev->SetTextureStageState(0,D3DTSS_COLOROP,D3DTOP_MODULATE );
m_pd3dDev->SetTextureStageState(0,D3DTSS_COLORARG1,D3DTA_TEXTURE);
m_pd3dDev->SetTextureStageState(0,D3DTSS_COLORARG2,D3DTA_DIFFUSE );
m_pd3dDev->SetTextureStageState(0,D3DTSS_ALPHAOP,
D3DTOP_SELECTARG1);
m_pd3dDev->SetTextureStageState( 0, D3DTSS_ALPHAARG1, D3DTA_TEXTURE );

m_pd3dDev->SetTexture( 1, m_pEmbossTexture );
m_pd3dDev->SetTextureStageState(1, D3DTSS_TEXCOORDINDEX, 1 );
m_pd3dDev->SetTextureStageState(1,D3DTSS_COLOROP,
D3DTOP_SELECTARG2);
```

```
m_pd3dDev->SetTextureStageState(1, D3DTSS_COLORARG1,
D3DTA_TEXTURE);
m_pd3dDev->SetTextureStageState(1, D3DTSS_COLORARG2,
D3DTA_CURRENT);
m_pd3dDev->SetTextureStageState(1,D3DTSS_ALPHAOP, D3DTOP_ADDSIGNED );
m_pd3dDev->SetTextureStageState(1,D3DTSS_ALPHAARG1, D3DTA_TEXTURE  |
D3DTA_COMPLEMENT );
m_pd3dDev->SetTextureStageState(1,D3DTSS_ALPHAARG2,D3DTA_CURRENT );

m_pd3dDev->SetRenderState( D3DRS_ALPHABLENDENABLE, TRUE );
m_pd3dDev->SetRenderState( D3DRS_SRCBLEND,  D3DBLEND_SRCALPHA );
m_pd3dDev->SetRenderState( D3DRS_DESTBLEND, D3DBLEND_ZERO );
m_pObject->Render( m_pd3dDevice );
```

Notice how we set the texture stage 1 to do an add while we are complementing the map.

The complex part of any emboss bump mapping algorithm is how to compute the light direction, and thus shift the u,v texture values to simulate bumps. We must begin by placing a coordinate system at the vertex and expressing the light direction in terms of those coordinates. The first vector we will use is the normal at the vertex. The second vector is a vector along either the u or v texture coordinate axes, tangent to the surface. The third vector, dubbed the binormal, is just the cross product between the normal and tangent vector. These three vectors conform a basis matrix, which can be used to convert the light direction to local coordinates. This new vector is said to be in the object's tangent space. By scaling it (depending on the amount of bumps we want to simulate), we can add its *X* and *Y* components to the u,v pairs, and thus generate a nice looking bump map effect.

Dot3 Bump Mapping

The Dot3 bump mapping method starts not with a heightfield as embossed bump mapping did, but with a normal map: a regular bitmap that encodes normals instead of RGB triplets. Then, to render the bump maps, we transform the light position to the tangent space, as we did with embossing. We then have one light vector for each vertex in the mesh. To render a triangle, the light vectors for each one of the three vertices are interpolated. Notice how this is not a color interpolation but a light vector interpolation.

Then, the bump map is combined with the interpolated light value for a given pixel. These are combined with a dot product as in the classic Lambert equation. This dot product is implemented as a special texture blending function.

Here is the sample code to perform Dot3 bump mapping on Direct3D 9:

```
// we compute a light vector
D3DXVECTOR3 m_vLight;
point p(0.5,1,0.5);
p.normalize();
m_vLight[0]=p.x;
m_vLight[1]=p.y;
m_vLight[2]=p.z;
// encode the vector into a double word
DWORD dwFactor = VectortoRGBA( &m_vLight, 10.0f );
// set the computed factor so the texture unit uses it
d3d_device->SetRenderState( D3DRS_TEXTUREFACTOR, dwFactor );
// set the texture (here goes the normal map)
texture->activate(0);
// operation: dot3
d3d_device->SetTextureStageState(0,D3DTSS_COLOROP,
D3DTOP_DOTPRODUCT3);
// first argument: the normal map
d3d_device->SetTextureStageState(0,D3DTSS_COLORARG1,
D3DTA_TEXTURE);
// second argument: the factor
d3d_device->SetTextureStageState(0,D3DTSS_COLORARG2,
D3DTA_TFACTOR);
```

Dot3 bump mapping has an advantage over embossing in that results look remarkably better. Additionally, Dot3 can handle specular highlights on the bump maps, whereas emboss only supports the diffuse component of lighting. Additionally, the code is remarkably simple.

Gloss Mapping

Gloss mapping is a variant of environment mapping that allows greater realism in your reflections. A new texture, the gloss map, encodes information about the reflectivity of the object's surface, so it is not constant along its surface. Some areas will be shiny, and others will be dull. A popular way to achieve this reflective result is to encode the gloss mapping information as the alpha channel of the base material.

Then, to render the glossiness, we start by rendering the base texture map with no alpha and modulating it with diffuse lighting information. We then multiply the gloss information by the specular or environment texture map. This results in a reflective component that varies along the surface. Then, we add this to the base texture as the specular component. Because more information was used to compute the result than in traditional environment mapping or specular highlighting, more realistic reflections and highlights are computed. Figure 18.7 shows a sphere with and without gloss mapping information.

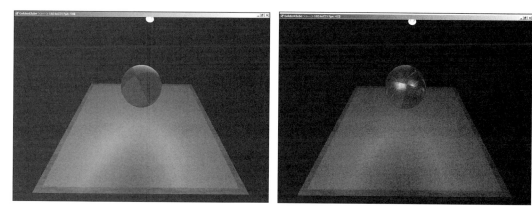

Figure 18.7   Gloss mapping.

In Closing

Lighting, as discussed in the previous chapter, is largely implementation independent. Most techniques have to do more with the physical laws of the world than with OpenGL or DirectX. Texturing, on the other hand, is a bag full of API-dependent tricks. Environment mapping, bump mapping, and more generally, texture combiners are very close to the metal, and thus research on API-specific methods is needed.

I suggest you complete this reading with a lengthy visit to a web site or package of your choice. The DirectX SDK is full of advanced texturing samples that cover all topics explained in this chapter as well as many new subjects. As for OpenGL programmers, both NVIDIA and ATI have well laid out developer sites, where interesting demos can be downloaded and new tricks learned.

Chapter 19

Particle Systems

"Electricity is actually made up of extremely tiny particles called electrons, that you cannot see with the naked eye unless you have been drinking."

Dave Barry, *The Taming of the Screw*

In previous chapters, we discussed how to represent many different environments in a computer game. From a dungeon to a vast plain along with its populating characters, we have explored how to decompose graphics into triangle arrays, so they can be efficiently rendered by the graphics subsystem. The more triangles we use, the richer and more engaging the representation. As a clear sign of devotion to triangles, remember the famous quote by one of the founding members of Pixar way back in the 1980s, "Reality is 80M triangles per second."

However, some effects are hard to imagine in terms of triangles. How many triangles does a bonfire have? And how about the mist that clings to a mountain top? And a tree? These are items we need to represent, but are nontrivial to express in terms of triangles. We tend to think in terms of simple solid structures inherited from platonic solids (cubes, spheres, and so on). But everyday life continually challenges this simplicity, making us think of creative ways of depicting its richness.

This chapter (along with subsequent chapters) tries to explore techniques designed to render "advanced" effects such as the ones just mentioned as well as many others. In this chapter, we will explore particle systems, which are a mathematical formalism that can be used to represent dynamic, complex behaviors such as smoke and waves. The next chapter will specifically deal with organic rendering techniques, covering most natural phenomena, either static or dynamic in essence. The following chapter will deal with the procedural paradigm, which is a powerful tool used to represent complex geometry in an efficient way.

Anatomy of a Particle System

A particle system is essentially a mathematical formalism used to describe phenomena that are

➤ Dynamic and time dependent

➤ Highly parallel with small individual components

➤ Complex

Examples of such behavior include smoke from a chimney, fire, birds flying in a flock, snowflakes, and hundreds of other phenomena. Particle systems are context insensitive, meaning they can be used to model very different situations. The particle system is a tool, but does not imply a specific use-case in itself. By changing some of its inner components, it can be suited to any problem, as long as it follows the global philosophy outlined earlier.

Particle systems were introduced in the early 1980s by Pixar (then part of the Lucasfilm special effects group) for the movie *Star Trek II: The Wrath of Kahn*. Specifically, particle systems were used to represent a chain-reaction explosion on the surface of a planet, so the planet changed from a dead, barren look to a full living ecosystem.

A particle system fundamentally consists of an array of particles, each one changing dynamically according to some established routines. You can model individual rain-drops reacting to gravity and wind, birds executing a simple AI routine, and so on. All particles have the same parameters controlling their look and behavior. But as they evolve in their ecosystem, each follows a slightly different evolution, and the desired complexity emerges naturally.

Local Versus Global Particle Systems

Particle systems can broadly be divided into two large groups, which I will refer to as local and global. A local system consists of a group of particles that behave as if each one was alone. Thus, interactions between particles are not taken into consideration, and all calculations are local to the current particle. On the other end of the spectrum, a global particle system involves particles that interact and react to each other. In these particle systems, the behavior of each individual particle depends in part on its own characteristics, but also on the interactions with the rest of the group.

Many times a local system is nothing but a simplification of a global system. For example, consider a group of fallen leaves from a tree, blown by the wind. If you want to model them accurately, you need to consider changes in the trajectory if two or more leaves collide, making the behavior of the single leaf dependent on the rest. Clearly, this would yield a global particle system. But many games prefer to ignore leaf collision and, by simplifying the simulation, implement it as a local particle system.

As you will soon discover, both groups have different advantages and problems, and require specific programming techniques. Obviously, global particle systems produce much more complex and interesting behavior. But richness does not come for free. Calculating the influence of the other particles will usually increase our computational costs significantly. So, global particle systems must be handled with care.

The Particle Data Structure

Defining the particle data structure means answering the "what" question: What are we modeling? Is it going to be fire, smoke, or water? Clearly, different phenomena will require different particle parameters.

When choosing the particle data structure, it is essential to create a parameter set that is both sufficient but not bloated. Given the parallel nature of particle systems, having superfluous parameters will increase the memory footprint, whereas having too few control parameters will degrade the system's visual quality.

Particle systems have traditionally dealt with fast moving items with no interaction between them. Be it explosion sparks, rain, or water, the underlying structures are almost identical. Here is the original particle structure taken from the seminal Reeves SIGGRAPH Paper (see references in Appendix E, "Further Reading"):

➤ Position

➤ Velocity (vectorial)

➤ Size

➤ Color

➤ Transparency

➤ Shape

➤ Lifetime

This structure was used to create some rather advanced effects in *Star Trek II: The Wrath of Kahn*. We can broadly divide the parameters into two different groups:

➤ Parameters associated with the behavior of the particle

➤ Parameters associated with the look of the particle

Behavior parameters should be sufficient to implement a compelling particle simulator. Thus, it is essential to analyze the kind of behavior we are trying to simulate, to understand which parameters are needed. The best place to gather this information is from physics handbooks, especially those dealing with dynamics for particles or rigid bodies. Study the forces you will apply to the particles. Do you need friction? Speed? Acceleration? Try to understand the role of global-scope constants. For example, it makes no sense to have each particle store the gravity constant. That value will be the same in all of them. On the other hand, the weight of each particle might be useful in some circumstances.

Once you have determined which behavior parameters your simulator needs, you will need to specify those parameters dealing with the look of the particle. Here the possibilities are almost endless. You will definitely need a particle color, blending mode, size, and texture identifier, but most particle systems need many more parameters. For solid particles, you might need to specify which mesh you will use to paint particle animation counters, halos, and dozens of other features. Here the best advice is to decouple the particle rendering from the simulation loop, so you can test painting a single particle in a separate program. This way you can refine the visual result and decide which parameters your particle renderer needs to convey the right look.

A Generic Particle System

Now that we have a global understanding of what a particle system is, let's take a closer look at how we can implement it. Consider the following class definition for a basic particle system:

```
class particlesystem
    {
    particle *data;
    int numparticles;
    public:
        void create(int);    // creates a system of n particles
        void recalc();
        void render();
    private:
        void spawn(int);    // spawns particle n
        void affect(int)    // affect particle n by outside forces
    };
```

Notice how we need a `spawn` and `affect` routine on a particle basis. These two routines implement the core of the system: how particles are born and what simulation process they undergo. These two routines can actually be part of a particle class, if needed, to further clarify the code.

Spawning Particles

Particles are created at some kind of emitter, which initializes their parameters. If we want our system to behave in any interesting way, the key is to generate each particle with slightly different initial values, so the behavior rules (which are shared by all particles) make each one look like a unique element.

A variety of emitters have frequently been used. The most well known is the point emitter, which generates all particles at a point in space, as in an explosion. But explosions are not born in a single point in space. In fact, only the Big Bang happened this way, and we're not even sure about that. Explosions in the real world have volume and shape, as particles of fire emerge from the exploding object. Thus, sometimes we will perturb the point, so particles are born in an area surrounding it, but not quite at the point. This is a very common approach in particle system creation: adding an amount of randomness so results do not look too regular and algorithmic. For example, for our point emitter, we would use something like this:

```
point pos(3,5,4); // particles are born in 3,5,4
pos.x += ((float)rand()%2000-1000)/1000;
pos.y += ((float)rand()%2000-1000)/1000;
pos.z += ((float)rand()%2000-1000)/1000;
```

The last three lines implement a distortion of one in any direction, positive or negative. So in fact the volume particles emerge from a one-sided cube centered at 3,5,4. This philosophy is so deeply rooted within this discipline that it even has a name: *jittering*, which describes the addition of controlled amounts of noise to reduce the algorithmic look of the simulation.

There are also other shapes of emitters. To simulate snow or rain, for example, you will probably use a 2D polygon aligned in the XZ plane. Here is the source code to compute such a polygon:

```
point pos(3,5,4); // particles are born in 3,5,4
pos.x += ((float)rand()%2000-1000)/1000;
pos.z += ((float)rand()%2000-1000)/1000;
```

In this case I have created a square, which is very common. Other 2D shapes could be implemented as well.

A third type of emitter is referenced with regard to the player's position. Imagine that you need to simulate rain. Quite likely, you will not fill the whole game level with hundreds of thousands of individual raindrops. It simply makes no sense because distant raindrops will not be visible. In this scenario, it would be great to generate rain right where the user can notice it most, which is directly in front of him. Thus, we generate rain in our regular coordinates, and then translate and rotate to the particle system's final position and rotation. Here is an example of how to generate these particles. I assume `fov` is the horizontal aperture of the camera, and `distnear` and `distfar` are the range of distances we want to fill with particles:

```
float dist=distnear+(distfar-distnear)*((float)rand()%1000)/1000;
float angle=fov*(((float)rand()%2000)-1000)/1000;
point p(dist*cos(angle),0,dist*sin(angle));
p.rotatey(camera_yaw);
p.translate(camera_position);
```

This code generates particles right in front of the camera, so they fill the screen but don't go anywhere else. Only the particles we really need are taken into consideration.

Another type of emitter is the screen-based emitter, which is used for particle effects that are computed in screen space, such as the trail of water left by a raindrop on the camera's surface. These particles are born anywhere, but are always referenced to the camera's viewport. So, generating them is a bit different. A 2D particle system is rendered with the 3D pipeline switched off, much like a sprite engine from the old days. The generation of the particles is not very complex; it is just particles on a 2D rectangle. Here is the code:

```
pos.x += SCREENX*((float)rand()%2000-1000)/1000;
pos.y += SCREENY*((float)rand()%2000-1000)/1000;
```

This code assumes that `SCREENX`, `SCREENY` hold the resolution in pixels on the screen. Obviously, most of the complexity of these systems is not in the spawning of particles, but in the actual rendering. You can see different types of emitters in Figure 19.1.

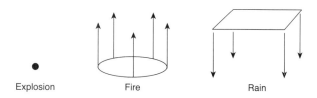

Explosion   Fire   Rain

Figure 19.1 Emitters for different effects.

Once we have the emitter, it is time to move on to the next parameters. Initial velocity should be determined. Some popular choices here are a directional velocity (all particles move in the same direction), a radial velocity (particles move away from center), rotational (as in a tornado), or random. Each of these should be implemented with a certain degree of jitter, so different particles have slightly different parameters and hence evolution.

Other parameters can be tuned as well: Color, alpha (very important if particles are to fade away as they die), texturing coordinates, and so on must all be set. Additionally, we need to establish the particle's age and life cycle parameters. These can be implemented in two ways: You can set the particle's age to zero and have a second parameter that is the time to live of the particle. At each simulation tick, you increase the age until the time to live (which is nothing but a counter) is reached, and the particle is killed and respawned elsewhere. Because simulation ticks are usually fixed in length, we get device-independent speed.

An alternative is to establish not the age, but the instant at which the particle was spawned. You would get that from the system with a call to timeGetTime(), store it, and then use it for age computations. Basically, at each loop you would recompute the current time with timeGetTime(), subtract the time of birth from this second value (thus computing the age in milliseconds of the particle), and compare it with the time to live, which is also a time period not only a loop counter as in the previous case. As usual, different programmers prefer one approach or the other for personal reasons.

Particle Behavior

If particle structures try to define what we are going to simulate, the behavior engine should attempt to mimic how that specific phenomena evolves over time. Will it be a physically based simulation, or will it be stochastic? The most common choice is to implement some kind of dynamics to the particles so they mimic real-world phenomena.

Let's take a look at some examples of increasing complexity. To begin with, imagine that we are to render a rain particle system, trying to get a convincing heavy rain effect. Raindrops move at a very high speed as they fall to the ground, so we can make the assumption that they are unaffected by wind or other external forces. Making a fast object change its direction is hard, because the force we need to supply to it increases with speed. Thus, our raindrops are spawned with an algorithm similar to those explained in the previous section, and we only need to recompute their position.

Now, from very basic physics you know that

```
Position = initial position + velocity*time
```

Taking this as a differential equation for a brief period of time, we can rewrite it to form

```
dPosition = Velocity*dt
```

where dPosition is the change in position, Velocity is the instantaneous velocity at a given point in time, and dt is the differential of time we want to evaluate position differences in. Here we are assuming that Velocity is valid all through dt seconds, which is generally false. We are taking one sample and generalizing it to a whole time interval. This makes these kinds of simulators, called *Euler Integrators*, very unstable in more complex systems. But for particle systems, these are the way to go because of their simplicity and elegance. So how do we convert this into running code? We substitute dt for the differential between successive simulation ticks and use the current velocity as the speed parameter. Now, we can incorporate basic Newtonian physics into the equation. Let's review how this might work, starting with the equation

```
F=m*a
```

which turns into

```
a=F/m
```

But still acceleration is the second derivative of position, as in

```
a=d²x/dt²
```

So now we have the basic relationships between cinematics (acceleration) and dynamics (forces). The basic laws of cinematics can then be rewritten as

```
v=dx/dt
a=dv/dt
```

And thus all we have to do is represent forces and compute accelerations based on them. Take, for example, gravity, as governed by the expression

```
f=m*g
```

where g=(0,-9.8,0). Other, more interesting forces can be represented as well. Here are the expressions for viscous drag, which is caused by a projectile trying to cross a medium that offers some resistance. Viscous drag is proportional to speed, so faster objects have a bigger force opposing them. In this equation, kd is a medium-dependent constant called the drag coefficient:

```
F  =  -kd  *  (dx/dt)  =  -kd  *  v
```

A third, interesting law governs the behavior of particles connected by elastic springs. Each spring has an ideal length, so if we compress it by moving the two particles closer to this rest length, the force will try to separate them. If we try to separate them beyond the rest length, the force will oppose that as well. This law is called *Hooks Spring Law* and is very interesting because it is the starting point of many interesting physics simulation techniques. Here is the complete equation:

$$ f = - \left[k_s \left(\| x_a - x_b \| - r \right) + k_d \left(v_a - v_b \right) \frac{x_a - x_b}{\| x_a - x_b \|} \right] \frac{x_a - x_b}{\| x_a - x_b \|} $$

It's an impressive piece of mathematics, but don't be put off by it. Our procedure will always be the same. Several types of forces are pictured in Figure 19.2. Here is the overall algorithm to compute physics-based particle systems:

1. Compute the sum of forces interacting with the particle at a given point in time.

2. Derive accelerations from forces.

3. Use time differentials to compute changes in position and velocity using Euler integration.

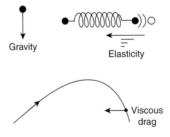

Figure 19.2 Some possible forces that could act on particles.

Here is, for example, the code required to implement a behavior engine that takes gravity and a constant lateral force (such as a wind vector) into consideration. This can be used to create a geyser kind of effect:

```
for (i=0;i<num_particles;i++)
   {
   elapsed_time=(timeGetTime()-time_last_call)/1000.0;    // in
seconds
   // first, compute forces
   point gravity_force=particle[i].weight*gravity;
   point wind_force=(...) // compute wind
   point total_force=gravity_force+wind_force;    // resulting
force on particle

   // second, derive accelerations
   point accel=total_force/particle[i].weight;

   // third, integrate
   particle[i].velocity+=accel*elapsed_time;

   particle[i].position+=particle[i].velocity*elapsed_time;
   }
```

So it is actually pretty easy to create particle-based physical simulations. However, many behaviors are defined aesthetically, not physically. Keep that in mind when you create your particle system. Take, for example, a smoke column. Smoke trajectories are really hard to simulate physically. The smoke's direction depends on temperature, wind, the chemicals contained in the smoke, and a host of factors we simply cannot take into consideration in a real-time game. So, smoke is usually simulated aesthetically, not physically. If you think about it, a smoke plume is basically a series of smoke particles (each rendered nicely with a smoke texture quad). These particles emit from a single point with a velocity in the positive vertical direction. As they rise, they are affected by complex forces, which makes the shape of the column somehow interesting but also hard to simulate. Here is a pretty popular smoke simulator:

```
for (i=0;i<num_particles;i++)
   {
   elapsed_time=(timeGetTime()-time_last_call)/1000.0;    // in
seconds
```

```
    // first, compute forces
    point wind_force=noise(particle[i].position);
    point raise_force(0,1,0);    // due to temperature smoke always
rises
    point total_force=wind_force;    // resulting force on particle

    // second, derive accelerations
    point accel=total_force/particle[i].weight;

    // third, integrate
    particle[i].velocity+=accel*elapsed_time;

    particle[i].position+=particle[i].velocity*elapsed_time;
    }
```

In this simulator, `noise()` is a call to the popular Perlin noise routine, which generates continuous noise in a 3D space. Noise allows us to create patterns of movement, which somehow look like smoke, swirling and rising from the ground. Obviously, this approach is purely aesthetics driven, but after all, games are an aesthetics-driven industry at the core.

Particle Extinction

Particles in a system are not meant to live very long. After their life cycle is depleted, they are deleted and respawned at the emitter. This usually means the particle has crossed the screen or performed a full cycle and can thus be reentered in a loop. Some particle systems, with explosions being the obvious example, will be nonlooping. Particles are created, live, die, and then the particle system as a whole is shut down. Even so, we will now focus on those systems where particles must be regenerated to understand the code required to do that.

Generally, a particle dies after its age surpasses its time to live. When this moment arrives, all we have to do is call the spawn routine again, passing this particle identifier as a parameter. By doing so, we get a new particle with fresh parameters where we had the old one. Thus, no memory deletion or reallocation is actually needed. All we do is recycle that position in the array for a new element.

From an aesthetics point of view, it is very important to fade particles out somehow as they approach their death. Failing to do so would make particle disappearance look annoying because bright particles would suddenly disappear. A number of techniques can be used to handle this situation properly. In a rain particle system, for example, raindrops are not killed by age, but are killed whenever they cross the ground plane. Thus, there is no possibility of particles "popping out" of the scene, because they will have crossed the ground floor in the frame right before their destruction.

Take a smoke column, for example. Here, we need to cleverly use alpha values to fade particles in and out. Particles will be opaque in their heyday and then will be born and die almost transparently. Notice that the same care we take with the death of the particles must be taken with their birth as well. We do not want particles to pop in suddenly out of nowhere. A nice trick to ensure that particles alpha blend properly when they enter and leave the stage is to modulate their alpha as a sin function, such as

```
alpha=sin(PI*age/maxage);
```

The argument to the sin call returns a floating-point value in the range from 0 to Pi. Then, the sin function evaluates to zero (thus, completely transparent) at these two values, and rises smoothly to 1 in between to represent the opacity at the particle's middle of life.

Rendering Particles

The believability of a particle system depends on rendering as much as it depends on the actual simulation of the behavior. We can change a mass of people to flowing water by just adjusting our particle rendering engine.

Given the tremendous amount of phenomena that can be modeled using particles, it shouldn't be surprising that many different rendering approaches exist. But there are some general tips to follow, which are covered in the following sections.

Compute Particles Cheaply

Rendering particles can become troublesome, especially when dealing with large numbers of elements. Don't forget we need to rotate and translate each individual particle so it faces the viewer and gives the proper illusion. Rotating has a cost, especially when you do it many times. We could choose to render particles one by one, rotating each one with a matrix stack consisting of rotations and translations. But because transforms can only be performed outside of rendering portions, we would need to render particles separately, and thus eliminate the option of sending them in batches, which is always more efficient. Thus, different methods will be used. A first approach is to align them to the camera yourself by designing a right and up vector, and then defining particles based on them. In a world with yaw only, a right vector (with regard to the camera and screen) can be defined as

```
point right(cos(yaw+pi/2),0, sin(yaw+pi/2));
```

And an up vector is simply

```
point up(0,1,0);
```

Then, a screen-aligned billboard of size S at position pos can be defined as

```
P1=pos-right*S-up*S;
P2=pos+right*S-up*S;
P3=pos+right*S+up*S;
P4=pos-right*S+up*S;
```

The preceding scheme is pictured in Figure 19.3.

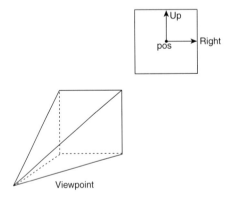

Figure 19.3 Computing the up and right vectors for a particle.

This method can be easily extended to a full camera with roll, pitch, and yaw. In this case, computing the vectors yourself is not a good idea, because you can get them from the modelview matrix, as shown in the following code:

```
glGetFloatv(GL_MODELVIEW_MATRIX, mat)
right.create(mat[0], mat[4], mat[8]);
up.create(mat[1], mat[5], mat[9]);
```

An even better alternative is to let the API align the billboards using hardware functionality. Most modern video cards can handle billboards internally, so all we pass through the bus are particle coordinates and not much else. The card also takes care of constructing the quads and rendering them to the screen. This provides much better results because we save bus resources and avoid transforms. This functionality is present in both OpenGL and DirectX under the form of Point Sprites. In OpenGL it is part of an extension, and in DirectX it is built into the core API.

Use Blending Modes Appropriately

Great expressive power is available if you learn how to unleash it. Many blending modes are available for you to experiment with and create unique looking systems. The two basic modes are the filtered and the additive blend. Filtered blend is defined by these alpha values:

```
SRC_ALPHA, ONE_MINUS_SRC_ALPHA
```

It provides the look of a semitransparent particle, like rain. The particle is not self-illuminating, so adding more and more layers will not make the scene look brighter. That can be achieved by additive blending, such as

```
SRC_ALPHA, ONE
```

So we do not filter the background, but add our components to it. This mode is used for anything involving light, fire, explosions, and so on. Be careful: Alpha values must be kept low, so as not to saturate the final image too soon and retain some color.

Animated Textures

Many particle systems need you to go one step beyond just animating particles using a high-quality simulator. Imagine a fireball, for example. Its dynamics are too fast and complex to render each particle as a static quad. Thus, we need to combine a good simulator with particle-level animation, so each particle has several frames of animation, usually stored in the same texture as tiles. Then, the particle will cycle through its animation frames during its life cycle, making the overall look much more dynamic.

If you choose to follow this path, just make sure particles are not in sync in their animation loops, or the effect will be completely destroyed. Different particles must be at different frames within the animation at any given point in time.

Chained/Hierarchical Systems

The dynamics of the real world often combine several stages to create a complex composite illusion. Take the blast created by a rocket firing, for example. Fire emerges from the exhausts, and then huge clouds of smoke and water vapor are generated. Additionally, small particles of ice separate from the main structure, following different trajectories. How can we characterize that? Is it a particle system? Quite clearly not, because there are several types of particles, each governed by different simulators with different rendering engines. But the system can be seen as a whole: a system of particle systems. Thus, we must design our particle systems so we can aggregate and chain them into groups. We need arrays of systems and message-passing policies that allow chaining to take place. For example, it is a good idea to add an "extinguish behavior" to the particles, which defines what actions are carried out whenever we need to respawn a particle. This behavior will be empty by default, but we could decide to create a particle of a different kind than this one extinguishes. Think of a fire element that, upon destruction, triggers a smoke system. This kind of overall architecture is necessary to create richer effects.

Visual Parameters as Functions of Time

All visual parameters are functions of time. Take a look at fire, for example. The core flame is usually blue, and as it moves away, it turns yellow, then white, and slowly vanishes. Realistic particle systems need time-varying parameters. Color and alpha are obvious, but there are others. The spin (speed of rotation), the frame in the animated texture, and so on create a much more convincing effect if time is entered into the equation. If each particle has a slightly different time-response curve, the effects will really improve.

Some Notes on Architecture

Some commonsense ways of coding particle systems have evolved through the years. Basically, two "patterns" exist, which are suitable in different scenarios. On one end of the spectrum, some teams code particle systems as a class hierarchy, so we have an abstract "particlesystem" class, from which specific particle system classes would be derived via inheritance. Particlesystem would declare virtual members such as recalc and render, which would be provided by each individual system or even by the particle class itself. Here is an example built using this technique:

```
class particlesystem
    {
    public:
    point position;
    particle *data;
    int numparticles;

    // methods executed from the base class particlesystem
        void create(int,point);    // creates a system of N particles
        void recalc();    // recalcs all particles

        // methods to be defined by the specific classes
        virtual void paint();    // paints the N particles.
        virtual void respawn(int);    // re-generates particle i
        virtual void affect(int);    // calculates the interaction
of particle i with the environment
    };

class rainfall: public particlesystem
    {
    public:
        // specific params
        point throwv;
        point pos;
        float initvel;
        int texid;
        double maxttl;
```

```
        double minttl;
        double maxvel;
        double minvel;
        double xrand;
        double yrand;
        double zrand;
        double movx;
        double movz;
        color ocol;
        color fcol;
        point wind;
        double density;

        rainfall()  :  particlesystem(){}
        // rewritten methods
        virtual void loadparams(char*,point);
        virtual void respawn(int);
        virtual void affect(int);
        virtual void paint();
    };
```

Using this approach allows us to arrange all systems in the game world in an array and access them linearly using a common interface. Each system can still be different, from the parameters to the physics simulator. But all those details are hidden from the programmer, who can access them using a homogeneous interface. Take a look at Figure 19.4 for a diagram of the data structure.

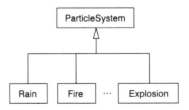

Figure 19.4 Hierarchical particle system, showing the abstract and the derived classes.

Another philosophy is to create a deep, complex particle system class, where individual systems are nothing but data-driven objects that parameterize the class in many ways. In this case, we would have parameters that would define almost anything, because all particle systems in our game would be implemented in the same class. We would need Boolean values to turn on or off specific forces, texture coordinates, and so on.

The advantage of this second method is simplicity. After all, many particle systems can be implemented from a central piece of code, possibly using some switch constructs along the way to select parameters like the type of emitter or velocity, and so on. Another advantage is that you can create a graphical editing tool that allows you to parameterize the particle system object, and thus easily test new particle system ideas from an artist/content developer perspective.

In the end, the difference lies not so much in raw speed, because both methods have advantages and disadvantages in this respect. It is more a problem of what you want. That is, do you want many systems that are very different from each other and share almost no code at all, or systems where we can recycle most of the source, and thus can be implemented in a single file that can be heavily parameterized?

Speed-Up Techniques

Any hardware is condemned to be performance limited, so our systems' goals must be reasonably limited.

But sometimes we can reach higher and faster by careful planning and analysis of the system we are to model. Many techniques can be used in order to speed up our calculations, and thus allow us to be able to create unique, complex particle systems. In this section, I will detail a variety of tips and tricks that can multiply the richness and quality of your results. Note, however, that there is no silver bullet in this advice. Only a deep knowledge of what you are modeling can help you determine which of these techniques might work best for you.

Avoid Malloc and Free

The first optimization for particle systems is based on the observation that allocating and freeing memory is a slow process. Thus, calls to memory management routines inside the system's loops should be avoided as much as possible. Although very efficient memory managers have a significant overhead for each allocation or deallocation of memory. They must scan the free blocks of memory, select the best-suited one (according to different policies), and so on. So, taking some time to plan your code is the best way to achieve top performance.

For example, freeing memory each time a particle dies (or allocating more memory for newborn particles) can have a significant performance hit, especially in those systems with large particle numbers or short life spans.

An alternative to `malloc` and `free` (or `new` and `delete`, if you lie in C++ land) must be found in order to avoid their cost. The easiest approach is to map our system to a static array of particles. Then, each time a particle gets killed, we will mark it (using one Boolean flag). This way the deletion routine can be skipped. We do not need to be allocating memory for new particles all the time. They are placed in the same array positions as dead particles instead. Using this technique, the particle system can contain a constant number of particles, avoiding calls to `malloc` and `free`.

From the previous discussion, you might think we need to loop the array to determine where to put a newborn particle. But it needn't be the case. One loop can recalculate, kill, and respawn in an efficient manner. Here is the code idea:

```
for each particle in the system
    if particle is dead
            respawn the particle[i]
        else
            recalc particle[i]
        end if
end for
```

Spatial Indexing

Spatial indexing (explained in detail in Chapter 4, "Design Patterns") allows us to quickly perform queries that have to do with spatial locations. Tests like calculating the distance from one point to a set of objects, selecting closest pairs in a spatial set, and so on can be accelerated considerably by using them. Thus, using a spatial index should allow us to speed up global particle systems significantly.

Remember that, essentially, a particle system with global effects has a worst-case cost of

```
O(# of particles^2)
```

This comes from the fact that each particle must be tested against the others to account for interdependencies. So, a spatial index allows us to keep track of neighboring relationships, reducing the cost to

```
O(# of particles*k)
```

where k is a constant that depends on the quality of the spatial index. For example, for a gridded, 2D system with a homogeneous distribution of the particles, we have

```
K= # of particles / (Xs*Zs)
```

where Xs and Zs are the number of cells in the grid in X and Z respectively. Clearly, a fine-grained grid can help a lot in reducing a particle system's recalculation cost.

LOD Particle Systems

Particle systems often consist of several hundreds or thousands of elements, each one requiring dynamic updates. Moreover, the methods used to render them are often costly (alpha blending, multipass techniques). But we can achieve significant improvements in performance by using the level-of-detail (LOD) paradigm.

Imagine a smoke plume from a campfire modeled using particle techniques. Viewed from a distance, we might be able to skip some calculations and still get a realistic result. Then, as we move closer, more and more particles can be spawned, and a better interaction model can be applied for extra realism.

Clearly, the system must be carefully tested to ensure a visual consistency along the approach. But the added performance will likely compensate for any small artifacts that might appear.

Now, let's take a look at LOD particle systems in a general manner. Clearly, there are two areas we can work on in terms of LODs. First, we could try to optimize the rendering code. Second, we could try to optimize the recalc/respawn loop.

Optimizing the rendering code for a particle system can be tricky. Additionally, given the speed of the current accelerators on the market, rendering is usually not the bottleneck. Updating the particles and creating new ones as the old ones die is significantly more expensive. Thus, I'll concentrate on the second technique.

Optimizing `recalc()` by means of LODs is relatively simple. We only need to define what will vary depending on the distance/resolution and how it will vary. The easiest technique is to vary the number of particles, interpolating from a basic particle system with only a few particles when we are far away, to a full-blown system when we are up close. The sequence we will follow will be

1. Calculate the ideal number of particles depending on distance.

2. Recalculate the existing particles.

3. If a particle dies, respawn it only if we are below our ideal particle number.

4. If we are still below our ideal particle number, scan the empty particles in the array to respawn accordingly.

So, we have an ideal system size that we converge on by means of not respawning particles (to decrease the size) or by creating new ones (to increase detail). A caveat on this technique is that it requires the viewer's speed to be slow compared to the respawn frequency of the particles.

As a counterexample, imagine a jet fighter simulator where we use this technique to simulate smoke coming from ground explosions. The plane "sees" the particle system five miles ahead, where it consists of about 10 particles only. Because the jet fighter is very fast, and the smoke plume is comparatively small, the plane can approach too fast for the system to create new particles, resulting in a poor-looking system.

Another way of optimizing recalculations involves simplifying the inner calculations performed for each particle. Some systems calculate complex equations to ensure a physically and visually correct look. But for distant systems, some calculations can be switched off, and thus save precious clock cycles. I will provide two examples here.

Imagine a physically based particle system, such as smoke plumes interacting with wind. Essentially, the plume rises using a sine wave to displace in X and Z, and some Perlin noise is added to the mix to provide a nice, rich swirling. Noise influence is increased with height, so the top of the plume is more chaotic.

But remember that Perlin noise is a costly function: Each evaluation requires nontrivial math such as trilinear interpolations and Spherical Linear Interpolators (SLERPs). Clearly, not the kind of math you want to do standing five miles away from the system. So, our decision could be to switch off the Perlin noise with distance.

A different example would be global or interactive particle systems, where each particle interacts with the others or with the environment to create a complex behavior. Many times, these interparticle interactions provide subtle detail, such as particle collisions, attractions, and repulsion: leaves falling and colliding with each other, raindrops colliding with the scenario, and so on. On the other hand, they are very costly. Remember that the classic particle `recalc` loop has a cost of

```
O(number of particles)
```

But an interactive system raises that to

```
O(# of particles * # of interactors)
```

We have seen how spatial indexing techniques can be used to reduce the second member of the cost equation. But many global or interactive calculations can be scaled down (or even completely eliminated) with distance. It is unlikely that the viewer will notice if the leaves are not colliding when standing sufficiently far away from the system.

Shader-Based Particle Systems

One of the best ways to speed up a particle system is to implement the expensive physics simulator on a shader (shaders are covered in Chapter 21, "Procedural Techniques"), so it can be executed in parallel to the CPU. This imposes some restrictions on what can actually be computed, but most effects can be achieved this way.

Shaders are an advanced subject, and covering them here would interfere with the structure of the book. But a complete section on particle systems and shaders can be found in Chapter 21. I suggest you browse that section to learn how to speed up the computation of a particle system using shaders.

In Closing

Particle systems are not hard to code and can greatly add to the visual appeal of a game if used well. They improve the presentation values and add a sense of activity, helping to convey realism to the player.

Besides, particle systems are very well suited to simulate organic and natural phenomena, from clouds to rain to smoke. In the next chapter you will learn about these complex phenomena, and many new uses for particle systems will be presented.

Chapter 20

Organic Rendering

KEY TOPICS

- Nature and Complexity
- Trees
- Grass
- Clouds
- Oceans
- In Closing

"A cloud is not a sphere, a mountain is not a cone"

Benoit Mandelbrot

Particle systems have probably helped widen your perception of what can be rendered in real time. But wait, there's more. There are some objects that cannot be expressed in terms of conventional geometry, nor are they well suited for representation by a particle system. Take a tree, for example: a towering oak with thousands of leaves, branches, and bark. How many different triangles do you need to render it in all its beauty? As anyone familiar with fractals knows, the answer depends on the resolution: How accurate do you need to be? Objects found in nature exhibit the property of fractal depth: an almost unlimited level of detail, which makes them really complex to handle in a real-time game. At some point, you will need to reach a compromise between visual appeal and a stable frame rate.

Thus, organic rendering is defined as the technique used to create realistic representations of nature using computer graphics. Notice that I am talking about rendering, not modeling. If you need to paint a car, most of the decisions are made at the modeling stage—for example, the number of triangles needed, textures, and so on. With nature and its infinitely subtle details, we need to transport part of the work to the rendering stage, applying specific algorithms to create good approximations of the natural world.

This chapter is devoted to the subject of organic rendering. It is a beautiful subject, and the results are often quite spectacular. Unfortunately, it is not a case of one-size-fits-all. Most algorithms work on a case-by-case basis, and although some general strategies exist, we will need to think in terms of very specific problems. I will cover different manifestations of nature one by one (trees, grass, clouds, and so on) and explore suitable algorithms for each.

Nature and Complexity

Clouds are not spheres, mountains are not cones, and the bark of a tree is not smooth. In one word, nature is complex. By complex I mean that the level of detail does not decrease as we take a closer look.

Take a wristwatch, for example. If you look at it from a couple of meters away, you will only notice its general shape. But as you move closer, details will appear. Notice, however, that details seem to stop at a certain scale. There is no single feature smaller than a few millimeters. If you were to view it through a microscope, you would see that the surface is not really smooth but full of ridges due to manufacturing. However, at least in apparent terms, there is a discontinuity in detail.

Now, compare a wristwatch to a leaf of a tree. The closer you look, the more details you see, even at the microscopic level. There's a continuous increase in detail as we increase the scale. It's an interesting property of natural elements that is shared by all animals, plants, water, clouds, and even terrain. This continuity manifests itself in two apparently different but similar scenarios: geometry and appearance. Using the example of a leaf again, you notice as you move closer the nerves, wrinkles, and so on but also tiny texturing patterns, subtle color changes, and more.

So, the first conclusion of this analysis implies that all methods devoted to nature rendering will have a level-of-detail (LOD) component, allowing us to approximate the varying level of detail found in the real world.

Trees

Tree rendering has only recently found its way into computer games. Golf simulators were among the first to try to convey the look of realistic trees (usually by simulating them with billboards). But many games today take place in outdoors scenarios, so trees are getting more popular.

Trees can be rendered in a variety of ways, and the decision on how to do this depends on the priority of the trees in the rendering pipeline. There are many different approaches, but each one offers a different cost-benefit relationship, so you need to analyze how many clock cycles or triangles you are going to devote to your scenario. In some action games, trees can just be a backdrop against which the gameplay occurs, and thus a simple, cheap method will be employed. In other scenarios, such as role-playing games (RPGs), the tree is part of the atmosphere, and thus more energy will be devoted to portraying them realistically.

I will cover the different rendering methods in detail, emphasizing the key characteristics (memory footprint, CPU usage, triangles, and so on) so you can make an informed decision for your game.

Billboards

A billboard is a screen-aligned quad that is used to substitute a complex, distant object with a high-resolution picture. As the viewer moves around, the billboard also rotates, so it always faces you. Billboards are great for distant trees because they allow you to represent a visually dense forest with just a few triangles.

As you have already seen, aligning a billboard with the screen is relatively straightforward. All you have to do is calculate world-space vectors, which, when projected, result in screen-aligned vectors, and then use them to render the primitive. These computations can easily be made from the modeling and projection matrices in your API of choice or directly by combining the player's position and rotation angles with some clever trigonometry.

If you decide to render trees with billboards, you should be aware of some techniques that might be helpful to increase the realism of the result. Try to use as many different textures as you can, so the landscape looks varied and not a repetition of the same tree.

If possible, pack all those tree textures in a large, single texture, so you can encapsulate the entire forest in a single rendering call, avoiding the ever-costly texture swap operations.

A second piece of advice: If you can afford it, apply a subtle screen-aligned skewing transform to the trees to convey animation. Make sure trees are phased out from one another, so the overall result gives a sense of chaos, which will help realism. Skewing can be implemented easily on billboards. It is just a matter of leaving the base vertices unchanged while translating the top vertices along the line defined by the screen-aligned horizontal vector, as shown in Figure 20.1.

Figure 20.1 Billboarded tree using a skew transform to simulate simple animation.

Another improvement technique is to play with colors and sizes a bit. You can either recolor textures so they look different or modify per-vertex color and modulate texture color slightly in the rendering pass. Whatever your choice, the idea is that no two trees should look exactly the same; they should vary in hue over a relatively broad spectrum. Also, play with sizes. Store one scaling transform for each tree, so you can display different size trees. Huge variations are not really required. Allowing a 10–15 percent deviation from the "standard" size is all you need to further break down the landscape patterns, and thus create a convincing scenario.

Billboards are great if you need to create a forest on a very limited resource platform. Thus, all the techniques previously explained are geared toward increasing the realism of the results, because this technique is pretty limited. Now let's explore some limitations and items to watch out for when using billboarded trees.

First and foremost, be very careful with viewing distances. As you probably know, billboards are not really meant to be viewed up close. They are flat, look pixelated, and if the billboard is close to the lateral edges of the screen, can look distorted.

The best alternative to correct a flat, pixelated look is to blend a faraway billboard representation with an up close version made by using a more involved method. Image-based rendering trees can be used as well as real geometry objects. I will go into more detail about these approaches as I explore each technique. The distortion issue is somewhat harder to deal with. Billboards are designed to always face the camera. Thus, if they are close to the viewer, a small camera movement will imply a large angular shift, so the billboard will rotate to accommodate the new player position and can sometimes look wrong.

Two solutions exist to solve this problem. The first option is to align the billboards not so they face the camera, but so they face the camera's viewing plane (see Figure 20.2). By doing this, distant billboards will still look correct (angular issues are negligible here). Closer instances will no longer rotate to face the viewer, and a more realistic look will be reached.

Figure 20.2   Billboards aligned with the camera (left) versus billboards aligned with the camera's viewing plane to correct distortion.

The second alternative is to allow a limited rotation over the camera's viewing plane. This is a middle-of-the-road solution that provides quite good results. Here, billboards will be computed as if they were facing the camera. Then, the angle between this representation and the viewing plane will be computed, and only a limited range of rotations will be allowed. This way trees can be oriented to the camera when they are distant, and closer trees do not suffer the rotation artifacts found in classical billboards.

Image-Based Methods

Traditional graphics programmers tend to have a predilection for triangles. All problems must boil down to triangle rendering and a (sometimes pretty complex) geometrical representation. But what if we forgot about that for a second? What if, instead of decomposing everything into triangles, we chose a different primitive? Image-Based Rendering (IBR) is the common denominator of many different techniques that do not try to create accurate geometrical representations of objects, but rather convey their visual appeal by using images. In the extreme case, a billboard is an IBR method. But many other IBR methods exist, yielding much better results.

Tree rendering is very suitable for IBR. Trees have huge geometric data sets, with a decent tree requiring well over 10,000 triangles. IBR, on the other hand, places the emphasis on textures, keeping triangle counts relatively low. As you will see in a moment, you can create relatively good-looking trees with about 20 triangles using some clever IBR techniques.

IBR techniques can also be scaled up or down to offer varying levels of detail. We will see how they blend naturally with billboards and can be easily integrated with geometry representations as well.

Parallel IBR Method

The Parallel IBR method is designed to accurately portray trees that are part of a background. The limitation is that we must either be static or moving in a parallel plane to the trees. Thus, it is a suitable method for adventures, most fighting games, and so on.

The main idea is to represent the complexity of a real tree with a hierarchical, layered billboard array. We would use one billboard for the tree trunk, and from there, a series of billboards connected by joints, much like a character in skeletal animation. Thus, we can animate the tree as if it were being blown by the wind by propagating motion through the hierarchy while keeping a very low triangle count. A good model of a tree using this method can take about 25 quads to render, so the method can be used for dense forests as well.

The main difficulty of this method is obtaining the billboard data so the resulting tree looks good. The method I would recommend requires a rendering package (3ds max, Maya, and so on) and any of the tree modeling plug-ins available for them. You start by modeling the tree with as much detail as you want. Remember that this is an IBR method, so more detail does not necessarily mean more complexity or lower frame rates. Thus, make sure the tree is as realistic as possible.

Then, you need to use clipping planes or Boolean operations to extract slices of tree geometry in Z direction and take snapshots of that geometry. The trunk can generally be stored in a single layer, and thus the tree foliage is where you must spend most of your time. Make sure large branches are hierarchically divided into several layers because this will allow finer animation later on. I suggest storing these layers using some meaningful naming convention because reconstructing the tree afterward can become tricky if you don't. For example, I encode the name as a series of letters, which represent the hierarchical disposition of a given layer as shown in Figure 20.3.

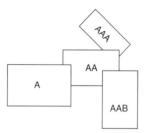

Figure 20.3   Naming for hierarchical branches.

The next step involves storing the "anchor point" for each joint between two layers. The anchor point is where we will link pieces together. A branch will rotate with respect to this spot, so detecting it correctly is essential for the realism of the complete scene. You should store these joint coordinates in 2D, referring to the current element's coordinate system, as shown in Figure 20.4.

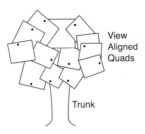

Figure 20.4   Orthogonal image-based trees with quads shown.

So our data set is now ready.

To render it, we must follow a skeletal animation approach. Each new billboard inherits movement from its parent and propagates downward to the children. As a rule of thumb, nodes closer to the root are generally larger and heavier. Thus, the range of movements of the different branches should increase slightly as we move away from the tree root and advance to the leaves.

Combining all the steps in this process generates extremely photorealistic trees. Note, however, that creating the data set is a tedious process, especially if you need to do it for several tree types to create a forest. Thus, it is recommended that you code some plug-ins for your modeler of choice, which makes life easier. An intuitive GUI can greatly simplify creating this method's data sets.

An extension to this mechanism uses parallel IBR for the leaves, which are usually stored in clusters, and real geometry (possibly with progressive meshes as explained in Chapter 21, "Procedural Techniques") for the trunk. This way we have trees we can move closer to, and if leaves are designed to incorporate not only the yaw but the pitch as well, we can look up from below.

Orthogonal IBR method

The parallel method explained in the previous section allows the creation of realistic trees for static or movement-limited players. They convey a great sense of parallax and volume, and can be animated. The downside is that we cannot look at the tree up close, nor rotate around it realistically. The reasons for these limitations lie in the texture resolution and in the fact that textures are screen-aligned, so rotating around them is impossible.

A new technique must be used for those cases requiring more flexibility. As in the previous case, this technique is somewhat similar to medical computerized axial tomography (CAT) scans, so slices of the tree must be taken.

But this time we will be able to rotate freely and, with some limitations, even stay in the shade of our trees.

The key difference is that this time we won't take parallel slices but will sample the tree in both the *XY* and *YZ* plane, so we get a series of evenly spaced texture maps. Then, we will paint them, reconstructing the proportions of the tree as in conventional volume rendering. To prevent the viewer from noticing the regular pattern, alpha-blending will be used to ensure a smooth transition between billboards aligned in both axes. This way we can view the tree from any distance and rotate around it. The more billboards you use, the better results you will achieve. However, demos with about 5–8 slices in each direction (resulting in a 20–32 triangle tree) look quite good. The only problem with this technique is that the trunk must usually be dealt with separately, because most of the time it will look wrong.

The other issue is that a viewer right below a tree shouldn't be allowed to look up, or the illusion of complexity will be lost completely. Pitch movement must thus be limited for this technique to achieve good results. A workaround to this situation is using not two axes but three axes: *XY*, *YZ*, and *XZ*. The *XZ* billboards will seldom be used except to solve the case where the viewer is placed below the tree. Then, the treetop would be sliced in horizontal layers, and the sense of volume and parallax will be preserved. But this solution is seldom implemented because it requires even more texture maps (IBR methods are all texture hungry). It is much simpler to restrict camera movement a bit.

As for the implementation, the orthogonal method starts like the parallel method: by modeling a very high-resolution tree using any plug-in or package. The tree can again be as complex as you want because we will not be using the geometry at all. The slicing process does not take place in the modeling package but in a preprocessor or at load time in the main application. The algorithm is as follows:

```
compute the bounding box of the tree
select the right number of slices
for each slice in XY plane
    place the camera in a fixed position along the Z axis
    initialize a front and back clipping plane so you restrict the
Zbuffer to the area you want to slice
    render the frame, save to disk (possibly scaling)
end for

for each slice in YZ plane
    place the camera in a fixed position along the X axis
    initialize a front and back clipping plane so you restrict the
Zbuffer to the area you want to slice
    render the frame, save to disk (possibly scaling)
end for
```

Note that the position of the camera is not really relevant, as long as it remains still over a rendering loop. The only difference it will make is on the size of the billboards, which will be scaled to suitable texture sizes afterward anyway.

Now you should have a series of RGBA images ready for rendering. As you can see, this preprocess is much simpler than the one required in the parallel method. For rendering, you must begin by rendering all images to a series of axis-aligned quads, so they reconstruct the geometry of the tree. Then, you must alpha-blend the quads depending on the angle to the viewer. Specifically, quads facing the viewer must be opaque, and as the quad moves away from the viewer, its transparency should increase. Tuning this code is essential for the illusion of volume, so a bit of trial and error is required. Once you achieve this, you should see the *XY* and the *YZ* billboards "taking turns," so as *XY* quads fade out, *YZ* quads fade in to create a continuous look of the tree volume. Sometimes the trunk will work out well with this technique, and sometimes you will need to use a regular mesh for the trunk because it will look layered. You can see the overall result depicted in Figure 20.5.

Figure 20.5   Final look of the tree with anchor points and texture maps shown.[1]

Orthogonal IBR trees look very convincing. But they have a downside. The hierarchical animation method we devised for parallel trees is not feasible here. Texture maps are evenly spaced and moving them would make the tree look like it was breaking. A minor improvement can be achieved by shearing the top vertices of the quads very subtly, so it looks like the treetop as a whole is moving. Sometimes you will even be able to manually add some extra quads to the treetops, so you can move them a bit and imitate animation. However, this technique works best with static trees.

Another downside to this technique in particular (and IBR in general) is that texture use simply skyrockets. A detailed, good quality tree will need a lot of good quality slices, and this means lots of memory will be used. Take, for example, a tree made of 8+8 slices; each one stored as a 32-bit 256×256 RGBA bitmap. Each bitmap will require 256KB of uncompressed memory for a grand total of 4MB for the whole tree. You might argue that these numbers are not that bad because we are not using any geometry in return. Although this is correct, 4MB per tree makes using this technique very hard in any mainstream game, where data sets must be kept to a minimum. Here is some advice to reduce the texture requirements:

---

1 Figure from Aleks Jakulin. "Interactive Vegetation Rendering with Slicing and Blending," *Eurographics 2000*. Used with permission.

- ➤ Do not store alpha values. Store transparency using the black color and generate transparencies by carefully selecting the blending function.

- ➤ Use palletized textures. Treetops are relatively uniform in color and can thus be successfully encoded in 256 colors.

- ➤ Use fewer and smaller slices depending on your viewing distance. If you will only see the trees from far away, maybe 4×4, 64×64 slices will be more than enough. A 4×4, 64×64 tree only takes up 256KB (using RGBA maps).

- ➤ If you combine this technique with a high-resolution, up close model, texture sizes can also be reduced because they will never be seen up close.

- ➤ Create different trees with the same texture map. Mirror the maps vertically or horizontally, use slight vertex color differences, and scale up or down to ensure that each texture map creates as many trees as possible.

Grass

We have seen how tree rendering is a matter of providing lots of detail to a single object using very little geometry. Grass rendering is a completely different story. Each blade of grass is relatively simple and can range from a single line to a few triangles. However, we must render thousands of them to convey the look of a real grass meadow. Here complexity does not lie in the specific object but in the numbers we will try to achieve. Unsurprisingly, grass rendering methods are quite different from tree algorithms.

We will explore a series of suitable algorithms for grass. Some of them will have specific limitations (not being able to animate the grass is a popular one). Only by knowing all of the algorithms in detail will you be able to select the one that suits you best.

Layered Grass

One approach to rendering grass is to compute grass via volume rendering. This is a very low-cost algorithm that produces quite good results. The idea is simple: Take an individual blade of grass. The blade will be vertical or almost vertical, and thus simplifying it with a straight vertical line is quite accurate. But how many blades of grass exist in an open meadow? The number can be in the hundreds of thousands, and we are clearly not going to paint that many lines. The cost would be prohibitive. We need an alternative way to tackle the problem, so we can keep the apparent complexity level while keeping an actual complexity level that's low enough.

Here is where the volume rendering concept kicks in. Instead of painting individual blades, we will sample the volume occupied by the whole grass meadow, and render blades as pixels on a texture. To do so, we will use volume elements (voxels), which will encode the grass blade layout as a volume function. Now, because we are simplifying grass by straight vertical lines, we lose the Y information, and we can compress our 3D voxel to just a 2D bitmap, which we will layer in Y to convey volume.

So, our algorithm is as easy as painting the same bitmap in several Y slices. Now, the bitmap is the complex part. For volume rendering, the bitmap will need to encode the XZ section of the blades of grass. This means an RGBA bitmap, where areas covered by grass are painted with alpha=1, and areas that are not supposed to have grass blades are painted with alpha=0. It is very important to space all grass elements evenly, so we cannot sense the tiling pattern in the grass.

The rendering is quite simple. Render the ground plane first. Then, render the same quad, shifting it along Y for each iteration. Between 5 and 20 quads will be needed to convey the sense of vertical continuity. As a rule of thumb, the number of layers should be correlated to the camera's pitch. A highly pitched camera sees the blades from above, and thus not many iterations are required. A camera that is almost parallel to the ground, on the other hand, will need a much higher number of iterations to generate the illusion of a continuous blade. Take a look at Figure 20.6 for an explanatory drawing.

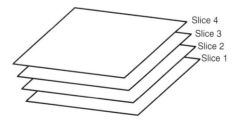

Figure 20.6   Layers of texture maps are used to render grass and convey parallax.

Thus, the method takes one texture map and as many quads as needed to depict the blades. We can even add animation by changing the grass texture coordinates slightly. In fact, this method has been recently coded for a variety of games and platforms.

Grass cannot be looked at closely, but the illusion is quite convincing, and the cost is definitely a plus.

Additionally, this method can be implemented in a single quad using a pixel shader. Here we would compute the angles from the player to each texel and sample the volume to generate the texture map. This way we would only be using one quad, which would work the projection details internally. Notice, however, that this shader approach is not necessarily a good idea. If we paint several quads using our first approach, we can have elements half immersed in the grass realistically, such as an animal in the middle of high grass or a football standing in the middle of a field. The shader method, by using just one quad to condense the information from the different quads, eliminates this possibility.

Statistical Distribution Algorithms

We will now explore the statistical distribution algorithm, which tries to convey the density of full grass meadows in real time. Because rendering all the grass is simply impossible, the method focuses on a radius surrounding the player and alpha-fades grass as distance increases so no pop in occurs. If the grass color blends well with the terrain, the eye is fooled, and the viewer assumes that the entire meadow is effectively covered by grass. Using this simple trick ensures that we are painting a constant number of triangles for the grass, which is key to any algorithm.

Geometry is painted using quadrilateral primitives; and each quad represents several blades of grass that are grouped together. This helps reduce the triangle impact, because grass will certainly need lots of geometry. With this technique, it is important to use a good rendering method (such as Vertex Array Range [VAR] in OpenGL or `DrawPrimitive` in DirectX). Unfortunately, grass is not composed of primitive strips, and indexing it will not help significantly, so a VAR of quads looks like a good choice.

At this point, the statistical part of the algorithm begins its work to ensure that undesired visible patterns are broken down as much as possible. The viewer must not notice how blades are grouped together, nor notice that the landscape is not full of grass. To achieve this, the best choice is to use a spatial Poisson distribution, which distributes a series of samples in the ground plane so that the XZ distance between any two randomly selected samples is never smaller than a given threshold. Poisson distributions are popular in computer graphics literature. They are used to sample areas in stochastic ray tracing for a similar effect.

Implementing a Poisson distribution is not simple. If we need a 100 percent accurate result, the method that will need to be used is called "dart throwing;" that is, successively adding elements to the spatial distribution randomly, and if the new element violates the Poisson distribution definition (and thus has another primitive closer than the desired threshold), eliminate it. By repeating this routine until the desired density is reached, we will obtain a perfect Poisson distribution. But for large surfaces this process can take ages to complete, so a near-Poisson method is used: Divide the surface in a square grid, place one element in each node, and apply a small random movement to it in both X and Z directions. This small movement is called *jitter* and ensures that no visible patterns occur. If the jitter is limited (for example, to half the grid size), we still comply with a Poisson distribution at a fraction of the cost. For grass creation, this method (see Figure 20.7) will be used.

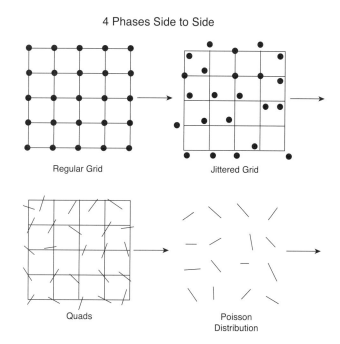

Figure 20.7   Statistical distribution of grass blades. Top left: Grid. Top right: Grid jittered to create a Poisson distribution. Bottom left: Quads added. Bottom right: Final result where all regular patterns have been eliminated.

Once the Poisson distribution has been evaluated, a rotation jitter must be introduced. Keeping all of the blade segments aligned certainly does not help convey a sense of chaos and naturalness. Thus, each quadrilateral will be rotated around the Y (vertical) axis. Here a plain random rotation will do the work perfectly, allowing a chaotic meadow to emerge.

A final step that further helps reduce visual artifacts is adding a scaling factor to the individual quads, so some quads are taller than others. A 30 percent deviation or so works well.

A note on rendering: As you have probably discovered, this is a fill-rate intensive method because many quads are required to convey the density of a real grassland. Thus, the rendering algorithm must be chosen carefully. Under OpenGL, using Display Lists is not a good idea because we will need to animate the blades and that requires resubmitting the list. A better move is to use server-side vertex arrays, which can be updated as needed. A particularly good strategy is to compute the Poisson distribution at load time and create an array with all the quad vertices, texture coordinates, and so on. The array will represent a square patch of grass, say, 10×10 meters. Then, you only animate the two top vertices of each quad through shearing and send the patch to graphics hardware using server-side arrays. This allows you to send the same array several times with a PushMatrix-Translate-PopMatrix, thus being able to fill a whole plain of grass by repeating the 10×10 pattern. The benefit is clear: You will only animate 10×10 meters of grass and use that sample to cover many miles.

Clouds

Many games use clouds and dynamic weather systems to convey an immersive gameplay atmosphere. In *Metal Gear Solid 2*, for example, part of the action takes place under very heavy rainfall, creating an oppressive feeling. Other games, like flight simulators, need clouds to offer the realism players are expecting from the game. Whichever the case, clouds are quite important in many genres. They can be simulated successfully using several methods, from the very simple for decorative clouds to the quite complex for games requiring clouds as part of their gameplay.

In one extreme, we can just use a skybox, a textured large object, which, once applied to sky textures, can become our sky. We will discuss this method in a moment. On the opposite end of the spectrum, we could implement a volumetric cloud system with properties such as density and temperature, so a plane can traverse a thunderstorm and the player can feel the turbulence. As usual, the choice will depend on the amount of clock cycles you are willing to devote to cloud simulation. Additional features rarely come at no cost.

Skyboxes and Domes

The easiest way to get a cloudy sky is to use a skybox or skydome. These are simply large boxes or hemispheres with normals looking inward, and a texture that tiles across the triangles representing the sky.

For a skybox, five quads are used. They are generally called top, front, back, left, and right; and each one has a unique texture, which blends seamlessly with neighboring quads. Because the quads are painted with no lighting at all, the seams between them are impossible to see, and the sky looks like a whole.

The only difficulty in creating skyboxes is obtaining the source pictures so they integrate perfectly. The best way to obtain them is to create them with a rendering package that has a procedural sky generator. One of the most popular packages is Terragen, which creates full landscapes with terrain, water, and skies.

Using Terragen, the method basically consists of defining a good-looking sky, and then placing a camera in the center of the scenario. Four renders are then performed at yaw angles of 0, 90, 180, and 270. And then another render is computed with the camera looking upward. A sixth render with the camera looking down can be useful for some applications, but most games use five images.

Once images are created with Terragen, it is all a matter of testing until they are properly laid on the five quads. Then, the sense of being in a box should disappear, and only a continuous sky should be visible.

Billboarded Clouds

Another technique that can be useful is using billboarded clouds, so each cloud can move and react independently. Clouds only need to be aligned to the viewer and moved very slowly. Billboarded clouds can be combined with a skybox easily, but the downside is that we cannot cross or enter the cloud. That would kill the illusion of volume because we would realize the cloud is nothing but a plane. We need a better system to create realistic cloud representations.

Volumetric Clouds

For those applications that need an extra-realistic look, a volumetric cloud model can be implemented, so the player can enter a thunderstorm, be immersed into volumetric fog, and so on. Be warned, though: Volumetric cloud systems require a significant amount of resources, both in the CPU and GPU, and thus can decrease the overall performance of your title.

There are a variety of volumetric cloud approaches. Thus, I will expose a generic cloud system that can be customized or extended to fit many uses.

The first component we will need is a data structure to hold the clouds. This can range from the very simple to the very complex. On the simple side, we could do a list of 3D points and radii, and implement the clouds as an isosurface that we would evaluate per frame. The cloudiness of a point in space would be computed using a variant of a field function. This approach can work well for systems with very few elements where the number of cloud generators is relatively small.

If we need a more accurate representation, we could divide our game world into a voxel structure, with each voxel node representing the cloud density at that point. Although voxel systems are sometimes rejected for their relatively large memory foot-print, a cloud system can be rendered efficiently using voxels at a reasonable cost. It all depends on selecting the right cell size. As an example, a 5×5 km scenario, sampled from the water level to 500 m in height (suitable for any city and most outdoors games) at a homogeneous resolution of 50 meters per sample (each sample being one byte) takes only 100KB. Clearly, voxel systems must be controlled carefully because they tend to grow, but that does not necessarily make them unfeasible.

For those situations where a voxel system is too expensive, a two-level fractal compressed cloud system can be implemented. Here the idea is to have a low-resolution voxel system and a "detail" voxel, which we place inside each of the larger voxel's cells, much like the recursion found in fractal systems. Because we will interpolate the detail voxel values according to the four corners of the larger cell, self-similarity will remain unnoticed, and a large cloud system will fit in any memory constraint.

As for the rendering portion of the algorithm, volumetric clouds are best treated as a very slow moving particle system. Cloud elements are just billboards with very low opacity value, and by layering them, we achieve the sense of density we are aiming for. We can even use a color table to ensure that clouds look realistic or even extract the color from a semivolumetric approach; that is, paint each element in a color proportional to the summation of cloud density above it. This way we can represent the gradation of colors found in the different kinds of clouds, from very pure cirrus layers to a dark gray thunderstorm.

Mark Harris from the University of North Carolina at Chapel Hill suggests using impostors to reduce the depth complexity and fill rate required to render the clouds. After all, don't forget we are talking about particle systems, and these take up lots of system resources. Creating a realistic cloud can take between 1,000 and 5,000 particles, and that's definitely not what you want to render on a per-frame basis: The cost is simply too high. Thus, we can condense clouds into IBRs, which is what impostors are all about. We render the cloud to a texture and use it until we have moved significantly, and thus we need to recompute the impostor. By using impostors, we are dramatically reducing the computational cost of our cloud system. All we need to do is establish an error metric that governs the moment when we will recompute the cloud.

Oceans

As with many organic effects, a low-quality ocean is easy to do, but good-looking results are really hard to achieve. In the end, it all depends on the amount of CPU cycles you can devote to rendering it. Will your game be a totally underwater experience such as *Ecco the Dolphin*, or will your sea play a secondary, purely decorative role? True-to-life oceans will be computationally expensive, so it is good practice to analyze your expectations before moving forward.

In its simplest form, an ocean is nothing but a textured, partially transparent plane. The texture will try to mimic the look and color of real water, so animating it will convey a higher sense of realism. But both the geometry of this water and its look are too simplistic. Oceans move and have complex interactions with light, which affect its appearance. Let's examine geometry and appearance in detail.

Realistic Ocean Geometry

To create realistic oceans, we will need to implement waves, sea spray, and so on. Several methods of increasing complexity have been devised through the years. One approach would be to use a simple sine wave as the wave function, thus creating a uniform wavy look. Be warned, though: Trigonometric functions are very expensive, so it's better to have them tabulated beforehand, thus avoiding costly computations for every frame.

Because oceans are rarely regular, a single sine wave will simply not cut it. Thus, two other approaches have surfaced. Using one approach, we can simulate ocean geometry by means of adding sine waves in an octave pattern, with each harmonic having double frequency and half amplitude. If we jitter these with some form of noise (Perlin noise, for example), the results will get better quickly. The second approach involves using mathematical models of the ocean, often implemented as particle systems: Each surface element is a particle connected by springs to neighboring elements. Then, using physically evolved models, we can simulate ocean dynamics efficiently. You can find an excellent overview of both methods, and a complete example of a mathematical ocean framework, in Lasse Staff Jensen and Robert Golias' Gamasutra article, quoted in Appendix E, "Further Reading."

Ocean Appearance

Pure water is transparent, and thus its real-world look is usually affected by several factors: reflections, color tints, light phenomena, and so on. In fact, the look of water is fundamentally defined by its interactions with light and other media, not as much by the water itself. Thus, to convey the sense of real water we will need to study how it interacts with its environment.

From an optics standpoint, water is a highly reflective, partially transparent material. Its internal color is very subtle and only appears in large bodies of water. It can vary depending on its chemical microcomponents such as algae and bacteria, but is generally in the blue green range. Water has an index of refraction that distorts our sense of size, making objects look bigger than real life. Additionally, both the reflection and the transparency are very sharply defined, as in most liquids. This means objects put into or reflected in water will still look focused, as opposed to stained glass, which is transparent but makes light rays bend randomly, producing a blurred look. Only when waters of different temperatures are mixed do blurry reflections and refractions appear.

Thus, the first step toward realistic water is using environment mapping to reproduce the reflective nature of its surface. Environment mapping is a very well understood technique, and its technical details are exposed in Chapter 18, "Texture Mapping." We can use both spherical and cube mapping, the latter offering better results at the price of higher texture costs. The choice, as usual, depends on the effect you want to achieve. For an open-ocean game, quite likely a spherical map of the sky will be just fine. But if you want true reflections (in a lake surrounded by trees, for example), cube maps will be a better choice. Just remember that if you plan on computing realistic reflections, you will need to recompute the cube map per frame (or every few frames), and thus the computational complexity will grow. Make sure reflected geometry is simple, so the render-to-texture pass can be performed with little cost. Another alternative is to use an LOD strategy, so the reflected models are scaled-down versions of the geometry. This can be very effective, especially if the reflection index is not very high, so the viewer will not notice any difference at all.

The transparency index of open-sea waters varies greatly depending on the chemicals of the water and the sun's intensity. Generally speaking, visibilities of about 15–20 meters are considered normal, which gives a transparency index of between 73 and 80 percent per meter (80% of the light entering a volume of water one meter wide effectively makes it to the other side, the rest is absorbed).

But absorption of light is just one of the consequences of water transparency. The other one is refraction: the bending of rays due to differences in the density of the different media. Light speed in open air is significantly faster than in denser media such as water, and thus light rays bend as they enter the liquid. This can successfully be simulated using shader techniques (explained in the next chapter). Notice, however, that most games totally ignore refraction because it is hardly visible in gameplay scenarios. The only examples would be games where players get to cross rivers, or other situations where they are partially immersed in water. A fully underwater game, for example, does not need to simulate refraction because all the action happens in the same medium (water), and thus no rays are bent.

One of the few exceptions to this rule is the phenomenon called caustics: light concentration due to refraction, which causes dancing patterns of light in the bottom of the sea. These are often visible in anything from lakes to underwater games.

Caustics

Caustics are produced whenever light travelling through different paths ends up converging on the same spot. Caustics appear because some semitransparent object acts as a lens, focusing the rays of light in a small area. The classic caustic example is the light spot caused by a lens on a sheet of paper or the apparently chaotic patterns formed by waves in the bottom of a swimming pool.

Unfortunately, realistic caustics are computationally prohibitive. They are usually computed using forward ray tracing with photon maps, which takes minutes or even hours to compute for a single frame. Thus, some simplifications must be implemented in order to approximate them in real time. We will see some algorithms that efficiently mimic the look of real caustics interactively. But none of them will really implement caustics analytically because the process would be too expensive. Let's begin by learning why.

In a realistic caustic simulation, a number of light rays are shot from the light sources in all directions. These rays or photons represent the amount of light being emitted by each lamp. Those rays directly hitting opaque objects are simply eliminated (whereas their lighting contribution is applied to the opaque object's surface). The vast majority of rays will thus disappear. But those rays hitting semitransparent objects such as glass or water will be propagated and entered into the new medium; their direction will change due to the difference in the speed of light between the "outside" medium (air, generally) and the "inside" medium (glass, water, and so on). This change of direction or bending is governed by Snell's Law, which states that:

```
Sin (incoming) / Sin (transmitted) = IOR
```

Snell's Law is depicted in Figure 20.8. These are the rays that will sometimes converge to create a caustic. Thus, we must follow them and assign them to surface points, so we can sum the contribution of the different rays and decide which pixels are affected by a caustic. The bad news is that this is a brute-force algorithm. We need millions of photons to reach a good level of realism, and that discards the technique for real-time use.

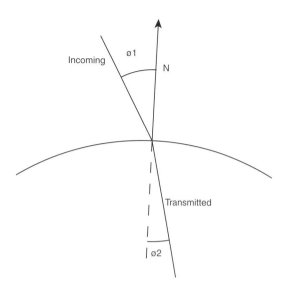

Figure 20.8   Snell's Law governs the bending of the rays as they cross media boundaries.

A different, more successful approach involves backward ray tracing using Monte Carlo estimation. Here, we start at the bottom of the sea, and trace rays backward in reverse chronological order, trying to compute the sum of all incoming lighting for a given point. Ideally, this would be achieved by solving the semispherical integral of all light coming from above the point being lit. But for practical reasons, the result of the integral is resolved via Monte Carlo sampling. Thus, a beam of candidate rays is sent in all directions over the hemisphere centered at the sampling point. In most cases, 16 rays per pixel suffice to achieve photorealistic results. Those that hit other objects (such as a whale, ship, or stone) are discarded. Then, rays that hit the ocean surface definitely came from the outside, making them good candidates. Thus, they must be refracted, using the inverse of Snell's Law. These remaining rays must be propagated in the air to test whether that ray actually emanated from a light source or was simply a false hypothesis. Again, only those rays that actually end up hitting a light source do contribute to the caustic, and the rest of the rays are just discarded as false hypotheses.

Monte Carlo methods are somewhat faster than regular forward ray tracing: They narrow the amount of rays to just a few million. But the number of samples still makes them too slow for real-time use. We can, however, simplify the backward Monte Carlo ray tracing idea to reach the desired results. We make some aggressive assumptions on good candidates for caustics, and thus compute only a subset of the arriving rays.

Specifically, we compute one ray per pixel. Thus, the method has very low computational cost, and produces something that very closely resembles a caustic's look and behavior, even though it is totally incorrect from a physical standpoint.

To begin with, we compute caustics at noon at the Equator. This implies the sun is directly above us. For the sake of our algorithm, we need to compute the angle of the sky covered by the sun disk. The sun is between 147 and 152 million kilometers away from Earth depending on the time of the year, and its diameter is 1.42 million kilometers. Half a page of algebra and trigonometry yield an angle for the sun disk of 0.53°.

The second assumption is that the ocean floor is located at a constant depth. Don't forget that the transparency of water is between 77 and 80 percent per linear meter. This means 20 to 27 percent of incident light per meter is absorbed by the medium (heating it up), giving a total visibility range between 15 and 20 meters. Logically, this means caustics will be formed easily when light rays travel the shortest distance from the moment they enter the water to the moment they hit the ocean floor. Thus, caustics will be maximal for vertical rays and will not be as visible for rays entering water sideways. This is an aggressive assumption but is key to the success of the algorithm. Notice, as a simple proof, that caustics are extremely popular in tropical, sandy beaches. These are usually close to the equator and are indeed very shallow. So it seems we are heading in the right direction.

Our algorithm works as follows: We start at the bottom of the sea, right after we have painted the ground plane. Then, a second, additive blended pass is used to render the caustic on top of that. To do so, we create a mesh with the same granularity as the wave mesh and one that will be colored per-vertex with the caustic value: zero means no lighting and one means a beam of very focused light hits the sea bottom. To construct this lighting, backward ray tracing is used. For each vertex of the mesh, we project it vertically until we reach the wave point located right on top of it. Then, we compute the normal of the wave at that point using finite differences. With the vector and the normal, and using Snell's Law (remember the IOR for water is 1.33333), we can create secondary rays that travel from the wave into the air. Now, all we have to do is check which rays actually hit the sun after leaving the water. To do so, we compute the angle between the ray and a vertical ray using the dot product. We know the sun is 0.53° across, but its halo can be considered as a secondary light source, most days covering an arc 10 times larger. Then, we use the angle to index a texture map, which encodes the luminosity of the caustic depending on the angle (see Figure 20.9).

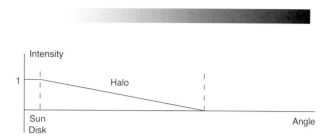

Figure 20.9 A texture map is used to bind ray angles to luminosities.

As a recap, the technique I have exposed basically converts a caustic computation problem into environment mapping, using the wave generator function to compute the texture coordinates. Luckily, the results (see Figure 20.10) are remarkably good.

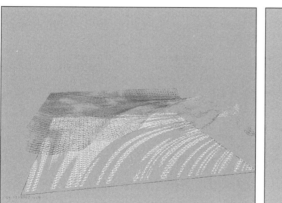 

Figure 20.10 Left: Wire frame vision, showing the samples at the bottom of the sea. Right: Solid view, showing the typical interference patterns found in caustics.

This technique can also be implemented using classic graphics programming. But it was designed from day one to be coded using pixel shaders for increased efficiency. To do so, we would compute the wave function and the backward ray tracing step in a shader, which also computes the derivative of the wave function. More details and a demo of this implementation can be found in the Gamasutra paper by Juan Guardado of NVIDIA and me, and is available on the Gamasutra web site."

In Closing

After reading this chapter, you may end up with a false impression that you have mastered nature rendering completely. If this is the case, I suggest you close the book, go for a walk, and then return to your reading when you are done. Go out to a meadow, river, or a park and take a look around. You will soon discover how nature's complexity is far from being tamed by graphics programmers, and some doubt it will ever be mastered. Given its fractal complexity, nature will always need more resources and more involved algorithms, effectively remaining one of the main challenges for programmers for years to come.

This chapter, along with the references provided in Appendix E, have just scratched the surface of what is certainly going to be an extensive subject in graphics programming. The more familiar you become with these subjects, the more competitive you will be.

Chapter 21

Procedural Techniques

"The process of preparing programs for a digital computer is especially attractive, not only because it can be economically and scientifically rewarding, but also because it can be an aesthetic experience, much like composing poetry or music."

Donald E. Knuth

Game development is an evolving science, and thus more sophisticated and efficient methods appear constantly. One clear sign of this evolution is the shift from explicit to implicit representations in many areas, such as AI, for example. In the old days, enemies were built directly into the game code using state machines or nested `if-else` structures. It was a clearly explicit, closed definition what you saw was what you got. Now, compare this explicit AI definition with a modern scripting system, where the AI is left as an open API so content integrators can work with it and tweak it separately from the main source files. Here the representation is implicit. Content integrators can bind any AI procedure (provided it follows some coding conventions) to the core game and use the result as a seamless whole. All areas of game programming have followed a similar approach, whether it's Digital Signal Processing (DSP) filters for audio or, as the subject of this chapter states, implementing graphics routines using shaders.

A *shader* is just a routine that implements part of the graphics processing tasks as a filter. Shaders emerged in the late 1980s as a fundamental component in Renderman, the seminal renderer/scene description methodology by Pixar. Today, most graphics cards support them on hardware, so boards can run shaders internally and thus increase the expressive potential found in fixed-function pipelines. Simply put, a shader implements an effect by means of a small program. This global philosophy is called the *procedural paradigm*: substituting part of the explicit data by implicit routines. It has surfaced in several areas of game development. Considering the importance of the presentation layer, it is not surprising that the graphics pipeline is where these kinds of methodologies can best be used.

Procedural Manifesto

A procedural model is a description of a system (graphics, audio, AI) using algorithms rather than explicit, precomputed data. Thus, a common characteristic of all procedural methods is the use of code (in many different languages). As the richness of the programming language grows, the expressive potential will grow as well, and the procedural representation will unleash all its flexibility.

Additionally, procedural methods are resolution independent by nature (see Figure 21.1). When you hard-code an AI routine or create a texture map in Photoshop, you are essentially locking down the level of detail. The complexity of the AI and the texture resolution are fixed. Procedural systems are resolution independent, so you can scale up and down without losing detail. All you have to do is provide finer granularity algorithms, which can scale when needed. The same way a fractal can have infinite detail, a procedural method can be arbitrarily detailed as well.

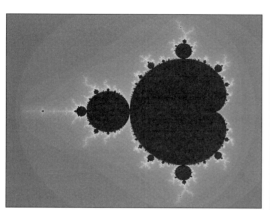 

Figure 21.1   View of the popular Mandelbrot fractal, a classic procedural model. Left: Overall view. Right: Zooming ×1000, a region showing the intricate, resolution-independent detail.

Another benefit of procedural techniques is *data amplification*: the capability to create high-complexity results from relatively simple input data sets so the procedure acts as a data amplifier. Again, fractals are a great example. A fractal terrain generator using midpoint displacement gets a quad as input, but can generate infinitely detailed mountains from it. Thus, the shader can sometimes not only filter and modify, but also create new detail as well.

Thus, procedural techniques are a great way to provide flexibility in game development. The learning curve might be the downside, but the overall balance is clearly positive. Games are both more flexible and easier to maintain because different team members have access to different game components.

Sometimes, procedural techniques are dealt with individually. We refer to vertex shaders, DSP routines for audio, Java scripts for AI, and so on. But it is important to understand that each of these (and many others) is nothing but a leaf of the same tree. The coding techniques might somehow differ, but the overall philosophy is the same.

Renderman

The procedural paradigm took the computer graphics scene by storm with the introduction of Renderman. Renderman's goals were to offer a description language suitable to work with huge data sets, so real-world, natural scenes could be created. To achieve this complexity, the graphics process was broken into two major tasks: shape determination, which worked on the incoming geometry, and shading, which determined the visual appearance of the geometry. Renderman's engineers soon discovered that setting all shading and shaping properties explicitly would be prohibitive, both in terms of the size of the data set and the work required to create them. Thus, they allowed parts of the graphics pipeline to be substituted by small programs that acted much like filters on the data. Mathematical functions could be used to displace geometry and thus create the illusion of wrinkles, fractals could be employed to create visually rich and scale-independent texture maps, and so on. Take a look at Figure 21.2 for a sampler of Renderman shaders.

Figure 21.2 Samples of Renderman shaders.

These user-provided programs were soon dubbed shaders because they were mainly used to create new texturing patterns and influence shading properties. However, there were six different types of shaders within Renderman:

- ➤ Light source shaders

- ➤ Volume shaders

- ➤ Transformation shaders

- ➤ Surface shaders

- ➤ Displacement shaders

- ➤ Imager shaders

Light source shaders are used to create sophisticated lighting effects. They receive the position of a light source and the direction of a surface point from the light. Then, they return the color of the light originating at the source and striking that point. A good example would be creating a light bulb that's surrounded by a fine metallic mesh. We can create a light shader that emits different lighting intensities depending on whether the surface point is occluded by the mesh or not. Other effects, such as spotlights and bizarrely shaped lamps, could be created in the same way.

Volume shaders are used to specify properties for volumes of space, such as fog. They receive the color, intensity, and direction of the light entering a volume and return the intensity and color of the light leaving that same volume.

Transformation shaders are more related to geometry than to the shading process itself. They allow developers to apply transformations (both on an object and vertex level) to the incoming data stream. Transformation shaders receive one point and return a transformed point after all required operations are performed. If we apply the transformation to the complete object, rigid body transforms are achieved. By working on a vertex level, we can specify deformations, bendings, and so on.

Surface shaders are used to specify the optical properties of surfaces: how they interact with light and so on. These shaders provide the best way to specify brilliance/metallic appearances as well as add bump maps. A surface shader often receives a point on the surface, the normal, and the lighting information. It then returns the reflected light. For example, bump maps can easily be added by perturbing the surface normal with some mathematical function (Perlin Noise would be very popular in this field), and then lighting the surface. Because the normal has been manipulated, the lighting will resemble that of an irregular surface.

Displacement shaders are a surface shader's older brothers; they are more powerful and complex to use. Surface shaders can create the illusion of an irregular surface by using bump mapping. This technique does not actually manipulate the surface, but instead manipulates its normal. So how can we build real protuberances? How can we create a moon surface full of craters? Displacement shaders are the tools for the job in this case. They receive a point on the surface and several other details (such as the normal, partial derivatives, and so on) and compute a new, displaced point. This can be used to create fractal mountains from a single quad, just by supplying the fractal function to the shader.

Imager shaders are used for color-based postprocessing. They receive floating-point pixel color values and return a set of values of arbitrary meaning as output. Thus, they can be used for effects like grayscale processing or color tinting, but also for other interesting applications. They can convert a vanilla RGB output into Hue-Saturation-Value (HSV) or any other format. They can produce most effects found in commercial image processing software, and so on.

Renderman shaders were written in a C-like language and included a great library of useful functions. As an example, here is a surface shader that computes Lambert-like lighting by multiplying the incident light vector by the normal:

```
surface IDez()
{
Ci = abs(normalize(N).normalize(I));
}
```

Notice how `Ci` is the result of the shader, which receives N and *I* as inputs (even if they are not passed as parameters). The syntax is not very different from regular C code except for the first token, which is used to specify the type of the shader. Now, here is a more involved example that computes a bubbly displacement using the cellular basis function described by Steven Worley in his popular SIGGRAPH paper (see Appendix E, "Further Reading," and Figure 21.3). In this code, we will be passing three parameters that control how the displacement is applied:

Figure 21.3   Worley basis functions used to produce several textures,
rendered using Renderman shaders.

```
displacement IDbubbly(float mult=5,Nzscale=1,Kd=0.2,bubsize=1)
{
normal Nn = normalize(N);
float a,b,c,bub;
float dist, shortest=10000;
point Po = transform("object",P)*mult;

/*true cell center, surrounding cell centers, noised cell center*/
point trucell, surrcell, nzcell;
vector offset;

setxcomp(trucell,floor(xcomp(Po))+.5);
setycomp(trucell,floor(ycomp(Po))+.5);
setzcomp(trucell,floor(zcomp(Po))+.5);

/*what is the shortest distance to a noised cell center?*/
for(a = -1; a<= 1; a+=1)
    {
    for(b = -1; b<=1; b += 1)
        {
        for(c = -1; c<=1; c += 1)
            {
            offset = vector(a,b,c);
            surrcell = trucell+offset;
            nzcell = surrcell + ((vector cellnoise(surrcell)
-.5)*Nzscale);
            dist = distance(Po,nzcell);
            if(dist<shortest) shortest = dist;
```

```
            }
        }
    }
bub = clamp(shortest,0,bubsize)/bubsize;
P+= Nn*(pow(bub,2)-1)*Kd;
N = calculatenormal(P);
}
```

Renderman shaders were compiled and stored as bytecode. Then, at render time, the appropriate shaders were executed as many times as needed to simulate the desired effects. Renderman shaders were never designed for real-time use. Render times were often in the "hours" magnitude per frame. Undoubtedly, shaders slowed down the rendering process, but the added flexibility and control made them a very interesting option. As a testament to Renderman's quality and flexibility, it is one of the leading rendering/scene description platforms used today, 15 years after its inception. The system gained widespread recognition with its use in movies like *The Abyss*, short films like *Luxo Jr.*, and especially *Tin Toy* by Pixar; and it continued producing an endless list of blockbusters that have benefited from the flexibility of Renderman's shading language.

In fact, you will soon see that Renderman has greatly influenced the way we perceive shaders today. In fact most real-time shading systems can be considered descendants of this cornerstone product.

Real-Time Shading Languages

The advent of powerful 3D graphics cards in the consumer market forever changed the way graphics were done. Very popular algorithms from the past were soon degraded, as the focus shifted from precomputed to real-time graphics. The 1990s were definitely exciting times for graphics programmers. The evolution has been huge, putting Moore's Law into question many times. Speed has increased astronomically, and today GPUs are probably more complex than the CPU.

But this quest for raw speed had its phases, too. It all began with simple rasterizers that did little beyond drawing triangles onscreen. Multitexturing was then introduced, mainly as a way to compute items like light maps and bump maps. The arrival of multitexturing marked a shift in the mind of most developers. Texture maps were no longer "pictures of a material we wanted to tile on the mesh": They were arrays of data with which we could do mathematical operations. Good examples are the normal maps used to encode bump mapping. With this change in attitude, APIs needed more powerful ways of specifying texture arithmetic, in other words, how different texture stages related to each other. Mechanisms like the register combiners were designed for this purpose. If you think about it, these were the first steps in the realm of programmable pipelines.

As hardware iterations have passed, graphics chip vendors have realized the potential of programmable pipelines and have incorporated more and more functionality into their systems. The concept of vertex versus pixel programs was established early on, and from there it was all a matter of adding programmability to the system. The first shading languages appeared, basically as a way to provide more flexibility to the register combiners mechanism. The syntax was a very crude assembly language. The current crop of languages, such as C for Graphics (Cg) or high-level shading language (HLSL) are nothing but interfaces to these assembly processors that allow programmers to work in a high-level, intuitive scenario.

There is a clear division in the way we can access the pipeline. We can still send data and let the API take care of everything by using the fixed-function pipeline. This way computations like transform, lighting, projection, shading, and texturing are automatically processed. On the opposite end of the spectrum, we have the programmable pipeline, which is the realm of vertex and pixel shaders. Notice that I've described these two as alternatives that are mutually exclusive. Both have unpredictable side effects. Under the programmable pipeline, we have to take care of everything, not only our particular effect. It is a black-or-white situation. In the fixed function, everything is done by the API. In the programmable pipeline, the API does nothing by itself (other than running shaders), and we must implement routines like projections inside our shader code. Luckily, some utility routines exist to help us out in this respect.

Current Languages

Unfortunately, there is no universal standard for real-time shading languages as of today (although I expect this issue to be resolved sometime soon). Different vendors are pushing forward different languages, which, in the end, have minimal differences.

This hurts the developer community and, as a result, the users, because the lack of an open standard prevents shaders from reaching widespread acceptance. Developers do not want to code different versions of their software, and different users have cards that might not be compatible with shaders. Let's take a look at what's currently available.

Cg

Cg is a high-level shading language introduced by NVIDIA for its GeForce family of accelerators. Cg has a syntax that is very close to C and allows the creation of procedural effects that are run directly on the hardware. The Cg compiler detects the accelerator type and produces hardware-specific microcode for your graphics card.

Cg shaders can work on vertices to perform custom geometry processing, create procedural texturing effects, or screen postprocesses. They can even be used in animation and skinning algorithms to reduce the CPU burden. The downside, at the present time, is that Cg is only supported by NVIDIA cards. Although the compiler is open-sourced, other manufacturers have not yet embraced it, so shaders written in Cg will, at least for now, be limited to GeForce-class cards.

Cg can be used in DirectX and OpenGL, so at least this language is a cross-API standardization effort.

HLSL

HLSL is Microsoft's take on shading languages in the context of DirectX. Thus, it is an API-specific language. Incidentally, HLSL and Cg syntax is identical. Microsoft and NVIDIA reached a common ground that they both respect, at least as of today. So, a shader in HLSL can be compiled with a Cg compiler, and vice versa.

HLSL is supported by ATI cards under DirectX as well.

GL2 Shading Language

For some time, a committee has been working on a proposal for OpenGL 2.0, which would be the first major revision to OpenGL. This revision would try to upgrade the API to current and next generations of accelerators. OpenGL has remained unchanged on a global level for more than 10 years now. One component of this new specification is the addition of a shading language, which would make programmable pipelines part of the GL2 standard. The shading language borrows most of its syntax from Renderman, which is a very good move toward an industry-wide standard. The GL2 shading language is supported by all vendors involved in the GL2 effort. As such, companies like ATI and 3D Labs have already announced their support for it.

Types of Shaders

As mentioned earlier, Renderman offered six types of shaders to application developers. However, the current crop of real-time shading languages only offer two types: vertex and fragment shaders. To understand the potential of each type, we must first review a general graphics pipeline. Vertices traverse five stages on their way to the graphics card:

1. Transformation converts vertices into their actual location if geometric transforms are specified. Vertices are projected to device coordinates, and texturing coordinates and colors are computed.

2. Primitive assembly and rasterization takes place. The graphics subsystem batches data in packets needed to create full primitives: A triangle needs three vertices, and so on.

3. The rasterization phase converts the complete primitive into a series of fragments. Fragments are the individual elements that make the representation of the object. Once converted into fragments, the fragment texturing and coloring phase starts.

4. Fragments are shaded and assigned texturing coordinates, depending on the per-vertex information.

5. Raster operations begin, which include depth testing, alpha-blending, stencils, and so on.

Vertex and fragment shaders allow you to program portions of that pipeline into a shader. Vertex programs, for example, are executed instead of the transformation step. As such, a vertex shader takes input data (vertices, texturing coordinates, colors, lights, and so on) and performs arbitrary transforms on them, making sure the output is projected to device coordinates. Thus, vertex programs can perform any kind of per-vertex processing: geometry animation, texture coordinate processing, coloring, lighting, and so on. Notice how, at this stage, we cannot talk about fragments, so all our work will be done on per-vertex data.

Fragment shaders, on the other hand, overwrite the fragment texturing and coloring phase. As a result, we receive texture coordinates and colors, and have the tools and power to generate procedural textures, and so on.

If you think about it, real-time shading languages are very different from an interface specification like Renderman. Shader types are a clear example. Where Renderman offered a high-level, very abstract shading language, newer languages offer very strict control on what can be done at each step in the graphics pipeline. Some of these limitations are imposed by the relatively restricted execution environment. We need scripts that run in real time, and that means our language will be limited sometimes.

A Collection of Shaders

We now know the basics about what shaders are and how to code them. The rest of the chapter is a collection of popular vertex and pixel shaders, so you can learn first-hand how some classic effects can be created. All the shaders in this chapter are coded using NVIDIA's Cg shading language. I have selected this tool for several reasons. It can compile on Macs, Linux, and Windows boxes.

In addition, it is supported by DirectX and OpenGL, and if the latest information is accurate, it can be used on an Xbox as well. Also, it is source compatible with Microsoft's HLSL and DirectX 9, and thus is probably the widest supported standard available for real-time shading.

> **NOTE**
> Check out NVIDIA's web site at `www.nvidia.com/view.asp?IO=cg_faq#platforms` for more information.

Geometry Effects

One of the easiest shader types can be used to implement geometry effects, such as simple animation, transforms, and so on. In this case, I have designed a Cg shader to create the illusion of wave movement in the sea. Because it is the first example, I will describe the creation process in detail.

We must first decide on the chain of responsibility in the program, or in simpler terms, what does what. Because shader languages cannot create vertices at the present time, all geometry and topology must be passed to the shader. Then, the shader will only transform vertex positions, so the wave effect is achieved. We will pass the sea as a grid with each "row" in the grid consisting of a triangle strip. The vertex program will have the following source code:

```
void waves (float3 position: POSITION,
float4 color: COLOR,
float2 texcoord: TEXCOORD0,
out float4 oPosition: POSITION,
out float2 oTexCoord: TEXCOORD0,
out float3 oColor: COLOR,
uniform float timevalue,
uniform float4x4 modelviewProj)
{
float phase=position.x + timevalue;
float amplitude=sin(phase);
float4 position=float4(position.x,amplitude,position.z,1);
oPosition=mul(modelviewProj, position);
oTexCoord=texCoord;
oColor=color;
}
```

This very simple shader starts by computing a wave front along the X axis. I have kept the simulation to a bare minimum so you can familiarize yourself with Cg's syntax. Notice how our shader receives traditional pipeline parameters such as the `position`, `color`, and `texcoord`. It also receives the `modelviewProj` matrix so we can implement the vertex projection portion. It can also receive user-defined parameters. In this case, it receives the time value that we will need to make the wave advance as time passes. On the opposite end, the shader returns those parameters marked with the reserved word `out`. In this case, we return a position, texturing coordinate, and color.

A much better water simulation can be created using the Cg language. But as our first shader, this one should do. Let's move on to more involved examples.

Lighting

Lighting can easily be computed in a shader. All we need to know is the lighting model we want to use, and then build the specific equations into the source code. In fact, lighting can be computed both at a vertex and fragment level. A vertex shader can compute per-vertex illumination, and the API of choice will interpolate pixels in between these sampling points. A fragment shader will compute lighting per pixel, offering much better results. We can also choose to implement more complex lighting effects, such as Bidirectional Reflectance Distribution Functions (BRDFs) (see Figure 21.4).

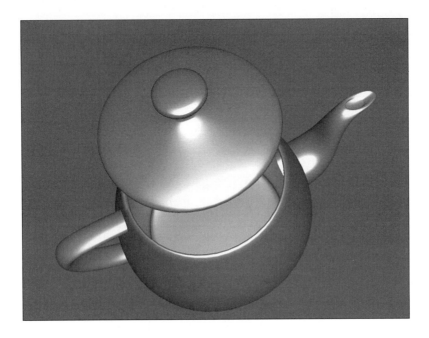

Figure 21.4   A shiny gold teapot implemented using a BRDF on a pixel shader.

Our first example will be a simple vertex shader that computes lighting per vertex using the classic ambient, diffuse, and specular equation. Because this model was already explained in Chapter 17, "Shading," we will focus on the shader:

```
void vertex_light        (float4 position   : POSITION,
float3 normal      : NORMAL,
out float4 oPosition : POSITION,
out float4 oColor      : COLOR,
```

```
uniform float4x4 modelViewProj,
uniform float3 globalAmbient,
uniform float3 lightColor,
uniform float3 lightPosition,
uniform float3 eyePosition,
uniform float3 Ke,
uniform float3 Ka,
uniform float3 Kd,
uniform float3 Ks,
uniform float  shininess)
{
// we will need these
float3 P = position.xyz;
float3 N = normal;

// Compute ambient term
float3 ambient = Ka * globalAmbient;

// Compute the diffuse term
float3 L = normalize(lightPosition - P);
float diffuseLight = max(dot(N, L), 0);
float3 diffuse = Kd * lightColor * diffuseLight;

// Compute the specular term
float3 V = normalize(eyePosition - P);
float3 H = normalize(L + V);
float specularLight = pow(max(dot(N, H), 0), shininess);
if (diffuseLight <= 0) specularLight = 0;
float3 specular = Ks * lightColor * specularLight;

// load outputs
oPosition = mul(modelViewProj, position);

oColor.xyz = ambient + diffuse + specular;
oColor.w = 1;
}
```

This code is pretty easy to follow. We compute the position and normal that are used all over, and then we simply implement the equations in order: ambient, diffuse, and specular. Now, this shader won't look very realistic on coarse geometry due to the interpolation done between per-vertex colors. For smoother results, a fragment shader must be used. Remember that fragment shaders are evaluated later in the pipeline in order for each fragment (which is somehow related to each pixel) to be rendered. Here is the source code, so we can compare both versions later. The illumination model is the same.

```
void fragment_light   (float4 position   : TEXCOORD0,
                               float3 normal     : TEXCOORD1,
out float4 oColor      : COLOR,

uniform float3 globalAmbient,
uniform float3 lightColor,
uniform float3 lightPosition,
uniform float3 eyePosition,
uniform float3 Ke,
uniform float3 Ka,
uniform float3 Kd,
uniform float3 Ks,
uniform float  shininess)
{
float3 P = position.xyz;
float3 N = normal;

// Compute ambient term
float3 ambient = Ka * globalAmbient;

// Compute the diffuse term
float3 L = normalize(lightPosition - P);
float diffuseLight = max(dot(L, N), 0);
float3 diffuse = Kd * lightColor * diffuseLight;

// Compute the specular term
float3 V = normalize(eyePosition - P);
float3 H = normalize(L + V);
float specularLight = pow(max(dot(H, N), 0), shininess);
```

```
if (diffuseLight <= 0) specularLight = 0;
float3 specular = Ks * lightColor * specularLight;

oColor.xyz = ambient + diffuse + specular;
oColor.w = 1;
}
```

The differences are minimal. Here we do not project vertices because we are not deciding where vertices go but instead how they are shaded. The lighting model is virtually identical, so both shaders should create similar pictures, with the latter having better quality than the former.

On the other hand, remember that the vertex shader will be executed once per vertex, whereas the fragment version will be run many more times. So performance does not necessarily have to be the same due to the different number of executions.

As a summary, lighting effects are really easy to put into shader code. The complex part is reaching the lighting equations, not coding them. Shaders are just an implementation of the equations. Because these equations tend to have lots of parameters, we need a mechanism to pass them to the shader. That's what the uniform keyword is for: It declares a parameter that comes from an external source (usually the C++ calling program). Then, after passing extra parameters to the shaders, all you need to do is compute the lighting expression in the shader. You can do so at the vertex shader level or in a fragment program. The latter offers better results at a higher cost, but most of the shader's source is the same.

Texture Mapping

Many texture mapping tricks are possible with shaders. Again, most of these techniques can be resolved at the vertex shader level or in a fragment program. Vertex shaders can change the mapping coordinates of a vertex, and thus full texture mapping can be implemented this way. Fragment shaders are a great place to compute procedural textures, which are computed not as texture coordinates, but actually shade each fragment with a mathematical function.

In this next example, I will compute a vertex shader that implements texture animation on the GPU. The idea is really straightforward. We have a global texture map that encodes several frames of a looping animation. Think of a flame with *n* subtextures encoded into one. We want to pass a timer to the shader so it automatically generates texture coordinates for the frame we are in. Here is the source code for this example:

```
void flames          (float3 position: POSITION,
float4 color: COLOR,
float2 texcoord: TEXCOORD0,

out float4 oPosition: POSITION,
out float2 oTexCoord: TEXCOORD0,
out float3 oColor: COLOR,

uniform float timevalue,
uniform float speed,
uniform float4x4 modelviewProj)
{
int frame=abs(speed/timevalue);
frame=frame%16;
int row=frame%4;
int col=frame/4;
float xCoord=row*0.25+texcoord.x*0.25;
float yCoord=col*0.25+texcoord.y*0.25;

oPosition=mul(modelviewProj, position);
oTexCoord=float2(xCoord, yCoord);
oColor=color;
}
```

Notice how the shader's source computes the frame we are at, and then translates that into row and column numbers to index our texture map, generating texturing coordinates for the flame.

The most interesting texture effects lie on the fragment program side. Having control on a per-texel basis gives us the flexibility we need to create unique textures. As an example, here is a fire generator by Damian Trebilco.

```
void fire (float4 Position : POSITION,
float3 Tex0      : TEXCOORD0,
float3 Tex1      : TEXCOORD1,
float3 Tex2      : TEXCOORD2,
float3 Tex3      : TEXCOORD3,
out float4 oColor    : COLOR,

uniform sampler2D FireMap,
                  uniform sampler1D LookupMap,
                  uniform float3 fireVar)
{
float4 currentIndex;
float index;

//Sample the four texture positions (The texture width is in the
z component)
currentIndex =f4tex2Dproj(FireMap, Tex0);
currentIndex +=f4tex2Dproj(FireMap, Tex1);
currentIndex +=f4tex2Dproj(FireMap, Tex2);
currentIndex +=f4tex2Dproj(FireMap, Tex3);

//Get the average
index=currentIndex.a *0.25;

//Decrease by a large amount for all initial values
if(index > fireVar.x)
    {
    index = index - fireVar.y;
    }
//When the limit is reached, drop off slower
else
    {
    index = index - fireVar.z;
    }

//Clamping the index is not really necessary unless a floating
point target is used
clamp(index,0.0,1.0);
```

```
//Look up the new color in the palette
oColor.xyz =h3tex1D(LookupMap,index);
oColor.w   =index;
}
```

This program requires some explanation. Fire was a popular effect in the demo scene in the late 1980s. It was computed by painting white pixels at the bottom of the screen, and then using a cellular automata-style routine to propagate the fire to the pixels above it. For each frame, each pixel was scanned, and its new color value was the average of the color values of the pixels located below it, as shown in Figure 21.5.

 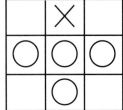

Figure 21.5 Cellular fire. Left: End result. Right: Explanation. To compute a fire sample at the position X in frame N+1, we average the values at pixels marked O at frame N.

Computing fire on a shader is very similar to this approach. We need the fragment program to receive the pixel to be shaded and the values of the pixels to be taken into consideration. To do so, we use a sampler, which is a Cg object that allows us to retrieve values from textures. The first four lines of the shader retrieve the indices of these four pixels. We then average these values, which causes the bleeding and vertical propagation fire effects are known for. Then, the `if` clause is added only to regulate the speed at which flames fade away: faster if above a certain threshold and slower afterward. However, fire does not work on RGB space, but instead works on index space, as in a palettized environment. Thus, we need to do a table lookup using a 1D sampler to retrieve the RGB values associated with the index we have computed for this point.

This effect is a very good showcase of how procedural textures are generated.

Particle Systems

Another application of vertex shaders is the computation of a particle system's behavior on the GPU. This is somewhat more complex because the parameter passing can be unintuitive. Imagine an explosion, for example: Particles fly off in all directions following straight lines from a central position. This effect can easily be built into a vertex shader because we can compute each particle's position from its initial values—pass position, velocity, and time elapsed to the shader—and it will take care of the rest. The equation would be

```
Pos=pos0 + vel0*t
```

We can use this same philosophy to compute any effect that depends on initial values only: pass these values and use the shader as an equation solver. Now, imagine that we have a somewhat more complex particle system, where each frame has a degree of uncertainty, so each iteration is computed from the preceding one. For example, imagine a column of smoke, which is affected per frame with Perlin Noise, like this:

```
pos.x=prevpos.x+noise(x,y,z)*0.01;
pos.y=prevpos.y+0.1;
pos.z=prevpos.z+noise(x,z,y)*0.01;
```

This is harder to lay down to code. Each shader iteration recomputes the position, which we would need to recover after the processing, so we can feed it to the next iteration, and so on. For the time being, this is not possible, so we will have to restrict ourselves to shaders based on initial conditions only. Here is, for example, the source code for a shader that computes the position and orientation of a particle emanating from an initial position, with a certain velocity:

```
void particle(float4 position: POSITION,
float4 color: COLOR,
float2 texcoord: TEXCOORD0,
float4 velocity: TEXCOORD1,
float4 initialpos: TEXCOORD2,
out float4 oPosition: POSITION,
out float2 oTexCoord: TEXCOORD0,
out float3 oColor: COLOR,
```

```
uniform float timevalue,
uniform float4x4 modelviewProj)
{
float4 newpos=initialpos+position+velocity*timevalue;
oPosition=mul(modelviewProj, newpos);
oTexCoord=texCoord;
oColor=color;
}
```

The code is straightforward. All we have to do is feed the shader with particle coordinates in the form displayed in the figure, and the shader will translate them to the initial position and animate them with time. We did not deal with alignment this time because it was explained in the previous shader example. By merging both, you will achieve a pretty interesting combined result (see Figure 21.6).

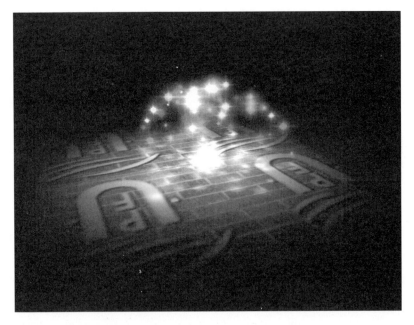

Figure 21.6 Particle system using shaders for simulation and DirectX `PointSprites` as the rendering primitive. Particles are blended additively.

Animation

Animation, whether it's vertex- or skeleton-based, is a CPU-hungry process. If we go the vertex path, we will need interpolations galore to make sure movements are smooth and we can store as few frames as possible. On the skeletal side, quaternion interpolations are just part of the problem. The real meat comes when we need to perform point-matrix multiplies, possibly blending different matrices per vertex to perform multiple bone influences.

Thus, it is not surprising that animating characters is one of the tasks shading languages can be devoted to. All will be achieved through vertex shaders, which will implement the animation algorithm of your choice.

In this example, you could implement keyframe interpolation using a vertex shader. The core interpolator is no big issue. Linear interpolation can be implemented with the following equation:

```
Position=positionA*(1-alpha) + positionB*alpha
```

where *positionA* and *positionB* are the two position endpoints and *alpha* is the interpolator. This transforms nicely into Cg code with the `lerp` function, which implements a linear interpolation:

```
Position=lerp(positionA, positionB, alpha);
```

The only problem with this approach is how to pass both positions to the vertex shader, which, if you recall, must act like a filter: receiving one set of vertices and transforming it. Currently, there is no way to pass both meshes, so we need some tricks to get this working. The trick we will use is to store the second mesh as texturing coordinates, so we can access them from within the shader. Specifically, we will pass a position, the regular `float2` set of texture coordinates, one color (`float4`), and a second set of texture coordinates (`float3`), which will hold the second position to interpolate. Take a look at the following code:

```
void keyframe (float3 positionA: POSITION,
float3 positionB: TEXCOORD1,
float4 color: COLOR,
```

```
float2 texcoord: TEXCOORD0,
out float4 oPosition: POSITION,
out float2 oTexCoord: TEXCOORD0,
out float3 oColor: COLOR,
uniform float alpha,
uniform float4x4 modelviewProj)
{
float3 position=lerp(positionA, positionB, alpha);
oPosition=mul(modelviewProj,float4(position,1));
oTexCoord=texCoord;
oColor=color;
}
```

That's just four lines really, and it saves developers a lot of headaches. All we need to do is compute the alpha value based on the distance between both key frames. Notice that the preceding code can handle both regular and unevenly spaced keys. We could enhance the code to pass extra data and drive a quadratic or cubic interpolator, but for most uses, linear is fine.

This approach can be adapted easily for facial animation using morphs. After all, we are just interpolating several facial expressions per vertex, so the preceding code, in all its simplicity, is definitely worth checking out. But other, more serious animation problems lie ahead. Wouldn't it be cool to implement a similar approach to skeletal animation? This is a much trickier case because the algorithm is more complex. Recall that skeletal animation (I'm talking about the multibone approach) is resolved in two phases. We first propagate matrices and store, for each vertex, the bones, and thus the matrices that affect it. We also store matrix weights, so we can blend them properly. As you can imagine, this is the cheap stage because the next one implies performing many point-matrix multiplies and blending the results together. Thus, it is the second phase what we would need to improve by coding the actual skinning code into a shader.

Now our animation code will need to receive, along with the vertex we are processing, the matrices that affect it and the corresponding weights. For simplicity, we will restrict the number of bones that influence a vertex to four, so we need to pass four matrices:

```
void skinning(float3 position    : POSITION,
float3 normal        : NORMAL,
```

```
float2 texCoord     : TEXCOORD0,
float4 weight       : TEXCOORD1,
float4 matrixIndex  : TEXCOORD2,

out float4 oPosition : POSITION,
out float2 oTexCoord : TEXCOORD0,
out float4 color     : COLOR,

uniform Light light,
uniform float4    boneMatrix[72], // 24 matrices
uniform float4x4  modelViewProj)
{
float3 netPosition = 0, netNormal = 0;

for (int i=0; i<4; i++)
    {
    float index = matrixIndex[i];
    float3x4 model = float3x4(boneMatrix[index+0],
boneMatrix[index+1],
                                  boneMatrix[index+2]);
    float3 bonePosition = mul(model, float4(position, 1));

    float3x3 rotate = float3x3(model[0].xyz, model[1].xyz,
model[2].xyz);
    float3 boneNormal = mul(rotate, normal);
    netPosition += weight[i] * bonePosition;
    netNormal   += weight[i] * boneNormal;
    }
netNormal = normalize(netNormal);

oPosition = mul(modelViewProj, float4(netPosition, 1));
oTexCoord = texCoord;
ocolor = Illuminate(light, netPosition, netNormal);
}
```

We then loop four times (one per matrix), accumulating each matrix contribution to the vertex and normal value. Notice how the call to `Illuminate` (which is not included for simplicity) computes shading based on these values. Then, for each matrix, the `TEXCOORD1` is used to specify its weight, and the `TEXCOORD2` is used to index it into a larger `bonematrix` array. The model variable holds the current bone influence matrix, which is then applied to the vertex and finally to the normal. Then, this `bonePosition` (the vertex position according to this bone) and `boneNormal` (the normal according to that same bone) are added, integrating weight on the equation. The equation is exactly the same as the one we used in our discussion on skeletal animation.

Procedural Texturing

One of the main uses for shaders in the movie industry is the creation of procedural textures. Here materials are not defined in terms of bitmaps but in mathematical functions that, when combined, produce aesthetically pleasing results. As a simple example, imagine a checkers pattern, each tile being one meter across. Here is the pseudocode for a shader that would compute this on the GPU, thus saving texture and CPU resources:

```
checkers (point pos)

if (trunc(pos.x) + trunc(pos.y)) is odd
        color=black
else color=white
```

As you can see, procedural textures are always implemented with pixel shaders, where the shader receives the point to texturize and computes output colors in return.

A good library of mathematical functions is essential for procedural textures to work. Most effects are achieved with operators like trigonometric functions, logarithms, and especially, controlled noise functions such as Perlin Noise (for more on this funcion, see the Perlin article listed in Appendix E). This function generates pseudorandom values over a 3D space, so values close in parameter space are close in their noise value; and faraway parameters yield uncorrelated outputs. Think of it as a band-limited, continuous and derivable noise.

Using Perlin Noise properly, you can implement most natural-looking materials, like wood, marble, or clouds. As an example that shows its capabilities, take a look at Figure 21.7, which was taken from a shader by Pere Fort. Here we are using Perlin Noise to compute an animated sun complete with coronas, surface explosions, and animation. The sun is really a quad, textured using a pixel shader.

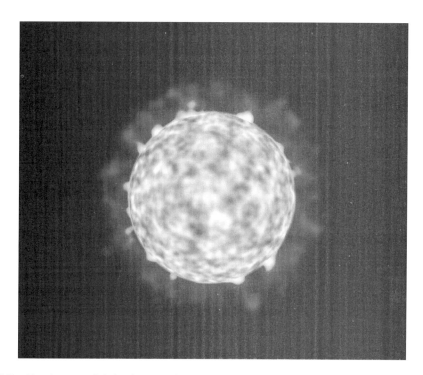

Figure 21.7   Flaming sun disk implemented as a quad with procedural Perlin textures on a pixel shader.

Here is the commented source code for this interesting effect, which somehow shows how real-time shaders can actually create some never-before seen effects in computer games. The source code is very lengthy, but I think it provides a clear vision of what the future holds for shading languages:

```
struct vp2fp
    {
    float4 Position  : POSITION;
    float4 TexCoord  : TEXCOORD0;
    float4 Param     : TEXCOORD1;
    float4 Color     : COLOR0;
    };



// INPUTS
// TexCoord : TEXCOORD0 = here we encode the actual coordinates
plus the time
```

```
// Param    : TEXCOORD1 = here we encode in x and y the angles to
rotate the sun

float4 main(vp2fp IN, const uniform sampler2D permTx, const uniform
sampler1D gradTx  ):COLOR
{
//distance vector from center
float2 d = IN.TexCoord.xy - float2(0.5f,0.5f);

//distance scalar
float dist = sqrt(dot(d,d)) * 2;

// Sun's radius
float radSun = 0.6f;
// Halo's radius
float radHalo = 1.0f;

float3 vCoord = IN.TexCoord.xyz;
float freq;

if(dist < radSun) // fragment inside the Sun
    {
    // freq inside the Sun is higher than outside
    freq = 64;
    // texture coords displacement in 2D
    vCoord.xy -= IN.Param.xy;
    // sphere function, with 70% depth
    vCoord.xy -= d*sqrt(radSun*radSun-dist*dist)*0.7f;
    }
else //fragment outside the Sun
    {
    // freq outside the Sun is half than inside
    freq = 32;
    // a little displacement (20%) of the halo while rotating the
sphere
    vCoord.xy -= IN.Param.xy*0.2;
    }
```

```
// sum of two octaves of perlin noise, second with half the freq
of the first
float4 total = 0f.xxxx;
total += (perlinNoise3_2D(vCoord*freq  , permTx, gradTx) +
0.7).xxxx*0.33f;
total += (perlinNoise3_2D(vCoord*freq/2, permTx, gradTx) +
0.7).xxxx*0.66f;

// after getting the result of the noise we can compute the
radius of the explosions
// we can use one dimension from the result to get a single
dimension perlin noise
float radExpl = (1 + total.x) * radSun * 0.6f;

// this generates a little halo between Sun and explosions, and
avoids some aliasing
if(radExpl < radSun*1.01f) radExpl = radSun*1.01f;

// filtering the colour of fragments
// first smoothstep makes explosions darker as the radius increases
// second smoothstep makes the halo darker as it becomes far from
the sun
dist = smoothstep(radExpl,radSun,dist)*0.5f +
smoothstep(radHalo,radExpl,dist) * 0.5f;

// transform black into red
// blue to 0 means obtaining yellow
// maintain the alpha input
total.rba = float3(total.x*1.8f,0.0f,IN.Color.a);

// ensure the ranges of the colors after all modifications
total.xyz = clamp(total.xyz,0,1);

// return all the modifications with the filter applied
return total*dist;
}
```

Special Effects

Lighting, animation, and texturing are popular areas for shader use. However, the shaders we have examined so far are very conservative shaders that are only a few lines long and implement simple effects. There are many interesting effects just waiting for you to code them. As an example, I will expose the shader code to compute toon shading on the GPU. For more on toon shading, take a look at Chapter 17, which covers shading techniques. Our implementation will strictly follow the algorithm exposed in that chapter. I have chosen a version that couples a vertex and a fragment shader. The vertex shader computes the texturing coordinates, and the fragment version performs the actual color blending. Both shaders are chained, so the output of the vertex shader eventually gets processed by the fragment shader. Here is the Cg code for the vertex shader:

```
void toonShading_v(float4 position : POSITION,
float3 normal     : NORMAL,

out float4 oPosition      : POSITION,
out float diffuseLight    : TEXCOORD0,
out float specularLight   : TEXCOORD1,
out float edge            : TEXCOORD2,

uniform float3 lightPosition, // Light Pos (in obj space)
uniform float3 eyePosition,   // Eye Pos (in obj space)
                 uniform float shininess,

uniform float4x4 modelViewProj)
{
oPosition = mul(modelViewProj, position);

// Calculate diffuse lighting
float3 N = normalize(normal);
float3 L = normalize(lightPosition - position.xyz);
diffuseLight = max(0, dot(L, N));

// Calculate specular lighting
float3 V = normalize(eyePosition - position.xyz);
float3 H = normalize(L + V);
specularLight = pow(max(0, dot(H, N)), shininess);
```

```
if (diffuseLight<=0) specularLight = 0;

// Perform edge detection
edge = max(0, dot(V, N));
}
```

The first portion of the preceding code does not really need an explanation. We compute the projected position, and then sequentially process diffuse and specular components. We then compute an edge value, which is zero if *V* dot *N* is less than or equal to zero. By doing so, we are detecting, with a zero value, those places where *V* and *N* are perpendicular, and thus, we are on the silhouette of the object to be rendered. We will need to pass that value to drive our fragment shader, whose source code follows. Notice how the vertex shader does not compute a per-vertex color or texture coordinate:

```
void toonShading_f (float diffuseLight  : TEXCOORD0,
                    float specularLight : TEXCOORD1,
                    float edge          : TEXCOORD2,

out float4 color : COLOR,

uniform float4 Kd,
uniform float4 Ks,
uniform sampler1D diffuseRamp,
uniform sampler1D specularRamp,
uniform sampler1D edgeRamp)
{
// Apply step functions
diffuseLight = tex1D(diffuseRamp, diffuseLight).x;
specularLight = tex1D(specularRamp, specularLight).x;
edge = tex1D(edgeRamp, edge).x;

// Compute the final color
color = edge * (Kd * diffuseLight + Ks * specularLight);
}
```

The shader is dead simple. We start by doing a table lookup based on the diffuse illumination value computed at the vertex stage, and then use this to drive a 1D texture lookup. This texture will be the typical discretized map, which usually has two or three shades: one for dark hues, one for mid-ranges, and one for well-lit zones. The second line does exactly the same thing for specular textures, and then edge is processed. For edge, the texture encodes the range of values that we want to assign to the black outline. The values coming from the vertex shader are in the range 0..1, but we need our silhouette to be perfectly divided into zones that are purely white and zones that are perfectly black. Thus, the edge texture lookup maps the continuous range 0..1 to two possible values, 0 for values below a fixed threshold (say, 0.2) and 1 in any other case.

The final equation is where all parts fall into place. The member inside the parentheses is just a regular lighting equation that uses the discretized values to modulate the diffuse (Kd) and specular (Ks) colors. We multiply this by the edge value, so edges that equal zero (thus, points in the silhouette) are shaded in black, and a nice outline is drawn.

This is just a simple example of what can be achieved by leveraging the power of vertex and fragment shaders, and especially by chaining them so they both work as stages of a whole process.

In Closing

Shading languages are probably the most significant development in recent years for real-time graphics. The ability to write special-purpose routines to handle effects directly on the GPU has a number of benefits that we are still discovering today. Just think about a few of these rewards: flexibility, expressive power, and integration with the movie industry. But it appears that the current crop of shading languages is just one step in the evolution. We are advancing in the right direction, but are not quite there yet. Most likely, advances in the shader arena will dominate our craft for years to come.

So, where can we turn when looking for a glimpse into the future? Who can offer guidance or ideas for new techniques? I must say the answer is probably hidden somewhere in the movie industry and in the Renderman software. Although it is true that offline shading languages such as Renderman and real-time languages such as HLSL or Cg are a completely different business, their goals are the same. Renderman has been around for some time now and has an expressive power, which is, as of today, superior to current real-time shading languages. By taking the time to learn new techniques, you will hopefully make real-time languages a more sophisticated solution in the years to come.

Chapter 22

Geometrical Algorithms

"Don't try to be like Jackie. There is only one Jackie....
Study computers instead."

Jackie Chan

This chapter is devoted to providing you with a collection of useful geometrical tests for computer games. Most of it deals with the subject of collision detection and response, which is of extreme importance for almost any game. However, there are many more techniques to explore. We need to detect the room the player is standing in, compute the sound propagation, and explore a myriad of other tests we will end up using on a day-to-day basis.

The structure of this chapter is thus a bit different from the rest of the book. It is a collection of articles on different geometric computations, so it can be browsed quickly to find what you are looking for.

Point Inclusion Tests

The first problem we will try to analyze is finding whether a 2D or 3D point lies within different types of bodies, from spheres to meshes of various types. This is an essential test for fields like AI or collision detection. From grenades to wall-following, almost every interesting algorithm needs, at some point in time, to deal with this kind of issue.

Point-in-Sphere

The simplest point inclusion test involves testing whether a point is actually inside a sphere. A sphere can be considered a generalization of a point. It is actually a point with a radius. Thus, given the sphere (as shown in Figure 22.1)

$$(X-Xc)^2 + (Y-Yc)^2 + (Z-Zc)^2 = R^2$$

and the point P

```
P= (px,py,pz)
```

P is inside the sphere if and only if

```
Inside= (sqrt ( (px-xc)² + (py-yc)² + (pz-zc)² ) < radius
```

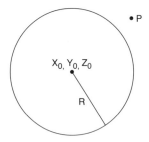

Figure 22.1 Graphical representation of point-in-sphere test.

Remember that square roots are expensive. Thus, an optimization could be

```
Inside= ( (px-xc)² + (py-yc)² + (pz-zc)² ) < radius²
```

as well as storing the radius squared to speed up computations.

Point-in-AABB

An axis-aligned bounding box (AABB) is a box whose support planes are aligned with the X, Y, and Z planes (see Figure 22.2). It is very popular for gross collision detection. An object is assigned an AABB, and as a first step in the collision detection process, we test for collisions with the box, not the object, providing an almost trivial rejection case for most tests.

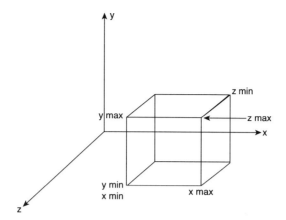

Figure 22.2   Graphical representation of an AABB.

Thus an AABB is defined by six planes, whose equations are

```
x-xmax=0
x+xmin=0
y-ymax=0
y+ymin=0
z-zmax=0
z+zmin=0
```

The test is as follows:

```
bool inside(point p)
{
if (p.x>xmax) return false;
if (p.x<xmin) return false;
if (p.y>ymax) return false;
if (p.y<ymin) return false;
if (p.z>zmax) return false;
if (p.z<zmin) return false;
return true;
}
```

Point-in-Convex Polygon

We can compute whether a point is inside a convex polygon (see Figure 22.3) by looping through the edges of the polygon and making sure the point is always in the same hemispace with regard to the edges. We start at the first vertex and compute the vector from the first to the second. Then, we build a new vector from the first vertex to the point we are testing and perform a cross product between these two vectors. With the original vector and the result of the cross product, we can compute a plane that includes the edge. Then, we just need to test which hemispace from the plane the point located to. Repeating this for each edge of the polygon and making sure all hemispace tests return the same sign, we detect whether the point is inside the polygon.

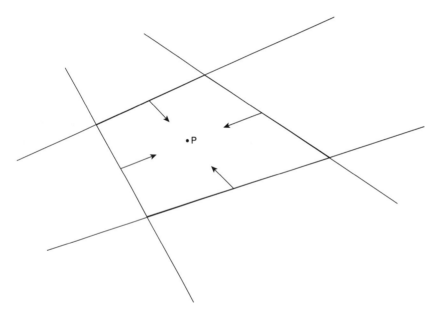

Figure 22.3 Convex polygon with all normals pointing inward.

Now, doing dot and cross products all over the place does not look very efficient. But all this can be precomputed. And after all, storing one plane per edge is just four floating-point values, which is a reasonable memory footprint. Here is the pseudocode in full. Notice how I assume normals to the polygon's faces are looking inward.

```
While we haven't done a full cycle
    Compute edge vector
    Use edge vector and normal to compute "up" vector using a
cross product
    Use edge and up to compute a plane
    If the plane value of point P is less than zero return false;
End while
Return true
```

Point-in-Polygon (Convex and Concave): Jordan Curve Theorem

Computing whether a point is inside a polygon in a general case is significantly harder than performing the test when assuming the polygon is convex. One of the main techniques used to do this involves using the Jordan Curve Theorem, which states that a point is inside a 2D closed polygon if and only if the number of crossings from a ray emanating from the point in an arbitrary direction and the edges of the polygon is odd. Think of a triangle, for example. If a point is inside the triangle, and you create a ray from that point in any direction, it will cross the triangle at exactly one point.

The elegance of the Jordan Curve Theorem is that it only needs the polygon to be closed, because open polygons do not clearly specify the notion of "in" and "out." Notice, however, that the algorithm works beautifully on convex, concave, or even malformed polygons as shown in Figure 22.4.

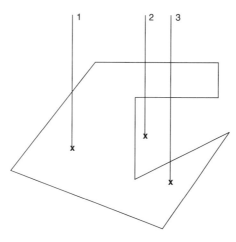

Figure 22.4 Jordan Curve Theorem with several different cases analyzed.

Thus, the algorithm can be described by the following pseudocode:

```
bool isinside(point p, polygon P)
choose an arbitrary direction... (1,0,0) is a good one
build ray r based on p and the direction
initialize count to zero
for each edge
        test ray-segment
        if crossed
                increase count
        end if
end for
return count is odd
```

So, the algorithm is O(n of edges), which is not too bad.

Point-in-Convex Object

Testing whether a point is inside a convex object is relatively straightforward and can be easily considered an extension of the point-in-convex shape test explained earlier. The 2D test works by checking the point against the line segments and making sure we are always in the same hemispace. In the 3D case, we will need to test for planes instead of line segments, but overall the approach is the same. A 3D point lies inside a 3D convex object if and only if the point is located in the same hemispace regarding the support planes of all the triangles of the object. Here is the algorithm in detail:

```
sign=sign of the point-plane test using the first plane of support
for each plane of support
    if sign is different than the point-plane test sign for the
next plane
        return false
end for
return true
```

Notice how we can perform early-bird detection because the test will return false as soon as one plane stops following the rule.

Point-in-convex object tests are very useful for collision detection. They can be efficiently performed on the convex hull of the objects we need to test. Their cost is O(number of planes), which can be greatly improved by adding a point versus bounding sphere test to discard most cases beforehand. For those cases returning a positive, we can choose between further refining the solution (if the object was actually concave) or using this simplified solution. Remember that the convex hull test can return a false positive for concave objects if the point lies in a cavity of the object. In this case, some games will require a higher precision result, and thus we will need to use an additional test to determine if there actually was a collision. A good option is to use the Jordan Curve 3D test, which is explained in the next section. But many games can use this simplified test based on convex objects with no problem at all.

Another option is to always decompose any concave objects into a set of convex objects, so this test can always be used safely. Although this strategy must be addressed carefully (sliding collisions do not work well in concave geometry), we can often avoid using a concave test, which will indeed be more costly.

If you need information on how to compute the convex hull of an object, check out the section "Computing a Convex Hull," at the end of this chapter, where a number of different strategies are presented.

Point-in-Object (Jordan Curve Theorem)

The 2D Jordan Curve Theorem explained earlier can be easily extended to 3D, thus obtaining a general point-object inclusion algorithm. The operation, again, would involve counting the intersections from the point along a ray in an arbitrary direction. If the number is odd, we are inside the object. If it is even, we are outside.

Point-in-Object (3DDDA)

The Jordan Curve method has a cost linear to the number of triangles, because we need to count intersections with a line segment. A different approach can greatly reduce this cost by increasing the memory footprint of the algorithm. It is called the 3D Digital Differential Analyzer (3DDDA). Its core idea is very simple. At load time, the process meshes, so data is stored in a 3D regular grid. Each grid cell will contain those triangles whose barycenter is located inside the cell. The grid size must be inversely proportional to the number of triangles in the mesh. So, when we need to find out whether a point is inside the mesh, all we have to do is follow the segment on a cell-by-cell basis, intersecting only with those triangles that lie in the cells we visit along the way. By doing so, we will end up testing a very low number of triangles, especially when compared to the whole mesh (see Figure 22.5).

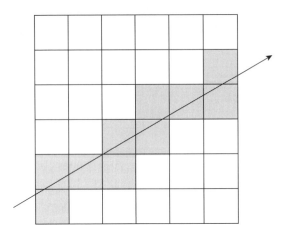

Figure 22.5 3DDDA, pictured. Visited cells are shaded.

Another improvement to this algorithm is to store one enumerated value per cell, which can be INSIDE, OUTSIDE, and DON'T KNOW. As we load the mesh, we perform our 3DDDA test stochastically in several positions of each cell and store the result. This way, whenever we need to test for point inclusion, we can save most tests. If the grid size is selected properly, most cells will be completely in or out, and thus the test will be free. For those cells that have a part inside and a part outside, we can use our regular 3DDDA code.

3DDDA was introduced by Fujimoto as a way to speed up ray-mesh tests in ray tracing. Assuming N triangles and a grid of Gx,Gy,Gz cells, and assuming triangles are spaced evenly, the cost of a 3DDDA run is $O(N/(Gx*Gy*Gz))$ for a single cell, and at most we scan max (Gx,Gy,Gz) cells along the way. So, cost is orders of magnitude below the previous test. Accelerations in the hundredths are not uncommon, with the downside being the large memory footprint left by 3DDDA.

Ray Intersection Tests

Finding which points lie inside which objects is not actually that hard. But its use is limited. The ray intersection test is much more powerful. For example, imagine a fast bullet and a collision detection routine with a relatively small target such as a can of soda. Because the can is relatively small and the bullet is incredibly fast, it could very well happen that on successive frames the bullet is on opposite sides of the soda can, but no single frame exists where the bullet is actually inside the can. Did the intersection happen? The only way to find out is to test the ray formed by the successive positions. If the ray intersected the can, the bullet hit its target.

Ray-Plane

Testing for intersection between a ray and a plane is easy (see Figure 22.6). All we have to do is analyze the ray in its parametric form:

```
X = org.x + dir.x*t
Y = org.y + dir.y*t
Z = org.z + dir.z*t
```

and the plane with the equation

```
AX + BY + CZ + D = 0
```

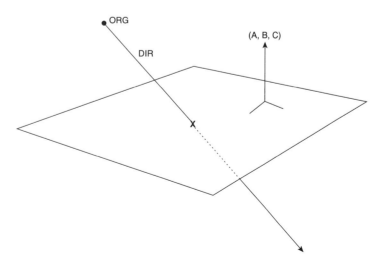

Figure 22.6 Ray-plane intersection test.

Half a page of algebra can prove that the preceding equations blend into

```
t = - (A*org.x + B*org.y + C*org.z + D) / (A*dir.x + B*dir.y +
C*dir.z )
```

Or, if you prefer a more compact notation (using the fact that (A,B,C) is the normal vector to the plane), you can say

```
t = - (n·org +D) / (n·dir)
```

Obviously, a ray parallel to the vector will return (n·dir)=0, because the dot product of perpendicular vectors equals zero. Thus, we must compute the denominator first, and if it is different from zero, use the numerator to actually compute the t parameter.

Remember that negative t values mean that the ray actually pierces the plane, but not in the direction expressed by the parametric equation of the ray. Actually, if we want the intersection to take place between two specific points in the ray, here is the usual routine:

```
compute dir as the vector from one point to the other
do not normalize dir
use the regular test
if the computed t value is in the range from zero to one
    the segment intersected the plane .end if
```

Ray-Triangle

Testing whether a ray intersects a triangle can be performed in a variety of ways. The most popular is not really a test on its own merit, but a composite of two other tests that have already been discussed. The routine would be as follows:

```
Compute the intersection between the ray and the support plane
for the triangle
If there is an intersection point, compute if that point is
actually inside the triangle using a triangle inclusion test.
```

Other solutions might be derived using linear algebra, but as far as cost is concerned, none of them offers a significant improvement over this one.

Ray-AABB Test

One of the best methods for detecting whether a ray intersects an AABB was introduced by Woo. It uses a three-step algorithm to progressively discard candidate planes, and thus performs costly computations on the minimum possible data set. The pseudocode of the algorithm is as follows:

```
From the six planes, reject those with back-facing normals
From the three planes remaining, compute the t distance on the
ray-plane test
Select the farthest of the three distances
Test if that point is inside the box's boundaries
```

Note that we are assuming we are outside of the object. If we were inside or normals were flipped for some unknown reason, step one would be negated. Thus, the overall test involves

> ➤ Six dot products to check the first step

> ➤ Three point-ray tests

> ➤ A few comparisons for the last step

Incidentally, the 4-step algorithm from the previous section can be used for object-oriented bounding boxes (OOBBs) with minor changes. The first three steps remain unchanged. The last one, however, becomes a bit more complex, as we cannot optimize some computations due to non-axial alignment of the box's support planes. Even so, Woo's algorithm would be a good solution for these cases.

Ray-Sphere Test

Let's now analyze the intersection between a ray and a sphere in 3D. Given the ray

```
R:
X = Rorg.x + Rdir.x * lambda
Y = Rorg.y + Rdir.y * lambda
Z = Rorg.z + Rdir.z * lambda
```

and the sphere defined by

```
(X-CenterX)2 + (Y-CenterY)2 + (Z-CenterZ)2 = Radius2
```

the intersection test can fail (if the ray misses the sphere), return one single solution (if the ray touches the sphere tangentially), or return two points (for a general collision). Whichever the case, the preceding equations are easily combined to yield

```
A*t2 + B*t + C = 0
```

where

```
A = Rdir.x2 + Rdir.y2 + Rdir.z2
B = 2* (Rdir.x2*(Rorg.x-CenterX) + Rdir.y2*(Rorg.y-CenterY) +
Rdir.z2*(Rorg.z-CenterZ))
C = (Rorg.x-CenterX)2 + (Rorg.y-CenterY)2 + Rorg.z-CenterZ)2 -
Radius2
```

In the preceding equation, *A* usually equals one because the ray's direction vector is normalized, saving some calculations.

Because we have a quadratic equation, all we have to do is solve it with the classic formula

```
-b +- sqrt (b2 - 4AC) / 2a
```

The quantity

```
B2 - 4ac
```

is referred to as the determinant. If it is negative, the square root function cannot be evaluated, and thus the ray missed the sphere. If it's zero, the ray touched the sphere at exactly one point. If it's greater than zero, the ray pierced the sphere, and we have two solutions, which are

```
-b + sqrt (b2 - 4AC) / 2a
-b - sqrt (b2 - 4AC) / 2a
```

Ray-Convex Hull

Computing the intersection test between a ray and a convex hull is easy. We loop through the different planes of the convex hull. If we reach the end of the list and all tests were negative (meaning both the first and second point in the ray lie outside the hull), we can stop our search. But what we are interested in are those cases in which a ray's origin has a different sign than the ray's destination. In these cases, we can be sure that a collision took place. Then all we have to do is test the segment and the plane, thus computing the effective intersection point.

Ray-General Object (3DDDA)

Computing the intersection point between a ray and a concave object is a complex issue. We can use the Jordan Curve Theorem, but because there can be several intersections, we need additional information in order to decide which one we should return. Thus, a good idea is to use a 3DDDA approach, starting from the cell closest to the origin of the ray and advancing in the direction of the ray. If one cell is OUTSIDE, we move to the next one with no test at all. When we reach the first cell where we get a DON'T KNOW value, we test for the ray with the triangles of the cell. This way the search space is small, and we can converge quickly to the point in space that marks the first collision between the ray and the general object. Again, the speed of the test has a downside of higher memory consumption.

Moving Tests

Imagine a game of snooker with balls moving around quickly. If we need to compute the interactions between the different balls efficiently and with precision, we cannot consider them to be static objects. We need to compute trajectories, making sure we detect both if a collision took place and when it took place. This is a relatively young field and only recent advances in real-time physics have made such computations possible.

Sphere: Sphere

We will now derive a test for moving spheres, which is very useful for moving objects. I will use it as an example of how to solve algebraic, restriction-based equations so we can compute collisions. You can adapt the following case for other shapes as well.

To begin with, here are the two expressions for two points moving in space. Each point is determined by its position when time=0 and its velocity vector:

```
pos_a=pos0_a + v_a*t
pos_b=pos0_b + v_b*t
```

Now, we can blend the two equations by computing the difference between them, that is, the vectorial difference between both positions:

```
pos_a-pos_b = dpos = (pos0_b-pos0_a)+(v_b-v_a)*t = dpos0 + dv*t
```

Now, let's square the equation:

```
dpos² = dpos0 + 2*dpos0*dv*t + dv²*t²
```

Expanding it to incorporate the *X*, *Y*, and *Z* terms, we get the following expression for the distance between the two sphere centers:

```
dist = sqrt        (dpos0.x² + dpos0.y² + dpos0.z² +
2*dpos0.x*dv.x*t + 2*dpos0.y*dv.y*t + 2*dpos0.z*dv.z*t + dv.x²*t²
+ dv.y²*t² + dv.z²*t²)
```

Figure 22.7 illustrates the situation described by the preceding equation. By grouping terms together, we reach the following expression:

```
dist = sqrt ( A + B*t + C*t²)
```

where

```
A = dpos.x² + dpos.y² + dpos.z² = |dpos|²
B = 2*(dpos.x*dv.x + dpos.y*dv.y + dpos.z*dv.z) = 2*(dpos dot dv)
C = dv.x² + dv.y² + dv.z²= |dv|²
```

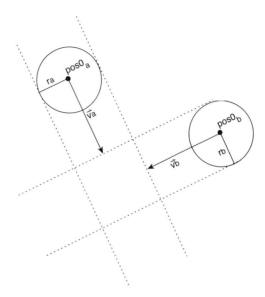

Figure 22.7 Moving sphere test.

If we forget about *dist*, and square both sides of the equation to compute *dist* squared instead, we get

```
dist² = A + B*t + C*t²
```

Now, let's incorporate the radii to check for a collision. A collision happens if, for any moment in time

```
dist = r1 + r2
```

where *dist* is the distance we were just working on, and *r1/r2* are the radii. Now, let's square the equation:

```
dist² = (r1+r2)²
```

This can now be blended with our earlier equation to produce

```
(r1+r2)² = A + B*t + C*t²
```

By rearranging terms so this equation fits with our quadratic solving formulas from school, we get

```
C*t2 + B*t + A-(r1+r2)2 = 0
```

or

```
C*t2 + B*t + A = 0
```

Assuming a change in the value of A, which right now is

$$A = dpos.x^2 + dpos.y^2 + dpos.z^2 = |dpos|^2 - (r1+r2)^2$$

The equation is solved by

```
t = -B +/- sqrt (B2 - 4AC) / 2A
```

So there is a collision if

```
B2 > 4AC
```

Then, we assume

```
B2= (2*(dpos dot dv))2 = 4*(dpos dot dv)2
4AC= 4* (|dpos|2 - (r1+r2)2) * |dv|2
```

The solution is that the collision occurs if the following is true:

```
4*(dpos dot dv)2 > 4* (|dpos|2 - (r1+r2)2) * |dv|2
```

or, for elegance:

```
(dpos dot dv)2 > (|dpos|2 - (r1+r2)2) * |dv|2
```

Point Versus Triangle Set Collision (BSP-Based)

Let's now explore one of the most popular ways of testing for collisions in a game level. The method takes advantage of the quick sorting behavior of a Binary Space Partition (BSP) tree to quickly find out where the player is standing.

Basically, we will traverse the BSP, selecting for each node the subnode in which the point is lying, according to the division plane. Remember that the planes we visit on our way to the leaf form a convex shape around the point. Logically, these planes are the closest ones to the viewer. So, all we have to do is a point versus polygon test to determine if we are actually lying in a valid region. Because the BSP will have divided the input set in half at each level, the total cost of the operation will be $O(\log_2 n)$, which is the number of levels in the BSP. Notice that we are assuming the division criteria is perfect, thus the BSP is a balanced tree.

Mesh Versus Mesh (Sweep and Prune Approach)

The last algorithm we will discuss for collision detection is very well suited for environments consisting of many different objects. This kind of problem usually requires $N \times N$ tests (all objects can collide with all other objects), which are costly and must always be avoided. Sweep and prune allows us to focus only on potential collision candidates, because most object interactions will be discarded in an early, low CPU cost stage.

The key idea is to detect bounding box overlaps (see Figure 22.8). Two bounding boxes overlap if and only if their intervals overlap in all three directions, X, Y, and Z. So, we build three lists and insert these intervals into them. By analyzing the intervals, we can quickly detect which boxes overlap and perform a fine-grained test to actually compute the collision point.

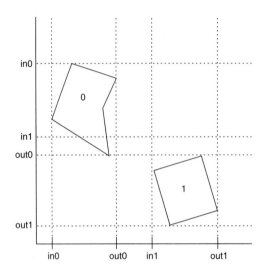

Figure 22.8 A diagram showing how sweep and prune creates intervals in the different axes.

Here is the full sweep and prune algorithm:

```
Construct 3 lists, one for each dimension.
For each object in the scene
    project each 3-dimensional bounding box onto the x,y and z
axes.
    Store these projected values as ENTRANCE or EXIT in the lists
End for
Each list contains the end-points of the intervals corresponding
to that dimension.
Sort lists by coordinate value to determine which intervals overlap
Scan the lists.
Store overlaps in X,Y and Z in a separate array
If an overlap occurs in three directions
    // fine collision algorithm goes here
end if
```

In general, such a sort will take O(n log n) time. However, we can reduce this time if we keep the sorted lists from the previous frame, changing only the values of the interval endpoints. Because there will be relatively small movements between frames, the lists will be nearly sorted, so we can sort in expected O(n) time using Insertion Sort.

Computing a Convex Hull

The convex hull of a set of points is the minimal convex object that encapsulates another object, either convex or concave. As a result, the convex hull of a convex object is itself, and convex hulls of concave objects are always bigger in volume than the original shape.

2D Solution

Several ways can be used to compute the convex hull of a set of points. In 2D, we would use the "rubberband method." This simple method computes the convex hull by using angular criteria. We start by searching the vertex in the mesh that has the minimal *X* value. Obviously, a vertex with a minimal coordinate value is always part of the convex hull. Then, we loop through the remaining vertices, looking for the vector that lies (angularly speaking) to one extreme of all the others. In other words, we must select the vertex from the set so that a segment from the original vertex to this newly added one has all other vertices located in the same hemispace. We then eliminate this new vertex and so on until we cannot add any further vertices, and we reach the starting point again.

3D Solution

Several algorithms have been proposed to create 3D convex hulls. One of the best is the Quickhull algorithm, which uses a divide-and-conquer approach. The idea is simple: Start with vertices that are part of the solution and recursively add new vertices to the solution, refining it. The implementation is quite complex.

1. Allocate a polyhedron that will hold the solution.

2. Compute the maximal simplex from the 3D vertex list. In a 3D case, we must find four points from the set that define the maximal volume tetrahedron, which will be part of our result. To compute the tetrahedron, follow these steps:

   a) Compute the points with maximum and minimum *X*, *Y*, and *Z* values.

   b) Build lines that connect the minimum and maximum distance points in each direction: Xmin to Xmax, and so on.

c) Select the longest line of the three. That's one edge of the tetrahedron.

d) Now, select the point (of the minimax set) that has the longest distance to the line. That point and the line define a triangle that is part of the solution.

e) Use the support plane of the triangle and detect the point of the minimax set that is farthest from the plane. The plane and the newly computed point define the tetrahedron, and thus the simplex.

3. Sort the points into those inside and outside of the tetrahedron. Delete those inside, because they are surely not part of the solution. Sort those outside into four groups, depending on which plane from the tetrahedron they lie outside of. If a point lies outside of more than one plane, place it randomly in one of them. Let's call these four sets the OUTSIDE set with regard to a face.

4. While there are faces in the convex hull whose outside set is not empty:

a) Find the point in the outside set that is farthest from the support plane.

b) Compute the horizon of the polyhedron as seen from the selected point. This is used to refine edges from our polyhedron that are not really part of the convex hull. To construct the horizon, we perform a depth first search starting at the triangle the candidate point lies in. At each step in the process, we cross one edge and visit the neighboring triangle. If it is visible, we cross another edge, and so on. Whenever the crossing of an edge leads to a nonvisible (in terms of the dot product between the normal and the viewpoint vector, as in culling) triangle, we store the offending edge as part of the horizon and stop the search. When the algorithm is over, we have a list of edges that are all part of the horizon.

c) Build a cone from the new vertex to the vertices on the horizon.

d) Divide the outside set into two new sets. Those points inside the cone will be deleted (because they are not part of the convex hull), whereas those outside are the new OUTSIDE set.

e) Iterate.

5. Now there are no vertices in any of the outside sets, and thus the convex hull is computed.

Quickhull is a complex algorithm. But in complexity lies efficiency. Quickhull runs in $O(n^2)$, whereas average case cost is close to $N*\log N$, which would be the optimal solution for this kind of problem.

Triangle Reduction

Another family of geometrical algorithms we will review is triangle reduction methods, which are used to create variable-resolution meshes from a base mesh. Although some games never use triangle reduction or use it at the modeling stage, many others find it useful to perform some kind of software triangle reduction. Some popular reasons for this are

➤ Selecting a level of detail for an object that can be up close or far away

➤ Using lower resolution meshes to compute shadows

➤ Tuning the game to the player's hardware capabilities at load time

Whichever your case, triangle reduction policies can be implemented either as a pre-process at load time, assuming computational cost is relatively unimportant, or as a real-time process, computing the reduced mesh in real time. Obviously, the algorithms will be different depending on your choice. Triangle reduction is not a simple process, and thus trying to compute a good multiresolution mesh in real time will definitely need some careful planning.

Vertex Collapsing

Vertex collapsing involves eliminating vertices from the base mesh using the criteria of coplanarity with neighboring vertices. It requires reconstructing the mesh once the vertex has been deleted.

Fundamentally, we will need to arrange geometrical data in memory so we can traverse the structure using both geometric and topological relationships. We will need to quickly determine which edges are connected to a certain vertex or compute by-face normals for a given face. The core of the algorithm for each vertex is to compare the per-face normals for those faces our original vertex belongs to. If the difference in the normals is below a certain threshold, we will delete the vertex from the data structure, and by traversing those edges that have actually survived, reconstruct the base mesh (see Figure 22.9). By iterative application, we will reach lower triangle rates, and thus higher performance.

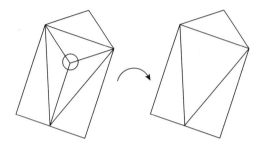

Figure 22.9 Vertex collapse. Left, original mesh. Right, mesh after the central vertex has been deleted.

Edge Collapsing

An interesting but similar approach works not on vertices, but on edges. An edge is shared by at most two triangles. Then, it is all a matter of detecting those edges whose neighboring triangles have a large index of coplanarity. If a certain threshold is met, we can delete the edge and weld the vertices at both sides of the edge together. To do so we remove the vertices at both ends of the edge and create a new one located in the midpoint between the two and on the axis formed by them. An example of edge collapse is shown in Figure 22.10.

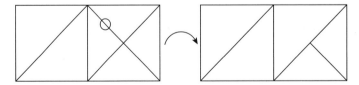

Figure 22.10 Edge collapse. Left, original mesh. Right, mesh after the highlighted edge has been deleted.

Progressive Meshes

One of the most popular real-time triangle reduction algorithms is progressive meshes, introduced by Hugues Hoppe in 1996. The algorithms we have seen so far are designed to build a low-resolution mesh from a base, high-quality model. Progressive meshes go one step beyond and allow real-time continuous level-of-detail (LOD), so we can increase and decrease triangle counts as needed and always have a model whose complexity is just right for each moment. All these benefits come from preprocessing the mesh so both the initial topology and constructive description are stored. Then, the run-time algorithm is simple, so it can be used for games.

Progressive meshes start with a base mesh, which is reduced, one edge at a time, using a variation of the edge collapse strategy outlined earlier. As we have already seen, given a mesh Mn, we can compute mesh $Mn-1$ by performing a one edge collapse. This removes one vertex and two faces exactly. Now, notice that we can revert the process and reconstruct Mn from $Mn-1$ if we store the information of the collapse: the positions of the two vertices and the connectivity of each one. This means the collapse operation is invertible. We will call the inverse operation a vertex split, because it takes one (collapsed) vertex and divides it in two.

Then, by sequencing vertex splits, we can represent any mesh by means of

> ➤ A low-quality mesh as an initial $M0$

> ➤ The ordered sequence of vertex splits we need to perform to move from $M0$ to the high-quality Mn

This is the core of the progressive mesh concept. We store a low-quality mesh and the constructive method to generate higher quality versions. Then, at runtime, we use these two structures to build a mesh that is just perfect for our needs. Meshes usually move closer or farther progressively, so we will just need to perform vertex splits or merges every few frames because sudden changes in resolution are not frequent. A series of progressive meshes is depicted in Figure 22.11, showcasing the progression from a high-quality mesh to a very low-resolution mesh.

Figure 22.11   Progressive meshes. The leftmost mesh is progressively reduced until the rightmost version is computed.

To build a progressive mesh, we must start with the high-quality version.

Progressive meshes suffer from much less popping than other methods. In the end, triangles are continually added, so the changes in appearance are very small. But sometimes we notice vertices moving, which can become a bit annoying. An improvement over the initial progressive mesh idea can be implemented to completely avoid those annoying pops and ensure an always-perfect appearance. The enhancement, called *geomorphing*, works by considering a vertex split as a continuous process, as opposed to a discrete one. When we need to split a vertex in two, we will do this progressively by beginning with two vertices that are located where the original one was, and then moving them along the axis until they reach the final position, providing a higher smoothness to our LODs.

Another, quite interesting advantage of progressive meshes comes from their suitability to the online medium. This representation makes meshes ideal for massively multiplayer games where content must be downloaded from a host in real time during the course of the game. Intuitively, imagine that a player is traversing the game world and happens to reach a zone he's never been to before, with new geometry pieces, like a castle, for example. Logically, the castle will appear from the horizon as we approach it. It is only a few pixels across and immersed in fog. Thus, we can begin by downloading *M0*, which is small and therefore efficient for transmission over a communications line. Quality will not be very good, but that's not necessary at this stage anyway. Then, we can start sending the sequence of vertex splits, so the player can always get the best representation as he moves closer to the new geometry piece. Transmitting vertex splits is very efficient because the amount of data involved is relatively small. Once we end the transmission of the whole sequence, we will have the final version of the castle persistently in memory and on our hard drive, because progressive meshes are lossless. This is one of the reasons progressive meshes work with low-quality meshes and vertex splits instead of working with high-quality versions and vertex merges. Many online games build their graphics pipelines around a progressive mesh processor for locations and items, and a terrain renderer that supports large data sets.

Nonconservative Triangle Reduction

All the algorithms we have seen so far belong to a global family called *conservative triangle reduction algorithms*. If you analyze them globally, they all start with the base mesh and try to detect unimportant elements, whether it's vertices, faces, edges, and so on. But does that really define a low-detail object? Not really. What defines a low-detail representation of an object is that, seen from the right distance, it looks very similar to the original version. Reducing triangles by selecting unimportant ones is just one of the ways to face the problem. We could simply choose to start from scratch and build a whole new mesh that represents the original one, but has fewer triangles. This new method does not guarantee we will preserve part of the original geometry data. In fact, we will generally throw it away and replace it with a totally new set of vertices, edges, and so on. This new representation will, however, look very similar to the original one when seen from a distance.

Nonconservative algorithms generally provide much better results, especially for dramatic triangle reductions where conservative algorithms fail to find unimportant data. If you need to reduce a mesh by 50 percent or more, it is likely that you will reach a point where all vertices will contribute to the object's shape, and trying to reduce even more will simply collapse some areas in the mesh and spoil the overall look. As an example, compare the four images in Figure 22.12. The top-left image is the original mesh, consisting of 1,366 triangles. The bottom-right image is the result of a nonconservative algorithm, reducing the mesh to only 21 triangles (that's 1.5% of the original cost). Notice how the algorithm has completely replaced the original object with a new one, whose shape more or less resembles it. A conservative algorithm used to that degree of reduction would simply have destroyed the object's appearance completely.

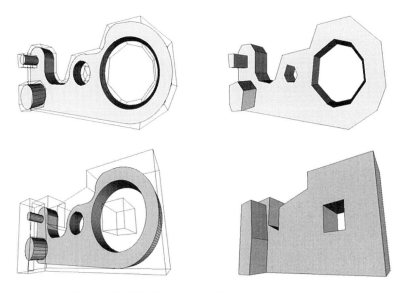

Figure 22.12   Nonconservative triangle reduction.

As an example of nonconservative triangle reduction, take the Trihedral Discretized Polyhedra Simplification (TDPS) algorithm presented by Andujar in his doctoral dissertation (reference and links in Appendix E, "Further Reading"). This algorithm reduces triangle counts by first analyzing the space occupancy and then rebuilding a new object based on this space occupancy information. Thus, it offers much better results, especially when trying to create dramatic triangle reductions. The core idea is quite simple: Construct an octree based on the space occupancy of the mesh. Octree nodes are marked as fully outside, fully inside, and on the edge. These last nodes are the ones we will recurse until a desired geometry detail level is reached. The octree stores data in the leaves as well as in the internal nodes. Looking at the leaves, we will discover the detailed space occupation information, and as we move closer to the root, shapes become coarser. Then, at runtime, a threshold is fixed so we can limit the depth of the octree traversal. We scan the octree, and as we reach the limit of our traversal with regard to the maximum threshold, we apply a marching cubes approach so we tessellate each cell into the minimum number of triangles, which is usually two. This way, a different threshold generates a different LOD, but all of them are based on space occupancy, not actual geometry. Check out the pictures in Figure 22.12 and notice how the shape-based triangle reduction policy delivers very good results where traditional decimation methods would fail.

In Closing

Geometry is the mortar from which good games are built. The methods explored in this chapter are just some of the most frequently used ones, but there are many more. The field of computational geometry is huge and always expanding. As games advance, surely new geometric tests will evolve. Be sure to check out Appendix F because there are many references to the materials covered in this chapter.

Appendix A

Performance Tuning

"Swifter, Higher, Stronger"

Olympic Motto

We are reaching the end of our journey. Our game is looking great. Performance, however, is poor. Our impressive graphics engine moves at a sluggish pace, making the final product unplayable. Too often, developers code with a high-end configuration in mind, and thus the complete product slows down in less powerful equipment. If this is your situation, time has clearly come for some performance tuning. Be prepared to spend long hours of hard work that will recover those lost frames-per-second and make your game come back from the land of the dead.

Analysis Techniques

Game code analysis is essential to ensure good performance. But analyzing code is like peeking thru a keyhole. You get very limited access to the interior, and it is hard to gather the relevant information. However, we need to find a way to shed some light on our code so we can visualize what goes on inside and, essentially, where our resources (CPU cycles, bus bandwidth, memory) are being spent. There are a number of techniques that have evolved through the years. They range from plain tricks to really involved solutions. However, all of them should give the applications programmer a clear picture of what is going on in each game loop, and what is taking away all the precious cycles.

In this first section, we will explore a variety of analysis and profiling techniques in detail. We will learn how to trace memory, time critical code sections, and extract important data from our code. In the next section, we will study how specialized tools can help us carry out this same task.

To begin with, let's specify the goals of our analysis. Fundamentally, we need to determine, for any given section of code:

- ➤ The time it takes to execute

- ➤ The memory it is consuming

By computing these values repeatedly through the code, we will be able to create full cost breakdowns: a complete picture of where clock cycles are spent and what is eating up all the RAM.

Timing

Computing the time it takes to run specific routines is relatively straightforward. All operating systems have an internal real-time clock that can be queried for the current time. The syntax might differ from one system to another, but the overall philosophy is the same. In the Win32 programming environment, for example, we can use the call:

```
long timeGetTime();
```

This call returns the amount of time, in milliseconds, elapsed since Windows booted. We have seen this call many times in the book already. You should also remember that by doing the following, we can compute the duration, in milliseconds, of any routine:

```
long t1=timeGetTime();
// here goes the code we need to time
long t2=timeGetTime();
long elapsed= t2-t1;
```

This is the easiest way to analyze time costs and, incidentally, one of the best. I recommend that you first always try to use timers when debugging long game loops. It is a good idea to break code down into sections and use `timeGetTime()` to take time samples, thus getting a clear portrait of how much each component takes to execute. For example, you could do the following:

```
long t1=timeGetTime();
recompute_logic();
long t2=timeGetTime();
```

```
compute_collisions();
long t3=timeGetTime();
render_walls();
long t4=timeGetTime();
render_AIs();
long t5=timeGetTime();
render_FX();
long t6=timeGetTime();

long timeFX=t6-t5;
long timeAI=t5-t4;
long timeWalls=t4-t3;
long timeCollisions=t3-t2;
long timeLogic=t2-t1;
```

By printing the different values to the screen (and adding other timers if needed), you can have an onscreen performance monitor that measures the different core components. Even better, you can convert them to percentage representation to see how the different pieces hold together in a graphical bar chart. This data will become priceless to ensure smooth performance. It will become trivial to detect which sections of a game level slow the engine down, who is responsible, and so on.

Then, whenever the team decides one section is too slow, it is all a matter of putting extra timers inside that section until you get an exact picture of who is responsible and how to fix it. Rigorous use of this policy has been very helpful in countless projects, because day-to-day coding frequently adds inefficient routines to games. Using the performance monitor (and saving the numbers daily in an Excel sheet, for example) is a good way to ensure that performance stays consistent through the end of the project.

A potential issue with this method is how to take timings on really fast routines. Software timers have limited resolution, and sometimes, this will make faster routines seem like they are taking zero time to execute. Win32's timeGetTime, for example, has a resolution of one millisecond. Although that is reasonably accurate for most uses, sometimes a higher resolution is desirable. After all, a game running at a stable 50 fps takes 20 milliseconds to render one frame. With that ballpark figure, it is not surprising that some components take less than one millisecond to execute, and thus cannot be measured with a call to timeGetTime.

The way to profile those components is to run them in batches, so we time not one execution but several at once. This way we can divide by the number of iterations afterward and get a better feel for the real time cost. This is really handy if you have to profile mathematical routines, simpler tests, and so on, which take less than one millisecond to execute. Here is an example:

```
long time1=timeGetTime();
for (i=0;i<iterations;i++)
    {
    // really important routine goes here
    }
long time2=timeGetTime();
double elapsed=(double)(time2-time1)/iterations;
```

After this sequence, `elapsed` holds the average duration of the routine in milliseconds. The larger the number of iterations, the less relevant the overhead of the `for` loop, and thus the more reliable the measure. Loop unrolling can often be used for more accurate measurements because sometimes the loop will introduce perturbations in the measurements.

You have to be careful with this approach, though, because the measurements will not be completely correct. Performance will be a bit on the optimistic side due to the fact that repeated calls can somehow take advantage of the code and data caches found in most modern-day CPUs, causing the code to execute faster than it would in normal conditions. But the result will provide a qualitative estimate of your code's speed.

Memory Footprints

Once you are in control of all the timing in your game loops, it is then time to begin profiling memory use. Measuring how much memory is spent in certain portions of your program is extremely important. Memory leaks can cause your software to malfunction, and bad memory management can sometimes yield worse than expected performance due to memory trashing. Optimizing for speed only is never a good policy. Memory management errors frequently render the game unplayable.

We will begin by analyzing the memory balance of a given call. By testing the total available memory before and after the call, we can perform a subtraction and discover how much memory was taken away (or returned) by the call. The approach is very similar to timing a critical portion of our code, as shown in the following code snippet:

```
long m1=available_memory();
// here goes the code to test memory for
long m2=available_memory();
long consumed_memory=m2-m1;
```

Unfortunately, the implementation details for such a mechanism are a little more complex than simple timing routines. In multitasking environments, memory can be taken away by another program, so using the available memory as an indicator can be tricky. Should we query for the total physical memory or the virtual memory available to this application?

A very popular technique is to go one step further and write our own memory manager, which keeps track of memory allocated and deallocated by the application. The most popular method is to overwrite the memory allocation calls. So instead of using the standard `new` and `delete` calls, a user-provided set is called, and memory is traced in the process. This is possible if you create a new set of calls and assign them to the standard namespace used by system calls. Here is an example:

```
using namespace std;    // overwrite the standard namespace calls

unsigned long usedmemory=0;    // Count of blocks allocated.
unsigned long maxusedmemory=0;    // Count of blocks allocated.
unsigned long minusedmemory=0;    // Count of blocks allocated.
int numallocations;
unsigned long maxallocations=0;    // Count of blocks allocated.


// User-defined operator new.
void *operator new(size_t blocksize)
{
numallocations++;
usedmemory+=blocksize;
```

```
if (usedmemory>maxusedmemory) maxusedmemory=usedmemory;
if (numallocations>maxallocations) maxallocations=numallocations;
return malloc(blocksize);
}
```

Notice how this operation stores some relevant information, such as number of undeleted allocations, total used memory, and so on. In addition, we call the C `malloc` function to ensure that memory allocation is actually performed. For completeness, here is the equivalent code for the `delete` operator:

```
void operator delete(void *pointer)
{
numallocations--;
usedmemory-=_msize(pointer);
if (usedmemory<minusedmemory) minusedmemory=usedmemory;
free(pointer);
}
```

Notice how we use the `_msize` function, provided with all C implementations, which tells us the allocated size of a given pointer. Thus, we can keep track of the number of open handles (undeleted memory blocks), total amount of memory, and so on.

Now all you have to do is display the memory allocation information at runtime. The number of blocks and total used memory should remain more or less stable. This is a clear sign that all calls to `new` have their corresponding `delete`. Additionally, as soon as objects are destroyed at application shut down, we should see a diminishing number of allocated blocks to finally end up with zero blocks and reserved memory. Any change in this behavior is most likely caused by a memory leak.

As a more involved solution, we can add functionality to the overloaded `new` and `delete` calls, so memory management is actually performed by the application. We would allocate a large memory pool at boot time and use our homegrown `new` and `delete` operators to manage it. This way we can implement a specific memory management scheme that increases performance for our title.

Knowing the memory access patterns of an application definitely gives the application programmer some advantage over the standard, multipurpose `new` and `delete` calls. In console titles, for example, it is very important to reduce internal fragmentation because memory is usually scarce. Thus, implementing the memory architecture manually provides an additional level of control.

Analysis Tools

So far we have seen how to profile our code manually, which gives us a great deal of information and control at the cost of long working hours. On top of that, some tools can help us monitor our code efficiently, detect critical zones, and keep an eye on memory use automatically. These tools are usually called *code profilers*, and they should help us visualize as much information about our code as possible. Many programming environments such as Borland's, Microsoft's Visual C++, and most others come with built-in profilers. Traditionally, these packages provide you with lots of different data: percentage of CPU use for each routine, call stacks, and so on. Microsoft's Visual C++ environment, for example, gives you complete information on the percentage of CPU time taken by each function in your code. It can also help you track down memory issues, such as leaks, and should be really helpful in your personal battle with bugs.

Beyond commercial profilers, some higher complexity tools can help us out in ensuring top performance for our game. A good example would be VTune by Intel (see Figure A.1), a code analyzer, optimizer, and memory checker. VTune is very helpful if you need to track your code closely. It has a built-in hotspot detector that can help us find and graphically represent where the CPU time is being spent. Then, there's the Code Coach, which analyzes your code and provides tuning advice oriented to increase its performance. Also, VTune comes with a host of assembly-language optimizers and analyzers. The dynamic assembly analyzer, for example, provides a thorough analysis of the dynamic behavior of your application, that is, cache use, branch prediction, branch target buffer, and so on. Remember, many clock cycles are lost at the micro-level because of bad dynamic policies. Nonsequential memory accesses stall the cache and so on.

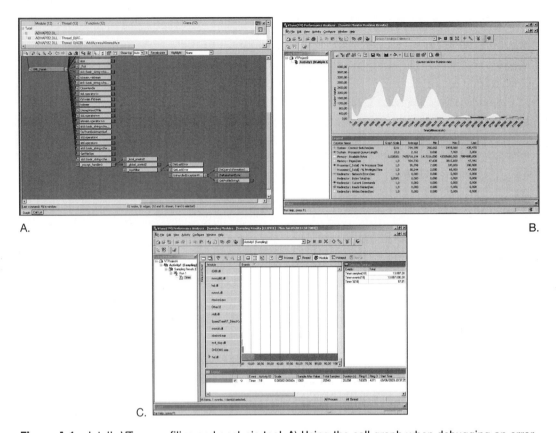

A.

B.

C.

Figure A.1   Intel's VTune profiling and analysis tool. A) Using the call graph when debugging an error
inside an XML parser. VTune shows us the offending call. B) The counter monitor showing
CPU load on an application. Notice it is very high when we are loading data and diminishes afterward. C) The module sampler showing an application making heavy use of the
DirectX Hardware Abstraction Layer (HAL).

Detecting Bottlenecks

Armed with our toolbox of analyzers and tools, it is now time to actually optimize that
piece of game code. Generally speaking, slow code is usually caused by a slower than
expected subsystem that drags the whole performance down. The same way a herd of
sheep advances as slowly as the slowest one, code is frequently dragged down by a
slow component that requires further optimization. That component is called the
bottleneck, and part of the solution begins by locating the offending code so we can
improve its performance and make a huge impact on the overall results. It makes no
sense to spend time optimizing code that's actually performing well.

Bottlenecks are usually located in one of four major areas: application, data transfer, geometry, and rasterization (see Figure A.2). The application stage runs the game logic, AI, collision detection, and so on. It is performed fully by the CPU, although some examples of hardware-accelerated collision detection are beginning to arise. Then, a data transfer phase is used to deliver data to the hardware using buses: geometry, textures, lights, and so on. Data transfer depends on many components. The CPU speed will determine the rate at which data is sent, the bus architecture and speed will tell us how much bandwidth we have to perform the transfer, and the graphics subsystem can provide a host of features that will significantly enhance or degrade performance. Once data is in the graphics subsystem, two stages are performed sequentially: First, the geometry stage illuminates and transforms data to screen coordinates. Second, rasterization actually paints pixels to the screen. These are the four mission-critical components for any game engine. However, there are other secondary sources of bottlenecks, such as audio, disk I/O, or input processing. But application, data transfer, geometry, and rasterization are the four main components, and thus most problems arise from them. These four account for most of the processing time, so we will end up optimizing those components that make a bigger impact. Input processing rarely takes a significant piece of the pie, so the potential for improvement is limited.

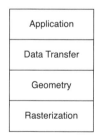

Figure A.2 The four stages suitable for optimization.

Now, let's see how to determine which component is the bottleneck. This is a trial-and-error process, albeit a very scientific one. You must vary the workload of the section you are analyzing while trying not to impact the rest of the code. Then, study how performance varies as the workload is modified. Alternatively, try to shut down all phases but the one you are analyzing and vary the workload of that phase to measure performance variations. Recall that we learned how to build performance monitors that graphically show us how much time is being spent in each portion of the code. Now, it is a matter of using them to detect slower than expected zones.

Application, for example, can be the bottleneck if your AI is too slow or collision detection is taking too long to execute. To detect these situations, all you have to do is attach the game logic to a `null` driver, so the geometry and rasterization stage are basically idle. For example, take all the calls that actually render geometry and deactivate them. Make sure any scene traversal operations (quadtrees, BSPs, and so on) are also inactive. Using a performance monitor such as the one explained in the "Timing" section, you should see all the geometry and the rendering calls consuming zero or very little resources. Does the performance increase, or does it basically stay unchanged? If no improvement is visible, your game logic is the bottleneck: Even with no graphics, in this case, performance stands still. In the next section, I will propose several ways of improving game logic performance.

Detecting a data transfer problem is a twofold process because we can be suffering a bottleneck transferring either textures or geometry (or both). To test for a texture bottleneck, simply replace your texture set with a different one where all textures are scaled down. Dividing texture size by a factor of two or even four is a good idea. Dividing by four means that you are transferring one sixteenth (or approximately 6%) of the initial volume of data. If performance increases, the application was texture bound, and we will need to work on ways to spend less time transferring textures. Do not forget that one image is not only worth a thousand words, but also costs a thousand words. Textures take lots of memory, and thus take a long time to transfer.

Detecting if the problem lies in the geometry transfer is a bit trickier. We could try to send fewer triangles down the pipeline because this would vary the workload at this stage. But as a side effect, we would be influencing the geometry stage as well (less vertices would be transformed and lit), so our analysis would not be very accurate. The best way to detect a geometry transfer problem is to vary not the number of primitives but the format. We can change colors from floats to unsigned bytes, simplify normal encoding, and so on. This way the geometry stage is actually processing the same amount of data, and all performance variation can surely be attributed to the change in the geometry transfer stage. If performance varies significantly, we need to work on optimizing this stage.

Detecting a geometry bottleneck is the hardest of all. It is difficult to isolate the geometry pipeline and profile it without causing undesired side effects to the neighboring phases. We might attempt one technique to stress test the geometry stage and end up affecting the rasterizer stage as well. Thus, indirect methods must be used frequently because a frontal assault to the problem is often not possible. Generally speaking, the geometry stage includes scene traversal, transforms, and lighting. Testing for lighting issues is relatively straightforward. All we have to do is remove some or all light sources from the scene and see how performance evolves. If it varies greatly, lots of time was spent in the lighting portion of the geometry stage, and that means we were lighting bound. This occurs frequently in older graphics cards or if we are using many light sources. Traversal and transforms are the hardest to test for. Altering this code will definitely affect the rasterizer stage because objects will change their state from visible to invisible. Thus, it is not easy to detect when our transform engine is simply taking up too many resources. As a first approach, we could profile the rasterizer and application separately and, if neither of them seems to be causing a bottleneck, we can be sure the geometry stage is responsible. A second alternative is to use carefully located timers, so we can take samples without affecting the rest of the code.

Additionally, testing for a bottleneck in the rasterizer stage is really straightforward. These bottlenecks appear whenever the graphics hardware has problems painting the amount of pixels we are feeding it with. Thus, the easiest way to test for such a scenario is to reduce the size of the window or graphics mode resolution. This causes the hardware to render fewer pixels. A significant performance gain is a clear signal that our rasterizer was dragging performance down, and thus needs optimization. An alternative method is to use a depth-complexity image, which will help us visualize the amount of overdraw we are suffering. Overdraw kills performance at the rasterizer stage because the same pixel gets painted many times. We will discuss how to build depth-complexity images in the section "Tuning the Rasterizer Stage."

General Optimization Techniques

We know our code is slow. We have identified the portion that is dragging performance down. Now, let's try to improve its performance by optimizing it. But first, a clarification is needed. Some years ago, all you needed to optimize game code was a thorough knowledge of assembly language. Compilers were not that good, and thus transforming the offending piece of code into hand-written assembly language magically boosted performance. Today's games are much more complex, and optimization generally comes from careful algorithmic analysis and not as much from down-to-the-metal coding. On the other hand, compilers have improved performance spectacularly, and thus there's less potential in hand coding your critical sections. Many times you will spend long hours figuring out the best assembly implementation, only to end up with more or less the same performance. Thus, let's start by reviewing some general techniques that should help you regardless of the nature of your code. In later sections, we will move on to optimization recommendations for each of the four phases.

Choose Your Enemy

Focus on small portions of code that take lots of resources. It makes no sense to spend time working on a linear piece of code. Evil hides in loops, especially when lots of iterations and complex processing goes on inside. So, begin by carefully selecting your optimization target. Optimizing is a time-consuming, mind-bending process, and it better pay off in the end. Recursion is also a great hiding place for slow code. Take a look at those tree building routines to make sure each recursion takes as little time as possible to execute.

Precompute Everything

Study your code carefully and detect values that are computed in complex arithmetic functions. Does your code use trigonometric functions, random numbers, or any other kind of complex mathematical routine? Try to tabulate those so the only processing that takes place inside the loop is the table lookup. Code such as the following example is going to consume more CPU cycles than you might expect:

```
float acc=0;
for (i=0;i<1000;i++)
    acc=acc+i*sin(x*i);
```

Substituting the sin call with a table lookup (and precomputing the sine function into that table) produces a five times speed increase on a regular PC. Hopefully, this simple example will show you the importance of avoiding expensive computations inside tight loops.

Simplify Your Math

Not all mathematical operators are equally fast. Traditionally, additions (or subtractions) were faster to compute than multiplies, which in turn were faster than divides. Today, performance varies greatly from one platform to another. On a regular PC, a divide costs one and a half times a multiply, so it is a good idea to check for performance on your target platform. The following two snippets perform the same task, but the second version only has 60 percent of the timing cost of the divide version:

```
float acc=1000;
for (long i=0;i<100;i++)
    acc=acc/2.0;

float acc=1000;
for (long i=0;i<100;i++)
    acc=acc*0.5;
```

Some operations that should be avoided at all costs are square roots, logarithmic operators, and so on. Try to simplify equations and, if you really need to use complex math routines, tabulate them beforehand.

Also, be especially careful with operations that require type conversion. Adding integers to floats and so on, means the CPU must perform type conversions internally, which takes time to compute. Try to plan your code so type changes are kept to a minimum.

Additionally, rearrange your math operations so you take advantage of the less-costly CPU instructions. Here are two simple examples:

```
a*b + a*c  a*(b+c); Gets rid of one multiply
b/a + c/a = (1/a)*(b+c); changes one division for one multiply,
which is usually cheaper.
```

The distributive, associative, and commutative laws of arithmetic can help you find the optimal representation for any expression, so the least computations need to be performed.

Store Data Efficiently

Using unneeded precision will significantly increase your memory footprint and will also have a clear impact on performance as well. Try to store data efficiently, using the minimum bits possible. Color interpolation is a good example. Too often, floating-point values are used for color representation, and in the end, colors end up being displayed on a CRT screen that actually does not support that much precision. Using bytes should suffice and decreases memory footprint by a factor of four. It also allows the CPU to use cheaper, byte-based operations or even things like Intel's MultiMedia eXtensions (MMX). As an example, imagine that you need to interpolate two vectors of color values. The original, float-based routine, would be the following, which requires two float multiplies and one float addition per cycle:

```
void interpolate_vector_float(float *v1,float *v2,float *v3,int
num,float alpha)
{
int i;

float alphainv=1-alpha;
for (i=0;i<num;i++)
    {
    v3[i]=v2[i]*alpha+v1[i]*alphainv;
    }
}
```

Note how we have precomputed `alphainv` before entering the loop to maximize performance. Then, a byte-based approach would be as follows:

```
void interpolate_vector_byte(unsigned char *v1,unsigned char
*v2,unsigned char *v3,int num,float alpha)
{
int i;

unsigned char balpha=(unsigned char)(alpha*255);
unsigned char balphainv=255-balpha;
for (i=0;i<num;i++)
    {
    unsigned int tmp=v2[i]*balpha+v1[i]*balphainv;
```

```
    tmp=(tmp>>8);
    v3[i]=tmp;
    }
}
```

Notice how we prepare both `alpha` and `alphainv` in bytes, so the interpolation is actually multiplied by 256. Hence, the right-shift we perform keeps data in bytes. As a result, the byte version is twice as fast as the float version, and the data set occupies one fourth of the original version. Sometimes the extra precision will be needed, but getting used to smaller data types improves the performance of your code.

Forget *Malloc()* and *Free()*

Memory allocation routines should be avoided at all costs inside game loops, which need to be optimal. `Malloc()` and `free()` incur a significant performance hit, which you simply cannot afford inside a tight loop. At load time, place all your memory allocation outside critical sections. Then, use static data or a homegrown memory manager to handle your memory needs during rendering. As a short example, take a look at the following innocent code:

```
for (long k=0;k<1000000;k++)
    int i=1;
```

Very simple, right? Now, take a look at this almost identical version:

```
for (long k=0;k<1000000;k++)
    {
    int *i=new int;
    int i=1;
    delete i;
    }
```

The first version took three milliseconds to run. The dynamic memory version took one and a half seconds. It is understandable because of the large number of calls, but still, keeping `malloc` and `free` (or `new` and `delete`, if you prefer) outside of critical loops is definitely part of any recipe for success.

Be Linear

Most modern CPUs come with built-in caches that make sequential access to memory extremely efficient. Every time an element is requested, the element is copied to cache memory along with all its memory neighborhood. This means subsequent linear accesses do not need to reach out for main memory, but instead can get the data from the fast cache memory. It takes a bit of coding discipline to traverse structures linearly, but it generally pays off in the long run: Less cache misses mean higher performance.

Watch Out for Pointers

This rule is a corollary of the previous rule. Often, large programs end up with layered data sets, where we can access attributes deep inside the structure by using pointer indirections (as shown in Figure A.3).

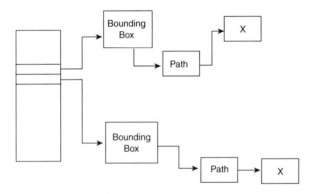

Figure A.3 Data structure showing the risk in highly branching structures and linear accesses.

In the figure, we have an array of pointers to objects called obj. Each object, in turn, has an attribute that stores a pointer to the object's bounding box. The bounding box has a pointer to the minimal-value point, and in addition, a point has a pointer to a float that stores its X-value.

Now, performing such an access can seem highly sophisticated, but it is not. Each indirection means the CPU must scan a completely different area in memory, so sequential accesses are destroyed. This means each indirection is a cache miss, which can stall the CPU and completely bog down performance.

How do we get rid of pointer indirections? Well, many times we can't. We simply need to jump around like a monkey on a tree. On the other hand, sometimes many indirections can be precomputed outside the loop. For example:

```
for( int i = 0; i < numPixels; i++ )
    {
    rendering_context->back_buffer->surface->bits[i] = some_value;
    }
```

can be rewritten as:

```
unsigned char *back_surface_bits = rendering_context->back_buffer-
>surface->bits;
for( int i = 0; i < numPixels; i++ )
    back_surface_bits[i] = some_value;
```

Application

Now we enter the arena of tuning specific subsystems, which is where most performance is hidden. We will begin by tuning the application/game logic phase. Among all the subsystems, this is the one that requires deeper knowledge about what the application is doing at each step. Let's face it, performance gains in the application stage rarely come from coding a routine straight into assembly. Algorithmic optimization can yield much better results. Rearranging data, simplifying some AI processes, and so on can produce significant speed increases.

My first suggestion is to use monitoring and profiling techniques to create a statistical chart of where time is being spent. Identify major subsystems and assign a percentage of CPU time to them. These will include collision detection, AI, network (for multiplayer titles), sound, input processing, and so on. Now focus on those subsystems that show the greatest potential. Optimizing everything is most likely unfeasible because of time constraints.

If your problem lies within the AI code, start by realizing that AI time is usually computed as:

```
Time=Time for Idle AI*number of idle AIs + Time for active
AI*number of active AIs
```

Typically, not all AI entities are active simultaneously. Those far from the viewer are in an idle state, which makes them consume less resources (think of an enemy located two miles away from the viewer). These AIs just need very quick routines that are used to discard them. Reducing the global number of AIs will definitely improve performance, but at the cost of sacrificing gameplay. Thus, my advice is to focus on three areas:

➤ Discarding idle AIs faster

➤ Discarding more AIs as idle

➤ Accelerating the active AI code

Thus, you can implement better spatial subdivision and indexing to ensure that the test that determines whether an AI is considered active or idle is faster. Dividing your world into chunks or zones and storing the AIs in each zone in the same structure, for example, ensures that the test can be done trivially. As you compute the active zones for graphics processing (by using portal rendering, BSPs, and so on), you are simultaneously determining which AIs will be activated. Any approach that has to do with manually scanning AI lists to find out which ones to keep on and off is inherently evil because performance will degrade if the number of AIs increases.

Another option is to lower the threshold at which you deactivate AIs. This makes the number of active (and hence CPU hungry) AIs lower and improves performance as well. You can either consider AIs as fully idle and fully active or implement an AI level-of-detail (LOD) policy. Using AI LODs involves creating several copies of the AI routine, which carry out the same actions with different levels of detail. In a game involving lots of AIs, such as a *3D RTS*, a good example would be a crossings processor. In our example, a fully active AI will have a path finding module, which will compute paths through the level, and a low-level crossing processor, which resolves those situations in which two units must cross each other. For a semiactive unit, we still need the path finding code (gameplay would be broken if these units could cross obstacles). But most likely, we will be able to shut down the crossing processor. We won't be watching distant units as closely, and after all, skipping a crossing (and simply running into each other) will probably not affect gameplay that much. This way we can reduce CPU cost.

An alternative option is to actually accelerate the cost of the high-detail, active AIs. This requires careful analysis and must be tackled on a case-by-case basis. Maybe your AI collision detection is too precise and slow, and can be sped up. Maybe the rule system has too many rules. Maybe the script interpreter is simply too slow. Again, know your code and try to make the most of it.

Another area within the application stage to watch out for is audio processing. The cost of this stage can skyrocket if you stack too many audio tracks, or the compression standard uses too much CPU resources. Formats like MP3 require complex codecs, which take up significant system resources. Some platforms will come with hardware-assisted decoders, but watch out for performance if you begin stacking sound layers. Under software emulation mode, performance decreases linearly to the number of channels.

Efficient Data Transfer

The data transfer stage can yield impressive improvement ratios and is relatively straightforward to optimize, making it an ideal target for us. Again, we will talk about techniques for geometry and textures separately because each deserves a different solution.

Texture optimization must always start with a serious diagnostic of where the problem comes from. To begin with, all textures should be in GPU memory whenever possible, and texture swapping must be kept to a minimum. Thus, start by computing the memory size of each texture map and end up with a complete texture budget that summarizes how much RAM your textures are consuming. Most likely, they will not fit in video memory; thus, swapping will be slowing your application down.

Then it is time to optimize texture formats, so less space is required for them. Take a look at your target platform and API: Which efficient internal representation formats are supported? Most APIs support many creative encoding formats that will reduce memory footprints. Using palletized maps is just one of the options, but you can also choose to implement texture compression algorithms, such as DXT, which store textures compressed in video memory. Another issue to watch out for is the abuse of alpha channels. A texture map that is to be used for alpha testing (not blending) should have no more than one bit for alpha. An interesting format is RGB5_A1, defined as five bits for R,G,B (providing 32 intensity levels for each component) and one bit for alpha. This format uses 16 bits per pixel, whereas encoding in traditional RGBA mode would take up 32. Some quality might be lost in the process, but 15 bits for color is perfectly appropriate for most textures.

Once the right format is found, it is time to work on texture sizes. The larger the map, the better the quality, but also the more memory it will take and the longer it will take to download to the graphics subsystem. Thus, it is very important to audit each and every texture to make sure it has the smallest possible size. Build a test application and test the same object with two textures, the original and one reduced in size. Consider the added quality versus reduced size equation, and make sure textures are as small as they can be but no smaller. We do not want texture maps to blur, but unnecessary detail will certainly hurt performance.

Sometimes, a large texture can be avoided with two smaller maps and some multipass trickery. In Chapter 18, "Texture Mapping," we discussed how a detail texture could be alpha-blended with the base map to create a large, nontiling texture map. This is very important in game consoles, where memory is a major concern. Using multitextured detail textures is an extremely popular way of offering great texture quality with low memory footprint.

Another issue to watch out for is the use and abuse of mipmapping. Mipmapping allows for better filtering by storing several prefiltered copies of the same texture map, each half the size of the previous one. Then, the one that more closely resembles the size of the onscreen primitive will be used. The good news is that quality is significantly increased. The downside is that a mipmapped texture map takes up double the memory of the original version, so mipmapping must be used with care. It only makes sense in games using large viewing distances, and many times, it can simply be avoided by using detail textures that fade away with distance.

Some additional advice on texture maps is to make sure you consolidate your texture lists. Too often, modeling packages apply the same texture to several objects, creating more than one texture identifier for the same map. If not treated with care, this may result in the same texture map being loaded into memory. This problem can always be avoided by using a preprocessing material list and storing unique identifiers only.

Once all these techniques are in place, you might however have to code a texture caching engine if your maps still do not fit in video memory. This way you can decide which texture maps are stored in video memory, so performance is maximized. Both simple and more involved solutions are usually available. In the simplest form, you will only need to assign priorities to texture maps, so the API's caching engine knows which maps should be prioritized into video memory. Under OpenGL, texture priorities are supported via the `glPrioritizeTextures` interface, which has the syntax:

```
void g|PrioritizeTextures( Glsizei n,const Gluint *textures,
const Glclampf *priorities)
```

Using this interface, we pass the number of textures to assign priorities to, an array with their texture identifiers, and a second array with values in the [0..1] range. Higher priority values mean higher probability of being stored in video memory, and a texture with priority set to zero will most likely never be stored in video memory. Similar functionality is available in DirectX using the following interface, which is a member of the `IDirect3DResource8` class:

```
DWORD SetPriority(DWORD PriorityNew);
```

This method can be applied to regular textures (`IDirect3DTexture8`), cube maps (`IDirect3DCubeTexture8`), volume textures (`IDirect3DVolumeTexture8`), and so on. Again, higher values are used to specify a texture that is to be stored in video memory, as often as possible.

Another, more involved solution is to manually build a texture cache engine from scratch, overriding the one supplied by the API. You can add a code layer to store a fixed amount of texture maps in video memory, and swap them in and out as needed. Both OpenGL and DirectX provide mechanisms to determine whether a given texture map is actually stored in video or system memory. Under OpenGL, the `glAreTexturesResident` call will take a list of texture identifiers as a parameter and return a list detailing which ones are currently stored in video memory. Under DirectX, the same functionality is available.

Tuning the geometry transfer must also start with an auditing phase: How much does each vertex weigh? Are you using the right format to ensure minimal download time? Colors as floats are often a waste, and unsigned bytes are perfectly valid. Other times, you will be able to precompute the lighting, so you will not pass per-vertex normals at all.

Another, more aggressive option is to send compressed data down the pipeline and expand it internally using a shader. Vertices can sometimes be sent as bytes, thus dividing the memory footprint by four. This approach would require a shader-based quantization/dequantization routine, which can only be implemented under some architectures.

The most powerful way of optimizing the geometry transfer is to work on a GPU-based cache memory, which ensures that geometry is transferred only when needed. Most modern accelerators allow developers to place geometry directly on GPU memory, so it is only transferred once and reused through many rendering loops. Under OpenGL, this is achieved by using Compiled Vertex Arrays or, even better, through proprietary extensions such as `Vertex_Array_Range` from NVIDIA or `Vertex_Array_Object` from ATI. Under DirectX, the same behavior can be triggered by working on the properties of the vertex buffer. For static geometry, we will use write-only vertex buffers and fill them only once. This tells the DirectX driver that data will not be updated at a later stage, and thus can be optimized. Similar tricks can be performed on dynamic memory as well, but be careful: Video memory is often slow to write, and thus careful planning is required. As an example, PC video memory is uncached; thus, the best way to get decent performance is to write it sequentially so you can make the most of the write combiners present in modern-day architectures. Therefore, it is common to work on a double-buffered level. One buffer stored in main memory is used to work on the geometry, and once data is ready, it is sent to video memory using block transfers to maximize performance. As usual, know your architecture to ensure that you do the right thing.

Tuning the Geometry Pipeline

The overall workload of the geometry stage is directly related to the amount of processed primitives (vertices, usually). It is also dependent on the amount of transforms to be applied, number of lights, and so on. Thus, being efficient in the way we handle these objects is the best way to ensure maximum performance.

We will begin by making sure the minimum number of transforms are applied to a given primitive. For example, if you are concatenating several transform matrices (such as a rotation and a translation) to the same object, make sure you compose them into one matrix, so in the end only one matrix is applied to vertices. Many modern APIs will perform this operation internally, but often we will have to combine hand-computed matrices ourselves. Remember that the following code duplicates performance because we have precomputed the resulting matrix manually:

```
matrix m1,m2;

for (I=0;I<1000;I++)
    {
    point transformedvertices[I]=m2*(m1*originalvertices[I]);
    }
```

It needs to perform 2000 point-matrix multiplies: 1000 to compute `m1*originalvertices[I]` and 1000 to multiply that result by `m2`. Rearranging the code to:

```
matrix m3=m2*m1;

for (I=0;I<1000;I++)
{
point transformedvertices[I]=m3*originalvertices[I];
}
```

duplicates performance because we have precomputed the resulting matrix manually. This kind of philosophy can be applied whenever we have hierarchical transforms. A good example is a skeletal animation system, where we need to concatenate one limb's local transforms to those of the ascendants in the skeletal hierarchy.

It is also a good idea to use connected primitives whenever possible because they send the same data using less primitive calls than unconnected ones. The most popular type of such primitives is triangle strips, which avoid sending redundant vertices that add no information and take up bus bandwidth. An object stored using triangle strips can require about 60–70 percent of the primitives from the original, nonconnected object. Any model can easily be converted to triangle strips by using any of the stripping libraries available (many of them are free). NVIDIA has been offering the NVTriStrip library and header files to the developer community for some time now. Usage is very straightforward, and a number of options are supported. We can choose to merge all strips in a long strip using degenerate vertices, we can optimize for vertex caches, and so on. Other triangle stripping options exist as well. Libraries, such as Brad Grantham's ACTC, do a remarkable job of consolidating triangle meshes and building strips from them. Download the latest release from `www.plunk.org/~grantham/public/ actc/index.html`.

Indexed primitives are also headed in the same direction. In any solid object, the same vertex will be sent many times through the geometry stage because it will belong to different, connected faces. Preindexing the mesh allows us to divide the object into geometry (that is, unique vertices that compose it) and topology (that is, face loops). Then, transforms can only be applied to the unique vertex list, which will be much shorter than the initial, nonindexed version. Remember that most APIs allow us to combine connected and indexed primitives for even better performance.

As far as lighting goes, many hardware platforms can only support a specific number of hardware light sources. Adding more lamps beyond that limit will make performance drop radically because any extra lamps will be computed on the software. Be aware of these limits and implement the required mechanisms so lamp number never exceeds them. For example, it doesn't makes sense to illuminate each vertex in the game level with all the possible lamps. Only a few of them will be within a reasonable distance to influence the resulting color. A lamp selection algorithm can then be implemented so closer lamps are used, and the rest, which offer little or no contribution, are discarded, thus making sure hardware lighting is always used.

Remember also that different kinds of light sources have different associated costs. Directional lights (which have no origin and only a direction vector, such as the sun) are usually the cheapest, followed by omni lights (lights located at a point in space, lighting equally in all directions). In addition, spotlights (cones of light with origin, direction, and aperture) are the most expensive to compute. Keep this in mind when designing your illumination model.

Tuning the Rasterizer Stage

Rasterization is where the raw power of the graphics subsystem is shown. However, some clever planning can significantly enhance performance here as well. Keep in mind that we are talking about drawing pixels onscreen. In an ideal world, we would paint each pixel exactly once so zero overdraw would be achieved. Under these circumstances, and assuming the screen is SX pixels wide and SY pixels high, we would be painting exactly $SX*SY$ pixels.

But this is seldom the case. We end up redrawing the same pixels over again, consuming fill rate and making the Z-buffer go mad in the process. To begin with, we need a diagnostic of the situation so we can understand how much overdraw there is in our rendering loop. Therefore, we need to compute a depth-complexity image (see Figure A.4), an image that graphically depicts how much overdraw there is.

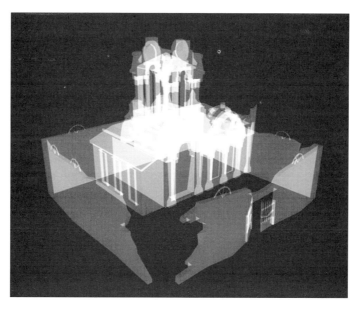

Figure A.4   Depth-complexity image.

To compute such an image, all we have to do is activate an additive blending function, such as glBlend(GL_ONE,GL_ONE), and render all primitives with texturing disabled and colored in plain white. The result will be an image brighter in those areas where overdraw exists. As areas get darker, it means we are rendering with less overdraw. Now, take a look at the picture in Figure A.4 and try to understand what is causing overdraw. Can you rearrange your code in such a way that overdraw is reduced? Turning culling on, for example, eliminates roughly 50 percent of all incoming triangles due to their alignment and will surely reduce overdraw. But what else can be done? Do you need to add specific occlusion-detection code? Maybe your hardware supports occlusion queries, and you can get that up and running in very little time.

Another factor that has an impact on rasterization speed is primitive Z-ordering. The way Z-buffers work, it is more efficient to send primitives front-to-back than the other way around. The reason becomes obvious if you focus for a second on a specific pixel of the screen. If you paint back-to-front, each new primitive is accepted, needs to be textured and lit, and updates the Z-buffer position. This means lots of overdraw. Now, if you start with the closest primitive, you will discard all subsequent primitives early in the pipeline because their Z-value will not make it to the Z-buffer. This means part of the lighting and texturing will be saved, and performance will increase. Sometimes it is not easy to sort all scene triangles front-to-back exactly, or it is too costly. But it is not that hard to do it roughly, achieving a significant increase in the process. If you use a BSP you can traverse it so you are rendering front-to-back. Quadtrees and octrees can also be treated this way. Portal systems can also be rendered front-to-back if you use the recursion level as your sorting mechanism. For example, paint rooms as you propagate calls through them, and you will ensure front-to-back ordering. None of these three approaches will perform total ordering, but making sure most triangles come in the right order will increase performance significantly.

You can also disable the Z-buffer completely for many large objects, thus increasing performance. A skybox, for example, will certainly be behind everything else. Therefore, it is safe to paint it first, with Z-buffer disabled. Keep in mind that large primitives take longer to render, and thus taking the skybox out of the way is a wise move. The same applies to onscreen menus and scoreboards, and generally speaking, all items that will definitely be closest to the player. These items will never be occluded, and thus can be rendered last, with Z-buffer disabled as well. Z-buffer testing and writing is expensive, so try to find ways to switch it off whenever possible.

Some algorithms, such as BSPs or some of the portal variants, order triangles internally, so there is no need to have the Z-buffer on. A call like `glDepthFunc(GL_ALWAYS)` will ensure that Z-values are updated, but no actual testing will take place.

Other Optimization Tools

Some products have been designed to assist you in the optimization and tuning process. There are code analyzers and profilers, which help discover both bottlenecks and slow sections in your code. There are also optimizers that simply try to write faster code using a variety of techniques.

An example of an optimization tool is Codeplay's VectorC. This package can automatically analyze your code and generate machine language, which is as close to optimal as possible. Usually, we would write our routine using a general-purpose compiler and, once we have detected a loop that is on the critical path to performance, use VectorC to write tighter code. VectorC can optimize for a variety of platforms (PCs and PS2s are supported) and specific processor types. Thus, a code snippet can be analyzed for a Pentium 4, an Athlon, or many other CPU types. Under specific tests on mission-critical routines, I have consistently seen VectorC outperform standard compilers by a factor of 25–40 percent.

In Closing

Optimization can sometimes be difficult, but it is definitely one of the most exciting areas in game development. With some careful planning, lots of coffee, and patience, you can dramatically improve code performance. Multiplying performance is often possible, making the unplayable become interactive. However, there are two key factors to successful optimization.

First, you need to learn to write efficient code as early in the coding process as possible and avoid waiting until the very end to actually profile your code. Monitoring your code every now and then, and taking timings to keep track of performance is a good way to make sure your code is relatively decent from day one. Writing "quick and dirty" solutions and trying to optimize them at the end of the development process is a bad idea. The task will become too daunting, and you will definitely get lost in the details.

Notice, however, that many optimization techniques make code less readable and harder to understand. Donald Knuth once said, "Early optimization is the root of all evil," and he was quite right. Focusing on extreme optimizations early on will surely degrade code clarity and elegance for the sake of raw speed. Pure optimization must thus be left for the end of the coding process. But writing code modules so they are more or less efficient from day one is the best way to ensure deadlines are met and performance evolves as expected. A final, raw optimization phase will make sure those mission-critical components are as efficient as possible.

Second, know your code. Analyze your code and understand what it does, and you will discover new ways to make it run faster. Optimizing code requires a deep understanding of your code's functionality and design. You must have this understanding in order to be able to make decisions that improve performance while maintaining the same great playing experience. You must deeply understand the cost breakdown of each routine from both a time and memory standpoint.

Appendix B

OpenGL

"Everything should be made as simple as possible, but not one bit simpler."

Albert Einstein

In this appendix I will provide you with a brief introduction to the OpenGL programming interface. This API, introduced in the early 1990s by Silicon Graphics, has been (and still is) an industry cornerstone because of its simplicity, elegance, and cross-compatibility. OpenGL is supported by many platforms, and its design methodology has become a guiding light for many APIs on different platforms.

Learning OpenGL provides a two-way benefit. First, OpenGL is available in numerous platforms. Second, most platforms that do not use OpenGL depend on APIs that have been heavily influenced by it, so having knowledge of OpenGL makes it really easy to learn most other APIs.

OpenGL is an excellent tool for anything from early-concept prototyping to independent game development and full title production. Being an open, platform-neutral standard, OpenGL enables you to connect with a huge user base, which provides information and code examples you can use to quickly get working.

Philosophy

OpenGL is a software interface to graphics hardware. It provides an abstraction model to the graphics subsystem, which allows programmers to code 2D and 3D graphics efficiently regardless of the specific hardware details. For the developer, OpenGL is nothing but a set of calls that allows the declaration of geometric objects, along with control mechanisms that determine how those objects are rendered.

OpenGL is also considered an immediate-mode API, meaning that declaring an object in OpenGL generally causes the object to be drawn. There are no persistent data structures or calls to simply declare geometry. Most OpenGL calls directly affect the contents of the frame buffer. This makes the API smaller and easier to learn. It also makes porting your application to OpenGL quite fast. You can still use all your object hierarchy because OpenGL does not force you to use any specific data structure. Only the rendering core must be OpenGL compliant.

OpenGL is also a platform-independent API. You can run OpenGL applications on anything from PCs to handhelds, game consoles, or parallel supercomputers, virtually without touching a single line of code. This is achieved by providing only the calls required for rendering. OpenGL does not handle tasks such as window management, memory allocation, and so on, which the application programmer must handle specifically for each operating system (OS). Then, you can choose between writing your own OS-dependent code to handle windows and memory blocks, or use any of the auxiliary libraries (such as GLUT, the OpenGL Utility Library Toolkit) that have spawned through the years, which allow you to forget about OS-dependent code.

OpenGL is a free, open standard. OpenGL was introduced by Silicon Graphics, but it is governed by an industry-wide Architecture Review Board, a committee formed by companies such as Microsoft, NVIDIA, Evans & Sutherland, and many others (obviously, SGI included). Features are added only when a broad consensus is reached, so the API remains elegant and free of vendor-specific calls. Sometimes specific vendors will implement proprietary features under the form of extensions. These are sets of calls that only work on some vendors' APIs, so they somehow break the elegance of the architecture. But as these extensions become popular, they are often incorporated into the next release, so we can say OpenGL is one of the most vendor-neutral APIs on the market.

Basic Syntax

OpenGL was designed to be very easy to learn and use. Thus, its syntax is relatively straightforward, and you can actually be coding within minutes. As an example, here is a very simple OpenGL code snippet:

```
glClearColor(0.0, 0.0, 0.0, 0.0);
glClear(GL_COLOR_BUFFER_BIT);
glLookAt(0, 0, -10, 0, 0, 0, 0, 1, 0);
```

```
glBegin(GL_TRIANGLES);
glColor3f(1,0,0);
glVertex3f(-1,0,0);
glColor3f(1,1,0);
glVertex3f(1,0,0);
glColor3f(0,0,1);
glVertex3f(0,1,0);
glEnd();
```

This relatively simple program draws a triangle on the screen. You can see the output in Figure B.1. But right now we will focus on learning the basic OpenGL syntax, and not so much on the triangle.

Figure B.1   White triangle over black background; "Hello world" for OpenGL.

As you will probably have discovered, all OpenGL calls start with the gl prefix. All words after gl use initial capital letters, and word separations are not separated by the underscore sign. Symbolic constants, on the contrary, use all caps and underscore each space. This makes command recognition simpler, for example:

glRenderMode   command

GL_TRIANGLES   symbolic constant

OpenGL explicitly indicates the parameter types in the function name. So, a call like this:

`glColor3f`

receives three parameters, each one of float type. Different calls receive different parameter sets. Moreover, some calls have variants depending on the parameters you want to pass. For example, to specify colors, you could use:

- `glColor3d`   Specifies colors as 3 doubles, RGB
- `glColor3f`   Specifies colors as 3 floats, RGB
- `glColor3ub`   Specifies colors as 3 unsigned bytes, RGB
- `glColor4d`   Specifies colors as 4 doubles, RGBA
- `glColor4f`   Specifies colors as 4 floats, RGBA
- `glColor4ub`   Specifies colors as 4 unsigned bytes, RGBA

This makes coding a bit more intuitive. Because OpenGL is available for many programming languages (C/C++, Pascal, Basic), it has its own generic types, so you can hide the specific types each language uses. For the C/C++ version of OpenGL, Table B.1 lists the parameter types.

Table B.1   Data Types and Suffixes for OpenGL Calls

OpenGL Type	Data Type	C Type	Suffix
Glbyte	8-bit integer	signed char	b
Glshort	16-bit integer	short	s
GLint, Glsizei	32-bit integer	long	i
GLfloat, GLclampf	32-bit floating-point	float	f
GLdouble, GLclampd	64-bit floating-point	double	d
GLubyte, GLboolean	8-bit unsigned integer	unsigned char	ub
Glushort	16-bit unsigned integer	unsigned short	us
GLuint, GLenum, GLbitfield	32-bit unsigned integer	unsigned long	ui

Additionally, most calls to OpenGL accept vectors to be passed as parameters. For example, the following two calls are completely equivalent:

```
glVertex3f(1.0, 0.0, 0.0);

float vertex_array[] = {1.0, 0.0, 0.0};
glVertex3fv(vertex_array);
```

Notice how the v suffix is used to indicate a vector is going to be passed. The numeric value then represents not the number of parameters, but the length of the vector.

So now we can review the preceding code and figure out what each line does. The first two lines specify the background color and clear the frame buffer to that value. Next, we define a camera with the gluLookAt call. Then, we declare a geometry object (a triangle), specifying its three vertices and a different color for each one. Let's now explore the rendering capabilities of OpenGL, to better understand how geometry is sent to the graphics hardware.

Immediate Mode Rendering

OpenGL decomposes any complex object into a series of simple primitives: points, lines, triangles, and so on. The reason for this is that graphics hardware is very good at rendering simple objects. Hardware routines for rendering triangles or lines are thousands of times faster than software implementations. More complex objects are unsupported because of the large variety (and hence algorithmic complexity).

Objects can be declared to OpenGL using a variety of rendering methods. Because we are just starting with OpenGL, I will cover only the simplest (and sadly, least efficient) rendering method, leaving more involved constructs for subsequent sections. The method we will be using is called immediate mode rendering, and involves sending the data to the hardware using many calls, one per element. Immediate mode rendering blocks are always started with the glBegin call, which specifies what kind of primitive we want to render, and should finish with a call to glEnd. The calls between Begin and End specify the geometric data. Remember that you can batch as many primitives as you want in a Begin-End construct: the more primitives, the better the performance. As a summary, here is a list of the geometric primitives available in OpenGL, along with how data is interpreted in each one. You can see a graphic representation of each primitive in Figure B.2.

➤ GL_POINTS Draws a point at each of the n vertices.

➤ GL_LINES Draws a series of unconnected line segments. Segments are drawn between v0 and v1, between v2 and v3, and so on. If n is odd, the last segment is drawn between vn-3 and vn-2, and vn-1 is ignored.

➤ GL_POLYGON Draws a polygon using the points v0, …, vn-1 as vertices. n must be at least 3, or nothing is drawn. In addition, the polygon specified must not intersect itself and must be convex. If the vertices don't satisfy these conditions, the results are unpredictable.

➤ GL_TRIANGLES Draws a series of triangles (three-sided polygons) using vertices v0, v1, v2, then v3, v4, v5, and so on. If n isn't an exact multiple of 3, the final one or two vertices are ignored.

➤ GL_LINE_STRIP Draws a line segment from v0 to v1, then from v1 to v2, and so on, finally drawing the segment from vn-2 to vn-1. Thus, a total of n-1 line segments are drawn. Nothing is drawn unless n is larger than 1. There are no restrictions on the vertices describing a line strip (or a line loop); the lines can intersect arbitrarily.

➤ GL_LINE_LOOP Same as GL_LINE_STRIP except that a final line segment is drawn from vn-1 to v0, completing a loop.

➤ GL_QUADS Draws a series of quadrilaterals (four-sided polygons) using vertices v0, v1, v2, v3, then v4, v5, v6, v7, and so on. If n isn't a multiple of 4, the final one, two, or three vertices are ignored.

➤ GL_QUAD_STRIP Draws a series of quadrilaterals (four-sided polygons) beginning with v0, v1, v3, v2, then v2, v3, v5, v4, then v4, v5, v7, v6, and so on. See Figure B.2. n must be at least 4 before anything is drawn, and if n is odd, the final vertex is ignored.

➤ GL_TRIANGLE_STRIP   Draws a series of triangles (three-sided polygons) using vertices v0, v1, v2, then v2, v1, v3 (note the order), then v2, v3, v4, and so on. The ordering is to ensure that the triangles are all drawn with the same orientation so that the strip can correctly form part of a surface. Figure B.2 should make the reason for the ordering obvious. *n* must be at least 3 for anything to be drawn.

➤ GL_TRIANGLE_FAN   Same as GL_TRIANGLE_STRIP except that the vertices are v0, v1, v2, then v0, v2, v3, then v0, v3, v4, and so on. See Figure B.2.

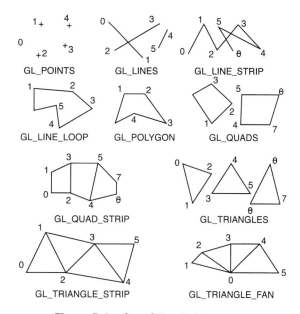

Figure B.2   OpenGL's primitive types.

Each vertex in a rendering batch can be assigned a color, texture coordinates, normal, and so on. To begin with, colors are specified with the glColor* family of calls. You must keep in mind that OpenGL colors are active after the respective glColor call, so you need to specify the color prior to sending the vertex to the hardware. Additionally, colors are persistent: All vertices in a batch will use the last declared color until a new one is assigned. For example, the following code paints a triangle:

```
glBegin(GL_TRIANGLES);
glColor3f(1,0,0);
glVertex3f(-1,0,0);
glColor3f(1,1,0);
```

```
glVertex3f(1,0,0);
glVertex3f(0,1,0);
glEnd();
```

The first vertex will be red (1,0,0). The second and third will be yellow. As an efficiency concern when using immediate mode rendering, remember to batch primitives together when you can. The following two code snippets, although similar, yield very different performance:

```
for (i=0;i<1000;i++)
   {
   glBegin(GL_QUADS);
   // paint a quad here
   glEnd();
   }

glBegin(GL_QUADS);
for (i=0;i<1000;i++)
   {
   // paint a quad here
   }
glEnd();
```

In the first case, we are painting 1,000 primitives and sending 2,000 OpenGL calls (each one with its overhead) to the pipeline, and that's not counting the rendering itself. In the second code snippet, we are sending one large batch of primitives and doing only two OpenGL calls. The second code snippet is significantly faster than the first. As you will soon see, there are very few reasons to break a primitive batch, and those reasons are usually performing a transform or changing the texture map. Other than that, we should create batches as big as possible.

Transformations

Imagine you are working on a space shooter and need to draw a fleet of starships. You have a ship model and need to render it several times to give the impression of a large fleet. Each individual ship is just an instance of the master ship, rotated and translated to a point in space.

As your first option, you could try to individually transform each vertex in the ship. You would need to implement rotation and translation matrices, and then manually apply them to the geometry. Although this task would not be very complex, it is hard to get the code right, especially if you plan to do transform chains. Luckily, OpenGL does this for you, so you can concentrate on other, more rewarding tasks. Transforms in OpenGL are really simple to use yet extremely powerful and flexible.

The key concept you must understand is that during the geometry processing, OpenGL applies several matrices to the incoming data. Data is initially transformed by a first matrix, which specifies model coordinates. This is called the modelview matrix and is used to perform object-level transforms such as in the previous starship example. To place each ship in its real location, we will specify a different modelview matrix for each one, so geometry is affected by that change as it crosses the pipeline.

A second matrix is used to specify how transformed (that is, affected by the modelview matrix) geometry is mapped to the screen. This is the projection matrix and is used to achieve perspective effects as well as complex camera lens deformations. If we change the projection matrix prior to sending a geometry block to OpenGL, the said geometry will be projected accordingly.

The last matrix we can modify is the texture matrix. This matrix is applied to texture coordinates right before rasterization. Thus, by applying a nonstandard texture matrix we can get animated texture effects: rotations, zooms, and so on.

Clearly, we need two types of calls. First, we need calls to specify which matrix we want to work with. Second, we will need calls that actually modify the selected matrix. For the matrix selection, the following call is used:

```
glMatrixMode(gluint matrixmode) ;
```

This call receives only one parameter, which can be any of the following symbolic constants:

- ➤ GL_MODELVIEW   Selects the modelview matrix

- ➤ GL_PROJECTION   Selects the projection matrix

- ➤ GL_TEXTURE   Selects the texture matrix

Once the right matrix has been selected, we can apply a wide range of transforms. This first call clears the currently selected matrix, so data traversing it remains unchanged:

```
glLoadIdentity();
```

To achieve this, the current matrix is initialized with an identity matrix (a diagonal of ones with all other positions initialized to zero). Remember that this call does not multiply the values of the current matrix but simply overwrites them.

The following call multiplies the currently selected matrix with a rotation matrix:

```
glRotatef(GLdouble angle, GLdouble axisx, GLdouble axisy, GLdouble
axisz);
```

The rotation matrix is specified by a rotation angle (in degrees) and an axis. You can see the geometric interpretation of this call in Figure B.3.

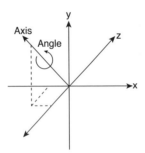

Figure B.3 How rotations work in OpenGL.

Specifying rotation with an angle and an axis might seem unintuitive. But once you master `glRotated`, you will discover its flexibility. If you need to perform simpler axis-oriented rotations, you can always simplify the call as follows:

```
glRotated (xangle, 1, 0, 0);
glRotated (yangle, 0, 1, 0);
glRotated (zangle, 0, 0, 1);
```

Translations are performed in a very similar way, using the `glTranslatef` call:

```
glTranslated(GLdouble dispx, GLdouble dispy, GLdouble dispz);
```

Here we only need to specify the displacement we want to apply, and the currently selected matrix is multiplied by this new translation matrix. Then, we can apply a scaling matrix with the following call:

```
glScaled(GLdouble scalex, GLdouble scaley, GLdouble scalez);
```

Notice how the scaling syntax allows both homogeneous and nonhomogeneous transforms. Also, keep in mind that you can actually scale by 0 (thus, eliminating one coordinate set). This is sometimes used in shadow algorithms: flattening the geometry to the ground level. However, avoid scaling by zero in all directions because your geometry would totally collapse.

Most transforms are specified using translations, rotations, or scales. But sometimes we will need extra flexibility. For example, imagine that you want to implement a shearing matrix or, even worse, that you need to manually apply a matrix you have computed. For these situations, OpenGL offers the following call:

```
glMultMatrixd (GLdouble *m);
```

This function passes a pointer to 16 consecutive values that are used as the elements of a 4×4 column-major matrix. This new matrix will multiply the currently selected matrix, so you can implement any transform that can be expressed as a matrix. Remember that matrices in OpenGL are represented in homogeneous coordinates.

Concatenation of Transforms

OpenGL transforms can be freely concatenated, so you can apply several transforms to the same geometry. This can be achieved by typing a series of transform calls. There are only two potential issues that you should be aware of.

First, OpenGL post-multiplies matrices. What this actually means for programmers is that you have to type transforms in reverse order. For example, if you need to place a starship in a 3D game and the ship has both a position and a yaw angle, you would do this:

1. Rotate the ship model (which would be centered at the origin).

2. Translate it to the final position.

In OpenGL, you must reverse these two matrices, so the code sequence would be

```
glTranslatef (…);
glRotatef (…);
```

This reverse ordering applies to all transforms that multiply the current matrix (glTranslate, glRotate, glScale, glMultMatrix). Thus, glLoadIdentity is not affected by this rule and should always be the first call in a transform chain.

Second, transforms are applied on a per-object basis and must thus be specified outside glBegin-glEnd sequences. Transforms placed inside geometry sections will probably be ignored or yield incorrect results.

Hierarchical Transforms

OpenGL provides functions to implement hierarchical transforms. For example, think of a tank with a turret and a cannon on top of it. The turret inherits the transforms for the tank body, and the cannon inherits both the transforms for the body and the transforms for the turret. These complex systems require chaining several transforms and being able to easily select which transforms are applied and where.

OpenGL implements hierarchical transforms through the glPushMatrix/glPopMatrix pair, whose use resembles the scope brackets in C code. PushMatrix opens a new scope or transform node, and PopMatrix closes it. A more involved explanation would be that PushMatrix makes a duplicate of the current matrix, so we can modify it freely while keeping a clean copy. PopMatrix eliminates the matrix at the top of the stack (usually a matrix we previously pushed in), so we can work with the matrix below that one.

As an example, here is the source for the tank renderer. I assume that the tank body must be translated and rotated with a yaw angle, that the turret only has a yaw angle, and that the cannon has a pitch:

```
glPushMatrix();
    glTranslatef(tankpos.x, tankpos.y, tankpos.z);
    glRotatef(tankyaw,0,1,0);
    // here I paint the tank
```

```
(...)
glPushMatrix();
    glTranslatef(turretpos.x, turretpos.y, turretpos.z);
    glRotatef(turretyaw,0,1,0);

    // here I paint the turret
    (...)
    glPushMatrix();
        glTranslatef(cannonpos.x, cannonpos.y, cannonpos.z);
        glRotatef(cannonpitch,1,0,0);
        // here I paint the cannon            (...)
    glPopMatrix();

glPopMatrix();

glPopMatrix();
```

The `PushMatrix`/`PopMatrix` paradigm offers all the flexibility you need to create hierarchical models. All you have to do is remember two very basic rules of thumb: Never place these constructs inside `Begin`/`End` sections, and always make sure you pop every matrix you push or, in other words, that you have exactly the same number of pushes and pops.

Camera Model

OpenGL draws primitives according to a user-definable camera model. You can specify a camera in very intuitive terms: position, aperture, and so on, and the geometry will automatically use that camera. Several cameras might be used. For example, a mini-map in the corner of a screen can use different camera parameters as the main scene. Additionally, you can select between different projection schemes: Perspective and orthographic are available, so you can choose your desired viewing algorithm. You can also completely override the camera and thus draw in window coordinates. This is especially useful when drawing in two dimensions, doing overlays for menus or interface elements, and so on.

An OpenGL camera is nothing but a series of transforms. The full scene is rotated according to the camera's orientation, then translated so the viewpoint is placed correctly, and an optional perspective transform is applied. But hand coding these transforms would be troublesome and prone to errors. Thus, the Open GL Utility Library (GLU) provides easy-to-use calls that take care of the camera operation. Overall, only two calls are required. The first call allows us to specify camera projection properties (aperture, aspect ratio, type of projection, and so on). The second is used to directly place the camera in our 3D world.

Let's now see how we can specify the camera's projection properties. Here is the call for perspective projection:

```
gluPerspective( GLdouble fovy, GLdouble aspect, GLdouble znear,
GLdouble zfar);
```

The first parameter indicates the field of view, in degrees, in the Y direction. The second parameter specifies the ratio between width and height. For example, a value of 1.3 implies that the camera's snapshot of the world is 1.3 times wider than it is tall. The last two parameters are used to initialize the Z-buffer. Both are strictly positive double values, specifying at which distance (in Z) the near and far clipping planes should be. Overall, these four parameters allow us to specify a view frustum completely, as shown in Figure B.4.

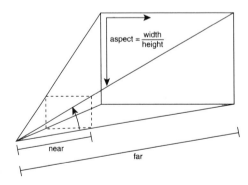

Figure B.4   Camera parameters and their geometric interpretation under OpenGL.

However, we need to place our 3D camera in space. This is easily achieved by using the call:

```
gluLookAt ( GLdouble eyex, GLdouble eyey, GLdouble eyez,
    GLdouble centerx, GLdouble centery, GLdouble centerz,

    GLdouble upx, GLdouble upy, GLdouble upz);
```

Although the parameter list looks impressive, this is a really straightforward call. The first three parameters indicate where the camera actually is. Then, the second triplet is used to specify the point in space the camera is pointing at. Notice we do not provide angles of rotation, but a target instead. The last triplet is used to specify a vector pointing up relative to the camera's orientation. This vector will be mapped to the vertical axis in the viewport and allows us to represent rolling cameras, like a plane in a twisting trajectory along its line of advance.

Now, it is essential that you realize that `gluPerspective` and `gluLookAt` are nothing more than a series of transforms encapsulated into comfortable calls. Thus, they affect the currently selected matrix as any `glTranslate`, `glRotate`, or `glMultMatrix` would do. As a result, you must be careful about the order of operations and the currently selected matrix. Failing to do so results in wrong textures, lighting, and so on. The following code is the way to properly initialize a camera under OpenGL:

```
glMatrixMode(GL_PROJECTION);
glLoadIdentity() ;
gluPerspective(…) ;

glMatrixMode(GL_MODELVIEW);
glLoadIdentity();
gluLookAt(…) ;
```

Again, remember that `gluPerspective` implements a projection model, whereas `gluLookAt` effectively places the camera, which is nothing but rotating and translating the scene accordingly.

Lighting

OpenGL offers an interface for hardware-accelerated, per-vertex lighting. This lighting must be supported by the hardware (hence the transform and lighting accelerator family). When implemented on hardware, OpenGL lighting provides good results at a relatively low cost.

Lighting is optional in OpenGL, and disabled by default. Thus, the first step in any lighting application is to effectively enable it, using the command:

```
glEnable(GL_LIGHTING);
```

Then, light sources and material properties for objects must be defined. Beginning with lights, OpenGL supports several types of luminaries. You can define infinite lights, which are supposed to be very far away and thus send parallel rays to the scene (the Sun would be a good example), or positional sources, which effectively are contained in a point in space. The latter can in turn exist under different incarnations. We can have omnidirectional sources, which emit light in all directions, or spot lights, which emit a cone of light in a certain direction. Additionally, positional light sources can have attenuation built in, so lighting intensity decreases with distance. A scene with OpenGL hardware lighting can be seen in Figure B.5.

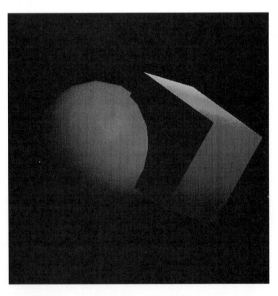

Figure B.5 Simple hardware lighting under OpenGL.

All these parameters are controlled with two calls only. The first one allows us to declare a new light source and has the syntax:

```
glEnable(GL_LIGHTx);
```

where *x* is the serial number of the luminaire. Values from 0 to 9 are mandatory, with some implementations supporting even more (at a higher computational cost). You can check the specific number of light sources supported by your implementation by accessing the integer constant GL_MAX_LIGHTS. Lights must be initialized with this call prior to assigning any parameters to them. Once a light has been initialized, the following call is used to define the light's properties:

```
glLight*(GLenum light, GLenum pname, GLenum param)
```

The preceding call has the *f*, *i*, *fv*, *iv* variants, so we can send a variety of parameter configurations to it. For example, here is how we would initialize a light's position:

```
GLfloat position = {0, 10, 0, 1};
```

```
glLightfv( GL_LIGHT0, GL_POSITION, position);
```

Notice that we are passing not a 3D point, but a 4D homogeneous coordinate in the form x,y,z,w. What this means in practical terms is that, for positional light sources, the parameter w will divide x,y,z, so it is a good idea to leave w=1. We can implement an infinite light source by storing w=0, and then using x,y,z to provide the unit vector for the light's direction.

Now, let's add some color attributes to the lamp:

```
GLfloat ambient[]= {0.2, 0.2, 0.3};
glLightfv( GL_LIGHT0, GL_AMBIENT, ambient);

GLfloat diffuse[]= {1, 1, 1};
glLightfv( GL_LIGHT0, GL_DIFFUSE, diffuse);

GLfloat specular[]= {1,1,1};
glLightfv( GL_LIGHT0, GL_SPECULAR, specular);
```

This rather simple example declares a positional, omnidirectional light source in OpenGL. I have also provided information on how to make it a directional light. Thus, it is now time to declare a spotlight. The previous code is still valid. All we have to do is send two additional `glLight` calls to specify the cone of light properties, as shown here:

```
GLfloat spotdir= {0,-1,0};
glLightfv(LIGHT0, GL_SPOT_DIRECTION, spotdir);
```

In the preceding example, we have defined our spotlight as pointing downwards in the vertical direction. The following line states that we want our spotlight to have an aperture of 25°, so the spotlight is completely defined:

```
glLightfv(LIGHT0, GL_SPOT_CUTOFF, 25);
```

We know where the light emanates from, the direction it is targeting, and the aperture of the cone.

A final addition to our lighting system is attenuation, which simulates the way light decreases in intensity as we move away from the emitter. OpenGL provides three attenuation options, which can be activated on a per-light basis. Obviously, a light must be positional for attenuation to work and can be both omnidirectional or a spotlight.

The attenuation equation used by OpenGL is as follows:

```
lightoutput=lightinput* ((1-constantfactor) +
linearfactor*distance + quadraticfactor*distance^2
```

We can specify three attenuation factors: one constant, which will be applied regardless of the distance from the lamp to the lit point; one linear with distance, which is applied linearly with distance; and one quadratic, which is multiplied by the distance squared. This approximation might seem complex, but in the real world, light attenuates with distance squared, right? However, units in the real world tend to have huge ranges (the Sun is millions of kilometers away, and a lamp can be one meter away). Computer graphics are hard to get right if we directly implement the real-world equation. Sometimes, you will not want attenuation. Most of the time, attenuation will be simulated with a linear decay factor, and other times (in space flight simulators, for example) a real-world quadratic factor will be used. Thus, it is handy to be able to use the three attenuation factors and even to combine them. As usual, the coding is really straightforward. The following line sets the constant attenuation factor:

```
glLighti(GL_LIGHT0, GL_CONSTANT_ATTENUATION, constantfactor)
```

A value of 1 produces no attenuation, and 0 would simply eliminate all scene lighting. The following code lines set the linear and quadratic attenuation factors, respectively:

```
glLighti(GL_LIGHT0, GL_LINEAR_ATTENUATION, linearfactor);
glLighti(GL_LIGHT0, GL_QUADRATIC_ATTENUATION, quadraticfactor);
```

It is good practice to first set the lights so lighting looks right, and only when we are happy with the results, start working on the attenuation factors. Setting a light in one step can be a tricky process.

Lights are useless without objects to interact with. Shiny objects behave in a certain way, some others are dull in appearance, and even surface color can determine how objects react to scene lighting. Thus, OpenGL supplies a set of calls that allow you to set surface properties in a way similar to setting lights.

To begin with, you must set surface colors. This is achieved with the `glMaterial*` set of calls. Here, for example, is the definition of a material somewhat similar to red plastic:

```
GLfloat ambient[] = {0.2, 0.1, 0.1, 1};
glMaterialfv( GL_FRONT, GL_AMBIENT, ambient);

GLfloat diffuse[] = {1, 0, 0, 1};
glMaterialfv( GL_FRONT, GL_DIFFUSE, diffuse);

GLfloat specular[] = {1, 0.8, 0, 1};
glMaterialfv( GL_FRONT, GL_SPECULAR, specular);

glMaterialf( GL_FRONT, GL_SHININESS, 25);
```

This definition works in harmony with OpenGL's rendering pipeline. Set the material right before sending the object to the pipeline, whichever rendering method you use, and the material will be applied to it. But remember that lighting uses information from the glNormal3f (or GL_NORMAL_ARRAY) to perform its computation. Be sure to specify those calls in your geometry declaration. Parameters are straightforward. For the color calls we specify color values as RGBA sets, and shininess is expressed as an exponent that scales the specular component: the larger the value, the more the surface will respond to specular highlights. If you want to learn more about the illumination process, you can find these equations explained in Chapter 17, "Shading."

Now you know how to enable OpenGL's lighting functionality. To complete this overview, I'll add a note on lighting performance. Some programmers tend to believe that hardware lighting comes at no cost on lighting-capable hardware. But performance degrades as you increase the lighting complexity. As an example, notice how the number of lights affects performance in Table B.2. Numbers are taken on an Athlon 1.3GHz PC with a GeForce3 card, running a benchmark application that renders spheres to the screen with a variable number of light sources. In case you are wondering, geometry is delivered to the hardware using display lists, which are explained in the "Display Lists" section later in this chapter.

Table B.2 Comparison Between Performance and the Number of Lights in a Scene, Using Simple Directional Lights

Number of Lights	Fps	Triangles/sec
0	105	20.3M
1	79	15M
2	71	13.6M
3	50	9.6M
4	38.5	7.4M

Moreover, cost also depends on the type of light. Directional light sources are faster to compute than spotlights, for example. Again, take a look at the results in Table B.3. Notice the performance hit when compared to Table B.2.

Table B.3 Comparison Between Performance and the Number of Lights in a Scene, Using Spotlights

Number of Lights	Triangles/sec Directional	Triangles/sec Spot
0	20.3M	15M
1	15M	7.3M
2	13.6M	6.8M
3	9.6M	5.78M
4	7.4M	4.48M

Notice how, under these conditions, directional light sources are approximately twice as fast to compute than spotlights. Thus, the best advice would be to time your code and understand the platform you are coding for to take advantage of its features. Rationalize the use of hardware lighting, so you can enjoy its benefits and avoid its limitations.

Texturing

From all the features available in OpenGL, textures is the one that provides the most impact on realism. A few triangles can become a gloomy scenario by selecting the right texture maps, and visual appeal is simply multiplied.

OpenGL implements textures on a per-primitive basis. You can specify which texture map should be applied to each triangle or quad, and how the texture should adapt to the object's geometry. Keep in mind, however, that OpenGL is not designed for textures to be applied manually. The best choice is to use a modeling package, apply textures with it, and then have OpenGL render those objects with the same texturing.

But before we can explore the texturing capabilities of OpenGL, we will take a look at how textures are loaded and stored by the API. To begin with, texture data can come from any file format such as TGA, JPEG, or any other. There is no restriction on the source of the material. All you have to do is load the data and deliver it to OpenGL so the API can manipulate it. This is usually called the *external format*. Keep in mind that once the texture map is loaded, it does not have to remain in user memory. OpenGL will copy the map to its own memory area, and further operations are performed directly inside the API, with no direct control of the texture.

Once in OpenGL's memory, texture data can be stored in a variety of ways: palletized, true-color, and so on. It also allows you to specify the texture map size or even to select the filtering algorithm to be applied. All these properties are called the *internal format* of the texture and determine how much memory each map will take.

As an example, here is the source code that takes a single TGA file, loads it into user memory, and delivers it to OpenGL to be used as a texture map. To make the code shorter, I will assume the texture is 256×256, RGBA. This way I can skip decoding the TGA header:

```
int LoadTexture(char *filename, int ident)
{
glBindTexture(GL_TEXTURE_2D,ident);

glPixelStorei(GL_UNPACK_ALIGNMENT,1);
glTexParameteri(GL_TEXTURE_2D,GL_TEXTURE_WRAP_S,GL_REPEAT);
glTexParameteri(GL_TEXTURE_2D,GL_TEXTURE_WRAP_T,GL_REPEAT);
glTexParameteri(GL_TEXTURE_2D,GL_TEXTURE_MAG_FILTER,GL_LINEAR);
glTexParameteri(GL_TEXTURE_2D,GL_TEXTURE_MIN_FILTER,GL_LINEAR);

FILE *f;

f=fopen(filename,"rb");
if (f==NULL)
    {
    // filename is wrong... probably file does not exist
    return -1;
    }

char *rgb=new char[Width*Height*Depth];
fread(rgb,sizeof(unsigned char),18,f);     // skip the header
fread(rgb,256*256*3,1,f);
```

```
glTexImage2D(GL_TEXTURE_2D,0,3,256,256,0,GL_RGB,GL_UNSIGNED_BYTE,rgb);
delete[] rgb;
return 0;
}
```

This is a significant amount of code, so let's go through it step by step. The call to glBindTexture tells OpenGL which texture map we will be working on. Texture maps are identified by nonnegative integers, so each texture map has a unique identifier. The glBindTexture is used whenever we want to work on a texture map, to initialize OpenGL's texture access routines.

The next five lines set some useful texture properties. The first one (glPixelStore) sets the unpack alignment, so data is byte aligned. Then, we use four lines to set the filtering and tiling properties of the texture map. The following lines tell OpenGL we want this map to repeat endlessly over the object's surface:

```
glTexParameteri(GL_TEXTURE_2D,GL_TEXTURE_WRAP_S,GL_REPEAT);
glTexParameteri(GL_TEXTURE_2D,GL_TEXTURE_WRAP_T,GL_REPEAT);
```

This way we can make copies of a small texture map over a large surface, as in a brick pattern covering a large wall. To achieve this, we will specify texture coordinates outside the standard (0,1) range to indicate repetition. An alternative would be to use GL_DECAL instead of GL_REPEAT. This would make the texture map appear only once, so any texture coordinate beyond the texture limit would not be painted.

As for the filtering, the following lines indicate how the texture must be filtered when magnified or minified:

```
glTexParameteri(GL_TEXTURE_2D,GL_TEXTURE_MAG_FILTER,GL_LINEAR);
glTexParameteri(GL_TEXTURE_2D,GL_TEXTURE_MIN_FILTER,GL_LINEAR);
```

In both cases, we indicate we want a bilinear filter to be applied, so texture maps look smooth when looked at from a distance or up close. Another possibility would be to use GL_NEAREST, which implements a nearest-neighbor policy. This is equivalent to switching off filtering capabilities.

After the texturing options have been set, it is time to load the texture data to a temporary buffer. In this rather simplistic example, I assume texture size and color depth are known. I have chosen the popular TGA file format, which basically uses an 18-byte long header and an RGB dump of the texture data. Thus, I can skip the header and load the data into a large temporary buffer.

Then, it is time to pass the texture to OpenGL so we can begin working with it. This is achieved by the `glTexImage2D` call, which has the following profile:

```
void glTexImage2D(GLenum target, GLint level, GLint internalformat,
GLint width, GLint height, GLint border, GLenum format, GLenum
type, void *pixels);
```

where `target` specifies the type of texture we are working with. Values can be `GL_TEXTURE_2D` for normal textures or `GL_PROXY_TEXTURE_2D`. The second option is used when we want to initialize an OpenGL texture map, but we don't want to fill it with data yet. Thus, all memory allocation and consistency checking is performed, but no data is read from pixels.

The level parameter is used for mipmapping and specifies the level of detail number. For regular textures, the parameter should be set to 0, and a value of N is the Nth mipmap reduction. Mipmapping is an advanced filtering option and is explained fully in Chapter 18, "Texture Mapping."

The third parameter is used to declare the internal format of the texture. It can be 1, 2, 3, or 4 to specify the number of components for each pixel. Thus, an RGB map would be 3. But you can achieve higher flexibility by using one of the following symbolic constants:

GL_ALPHA	GL_LUMINANCE4	GL_LUMINANCE6_ALPHA2
GL_ALPHA4	GL_LUMINANCE8	GL_LUMINANCE8_ALPHA8
GL_ALPHA8	GL_LUMINANCE12	GL_LUMINANCE12_ALPHA4
GL_ALPHA12	GL_LUMINANCE16	GL_LUMINANCE12_ALPHA12
GL_ALPHA16	GL_LUMINANCE_ALPHA	GL_LUMINANCE16_ALPHA16
GL_LUMINANCE	GL_LUMINANCE4_ALPHA4	GL_INTENSITY

GL_INTENSITY4	GL_RGB5	GL_RGBA4
GL_INTENSITY8	GL_RGB8	GL_RGB5_A1
GL_INTENSITY12	GL_RGB10	GL_RGBA8
GL_INTENSITY16	GL_RGB12	GL_RGB10_A2
GL_RGB	GL_RGB16	GL_RGBA12
GL_R3_G3_B2	GL_RGBA	GL_RGBA16
GL_RGB4	GL_RGBA2	

The next two parameters are straightforward and indicate the width and height (in pixels) of the texture map. Some graphics cards are limited to square textures, others require power-of-two sizes, and still others limit texture sizes to 256 in both directions. Unless you are sure about your graphics card, a 256×256 texture map is always a safe bet.

Then, we can specify how many pixels the texture should have as a border. This is added to the size of the texture, but most of the time this parameter should simply be set to zero.

To apply textures to OpenGL primitives we must specify their texture coordinates, which determine the orientation, sizing, and so on of the material on the primitive. Texture coordinates are specified in U,V values, which are interpreted as the position of the texture map corresponding to a given point in 3D space. Then, texture mapping stretches the map so that each vertex gets its corresponding texture coordinate, and those pixels in between get interpolated smoothly. Except for very simple demos, texture coordinates are meant to be taken from a modeling package because placing them by hand is a tedious process, especially in complex objects with elaborate texture designs.

Texture coordinates are thus stated per vertex, right before the vertex is declared. There is no priority between calls to texturing and coloring routines, but they must take place before their corresponding vertex for OpenGL to work properly. Texture coordinates are specified with the call:

```
glTexCoord*(....);
```

This call sets the texture coordinates for the current vertex. It allows several syntax variants, although the most popular incarnation is

```
void glTexCoord2f(float u, float v);
```

Here we are passing the texture coordinates as float values. As a complete example, the following code shows the "right" way of rendering a textured quad, which stretches a single texture map to cover all its surface:

```
glBindTexture(GL_TEXTURE_2D,materialid);
glBegin(GL_QUADS);
glColor3f(1,1,1);
glTexCoord2f(0,0);
glVertex3f(-1,-1,0);

glColor3f(1,1,0);
glTexCoord2f(1,0);
glVertex3f(1,-1,0);

glColor3f(1,0,1);
glTexCoord2f(1,1);
glVertex3f(1,1,0);

glColor3f(0,1,1);
glTexCoord2f(0,0);
glVertex3f(-1,1,0);
glEnd();
```

Notice how we bind the desired texture map outside the Begin/End construct. Failing to do so will make OpenGL ignore the call. In addition, you can combine texture mapping with colors to achieve a modulation effect. The incoming texture color will be multiplied with the per-vertex color (using interpolation when needed). This is especially useful in software illumination algorithms. We would apply base (unlit) textures to geometry primitives and modulate them with information from the software illumination stage.

Working in RGBA Mode

OpenGL can work in both RGB or RGBA mode. Under the new RGBA mode, transparencies can be encoded as a fourth component, so colors are blended together depending on their assigned alpha values. As a rule of thumb, an alpha of 0.0 means totally transparent, whereas an alpha of 1 means totally opaque.

But working with alpha values is a bit more involved than that. Water, glass, and fire are all semitransparent, but their optical properties are very different. Luckily, OpenGL supplies us with a set of calls that can simulate many different phenomena. Let's do an overview of OpenGL's RGBA functionality, and then look at some specific examples.

OpenGL offers two subsets of RGBA calls: blending or testing. Alpha blending refers to the color mixing process that takes place between translucent materials, such as stained glass. The resulting color is a combination of the colors of the different surfaces. Alpha testing, on the other hand, is a binary process by which a pixel is either fully opaque or fully transparent, so no blending takes place. A good example of alpha testing is a fence, where the geometry is just a quad with an alpha-tested texture map laid on top. Alpha testing is significantly faster than alpha blending because many fragments can be rejected early in the pipeline, and the remaining fragments do not have to compute pixel arithmetic (as opposed to the blending routine in the alpha blending mode).

Whichever the case, both alpha blending and testing must be enabled and disabled by using the following OpenGL tokens:

```
glEnable(GL_BLEND);      (...)    glDisable(GL_BLEND);
glEnable(GL_ALPHA_TEST);    (...)     glDisable(GL_ALPHA_TEST);
```

All code within an `Enable/Disable` scope will be treated accordingly. Let's first examine OpenGL's alpha testing routines. You first need to supply a texture that has an alpha channel. Then, you can tell OpenGL to accept or discard fragments depending on their alpha value. The syntax is as follows:

```
glAlphaFunc(glenum type, glfloat threshold);
```

The first parameter indicates the type of test we will perform, and the second parameter is a threshold value that is usually related to the type of test. For example, the following line sets a threshold value of 0.5, and tells OpenGL that fragments greater than that value should be painted; and fragments with alpha values lower than or equal to 0.5 should be discarded:

```
glAlphaFunc(GL_GREATER,0.5);
```

Alpha values for the test can either be passed per pixel, as part of an alpha channel bundled with the texture map, or per vertex in a `glColor4f` call. In the latter case, per-vertex alpha values are modulated by per-pixel texture values, so the resulting alpha value is passed through the test.

Alpha blending is a much slower and complex process, but results are very attractive. Here we will need to specify alpha values, either per vertex or per pixel, and a blending equation that determines how translucent objects will interact. The blending equation is specified with the following call, which determines how the source and destination fragments are combined:

```
glBlendFunc(glenum src, glenum dest);
```

Source means whatever graphic primitive you are about to paint. It is the source of new data. Destination is where the new data will be added—thus, the contents of the frame buffer. The two parameters allow you to specify what computation will be performed every time a source fragment is combined with a destination. Possible values for both parameters are

```
GL_ZERO

GL_ONE

GL_DST_COLOR

GL_ONE_MINUS_DST_COLOR

GL_SRC_ALPHA

GL_ONE_MINUS_SRC_ALPHA
```

GL_DST_ALPHA

GL_ONE_MINUS_DST_ALPHA

GL_SRC_ALPHA_SATURATE

The trick here is to learn which parameter combination is needed to render certain effects. To make your life easier, I'll now cover the most widely used combinations. Many times you will need to create semitransparent objects such as glass or clouds, which filter light but do not act like light sources. For this case, the parameter combination is

glBlendFunc(GL_SRC_ALPHA,GL_ONE_MINUS_SRC_ALPHA);

so that you pass alpha values to primitives you want to render transparent. Another typical scenario is rendering objects that, being semitransparent, do add illumination to a scene. Some examples are a bonfire, a lens flare effect, or a laser beam. In these cases, what you need is an additive blend, which is achieved by

glBlendFunc(GL_SRC_ALPHA,GL_ONE);

Many interesting effects can be created with more exotic parameter combinations. Make sure you understand the two examples provided in this section, and you will be able to think of new uses yourself.

Display Lists

Painting primitives using immediate mode is simple to code, but results in poor performance. We use lots of calls to deliver the geometry, thus fragmenting the bus usage. Luckily, OpenGL has better ways of handling geometry. Generally speaking, two global methods exist (each with some variants): display lists and vertex arrays. In this section we will explore display lists. In the next section we will cover vertex arrays.

Immediate mode commands are sent to the graphics hardware individually. They have to cross the bus, which is by no means a wide, empty road. In fact, it is better to imagine it as a very narrow road with lots of traffic. But graphics hardware has its own readily accessible memory pool. That's where the framer buffer and Z-buffer live, and where textures are held. Luckily, that's where display lists are stored too. A display list is a sequence of OpenGL commands that have been transferred to the server side (the graphics card), so they can be executed locally. Notice that display lists are not just geometry blocks. They really store OpenGL command sequences, much the same way in which many desktop applications allow you to create macros.

Display lists have the obvious advantage of being extremely efficient. No bus overhead is introduced, and thus rendering speed is maximal. But there is a downside to all this: Declaring a display list and placing it in the video card is a time-consuming process, so data cannot be dynamically refreshed. Display lists are great to hold static geometry that does not change during the game's life cycle, but they yield poor performance on dynamic data. As you will soon see, some types of vertex arrays can help with dynamic geometry.

Another caveat of display lists is that they are placed in the graphics card memory if there's memory available. Because there is a limited amount of video memory, the memory display lists use is also limited. If we didn't limit their memory, we would lose their speed because they would have to be stored in system memory.

Working with display lists involves a three-step process:

1. You need to create an identifier for the list. Identifiers are strictly positive integers, created with the call:

   ```
   int glGenLists(int range)
   ```

   This call allocates a number of previously unallocated display lists, as specified with the *range* parameter. The integer returned is the index that marks the beginning of a contiguous block of empty display list identifiers. For example, the call:

   ```
   int k=glGenLists(3);
   ```

   returns

   ```
   k=5
   ```

   This means we have three lists allocated with the identifiers 5, 6, and 7. If the requested number of lists is not available, the call returns 0.

2. Once we have a newly created display list, it is time to fill it with OpenGL commands. This can easily be achieved with the command pair:

```
glNewList(int listid, GLenum type);
glEndList();
```

The first call opens the display list. All OpenGL commands beyond this point (until reaching the `glEndList` call) are stored to the list identified by the first parameter. Notice that the list must be created with a previous call to `glGenLists`, or we might overwrite other lists. The second parameter specifies whether the commands to be packed to the list must only be stored as a display list or be executed as well. The possible values are

➤ `GL_COMPILE`   Compiles commands to display list, but does not execute them

➤ `GL_COMPILE_AND_EXECUTE`   Compiles commands to display list and executes them

This allows display list creation to be performed at boot time or in the middle of a rendering loop. But `GL_COMPILE` is the most common option.

3. Our display list is ready after the call to `glEndList`. From that moment, we can execute the code contained in the list with a single OpenGL call, which is

```
glCallList(int listid)
```

This call runs the list we pass as a parameter.

Vertex Arrays

We have seen how a display list offers very good performance for static geometry. Storing data in the GPU saves bus time and makes rendering faster on those cards that accelerate display lists.

Vertex arrays (VAs) use a totally different approach to offer increased performance over immediate mode. Some types of VAs will be faster than display lists, others slower. Even worse, performance will vary depending on the graphics card, so display lists might outperform VAs in some hardware configurations but not be as fast as VAs in others. However, VAs have an added advantage over display lists: They are designed to work with both static and dynamic geometry, so using VAs is the best way to get good performance on dynamic meshes.

A VA, as the name implies, is an array full of vertex data. VAs can contain vertex coordinates, colors, texture coordinates, normals, and indices to indexed meshes. Data can be organized in a single array (interleaving the different types of data) or by using several arrays, one per data type. Additionally, most data types are indeed optional. You need to specify vertex coordinates, but other than that, you can choose whatever else you want to represent. For example, you can have two arrays (one for vertices, one for colors) or a single array interleaving vertices, texture coordinates, and colors.

VAs are allocated in user memory space and filled with data by the user. They can be freely modified, so they are both valid for static and dynamic data. Then, they can be sent to the GPU with a single OpenGL call. This is key to their efficiency. By sending the entire array at once, the graphics drivers can optimize this block transfer, thus reaching better performance than immediate mode rendering.

VAs were progressively introduced in OpenGL as extensions. Several flavors exist, and some of them are still supported only as vendor-specific extensions. Generally, there are three types of VAs: regular, compiled, and server side.

Regular VAs enable you to define arrays of geometric data in user memory. The data is then sent efficiently through the bus on a frame-by-frame basis. Performance comes from block-transferring all the data in a single (or very few) call(s).

Compiled VAs extend regular VAs by allowing, under certain circumstances, reuse of the arrays on the graphics card, much like cache memory. The VAs are sent once and can be rendered many times from local memory. This makes them faster than regular VAs, especially for static data.

Server-side VAs allow VAs to be defined not in user memory, but directly on the graphics card. This way the rendering does not need to access the bus at all, and performance reaches its maximum. Some specific functions must be defined in order to allocate this special type of memory, but once we have gained access to it, we can render primitives efficiently and still be able to dynamically change the vertex data as needed. Server-side VAs are still implemented with vendor-specific extensions to OpenGL (as of OpenGL 1.4). In the near future, they might get a broader implementation. But today they exist under two commercial names depending on the hardware's manufacturer: Vertex Array Range (VAR) on NVIDIA cards and Vertex Array Object (VAO) for ATI. Both share the same philosophy, but each one has specific advantages and disadvantages.

Using Regular Vertex Arrays

Regular VAs are easy to understand and code because they resemble the data structure you would normally use to store geometric data. As an example, let's examine the simplest VA: a noninterleaved, nonindexed VA of vertices, colors, and texture coordinates. Here is the code:

```
// data structure definition
int numfaces=64;
float *vtx=new float[numfaces*9];
float *texcoords=new float[numfaces*6];
unsigned char *colors=new float[numfaces*9];

// here you would fill the arrays as needed... type your own code

// rendering code
glEnableClientState(GL_VERTEX_ARRAY);
glVertexPointer(3,GL_FLOAT,0,&( vtx[0]));

glEnableClientState(GL_TEXTURE_COORD_ARRAY);
glTexCoordPointer(2,GL_FLOAT,0,&( texcoords[0]));

glEnableClientState(GL_COLOR_ARRAY);
glColorPointer(3,GL_UNSIGNED_BYTE,0,&( colors[0]));

glDrawArrays(GL_TRIANGLES,0,3*numfaces);
```

There are three key steps to using VAs. You first need to declare them. They are just user-defined arrays, so they can be filled using conventional C/C++ code. In the second step, once they are declared and filled, you must enable the required arrays and pass a pointer so OpenGL has access to the data. Here the calls always have the same syntax:

```
gl*Pointer(int num, GLenum type, int stride, void *data)
```

The first parameter indicates how many components each element consists of. For example, a color as RGB has three components, a texture coordinate has two (*U* and *V*), and so on. The second parameter is the type of each component. This can be any of the generic OpenGL types, with the following restrictions:

- ➤ **Vertices**: `GL_FLOAT`, `GL_DOUBLE`

- ➤ **TexCoords**: `GL_FLOAT`, `GL_DOUBLE`

- ➤ **Normals**: `GL_FLOAT`, `GL_DOUBLE`

- ➤ **Color**: `GL_FLOAT`, `GL_DOUBLE`, `GL_UNSIGNED_BYTE`

The third parameter (`stride`) is used to create interleaved arrays. It specifies the number of array positions between the end of an element and the beginning of the next one. In a noninterleaved array elements follow each other in a sequence, thus 0 is used. For interleaved arrays, positive integers specify the spacing between elements. Additionally, the fourth and last parameter passes a pointer to the array data. Notice that you can pass a pointer to the beginning of the array as in the previous example or set the beginning of the array at some other point by using:

```
glTexCoordPointer(2,GL_FLOAT,0,&( texcoords[34]));
```

The third step in rendering a VA is effectively drawing the data using the specified arrays. Here the syntax for `glDrawArrays` again needs an explanation. The first parameter tells OpenGL which rendering primitive to use. The second parameter specifies the starting point from the arrays (in elements). For the third parameter, you must specify the number of elements to render.

Notice that the final parameter generally specifies the number of vertices to render, and hence the multiplication in the preceding code, because each triangle has three vertices. A similar approach can be used to render `GL_POINTS`, `GL_LINES`, and so on. A very good option is to draw arrays of triangle strips because these are usually very tightly packed (the first triangle takes three vertices and each subsequent triangle only takes one extra vertex).

The combination of VAs and triangle strips yields optimal performance. But we can further improve it by organizing data in the arrays in a different way. When drawing geometry, whether it's plain triangles or triangle strips, we will sometimes repeat a vertex because two faces might be sharing some vertices. This is especially important in arrays of GL_TRIANGLES, but can also happen with strips. We are wasting precious bandwidth resending vertex coordinates (along with normals, colors, and so on, which will probably be repeated as well). To prevent this and ensure optimal geometry packing, we can add a new array (the index array), which allows us to send each vertex exactly once.

Compiled Vertex Arrays

A compiled VA is just a regular VA that we can sometimes cache on the server side for repeated calls. Static geometry that gets rendered frequently, such as interfaces, static objects, and so on, can greatly benefit from its performance. Unfortunately, compiled VAs are available only in some newer hardware, so they must be handled with care.

Server-Side Vertex Arrays

Along with display lists, server-side VAs offer top performance in most rendering pipelines. As mentioned earlier, display lists have the shortcoming of being limited to static geometry because their initialization process is slow. Server-side VAs overcome this limitation, and thus can be used for dynamic data as well. As usual, benefits don't come completely free. Some programming details of server-side arrays are a bit unintuitive and reaching top speed using them might take some time and careful programming. Because server-side VAs are completely vendor specific, I will explore both NVIDIA's and ATI's approach, and hint at a common interface that should be available when this book hits store shelves. For now, take a look at Figure B.6 for a diagram of the difference between regular and server-side VAs.

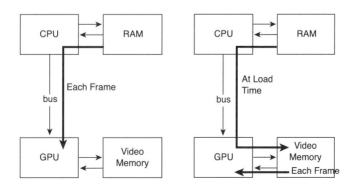

Figure B.6   Regular VAs (left) use the system bus per-frame, whereas server-side systems, such as VAR, VAO, and vertex buffer object (VBO), store data on the GPU side.

Vertex Array Range

VARs are offered on NVIDIA cards starting with the GeForce2. The technology is based on regular VAs, with the added benefit of being able to allocate the arrays both in video or in Accelerated Graphics Port (AGP) memory. Video memory is scarce because it is the memory available on the graphics card. Keep in mind that a graphics card must allocate, among other structures, the double-buffered frame buffer, the Z-buffer, texture maps, and so on. So, we can use available video memory to allocate a VA there. AGP memory, on the other hand, is just regular system memory, which has the special property of being easily accessed by the video card using the AGP bus. AGP memory is more plentiful and can offer similar performance to video memory, especially in systems with fast AGP buses.

To work with VARs, you basically request a block of memory in the GPU (either AGP or video memory). Then, you can create a different set of arrays in user memory space and fill those with data. Whenever you want to update the version on the GPU, all you have to do is block-copy data to the VAR declared in GPU space. It is very important not to access VAR memory in any way other than by doing a block-copy (memcpy), because VAR memory is slow to write.

Specifically, video memory is slow in all systems except those supporting Fast Writes. Only in these systems will write performance be good. But a good rule of thumb is to use video memory for static geometry that is used very frequently. This way you can maximize VAR speed and avoid the relatively poor video memory write performance. AGP memory, on the contrary, can be used for dynamic data. But remember that AGP memory is uncached, so random access is cost-prohibitive. Hence, the reason to work with regular, cached system memory and then block-copy data to AGP space is to write sequentially, taking full advantage of the write combiners.

Vertex Array Object

VAOs are ATI's version of server-side VAs. Like VARs, they allow programmers to declare a VA in video memory for improved performance. Unlike VARs, a VAO cannot reside in AGP memory.

Vertex Buffer Object

VBOs are the vendor-independent variant of server-side VAs. Supported by all major card vendors, they provide a common interface to declare buffers on video memory, so we can fill them with data, modify them, and render them efficiently. At the time of this writing, the specification has been approved and an implementation of the mechanism should surface soon. Quite likely, they will supersede both VARs and VAOs.

The main difference between VBOs and previous iterations is that VBOs allow developers to specify how are they going to use the buffer, so the API can make proper optimization choices. To declare a buffer, the following call must be used:

```
glBufferDataARB(target, size, *data, usage)
```

The first parameter must be `ARRAY_BUFFER_ARB`. The second is the size of the buffer in bytes. The third is the data to be mapped to the server-side buffer. The fourth parameter is where the usage is specified, with nine different usage patterns. Basically, the buffers can be characterized in three categories. They can be used for streaming (specify once, render once, as in a regular VA), for static geometry (specify once, render many times the same data, much like VARs), or for dynamic geometry (specify many times, render many times). Using a second criterion, buffers can be used to draw geometry, to read it back from video to CPU memory, or to copy it repeatedly onto GPU memory (for example for shader use). Then, by merging these two classifications, nine usage patterns emerge as shown in Table B.4.

Table B.4   Usage Patterns

	Draw	Read	Copy
Stream	ARB_STREAM_DRAW	ARB_STREAM_READ	ARB_STREAM_COPY
Static	ARB_STATIC_DRAW	ARB_STATIC_READ	ARB_STATIC_COPY
Dynamic	ARB_DYNAMIC_DRAW	ARB_DYNAMIC_READ	ARB_DYNAMIC_COPY

Overall, the system provides very fine-grained control over geometry and somehow resembles similar mechanisms found in DirectX.

OpenGL Extensions

You can achieve pretty spectacular results using standard OpenGL calls. You can also be sure that as soon as newer hardware features become mainstream, you will be able to use them in your OpenGL programs. However, graphics hardware evolves at a rapid pace, sometimes outpacing OpenGL. Features must be implemented in a variety of cards before they are fully integrated into the standard, so frequently it takes some time for the newer features to become available in the API.

Thus, sometimes you will purchase a new graphics card and some of its cutting-edge features will not be available in OpenGL. You could wait until the next OpenGL release, but that is simply not practical: It can take months or even years because some features are only supported by one vendor, and thus never make it to the standard.

Luckily, there is a better option. Because OpenGL is a standard, all adapters must conform to it and support all features. However, there is a caveat for those cases in which a certain feature must be exposed, but only for specific adapters. It is called the *extension mechanism*, and it allows developers to access cutting-edge features found in newer chips just weeks after the chip debuts.

An OpenGL extension is a set of calls that implement vendor-specific functionality, and thus is not considered part of the standard. Any graphics adapter can choose to implement that extension or not, and the applications programmer must check whether the extension is available prior to executing it. As an example, some graphics cards support stereo viewing, so you can plug special glasses into your computer and visualize 3D graphics realistically. Clearly, this feature is vendor specific, and other cards might not be interested in it at all. But programmers need to be able to access this functionality from their OpenGL programs. So the adapter's manufacturer creates an OpenGL extension, and thus programmers can access this feature.

Efficiency Considerations

All graphics APIs, and OpenGL is no exception, need tuning in order to get the best performance. We have seen how much of a difference we can make by sending triangle strips down the graphics pipeline instead of ordinary triangles. But there's more to efficiency than that. In this section, I will provide a listing of practices that should help you increase the performance of any OpenGL application.

Geometric Representation

To achieve top performance, you must use efficient geometry formats. Painting triangles with `glBegin(GL_TRIANGLES)` is simply not enough to achieve decent performance. Here are some geometry representation hints to speed up your application.

Use strips or fans as much as you can. They use less memory to represent the same amount of geometry. You can use utilities to stripify geometry for you, such as NVTriStrip from NVIDIA.

Use indexed primitives. This saves memory and avoids repeating the same vertices. A cube's memory footprint, for example, can be divided in two by indexing its faces properly. Creating indexed primitives is relatively straightforward as a preprocess: Get your incoming vertex list and every time you encounter a vertex you haven't encountered before, add it to the index table. Then, build the face loops by indexing them to the index list.

Use compact representations. For example, you can write:

```
glColor3d(1,1,1);
```

Storing colors as doubles is a performance killer. Most cards use floats internally, so you are wasting bandwidth. The following call is even more inefficient:

```
glColor3f(1,1,1);
```

Most computer screens work in 24-bit RGB color, so each pixel uses three bytes. Thus, a representation like the following offers the same visual quality while dividing memory use by a factor of four. Less memory implies less bus impact and higher performance.

```
glColor3ub(255,255,255);
```

Send as little data as possible. Imagine that you need to send a VA of 1000 triangles, all of them of equal color (white, for example). You can fill a color array with copies of that color or, even better, write:

```
glColor3ub(255,255,255);
glEnableClientState(GL_VERTEX_ARRAY....);
glDrawElements(...)
```

Repeated components do not need to be sent to the pipeline for each primitive. You can save lots of precious bandwidth by using a single call.

Geometry Rendering

Another item to watch out for is geometry rendering. Some paths into graphics chips are faster than others, and thus knowing how to deliver geometry to the hardware efficiently is key to achieving top performance.

For example, immediate mode rendering (`glBegin(GL_TRIANGLES)`) is painfully slow when compared to faster alternatives such as VAs. Thus, immediate mode rendering should be avoided at all costs, even for simple interface elements.

You have three alternatives. First, you can use display lists. Display lists offer good performance, but list setup is a slow process, so data cannot be animated. But for static geometry (interfaces and menus are a good example), they are an excellent rendering method. Second, VAs allows you to modify geometry on the fly. VAs are stored in the application's memory space, so you should try to batch primitives together in sequences of at least 100 elements. Then, render those using VAs or display lists. On most cards, the "sweet spot" where you can achieve maximum rendering speed is around 1,000 triangles.

A third, more involved alternative is to create a complete memory manager and take advantage of any special hardware available. Try to allocate very frequent geometry in video memory and take advantage of AGP buses to transfer it efficiently.

Avoid Unneeded State Changes

OpenGL is very sensitive to state changes. Every time you turn lighting on and off, change the active texture map, and so on you are incurring a performance hit. Thus, a series of measures need to be taken to ensure your rendering pipeline is as efficient as possible.

First, you can sort your objects by texture and render them with an efficient method (display lists or VAs). When sorting by texture, you ensure the minimum number of texture swaps and also allow longer primitives.

Second, make sure you are rendering with the minimum state available. Blending usage, for example, should be kept to a minimum because it is computationally expensive. Render all blended primitives together and disable blending as soon as you are finished. The same applies to lighting or to any other rendering option that might slow down your code.

Discard Early

The key to performance under OpenGL is not really about painting triangles fast: It is about not painting triangles even faster. Determining what should really be drawn accurately is the best way to ensure good performance. Don't let the hardware clip geometry for you. To discard a triangle it will already have crossed the bus, wreaking havoc with your performance. Detect unseen geometry as fast as you can. You can perform hierarchical, per-object clipping, you can cluster-cull back-facing geometry, and some cards can even help you determine occlusions before the real geometry is actually sent to the pipeline. Examine your target platform closely, so you know how to avoid doing more work than is really needed. In Chapter 12, "3D Pipeline Overview," we discussed some popular methods to reduce the rendered data set.

In Closing

Covering OpenGL in a single chapter is impossible. However, this chapter has provided you with all the information required to begin coding OpenGL programs. You know how to render geometry efficiently, how to control the camera, and how to achieve realistic effects using textures and lighting.

Throughout the book, OpenGL code has been used frequently to illustrate some coding principles. That code expands the contents of this chapter, so you can delve into OpenGL's more advanced features such as multipass rendering and vertex/pixel programs.

For those interested in more material dealing with OpenGL, see the official OpenGL web site at `www.opengl.org`. There you will find hundreds of code samples as well as the full documentation of the API. Particularly useful are the main pages, which can be browsed online and provide an alphabetic reference for all OpenGL calls.

Appendix C

Direct3D

This appendix provides a brief introduction to the Microsoft DirectX technology for rendering 3D graphics. A full-blown tutorial of the API would require hundreds of pages and is by no means the goal of this book. However, I felt it was important to offer some preliminary information, so you can get coding soon. Thus, this appendix only attempts to cover the essentials of Direct3D: its main components, how to work with them, and so on. Other chapters in the book provide more involved examples for specific applications.

History

Since the advent of PC computers and before the release of Windows 95, PC games were coded under DOS. Developers had direct access to the hardware, which wasn't as powerful as it is today: no 3D cards, no sound, just a plain CPU and memory mapped frame buffer. Logically, many tips and tricks emerged from the game development community as a way to achieve top performance under this not-so-powerful hardware. All critical routines, for example, were systematically coded in hand-optimized assembly language: rendering cores, block data transfers, and many other tasks could be sped up by many orders of magnitude with some clever planning and deep hardware knowledge. These were the years when each graphics programmer kept his `PutPixel` routine, counted down to the clock cycles, a trade secret.

But there was more than putting pixels onscreen quickly. Another interesting technique was to overwrite the interrupt vector, and thus have greater control over tasks like keyboard input, timer control, and so on. By replacing specific interrupt handling routines using your own code, you could ensure very low-level access to any system event, from a key press to the internal PC timer, which ticked, if memory does not fail me, 18.2 times per second. This was a dangerous trick because any mistake in your code would leave the PC in an unstable state, often ending in a black screen and a reboot.

Under this context, Windows 95 was launched. Unlike Windows 3.1, Windows 95 was a full-blown 32-bit operating system that loaded at boot time, so everything had to be done from within the OS interface. Gone were the days of using DOS for playing games and typing "win" whenever we wanted to use Microsoft Word. As you can imagine, Windows 95 wasn't very popular with game developers in the early days. Low-level access to the hardware was restricted, and this meant a lot to game developers. The only games that could be played within the main OS interface were relatively simple, mine-sweeper-like games.

Thus, Microsoft decided to create a specific set of tools to allow game developers to code cutting edge games under Windows 95. These tools allowed access to devices the developers were asking for while keeping the system relatively safe. Luckily, these were the years when graphics cards grew up and became 3D accelerators, and audio boards were already mainstream. So, did developers need to access the frame buffer anymore? Well, not as much as years before. In fact, what was required was an intermediate, standard layer of code that exposed the continuous advances of the hardware to developers, so they could use it without directly accessing it. This layer would "understand" the different hardware configurations, and simply map calls to the hardware when possible.

This new product was initially called the Game Software Developer's Kit (SDK) and, as it began to slowly spread around the community, it was renamed DirectX. The first iterations (until DirectX 5) were highly experimental. Microsoft was internally evolving the product and incorporating suggestions from the game developers. Microsoft fought an uphill battle with game developers to convince them that the newborn API was in fact a pretty good idea. These were the years of some pretty crude flames in the famous DirectX versus OpenGL battle. Some developers criticized Microsoft for creating a new API (which for years was rather poor) when a stable, elegant API was already available. Whatever your opinion, the fact is that DirectX's design was greatly improved, having borrowed many ideas from OpenGL. Let's not forget that OpenGL is just a 3D API, whereas DirectX is much more. In fact, some modern games use DirectX for everything but graphics, preferring OpenGL for rendering tasks.

DirectX was updated often (more or less once a year), so each new iteration provided new calls for the newest features present in hardware. Whether it was painting a triangle or reading the joystick input, DirectX mapped new functionality through its API in a matter of months. From version 6 and later, DirectX became a rather good API and finally won widespread acceptance, especially as 3D cards became more and more popular.

Currently, DirectX is the dominant API for PC game development. It is also the driving force in Microsoft's Xbox, which is coded in a special version of DirectX 8. In the PC arena, OpenGL still retains a following of developers. In the end, it is all a matter of preference because both APIs are just interfaces to the hardware, and thus the functionality is nearly identical.

Many DirectX APIs were used in different chapters throughout this book. A complete summary of where they can be found is at the end of this chapter. Thus, we will only focus on Direct3D now, which incidentally is the only API we haven't devoted space to.

Booting Direct3D

The first step any Direct3D application must perform is to create the Direct3D object, from which all other objects are generated. The Direct3D object is thus a bit like the factory design pattern. Once we have created it, we can extract new interfaces from it easily. Let's take a look at the code required to properly initialize Direct3D.

The structures we will need are as follows:

```
LPDIRECT3D8 g_pD3D = NULL; // Used to create the D3DDevice
LPDIRECT3DDEVICE8 g_pd3dDevice = NULL; // Our rendering device
HWND hWnd;       // window handle, already initialized
```

Now, let's review the calls required to actually create the Direct3D object. To do so, we need to pass the symbolic constant D3D_SDK_VERSION as a parameter, so Direct3D can make sure the application is built against the right set of header files. The code would be

```
g_pD3D = Direct3DCreate8( D3D_SDK_VERSION );
if (g_pD3D==NULL) return false;
```

We now need to create the Direct3D-compatible device that will be used to generate the graphics. This is a three-step approach. First, we query the system so we can get information on the display mode, window characteristics, and so on. Second, we fill the D3DPRESENT_PARAMETERS structure with the settings we want to include in our device, and third, we create the device. The following code gets the current display mode:

```
D3DDISPLAYMODE d3ddm;

if(FAILED(g_pD3D->GetAdapterDisplayMode(D3DADAPTER_DEFAULT,
&d3ddm)))
          return false;
```

Now, let's fill the presentation parameters structure, which is used to create the D3DDevice. Most parameters are unused and thus can be zeroed out. We set Windowed to TRUE, because we want to do D3D in a window, and then set the SwapEffect to discard, which is the most efficient method of presenting the back buffer to the display. We then request a back buffer format that matches the current desktop display format:

```
D3DPRESENT_PARAMETERS d3dpp;
ZeroMemory( &d3dpp, sizeof(d3dpp) );
d3dpp.Windowed = TRUE;
d3dpp.SwapEffect = D3DSWAPEFFECT_DISCARD;
d3dpp.BackBufferFormat = d3ddm.Format;
```

Notice how we have requested a windowed application, which runs in the same graphics mode as the host. By doing so, Direct3D inherits the window size from the main application. Now we are ready to actually create the device with the CreateDevice call. Here we are using the default adapter (most systems only have one unless they have multiple graphics hardware cards installed) and requesting the Hardware Abstraction Layer (HAL) (which is specifying that we want the hardware device rather than a software device). Software vertex processing is specified because we know it will work on all cards. On cards that support hardware vertex processing, though, we would see a big performance gain by specifying hardware vertex processing.

```
if(FAILED(g_pD3D->CreateDevice(D3DADAPTER_DEFAULT,
D3DDEVTYPE_HAL,
hWnd,
D3DCREATE_SOFTWARE_VERTEXPROCESSING,
```

```
&d3dpp, &g_pd3dDevice ) ) )
    {
    return false;
    }
```

The first parameter tells Direct3D we want to use the default graphics adapter. This is not important in most cases because we will probably only have one video card. But for systems with more than one video board, the first parameter is the ordinal number of the card: 0, 1, 2, and so on. The second parameter tells Direct3D to use the HAL. This means we will perform hardware rendering, which is the most common option. Other options are D3DDEVTYPE_REF for the reference rasterizer and D3DDEVTYPE_SW for software rendering. The third parameter is the window handle to the application. In the fourth parameter, we need to specify the kind of vertex processing will we use. We can choose between software vertex processing (as in the preceding example), hardware, or mixed. Right after the vertex processing options, we need to state which presentation parameters our device will be using. In the example, that data comes from the D3DPRESENT_PARAMETERS structure we just initialized. For completeness, here is the format of the structure:

```
typedef struct _D3DPRESENT_PARAMETERS_ {
    UINT                      BackBufferWidth;
    UINT                      BackBufferHeight;
    D3DFORMAT           BackBufferFormat;
    UINT                      BackBufferCount;

    D3DMULTISAMPLE_TYPE      MultiSampleType;

    D3DSWAPEFFECT      SwapEffect;
    HWND                      hDeviceWindow;
    BOOL                      Windowed;
    BOOL                      EnableAutoDepthStencil;
    D3DFORMAT            AutoDepthStencilFormat;
    DWORD                     Flags;

    UINT                          FullScreen_RefreshRateInHz;
    UINT                          FullScreen_PresentationInterval;

} D3DPRESENT_PARAMETERS;
```

As you can see, there's lots to explore and set, like initializing the stencil buffer or controlling the number of backbuffers. The call to `CreateDevice` ends the boot process and leaves us with a brand-new, ready to use Direct3D device where we can send our geometry. Here is the complete code so you can copy and paste as needed:

```
LPDIRECT3D8 g_pD3D = NULL; // Used to create the D3DDevice
LPDIRECT3DDEVICE8 g_pd3dDevice = NULL; // Our rendering device
HWND hWnd;   // window handle, already initialized

g_pD3D = Direct3DCreate8( D3D_SDK_VERSION );
if (g_pD3D==NULL) return false;


D3DDISPLAYMODE d3ddm;

if(FAILED(g_pD3D->GetAdapterDisplayMode(D3DADAPTER_DEFAULT,
&d3ddm)))
        return false;


D3DPRESENT_PARAMETERS d3dpp;
ZeroMemory( &d3dpp, sizeof(d3dpp) );
d3dpp.Windowed = TRUE;
d3dpp.SwapEffect = D3DSWAPEFFECT_DISCARD;
d3dpp.BackBufferFormat = d3ddm.Format;

if(FAILED(g_pD3D->CreateDevice(
D3DADAPTER_DEFAULT,
D3DDEVTYPE_HAL,
hWnd,
D3DCREATE_SOFTWARE_VERTEXPROCESSING,
&d3dpp, &g_pd3dDevice ) ) )
    {
    return false;
    }
```

Now, let's take care of some geometry.

Handling Geometry

Geometry processing in DirectX can be achieved in a variety of ways. In fact, different methods have been used as the API has evolved through several versions. Luckily, this has led to a stable, intuitive method, which is the one featured in DirectX 9, and the one we will be focusing on. The method consists of using vertex buffers, which are just user-provided arrays of data (vertex coordinates, texture coordinates, colors, and so on) batched together for rendering. A vertex buffer can be defined in user or graphics/AGP memory, be assigned a vertex shader for custom procedural effects, and so on.

We will begin by analyzing how to declare a vertex buffer. This is achieved by using the `CreateVertexBuffer` call, which has the following interface:

```
HRESULT CreateVertexBuffer(UINT Length,DWORD Usage,DWORD FVF,
D3DPOOL Pool,IDirect3DVertexBuffer8** ppVertexBuffer);
```

There are many calls that share this same (or relatively close) syntax in Direct3D. Creating indices, textures, and so on is all handled in a similar manner. Here is the run-down of the parameter list: The first parameter should contain the length of the buffer to be created, in bytes. The second parameter can be used as a hint to Direct3D about the use we are creating the index array for. Items like point sprites and N-patches are specified here, but if we just want to render regular geometry, we can store a zero value here. The third parameter declares the Flexible Vertex Format (FVF) to be used with this specific vertex buffer. FVFs are used to declare the data structure that will hold your vertices. Will you store vertex coordinates only, or will colors be added? Will you be incorporating texture coordinates and, if so, which data type will be used to encode them? All this is encapsulated in the FVF. A complete example is provided later in this section. After that, we need to state the kind of memory management we want for our buffer. Our vertex buffer can be stored in regular system RAM or, if our hardware supports it, directly in the video card. By doing this, we can ensure fast access to the rendering core and increased performance. Valid parameters are `D3DPOOL_DEFAULT`, which should be used to let Direct3D choose the most adequate storage options; `D3DPOOL_MANAGED`, which is used to store data in device memory to ensure optimal performance; or `D3DPOOL_SYSTEMMEM`, which stores data in regular system RAM. See the next section on geometry optimization for more on setting these parameters. The last parameter is just a pointer to the newly declared vertex buffer.

Now, we will use the DrawPrimitive to actually render the geometry. But we need to start by setting the stream source so any subsequent DrawPrimitive is coupled with the vertex buffer and the call knows where to get data from. This is achieved with the SetStreamSource call. The following is a complete example:

```
g_pd3dDevice->SetStreamSource( 0, g_pVB, sizeof(CUSTOMVERTEX) );
g_pd3dDevice->DrawPrimitive( D3DPT_POINTLIST, 0, NUMVTX );
```

The first parameter to SetStreamSource is the identifier of the logical stream to Direct3D, starting from 0 and reaching a value of numstreams-1. The second parameter is the vertex buffer, whereas the third parameter is used to specify the stride between two contiguous elements. In this case, it's the size of the CUSTOMVERTEX structure that is defined by our FVF. Once we execute this line, subsequent DrawPrimitive calls will know where to gather data from. The syntax for the DrawPrimitive call is

```
HRESULT DrawPrimitive(D3DPRIMITIVETYPE PrimitiveType, UINT
StartVertex,
   UINT PrimitiveCount);
```

The first parameter states the type of primitive to render. Valid types are

➤ D3DPT_POINTLIST   Renders the vertices as a collection of points.

➤ D3DPT_LINELIST   Renders the vertices as a list of line segments. Lines are built with vertices 0 and 1, 2 and 3, and so on. The number of vertices must be greater than two and even for this method to work.

➤ D3DPT_LINESTRIP   Renders the vertices as a single polyline. A line sequence will be created from vertices 0 to 1, 1 to 2, and so on.

➤ D3DPT_TRIANGLELIST   Renders the specified vertices as a sequence of triangles. Each group of three vertices defines a separate triangle. Backface culling is affected by the current winding-order render state.

➤ D3DPT_TRIANGLESTRIP   Renders the vertices as a triangle strip. Vertices 0, 1, and 2 form the first triangle, and then each new vertex (along with the previous two in the sequence) form the next one. The backface culling flag is automatically flipped on even-numbered triangles.

➤ D3DPT_TRIANGLEFAN   Renders the vertices as a triangle fan: Vertex 0 is the center of the fan, and vertices 1, 2, 3, and 4 define its outer edge.

The second and third parameter to `DrawPrimitive` tell Direct3D which position in the vertex buffer we should start streaming data from and how many primitives to send down the pipeline. This is useful to render not the complete primitive, but part of it (for example, the part that uses a unique material identifier).

Indexed Primitives

`DrawPrimitive` can only work with nonindexed primitives. For indexed primitives, `DrawIndexedPrimitive` must be used. However, we need to first learn how to create an index buffer, so we can couple that with the actual geometry. The process starts with a call to:

```
HRESULT CreateIndexBuffer(UINT Length,DWORD Usage,D3DFORMAT
Format,
   D3DPOOL Pool,IDirect3DIndexBuffer8** ppIndexBuffer);
```

This call creates the array of indices. The syntax is very similar to the `CreateVertexBuffer` call. The only difference is the third parameter. For the `CreateVertexBuffer` call, this parameter specifies the FVF to be used. This makes no sense in index buffers. But there is a parameter that is somehow similar: The `Format` parameter allows us to specify the format of the index buffer so memory footprint is reduced. Valid parameters are `D3DFMT_INDEX16` for 16-bit indices and `D3DFMT_INDEX32` for their 32-bit counterparts.

Now, we need to provide Direct3D with both a vertex and index buffer. The index buffer will contain the topology information (face loops), whereas the vertex buffer will hold the geometrical information, such as vertices, colors, and mapping coordinates.

Then, the `DrawIndexedPrimitive` is used to render the geometry. The syntax is

```
HRESULT DrawIndexedPrimitive(D3DPRIMITIVETYPE Type,
    INT BaseVertexIndex,
    UINT MinIndex,
    UINT NumVertices,
    UINT StartIndex,
    UINT PrimitiveCount
);
```

The first parameter defines the type of geometry to handle, from points to triangle strips and fans. The second and third parameters are used to specify the starting point in both the vertex and index buffers. Then, we use the remaining parameters to specify the number of vertices, the first index, and the number of indices to be processed, respectively.

User Pointer Primitives

Creating and filling a vertex buffer with data is only one of the ways to render geometry in DirectX. Sometimes, especially for testing purposes, you will simply want to allocate a memory buffer in user memory space and tell DirectX to render its contents without the burden of locking and copying it to the APIs space.

Logically, working with user memory pointers requires less effort from the programmer. There is no need for vertex buffers, locking, and so on. But this ease of use comes at a performance cost. Sometimes, data in user memory won't be copied to the graphics subsystem, and thus it will be hard to reach maximum performance. But for some cases, like geometry that changes on a frame-by-frame basis, the copy and lock operations might also be imposing a significant penalty, so user memory primitives will be the way to go.

User memory primitives are exposed through the `DrawPrimitiveUP` and `DrawIndexedPrimtitiveUP` calls. Here is the syntax for `DrawPrimitiveUP`:

```
HRESULT DrawPrimitiveUP(D3DPRIMITIVETYPE PrimitiveType,
UINT PrimitiveCount, const void *pVertexStreamZeroData,
UINT VertexStreamZeroStride);
```

As usual, the first parameter should contain the primitive type, which is the same as in regular `DrawPrimitive` calls. Then, we need the primitive count, which also has the same geometric interpretation as in the classic `DrawPrimitive`. As a third parameter, we will need a pointer to the data. We didn't use a pointer on `DrawPrimitive` because we passed the vertex buffer instead, so that is the main difference between the two calls. In addition, we will need to specify the stride. Note, however, that the pointer must still use DirectX's conventions for vertex structures. The structure of the data must be exactly the structure used in vertex buffers.

Indexed primitives can also work this way. In this case, the call is

```
HRESULT DrawIndexedPrimitiveUP(D3DPRIMITIVETYPE PrimitiveType,
UINT MinVertexIndex, UINT NumVertexIndices, UINT PrimitiveCount,
const void *pIndexData, D3DFORMAT IndexDataFormat, CONST void*
pVertexStreamZeroData, UINT VertexStreamZeroStride);
```

The parameters in the preceding call are also very similar to the regular
`DrawIndexedPrimitive` call. The only difference is the pointer to the index buffer
on parameter five and the pointer to the vertices on parameter seven. Other than that,
it works exactly like `IndexedPrimitive`.

Efficient Geometry Delivery

Direct3D offers some mechanisms to control how vertex buffers are delivered to the
hardware. By knowing these mechanisms, we can ensure optimal performance. To
begin with, we need to know how to declare a vertex or index buffer so it is always
stored in video memory. This is achieved at creation time. For example, the following
call gives Direct3D many cues about where to store the vertex buffer:

```
CreateVertexBuffer(size, D3DUSAGE_WRITEONLY, fvf, D3DPOOL_MANAGED ,
buffer);
```

First, we specify the buffer as write-only, so geometry stored there will never be animated or modified in any way. This is a good thing to do with all your static geometry
because it tells Direct3D that no updates to the data will be required, and thus it can
be transferred to the most efficient memory region available. Second, notice the parameter `D3DPOOL_MANAGED`, which tells Direct3D to make sure the vertex buffer is placed
wherever performance is best. Combining these two parameters is the best way to
ensure efficient rendering because data will be pulled from video or AGP memory
directly, skipping the bus.

Another interesting option is checking for hardware vertex processing capabilities—
texturing and lighting (T&L), shaders, and so on—so we can take advantage of them
in our application. DirectX allows us to check for hardware vertex processing compli-
ance when we create the device. This is achieved by using the call:

```
if(FAILED(g_pD3D->CreateDevice(
D3DADAPTER_DEFAULT,
D3DDEVTYPE_HAL,
hWnd,
D3DCREATE_HARDWARE_VERTEXPROCESSING,
&d3dpp, &g_pd3dDevice ) ) )
    {
    return false;
    }
```

Additionally, remember to use the most efficient delivery methods. Indexed, stripped coordinates are the way to go because vertex and index buffers will save precious memory, and fewer vertices will need to cross the pipeline.

Flexible Vertex Formats

Vertex buffers in Direct3D can encapsulate very different information, from vertex coordinates to texture coordinates and colors, and some other exotic data types such as weights for animation matrices. All this is elegantly built into the API using FVF, which is a mechanism to declare the format of a buffer so Direct3D knows how to handle it.

Fundamentally, vertices in Direct3D are defined as arrays of structs. Each struct is one vertex, and we can define the internals of that struct. The FVF informs Direct3D of our chosen format. For example, the following code tells Direct3D we have a vertex format that encapsulates position information (D3DFVF_XYZ), normals, and one set of texture coordinates:

```
struct D3DVERTEX
    {
    D3DXVECTOR3 p;
    D3DXVECTOR3 n;
    FLOAT tu, tv;
    static const DWORD FVF;
    };
const DWORD D3DVERTEX::FVF = D3DFVF_XYZ | D3DFVF_NORMAL |
D3DFVF_TEX1
```

However, the "flexible" in the FVF allows much more than this. Take a look at the next declaration:

```
dwFVF = ( D3DFVF_XYZ | D3DFVF_NORMAL | D3DFVF_DIFFUSE |
    D3DFVF_SPECULAR | D3DFVF_TEX2 );
```

This FVF incorporates vertices and normals, two sets of texture coordinates, and both a diffuse and specular color. This makes it useful for per-vertex lighting using hardware lights, which will interact with the FVF's diffuse and specular color.

There are many FVF combinations; each suited for specific purposes. The best way to learn about them is to take a look at the DirectX SDK documentation, which lists them and in most cases provides use examples. For completeness, the diagram in Figure C.1 shows all possible FVF combinations.

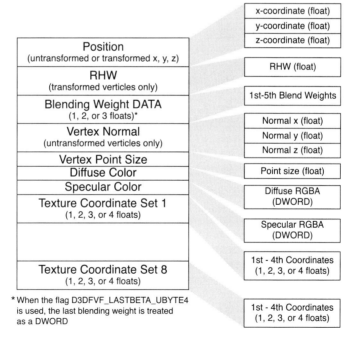

Figure C.1 The FVF framework with all possible values listed.

Matrices, Cameras, and Transforms

Direct3D can apply geometric transforms to incoming data. If the hardware supports
hardware transform and lighting, performance will be very good because computations
will be processed on the GPU. Older boards will perform software transforms.

As with OpenGL, the camera is just a special-case transform, which can be accessed
comfortably with some macro operations. Similarities with OpenGL do not end there.
Under Direct3D, we have a projection matrix (which controls the way data is projected
from a 3D game world to a 2D screen) and a modelview matrix, which controls the
camera placement with regard to the scene. In addition, Direct3D supports a third
transform called the world transform, which is used to apply local transforms to
objects in the scene.

To begin with, here is the source code required to place a camera in the game world.
First, we set our viewing matrix:

```
D3DXMATRIX matView;
D3DXMatrixLookAtLH(&matView,
&D3DXVECTOR3(x,0,z),
&D3DXVECTOR3(x+cos(yaw),0,z+sin(yaw)),
&D3DXVECTOR3(0,1,0));
g_pd3dDevice->SetTransform( D3DTS_VIEW, &matView );
```

Notice how we have implemented the classic first-person shooter camera: a position
and a yaw vector. Now we need to specify the projection matrix as well. So, we set the
field of view, the aspect ratio, and the near and far clipping planes:

```
D3DXMATRIX matProj;
D3DXMatrixPerspectiveFovLH( &matProj, D3DX_PI/4, 1.3, 1, 10000 );
g_pd3dDevice->SetTransform( D3DTS_PROJECTION, &matProj );
```

Once we have done this, we only need to learn how to specify hierarchical transforms
in our game geometry. These are specified by a set of calls in the DIRECT3DX utility
library, which is DirectX's counterpart to the GLU in OpenGL. Each function call
returns a specific matrix, which can be multiplied by our world matrix. We start with
the following call, which resets the world matrix:

```
D3DXMATRIX matWorld;
D3DXMatrixIdentity(&matWorld);
```

Then, we can use any of the following:

```
D3DXMatrixRotationX, D3DXMatrixRotationY, D3DXMatrixRotationZ
D3DXMatrixTranslation
```

Direct3D also supports some exotic matrices, such as a roll, pitch, and yaw matrix that is specified by the following code, which can be handy for flight simulators:

```
D3DXMATRIX* D3DXMatrixRotationYawPitchRoll(
   D3DXMATRIX* pOut,
   FLOAT Yaw,
   FLOAT Pitch,
   FLOAT Roll,
);
```

As you might expect, matrices can be stacked hierarchically, so complex coordinate systems can be built. All we have to do is compose matrices to achieve the desired result. Take a look at the following example in which we render a robot arm with three transforms: one for the shoulder, one for the elbow, and one for the wrist:

```
D3DXMATRIX matWorld;
D3DXMatrixIdentity(&matWorld);
g_pd3dDevice->SetTransform( D3DTS_WORLD, &matWorld );

// compute shoulder transform here

g_pd3dDevice->SetTransform(D3DTS_WORLD, shoulder_transform);

// render the upper arm, compute elbow transform

g_pd3dDevice->MultiplyTransform(D3DTS_WORLD, elbow_transform);

// render the lower arm, compute wrist transform
```

```
g_pd3dDevice->MultiplyTransform(D3DTS_WORLD, wrist_transform);
```

```
// render the robot arm
```

DirectX supports matrix concatenation much like OpenGL, so we can express a complex transform in terms of a series of simpler operations.

Working with Texture Maps

It is simple to add texture mapping to our Direct3D code. All we have to do is learn how to select the right texture map from a file and how to specify mapping coordinates for the geometry.

To begin with, we can load a texture map from a file by using the code:

```
LPDIRECT3DTEXTURE9 g_pTexture = NULL;
```

```
D3DXCreateTextureFromFile(g_pd3dDevice,"image.bmp", &g_pTexture));
```

Textures can be loaded using the Direct3D utility library. We need to specify a previously initialized Direct3D device object, the file we want to load (.bmp, .dds, .dib, .jpg, .png, and .tga. are all supported), and the texture object that will encapsulate the map from that moment on.

Then, we need a call to specify which is the current texture, so the renderer applies that one to subsequent geometry. This is achieved with the call:

```
g_pd3dDevice->SetTexture( 0, g_pTexture );
```

The first parameter is the stage that the texture will be assigned for. The first stage is 0, and so on. Texture stages are useful for multitexturing.

Then, all we have to do is specify an FVF that includes texture coordinates. This way our objects will appear fully textured. This is achieved by using a line like:

```
#define D3DFVF_GEOMETRY (D3DFVF_XYZ | D3DFVF_NORMAL | D3DFVF_TEX1 )
```

and the corresponding structure:

```
struct GEOMETRY
{
    D3DXVECTOR3 p;
    D3DXVECTOR3 n;
    FLOAT tu, tv;
};
```

A final observation is that texture mapping can be switched on and off depending on what you want to do. This is achieved with a call to `SetRenderState`, which is explained in the next section.

Lighting

DirectX has powerful lighting capabilities, which are especially useful on platforms supporting hardware lighting. We can set the type of light we want to use, its position, color, and several other parameters. Notice, however, that this is per-vertex lighting. We will be illuminating the processed vertices, and interpolation will be used to illuminate the pixels in between successive vertices. If you want to do per-pixel illumination, you need to use techniques such as light mapping, which is covered in detail in Chapter 17, "Shading."

Direct3D shading is accessed using very intuitive methods. We only need to define the light sources and their properties, and how each surface material will respond to them. To begin with, the core of Direct3D's lighting capabilities lies in the D3DLIGHT9 structure, which has the following attributes:

```
typedef struct _D3DLIGHT9
{
    D3DLIGHTTYPE Type;
    D3DCOLORVALUE Diffuse;
    D3DCOLORVALUE Specular;
    D3DCOLORVALUE Ambient;
    D3DVECTOR Position;
    D3DVECTOR Direction;
```

```
        float  Range;
        float  Falloff;
        float  Attenuation0;
        float  Attenuation1;
        float  Attenuation2;
        float  Theta;
        float  Phi;
} D3DLIGHT9;
```

The first parameter is the type of light source we want to use. Point lights, spotlights, and directional lights are all supported. Then, we have three color values to specify: the ambient, diffuse, and specular components of the light color. We can then specify the position (for point and spotlights) and direction (for directional and spotlight only) vectors. The next parameters are specific to spotlights. Range is used to control how light decays with distance. Points located further than range from the light source will not receive any light. Falloff represents the amount of decay between a spotlight's internal and external cones. Then, the three attenuation parameters are used to describe an envelope of the light's attenuation depending on distance. Basically, attenuation is computed as the sum of a cubic polynomial over the distance from the point being lit to the light source: Attenuation 0 is independent to distance, attenuation 1 is linear to distance, and so on. By using these values, we can implement exotic attenuation curves. As a summary, here is the law that describes how the parameters interact:

```
Atten = 1/( attenuation0 + attenuation1 * d + attenuation2 * d2)
```

Notice that directional lights have attenuation set to one regardless of the distance to the lamp and are thus not attenuated. For all other light types, points beyond the range are attenuated by a value of zero, and thus no light is ever received.

Additionally, theta is the angle, in radians, of a spotlight's inner cone—that is, the fully illuminated spotlight cone. This value must be in the range from 0 through the value specified by Phi, which is the angle, in radians, that defines the outer edge of the spotlight's outer cone. Points outside this cone are not lit by the spotlight. This value must be between 0 and pi. Take a look at Figure C.2 for a clarifying diagram.

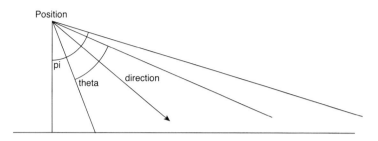

Figure C.2 Structure and parameters of a spotlight in DirectX.

Let's take a look at a working example in which we define a spotlight:

```
D3DXVECTOR3 vecDir, vecPos;
D3DLIGHT9 light;
ZeroMemory( &light, sizeof(D3DLIGHT9) );
light.Type        = D3DLIGHT_SPOTLIGHT;
light.Diffuse.r   = 1.0f;
light.Diffuse.g   = 1.0f;
light.Diffuse.b   = 1.0f;
vecDir = D3DXVECTOR3(0,-1,0);
D3DXVec3Normalize( (D3DXVECTOR3*)&light.Direction, &vecDir );
VecPos = D3DXVECTOR3(0,10,0);
D3DXVec3Normalize( (D3DXVECTOR3*)&light.Position, &vecPos );
light.Range       = 1000.0f;
light.Phi=1;
light.Theta=0.8;
g_pd3dDevice->SetLight( 0, &light );
g_pd3dDevice->LightEnable( 0, TRUE );
g_pd3dDevice->SetRenderState( D3DRS_LIGHTING, TRUE );
```

Notice how we end the sequence by sending the newly created light to the Direct3D device. In addition, we must enable lighting and activate the lighting render state for lights to be taken into consideration.

But we also need to set materials: Light interaction with vertices requires the latter to be assigned a material, so we can simulate how light bounces on different kinds of surfaces. This is achieved with the following D3DMATERIAL9 structure:

```
typedef struct _D3DMATERIAL9 {
    D3DCOLORVALUE Diffuse;
    D3DCOLORVALUE Ambient;
    D3DCOLORVALUE Specular;
    D3DCOLORVALUE Emissive;
    float Power;
} D3DMATERIAL9;
```

As with lights, the first three parameters are used to specify the color of the surface. In case the surface and light colors are different, lighting equations will blend the two. The last parameter is the typical exponent found in all specular highlights equations, which helps simulate different smoothness levels. Lower values can be used for rough materials, whereas higher values represent polished surfaces like metals or plastic. Setting a material is not very different from setting lights, as you can see in the following example:

```
D3DMATERIAL9 mtrl;
ZeroMemory( &mtrl, sizeof(D3DMATERIAL9) );
mtrl.Diffuse.r = mtrl.Ambient.r = 1.0f;
mtrl.Diffuse.g = mtrl.Ambient.g = 1.0f;
mtrl.Diffuse.b = mtrl.Ambient.b = 0.0f;
mtrl.Diffuse.a = mtrl.Ambient.a = 1.0f;
mtrl.Emissive= 5.0f;
g_pd3dDevice->SetMaterial( &mtrl );
```

A final comment on Direct3D's lighting is that often you will need to know the number of light sources supported by the device you are using. If your light number goes beyond that limit, illumination will be computed on the software driver, with the predictable loss of performance. Then, to detect the number of lights supported by the hardware, we only need to read the MaxActiveLights attribute of the D3DCAPS9 structure. Here is the source code for such a query:

```
D3DCAPS9 caps;
GetDeviceCaps(D3DADAPTER_DEFAULT,D3DDEVTYPE_HAL,&caps);
int num=caps.MaxActiveLights;
```

Render States

DirectX encapsulates many rendering options elegantly in a single interface: the render states. This consists of a single call that can modify dozens of rendering settings, such as fog, alpha-blending and testing, and so on. This way coding is greatly simplified. For example, here is the line required to set alpha-blending:

```
pd3dDevice8->SetRenderState(D3DRS_SRCBLEND, D3DBLEND_SRCALPHA);
pd3dDevice8->SetRenderState(D3DRS_DESTBLEND, D3DBLEND_ONE);
```

A similar call can be used to specify parameters like the point size, with the line:

```
pDevice9->SetRenderState(D3DRS_POINTSIZE, 5);
```

Render states are documented thoroughly in the DirectX SDK. They are listed in the D3DRENDERSTATETYPE structure. Just remember that some state changes are costly and should thus be handled with care.

The Extension Library

Direct3D's core provides tons of functionality to application developers. But it is an immediate-mode API at heart, so functionality is basically geared toward rendering. Most persistent data structures and complex algorithms are omitted from the API for elegance and simplicity. But that does not imply that we have to code these manually. In the most recent iterations of Microsoft's API, an additional library called the extension library has grown from a simple collection of frequently used routines to a full-blown set of objects and functions, which make programming games much easier. Need progressive meshes? Animation controls? All are included within the Direct3DX extension library. In this section, we will review what's available for developers in version 9.0.

ID3DXMesh

The ID3DXMesh interface provides access to triangle meshes. Many game developers prefer to keep full control over their mesh representation and rendering. However, after taking a look at the features included in this interface, you might want to think twice.

Many popular algorithms are included, so you can get working with little or no coding at all. Routines like X file loading, generating indexed meshes, stripping data, and sorting by texture identifier are all supported internally. For example, assuming an ID3DXMesh object, the following code generates triangle strips from it:

```
D3dxmesh->Optimize(D3DXMESHOPT_STRIPREORDER | D3DXMESHOPT_COMPACT
| D3DXMESHOPT_ATTRSORT, PrevAdj, PostAdj, FaceMap, VertMap,
newmesh);
```

This code returns a second mesh (newmesh) based on the original one, making sure data is converted to strips, unused vertices are deleted, and faces are sorted by attributes to minimize state changes. PrevAdj and PostAdj are the input and resulting adjacency lists, whereas FaceMap and VertMap are indices to faces and vertices.

ID3DXPMesh

Progressive meshes (see Chapter 22, "Geometrical Algorithms") are one of the most powerful paradigms to represent level-of-detail (LOD) geometry. They allow us to scale the number of triangles up or down with very little CPU impact, thus making them ideal for video games. But progressive meshes are hard to get right. Luckily, the extension library has an interface to support them internally, so you do not have to worry about the algorithm's specifics. The interface is equivalent to ID3DMesh, but includes specific calls to change the object's level of detail. In this case, the calls are as follows, which set the number of faces to be used by the progressive mesh engine:

```
ID3DXPMesh->SetNumFaces(DWORD faces);
```

Due to the nature of these meshes, we may not get a mesh with the exact triangle count we request, but it will definitely be close.

ID3DXFont

The ID3DXFont interface provides font rendering capabilities, so we can access TrueType fonts and use them within our application. Fonts are created using the following code:

```
HRESULT D3DXCreateFont(              LPDIRECT3DDEVICE9 pDevice,
     HFONT hFont,
     LPD3DXFONT *ppFont
);
```

The first parameter is the Direct3D object, the second is the font object information encapsulated in an HFONT interface, and the third returns the newly created font. Then, all we have to do is render text to the screen by using the following line:

```
INT DrawText(LPCSTR pString, INT Count, LPRECT pRect, DWORD
Format,
D3DCOLOR Color);
```

We pass the string, the number of characters to be rendered, a rectangle defining the position and size of the characters, a format string that can be used for justification and so on, and a color.

Animation Helpers

Direct3DX provides not one but several animation-oriented objects. When combined, these can help us code complex animation routines with little effort. An ID3DXAnimationController allows the user to define blending parameters when transitioning from one animation loop to another. The ID3DXAnimationSet allows you to work with a set of interpolators that can be used to compute animation in a multinode system. The GetInterpolatorByIndex, for example, receives an unsigned integer as its first parameter and returns as a second parameter the interpolator defined by that identifier. Then, the following call from the ID3DXInterpolator class allows you to, given an interpolator and a time value, retrieve rotation, translation, and scaling vectors that represent the state of the node at that time:

```
HRESULT GetSRT(DOUBLE Time, D3DXVECTOR3 *pScale, D3DXQUATERNION
*pRotate, D3DXVECTOR3 *pTranslate);
```

Notice how rotations are implemented via quaternions to avoid gimbal locking.

The `ID3DXKeyFrameInterpolator` interface inherits from the previous interface and provides extra interpolation controls for keyframed skeletal animation. We can retrieve the number of rotation, scaling, and translation key frames, and so on.

Additionally, the `ID3DXSkinInfo` interface can be used to implement weighted matrices for skeletal animation. We can define and retrieve bone influences, attach bones to vertices, and compute the resulting mesh after skinning is computed. The following call receives the list of matrices that represent bone transforms, as well as a list containing the inverse transpose of these matrices:

```
HRESULT UpdateSkinnedMesh(                    CONST D3DXMATRIX
*pBoneTransforms,
      CONST D3DXMATRIX *pBoneInvTransposeTransforms,
      PVOID pVerticesSrc,
      PVOID pVerticesDst
);
```

The third and fourth parameters represent the input and output vertex list.

Interestingly, all the animation controllers and interfaces can be tied to D3DX meshes, so we can load meshes and skin them afterward.

In Closing

This appendix has provided you with a global overview of DirectX and how to program the Direct3D graphics API. For further information, take a look at the specific chapters where we touched on popular subjects such as animation, sound, input processing, and so on using this Microsoft API. To make life easier, here is a listing of those chapters:

- ➤ DirectInput was thoroughly explained in Chapter 5, "User Input."

- ➤ Light mapping was discussed in Chapter 17, "Shading."

- ➤ More texture mapping tricks and tips can be found in Chapter 18, "Texture Mapping," including cube maps and bump mapping.

- ➤ Shader effects were explained in Chapter 21, "Procedural Techniques."

Appendix D

Some Math Involved

This appendix is meant to be a review of many mathematical formulas and equations that are used continually in game programming. You will find an overview of trigonometry, vector math, matrices, and so on. I suggest you make sure you understand the following pages thoroughly before reading the more involved chapters on geometry tests. These pages should help you refresh some useful math concepts that will be repeatedly used in the book.

Distances

There are a number of distance-related computations, measures, and indices that can prove useful in your game programming.

Distance Between Two Points

The easiest way to compute the distance between two points is to use the Euclidean distance metric. Given P and Q in a 3D world, the distance is computed by:

$$distance = \sqrt{(p.x - q.x)^2 + (p.y - q.y)^2 + (p.z - q.z)^2}$$

Computing square roots can be costly. Moreover, in some cases (such as spatial sorting by distance), you will not need the distance itself, but just a way to measure objects according to their distance. In this case, you can override the square root and use the expression:

```
distance_squared = (p.x-q.x)²+(p.y-q.y)²+(p.z-q.z)²
```

A third method is to use Manhattan distance metrics, which are defined as:

```
distance_manhattan = abs(p.x-q.x)+abs(p.y-q.y)+abs(p.z-q.z)
```

Manhattan distances are the 0-level Euclidean norm, defined by the general expression:

$$dis\,tance\_norm = \sqrt[n]{(p.x - q.x)^n + (p.y - q.y)^n + (p.z - q.z)^n}$$

Manhattan distances are used as very fast pseudodistances, especially to cull away distant objects. It is a very cheap test that can help us discard irrelevant primitives (both in terms of logic and presentation).

Distance Between Two Lines

Given two lines R and S in (origin, direction vector) form, we can compute the minimum distance between them easily. The lines have the following expression:

R:

$$\left.\begin{array}{l} X = Rorg.x + Rdir.x * \lambda \\ Y = Rorg.y + Rdir.y * \lambda \\ Z = Rorg.z + Rdir.z * \lambda \end{array}\right\}$$

S:

$$\left.\begin{array}{l} X = Sorg.x + Sdir.x * \mu \\ Y = Sorg.y + Sdir.y * \mu \\ Z = Sorg.z + Sdir.z * \mu \end{array}\right\}$$

These are the parametric equations of the lines, and they are very easy to construct from game data structures. The distance between them is computed with the following:

$$dis\,tance = \frac{(Rdir * Sdir) * (Rorg \cdot Sorg)}{|Rdir * Sdir|}$$

This formula can be somehow sped up. For crossing lines, the numerator will always be zero, and thus we can save the division and modulo operations in the denominator.

Distance from a Point to a Line

The distance from a point P to a line in parametric form (defined by Org and Dir) can easily be computed with the following:

$$distance = \frac{dir * (org \cdot P)}{|dir|}$$

By storing a normalized direction vector, we can save the divide, thus speeding up the computation.

Distance from a Point to a Plane

Distance from a point P to a plane in 3D space can be computed easily using the normal distance to origin plane representation. A plane can be represented as:

```
N.x*X+N.y*Y+N.z*Z+D=0
```

where N is the normal to the plane and D is the minimum distance from the plane to the origin. Assuming this representation, the distance is computed as follows:

$$distance = \frac{N.x * P.x + N.y * P.y + N.z * P.z + D}{|N|}$$

As usual, keeping the plane's normal as a unit vector speeds the formula, so we can save the modulo and division in the denominator.

Distance Between Two Planes

Finding the distance between two planes is pretty straightforward:

1. Test if the two normal vectors are the same; if they are, the planes are parallel. If they are not, distance is 0 (they intersect).

2. Select a point in one of the planes.

3. Perform point-plane distance as shown earlier using that point and the opposite plane.

Trigonometry

Given a right triangle (see Figure D.1), the following can be defined:

$$\sin(\alpha) = \frac{opposite}{hypotenuse}$$

$$\cos(\alpha) = \frac{contiguous}{hypotenuse}$$

$$\tan(\alpha) = \frac{contiguous}{opposite}$$

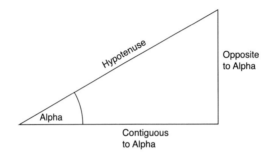

Figure D.1 Right triangle, showing the relationship between hypotenuse, contiguous, and opposite edges.

And here are some obvious relationships regarding trigonometric constants:

$$\sin^2(\alpha) + \cos^2(\alpha) = 1$$
$$\sin(\alpha) = \cos(\beta)$$
$$\cos(\alpha) = \sin(\beta)$$

Vector Math

This section provides a quick review of vector math.

Modulo

The modulo of a vector can be defined as its length and is computed by:

$$|p| = \sqrt{px^2 + py^2 + pz^2}$$

Dot Product

The dot product is an operation that, given two vectors, returns a floating-point value. It is usually depicted as:

```
u•v
```

And it is computed as follows:

```
u•v=ux*vx+uy*vy+uz*vz
```

Dot products are extremely popular in geometric tests. They can be computed on arbitrary vectors, but it is common to see them related to normalized (modulo-1) vectors. When applied to unit vectors, the dot product can be interpreted as the cosine of the angle between the two vectors being multiplied. Thus, the dot product of two parallel vectors equals one, and the dot product of two orthogonal (perpendicular) vectors equals zero.

Cross Product

The cross product is an operation that, given two vectors, returns a third vector. It is usually expressed as:

```
u * v
```

And is computed as follows:

$$u * v = \left(\begin{vmatrix} uy & uz \\ vy & vz \end{vmatrix}, - \begin{vmatrix} ux & uz \\ vx & vz \end{vmatrix}, \begin{vmatrix} ux & uy \\ vx & vy \end{vmatrix} \right)$$

The members between vertical braces are the determinants of those matrices. I will define determinants in a second. For now, suffice it to say that the preceding equation can be expressed as:

```
u*v=(uy*vz-uz*vy,uz*vx-ux*vz,ux*vy-uy*vx)
```

which can be easily understood. But notice how cross products are more expensive to compute than the dot version. Their geometric interpretation is, however, at least as interesting. Given two unit vectors, the cross product returns a third vector that is perpendicular to the plane formed by the two initial vectors.

Matrices

Matrices are powerful operators in algebra. They represent operations on vector spaces and are used everywhere in signal processing to represent geometrical transforms and to solve series of equations. In a general form, a matrix is an N×M construct such as:

$$\begin{pmatrix} a11 & a12 & ... & a1n \\ a21 & a22 & ... & a2n \\ ... & ... & ... & ... \\ am1 & am2 & ... & amn \end{pmatrix}$$

Matrices can be added, multiplied, transposed, and inverted. The following sections contain some examples for 3×3 matrices.

Matrix Addition

Adding two matrices is as easy as adding their cells one by one, as shown in the following example:

$$\begin{pmatrix} a11 & a12 & a13 \\ a21 & a22 & a23 \\ a31 & a32 & a33 \end{pmatrix} + \begin{pmatrix} b11 & b12 & b13 \\ b21 & b22 & b23 \\ b31 & b32 & b33 \end{pmatrix} = \begin{pmatrix} a11+b11 & a12+b12 & a13+b13 \\ a21+b21 & a22+b22 & a23+b23 \\ a31+b31 & a32+a32 & a33+b33 \end{pmatrix}$$

Two matrices must be equally sized for addition to be possible.

Matrix Transposition

Some matrix and geometry operations require finding the transpose of a given matrix, which is defined as its mirror using the diagonal as the reflection axis, as shown here:

$$\begin{pmatrix} a11 & a12 & a13 \\ a21 & a22 & a23 \\ a31 & a32 & a33 \end{pmatrix}^r = \begin{pmatrix} a11 & a21 & a31 \\ a12 & a22 & a32 \\ a13 & a23 & a33 \end{pmatrix}$$

Matrix-Matrix Multiplication

To multiply two matrices, their cell values must be multiplied using the following rule: To compute the cell at row X, column Y, we must perform the dot product of the X row from the first matrix with the Y column from the second matrix. Matrix multiplication is not commutative, so $A*B$ is not necessarily equal to $B*A$. For a 3×3 case, here is the compact notation:

$$\begin{pmatrix} a11 & a12 & a13 \\ a21 & a22 & a23 \\ a31 & a32 & a33 \end{pmatrix} * \begin{pmatrix} b11 & b12 & b13 \\ b21 & b22 & b23 \\ b31 & b32 & b33 \end{pmatrix} = \begin{pmatrix} (a1_{col} \cdot b_{row} 1) & (a1_{col} \cdot b_{row} 2) & (a1_{col} \cdot b_{row} 3) \\ (a2_{col} \cdot b_{row} 1) & (a2_{col} \cdot b_{row} 2) & (a1_{col} \cdot b_{row} 3) \\ (a3_{col} \cdot b_{row} 1) & (a3_{col} \cdot b_{row} 2) & (a3_{col} \cdot b_{row} 3) \end{pmatrix}$$

So, for example, the element (1,2) from the result arises from taking the first row from A (hence, a1col, which means row 1, all columns) and multiplying it by the second column of B (brow2, meaning all rows from the second column of B).

A special case of matrix multiplication is applying a matrix to a vector, which is just a single-column matrix. Here is an example for a 3×3 matrix and corresponding vector:

$$\begin{pmatrix} a11 & a12 & a13 \\ a21 & a22 & a23 \\ a31 & a32 & a33 \end{pmatrix} * \begin{pmatrix} px \\ py \\ pz \end{pmatrix} = \begin{pmatrix} (a1_{col} \cdot p) \\ (a2_{col} \cdot p) \\ (a3_{col} \cdot p) \end{pmatrix}$$

Determinant of a Matrix

The determinant of a matrix is a numeric value that is computed from the matrix's cells. It is extremely important because other operations rely on this value. As you will soon see, the determinant is tightly coupled to the inverse of a matrix, which is very important for geometry. The determinant is only defined for square matrices and is represented by two vertical braces. For a general-sized matrix, it must be defined recursively. Here are the formulae for 2×2 and 3×3 cases:

$$\begin{vmatrix} a11 & a12 \\ a21 & a22 \end{vmatrix} = a11*a22 - a12*a21$$

$$\begin{vmatrix} a11 & a12 & a13 \\ a21 & a22 & a32 \\ a31 & a23 & a33 \end{vmatrix} = a11*a22*a33 + a31*a12*a32 + a13*a21*a23 -$$

$$(a31*a22*a13 + a11*a23*a32 + a21*a12*a33)$$

Inverse of a Matrix

The inverse of a matrix A, represented by A^{-1}, is a matrix such that $A*A^{-1}=Id$, where Id is the identity matrix defined as:

$$Id = \begin{pmatrix} 1 & ... & 0 \\ ... & 1 & ... \\ 0 & ... & 1 \end{pmatrix}$$

The inverse of a matrix is very useful for geometrical transforms. But not all matrices have inverses. A matrix A must have a nonzero determinant for the inverse to exist. In this case, the inverse is defined as follows:

$$M^{-1} = \begin{pmatrix} \dfrac{adj(M11)}{|M|} & \dfrac{adj(M12)}{|M|} & \dfrac{adj(M13)}{|M|} \\ \dfrac{adj(M21)}{|M|} & \dfrac{adj(M22)}{|M|} & \dfrac{adj(M23)}{|M|} \\ \dfrac{adj(M31)}{|M|} & \dfrac{adj(M23)}{|M|} & \dfrac{adj(M33)}{|M|} \end{pmatrix}$$

where $adj(M_{ij})$ denotes the adjoint for the element at row i, column j. The adjoint is the determinant of a special matrix that is constructed from M as follows: Take the submatrix from the original one so that the row and column denoted disappear, and the rest remains the same. Then, the signs for the newly created matrix must be swapped as follows:

$$\begin{pmatrix} + & - & + \\ - & + & - \\ + & - & + \end{pmatrix}$$

For example, adj(M_{23}) for a 3x3 matrix would be as follows:

$$adj\,(M_{23}) = \begin{vmatrix} -m11 & -m12 \\ -m31 & -m32 \end{vmatrix} = \begin{vmatrix} -m11 & -m12 & ... \\ ... & ... & ... \\ -m31 & -m32 & ... \end{vmatrix}$$

Matrices for Geometry

Matrices are a compact and powerful tool used to describe geometrical transforms. In computer graphics and geometry in general the most popular form of matrix is the 4×4 homogeneous matrix, which is expressed as:

$$\begin{pmatrix} ux & vx & wx & tx \\ uy & vy & wy & ty \\ uz & vz & wz & tz \\ 0 & 0 & 0 & 1 \end{pmatrix}$$

The 3x3 top-left submatrix represents, in column order, the three basis vectors we want to implement. The fourth column labeled Tx, Ty, and Tz is the translate component. Given a point P, applying a transform simply means right-multiplying by the matrix while adding a trailing 1 to the point to add the translate component. Let's see this in detail:

$$\begin{pmatrix} ux & vx & wx & tx \\ uy & vy & wy & ty \\ uz & vz & wz & tz \\ 0 & 0 & 0 & 1 \end{pmatrix} * \begin{pmatrix} px \\ py \\ pz \\ 1 \end{pmatrix} = \begin{pmatrix} px*ux + py*vx + pz*wx + tx \\ px*uy + py*vy + pz*wy + ty \\ px*uz + py*vz + pz*wz + tz \\ 1 \end{pmatrix}$$

Then, by specifying the different transforms by means of these matrices, we can apply geometric transforms such as rotations, scalings, shearings, and so on to the incoming vertices. Let's review some popular transforms and their associated matrices.

Translation

Translations can be easily expressed in terms of homogeneous matrices. The translation (Tx, Ty, Tz) is applied as follows:

$$\begin{pmatrix} 1 & 0 & 0 & tx \\ 0 & 1 & 0 & ty \\ 0 & 0 & 1 & tz \\ 0 & 0 & 0 & 1 \end{pmatrix}$$

Remember that translating is essentially adding. Thus, the neutral translation is translating by zero in X, Y, and Z.

Scaling

Scaling can be implemented in both homogeneous and nonhomogeneous terms. Whichever the case, the general scaling operation (Sx, Sy, Sz) is applied by a matrix like this:

$$\begin{pmatrix} sx & 0 & 0 & 0 \\ 0 & sy & 0 & 0 \\ 0 & 0 & sz & 0 \\ 0 & 0 & 0 & 1 \end{pmatrix}$$

Always remember that scaling is fundamentally a multiplication operation. Thus, the identity operation is not zero as in translation, but one. Scaling by $(0,0,0)$ will collapse all your geometry, and quite likely generate some trouble in your graphics card.

Rotation

Rotation is a bit more complex than translating or scaling. It involves a bit more than adding or multiplying. We can define rotations around a canonical axis such as X (often called pitch), Y (often called yaw), and Z (often called roll). We can also define them around an arbitrary axis. We can also concatenate these matrices to perform compound rotations. Thus, there are different types of matrices we must become familiar with. To begin with, here are the roll, pitch, and yaw matrices:

Roll:

$$\begin{pmatrix} \cos(\alpha) & -\sin(\alpha) & 0 & 0 \\ \sin(\alpha) & \cos(\alpha) & 0 & 0 \\ 0 & 0 & 1 & 0 \\ 0 & 0 & 0 & 1 \end{pmatrix}$$

Pitch:

$$\begin{pmatrix} 1 & 0 & 0 & 0 \\ 0 & \cos(\alpha) & -\sin(\alpha) & 0 \\ 0 & \sin(\alpha) & \cos(\alpha) & 0 \\ 0 & 0 & 0 & 1 \end{pmatrix}$$

Yaw:

$$\begin{pmatrix} \cos(\alpha) & 0 & -\sin(\alpha) & 0 \\ 0 & 1 & 0 & 0 \\ \sin(\alpha) & 0 & \cos(\alpha) & 0 \\ 0 & 0 & 0 & 1 \end{pmatrix}$$

Basis Matrices

A more general type of matrix can be used to define a basis function for an arbitrary coordinate system. Imagine that you have a character who is holding an item in his hand. In order to paint the item in place, you have two alternative options. First, you can describe its position and then determine its orientation by means of roll, pitch, and yaw matrices. Second, you can give the same position as in the first option, but supply the vectors that define the X, Y, and Z axis local coordinate system for the hand (see Figure D.2). This is especially useful for hierarchical animation. In a simpler case, if you are to paint a car in a rally game and the car must adapt to the terrain, you will not have the slope in terms of roll, pitch, and yaw. Quite likely, you will have the normal of the terrain and the direction the car is advancing toward.

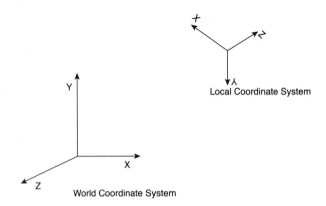

Figure D.2 Local versus world coordinate systems.

The normal is the Y vector of the local coordinate system, and the advance direction takes the place of the Z vector. By computing the cross product between Y and Z (both converted to unit vectors), we will unveil an X vector, which will in fact emerge from the position of the driver and exit the car laterally, as shown in Figure D.3. Those three vectors are the basis that defines the local coordinate system for the car.

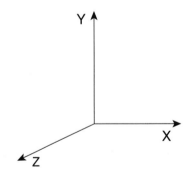

on the up-right axis (the rotated one) I need a car so it's oriented with the Y vector going through its roof, and the advance direction in X. So it must be upside down and looking left.

Figure D.3 Car showing the different coordinate systems.

Then, you can paint the car in its position and orientation by using basis matrices instead of simpler rotations and transforms. They are just plain homogeneous matrices that you will need to multiply all your vertices for. Given the three vectors defining the basis and the position vector, there are two important transform matrices.

The first matrix transforms from the world coordinate system into the object's coordinates. In other words, given a point above the car (in relative terms), such a matrix would allow us to know how high the point is from the car, even when the car is on a slope. The second matrix is the reverse process: Given a point in the car's coordinate system, it converts the point into world coordinates using the car's basis orientation matrix. For example, if we have a car in canonical orientation (Y meaning above and X meaning forward, for example) and want to place it in a point in space and in specific orientations, this is the matrix we would use.

For both matrices, we start with the basis of the space we want to move to. In this case, we create a 3×3 matrix whose columns are the new X, Y, and Z axes. Here is that matrix:

$$B = \begin{pmatrix} e_1 x & e_2 x & e_3 x \\ e_1 y & e_2 y & e_3 y \\ e_1 z & e_2 z & e_3 z \end{pmatrix}$$

So the basis is formed by the vectors e_1, e_2, and e_3, representing the X, Y, and Z axes respectively.

Then, the reverse transform is defined as:

$$RT = \begin{pmatrix} e_1 x & e_2 x & e_3 x & tx \\ e_1 y & e_2 y & e_3 y & ty \\ e_1 z & e_2 z & e_3 z & tz \\ 0 & 0 & 0 & 1 \end{pmatrix}$$

where the top-left submatrix is B, and the rightmost vector is the translation from the old origin to the new one. This transform is usually called the *rigid-body transform* because it allows us to place a rigid body in space given the three orientation axes and a new origin.

The direct transform is then defined using the inverse we defined earlier. Specifically, it is defined as:

$$DT = \begin{pmatrix} B^{-1} & B^{-1}T \\ 0 & 1 \end{pmatrix}$$

Incidentally, if the basis B is orthonormal (column vectors are normalized, and they are mutually orthogonal), the inverse can be easily computed as, in this case, $B^{-1}=B^{T}$.

Concatenation of Transforms

The previous ideas can be extended by concatenating change-of-basis matrices so we can build hierarchical transforms. Imagine that we want to place a sword in the hand of a soldier who is in turn riding a horse. To do so, we would:

1. Transform to the horse's reference system

2. Transform to the rider's reference system

3. Transform to the hand

4. Place the sword

5. Detransform the sword

6. Detransform the hand

7. Detransform the rider

8. Detransform the horse

These are, respectively, reverse transforms (to reach the sword) and direct transforms (to get back). Thus, the composite transform would look something like this:

$$\text{Position(sword)} = RT_{(horse)} * RT_{(rider)} * RT_{(hand)} * \text{Transform}_{(sword)} * DT_{(hand)} * DT_{(rider)} * DT_{(horse)}$$

Appendix E

Further Reading

"Outside of a dog, a book is a man's best friend. Inside of a dog, it's too dark to read."

Groucho Marx

No book about game programming would ever be complete without some pointers to additional learning resources. Game programming is an involved science that stands on the shoulders of many different subject areas. This appendix provides you with a full bibliography, sorted by chapter. This way you can find more information on the subjects in which you are most interested.

Chapter 1: Chronology of Game Programming

Baer, Ralph H., and Leonard D. Cope. Manually programmable video gaming system. United States Patent 4,355,805. October 26, 1982.

Burnham, Van. *Supercade: A Visual History of the Videogame Age, 1971–1984*. Cambridge: MIT Press, 2001.

DeMaria, Rusel, and Johnny L. Wilson. *High Score! The Illustrated History of Electronic Games*. New York: Osborne/McGraw-Hill, 2002.

Nintendo 64. United States Patent 6,331,856.

Chapter 2: Game Architecture

Brooks, Frederick P. Jr. *The Mythical Man-Month*, 2nd ed., Addison-Wesley, 1995.

Llopis, Noel. *C++ for Game Programmers*. Charles River Media, 2003.

Rollings, Andrew, and Dave Morris. *Game Architecture and Design*. Scottsdale, AZ: The Coriolis Group, 1999.

Chapter 3: Data Structures and Algorithms

Knuth, Donald E. *The Art of Computer Programming*. vols. 1–3, Addison-Wesley, 1998.

Musser, David R., and Atul Saini. *STL Tutorial and Reference Guide: C++ Programming with Standard Template Library*. Addison-Wesley, 1996.

Nelson, Mark. *C++ Programmer's Guide to the Standard Template Library*. IDG Books Worldwide, 1995.

Penton, Ron. *Data Structures for Game Programmers*. Premier Press, 2002.

Chapter 4: Design Patterns

Gamma, Erich, Richard Helm, Ralph Johnson, and John Vlissides. *Design Patterns*. Addison-Wesley, 1995.

Chapter 5: User Input

DirectX SDK samples.

Chapters 6, 7, and 8: Fundamental AI Technologies, Action-Oriented AI, and Tactical AI

AI Depot (very good articles on path finding and other techniques). Available at www.ai-depot.com.

Anglim, Simon, et al. *Fighting Techniques of the Ancient World: Equipment, Combat Skills, and Tactics*. Greenhill Books, 2002.

Connolly, Peter. *Greece and Rome at War*. Greenhill Books, 1998.

Forgy, C.L. "Rete: A Fast Algorithm for the Many Pattern/Many Object Pattern Match Problem." *Artificial Intelligence* 19 (1982): 17–37.

Funge, John David. *AI for Games and Animation.* AK Peters, 1999.

Goldsworthy, Adrian. *Roman Warfare.* Cassell & Company, 2000.

Miranker, Daniel P. *TREAT: A New and Efficient Match Algorithm for AI Production Systems.* Morgan Kaufmann Publishers, 1990.

Osprey Publishing books. An infinite source of accurate military information for the computer strategist.

Reese, Bjorn. Home page (navigation algorithms). Available at www.red3d.com/breese/navigation.html.

Reynolds, Craig. Home page (boids, group dynamics). Available at www.red3d.com/cwr.

Russel, Stuart J., and Peter Norvig. *Artificial Intelligence: A Modern Approach.* Prentice Hall, 2002.

Woodcock, Sean. Home page (everything game AI). Available at www.gameai.com.

Chapter 9: Scripting

Aho, Alfred V., Ravi Sethi, and Jeffrey D. Ullman. *Compilers: Principles, Techniques, and Tools.* Addison-Wesley, 1986.

De Figueiredo, L. H., R. Ierusalimschy, and W. Celes. "Lua: An Extensible Embedded Language." *Dr. Dobb's Journal* 21, no. 12 (December 1996): 26–33.

Ierusalimschy, R., L. H. de Figueiredo, and W. Celes. *Reference Manual of the Programming Language Lua 4.0.* Available at www.lua.org/manual/4.0.

Liang, Sheng. *The Java Native Interface: Programmer's Guide and Specification.* Addison Wesley Longman, Inc., 1999.

Riley, Sean. *Game Programming with Python.* Charles River Media, 2003.

Chapter 10: Network Programming

Blow, Jonathan. "A Look at Latency in Networked Games." *Game Developer* 5 (July 1998): 28–40.

Comer, Douglas E., and David L. Stevens. *Internetworking with TCP/IP Vol. III Client-Server Programming and Applications-Windows Sockets Version*. Prentice Hall, 1997.

Levine, David, Mark Wirt, and Barry Whitebook. *Practical Grid Computing for Massively Multiplayer Games*. Charles River Media, in press.

Chapter 11: 2D Programming

Game Programming Gems (all of the books in the series). Charles River Media.

LaMothe, Andre. *Tricks of the Windows Game Programming Gurus*. Sams, 1999.

Pazera, Ernest, and Andre LaMothe. *Isometric Game Programming with DirectX 7.0*. Premier Press, 2001.

Chapter 12: 3D Pipeline Overview

Akenine-Möller, Tomas, and Eric Haines. *Real Time Rendering*. AK Peters, 2002.

Eberly, David H. *3D Game Engine Design: A Practical Approach to Real-Time Computer Graphics*. Morgan Kaufmann, 2001.

Game Programming Gems (all of the books in the series). Charles River Media.

Morley, Mark. *Frustum Culling in OpenGL*. A tutorial. Available at www.markmorley. com/opengl/frustumculling.html.

Chapter 13: Indoors Rendering

Abrash, Michael. Michael Abrash's Ramblings (*Quake 3* visibility, lighting, and so on). Available at `www.bluesnews.com/abrash`.

Perez, Adrian. "Peeking through Portals." *GameDeveloper* 2 (March 1998).

Teller, Seth Jared. "Visibility Computations in Densely Occluded Polyhedral Environments." University of California at Berkeley. Available at `http://sunsite. berkeley.edu/NCSTRL`.

Chapter 14: Outdoors Algorithms

Blow, Jonathan. "Terrain Rendering at High Levels of Detail." Paper for the Game Developers Conference 2000, San Jose, CA.

Duchaineau, Mark, Murray Wolinsky, David E. Sigeti, Mark C. Miller, Charles Aldrich, and Mark B. Mineev-Weinstein. "ROAMing Terrain: Real-time Optimally Adapting Meshes." Available at `www.llnl.gov/graphics/ROAM/roam.pdf`, 1997.

Lindstrom, Peter, David Koller, William Ribarsky, Larry F. Hodges, Nick Faust, and Gregory A. Turner. "Real-Time, Continuous Level of Detail Rendering of Height Fields." ACM SIGGRAPH 1996 (August 1996): 109–118.

Snook, Greg. *Real-Time 3d Terrain Engines Using C++ and DirectX*. Charles River Media, 2003.

Turner, Bryan. "Real-Time Dynamic Level of Detail Terrain Rendering with ROAM." `http://www.gamasutra.com/features/20000403/turner_01.htm`, April 3, 2000.

Ulrich, Tatcher, "Super-size it! Scaling up to Massive Virtual Worlds." (course notes) SIGGRAPH 2002.

Chapter 15: Character Animation

Ekman, P. and Friesen, W.V. *Facial action coding system: A technique for the measurement of facial movement.* Palo Alto, CA: Consulting Psychologists Press (1978).

Parke, Frederic I., and Keith Waters. *Computer Facial Animation.* AK Peters, 1996.

Watt, Alan, and Mark Watt. *Advanced Animation and Rendering Techniques: Theory and Practice.* Addison Wesley, 1992.

Chapter 16: Cinematography

Ablan, Dan. *Digital Cinematography & Directing.* New Riders Publishing, 2002.

Kuipers, Jack. *Quaternions and Rotation Sequences: A Primer with Applications to Orbits, Aerospace, and Virtual Reality.* Princeton University Press, 2002.

Chapter 17: Shading

Gooch, Bruce, and Amy Ashurst Gooch. *Non-Photorealistic Rendering.* AK Peters, 2001.

Kilgard, Marc. "Shadow Mapping with Today's OpenGL Hardware." Game Developer's Conference, 2000.

Meier, Barbara J. "Painterly Rendering for Animation." SIGGRAPH 1996.

Reeves, William, David Salesin, and Robert Cook. "Rendering Antialiased Shadows with Depth Maps." SIGGRAPH 1987.

Segal, Mark, et. al. "Fast Shadows and Lighting Effects Using Texture Mapping." SIGGRAPH 1992.

Williams, Lance. "Casting Curved Shadows on Curved Surfaces." SIGGRAPH 1978.

Chapter 18: Texture Mapping

Blow, Jonathan. "A Texture Cache." Game Developer's Conference, 1998.

Chapter 19: Particle Systems

Reeves, William T. "Particle Systems—A Technique for Modeling a Class of Fuzzy Objects, Computer Graphics." 17:3 pp. 359-376, SIGGRAPH 1983.

Witkin, Andrew, and David Baraff. "Physically Based Modeling: Principles and Practice." (online SIGGRAPH 1997 course notes). Available at `www-2.cs.cmu.edu/~baraff/sigcourse`.

Chapter 20: Organic Rendering

Jakulin, Aleks. "Interactive Vegetation Rendering with Slicing and Blending." Eurographics 2000.

Staff Jensen, Lasse, and Robert Golias. "Deep Water Animation and Rendering." Gamasutra. Available at `www.gamasutra.com/gdce/2001/jensen/jensen_01.htm`.

Chapter 21: Procedural Techniques

Apodaca, Anthony A., and Larry Gritz. *Advanced RenderMan: Creating CGI for Motion Pictures.* Morgan Kaufmann, 1999.

Cook, Rob L. "Shade Trees." SIGGRAPH 1984.

Ebert, David, et al. *Modeling and Texturing: A Procedural Approach.* 3rd ed. Morgan Kaufmann, 2002.

Fernando, Randima, and Mark J. Kilgard. *The Cg Tutorial: The Definitive Guide to Programmable Real-Time Graphics.* Addison Wesley, 2003.

Lecky-Thompson, Guy. *Infinite Game Universe: Mathematical Techniques.* Charles River Media, 2001.

NVIDIA Corporation. Cg specification. Available at `www.cgshaders.org`.

Perlin, Ken. "An image synthesizer." SIGGRAPH 1985.

Proudfoot, Kekoa, William R. Mark, Svetoslav Tzvetkov, and Pat Hanrahan. "A Real-Time Procedural Shading System for Programmable Graphics Hardware." SIGGRAPH 2001.

Upstill, Steve. *The Renderman Companion: A Programmer's Guide to Realistic Computer Graphics.* Addison-Wesley, 1990.

Worley, Steven. "A cellular basis function." SIGGRAPH 1996.

Chapter 22: Geometrical Algorithms

Andujar, C. "Octree-based Simplification of Polyhedral Models," Ph.D. thesis. Available at `http://www.lsi.upc.es/~andujar/`.

Farin, Gerald, and Dianne Hansford. *The Geometry Toolbox for Graphics and Modeling.* AK Peters, 1998.

Graphics Gems (all of them). Morgan Kaufmann.

Hoppe, Hugues. "Progressive Meshes." SIGGRAPH 1996.

Appendix A: Performance Tuning

Abrash, Michael. *Zen of Code Optimization: The Ultimate Guide to Writing Software That Pushes PCs to the Limit.* The Coriolis Group, 1994.

Game Programming Gems (all of them). Charles River Media.

Appendix B: OpenGL

Woo, Mason, Jackie Neider, Tom Davis, and Dave Shreiner. OpenGL Architecture Review Board. *OpenGL(R) Programming Guide: The Official Guide to Learning OpenGL, Version 1.2.* 3rd ed. Addison-Wesley, 1999.

Appendix C: Direct3D

Walsh, Peter, and Adrian Perez. *Advanced Game Programming with DirectX 8.* Wordware Publishing, 2001.

Appendix D: Some Math Involved

Dunn, Fletcher, and Ian Parberry. *3D Math Primer for Graphics and Game Development.* Wordware Publishing, 2002.

Lengyel, Eric. *Mathematics for 3D Game Programming and Computer Graphics.* Charles River Media, 2002.

Index

Symbols

C

U

V

inform IT

YOUR GUIDE TO IT REFERENCE

New Riders has partnered with **InformIT.com** to bring technical information to your desktop. Drawing from New Riders authors and reviewers to provide additional information on topics of interest to you, **InformIT.com** provides free, in-depth information you won't find anywhere else.

Articles

Keep your edge with thousands of free articles, in-depth features, interviews, and IT reference recommendations—all written by experts you know and trust.

Online Books

Answers in an instant from **InformIT Online Books'** 600+ fully searchable online books.

POWERED BY
Safari

Catalog

Review online sample chapters, author biographies, and customer rankings and choose exactly the right book from a selection of over 5,000 titles.

New Riders

VOICES THAT MATTER

HOW TO CONTACT US

VISIT OUR WEB SITE
WWW.NEWRIDERS.COM

On our web site, you'll find information about our other books, authors, tables of contents, and book errata. You will also find information about book registration and how to purchase our books, both domestically and internationally.

EMAIL US

Contact us at: **nrfeedback@newriders.com**

- If you have comments or questions about this book
- To report errors that you have found in this book
- If you have a book proposal to submit or are interested in writing for New Riders
- If you are an expert in a computer topic or technology and are interested in being a technical editor who reviews manuscripts for technical accuracy

Contact us at: **nreducation@newriders.com**

- If you are an instructor from an educational institution who wants to preview New Riders books for classroom use. Email should include your name, title, school, department, address, phone number, office days/hours, text in use, and enrollment, along with your request for desk/examination copies and/or additional information.

Contact us at: **nrmedia@newriders.com**

- If you are a member of the media who is interested in reviewing copies of New Riders books. Send your name, mailing address, and email address, along with the name of the publication or Web site you work for.

BULK PURCHASES/CORPORATE SALES

The publisher offers discounts on this book when ordered in quantity for bulk purchases and special sales. For sales within the U.S., please contact: Corporate and Government Sales (800) 382-3419 or **corpsales@pearsontechgroup.com**. Outside of the U.S., please contact: International Sales (317) 428-3341 or **international@pearsontechgroup.com**.

WRITE TO US

New Riders Publishing
800 East 96th Street, 3rd Floor
Indianapolis, IN 46240

CALL/FAX US

Toll-free (800) 571-5840
If outside U.S. (317) 428-3000
Ask for New Riders
FAX: (317) 428-3280

New Riders

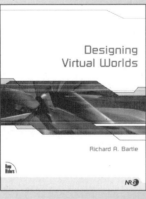